LEARNING

LEARNING

BEHAVIOR AND COGNITION

Second Edition

David A. Lieberman
University of Stirling
Scotland

Brooks/Cole Publishing Company
Pacific Grove, California

PSYCHOLOGY EDITOR: Kenneth King
EDITORIAL ASSISTANT: Gay Meixel
PRODUCTION: Cecile Joyner, The Cooper Company
PRINT BUYER: Diana Spence
PERMISSIONS EDITOR: Robert Kauser
DESIGNER: Carolyn Deacy
COPY EDITOR: Peggy Tropp
TECHNICAL ILLUSTRATOR: Alexander Teshin and Associates
COVER DESIGNER: Carolyn Deacy
COVER: Robert Hudson, *Out of the Blue* (1980–81). Acrylic on canvas with wooden chair, plastic tree, wood, and steel tubing, 96⅜ × 180⅞ × 27¾″. San Francisco Museum of Modern Art, purchased with the aid of the Byron Meyer Fund.
COMPOSITOR: Bi-Comp, Inc.
PRINTER: Arcata Graphics/Fairfield

This book is printed on acid-free recycled paper.

4 5 6 7 8 9 10

Library of Congress Cataloging-in-Publication Data

Lieberman, David A.
    Learning: behavior and cognition / David A. Lieberman.—2nd ed.
        p.   cm.
    Includes bibliographical references (p.   ) and index.
    ISBN 0-534-17400-0
    1. Learning, Psychology of.   2. Paired-association learning.
3. Conditioned response.   4. Human information processing.
I. Title.
BF319.5.P34L543   1992
153.1′526—dc20   92-29940

TO MY FAMILY,
WHOM I LOVE VERY MUCH

CONTENTS

CHAPTER FOUR

PRINCIPLES AND APPLICATIONS 110

CHAPTER FIVE

THEORIES OF CONDITIONING 146

PART IV

THEORETICAL PROCESSES IN ASSOCIATIVE LEARNING

CHAPTER TEN

LEARNING IN AN EVOLUTIONARY CONTEXT 360

CHAPTER ELEVEN

WHAT IS LEARNED? ASSOCIATIVE VERSUS COGNITIVE THEORIES OF LEARNING 394

CHAPTER TWELVE

How Is It Learned? An Information-Processing Model 428

CHAPTER THIRTEEN

Is Associative Learning Simple or Complex? 486

PREFACE

I find research on learning exciting. The topic is of profound importance—almost every aspect of our behavior is guided by learning—and there can be wonderful pleasure when researchers' efforts to penetrate the complex and tangled surface of human behavior yield glimpses of the elegant processes lying underneath. Tackling learning may not be quite as physically stimulating as trying to climb Everest, but the intellectual challenge is every bit as exhilarating.

In writing this text, I have tried to communicate the challenge facing learning researchers, and the excitement and beauty of their voyages of discovery. The purpose of this preface is to explain some of the assumptions that guided my efforts and also some of the features of the resulting text that perhaps make it distinctive.

Intellectual stimulation. One of my fundamental goals was to present ideas in a way that would be intellectually *rigorous* and *stimulating*. In planning any text, one of the most difficult issues is how to balance the need for broad coverage against the dangers of superficiality—of losing students in a forest of facts. My own bias is against the handbook approach. I think students gain more from a deep understanding of fundamental ideas than from a superficial familiarity with a much larger set of facts. In writing this text, therefore, I have tried to identify the most important issues in associative learning and present them in depth, rather than providing shallower coverage of all issues.

One example of this approach is in my treatment of experimental design. If students are to be helped to think critically, it is vital that they understand the logic of experiments, rather than just memorize their conclusions. For this reason, I have emphasized the logic of experimental analysis throughout this text. Chapter 1 provides an introduction to the experimental method: what are the advantages and disadvantages of experiments, why do learning researchers sometimes use animals, and so on. In subsequent chapters, I have continued this approach by analyzing selected experiments and methodological issues in depth, while giving briefer summaries of other studies.

I have taken a similar approach to presenting theories, concentrating on presenting a small number in depth rather than providing more superficial coverage of them all. In the case of classical conditioning, for example, I have focused on the theory I consider to be the most important: the Rescorla-Wagner model. Through extensive analysis of this model, I have tried to convey a feeling for how theories can be used to explain known phenomena and to generate novel and sometimes counterintuitive predictions. This material is not easy, but I have tried to present the material as clearly and as simply as I could, and in my experience students feel that the model's importance makes the effort it requires worthwhile.

Where this selective approach has meant that coverage of some issues has had to be curtailed, I have provided references that the interested reader can consult for more information.

Practical applications.   A second goal was to present learning in a way that would be *interesting*. I think students sometimes find learning boring because of an understandable difficulty in seeing the relevance of experiments on rats to the problems they face in their daily lives. It is not enough for teachers and textbooks to assert that laboratory research is relevant: This relevance has to be demonstrated. I have done this by interweaving material on laboratory research and practical applications throughout the text. Applications of learning principles are not only fascinating in themselves but also provide a critical test of the validity of laboratory principles. Material on applications thus provides a sense not only of how much has already been achieved but of what remains to be discovered.

Among the practical issues examined in the text are how rewards and punishments subtly shape our lives (why is it, for example, that students often have so much difficulty in forcing themselves to study, when there appear to be such massive rewards contingent on good grades—entrance to graduate school, a good job, and so on); how classical conditioning affects emotions such as fear and sexual arousal; how learning principles can be used to overcome phobias and cigarette smoking; but also the need for caution in applying learning principles (for example, how rewards for doing homework can sometimes reduce interest in studying rather than enhance it).

The conflict between associative and cognitive theories of learning.   Perhaps the single most important factor shaping the development of research on learning has been the tension between associative and cognitive interpretations. Where associative theorists believe that complex learning can be understood in terms of fundamentally simple associative mechanisms (in Estes' classic phrase, learning is viewed as a sort of mental chemistry), cognitive theorists assume that the fundamental processes are much richer and more complex.

Given the central role of the conflict between these views in the development of the field, I have devoted considerable space to explaining the two views and tracing their evolution under the pressure of accumulating evidence. The alternative conceptualizations are first introduced in Chapter 2, and then analyzed more intensively in Chapter 11, which describes the conflict between S-R and cognitive theories of what is learned, and how the views of the two sides gradually converged. The chapter concludes by exploring the possibility that both sides may have been right, as learning may involve both relatively simple habits and more complex expectations. (This view has recently found powerful echoes in research on human cognition, with the emergence of distinctions between controlled and automatic processes, and between procedural and declarative memories.)

Chapter 12 then traces the development of information-processing models of learning, and examines how principles of memory and attention developed in research on human cognition can also be used to explain many aspects of associative learning. This approach represents a synthesis of cognitive and associative approaches to learning: The emphasis on explanatory processes such as memory and attention is clearly cognitive, but the models retain the assumption of associative theories that seemingly complex phenomena can be understood in terms of simple underlying processes.

Finally, Chapter 13 introduces one of the most exciting recent developments in psychology, *neural network models*. These models provide a new synthesis of associative and cognitive approaches: Learning is still seen as involving cognitive processes of considerable complexity, but these are in turn explained in terms of simple associative processes at a neural level. In the few short years since these models first appeared, they have already had impressive success in accounting for instances of learning ranging from classical conditioning in slugs to language learning in humans. The chapter examines some of this evidence, and considers the potentially revolutionary implications of neural network models for our understanding of learning and the mind.

Key changes to the second edition. The second edition involves many changes designed to improve existing material or incorporate new material (an expanded section on the conditioning of autonomic responses to insulin, heroin, and viruses is one example). The largest of these changes involves greatly expanded coverage of the biological bases of learning. Animals and humans do not start life with totally blank minds—John Locke's famous *tabula rasa*. Many thousands of years of evolution have endowed us with built-in reactions to important events, and learning occurs within the boundaries of this biological inheritance. In this edition, I have given greater emphasis to this biological context, and Chapter 10 has been entirely devoted to the role of evolution in shaping learning. The chapter begins with an introduction to the concepts of evolution, and it then traces how the pressures of natural selection have molded learning processes to fit the needs of different species and situations.

Imprinting and song-learning are used to illustrate the diversity of learning, along with examples from classical conditioning and reinforcement. It is now abundantly clear that the general process view of learning is wrong—learning is not uniform in all species and situations—but the chapter concludes by exploring the possibility that the observable differences in learning may represent variations on a small number of common themes.

Aids to studying. In order to help readers to absorb the sometimes challenging material in each chapter, an extensive *Summary* is provided at the end of each chapter. In addition, there is a *Selected Definition* section that reviews the main concepts introduced in the chapter, and a series of *Review Questions*. If a student can answer these questions, he or she can be confident that they have understood the main concepts and themes of the chapter.

Acknowledgments. I hope that this text is both challenging and interesting, and that it provides a sense of the importance and excitement of research on learning. If the text achieves any of these aims, credit will be due to many individuals. One is Ralph Haber, who provided warm encouragement and support when I first contemplated what to me was the awesome prospect of writing a text. I am also grateful to many friends and colleagues who have read and commented on the manuscript at various stages of its preparation. For the first edition, Tony Dickinson of Cambridge University, Vin LoLordo of Dalhousie University, and Glyn Thomas of Birmingham University were all kind enough to read the entire manuscript. I also received helpful comments from Pete Badia of Bowling Green State University, David L. Brodigan of Carleton College, John Capaldi of Purdue University, Alexis C. Collier of Ohio State University, Robert L. Greene of Case Western Reserve University, Nancy K. Innis of the University of Western Ontario, Donald F. Kendrick of Middle Tennessee State University, Steve Maier of the University of Colorado, Mary Jane Rains of the University of Wisconsin, Stout, and Mark Rilling of Michigan State University.

In preparing the second edition, I was helped by comments from Pamela Jackson-Smith of the University of Utah, Michael E. Rashotte of Florida State University, and Gene D. Steinhauer of California State University at Hayward, who read the first edition and offered suggestions for how it could be improved. Bill McGrew and Cliff Henty of the University of Stirling then provided helpful comments during the preparation of Chapter 10, and Michael S. Fanselow of the University of California at Los Angeles and Sandra J. Kelley of the University of South Carolina at Columbia, were both kind enough to comment on the entire revision.

I believe the text benefited substantially from the comments of all of these reviewers, and I am grateful for their efforts. I did not always follow their advice, however, and, accordingly, they should not be held responsible for any errors or omissions that remain.

In a slightly different context, I am again grateful to Mike Rashotte of Florida State University. I prepared a considerably expanded Test Manual to accompany this edition, and Mike was kind enough to allow me to incorporate some of the exam questions he used in his course in the Manual.

I would also like to thank the production staff at Wadsworth, as well as Peggy Tropp, who acted as copy editor, and Cecile Joyner of the Cooper Company who was a very helpful production editor. It has been a pleasure working with all of you.

Perhaps my greatest debt, though, is to Ken King, the psychology editor at Wadsworth. From the beginning, he understood what I was trying to do and strongly supported me in working to achieve it, even in cases such as the Rescorla-Wagner model, where my approach differed substantially from that of existing texts. I am grateful for his support, encouragement, and acute insights; I do not think I could have had a better editor.

INTRODUCTION

CHAPTER ONE

SOME BASIC ASSUMPTIONS

In the old television series *Dragnet,* police sergeant Joe Friday was forever being confronted by incoherent witnesses to a crime. He would stoically endure their babbling until, his patience finally exhausted, he would interrupt, "We want the facts, Ma'am, just the facts." Psychologists too want the facts, but, with experience, they acquire a certain wary respect for the problems involved in determining facts.

What is a fact? Of course everyone knows what a fact is; a fact is . . . , well . . . it's a *fact,* something that everyone knows to be true. Or is it? Was it a fact that the earth was flat because everyone before Columbus believed it to be so? Or that the earth was the center of the universe before Galileo single-handedly moved it into orbit around the sun? And if we cannot be sure of the truth in cases as obvious as these ("Can't you feel that the earth is still? Can't you see that the sun is moving?"), how much more difficult must it be when the truth is more obscure, and when experts can't even agree among themselves? If one scientist claims that the moon is composed of blue cheese, and a colleague tartly replies, "So's your mother," how are we to decide which of their scientific views is correct?

In older sciences, such as physics and chemistry, disputes over scientific facts are less obvious: Over the years, basic concepts such as the atom and gravity have become firmly established; only after considerable training to learn dispute-free "facts" are new initiates to the profession gradually introduced to the ambiguities and uncertainties of current research. In psychology, which is a relatively new science, these disputes cannot be obscured so easily: The dividing line between "old established facts" and "new controversial hypotheses" is less clear, and there is not as comforting a bedrock of certainty and accomplishment to support a student when he or she feels overwhelmed by conflicting claims. Consider such a relatively simple problem as the use of corporal punish-

3

ment: Is corporal punishment an effective and ultimately humane way to eliminate a person's harmful behavior, or is it a barbaric relic of our primitive past? There is evidence to support both views, and it can be more than a little frustrating to try to analyze the polemics of each side, and more than a little tempting to give up in disgust, crying "a plague on both your houses."

In their attempts to resolve such disagreements—to decide what is a fact and what is not—psychologists have relied on a number of assumptions. These assumptions are now so well accepted that psychologists rarely question them; this does not necessarily mean, however, that the assumptions are correct. In this chapter we will examine these assumptions in some detail. It is perhaps worth emphasizing in advance that the assumptions we will be examining really are assumptions, slowly developed over several centuries within a particular cultural and scientific tradition, and indeed not universally accepted even among psychologists. There are good grounds for you to approach these assumptions with a healthy skepticism and to form your own views of their validity. The better you understand these assumptions, however, the better you will understand why research on learning has followed the paths that we will be tracing in subsequent chapters.

One purpose of this chapter, then, is to examine the methodological assumptions that have guided psychological research: why psychologists rely on experiments to understand learning, and the logic that guides them in designing these experiments. Before considering how to do research, however, we will begin by focusing on an even more fundamental issue: Why study learning in the first place?

1.1 WHY STUDY LEARNING?

Why do psychologists study learning? One reason is simply curiosity; a second reason is the belief that a better understanding of how people learn will inevitably lead to a wide range of important practical applications. On the surface, both reasons may seem straightforward, but each has proved contentious.

At times, we value curiosity unreservedly; a child's open curiosity, for example, enchants us. On the other hand, we are often suspicious of curious academics who choose to spend their lives studying courtship patterns among Pacific Island natives, the use of imagery in the novels of Thomas Hardy, or the mechanisms of learning in white rats. Are these really appropriate activities for grown men and women? In the 1970s, Senator William Proxmire of Wisconsin became famous (or notorious, depending on your point of view) for publicizing what he considered egregious misuse of public funds to support such research; he called it his "Golden Fleece of the Month" award. Popular references to "ivory towers" and "the sheltered groves of academe" similarly convey our uneasiness about individuals motivated solely by curiosity.

Despite this public ambivalence, curiosity is one of the strongest motives for psychological research. When applying for grants, however, psychologists are rather more likely to emphasize a second motive: the practical value of knowledge about behavior. The better we understand how people learn, for example, the better able we will be to help them learn appropriate behaviors and eliminate inappropriate ones. This belief, in turn, rests on three further assumptions:

1. Behavior is lawful; that is, it is governed by laws.

2. If the laws of behavior are known, behavior can be controlled.

3. The capacity to control behavior is desirable.

All of these assumptions are controversial, and in the following sections we will examine each of them in some detail.

Is Behavior Lawful?

Determinism.   Within science, a law is essentially a statement of the form "If A, then B." That is, if some condition A exists, we predict that event B will occur. The statement "The sun rises every morning," for example, predicts that if it is morning, then the sun will rise. Similarly, Einstein's famous equation $E = mc^2$ says that if m had a value of 1 and c had a value of 2, then the value of E would be 4 (the real value of c is rather greater). The assertion that behavior is lawful, therefore, is essentially a claim that behavior is predictable: Whenever a certain set of conditions arises, the same behavior will always follow.

The belief that behavior is lawful—that how we behave is entirely determined by our environment and our genetic inheritance—is known as **determinism.** According to determinists, all behavior is determined by our current environment and our past experience. Your decision to go to college, for example, will have been determined by factors such as the educational background of your parents, the grades you received at school, the economic advantages of a degree, and so forth. Together, these factors made it inevitable that you would eventually choose to go to college, whether or not you were consciously aware of their influence.

Dramatic advances in sciences such as physics and chemistry have made us more comfortable with the idea that nature is inherently orderly, even though our ignorance may sometimes make it appear capricious. But is the behavior of a living organism just as lawful, just as determined, as the orbit of a rocket or the ticking of a clock? Are we really just helpless pawns in the grasp of environmental and genetic forces beyond our control?

Free will.   Within Western civilization, strict determinism of this kind has generally been rejected. Humans, according to most Western religions, are fundamentally free: Each individual has the power to determine his or her own actions; it is this **free will** that makes each person responsible for his or her actions and provides the basis for our ethical concepts of morality and responsibility. Aside from formal religious teachings, however, there is a deep strain within all of us that resents the notion that we are only insignificant links within a causal chain, like billiard balls hurtling blindly through space, propelled by forces we cannot resist. This image is not only demeaning, it is also contrary to our everyday experience. When we make decisions—whether simple ones about what clothes to wear or more complex ones such as what career to follow—we feel no sense of compulsion, of constraint. We can do what we want, go where we want, choose what we want. Where is this mysterious determinism if we are so evidently free to choose?

This sense of our ultimate freedom, of our capacity to defy all manner of control and manipulation, was eloquently expressed by Dostoevsky:

> Out of sheer ingratitude man will play you a dirty trick, just to prove that men are still men and not the keys of a piano. . . . And even if you could prove that a man is only a piano key, he would still do something out of sheer perversity— he would create destruction and chaos—just to gain his point. . . . And if all this could in turn be analyzed and prevented by predicting that it would occur, then man would deliberately go mad to prove his point.

(Quoted in Skinner, 1955, p. 49)

Us versus them. Is the idea of determinism really as foreign to us as this quote suggests? Certainly many of us believe our own behavior is a result of free will, yet we constantly act as if the behavior of others is strongly determined. Advertisers, for example, spend billions of dollars annually in the belief that consumer choices among competing products are the result not simply of rational evaluations, but of profound—and manipulable—unconscious processes. Our choice of a car, for example, is thought to be determined not simply by compression ratios or camshaft differentials, but by whether a pretty girl is pictured next to it in an advertisement, and by the powerful and masculine connotations of its name (Maverick, Jaguar, Cougar, and so on). Some research, moreover, suggests that advertisers may be justified in their belief. In one experiment by Smith and Engel (1968), 120 adults were shown a picture of a car with or without a sexy redhead, in black lace panties and a sleeveless sweater, standing next to it. When asked to evaluate the car on a number of dimensions, those who saw it with the model standing next to it rated it as significantly more appealing and better designed. They also estimated it to be more expensive (by an average of $340), faster (by 7 mph), and less safe. When a subset of the subjects were later asked if their ratings had been influenced by the presence of the model, however, 22 of the 23 subjects interviewed denied it. One respondent claimed, "I don't let anything but the thing itself influence my judgments. The other is just propaganda." Another commented, "I never let myself be blinded by advertising; the car itself is what counts." We are all convinced that it is only other people, not we, who are influenced by advertising; but the evidence suggests that most, if not all, of us actually are influenced.

Parental attitudes provide another example of the belief that other people's behavior is powerfully determined by their environment. Few parents simply ignore their children in the belief that all will work out for the best in the end. Rather, most parents believe passionately in the importance of a good environment for their children's development and do their best to ensure such an environment. The intensity of this belief is often revealed most clearly in the presence of a perceived threat to that environment, such as pornography, television violence, or most poignantly, racial integration in the schools. When black children in the United States were bused to all-white schools for the first time in the 1960s, picketing white mothers cursed and spat at them. These mothers' fury was fueled by their belief that racial integration would have devastating consequences for their children. This fear was mistaken, but its intensity reflected an underlying assumption that the school environment plays a powerful role in determining a child's development.

The actions of government leaders similarly attest to our faith in the lawful determination of behavior. Whether or not that faith is justified, government leaders continually legislate in the belief that their efforts will have a predictable effect on people's behavior. They adopt deficit spending because it is expected to encourage consumers to spend more and thus avert a recession. They decree penal codes in the belief that the threat of punishment will act as a deterrent to crime. And they accept the horrible destructiveness of war in the belief that the bloodshed will deter future aggressors. (World War I was meant to "make the world safe for democracy"; it was "the war to end all wars." The Vietnam conflict would ensure "a generation of peace.") All of these actions are based on the belief that the behavior of others can be controlled.

Whatever our belief in our own free will, then, in our everyday lives most of us seem to expect other people to react in reasonably predictable ways to our behavior. However much we may dislike some powerful bully, for example, we don't simply walk over to him and punch him in the nose, because we know very well that his reaction will not be random, but intensely and unpleasantly predictable. Even Dostoevsky, at the very moment when he most emphatically proclaimed that humans, out of sheer perversity, would defy all controls, was implicitly assuming that this behavior was predictable—that a human being's reaction to controls would always be one of defiance rather than of passive acceptance.

Any evidence that behavior is predictable does not, of course, prove that it is always predictable. There are many behaviors we cannot predict, from serious ones such as which children, on growing up, will commit mass murders, to mundane ones such as which desserts people will order in restaurants. The issue is how to interpret such breakdowns in predictability. For proponents of free will, these breakdowns are evidence that behavior is not completely lawful; for determinists, they are evidence that we do not yet understand the lawful relationships involved. There is no way to prove which side is right; they are simply different assumptions about the nature of the world. For our current purposes, the important point is that both sides agree that the environment exerts a strong influence on behavior, however much they disagree over whether that influence is total.

Can Behavior Be Controlled?

Insofar as we can identify lawful relationships between our environment and behavior, will we be able to use this knowledge to control people's behavior? Up to a point, this conclusion follows axiomatically: If we know that condition A reliably produces behavior B,

$$A \longrightarrow B$$

then we can produce behavior B simply by establishing condition A. In practice, though, this is not always easy. If we discovered that individual tutoring was the most effective form of education, for example, it would not necessarily follow that society could afford to provide every student with her or his own tutor. In general, though, it seems fair to say that an increase in our understanding of the laws governing behavior would also increase our ability to control such behavior.

Is Controlling Behavior Desirable?

One argument for studying learning, then, is that such study can lead to a significant enhancement of our capacity to control people's behavior. Stated in these terms, however, it is not immediately obvious that such an enhancement is desirable. Do we as individuals, or as an organized society, have the right to control how other people behave?

To answer this question, we first need to define more carefully what we mean by the word *control*. In normal usage, *control* often implies some form of coercion or physical force, as in controlling a dog with a leash. In the field of psychology, however, to say that a stimulus controls a behavior simply means that it determines that behavior, or makes it more likely. A red light, for example, controls a driver at an intersection just as surely as a leash controls a dog. In asking whether behavior should be controlled, therefore, we are concerned not simply with naked physical force but with a much wider array of behavioral influences, ranging from higher pay as an inducement for taking a dangerous job, to appeals to conscience for donating to a charity.

Skinner's view.   Given this broader definition, is it right for us to use the principles of learning to control other people's behavior? According to B. F. Skinner (1955, 1971), it would be pointless to debate whether to control behavior, because behavior is already controlled. One striking example of such control involves young children, whose routine may be strictly regimented from the moment they wake up until the moment they go to sleep. The foods they eat, the times they study, the programs they watch on television, and the friends they play with all may be regulated by their parents. Sometimes this control may be exercised through rewards, sometimes through punishments. Whatever the technique, the result is often strict parental control over what a child may or may not do.

As we grow older, direct parental control diminishes and we become increasingly responsible for our actions. The question is, are we really becoming freer, or are the controls simply becoming more subtle? How many high school students, for example, would choose to spend a beautiful spring day hunched over their desks memorizing the periodic table for a chemistry class, if they were really free to act as they wished? Students who dutifully memorize tedious material do so not out of a love of learning but because of powerful social pressures. Doing well at school may earn praise from parents and teachers, respect from peers, and admission to a prestigious university, whereas failure may have serious social consequences. Although a college student may have much greater freedom in selecting courses and scheduling study time, similar pressures are still at work. No matter how much students may prefer courses in literature over calculus, for example, or how much they would prefer to read an interesting article rather than write a lab report, the constant pressure for grades still largely determines their allocation of time.

If schools represent one powerful agency of social control, an even more potent and widespread source is the government. The government is constantly controlling our behavior, both directly and indirectly, using powerful legal sanctions to win our compliance, if not always our enthusiasm. A thrifty person who might choose to risk his or her life rather than surrender a wallet with 20 dollars in it to a thief will hand over many times that amount to the Internal Revenue Service rather than risk incurring their wrath. Perhaps the most striking example of how powerfully the government can control our behavior, however, is the military draft. The disadvantages of army life even during peacetime include long periods away from family and friends, harsh and austere living conditions, and strict discipline; during a war, the conditions are infinitely worse. Presumably nothing is more important to people than their own lives, and literature and history bear eloquent witness to the fierce struggles of individuals for survival in the most hostile environments. Yet when ordered by their governments to risk their lives in conflicts they may not understand or agree with, millions of men quietly enter the army without open protest. During the American involvement in Vietnam, for example, many soldiers believed the war to be futile and deeply feared death, but they allowed themselves to go to battle, and they obeyed the orders of their officers, even when the likelihood of being killed was great.

Existing controls: the Milgram experiment.   The extent to which such obedience may be ingrained within us was dramatically illustrated in a series of experiments by Stanley Milgram (1963, 1974). Subjects were told that they were participating in a study on the effects of peer-delivered punishment on learning. They were asked to use electric shock to punish their partners whenever they made an error on a memory problem. The intensity of the shock was controlled by a series of 30 switches, ranging from 15 to 450 volts, and the experimenter instructed subjects to increase the intensity of the shock after every error by the partner, who was in an adjoining room. Unknown to the subject, the partner was actually a confederate of the experimenter and never received the shocks.

Milgram had hoped to use the highest shock intensity his subjects were willing to administer as a measure of their obedience to authority—in this case, a scientist in a white lab coat. The astonishing result, which Milgram had not anticipated, was that there were essentially no limits to his subjects' obedience. Most of them continued to administer shocks even when their partners pounded on the wall and refused to answer any questions and when the switch on the shock control panel was labeled *450 volts . . . Danger: Severe Shock.* His subjects became extremely upset as the experiment continued, some laughing hysterically and pleading with the experimenter to let them stop, but almost all continued to administer shocks when ordered to do so. One observer reported:

> I observed a mature and initially poised businessman enter the laboratory smiling and confident. Within 20 minutes he was reduced to a twitching, stuttering wreck, who was rapidly approaching the point of nervous collapse. He constantly pulled on his earlobe, and twisted his hands. At one point he pushed his fist into his forehead and muttered: "Oh, God, let's stop it." And yet he continued to respond to every word of the experimenter, and obeyed to the end.

(Milgram, 1963, p. 377)

It would be comforting to think that this willingness to obey authority was somehow anomalous—that people would not really obey authority in this way outside the laboratory—but, if anything, history suggests the opposite. One recent example comes from the My Lai massacre in South Vietnam, in which American soldiers killed hundreds of defenseless women and children. Perhaps the most surprising aspect of this tragedy was not the killing itself but the public's reaction to it. According to polls, almost 75 percent of those interviewed believed that there should be no punishment of the soldiers involved if they had acted under orders. Social control of our behavior is perhaps not as unacceptable to us, nor as unlikely, as we sometimes think.

One of the most insidious features of these controls is that they are so often invisible to us. We quickly recognize, and resist, attempts to control our behavior through coercion or punishment, but we are much less sensitive to manipulation through rewards. Imagine, for example, that a professor wanted subjects for a dangerous drug experiment and threatened to fail anyone in the class who wouldn't participate. The students would immediately recognize this as an outrageous abuse of his position and vigorously resist participation. If, however, the professor used rewards, perhaps promising participants bonus points—an example that may not be altogether unfamiliar to you—the students would offer little objection. There are, of course, important differences between these two forms of control that should not be ignored, but the important point in the present context is that they are both forms of control: In both cases, the professor is manipulating some aspect of the students' environment in order to produce a desired change in their behavior.

It is not that our behavior hasn't been controlled, argues Skinner, but that past controls have often been haphazard as well as hidden, thus giving us the *illusion* of freedom. Advances in behavioral technology, however, are making more effective control inevitable, and Skinner argues that we must begin to plan rationally the best use of these techniques if they are not to be appropriated and perverted by powerful elites. "We are all controlled by the world in which we live, and part of that world has been and will be constructed by men. The question is this: Are we to be controlled by accident, by tyrants, or by ourselves in effective cultural design?" (Skinner, 1955, p. 56).

Ends and means.   Up to a point, Skinner's arguments are persuasive. We are constantly controlling other people's behavior, even if only by smiling at them, so there seems little point in debating whether any control is acceptable. Serious issues remain, however, about which forms of control are morally acceptable and the ends to which they should be directed. To illustrate the kinds of problems that can arise, we will consider two examples. The first involves the extent to which education should focus on obedience; the second involves the morality of coercing psychiatric patients to participate in treatment.

Several early studies in education examined whether the principles of reward developed in the laboratory could be successfully applied to improve children's performance in school. The children in these studies were encouraged by a teacher to stay in their seats and work quietly; the teacher praised them when they did so. On the surface, these studies did not seem objectionable, but they were criticized in a provocative paper by Winett and Winkler (1972) for their choice of target behavior. In an article entitled "Current Behavior Modification in the Classroom: Be Still, Be Quiet, Be Docile," the authors noted that most of these early studies concentrated almost exclusively on rewarding children for sitting still and working quietly. They suggested that education might be more effective as well as more enjoyable if children were also encouraged to move around, talk with friends, and so on. Furthermore, they suggested that a more productive strategy than treating children as the passive target of control by the teacher would be to involve them in planning the reward program, including the behaviors to be changed and the rewards to be used.

Underlying this debate is a conflict over values: To what extent should education encourage children to be obedient rather than independent? There is no "right" answer to this question. Societies, and people within a society, weigh these values differently and thus may reach different conclusions. The example illustrates, however, that even seemingly straightforward attempts to modify behavior may implicitly involve subtle value judgments.

Assuming some consensus concerning the goals of a behavioral program, further difficulties may arise in choosing the methods to implement them. To illustrate this point, suppose you were on the board of governors of a state psychiatric hospital and your chief psychologist came to you for permission to implement a new therapeutic program for chronic schizophrenic patients. The staff psychologists have tried all available treatments without success, and unless a more effective treatment can be found, the patients are almost certain to spend the rest of their lives in the hospital.

Your chief psychologist proposes trying a new treatment in which patients are rewarded for engaging in appropriate behaviors such as getting out of bed, dressing themselves, and talking to other patients. The program has been tried elsewhere and has, reportedly, produced substantial improvement, with many patients recovering sufficiently to be discharged from the hospital (for example, Paul & Lentz, 1977).

However, for many of the patients in your particular hospital, very few rewards are effective, and the chief psychologist is now requesting permission to use food as a reward. According to the proposed plan, if patients engage in the desired behaviors, they will be given access to meals as a reward; if not, they will be deprived of meals for up to three days. (Although it is an unpleasant solution, such a regimen is not physically damaging.)

Would you give your chief psychologist permission to proceed? The argument in favor is that this approach may be the only chance these patients will have to lead normal lives; if you refuse, you may be condemning them to confinement in a hospital for the rest of their lives. Furthermore, maintaining a patient in a psychiatric hospital is expensive, and, in a state hospital, expenditure for this purpose may reduce the funding available for other medical programs and equipment (such as the latest brain-scan machines) that could save lives. On the other hand, is it morally acceptable to force patients to participate in a rehabilitation program against their will? If we accept the principle that society can force individuals to participate in a rehabilitation program in order to save money, there is a danger that this principle might eventually be extended to other, less palatable programs. For example, we could argue that it would be equally justifiable to kill severely handicapped children at birth, on the grounds that the funds required to care for them could be better used in saving the lives of others.

Again, there are no easy answers to such ethical dilemmas. (For further discussion, see Wexler, 1973; O'Leary, Poulos, & Devine, 1972.) It may be the case, as Skinner argues, that control of human behavior is inevitable, but it should be clear that difficult issues can arise concerning both the ends to be achieved and the means to be used. People do not like to feel controlled or manipulated (see Lefcourt, 1973), and psychologists need to understand and to respect such feelings in planning practical applications. On the other hand, it would be a mistake to exaggerate these difficulties. Serious ethical issues sometimes arise, but most applications of learning principles—such as teaching children with learning disabilities to read, finding ways to make education more fun, and helping people with problems such as alcoholism or obesity—are wholly desirable.

We have seen that psychologists study learning in part out of curiosity and in part with the expectation of gaining important practical applications. This expectation rests on the assumptions that behavior is lawful, that knowledge of these laws would increase our capacity to control behavior, and that this increase is desirable. There is considerable agreement that behavior is at least partially lawful—that the environment in which we find ourselves can substantially alter how we behave. If we could discover the laws relating behavior to the environment, there seems little doubt that our capacity to control behavior would increase, which leads us to consider the morality of such control. As Skinner argued, society already controls our behavior, so the real issue is not whether to control behavior, but how to control it—to what ends and with what means? Serious ethical issues still arise in choosing ends and means, but on the whole it seems likely that a better understanding of how people learn would allow a wide range of beneficial applications.

1.2 HOW SHOULD WE STUDY LEARNING?

The assumptions reviewed in the preceding section suggest that an understanding of the principles of learning might lead to important practical benefits. How, then, should we go about discovering these principles?

Authority

Historically, the most common answer to the problem of obtaining knowledge has been to consult an authority. Over the centuries, reliance on authorities has been a constant feature of human society, and defiance of such authorities has often been at the risk of life and limb. In ancient Greece, the heresies of Socrates led to his being poisoned with hemlock. Fifteen centuries later, Galileo's challenge of the teachings of Socrates and Aristotle (which, ironically, had become dogma) almost led to his being burned at the stake. The stifling effects of medieval orthodoxy were humorously but accurately satirized in a story by Francis Bacon, written in 1605:

> In the year of our Lord 1432, there arose a grievous quarrel among the brethren over the number of teeth in the mouth of a horse. For 13 days the disputation raged without ceasing. All the ancient books and chronicles were fetched out, and wonderful and ponderous erudition, such as was never before heard of in the region, was made manifest. At the beginning of the fourteenth day, a youthful friar of goodly bearing asked his learned superiors for permission to add a word, and straight-away, to the wonderment of the disputants, whose deep wisdom he sore vexed, he beseeched them to unbend in a manner coarse and unheard-of, and to look in the open mouth of a horse and find answer to their questionings. At this, their dignity being grievously hurt, they waxed exceedingly wroth; and, joining in a mighty uproar, they flew upon him and smote him hip and thigh, and cast him out forthwith. For, said they, surely Satan hath tempted this bold neophyte to declare unholy and unheard-of ways of finding truth contrary to all the teachings of the fathers. After many days more of grievous strife the dove of peace sat on the assembly, and they as one man, declaring the problem to be an everlasting mystery because of a grievous dearth of historical and theological evidence thereof, so ordered the same writ down.
>
> (Quoted in Munn, 1961, p. 4)

Lest you think this attack on authority to be unfounded or unduly harsh, consider the advice of the respected seventeenth-century German physician John Loselius, on the proper treatment of gout:

> Shave with a razor the hair off both legs, and at the same time cut the nails off hands and feet. This should be in the spring when the sap is flowing, and the day before the new moon. Make a hole right into the heartwood of a poplar or oak tree and insert the hair and nails. Stop it tight with a plug made of a branch of the tree, and the transplantation is perfect. Cut off close to the tree that part of the plug that sticks out, and the next day plaster the place well with cow dung. If the patient does not in the next three months feel the malum again, he can credit it to the tree.
>
> (Quoted in Roueche, 1954)

In our more skeptical era, the power of authority is no longer as absolute as it once was. Yet such authoritarian nonsense is not the exclusive province of the past. Twentieth-century medicine and science have had more than their share of absurdities, including such nightmares as prefrontal lobotomies, a widely accepted treatment for certain mental disorders involving the surgical removal of a substantial section of the brain, thereby curing patients by reducing them, in some cases, to vegetables. It should be clear that authority, whether religious, medical, or scientific, is not the last word. Indeed, even authors of textbooks have been known to err!

Introspection

An alternative means of gaining knowledge has been **introspection**, a person's examination of his or her own thoughts or feelings. We all introspect on occasion, and literature abounds with references to people "searching their souls" or "plumbing the depths of their hearts" in an attempt to understand themselves. The first systematic application of this technique, however, was the work of a German psychologist of the late nineteenth century, Wilhelm Wundt. The essence of Wundt's technique was extremely simple: Subjects were exposed to a stimulus and then asked to report the sensations aroused by it. In actual practice, however, this technique required long and arduous hours of training. It was important, for example, that a subject report not simply what he or she saw (such as a chair), but the exact sensations the object elicited, the quality and intensity of such sensations, how they changed over time, and so on.

This precise analysis of sensations is not easy. A naive observer exposed to a brightly lighted piece of coal and a dimly lighted paper, for example, will invariably report that the coal appears darker, even though physically it may actually be reflecting far more light. Observers in such cases are not reporting what they actually see but what they expected to see. Wundt's subjects underwent extended training to overcome this and similar errors. Once the observers were properly trained, Wundt hoped to use their reports to analyze the complex patterns of human thought into their constituent elements and then discover the laws by which these elements are combined to produce the richness and variety of mental life.

Though the rigorous demands of Wundt's technique now seem somewhat daunting, the underlying logic has great intuitive appeal. If we want to understand the processes of learning, what better way is there than by studying these processes at work within our own minds? In the end, we must all rely on the judgment of our senses—it is a brave person who strides forward when his or her eyes tell of an abyss ahead. In the same way that our peripheral senses provide us with our most reliable information about the external world, introspection would seem to be the best guide to the world of the mind.

The limits of conscious awareness.   Yet, despite its obvious attractions, introspection gradually fell into progressively greater disrepute, until eventually it almost disappeared from psychology. One reason for this collapse was that even as Wundt was painstakingly beginning to train his subjects, a Viennese physician named Sigmund Freud was developing his revolutionary theories—theories that, in an offhand way, were ultimately to destroy the rationale for introspection. Freud exposed for the first time the Byzantine world of the unconscious, its primitive swirl of emotions hidden from consciousness behind powerful defensive barriers. This metaphor of hidden, subterranean forces had devastating implications for introspection, attacking its very foundations: a faith in the accessibility of all thought to conscious analysis. Unless every aspect of human thought and emotion could be observed and analyzed, introspection could at best provide only an incomplete and fragmented picture of the causal mechanisms of behavior. And Freud's theories suggested that consciousness was but the visible tip of the iceberg, with vast areas of the mind forever hidden in the murky depths of the subconscious.

Freud's theories suggested for the first time that there might be severe limits to the power of conscious analysis, but it seems likely that these limits would have become apparent in any case. Consider, for example, what happens when you try to prove a geometry theorem. You may struggle for minutes or even hours, doggedly searching for a solution, when suddenly the correct answer occurs to you. What happened exactly? How did you suddenly pass from a state of complete and utter confusion to one of confidence in the right answer? Clearly some important mental processes intervened between these two states, but, introspectively, all is a blank, your mind an empty vacuum from which the correct solution emerged as if by spontaneous generation. To take an even more homely example, how is it that we are able to control and coordinate our bodily movements? Try, for example, to introspect as you repeatedly flex your thumb. Concentrate intensely and try to feel every sensation. You may be able to feel your thumb's movement, but can you feel the command that initiates that movement? What is making your thumb move? What is the link between your eyes scanning this page and the actual flexing of your thumb in that far-off extremity? Our inability to trace the processes involved even in such simple acts as thumb flexing suggests serious limits to the usefulness of introspection in analyzing complex thought and learning.

The problem of confirming reports.   Considerations such as these suggest that introspection can at best play only a limited role in helping us understand behavior. It would seem, however, that we should at least be able to use introspection in analyzing that fraction of our experience that is accessible to consciousness. Again, however, critics have raised serious objections to the use of introspection even in this limited domain. The problem, fundamentally, is one of confirmability: How are we to confirm the accuracy of an introspective report when it is based on private events that are inaccessible to any outside observer? If a person says she or he is feeling angry, for example, how do we know whether the person is really feeling anger or fear, or perhaps some subtle combination of the two?

It may seem churlish to question the honesty of such a report (isn't a person the best judge of her or his own feelings?), but studies of perception in other situations suggest a need for greater caution. Just as our visual senses may not be flawless—the moon is *not* larger at the horizon, and desert oases glimpsed from afar have a dismaying tendency to recede as we approach—so, too, introspection may yield data that are not necessarily accurate.

The problem of evaluating observers' reports is not, of course, unique to introspection. A person who says he feels hungry is really no different from a scientist who reports seeing a rat or, for that matter, a flying saucer. Each of these statements is simply a report of subjective experience; the fact that the stimulus for one example originated outside the body rather than inside it does not give the former report any greater validity. Whatever the original stimulus for these reports, we are faced with the problem of evaluating their accuracy—that is, evaluating how closely the original events and the verbal reports correspond.

Reports of external events can be confirmed by establishing either their reliability (for example, by comparing the reports with those of other observers in the same situation) or their consistency with other data (for example, radar reports in the case of flying saucers). In the case of introspective reports, however, confirmation is not quite so easy. To start with, how are we to estimate the reliability of an introspective observer when no other observer can detect the private events on which the report is based? We might expose two observers to the same external stimulus, in the hope that it will produce essentially identical experiences in both observers, thus allowing comparison of their reports, but what if their accounts differ? Imagine, for example, that we show two observers a colored card, and one observer says the card is green while the other insists it is red. How can we tell which observer is correct, or whether neither or both are correct? (Color blindness may produce different but equally valid sensations.)

Nor is this dilemma simply academic, for precisely such disagreements arose as different schools of introspectionists clashed. In the classic controversy over "imageless thought," for example, there were angry debates as to whether thinking is necessarily accompanied by imagery, with the two sides reporting opposite results. Oswald Külpe argued for the existence of imageless thought by pointing to abstract words such as *meaning*, which, he claimed, produce no conscious image. The psychologist Edward Titchener, on the other hand, insisted that if you introspected carefully enough, even the most abstract words would produce images. In the case of *meaning*, for example, he reported seeing "the blue-grey tip of a kind of scoop which has a bit of yellow about it (probably a part of the handle) and which is digging into a dark mass of what appears to be plastic material" (Titchener, 1915, p. 519). This image had its origins, he suggested, in injunctions from his youth to "dig out the meaning" of Latin and Greek phrases.

Evaluation.   The realization that much of the mind's functioning is unconscious, coupled with the difficulty of reliably observing even those areas that ostensibly are conscious, led eventually to the virtual abandonment of introspection as a scientific technique. Do not conclude that introspection is totally without value. It is still a fertile, if informal, technique for generating hypotheses about the causes of behavior, and it can sometimes provide confirmable information that can be highly valuable. (See, for example, Lieberman, 1979.) For the most part, however, psychologists have abandoned introspection as a systematic technique for acquiring knowledge.

In thus rejecting introspection, we must admit that we seem to be turning our backs on much of the richness and fascination of the mental world—indeed, of the entire world, for what else does any of us directly know or experience besides the workings of our own minds? It is perhaps worth emphasizing, therefore, that this rejection was not prompted by petulance, or by a Calvinistic desire to make psychology seem cold or dreary. Psychology originated as a branch of philosophy, and for centuries it was concerned exclusively with the contents and processes of the mind. These genuinely fascinating problems were finally put aside only when psychologists became convinced that direct study of the mind was futile so long as observers could not reach agreement on even its most elementary properties. In domains where agreement is obtainable, introspection can still serve as a useful tool; but for the substantial areas of mental functioning that are unconscious, it can play little role.

As psychologists lost faith in efforts to observe the mind directly, they turned instead to objective observations of behavior. An objective observation, in this sense, is simply one on which all observers can agree. "The sun set at 5:08," for example, is an objective report, because it is at least potentially confirmable by independent observers, whereas "I felt hungry at 5:08" is not an objective report. Note that an objective report is not necessarily any more valid than a subjective one: Subjective reports may be quite true (if, for example, I really was hungry at 5:08), and, conversely, objective reports may be quite false (the sunset might have been an optical illusion that deceived everyone). By focusing on behavior that could be described objectively, however, psychologists hoped at the very least to be able to agree on their data, thus allowing theories to be evaluated in terms of solid evidence rather than by the eloquence or authority of the opposing theorists. The advantages of consensus could only be purchased at a price—the exclusion of most introspective evidence from the subject matter of psychology—but the bargain seemed a good one to psychologists weary of decades of futile controversy.

1.3 THE EXPERIMENTAL METHOD

The new concern with behavior was accompanied by an increasing emphasis on experimentation. Instead of passively observing behavior in the hope of noticing what antecedent conditions might have caused it, the essence of the experimental approach is to actively manipulate those conditions. The aspect of the environment that we manipulate is called the **independent variable**, and the behavior we observe is called the **dependent variable**. In outline, then, the experimental method consists simply of manipulating some independent variable and observing its effect on some dependent variable. A consistent relationship between them—for example, environmental variable A is always followed by behavior B—is called a **law**.

If experimentation were really so simple, discovering the laws of behavior should be easy: All we would have to do would be to manipulate our independent variables, observe their effects, and combine the resultant laws into a comprehensive account of behavior. The problem is that *we must manipulate only one independent variable at a time*. If several independent variables changed simultaneously (see Figure 1.1), then it would be impossible to say which one was responsible for the resulting behavior. As we shall see, however, it is extraordinarily difficult to ensure that only one independent variable changes at a time.

A Hypothetical Experiment

To illustrate the kinds of problems that can arise, consider the following example. Suppose that a psychologist reported a new and highly effective treatment for severe depression. The fundamental cause of depression, she argued, was a lack of self-confidence. Therefore, what psychologists need is a way of bolstering people's self-confidence. To this end, she arranged for her patients to participate in weekend expeditions in which they engaged in demanding physical sports—mountaineering, canoeing, sailing, and so on—and found that they could overcome difficult problems. At the end of one year's treatment, she reported, 93 percent of the participants in her program were substantially or fully recovered.

On the basis of this evidence, would you conclude that the new therapy

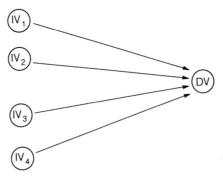

F I G U R E 1.1   Four independent variables (IVs) simultaneously influencing a dependent variable (DV).

was effective? According to the logic of the experimental method, you would first need to satisfy yourself that no other variable had been present that could have accounted for the observed improvement. In the following section, we will consider several alternative explanations, but before proceeding to that section you may find it fun to see how many of these explanations you can think of by yourself. Assume that you had conclusive evidence that patients who received the treatment improved; what other evidence would you want before you would recommend this expensive treatment to a friend who is severely depressed?

The Search for Alternative Explanations

Time.   One independent variable that could account for the improvement observed in this study is the building of self-confidence, but another variable is simply the passage of time. Depression is rarely a permanent condition, and the patients might have improved just as much had they simply been left alone for one year.

In situations in which more than one independent variable is present, the simplest way to determine the effects of one of these variables is to physically eliminate the others. If you found that an injection of penicillin and Aureomycin was effective in treating flu, for example, then, to evaluate the contribution of penicillin on its own, you could remove Aureomycin from the injection. This elimination strategy, however, cannot be applied to our depression example because there is no way of "eliminating" time: Patients cannot be given confidence-boosting experiences without time also passing.

In cases in which an unwanted variable cannot be eliminated physically, its effects may instead be neutralized through the use of an appropriate control group. To eliminate time as a factor, we could arrange for a control group that receives only the passage of time (that is, is left untreated for a year). In effect, both treatment and control groups would receive the time variable, but only the experimental group would receive the treatment in which we are primarily interested.

experimental group: time + confidence building
control group: time

If at the end of the year the experimental group showed substantially more improvement, this difference could not be explained by the passage of time, since both groups received equal exposure to this variable. This design, in other words, controls for the effect of time by arranging for it to affect both groups equally: If the groups still differ, some factor other than time must be at work.

Subject expectations.   Suppose, then, that we ran our proposed experiment and found that the experimental group still improved substantially more: Could we now conclude that confidence building is an effective treatment for depression? Again, the answer is no, because other independent variables are present in the experimental group and could account for the improvement. One such variable is subject expectations. When subjects are asked to participate in a treatment program, they typically assume that the treatment is likely to be effective; otherwise, the experimenter would not waste time investigating it. Such expectations of improvement may themselves be sufficient to produce improvement. In the field of medicine, for example, studies of cold medicines have repeatedly shown that most of the popular remedies have no direct effect; it is the fact that patients expect to improve that underlies any improvement, with placebos (pills that have no active ingredients) being just as effective as commercial products that do have active ingredients.

Another example of the importance of subject expectations comes from studies of hypnosis, in which hypnotized subjects can often perform quite remarkable feats such as lying rigid between two chairs while supporting a great weight, or withstanding intense pain. Most, if not all, of these feats have been found to be due to subjects' expectations: When subjects believe that they can do something, this belief allows them to perform feats that normally would be beyond their ability. When nonhypnotized subjects are told that they really can perform these feats, their performances match those of hypnotized subjects (Barber, 1976).

In our depression experiment, then, subjects might have improved simply because they expected to, rather than because of any real increase in self-confidence engendered by sailing, climbing, and so on. To control for this possibility, we could redesign the study so that all subjects would expect to improve equally, whether or not they received the experimental treatment. We might rerun the experimental group but compare it with a control group that also receives a highly plausible treatment (for example, weekly injections of vitamins, explained on the basis that vitamin deficiency plays a crucial role in depression). If the only factor in this experiment is expectation of improvement, both groups should improve equally. If we again found substantially greater improvement in the experimental group, could we now conclude that confidence building is an effective therapy for depression?

Experimenter expectations.   You may not be altogether surprised to hear that the answer is again no. Although our experimental and control groups are matched in terms of subject expectations, they may still differ in terms of experimenter expectations. That is, the experimenter who ran the study might have believed in the importance of self-confidence, and thus expected the experimental group to improve more.

At this point you could be forgiven if you were beginning to feel exasper-

ated. We seem to be nitpicking. Even if an experimenter did expect one group to do better than another, could this really have determined the outcome of the experiment? Surprisingly, the answer is yes. In an experiment by Rosenthal (1966), for example, subjects were shown pictures of faces and asked to rate them in terms of whether they appeared to be of successful people. (The rating scale ranged from -10 for faces of people thought to be very unsuccessful to $+10$ for faces of people looking very successful.) Each group of about a dozen subjects was read standard instructions and then shown slides of the different faces. The study used different experimenters for the different groups, and these experimenters were led to expect different outcomes. One group of experimenters was told that they were being given a special set of subjects who would probably produce positive scores, whereas a second group of experimenters was led to expect negative scores. In fact, subjects were assigned to the experimenters at random. Under these circumstances, could experimenter expectations make any difference? The results were that they did: Experimenters expecting positive results obtained significantly higher scores than did those expecting negative results. Thus, despite the fact that all subjects saw the same faces and were read the same instructions, their ratings of the faces were strongly influenced by what their experimenters expected.

How could an experimenter's expectations affect a subject's evaluation of a picture? We know very little about the underlying processes, but some evidence suggests that subtle cues from the experimenter may be involved. One of the classic examples of such cues is the case of Clever Hans. (See Pfungst, 1965.) Hans was a horse that lived on a farm in Germany at the turn of the century. Hans wasn't an ordinary horse, though: He was the only horse in Germany that could add! When asked the sum of two plus two, for example, Hans would slowly begin to tap the ground, one, two, three, four . . . and then stop. Nor was this simply a trick he had memorized, because he could add virtually any numbers, and it didn't even matter who asked the question. Moreover, addition wasn't his only skill: He was equally proficient at subtraction and, incredibly, multiplication and division. An obvious explanation for his prowess was some sort of signal from his master, but when a blue-ribbon panel of experts convened to investigate Hans's extraordinary powers, they found that the master's absence had no effect on Hans's performance.

The explanation for Hans's apparent genius was eventually discovered in a brilliant series of experiments by Oscar Pfungst, a German psychologist. Pfungst found that Hans's accuracy was considerably reduced if the person who asked the question didn't know the correct answer. Furthermore, the further away the questioner stood, the less accurate was Hans's answer. Finally, putting blinders around Hans's eyes totally destroyed his performance. Clearly, Hans could answer questions only if he could see someone who knew the correct answer. But what possible visual cues could the questioner have been providing? The answer, Pfungst discovered, was that questioners tilted their heads

slightly forward as they finished their questions, and this was Hans's cue to begin tapping. As the tapping approached the correct answer, the observers tended to straighten up in anticipation, and this slight tensing was Hans's cue to stop. Hans was extraordinarily sensitive to such cues, responding to the raising of eyebrows or even the dilation of nostrils, and Pfungst was eventually able to control Hans's tapping completely by producing these cues deliberately. Hans truly was an extraordinary horse, but his genius lay more in his powers of observation than in any arithmetic ability.

And now, at long last . . .   Let us now return to our depression experiment. Suppose that we redesigned our experiment yet again to ensure that the experimenter who ran the study expected both groups to improve equally, and we again found substantially greater improvement in the experimental group. Now, at long last, would we have proved that building self-confidence is an effective treatment for depression? Yet again, the answer is no. Why not? What other variable could possibly have been present? It is not easy to identify other variables, but the fact that we can't identify alternative explanations doesn't prove that there aren't any. The blue-ribbon panel was unable to find any plausible explanation for Hans's dazzling performance, but that didn't prove that it was the result of a genuine mastery of arithmetic. In a similar vein, for centuries naturalists were unable to explain the mysterious ability of bats to navigate in total darkness, but that didn't prove that it was the result of some occult power. (The discovery of radar in the 1930s eventually led to the solution.) An experiment, in other words, can never *prove* that a particular explanation is correct, because it is always possible that some alternative explanation will eventually be found.

The Nature of Scientific Progress

We started with a seemingly simple experiment, but the more we analyzed it, the more alternative explanations for its outcome we identified. This is always the case. The goal of the experimental method is to change only one independent variable at a time, but this ideal can never be fully realized. We can control for the effects of particular variables, such as time and subject expectations, but there are always changes that we cannot control—fluctuations in humidity, the occurrence of sunspots, the death of an earthworm in China. The fact that we cannot control for all possible variables has some important implications for the nature of scientific progress.

The slowness of scientific progress.   One implication concerns the slowness and confusion with which science sometimes progresses. A popular image of science has the scientist in an antiseptic white lab coat, progressing inexorably through rigorous analyses. In practice, scientific progress is often much more

confused and halting. As we have seen, it is impossible to control for all possible variables; we can only control for those variables that seem most important. Our notions of what variables are important, however, are often wrong. For example, one of the most dangerous things a woman in Victorian England could do was enter a maternity hospital; many thousands of women died every year after giving birth. When Joseph Lister suggested that doctors could prevent these deaths if they washed their hands with soap, his proposal was greeted with incredulity: How could washing hands with boiled-down animal fat prevent a woman from dying? Now, with our greater understanding of the existence and nature of germs, his suggestion makes sense, but at the time it seemed utterly preposterous. Similarly, in the case of Clever Hans, few would have believed beforehand that a horse could be so sensitive to minute changes in people's postures.

There is thus a built-in Catch-22 to scientific progress: To discover scientific laws, you must control all important variables; unfortunately, you can only identify what variables are important if you already know the laws. This problem is not insurmountable. We just have to plug away, identifying important variables as best we can in experiments that may initially lack important controls. This bootstrapping process means that progress may initially be slow and frustrating as we struggle to identify the important variables.

The need for humility.   A second implication of the difficulty of controlling all variables is the need for some caution, and even humility, in interpreting experimental evidence. However certain we may be that a particular explanation is correct, it is always possible that it will eventually be superceded by a better explanation. The astronomer Ptolemy, for example, believed that the earth was the center of the universe, with the sun and stars revolving around it. Using a model based on this assumption, he was able to predict the movements of the planets through the sky with remarkable success. His model was sufficiently accurate to allow sailors to use it to navigate the seas for more than 1400 years, even though we now know that his theory was totally wrong. Similarly, Newton's theory of gravity has been one of the cornerstones of modern physics, but this did not prevent Einstein from developing a theory of relativity that fundamentally recast some of Newton's most basic assumptions about the nature of time, space, and gravity. In interpreting scientific evidence, then, we need to recognize that even the best scientific explanations may be wrong—or, at any rate, incomplete.

The artificiality of experiments.   A third implication of our analysis concerns the inherent artificiality of experiments. To isolate the effects of one variable, you need to hold others constant, but the more you control the environment, the less like real life it becomes. The underlying strategy is summarized in Figure 1.2: You start with a complex environment and, by *analysis*, try to break

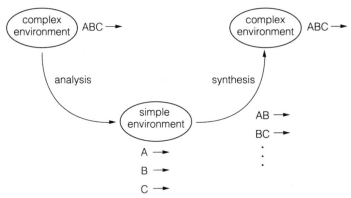

F I G U R E 1.2   Using the experimental method, the experimenter analyzes a complex environment to isolate variables and then synthesizes the variables in progressively more complex combinations.

this complex environment into simpler ones so you can study the effects of constituent elements (A, B, C, and so on) one at a time. Then, once you have determined the effects of each variable on its own, you use the method of *synthesis* to begin recombining them, studying what happens when two or more variables act together (AB, ABC, and so on). The scientific method thus proceeds by first analyzing complex environments into simpler ones, then gradually returning to the more complex environment that was the original focus of interest.

In the case of psychology, most research is still analytical, with the result that it is very easy to feel depressed by its artificiality. "It's all so meaningless," you might say. "What does the behavior of a student in an artificial laboratory setting have to do with real life?" The answer lies in the assumptions we have been tracing in this chapter. If behavior is lawful, and if the best way of discovering these laws is through well-controlled experiments, then eventually the principles discovered in these artificial settings will help us understand behavior in the more complex conditions of the real world.

In other sciences, this faith in the experimental method has paid off handsomely. In genetics, for example, Gregor Mendel discovered the principles of genetics by studying how the color of pea flowers determined the colors of their progeny. In one sense, his experiments were highly artificial: Peas and humans would seem to have little in common. By studying the transmission of traits in this simple setting, however, geneticists have been able to identify genetic principles that also apply to the vastly more complex genetic system of humans, an advance that has already made possible test-tube babies, as well as significant progress toward the cloning of humans from single cells. In less than 100 years, we have moved from the investigation of the garden pea to an understanding of some of the most profound mysteries of human life.

1.4 THE USE OF ANIMALS

Having decided to study the laws of learning, and to do so through careful experimentation, we now come to the question of what species to study. If our goal is to understand human behavior, the answer might seem obvious: We should study humans. Given the blinding clarity of this logic, why have psychologists often studied animals instead?

The Advantages to Using Animals

Control of the environment.   The reasons that psychologists study animals are complex, but all are rooted in the problems of experimental control discussed in the last section. We said then that one of the crucial problems in psychological research is to manipulate only one independent variable at a time while holding all others constant. In practice, this requires extensive control over the subject's environment. For both moral and practical reasons, such control is easier to attain with animal subjects than with human subjects.

For example, one problem of considerable importance in human behavior concerns the effects of a child's early environment on her or his development. Freudians have long argued that the first years of life may be crucial in determining personality. More recently, educators have suggested that early sensory and social deprivation may be an important factor in the poor school performance of some children (particularly from underprivileged homes) and have urged governments to invest in compensatory childcare programs for young children. How are we to determine whether the role of early experience is really so crucial and, if so, which aspects are most important? To determine the importance of early sensory experience, for example, should we run controlled experiments in which half the children are reared normally while the other half are permanently confined to a barren environment, devoid of all stimuli? Similarly, to determine the importance of a mother's role in a child's normal development, should we compare children reared with their mothers to children taken away from their mothers and reared with no mother substitutes? Such experiments would hardly be humane or practical. The questions involved are of critical importance, with serious implications for the future structure of our schools and even our families, but the experiments necessary to answer such questions are clearly unacceptable.

Using animals as subjects, however, psychologists have conducted experiments to answer precisely these questions, with often fascinating results. Harry Harlow, for example, has reported a series of experiments in which infant rhesus monkeys were reared in varying degrees of social isolation. When taken away from their mothers immediately after birth and reared in total isolation, these infants became highly neurotic, spending much of their time huddled in corners, rocking back and forth and sucking their thumbs. Furthermore, this

pattern of disturbed behavior persisted into adulthood, and most were unable to function normally in a group, or even to mate.

These early studies supported the critical role of early experience in social development, and in later experiments Harlow and others isolated some important variables. The presence of the mother, for example, is not necessarily critical; infants taken away from their mothers but reared with other infants show significantly less disturbance (Harlow & Harlow, 1965). Another finding, with poignant social implications for certain humans, is that male rhesus monkeys, which normally play an insignificant role in child rearing, can, if necessary, replace the mother with no apparent ill effects to either child or father (Mitchell & Brandt, 1972).

A similar line of experiments has examined the role of early sensory experience in the development of rats. Some rats were reared in "enriched" environments that included other rats and a variety of toys, platforms, colors, and sounds; other rats were reared in "deprived" environments that lacked these stimuli. It was found that animals reared in the enriched environments developed larger brains (Rosenzweig, 1984), with considerably more complex interconnections among their neurons (Turner & Greenough, 1985). These results suggest that early stimulation plays a critical role in the brain's development and thus in our capacity for learning in later life.

Simpler systems.   One advantage of using animals as subjects, then, is that we can more easily control their environments and thus determine which variables are important. A related advantage is that of studying simpler systems. To isolate the effects of a single variable, one strategy is to control the environment so that few variables will be present; an alternative strategy is to study a simpler system, in which fewer variables exert an influence. Suppose, for example, that you wanted to understand the principles of electronics. You would obviously find it easier to understand these principles if you began by studying a transistor radio rather than a giant computer: The simpler the system, the easier it is to understand its operations. Thus, scientists were able to isolate the fundamental principles of genetics by first studying two lower life forms—the fruit fly and the pea—that offer simpler systems. If, instead, they had first tried to understand these principles in a more complex system—for example, the inheritance of human intelligence, which is almost certainly influenced by many thousands of genes—it is unlikely that they would yet have learned much at all about the principles of genetic transmission.

The simpler the system, the easier it is to determine its fundamental principles. Determining the principles of behavior in animals, however, can help us to understand human behavior only if these principles are similar. Is this assumption justified? Do the principles of learning in rats or even monkeys have any relevance for human behavior?

Is Animal and Human Behavior Similar?

Throughout history, the notion that animals and humans are similar would have been met with indignation and disbelief, but in 1859 Charles Erasmus Darwin published a book that for the first time challenged the complacent view of human beings that they are the unique culmination of creation. Darwin dared to suggest that human beings are not unique, that they are only one of many species of animals on Earth, all shaped by the same environmental forces and evolved from the same common ancestors. It follows that, if humans and other animals are so closely related, important similarities must exist between them.

Biologically, the proof was not long in coming; indeed, much of it had already been assembled. Despite the incredible diversity of animal species (there are now thought to be more than three million species, ranging in size from virtually invisible microorganisms to the mammoth blue whale, whose tongue alone weighs more than an elephant), the underlying biological principles are surprisingly similar. Our understanding of human neurophysiology, for example, is built largely on the pioneering work of Hodgkin and Huxley on the giant squid. Similarly, our understanding of human vision is based on Hartline and Ratliff's investigations of the eye of the horseshoe crab, a primitive species almost unchanged from primordial times. And when we begin to examine species more closely related to humans, the similarities become even greater. The basic principles of digestion, vision, respiration, locomotion, and so forth are, for all practical purposes, identical across the various mammalian species. Indeed, it is precisely because of this fundamental equivalence that modern medicine has been able to develop so quickly. The drugs and surgical techniques upon which our lives now depend were generally pioneered not with people, but with mice, monkeys, and the famous guinea pig—that much put-upon rodent whose name has become synonymous with the concept of experimentation.

Tool use.   For post-Darwin scientists, there seemed little question of the fundamental similarity of animals and people, at least in terms of physical construction. Behaviorally, on the other hand, this similarity was less obvious. Even if humans had once been a simple ape, so the argument went, they had long since begun a unique evolutionary path that left them the only animal capable of using tools, of transmitting culture, and of symbolic communication. More recently, however, evidence has accumulated that human beings are not unique even in these areas. Chimpanzees, for example, use twigs to reach into termite nests and gather the tiny insects to eat. Nor is this use of tools fortuitous: If an appropriate twig is not available, the chimp will modify one until it is of the correct size and shape (Goodall–van Lawick, 1968).

It might be argued that only higher primates such as chimpanzees have the capacity to use tools, but even this no longer appears to be true. On the

Galapagos Islands, where Darwin did much of his research, there is a finch that faces a problem similar to that of the chimpanzee. The finch likes to eat insects that live under the bark of trees; although it can drill a hole through the bark, its beak is not long enough to catch its prey. The finch solves this problem by searching for a cactus spine and then, holding it in its beak, poking the spine around the hole. When the surprised insect emerges, the finch drops the spine and quickly eats the insect. And, like the chimpanzee, the finch is selective in its approach, rejecting spines that are not the right size for the hole it wishes to attack (Millikan & Bowman, 1967). As these and other instances of tool use and even culture were reported (Miyadi, 1964), it became increasingly clear that humans are not unique even in these abilities, although we still seemed to be the only animals with a sophisticated language and the intellectual capacities that language implies.

Language.   Perhaps the final step in the evolution of our species' self-image stemming from Darwin may have begun in 1969 with the publication in the journal *Science* of an article by Allan Gardner and Beatrice Gardner. The article reported their efforts over the preceding two years to teach a baby chimpanzee named Washoe to use sign language. The results were dramatic. Washoe quickly learned a great many signs and used them reliably in a wide variety of situations. The sign for *dog*, for example, was elicited by a wide variety of dogs, both alive and in pictures, and even by the barking of a dog that could not be seen. (See also Savage-Rumbaugh, 1986.)

Problem solving.   The degree to which the linguistic skills of Washoe and other chimpanzees resemble those of humans is controversial. (See Terrace, 1985; Gardner & Gardner, 1985.) There is little doubt, however, that the cognitive capacities of chimpanzees and other animals are far greater than was previously believed.

In one experiment, for example, Premack and Woodruff (1978) showed Sarah, a chimpanzee, videotapes of humans struggling to solve a problem. In one of those situations, illustrated in Figure 1.3, a man is trying to escape from a locked cage. After the videotape was over, Sarah was shown a set of pictures suggesting possible solutions—for example, a picture of a key and of an irrelevant object such as an electric plug—and asked to choose one; the experimenter remained outside the room, so as not to influence her choice. The result was that Sarah chose the correct solution every time. In a second experiment, the choices were made more difficult; for example, a phonograph was not working, and Sarah was shown pictures of a plug attached to a wall, an unattached plug, and an attached plug that had been cut. Again, Sarah's performance was essentially perfect; she chose the correct solution for 11 out of 12 problems.

To solve these problems, Sarah had to understand the nature of the problem confronting the person, the correct solution, and the fact that she was

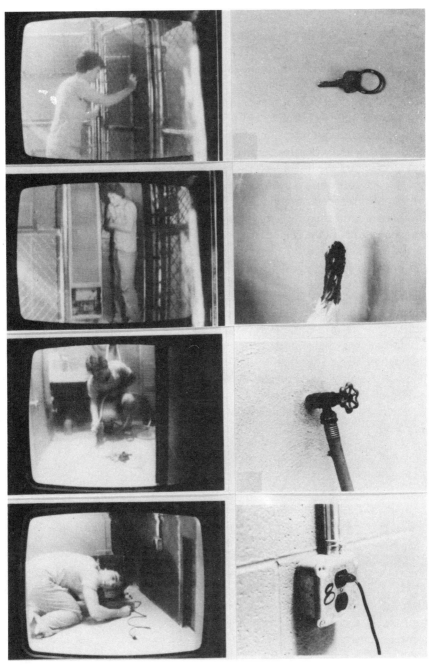

FIGURE 1.3 The pictures on the left are taken from four videotaped enactments of problems: trying to escape from a locked cage, shivering after struggling with a malfunctioning heater, attempting to wash a floor with no water emerging from the hose, and trying to play a phonograph. After seeing each of these 30-second videotapes, the chimpanzee was offered a choice between two of the four pictures shown on the right: a key, a lit torch, a hose connected to a faucet, and a plug connected to a wall socket. (Premack & Woodruff, 1978)

being asked to provide a solution. (After all, the pictures could have been presented simply to determine which one she liked best.) The solutions had never been taught deliberately to Sarah; she could have learned them only by observing routine activities in the laboratory. Sarah's performance under these conditions suggests a remarkably high level of intelligence.

Nor is a sophisticated capacity for learning confined to primates. Pigeons, for example, are capable of learning complex concepts (see Chapter 13), and many species are capable of feats of memory that would put most humans to shame. Clark's nutcracker, for example, is a species of finch that hides seeds in caches during the summer and then retrieves them during the winter. It typically hides from 5,000 to 10,000 caches each summer and is able to remember the locations of these caches with almost uncanny accuracy (Vander Wall, 1982).

This does not mean that humans are indistinguishable from other species, nor that all or even most research into learning should be done with animals. Humans are unique, and it would be foolish to expect to gain a complete understanding of people from the study of pigeons or white rats. Because humans and other species have shared millions of years of evolution in common, however, it would be surprising if they were not similar in important respects, and the available evidence supports this assumption.

Ethical Issues

We have seen that the use of animal subjects in experiments can have significant advantages. Because of the possibility of more stringent control over the environment, we can analyze phenomena in animals that, for moral or practical reasons, might otherwise be inaccessible. Insofar as the learning processes in animals are simpler, this can actually be an advantage, since we can more easily analyze these processes. On the other hand, the similarity of animal and human behavior means that we must take seriously the ethical issues raised by the use of animals in experiments. If animals are similar to us in intelligence, and presumably also in feelings, how can we justify confining them in cages and, in some cases, subjecting them to painful stimuli such as electric shock?

One view is that such research cannot be justified, because animals are living creatures with just as much right to life and freedom as humans have. This position is attractive in its strong value for all life, but few people hold it in its pure form. Suppose, for example, that you had a child who contracted rabies, and that the only way to obtain a vaccine to save the child's life required killing a mouse. Would you do it? Very few people faced with this dilemma would not choose to save the child, implicitly valuing a child's life above that of a mouse.

Rightly or wrongly, then, most people do value human welfare above that of animals, but this does not imply that animal life is worthless. Thus, the

problem remains of deciding whether the benefits of particular experiments with animals outweigh the cost to the animals. To assess this, we need some method of quantifying both the benefits and the costs; in practice, though, this is difficult if not impossible. Suppose, for example, that we wanted to assess the cost to the subjects of an experiment on the effects of punishment. How could we decide how much pain a rat would experience if it were given an electric shock? What if we substituted a fish or a cockroach as the experimental subject? Do they also feel pain? If so, is it more or less than that experienced by the rat?

If it is difficult to find any objective way of assessing the costs of animal research, it can be equally difficult to assess its benefits. In our hypothetical rabies example, we assumed that killing the mouse would save the life of the child, but the benefits of experiments are rarely this predictable. Experiments that seem minor at the time they are performed may eventually have momentous theoretical and practical benefits. In a study by Comroe and Dripps (1977), for example, physicians were asked to rate the ten most important advances in cardiovascular and pulmonary medicine and surgery that had benefited their patients. A total of 663 studies were found to have been crucial in leading to these breakthroughs; 42 percent of them involved experiments that, at the time they were reported, seemed totally unrelated to the later clinical application. When doing basic research, it is difficult to predict what benefits may eventually be derived from enhanced understanding of a fundamental mechanism.

In deciding whether a planned experiment is justifiable, then, it is difficult to assess either the costs to the animals used or the long-term benefits that might accrue. There are no simple guidelines; all we can say here is that an assessment of the benefits to be gained depends heavily on the validity of the assumptions discussed in this chapter. If behavior is lawful, if experimental research is the best way to discover these laws, and if animal and human behavior is similar in important respects, then research on animals may play an important role in increasing our understanding of human behavior and thus alleviating human suffering.

1.5 VARIETIES OF LEARNING

There is one final question that needs to be addressed—namely, what this book is about. This may seem fairly obvious; its title, after all, is *Learning*. The problem is that learning is such a vast topic; it affects almost everything we do—from learning to tie our shoelaces when we are young to studying chemistry at college or learning how to make friends. It is thus impossible to cover every aspect of learning in a single course, and it has become customary to study different aspects in different courses: Courses on developmental psychology deal with one aspect, courses on educational psychology with another, courses on memory and cognition a third, and so on.

Within this division, courses on learning generally concentrate on a particular form of learning called *associative learning*. To explain what associative learning is, we will begin by examining what we mean by the broader term *learning*.

Reflexes and Learning

Some stimuli always elicit the same reaction. If you accidentally touch a hot pan, for example, it will make you pull your hand back every time; if a sudden gust of wind hits you in the eye, it will make you blink every time. In cases like this, in which a stimulus always elicits the same response, we call the stimulus-response relationship a **reflex**.

Habituation.   Our definition of a reflex states that the stimulus always elicits the same response, but under some conditions the strength of a reflexive response may change with experience. Suppose, for example, that you were quietly studying in your room one day when you suddenly heard a deafening noise—a particularly hideous burglar alarm in the building next door to you had just gone off. This sudden, intense noise would almost certainly make you jump, a reaction that is known as the startle reflex. The first time it happened, your reaction would be very intense, but if it happened again five minutes later, you would probably react less strongly; a third repetition would produce even less of a reaction, and so on. This decrease in the strength of a reflex when the stimulus is repeated a number of times is called **habituation**; it is a common characteristic of reflexes, especially when the stimulus is repeated within a relatively short period of time.

One experiment illustrating habituation was reported by Davis (1974). He placed rats in a cage that was mounted on springs, so that if they made a sudden movement he could measure the magnitude of this movement by measuring the movement of the floor. He then presented a loud tone to the rats a number of times. As shown in Figure 1.4a, he found that the tone initially produced a strong startle response, but that the magnitude of this response decreased over successive presentations.

Why do our reactions to stimuli sometimes habituate when the stimuli occur repeatedly? One possible explanation might be that the muscles involved in the response become fatigued with repeated use. Although muscle fatigue certainly can happen, it is easy to show that fatigue is not the cause of habituation by introducing a new startling stimulus. Suppose, for example, that after you had grown accustomed to the endlessly malfunctioning burglar alarm, you suddenly heard an explosion: You would probably jump just as energetically as when you first heard the burglar alarm. Your failure to respond to the alarm was not due to an inability to respond; rather, you became habituated to the particular stimulus that was repeated.

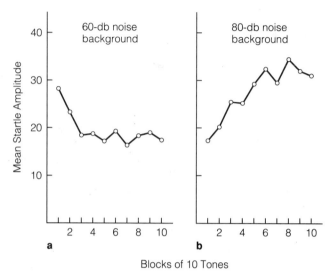

F I G U R E 1.4 Magnitude of the startle response of rats to successive presentations of a tone: (a) tone presented against the background of a 60-dB noise; (b) tone presented against the background of an 80-dB noise. (Davis, 1974)

A second possible explanation for a reduction in responding could be fatigue in the sensory system, or what is more properly called *sensory adaptation*. If a bright light were repeatedly flashed in your eye, for example, this would cause a decrease in the capacity of your sensory receptors to respond. Again, it is fairly easy to show that this is not what is involved in habituation. Suppose, for example, that your neighbor's burglar alarm went off every five minutes on the dot, and after several hours you had become so thoroughly habituated to this stimulus that you barely heard it any more. If it now went off 30 seconds after the previous alarm, you would almost certainly jump again: You had become habituated to the alarm's going off at a particular time, but if the alarm went off at an unexpected time it would again elicit a startle response.

Learning.　Habituation, then, is not due to fatigue in either the senses or the muscles; by elimination, it seems to involve some sort of change in the nervous system that links them. Specifically, habituation seems to involve learning that a potentially dangerous stimulus is not, in fact, followed by any harmful experience, and thus that we can safely ignore the stimulus.

Changes in behavior of this kind illustrate what we mean by learning. It is difficult to define learning precisely, but one simple definition would be a change in behavior due to experience. As sometimes happens with simple definitions, however, this one quickly runs into difficulties.

One problem, as we have already seen in our discussion of habituation, is that there are some changes due to experience that are really not what we mean by learning. If your behavior changed because you had not eaten for several hours, for example, this would not really be what we mean by learning, nor would changes due to impairments in your sensory or motor capacities. What we really have in mind are experiences that result in the storage of information in your brain, but a definition in these terms would be of little practical value because we almost never have direct information about what is stored in the brain; we can only infer learning by observing changes in overt behavior.

A further problem arises from the requirement of a change in behavior. In reading this page, hopefully you have learned something, even though at the moment there may not be any visible change in your behavior; the change might not be revealed until you took an exam. This example suggests that although we need a change in behavior before we can know that learning has occurred, what we mean by learning is not really the change in behavior, but rather the processes that led to this change in behavior.

To deal with these problems, we will redefine **learning** as a change in our *capacity* for behavior due to particular *kinds* of experience. This definition is regrettably more cumbersome, but it does come somewhat closer to what we generally have in mind when we talk about learning.

Sensitization. We are now ready to define associative learning, but before leaving the startle reflex we want to point out one more property of this response that will have implications for us later. In habituation, repeated presentations of a stimulus cause a reduction in the magnitude of the reflexive response. Sometimes, however, the response becomes *stronger* with repetition. An increase in the strength of a reflexive response when a stimulus is repeated is called **sensitization**. This phenomenon, too, is illustrated in Davis's (1974) experiment. In one of his conditions (the one shown in Figure 1.4a), the tone was presented against a relatively quiet background. In a second condition, however, the tone was presented against a noisier background—an 80-dB noise, instead of the gentler 60-dB noise used in the first condition. Under the louder condition, the startle response to the tone actually became stronger over successive presentations (Figure 1.4b).

Why should the presence of a loud background noise reverse the habituation effect of repeating a stimulus? Groves and Thompson (1970) have provided a possible explanation in terms of the general arousal level of the body. When we are asleep, our arousal level is low, and any stimulation will produce only a muted response. When we are awake, we respond to stimuli more strongly, and the more aroused we are, the more vigorously we tend to respond. When a loud noise was present, its continued presence caused a steady increase in the rats' level of arousal, and this in turn amplified their response to the tone. Thus, instead of diminishing, the level of response increased. You might imagine the same thing happening to you in our studying example, if there were only a few hours to go before your exam. As time passed, you might become increasingly tense, and the irritating effects of the burglar alarm, instead of diminishing, might become increasingly unbearable. Thus, although a reflexive response to a stimulus normally becomes weaker when the stimulus is repeated (habituation), under certain circumstances it will become stronger (sensitization).

Associative Learning

In the case of sensitization and habituation, learning occurs as a result of the presentation of a single stimulus. (However, see Whitlow & Wagner, 1984.) A more elaborate form of learning occurs when two events occur together and we learn about the relationship between them. If we use the symbol E_1 to represent one event and E_2 to represent the second event, then in **associative learning** we learn about the association or relationship between the two events:

$$E_1 \longrightarrow E_2$$

In some cases, the relationship may not be particularly important to us: for example, learning that sudden storms during the day are sometimes followed by rainbows, or that the mailman always comes around 9:30 in the morning. Where E_2 is an event that matters to us, however, learning to identify an event that regularly precedes it can be vital. The preceding event may be its cause, or, if it is a reliable predictor, it may at least allow us to identify when or where the important event is likely to occur, thus giving us the opportunity to take appropriate action. If you live by hunting, your survival depends on learning where your prey is most likely to be found and the stalking behaviors that will allow you to approach it without being detected; if you are a child, your happiness depends on learning which of your behaviors make your parents angry and which make them happy; as an adult, you need to learn the social skills that make lasting friendships more likely and the professional skills that will determine your chances of promotion. In all these cases, you need to learn which stimuli or responses make the outcomes you desire more likely.

Psychologists have proposed a number of theories about how this learning occurs. One view suggests that when events occur together we almost literally associate or bond them together in our minds, so that in future the occurrence of one of these events will automatically elicit the other. If you eat at 6:00 every evening, for example, then as 6:00 approaches you may find that you automatically become hungry and begin to think about food. If you behave in a way that makes a friend smile, that person's smile may automatically and unconsciously alter your behavior.

Dickinson (1980) and others have suggested an alternative framework that views associative learning as a knowledge-acquisition process. Each of our worlds is enormously rich and complex; we are inundated by sights, sounds, and other experiences. Associative learning is the process by which we identify the causal or predictive relationships that are embedded within this flux of events. In Dickinson's phrase, only if we can understand the "causal texture" of the world around us do we have any chance of influencing the events that matter to us. This is not to say that associative learning is all that is involved— complex cognitive and emotional processes may influence how we use the knowledge that we have acquired in deciding how to behave—but associative learning provides the foundation of knowledge on which these decisions are based.

Whichever of these views we adopt—whether we view associative learning as the formation of relatively simple, automatic associations, or as a more sophisticated process for acquiring knowledge about causal relationships (or both!)—we will see that associative learning does play a critical role in shaping our behavior. We will also see that experimental research has substantially improved our understanding of the principles of associative learning, and that these principles have been applied in situations as diverse as helping students to study more effectively, teaching athletes to play tennis better, and helping people to overcome phobias and addictions.

One reason for studying associative learning, then, is its practical importance. A second reason is that it is a relatively simple form of learning. As we argued in an earlier section, it is usually much easier to understand the operations of a complex system if we first study its principles in a simpler system. By studying the principles of learning in relatively simple situations, psychologists have hoped to be able to understand processes that also play a central role in far more complex situations.

We shall consider the relationship between associative learning and more obviously complex forms of learning such as concept learning and language learning in later chapters, especially Chapter 13, but it is worth emphasizing at this point that associative learning is only *relatively* simple. When a rat learns to press a bar to obtain food, for example, this may seem so simple a form of learning that there is virtually nothing to say about how it occurs, but we will find that the principles of learning involved are almost unimaginably more complex than they initially appear. After almost 100 years of research, we are still only beginning to understand how rats and humans manage to learn even the simplest relationships.

This book, then, will be about associative learning—in particular, two forms of associative learning known as classical conditioning and instrumental conditioning. We will leave their introduction, however, to Chapter 2.

1.6 SUMMARY

The focus of this text is associative learning—the learning that occurs when two events are paired together. In subsequent chapters, we will be looking at the principles of associative learning, how these principles can be applied practically (for example, how rewards and punishments can be used more effectively), and theories about the nature of the underlying processes. In this first chapter, we began by examining the assumptions that underlie the research we will be discussing, starting with the reasons that psychologists study learning in the first place.

One reason is simple curiosity: Psychologists are curious to know how people learn and find pleasure in understanding the mechanisms better. A second, more practical motivation is the belief that an understanding of how people learn will inevitably lead to important applications. This belief, in turn, rests on three assumptions: that behavior is lawful, that knowledge of these laws would increase our capacity to control behavior, and that this increase would be beneficial.

The first assumption—that behavior is lawful—arouses ambivalent feelings. Few of us are willing to accept our own behavior as entirely determined or lawful: We feel free to behave as we choose. At the same time, we recognize the powerful control that the environment exerts over the behavior of others. There is probably a consensus that the environment controls our behavior in important respects, but disagreement remains as to the extent of this control.

Insofar as behavior is lawful, discovery of these laws would almost certainly increase our capacity to control behavior. Whether this increase is desirable is again controversial. Skinner has argued that it is pointless to debate whether to control behavior, because we already do so; Milgram's research on obedience suggests the extent to which such controls already exist. If some degree of social control is inevitable, however, difficult issues may nevertheless arise in deciding our goals and the means for pursuing them. Most applications of learning principles are entirely benign, but in planning such applications we need to be sensitive to the ethical and political issues that can arise.

If we accept the goal of discovering the laws of learning, the next question is inevitably how to go about doing so. One attractive option is introspection—carefully observing our own mental processes in order to discover the laws governing our thoughts. Introspection was the main tool of psychologists in the nineteenth century, but it quickly fell into disfavor as introspectionists discovered that much of the mind's functioning is unconscious and thus hidden from introspective analysis. Moreover, even where mental processes were accessible to consciousness, subjects' introspective accounts often conflicted sharply. At best, therefore, introspection could provide only a limited account of why people behave the way they do, and psychologists turned instead to objective observations of overt behavior. In particular, emphasis shifted to experiments in which one aspect of the environment (the independent variable) was manipulated in order to assess its effects on some aspect of behavior (the dependent variable). A systematic relationship between the independent and dependent variables would then define a law.

In outline, the experimental method is almost trivially simple: To discover the laws of behavior, all we have to do is manipulate some aspect of the environment and observe its effects on behavior. The problem is that it is difficult to manipulate only one independent variable at a time. If several variables change simultaneously, it is not possible to determine which one was responsible for any observed change in behavior. One solution is to physically control the environment to minimize the number of variables present; when this is not possible, the experimenter can control for the effects of extraneous variables through comparison with control groups. Thus, if we wanted to determine the effects of variable A on learning but could not prevent the presence of variable B, we could compare an experimental group receiving AB with a control group receiving only B. If the experimental group learns faster, this difference in performance must be due to variable A.

In practice, it is impossible to control all possible variables; we can only control for those that seem most important. There is thus a built-in Catch-22 to scientific progress: To discover scientific laws, we need to control all important variables, but we can only identify the important variables if we already know the scientific laws! This problem can be overcome gradually through trial and error, but the result is that scientific progress is often frustratingly slow.

A further implication of the impossibility of controlling all variables is the need for some caution and humility in interpreting experimental evidence: However convincing the evidence may seem, it is always possible that an alternative explanation will eventually be discovered. Finally, the need to control the environment as fully as possible means that experiments are inevitably artificial: The more stringently we control the experimental environment, the less it will resemble the natural environment. Progress in other sciences, however, suggests that once we have analyzed the effects of individual variables in artificial environments, we can then synthesize their combined effects in progressively more complex and realistic settings.

The importance of controlling the experimental environment is the main reason for the use of animals in psychological experiments, because it is much easier to control the experimental and preexperimental environment of animals. Also, because animals are simpler than humans, it is easier to isolate the effects of single variables on their behavior. These advantages, however, are only meaningful if the principles of learning in animals and humans are similar. (There would be little point to discovering the laws of learning in animals if they bore no relation to those in humans.) The extent of the similarity of animal and human learning remains an open question, but research in recent decades has made it clear that animals have a surprisingly sophisticated capacity for thinking and learning. This does not mean that learning can only be studied in animals; nor does it mean that the principles of learning in animals are always identical to those in humans. It does suggest, though, that animal experiments can be useful as we try to understand the undoubtedly more complex learning processes of humans.

The evidence for similarities in animal and human learning also sharpens the ethical dilemma of using animals in research: If animals resemble us in intelligence and perhaps in feelings, do we have the right to force them to participate in experiments? There is no easy way to balance the benefits of animal research against the costs to the animals, but our calculation of the benefits will depend critically on the validity of the assumptions reviewed in this chapter: If behavior is lawful, and if the best way to discover these laws is through controlled experimentation, then it is likely that animal experiments will ultimately lead to important practical applications. The evidence in subsequent chapters will help you to form your own views of the validity of these assumptions.

We concluded our introduction to associative learning by examining what we mean by learning. Some stimuli always elicit the same response—this fixed relationship is called a reflex—but sometimes the response to a stimulus changes as a result of experience. For example, the first time you hear a loud noise it may make you jump, but if the noise is repeated your startle response may habituate. If this decrement occurred because you could no longer hear the noise, or because your muscles were too tired to contract properly, we would attribute the change to sensory or muscular fatigue; but if the change reflected the storage of some sort of information in your brain—for example, that the noise had occurred 10 times with no harmful consequences following—then it would be an example of learning. We defined learning more formally as a change in the capacity for behavior due to certain kinds of experience. (The limitation to certain kinds of experience allows us to exclude changes due to motivational shifts or to sensory or motor fatigue.)

In subsequent chapters, we will be focusing on associative learning, in which we learn about the relationship between two events that occur together. Such learning is of particular interest if the second event is one that is important to us and we need to be able to identify its causes in order to take appropriate action in the future. We will be focusing more specifically on two forms of associative learning—classical conditioning and instrumental conditioning—in part because of their importance in determining our lives, but also because understanding these processes may help us to understand learning in far more complex situations.

Selected Definitions

Determinism The belief that all behavior is caused by either environmental or genetic factors.

Free will The power that people have to determine their own actions, regardless of any external pressures.

Introspection A person's examination of his or her own thoughts or feelings.

Independent variable The aspect of the environment that an experimenter manipulates during an experiment.

Dependent variable The observable behavior that occurs as a result of manipulation of the independent variable during an experiment.

Law A consistent relationship between the independent and dependent variables in which the occurrence of some condition A always leads to outcome B.

Reflex A stimulus-response relationship in which a stimulus reliably elicits the same response innately, without prior experience.

Habituation A decrease in the strength of a reflex due to repeated presentations of the stimulus by itself.

Learning A term devised to embarrass learning psychologists, who tie themselves into knots trying to define it. We have defined it as a change in our capacity for behavior due to particular kinds of experience.

Sensitization An increase in the strength of a reflex due to repeated presentations of the stimulus by itself.

Associative learning Learning about the association or relationship between two events that occur together.

Review Questions

1. Is behavior governed by laws? What are the arguments for and against this view?

2. Is controlling another person's behavior ethical?

3. What developments undermined the use of introspection in psychology?

4. How do experiments control for unwanted variables?

5. What are the strengths and weaknesses of the experimental method?

6. Why do psychologists believe that the results of experiments carried out in highly artificial laboratory settings can tell us anything about behavior in the real world?

7. What are the arguments for and against the use of animals in psychological research?

8. Why is learning difficult to define?

C H A P T E R   T W O

AN INTRODUCTION TO ASSOCIATIVE LEARNING

A dog stands motionless in the middle of a room, immobilized by a leather harness. The room is very quiet, all outside sound being blocked by one-foot-thick concrete walls. A bell rings, and the dog turns toward the bell but otherwise shows little reaction. Five seconds later, the dog is presented food powder through a long rubber tube. The silence returns. Ten minutes pass; the bell sounds again and, as before, is followed by food. Ten more minutes pass. Again the bell sounds, but this time the dog begins to move restlessly in its harness, saliva dripping from its mouth. As the trials continue, the dog becomes increasingly excited at the sound of the bell, with more and more saliva flowing into a tube that has been surgically implanted in the dog's mouth. The saliva flows through the tube into an adjoining room where technicians record the number of drops.

When word of this experiment reached other scientists, the news was greeted with tremendous excitement. Within a few years, the experimenter, Ivan Petrovich Pavlov, was known to virtually every psychologist in the world. Within a few decades, his research had become perhaps the best known in the history of science, ranking with the legendary fall of an apple onto Isaac Newton's head.

Why all the excitement? What was so interesting about the fact that a dog could be trained to salivate? The answers to these questions have their roots deep in the history of Western intellectual thought, and we will need to explore that history briefly to understand the reaction to Pavlov's experiments.

2.1 THE ASSOCIATIVE BACKGROUND

Associations in the Body

Early explanations of human behavior were generally religious in character. Human behavior was seen as unpredictable, determined by fate or the whim of the gods. The advent of Christianity produced significant changes in these beliefs, but behavior was still seen as fundamentally unpredictable. Individuals were believed to have free will because they had souls. For almost 1700 years there were few significant departures from this theme, until the publication in 1650 of *The Passions of the Soul* by René Descartes. Descartes was a brilliant mathematician (Cartesian geometry was named after him), but he was also an outstanding philosopher, of such eminence that he was invited to Sweden to serve as the personal tutor to Queen Christina, then one of Europe's most powerful monarchs. He wanted to decline the queen's invitation politely, but she dispatched a warship to collect him, and he apparently found the honor too great to refuse. Conditions, however, proved less than ideal: Classes were held at five o'clock in the morning, in the unheated library of the castle. It was apparently an unusually rigorous winter even by Swedish standards, and Descartes died of pneumonia, at the age of 54, before the winter ended (Boring, 1950).

Aside from its somber implications for those contemplating careers in philosophy, Descartes's life is important to us because he was the first major figure in Western civilization to offer a detailed, mechanistic explanation for human behavior. According to Descartes, our senses and muscles are connected by a complex network of nerves, and it is the flow of "animal spirits" through these nerves that makes possible the instinctive reactions necessary for survival. If a person were to step into a fire accidentally, for example, the nerves in the foot would be stimulated and would transmit this excitation to the brain. The brain would then release animal spirits into the nerve, which flow back to the calf muscle and cause it to swell, resulting in the foot's withdrawal from the flame. (See Figure 2.1.) This simple mechanism—a receptor activating a muscle via a direct, innate connection—Descartes called a reflex, and he proposed that these reflexes underlie all automatic, involuntary reactions.

Voluntary behavior, however, was an entirely different matter. Descartes was a dualist, believing that the body and the mind exist in two entirely separate spheres. He believed that the body is physical and can be understood in terms of simple physical mechanisms, whereas the operations of the mind are controlled by the soul, a spiritual force that is independent of the physical universe. How then, you might ask, is the mind ever able to influence the body's operations, as, for example, in voluntary movements such as turning a page? The answer, according to Descartes, was that the soul was localized in an

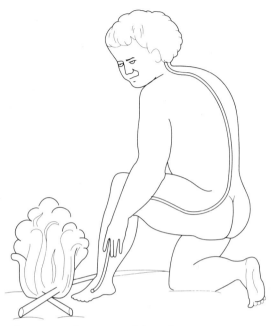

F I G U R E 2.1   Descartes's illustration of the reflex arc.

area of the brain known as the pineal gland, * and this gland was also a reservoir containing animal spirits, the physical fluid that produced the contractions of the muscles. By tipping the pineal gland in the desired direction, the soul was able to decant these fluids into the appropriate nerve, where they would flow to the appropriate muscle and initiate whatever movement was desired.

Associations in the Mind

Descartes's analysis showed how seemingly complex movements of the body could be explained in terms of the same simple mechanisms that governed machines, but he was not prepared to allow a similar determinism in the operation of the mind. This audacious step was first taken some 40 years later by an English physician named John Locke, secretary to the Earl of Shaftes-

---

* Descartes's choice of this seemingly minor organ for such a lofty role was by no means arbitrary. He knew that most of our sensory organs come in pairs—two eyes, two ears, and so on—and yet we perceive only one unified image. It was obvious, therefore, that all of our senses must converge on one center, where their disparate impressions can be blended together. And since the pineal gland, by virtue of its location in the exact midline of the brain, was the only organ not duplicated in the left and right hemispheres, Descartes concluded not unreasonably that it must be the seat of the soul.

bury. As was the custom of those times, Locke met weekly with educated friends to discuss current issues in areas such as science and theology. At one of these meetings, the disagreements became particularly intense, and it puzzled Locke that intelligent men could hold such different opinions regarding the same basic facts. He resolved to prepare a brief paper for the next meeting analyzing how each of us forms our ideas of the world and why our ideas are so different. Twenty years later, he finally completed this analysis, and it was published as a lengthy book, *An Essay Concerning Human Understanding*. The ideas in this essay were elaborated by later philosophers such as David Hartley and James Mill; together, these ideas form the doctrine that has become known as British Associationism.

The British Associationists.   According to the Associationists, thought is simply a succession of ideas through our minds, so that the basic unit of all thought is the idea. Descartes had believed many of our ideas to be innate, but Locke argued that our minds at birth are a tabula rasa, or blank slate. Any ideas we may have, he said, could only be acquired through experience. Locke suggested that any sensations that occur together will become associated so that if one of these sensations later recurs it will automatically elicit the second sensation. A stone, for example, produces a variety of visual and tactile sensations, which become associated through repeated pairings. It is this compound sensation (associated sensations) that forms our idea of a stone.

Ideas, in other words, are nothing more than sensations that have become associated together. This process of association also explains the sequence in which ideas occur to us.

> Our ideas spring up, or exist, in the order in which the sensations existed, of which they are the copies. This is the general law of the "Association of Ideas". . . . Of the successive order of our ideas, many remarkable instances might be adduced. Of these none seems better adapted to the learner than the repetition of any passage, or words; the Lord's Prayer, for example, committed to memory. In learning the passage, we repeat it; that is, we pronounce the words, in successive order, from the beginning to the end. The order of the sensations is successive. When we proceed to repeat the passage, the ideas of the words also arise in succession, the preceding always suggesting the succeeding, and no other. Our suggests father, father suggests which, which suggests art; and so on, to the end. How remarkably this is the case, anyone may convince himself, by trying to repeat backwards even a passage with which he is as familiar as the Lord's Prayer.
>
> (James Mill, *Analysis of the Phenomena of the Human Mind*, 1829)

The laws of association.   The concept of association can thus explain not only the existence of ideas but the order in which they occur. The fundamental principle underlying the formation of associations was **contiguity,** which stipulates that associations are formed between events that occur together. In the Lord's Prayer, the word *our* is followed by *father*, and as a result an association is formed between them. The word *which* also follows soon after, but the longer delay between *our* and *which* means that *our* is associated more strongly with *father* than with *which*, so that *our* is more likely to make us think of *father*.

A second principle of association was *frequency:* The more often two words occurred together, the more strongly they would be associated. The Lord's Prayer again provides an example: The more often we hear it, the more strongly we associate the words, and thus the better we recall it.

A third principle determining the strength of an association was said to be the *intensity* of the feelings that accompanied the association.

> [*The ideas*] *which naturally at first make the deepest and most lasting impression are those which are accompanied with pleasure or pain. . . . A man receives a sensible injury from another, thinks on the man and that action over and over, and by ruminating on them strongly or much in his mind, so cements those two ideas together that he makes them almost one; never thinks on the man, but the pain and displeasure he suffered comes into his mind with it, so that he scarce distinguishes them, but has as much an aversion for the one as the other.*

> (John Locke, *An Essay Concerning Human Understanding*, 1690)

Thus, by the nineteenth century, the historical groundwork was in place for a theory of human behavior based on the fundamental notion of the association. Descartes had shown how the movements of the body could be explained in terms of simple associations, or connections, between senses and muscles, and the British Associationists had extended his analysis to the mind, showing how thought could also be explained in terms of associations between ideas, and how ideas could in turn be analyzed into associations among sensations. The key to understanding human behavior, therefore, seemed to lie in an understanding of how associations come to be formed.

Associations in the Brain

This belief in the importance of associations was further reinforced as physiologists began to understand how the brain works. In discussing this knowledge, we will temporarily abandon our historical approach and present an overview of our current understanding of the brain's operations, rather than the picture as it existed in Pavlov's time. This updated review will allow us to introduce information that will be useful in later chapters, but will not greatly distort the situation that existed in Pavlov's era, when scientists already knew the broad outlines if not all the details.

The neural basis of behavior. Consider again Descartes's example of a man pulling his foot out of the fire. How is this movement actually produced? Descartes was right that there is a sense in the foot that will detect heat, and that it is connected via a nerve to the muscles that will withdraw the foot, but the properties of this nerve are somewhat different from those he imagined. Far from being hollow tubes that carry animal spirits, nerves are composed of cells, called **neurons** that are specialized to carry electrical signals. Figure 2.2 shows a schematic representation of a typical neuron. The neuron consists of a set of branching tendrils, called **dendrites**, that receive information from other neurons; a *cell body*; a long section called an *axon*; and, at the end of the axon, a set of *terminals* that make contact with the dendrites of other neurons. A neuron can be thought of as a battery that produces electrical energy, together with a wire that carries this energy somewhere else. The cell body is, in effect, the battery that produces an electrical signal; this signal is then conveyed along the axon, which is the wire, until it reaches another neuron. As shown in Figure 2.3, there is a very small space called the **synaptic gap** between the terminals of one neuron and the dendrites of another. When the electrical signal arrives at the terminals of the first neuron, it causes the release of chemicals called **neurotransmitters** that are stored in the terminals. These neurotransmitters move across the synaptic gap to the second neuron, where their arrival stimulates that neuron to produce an electrical signal, and so on.

In our fire example, the fire would stimulate a sensory receptor in the skin, inducing electrical activity in a very long *sensory neuron* that would carry an electrical signal from the foot to the spinal cord. (See Figure 2.4.) The signal would then be transmitted via an *interneuron* in the cord to a *motor neuron*, which would then convey the signal to a muscle in the calf. The arrival of the impulse would trigger electrical activity in the muscle, causing it to contract, thereby pulling the foot out of the fire. This account is oversimplified in that postural reflexes actually involve the integrated activity of many mus-

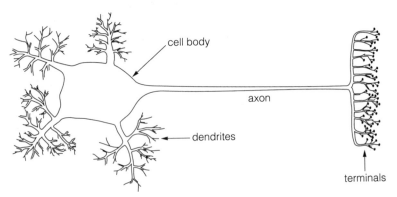

F I G U R E 2.2   Schematic representation of a typical neuron.

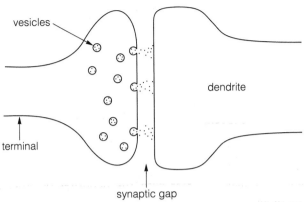

F I G U R E 2.3   Illustration of the synaptic gap between the axon terminal of one neuron and the dendrites of a second neuron. The axon terminal contains neurotransmitters stored in structures called *vesicles*. When an electrical impulse arrives at the terminal, it causes the release of these neurotransmitters which then move across the synaptic gap and induce electrical activity in the second neuron.

cles: Raising a leg requires compensatory adjustments elsewhere to ensure that the body does not fall over! Nevertheless, there really are simple reflexes of the type we have described in which only three neurons—a sensory neuron, an interneuron, and a motor neuron—combine to produce a reflexive response. Indeed, there are even simpler reflexes involving only a direct connection between a sensory and a motor neuron. Thus, although the details of how neurons carry messages differ from those proposed by Descartes—the mecha-

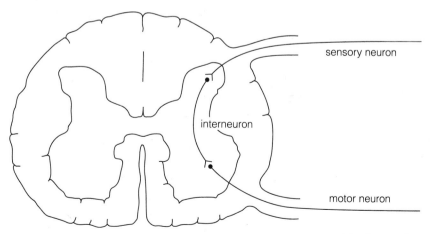

F I G U R E 2.4   Simplified illustration of a reflexive connection within the spinal cord.

nism is electrical rather than hydraulic—in its broad outlines the system is surprisingly similar to the one he portrayed.

What, then, of voluntary behavior? Suppose, for example, that a doctor asked you to raise your foot during an examination. How would you do it? Voluntary movements of this kind involve the brain, which is a massive collection of neurons—approximately 10 *billion* neurons—organized into complex subsystems. Different sections of the brain are specialized to carry out different functions: One system deals with vision, another controls eating, a third is responsible for language, and so on. Higher cognitive functions such as thought and language are largely concentrated in the outer layer of the brain called the **cerebral cortex**. If the cortex is damaged or anesthetized, we generally lose conscious awareness. Conversely, electrical stimulation of the cortex can produce conscious experiences. A Canadian neurosurgeon, Wilder Penfield, exposed the cortex of epileptic patients in the course of operations to treat their conditions. He found that if he stimulated certain areas of the cortex with very small electrical currents, his patients would report experiences such as hearing someone call their name or standing on a railway platform waiting for a train (for example, Penfield, 1958).

Returning to our foot-raising example, the doctor's words would trigger receptors in your ear which would transform them into a series of electrical impulses that would then be conveyed to the auditory area of the brain. This region, as most others, consists of an almost unimaginably dense web of interconnected neurons; a single neuron within the cortex may receive inputs from as many as 50,000 other neurons. Eventually, a set of signals would be conveyed to the motor cortex, and from there to the spinal cord and then to the leg muscles. Thus, in contrast to reflexes, which may involve just a single connection between a sensory and a motor neuron, more complex activities such as language and voluntary movement may involve the transmission of electrical signals within a network of many millions of neurons.

The neural basis of learning.   The picture of the brain we have painted so far might seem to suggest that our behavior should always be exactly the same, because a particular sensory input would always be routed through the same neurons to the same muscles. The reason that this does not happen is that the connections between neurons in the brain are not fixed: The strength of these connections can be altered by experience. Our understanding of how neural connections are altered is still at a very preliminary stage, but it appears that one of the mechanisms is a permanent increase in the number of neurotransmitters released by a neuron when an electrical impulse arrives at its terminal. The result is that activity in this neuron will thereafter be more likely to produce activity in the second neuron. Thus, although learning in the brain is almost certainly a very complex activity, if for no other reason than the vast number of neurons involved, at a cellular level learning is now thought to depend on simple changes in the strength of the connections between individual neurons. It is the strength of these connections that determines how electrical impulses are routed through the brain, thereby determining every aspect of our behavior.

We can now return to our historical argument. By the end of the nineteenth century, introspective and physiological evidence both suggested that much if not all of the mind's operations might be explicable in terms of simple associations, so that if we could understand how associations are formed, we might have the key to understanding the mind. Philosophers' attempts to identify the principles of association, however, had become bogged down. Different philosophers had suggested different principles, but because these principles were derived from introspection, there was no obvious way to decide which of the alternatives was correct. If only there were an objective method for studying the formation of associations . . . .

2.2 CLASSICAL CONDITIONING

Ivan Petrovich Pavlov was born in a small village in Russia in 1849. His early years were spent preparing for the priesthood at the local church school. His plans eventually changed, and in 1870 he walked hundreds of miles across Russia to enroll in St. Petersburg University as a student of physiology. His particular interest was in the physiology of digestion, and he developed ingenious surgical procedures for the measurement of salivary and gastric secretions in dogs.

Saliva is secreted normally by special glands within the cheek and then carried by ducts to the cheek's inner surface. By surgically redirecting one of these ducts, Pavlov was able to divert the saliva to the external surface of the cheek, where it could be collected through a connecting tube and then analyzed. Using this surgical preparation, known as a *fistula*, Pavlov found that salivation was an automatic, reflexive response that was elicited whenever food came into contact with the mucous membranes of the mouth.

After his dogs had been tested for several sessions, Pavlov noticed a strange phenomenon: The dogs began to salivate not only when food was placed in their mouths but also at other times. Many scientists would either have ignored this salivation, considering it irrelevant, or sought actively to prevent it, because its occurrence would contaminate their measures of the pure reflex to food. Pavlov, however, was fascinated. If salivation is a reflexive response, lawfully elicited only by very specific stimuli such as the presence of food in the mouth, why should it suddenly begin to occur in the absence of these stimuli?

Pavlov noticed that the occurrence of this "extra" salivation was not simply random, but apparently in response to particular stimuli such as the sight or sound of the experimenter's approach. Was it possible that the dogs had come to associate these stimuli with the delivery of food, and that this was why they were now salivating? Or, in Pavlov's terminology, that in addition to the innate or *unconditioned reflexes* with which every animal was born, they were able to form new, *conditioned reflexes*?

Pavlov's Conditioned Reflexes

Excited by the possibility of studying how new connections were formed within the brain, Pavlov abandoned his research on digestion, even though it had already made him world famous and was soon to earn him the Nobel prize. Instead, he set out to study how these new associations were formed by deliberately pairing stimuli with the presentation of food and observing how the conditions of pairing influenced the development of salivation.

Controlling the conditions.   Pavlov recognized from the outset that the task was not going to be an easy one: The brain was an enormously complex organ, sensitive to countless stimuli from the outside world, so that the effects in which he was interested might easily be lost in the flood of stimuli constantly washing over his subjects.

> *Unless we are careful to take special precautions the success of the whole investigation may be jeopardized, and we should get hopelessly lost as soon as we began to seek for cause and effect among so many and various influences, so intertwined and entangled as to form a veritable chaos. It was evident that the experimental conditions had to be simplified, and that this simplification must consist in eliminating as far as possible any stimuli outside our control which might fall upon the animal.*
>
> (Pavlov, 1927, p. 20)

To achieve this, Pavlov conducted his initial studies in an isolated room, where no one but the experimenter was allowed to enter. This precaution, however, proved inadequate, as even the slightest movement of the experimenter, such as a blink, was enough to distract the dogs. Pavlov tried placing the experimenter outside the room, but this did not solve the problem, as the dogs continued to be affected by stimuli such as the footsteps of passersby and even a cloud that temporarily reduced the amount of light coming in the window. Finally, Pavlov was driven to designing a completely new laboratory which, with the aid of a "keen and public-spirited Moscow businessman," he had built in St. Petersburg.

The laboratory looked like a fort, with walls more than a foot thick, encircled by a trench filled with straw to reduce vibrations. The actual test rooms were widely dispersed through the building to minimize distracting

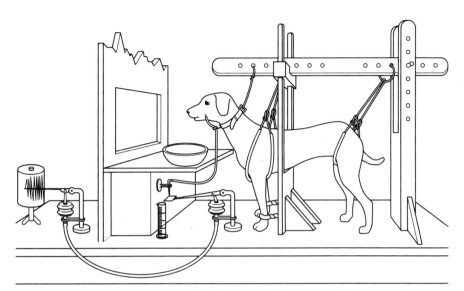

F I G U R E 2.5   Apparatus used in Pavlov's study of salivary conditioning in dogs. Saliva flowed through a tube connected to the dog's cheek and traveled to another room where it could be recorded. (After Yerkes & Morgulis, 1909)

noises. Figure 2.5 illustrates a typical test room. The dogs were strapped into loose-fitting harnesses to reduce movement, and any salivation was carried off through a tube to an experimenter in an adjacent, soundproof room. With the aid of a variety of electrically operated signal devices, Pavlov was now able to control almost completely any external stimuli that reached his subjects, and thus was ready to make a systematic study of how associations were formed.

A typical experiment.   We can illustrate the quality of the results Pavlov now obtained with an experiment by one of his students. Anrep (1920) first presented his dogs with a tone by itself, and found that it had no effect on salivation. He then paired the tone with food: The tone was sounded for five seconds; then, two seconds later, food was presented. Each of these tone-food pairings was called a **trial,** and Anrep presented a trial every few minutes. (The actual time between trials varied between 5 and 35 minutes.) On an average of once every ten trials, the tone was presented by itself for 30 seconds so the experimenter could measure the amount of salivation elicited solely by the tone.

The results for two subjects are shown in Figure 2.6, where we can see that the magnitude of salivation on the test trials gradually increased from 0 drops to a maximum level, or *asymptote,* of about 60 drops after 30 pairings. One striking feature of these results is the smoothness and regularity of the learning curves. It normally requires averaging the results of many subjects to

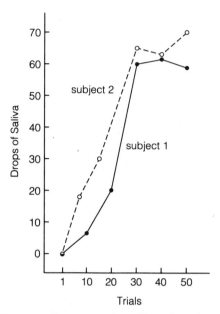

F I G U R E 2.6   Salivary conditioning in dogs. (Data from Anrep, 1920)

eliminate random variations and produce curves of this smoothness, but be-cause of the extraordinary control Pavlov achieved over the environment, he and his colleagues were able to produce beautifully clear and uniform data even in single subjects. Even more dramatic evidence of the underlying lawfulness of behavior in this situation is the similarity of the learning curves of the two subjects: Even though the subjects were tested separately, their behavior was virtually identical on trial after trial.

Pavlov called the salivation elicited by the food an **unconditioned re-sponse (UR)**, because no training was necessary to establish it, whereas the salivation to the tone was a **conditioned response (CR)**—that is, a response that occurs as a result of some training. Similarly, the food was an **uncondi-tioned stimulus (US)** for salivation—that is, a stimulus that elicits a response without training. The tone was a **conditioned stimulus (CS)**—a stimulus that, through training, elicits a response.* The entire procedure, in which the pairing of a CS with a US results in an increase in responding to the CS, has come to be known as Pavlovian or **classical conditioning**.

---

* Pavlov actually used the term *conditional response*, because the occurrence of the response was conditional on previous pairings of the CS and the US. The term was mistranslated as *conditioned response*. Some authors are now returning to Pavlov's original terminology, referring to conditional and unconditional stimuli and responses.

An Associative Analysis

Pavlov repeated this basic experiment with a variety of other conditioned and unconditioned stimuli, and in every case he found that the response originally elicited by the US was transferred to the CS that preceded it. To explain this result, Pavlov assumed that the presentation of any stimulus would result in activity in a particular set of neurons or "center" within the brain, so that presentation of the CS would activate one center and presentation of the US would activate another center. (See Figure 2.7.) Whenever activity in one center was followed by activity in another center, Pavlov proposed, the neural connection between these centers would be strengthened. For example, if a tone was paired with food, the association or connection between the tone and food centers would be strengthened, so that the next time the tone was presented, activity in the "tone" center would be transmitted via this new connection to the "food" center and from there via an innate pathway to the salivary glands. The amount of salivation, therefore, provided a simple and objective measure of the strength of the association.

Second-order conditioning.   Further research suggested that the associative process involved was a totally general one in which *any* stimuli that were presented together could be associated. It wasn't even necessary for either of

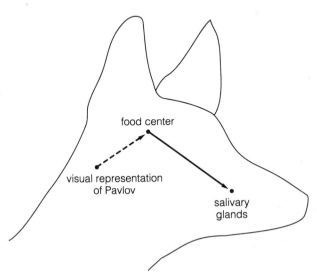

F I G U R E 2.7   Pavlov's view of the connections involved in classical conditioning. If the sight of Pavlov preceded food, the visual representation of Pavlov in the dog's brain would be connected to the food center (the broken line). Excitement in the food center would then be transmitted via an innate pathway (solid line) to the dog's salivary glands.

these stimuli to elicit an unconditioned response. In an experiment by one of Pavlov's associates, Dr. Frolov, for example, salivation was conditioned by pairing a black square with a metronome, even though neither was an unconditioned stimulus for salivation. This strange feat was made possible by a preliminary phase in which the metronome was paired with food. Once the metronome elicited salivation reliably, food presentations were discontinued and the experimenter began pairings of the square and metronome.

1.   metronome ⟶ food
2.   black square ⟶ metronome

After several trials, the black square also began to elicit salivation, even though it had never been followed by food. Pavlov called this phenomenon **second-order conditioning** and considered it to be the outcome of a double associative chain, from the square to the metronome, and then from the metronome to food. (See Rescorla, 1980, for an alternative interpretation.) Though second-order conditioning was not easy to establish, its existence suggested that associations might be formed between any stimuli that were contiguous.

Sensory preconditioning. Further support for the generality of the associative process involved was to come from later research on **sensory preconditioning**. In this phenomenon, two neutral or weak stimuli are first presented together and one of them is then paired with an unconditioned stimulus. The result is that responding is conditioned not only to the conditioned stimulus but also to the stimulus that was paired with the conditioned stimulus during the first phase. In the first clear demonstration of sensory preconditioning, Brogden (1939) gave dogs preliminary trials in which a buzzer was paired with a light. Then, in the conditioning phase, he paired the light with a mild shock to the paw, which elicited leg flexion.

1.   buzzer ⟶ light
2.   light ⟶ shock

Finally, Brogden presented the buzzer by itself on a test trial and found that it elicited leg flexion.

The most plausible explanation for this result is that when the buzzer was paired with the light during the preconditioning phase, an association was formed between them. During conditioning, a second association was formed between the light and the shock. When the buzzer was presented during testing, excitation was transmitted from the representation of the buzzer to the light, and from there to the shock. Or, in cognitive terminology, the dogs learned that the buzzer meant light and that the light meant shock, so that when they heard the buzzer during the test phase they expected the shock to follow.

We now know that sensory preconditioning occurs with a wide range of stimuli. Lavin (1976), for example, demonstrated that the pairing of two flavors results in an association being formed between them. It thus appears that associative learning does not require that either stimulus elicit a response, or at any rate a response more pronounced than that involved in normal perception: The fact that two stimuli occur contiguously may be sufficient for the stimuli to become associated.

A general process.   By investigating the conditioning of salivation, therefore, Pavlov could study how associations were formed throughout the brain. In the case of salivation, the stronger the association that was formed between the tone and food centers, the more presentation of the tone would stimulate the food center, and thus the more the dogs would salivate. By measuring the amount of salivation, therefore, Pavlov could assess the precise strength of the association within the brain, and thus could begin to determine the laws that governed the formation of such associations. And if, as Pavlov believed, education and training are "nothing more than the results of an establishment of new nervous connections" (Pavlov, 1927, p. 26), then by studying how dogs learn to salivate he could discover the principles that underlie all learning.

This claim may at first strike you as dubious, if not preposterous. Can the richness of human thought really be based on the same simple mechanisms that cause a dog to salivate in anticipation of food? We will consider this claim further shortly, but first we will introduce another procedure that was to play a major role in the investigation of associative learning.

2.3 Instrumental Conditioning

Reinforcement

At almost exactly the same time that Pavlov was watching his dogs salivate, a graduate student at Columbia University was intently watching cats struggling to escape from a wooden crate. The student's name was Edward Lee Thorndike, and we will again introduce our discussion of his research by examining its historical antecedents.

Are animals intelligent?   Thorndike's research, like Pavlov's, had its roots in the history of Associationism, but its most immediate antecedent was the publication of Charles Darwin's *Origin of the Species*. Darwin's theory of evolution had proposed that man was but one animal species among many, and this claim triggered a surge of interest in the intelligence and reasoning powers of animals. If Darwin was right, if we are closely related to other animal species, then the traditional view that animals are dumb brutes becomes far less attractive. After all, if our close relatives were dumb, what might that imply about us?

To lay the basis for a more realistic judgment, a contemporary of Darwin named George Romanes collected observations of animal behavior from reliable observers around the world. When published, the material in Romanes's *Animal Intelligence* seemed to strongly support Darwin's thesis, as anecdote after anecdote revealed impressive powers of reasoning. The following account of the behavior of captive monkeys in Paraguay—drawn, as it happens, from one of Darwin's own books—is representative:

> *Rengger, a most careful observer, states that . . . after cutting themselves only once with any sharp tool, they would not touch it again, or would handle it with the greatest caution. Lumps of sugar were often given them wrapped up in paper; and Rengger sometimes put a live wasp in the paper, so that in hastily unfolding it they got stung; after this had once happened, they always first held the packet to their ears to detect any movement within.*
>
> (Romanes, 1882)

These observations, and others like them, provided persuasive evidence that animals possessed intelligence and reasoning power of an impressively high order. But were these observations trustworthy? Thorndike thought not. In the first place, he doubted the accuracy of some of the anecdotal material.

> *One has to deal not merely with ignorant or inaccurate testimony, but also with prejudiced testimony. Human folk are . . . eager to find intelligence in animals. They like to. And when the animal observed is a pet belonging to them or their friends, or when the story is one that has been told as a story to entertain, further complications are introduced. Nor is this all. Besides commonly misstating what facts they report, they report only such facts as show the animal at his best. Dogs get lost hundreds of times, and no one ever notices it or sends an account of it to a scientific magazine. But let one find his way from Brooklyn to Yonkers and the fact immediately becomes a circulating anecdote. Thousands of cats on thousands of occasions sit helplessly yowling, and no one takes thought of it or writes to his friend, the professor; but let one cat claw at the knob of a door supposedly as a signal to be let out, and straightaway this cat becomes the representative of the cat-mind in all the books.*
>
> (Thorndike, 1898, p. 4)

Thorndike's Law of Effect.   Anecdotal observations, then, may not be accurate, and, even when they are, they may not be representative. The animal's

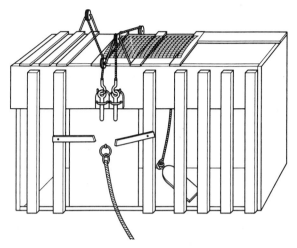

F I G U R E 2.8   Thorndike's puzzle box. (Thorndike, 1911)

success may have been due to chance, rather than to any powers of rational analysis. "To remedy these defects," Thorndike (1898) argued, "experiment must be substituted for observation and the collection of anecdotes. Thus . . . you can repeat the conditions at will, so as to see whether or not the animal's behavior is due to mere coincidence." Thorndike, therefore, began to study learning in animals systematically, using an apparatus that he called a puzzle box. Basically, it was little more than a wooden crate with a door that could be opened by a special mechanism, such as a latch or rope (Figure 2.8). Thorndike placed a dish containing food outside the box but visible through its slats, then put the animal to be tested inside and observed its reactions.

When a hungry cat was placed in the box, Thorndike found that it would initially scramble around the box, frantically clawing and biting at the sides of the apparatus in order to escape and reach the food. After approximately 5–10 minutes of struggling, the cat would eventually stumble upon the correct response and, upon finding the door open, would rush out and eat the food. According to Romanes's anecdotes, this success should have led to the immediate repetition of the successful response on the following trial. Instead, Thorndike found that the animal generally repeated the frantic struggling observed on the first trial. When the cat finally did repeat the correct response, however, the _latency_ of this response—the time from being put in the box to performing the response—was generally shorter than it had been on the first trial, shorter still on the third trial, and so on. Figure 2.9 presents representative records of the performance of two cats. Progress in both cases was gradual and marked by occasional reversals, but on average the time to escape became progressively shorter as training continued.

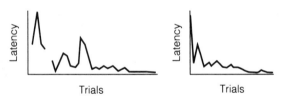

F I G U R E 2.9   Changes in the latency of escape from the puzzle box over trials for two of Thorndike's cats. (Thorndike, 1911)

What was the explanation for the improvement in the cats' performance? The gradual nature of the improvement convinced Thorndike that the cats had not formed a rational understanding of the situation. Rather, he argued, the food reward was gradually stamping in an association between the box cues and the escape response:

> *The cat does not look over the situation, much less think it over, and then decide what to do. It bursts out at once into the activities which instinct and experience have settled on as suitable reactions to the situation "confinement when hungry with food outside." It does not ever in the course of its successes realize that such an act brings food and therefore decide to do it and thenceforth to do it immediately from decision instead of impulse. The one impulse, out of many accidental ones, which leads to pleasure, becomes strengthened and stamped in thereby, and more and more firmly associated with the sense-impression of that box's interior. Accordingly it is sooner and sooner fulfilled.*
> (Thorndike, 1898, p. 45)

Thorndike repeated this experiment with other responses and also with other species, including chicks, dogs, and monkeys. The basic pattern of the results was almost always the same: a gradual improvement over many trials. This uniform pattern suggested that the gradual strengthening effect of rewards was not confined to a single situation or species, but represented a general law of behavior, which Thorndike formalized as the **Law of Effect**:

> *Of several responses made to the same situation, those which are accompanied or closely followed by satisfaction to the animal will, other things being equal, be more firmly connected with the situation, so that, when it recurs, they will be more likely to recur. . . . The greater the satisfaction . . . the greater the strengthening . . . of the bond.*
> (Thorndike, 1911, p. 24)

I can't get no satisfaction.   When Thorndike's findings were published, they aroused considerable interest, as they not only suggested a fundamental law of learning but also provided a simple method for studying it. A number of aspects of his work proved controversial, however, including his use of the subjective term *satisfaction*. Since we can't see into the mind of a cat, how can we know whether it is experiencing satisfaction? This difficulty in assessing satisfaction makes the Law of Effect potentially circular: A response will increase if it is followed by a satisfying outcome, but the only way we know whether the outcome is satisfying is if the response increases.

In fact, Thorndike was aware of this problem, and he proposed an independent and objective test for determining whether a consequence was satisfying:

> By a satisfying state of affairs is meant one which the animal does nothing to avoid, often doing such things as attain and preserve it.
>
> (Thorndike, 1911, p. 245)

In other words, if a cat repeatedly tries to obtain food in one situation—for example, by jumping up onto a table where it is kept—then by definition this food must be satisfying, and the Law of Effect now allows us to predict that the food will also be an effective reward for other behaviors, such as escaping from the puzzle box. Meehl (1950) later labeled this property of rewards *transituationality*.

Thorndike's objective definition of satisfaction saves the Law of Effect from circularity, but the term still bothered learning theorists because of its subjective connotation that a reward is emotionally satisfying. An experiment by Sheffield, Wulff, and Backer (1951) illustrates the dangers. To study what events are rewarding, they used an apparatus called a straight-alley maze, which consists of a start box and a goal box connected by a long alley. (See Figure 6.1c, p. 196.) To find out if a stimulus is rewarding, the stimulus is placed in the goal box and the subject in the start box, and the experimenter records how long it takes for the subject to run to the goal box. If the stimulus is rewarding, it should strengthen the response of running, and the speed of running down the alley should thus increase over trials.

The experimenters used male rats as subjects and a receptive female in the goal box as the reward. The normal copulatory pattern in rats consists of a series of 8–12 intromissions and withdrawals by the male until it finally ejaculates. When the male reached the goal box, the experimenters allowed it two intromissions, and then abruptly removed it from the goal box before it could ejaculate. It is not obvious that this sequence would be particularly satisfying for the male, but it proved to be a very powerful reward, because the males' speed of running down the alley increased over trials by a factor of eight!

Such evidence makes it at least questionable whether all events that strengthen behavior are emotionally satisfying, and it has led learning theorists to prefer the more objective term *reinforcer* to *reward*. A **reinforcer** can be defined as an event that increases the probability of a response when presented after it. Similarly, we can define **reinforcement** as an increase in the probability of a response due to the presentation of a reinforcer following that response.

Punishment

The statement of the Law of Effect quoted earlier is an abbreviated one; in Thorndike's full statement, he suggested not only that satisfying events would stamp in connections but also that unpleasant consequences would weaken connections. If a kitten was clawed every time it approached a neighbor's cat, for example, it would soon learn not to enter that cat's territory while it was around. This is an example of **punishment**, in which a response that produces an aversive or punishing consequence is reduced in frequency. If we represent the response by R, a positive or reinforcing consequence by S^R, and an aversive consequence by S^{av}, then these two forms of learning can be represented as follows:

$$\text{Reinforcement:} \quad R \longrightarrow S^R$$
$$\text{Punishment:} \quad R \longrightarrow S^{av}$$

Although reinforcement strengthens behavior and punishment weakens it, they are similar in that in both we need to learn about the relationship between our behavior and its consequences. This similarity, and the implication that the underlying mechanisms of learning might also be similar, has led psychologists to classify these forms of learning together as instances of **instrumental**, or **operant**, **conditioning**. Both terms emphasize that the response produces a consequence: The response can be said to be *instrumental* in producing the consequence, or to *operate* on the environment to produce the consequence.

Instrumental and Classical Conditioning

Instrumental conditioning can be distinguished from classical conditioning on the basis of the procedures used to produce it. In classical conditioning, a stimulus is followed by a stimulus; a tone, for example, is followed by food. In operant conditioning, a *response* is followed by a stimulus; opening the puzzle box door, for example, is followed by food. If we use the symbol S^* to stand for an important event such as food, then classical and instrumental conditioning can be represented as follows:

$$\text{Classical conditioning:} \quad S \longrightarrow S^*$$
$$\text{Instrumental conditioning:} \quad R \longrightarrow S^*$$

From the experimenter's point of view, the distinction between classical conditioning and instrumental conditioning is a simple one: It depends on whether a stimulus such as food is presented following a stimulus (classical conditioning) or a response (instrumental conditioning). In practice, distinguishing between the two forms of learning can sometimes be complex, but we will defer consideration of this problem to Chapter 9.

Given the number of terms we have now introduced, it may be helpful to pause to review these terms and the relationships among them. (See Figure 2.10.) In Chapter 1, we defined associative learning as the learning that takes place when two events occur together and we learn about their association or relationship:

$$E_1 \longrightarrow E_2$$

Conditioning is a form of associative learning in which E_2 is an important event. There are two forms of conditioning: classical conditioning, in which the important event follows a stimulus; and instrumental conditioning, in which the important event follows a response. Finally, instrumental conditioning can be further divided into reinforcement and punishment, depending on whether the consequence strengthens the preceding response or weakens it.

As we noted in Chapter 1, one reason for studying classical and instrumental conditioning is that these forms of learning play a major role in shaping our lives. In later chapters we will be examining the principles that affect conditioning and how these principles can be practically applied. The practical

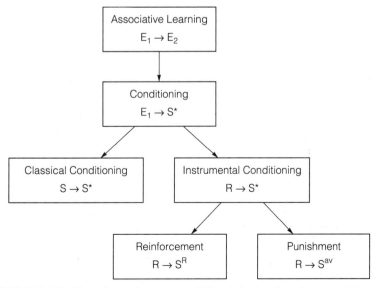

F I G U R E 2.10   The relationships among different forms of conditioning. S^* represents an important event, S^R a reinforcer, S^{av} an aversive stimulus.

importance of reinforcement and punishment are perhaps obvious, needing little further comment here, but it may be less obvious why classical conditioning matters. Salivation, for example, hardly seems one of the most important activities in which we engage. (If we lacked salivary glands, of course, our feelings about this might be different.) Salivation takes on considerably greater significance, however, if we recognize that it is an involuntary response: You cannot control the flow of your saliva in the same way you can raise your arm or waggle your fingers. If Pavlov could make a dog salivate whenever he wanted it to, an obvious question is whether classical conditioning could be used to control other involuntary responses as well. Could people learn to control their blood pressure and heart rate, or to control emotions such as anger and fear?

In our discussion of classical conditioning, we will see that classical conditioning does affect crucial aspects of our behavior, including what foods we eat, what stimuli we find sexually exciting, and how strongly drugs such as alcohol and heroin affect us. On the other hand, we will find that some of the more lurid fears of how classical conditioning can be used to brainwash people are not justified: Classical conditioning procedures cannot be used to turn innocent people into assassins, as imagined by some novelists, nor even to convert children watching television into fanatical consumers of corn flakes.

2.4 IS ASSOCIATIVE LEARNING SIMPLE?

One of the main concerns of this text, then, will be with identifying the principles of conditioning and examining how these principles can be practically applied. A second major concern will be with theoretical questions about the nature of the learning processes that underlie these principles. In this section we will introduce some of these theoretical issues.

Theories of Learning

Principles versus processes. The distinction between principles and processes can sometimes be confusing, and it may help to introduce this distinction with an example from another field. Biologists have shown that mammals will behave in such a way as to maintain their body temperatures within a narrow range; this is an empirical generalization, or principle, that summarizes behavior in a variety of situations. How mammals achieve a steady temperature, however, varies among species: Dogs, for example, will pant to cool their bodies when they become overheated, whereas humans will sweat. The fact that both species act to maintain a constant temperature is an empirical generalization, or *principle*; the behavioral mechanism that produces this outcome is called a *process*.

Similarly in the case of learning, reinforcement is at one level an empirical principle: When food or other reinforcers are presented, the observable result is an increase in the probability of the preceding response. However, there are different possible internal processes that could produce this outcome, and theories of learning are concerned with identifying the processes that are actually involved.

Associative versus cognitive theories of learning.   As we shall see, many theories about the nature of these learning processes have been proposed, but most fall into one of two broad camps: associative theories and cognitive theories. Before looking at these two approaches, however, we first need to distinguish between two very different usages of the term *associative*. At one level, we will be using the term in a purely descriptive sense to refer to the learning that occurs when two events are paired together. However, we will also sometimes use the term *associative* to describe the process that produces this observable learning. We can illustrate this distinction with the behavior of Thorndike's cats. At the descriptive level, this is an instance of associative learning because the cats were learning something about the association, or relationship, between pressing the latch and obtaining food. However, as Thorndike noted, there are at least two ways in which the observable improvement in the cats' performance could be explained: The cats developed a conscious awareness of the relationship between their behavior and the door opening; or food stamped in an association between the box and the successful response, so that the stimulus of the box would thereafter elicit the response automatically. The gradual nature of the improvement led Thorndike to support the associative explanation. Similarly, Pavlov proposed an associative explanation of classical conditioning, in which pairings led to the formation of an association between the CS and US centers in the brain.

A common theme of these and other associative theories is that events activate some sort of center or representation in the brain, and that learning involves the formation of associations between active centers. Pavlov's and Thorndike's explanations differed in the centers that were being associated— Pavlov thought that two stimulus centers were being associated, Thorndike that a stimulus center was associated with a response center—but both assumed that learning involved the formation of simple associations, so that activity in one center would automatically be transmitted to the other.

Cognitive learning theorists reject this view. The word *cognition* refers to thinking, and cognitive theorists believe that learning involves complex thought processes rather than simple associations. Even in a relatively simple situation, such as learning that a tone is followed several seconds later by food, cognitive theorists assume that subjects must attend to the tone when it is first presented and then must recall this presentation when they receive food. Thus, even the simplest learning situations involves cognitive processes such as memory and attention, as well as potentially even more complex processes. (See Chapters 12 and 13.)

In essence, the disagreement between associative and cognitive theorists concerns whether learning involves fundamentally simple processes, such as the formation of associations, or more complex processes such as memory. This disagreement has given rise to one of the most enduring controversies in psychology, and we will encounter it repeatedly in subsequent chapters. Because of the importance of this debate for understanding learning, however, we shall try to provide a preliminary feel for the issues involved by looking at one of the first skirmishes in the war, waged over the behavior of the cats in Thorndike's puzzle box.

Trial-and-Error Learning Revisited

Kohler's insightful analysis.   As we have seen, Thorndike considered the possibility that his cats understood the relationship between pressing the latch and the door's opening, but the gradual nature of their learning convinced him that learning was due to the gradual formation of associations rather than a sudden insight into the nature of the problem. This conclusion, however, was soon challenged by the Austrian psychologist Wolfgang Kohler. Learning in animals, Kohler argued, typically involved an intelligent appreciation of the relationship between responding and reinforcement; the apparent stupidity of the cats in Thorndike's puzzle boxes was a reflection not so much on the cats' intelligence as on Thorndike's! In particular, Kohler argued that Thorndike's tasks were too difficult because the causal relationships were concealed. The physical connection between the release mechanism and the door was in most cases not visible to the animals, so they could not directly perceive the relationship. If the relationship was made visible, Kohler suggested, animals would behave far more intelligently.

In one test of this prediction, Kohler (1927) provided a chimpanzee with a stick in her cage and then placed a bunch of bananas outside the cage just beyond her reach:

> She grasps at it, vainly of course, and then begins the characteristic complaint of the chimpanzee: she thrusts both lips—especially the lower—forward, for a couple of inches, gazes imploringly at the observer, utters whimpering sounds, and finally flings herself on the ground on her back—a gesture most eloquent of despair. . . . Thus, between lamentations and entreaties, some time passes, until—about seven minutes after the fruit has been exhibited to her—she suddenly casts a look at the stick, ceases her moaning, seizes the stick, stretches it out of the cage, and succeeds, though somewhat clumsily, in drawing the bananas within arm's length. . . . The test is repeated after an hour's interval; on this second occasion, the animal has recourse to the stick much sooner, and uses it with more skill; and, at a third repetition, the stick is used immediately, as on all subsequent occasions.

(Kohler, 1927, pp. 32–33)

This abrupt change in behavior, Kohler concluded, revealed a sudden *insight* into the problem.

We thus have two very different interpretations of animal learning: that it is a slow, gradual process based on associations, or the product of a rational appreciation of relationships. Each side, moreover, could summon persuasive evidence in its support: the very gradual improvements observed in Thorndike's puzzle boxes and other laboratory settings versus the sudden insights observed by Kohler. The situation was summarized with amusement by the philosopher Bertrand Russell:

> All the animals that have been carefully observed have all displayed the national characteristics of the observer. Animals studied by Americans rush about frantically, with an incredible display of hustle and pep, and at last achieve the desired result by chance. Animals observed by Germans sit still and think, and at last evolve the solution out of their inner consciousness.

(Russell, 1927, pp. 32–33)

An associative rejoinder.   Can we explain why Kohler's chimpanzees learned so much faster than Thorndike's cats? One possibility is simply that chimpanzees are smarter than cats, and there may be some truth to this, though in experiments where species such as cats and chimpanzees are presented with problems of equivalent difficulty, their performances are surprisingly similar. (For a review, see Macphail, 1982.)

An alternative explanation is suggested by the results of an important experiment by Harry Harlow (1949). Harlow gave a group of rhesus monkeys a discrimination problem involving two objects. If the monkey chose the correct object, it was allowed to keep the food that had been hidden underneath it. A screen was then lowered, the objects randomly repositioned, and the screen raised to begin a new trial. After 50 trials, a second problem was introduced involving new objects, and so on for a total of 344 problems.

Average performance over the first six trials for each problem is shown in Figure 2.11. The curve labeled *problems 1–8* shows performance averaged over the first eight problems. Preference for the correct object started at chance (50 percent) on the first trial and then gradually increased; even after five trials, though, the monkeys were selecting the correct object on only about 75 percent of the trials. Over succeeding problems, however, performance improved slowly but steadily until, by the end of training, subjects were choosing the correct object 98 percent of the time after only a single trial.

Harlow called this gradual improvement over problems "learning how to learn," or **learning set**, and suggested that it could account for the discrepancy between Thorndike's results and those of Kohler. In Harlow's experiment, as in Kohler's, subjects solved problems after only a single trial, but this apparently insightful behavior arose through the same sort of gradual learning that Thorndike had observed. (See also Epstein, Kirshnit, Lanza, & Rubin, 1984.) Per-

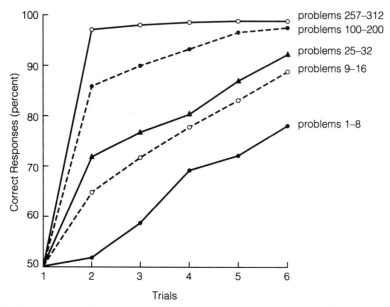

FIGURE 2.11   The formation of learning sets in rhesus monkeys. Each curve shows performance averaged over the sequence of problems indicated by number. (Adapted from Harlow, 1949)

haps, then, the insightful behavior of Kohler's chimpanzees had also been acquired through experience. His animals had been reared in the wild, and they could have had considerable experience in manipulating sticks before they were captured. As predicted by this analysis, Birch (1945) found that chimpanzees reared in captivity had great difficulty with Kohler's stick problem; only two of his six subjects managed to solve it within 30 minutes. When the chimpanzees were then allowed to play with sticks in their home cages for three days before being returned to the test situation, they all solved the problem within 20 seconds.

More recent studies of tool use in primates are also consistent with this analysis. For example, Boesch and Boesch (1984) observed chimpanzees in the wild learning to use stones and wooden clubs to crack open very hard nuts. Young chimpanzees learn the technique by observing how their mothers do it, but the acquisition of this skill stretches over a period of many years, as the young chimpanzees slowly become more proficient and the proportion of their efforts that are successful increase. Thus, Kohler's chimpanzees may not have been any brighter than Thorndike's cats; they may simply have benefited from past experience with similar problems.

Evaluation.   The fact that the use of sticks by Kohler's chimpanzees *can* be explained in terms of the gradual strengthening of associations, of course, does not necessarily mean that this explanation is correct; the behavior could also have been due to a sudden insight, as Kohler's description suggests. (After all, two of Birch's six subjects did manage to solve the problem quickly, even though they had no previous experience with sticks.) We will not try to resolve this question here. The issues involved are complex, and it will take us three entire chapters (Chapters 11, 12 and 13) to review the evidence and decide whether associative or cognitive theories offer a better account of learning. Our only purpose here is to introduce the issues and provide a preliminary indication of how experimenters have tried to test the two theories. You may find it interesting at this point to make a note of your own beliefs about whether associative learning is basically associative or cognitive. Whichever view you currently hold, you may find it challenged by some of the evidence to be presented.

2.5 SUMMARY

The first attempt to explain human behavior in terms of lawful principles was by Descartes, who attributed involuntary movements of the body to simple connections—which he called reflexes—between sensory receptors and muscles. The British Associationists extended Descartes's argument by proposing that thinking was also controlled by simple principles. Ideas were formed through associations between sensations, and thought was guided by associations between ideas that had previously occurred together. The idea that associations were critical in regulating behavior received further support when physiological research revealed that activity in the brain is determined by the transmission of electrical signals between cells called neurons, and thus that the strength of the connections between neurons is ultimately the crucial factor determining all behavior and thought. If we could understand the processes involved in the formation of associations, therefore, we might have the key to understanding human behavior.

It was this belief that explained much of the excitement over Pavlov's discovery of the conditioned reflex. Pavlov found that if a tone (the CS) was paired with food (the US), dogs would eventually salivate to the tone just as they had to the food. To explain this result, Pavlov suggested that the CS and US each triggered activity within some region of the dog's brain, and that when two centers within the brain become active within a short period of time, the connection between these centers is strengthened. The associative process involved appeared to be a general one, as research on second-order conditioning and sensory preconditioning suggested that associations could be formed between any stimuli that occurred together. Thus, by studying how salivation was conditioned, it might be possible to discover the laws governing the formation of all associations.

A second procedure for studying the formation of associations was developed by Thorndike. Darwin's theory of evolution had produced great interest in the intelligence of animals, and Thorndike set out to develop an objective procedure for assessing learning and intelligence. In his most famous experiment, he placed hungry cats in a puzzle box with a dish of food outside, and recorded how long it took the cats to open the door and obtain the food. He found that the latency of the escape response was reduced over trials, but the gradual nature of this reduction suggested to him that the cats' learning was based not on an intellectual appreciation of the situation, but rather on the gradual stamping in of an association between the stimulus of the box and the escape response. He found the same pattern of trial-and-error learning when he required other responses to open the door, and also in other species. These results led him to formulate the Law of Effect, which said that the connection between a stimulus and a response will be strengthened if the response is followed by a satisfying outcome, and weakened if followed by discomfort. Because the term *satisfaction* seemed potentially misleading, later psychologists used the term *reinforcer* instead of reward.

The Law of Effect proposed not only that rewards would strengthen responses but that punishments would weaken them. Because reinforcement and punishment both involve a change in the strength of a response as a result of its consequences, they are classified together as instances of instrumental conditioning. In order to provide students with yet more terms to memorize, classical and instrumental conditioning are themselves categorized as instances of associative learning, in which we learn the association or relationship between two events that occur together.

We appear to be able to associate virtually any stimuli that occur together—words, tastes, and so on—but psychologists have been particularly interested in studying classical conditioning and instrumental conditioning because of the powerful role they play in shaping our behavior. This role is particularly obvious in the case of reinforcement and punishment, but we shall see that classical conditioning also plays a key role in determining how we behave.

There are two major classes of theories about the nature of the learning processes involved in conditioning. Associative theories suggest that conditioning is a basically simple process involving the formation of associations between events that occur together, so that in future the occurrence of one of these events will automatically activate the other. Cognitive theories suggest that even the simplest learning situations require cognitive processes such as memory, attention, and abstraction—the same cognitive processes that we use in solving far more complex problems.

One clash between the two views came in trying to understand the slow learning observed in Thorndike's puzzle box: Whereas Thorndike attributed this to the gradual formation of associations, Kohler argued that it was because the construction of the box concealed from subjects the physical connection between the latch and the door. When Kohler gave chimpanzees the opportunity to obtain food outside their cage by using sticks, he found that they solved the problem not through gradual improvements but through sudden flashes of insight. However, Harlow later reported that the ability of monkeys to solve problems in a single trial was based on the gradual development of what he called learning sets, and more recent research suggests that the ability of chimpanzees to use sticks may be the product of extensive experience. It is thus not clear whether the insightful behavior of Kohler's chimpanzees truly reflected sophisticated cognitive processes, or, together with the work of the British Associationists, is another illustration of how seemingly complex thought may be based on the gradual strengthening of associations.

We shall encounter this conflict between associative and cognitive interpretations of learning repeatedly in later chapters, and we will trace the evolution of these views—still not complete—toward a consensus. One point worth noting here is the shared belief of both sides that associative learning does not differ from more complex forms of learning nearly as much as appearances might suggest. Consider the tasks of learning to ride a bicycle and mastering Einstein's theory of relativity. There can be little doubt that the latter task is much more difficult, but both associative and cognitive theorists believe that the two tasks nevertheless share important similarities. According to the associative view, this is because the simple associative processes involved in learning to ride also play a key role in more demanding tasks. (For evidence on the importance of simple associations in complex tasks, see the discussion of the Rescorla-Wagner model in Chapter 5 and of neural network models in Chapter 13.) According to cognitive theorists, it is because many of the cognitive skills required for thinking are also involved in seemingly simpler tasks such as learning to ride. In understanding atomic physics, cognitive processes such as memory, attention, and abstraction are important, but these processes also play an important role in the seemingly simple task of learning to ride a bicycle: Learners must learn which aspects of body position to attend to, remember their experiences, and abstract from their successful experiences the common elements or strategies that produced this success. Thus, although learning physics is undoubtedly harder, cognitive theorists believe that complex cognitive processes are involved in both. * In sum, whether we view associative learning as simple or complex, an understanding of the processes involved is likely to have significant implications for our understanding of learning in other situations.

---

* If the task of learning to ride a bicycle still seems absurdly easier to you, imagine trying to build a robot capable of mastering the skill—no one has come close to solving the problems involved. Many of the skills that seem trivial to us—reading handwriting, walking around a room without bumping into furniture—are still beyond even the most sophisticated computers.

Selected Definitions

Contiguity A fundamental principle believed to underlie the formation of associations. This principle stipulates that events that occur together become associated.

Neuron A cell in the body specialized to produce and transmit electrical impulses.

Dendrites Fibers that branch out from the cell body of a neuron to make contact with other neurons.

Axon The elongated section of a neuron which transmits an electrical impulse generated in the cell body to other neurons or muscles.

Synaptic gap The very small space that separates the axon terminals of one neuron from the dendrites of a second neuron. Neurotransmitters flow across this gap to transmit signals from the first neuron to the second one.

Neurotransmitters Chemicals that are stored within the terminals of a neuron. When an electrical signal arrives at the terminal, it causes the release of neurotransmitters which then move across the synaptic gap to stimulate another neuron.

Cerebral cortex The outer section of the vertebrate brain. It is the center of higher functions such as thought and language.

Trial In a learning experiment, a discrete opportunity for a subject to learn. In classical conditioning, a single pairing of a CS and a US is called a trial. In instrumental conditioning, a single opportunity for a subject to make a response—for example, for a cat to escape from a puzzle box or a rat to run through a maze—is also called a trial.

Maze experiments are sometimes called *discrete-trial* procedures because there is a clearly demarcated period during which the subject is given the opportunity to make a single response. In a *free-operant* experiment, by contrast, once subjects are introduced into the experimental situation—for example, a rat is placed in a box containing a lever—they are allowed to respond whenever they wish during an experimental session. (See also Chapter 6.)

Unconditioned stimulus (US) A stimulus that elicits a response without training.

Unconditioned response (UR) The response elicited by an unconditioned stimulus.

Conditioned stimulus (CS) A stimulus that, through pairing with an unconditioned stimulus, elicits a response.

Conditioned response (CR) The response to a conditioned stimulus caused by pairings of the CS with a US.

Classical conditioning An increase in the probability of a response to a conditioned stimulus (CS) due to pairings of that stimulus with an unconditioned stimulus (US). Older definitions of conditioning required that the response to the CS be the same as the response to the US, but it is now clear that these responses sometimes differ.

Rescorla (1988) has proposed defining classical conditioning more broadly as the learning of relationships among events. We prefer the term *associative learning* for the broader case, with classical conditioning restricted to instances of associative learning in which both events are stimuli and the second stimulus elicits an unconditioned response (or, in the case of second-order conditioning, the second stimulus elicits a conditioned response).

Second-order conditioning   Learning that takes place as a result of pairing a stimulus with a previously conditioned stimulus.

Sensory preconditioning   A procedure in which two neutral stimuli are presented together and then one of them is paired with an unconditioned stimulus. The typical result is that responding is conditioned not only to the conditioned stimulus but also to the stimulus paired with it during the preconditioning phase.

Latency   The time from when a response becomes possible until it actually occurs. In a puzzle box, for example, the latency of the escape response is the time from when the animal is placed in the cage until it escapes.

Law of Effect   Thorndike's statement that the presentation of a reward would strengthen the connection between the response that preceded it and the stimuli present at the time.

Reinforcer   An event that increases the probability of a response when presented after it.

The term *reinforcer* is also sometimes used to refer to a US, because the presentation of a US following a CS also leads to a strengthening of a response, in this case the conditioned response. A US such as shock, however, will not strengthen whatever response it follows in the same way as food does, and in this text we will reserve the term *reinforcer* for events that have this transituational capacity to strengthen almost any response they follow. For further discussion of the issues involved in distinguishing classical conditioning from reinforcement, see Chapter 9.

Reinforcement   The presentation of a reinforcer following a response, or the increase in response probability that results from this presentation.

Punishment   A subtype of instrumental learning in which the consequence is usually aversive and results in a decreased likelihood of a given response.

Instrumental conditioning (or **operant conditioning**)   A type of associative learning in which an important event follows a response, resulting in a change in the probability of the response.

Learning set   An improvement in the speed of solving problems due to previous experience with similar problems. This phenomenon is also called "learning how to learn."

Review Questions

1. Why did Pavlov's research attract so much attention?

2. What were the laws of association according to the British Association-ists?

3. Why is the organization of the brain consistent with Pavlov's view that all learning is "nothing more than the results of an establishment of new nervous connections."

4. What is the difference between second-order conditioning and sensory preconditioning?

5. Why didn't Thorndike trust anecdotal observations? How did he study learning instead?

6. What is the Law of Effect? What objections have been raised to it?

7. How do classical conditioning and instrumental conditioning differ? What are the different forms of instrumental conditioning?

8. What is a learning process?

9. What is associative learning? How do associative and cognitive theories of associative learning differ?

10. What evidence suggests that associative learning is a gradual, trial-and-error process? What evidence suggests that it is a sudden, insightful process?

CLASSICAL CONDITIONING

FOUNDATIONS OF CONDITIONING

W e have seen that Pavlov's research aroused interest partly because of its potential as a tool for studying the formation of associations, but also as a possible technique for controlling behavior. If salivation could be controlled, what about other involuntary behaviors such as heart rate and blood pressure, or emotions such as fear and ecstasy? In this chapter we will begin to address these issues. We will start by returning to Pavlov's laboratory, to see what else he learned about the properties of classical conditioning. We will then turn to Western efforts to build on his work and determine what range of behaviors could be classically conditioned.

3.1 PAVLOV'S DISCOVERIES

Once Pavlov had developed a reliable procedure for investigating conditioning, he embarked on an extensive series of experiments to study this process. Together with his colleagues, he built an extraordinarily detailed picture of the basic processes of classical conditioning. Indeed, there was a time in the 1950s when it could still be argued plausibly that every single major fact about conditioning had been anticipated by Pavlov some 50 years earlier. We cannot begin to convey the richness of Pavlov's work in the space available, but we shall summarize briefly some of his most important findings.

Extinction

For Pavlov, the real importance of conditioning was its role in adapting behavior to the environment. Some features of an animal's environment are relatively constant over its lifetime, and in coping with these static features unlearned reflexes may be adequate. Other features of the environment, however, may fluctuate, and an animal's chances of survival will be enhanced if it can adjust its behavior to the new circumstances. Grizzly bears, for example, feed on salmon; but the rivers contain salmon only during the brief migration season of that fish. If a bear visits a river one day and finds it teeming with salmon, it clearly will have a better chance of survival if it can learn that the river is a good source of food and therefore return the next day. Once the salmon migration is over, however, a river that was once full of fish may become empty. What happens to an established association when a CS no longer reliably signals the US?

The answer is shown in Figure 3.1, which presents the results of an experiment in which a previously conditioned stimulus was presented a number of times without the US. The result was that the conditioned response gradually disappeared, a phenomenon referred to by Pavlov as **extinction**. While answering one question, however, this result raised another question— namely, *why* did the response disappear? If a neural connection had been established in the brain between the CS and the US, could this connection have been obliterated simply by presenting the CS by itself a few times?

To Pavlov, this was implausible. There was no physiological evidence that neural connections suddenly disintegrated in this way, and observations of the dogs' behavior also suggested that the connections formed during conditioning were still present after extinction. If, for example, an interval of time was allowed to elapse after extinction had been completed, and if the CS was then presented again, the previously extinguished response would suddenly

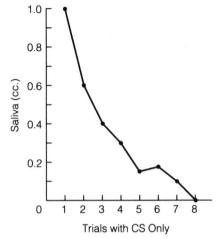

F I G U R E 3.1   Extinction of a conditioned response when the conditioned stimulus is presented by itself. (Data from Pavlov, 1927)

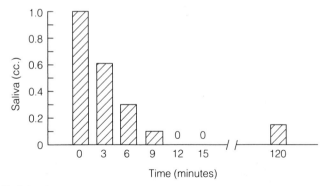

F I G U R E 3.2   Spontaneous recovery of an extinguished response. (Data from Pavlov, 1927)

reappear. Figure 3.2 shows that after a series of extinction trials in which salivation was progressively reduced to zero, the CS was reintroduced after a lapse of two hours and again elicited a significant amount of salivation. This **spontaneous recovery** of the response was only temporary; with further presentations of the CS, the recovered response would again be rapidly extinguished. The recovery clearly suggested, however, that a connection still existed between the CS and the response.

The concept of inhibition.   If the CS were still associated with salivation, why had the dog stopped salivating during the earlier extinction trials? The answer, according to Pavlov, was not that the old, excitatory connection had been destroyed, but that the CS had also acquired the capacity to inhibit responding. In an elaboration of Pavlov's ideas proposed by Konorski (1948), pairing of the CS and US was assumed to establish an excitatory connection between the corresponding brain centers, so that activation of the CS center would be transmitted to the US center. If the CS were then presented on its own, an inhibitory connection would be established between the centers so that activity in the CS center would now block or inhibit activity in the US center as well as excite it.

During Pavlov's time, no direct evidence was available for the existence of inhibitory connections in the brain, but we can clarify Pavlov's concept using physiological evidence that has become available since then. Suppose that we were able to isolate in the brain the three neurons shown in Figure 3.3. Neurons A and B both terminate at neuron C. To assess their relationships, we can stimulate activity in neurons A and B with an electrical current and observe the effects on neuron C by means of a recording electrode inserted into that neuron. Normally, the electrical potential inside a neuron remains at a constant level, but whenever an electrical signal is transmitted through the

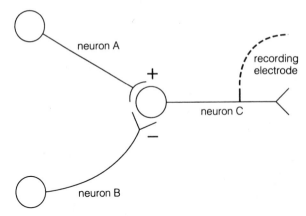

F I G U R E 3.3 Hypothetical arrangement of three neurons to illustrate inhibition. A tiny metal electrode inserted into the axon can record the passage of electrical impulses along the axon. The plus sign indicates an excitatory connection, as activity in neuron A increases activity in neuron C; the minus sign indicates an inhibitory connection, as activity in neuron B reduces activity in neuron C.

neuron there is a brief, sharp change in potential. These neuron impulses appear in recordings as vertical "spikes."

Suppose that we first stimulate neuron A for 10 seconds and find that neuron C becomes active for as long as neuron A is stimulated, producing an intense burst of spikes (Figure 3.4, trial 1). The electrical activity in neuron A is clearly being transmitted in some way to neuron C, implying an excitatory connection between them. Now suppose that we stimulate neuron B and find no effect on neuron C (Figure 3.4, trial 2). One possible interpretation of this result is that the connection between neurons B and C is defective, so activity B is not being transmitted. Suppose, however, that we now stimulate A and B together and observe significantly less activity in neuron C than when neuron

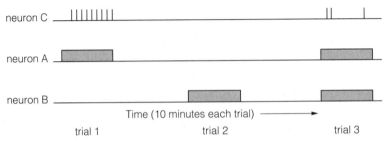

F I G U R E 3.4 A hypothetical record of electrical activity in neuron C. The shaded bars indicate when neurons A and B are being stimulated; the transmission of an electrical impulse in neuron C is represented by a vertical line or "spike" in the upper record. (Each vertical line is a single impulse.)

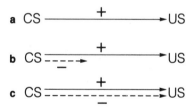

F I G U R E 3.5   Pavlov's view of the development of inhibitory connections during extinction: (a) By the end of conditioning, an excitatory connection has been formed between the CS and US (solid line). (b) Presentation of the CS by itself produces a new, inhibitory connection (broken line). (c) With repeated presentations of the CS by itself, the inhibitory connection becomes stronger (represented by a longer broken line).

A was stimulated on its own (Figure 3.4, trial 3). Clearly, neuron B does have an effect on neuron C, but that effect is to prevent or inhibit activity; when neuron B is active, other neurons have greater difficulty in triggering neuron C into action. Inhibitory neurons, in other words, do not themselves produce activity in the neuron they inhibit, but prevent that neuron from being stimulated by other neurons.

During conditioning, Pavlov argued, an excitatory connection is established between the CS and US (Figure 3.5a); during extinction, a parallel inhibitory connection is developed (Figure 3.5b). As the inhibitory connection becomes stronger, it is increasingly effective in preventing the response until eventually, when the excitatory and inhibitory tendencies are equally balanced, the conditioned response is no longer elicited (Figure 3.5c). As to the spontaneous recovery of the response, Pavlov assumed the inhibitory process to be more unstable or fragile than the excitatory process. The inhibitory connection would thus be more likely to decay with the passage of time and, hence, no longer able to block the response completely. (For discussion of alternative explanations, see Mackintosh, 1974; Thomas & Sherman, 1986.)

Conditioned inhibition.   Direct evidence for the existence of inhibition came from the phenomenon of **conditioned inhibition**—the tendency of a stimulus to block, or inhibit, responding as a result of previous training. The training procedure used by Pavlov was to alternate between trials in which the CS+ (positive stimulus) was paired with food and trials in which the CS+ and the CS− (inhibitory stimulus) were presented together without food. The CS− signaled that food would not be forthcoming and acquired the capacity to inhibit salivation. Suppose, for example, that we conditioned salivation to a metronome, but that on certain trials we presented a whistle simultaneously with the metronome and did *not* present food.

$$\text{metronome} \longrightarrow \text{food}$$
$$\text{whistle} + \text{metronome} \longrightarrow$$

After a series of such trials, subjects would respond vigorously when the metronome was presented by itself, but not when the metronome was presented in conjunction with the whistle. The reason, according to Pavlov, was that pairing the metronome with food had resulted in the establishment of an excitatory connection between the corresponding neural centers, whereas pairing the whistle with no food had resulted in an inhibitory connection between the whistle and food. When the metronome was presented by itself, it excited the food center and thus elicited salivation; but when the whistle was also presented, it inhibited the food center, with the net result that no response was elicited.

As a further test that the whistle was truly inhibitory, Pavlov combined it with other conditioned stimuli. In one experiment, a tactile stimulus was paired with food until it reliably elicited salivation, and then the whistle was presented at the same time.

whistle + tactile stimulus $\longrightarrow$?

The results are shown in Table 3.1, which is taken from Pavlov's published account. The tactile stimulus presented by itself elicited vigorous salivation; whenever the whistle was added, however, salivation ceased almost entirely. In another experiment, Pavlov presented a conditioned inhibitory stimulus with food and again found a reduction in salivation. Although alternative explanations for these results are possible, subsequent experiments have confirmed Pavlov's interpretation: Conditioned stimuli can acquire the capacity to inhibit a response as well as to elicit it. (For reviews, see Mackintosh, 1983; Williams, Overmier, & LoLordo, 1992.)

Returning to the phenomenon of extinction, it is now widely accepted that during conditioning an excitatory connection is formed between the CS and the US, and during extinction a second, inhibitory connection is added. As extinction trials continue, the inhibitory connection becomes progressively stronger until, eventually, it equals or exceeds the excitatory tendency in strength and responding ceases.

TABLE 3.1   A Test for Conditioned Inhibition (Data from Pavlov, 1927, p. 77)

Time	Stimulus Presented for One Minute	Drops of Saliva During One Minute
3:08 P.M.	Tactile	3
3:16 P.M.	Tactile	8
3:25 P.M.	Tactile + whistle	<1
3:30 P.M.	Tactile	11

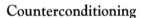

Counterconditioning

In addition to extinction, Pavlov discovered another way to eliminate a conditioned response, which was to pair the CS that elicited it with a US that elicited a different response. If the new response is incompatible with the old one, so that only one of them can occur at a time, then the more strongly the new response is conditioned the less likely it is that the old response will occur again. This technique has come to be known as **counterconditioning**. Pavlov provided a particularly dramatic demonstration of its power by showing that it could be used to suppress even unconditioned responses. In one experiment, he used an electric shock that normally elicited violent escape reactions and repeatedly followed it with presentations of food. Provided that the intensity of the shock employed was not too severe, he found that the dogs' normal defensive reactions were eventually suppressed almost entirely. Rather than jumping or showing any signs of discomfort on being shocked, a dog's only visible reaction was "turning its head to where it usually received the food and smacking its lips, at the same time producing a profuse secretion of saliva" (Pavlov, 1927, p. 30).

Stimulus Control

Pavlov recognized that the brain must cope with an enormous range of stimuli, detecting differences between even very similar stimuli so that each can elicit the appropriate response, but also in some cases grouping stimuli together so that minor variants of a stimulus will still elicit the same response. One of the topics he investigated, therefore, was how variations in the conditioned stimulus affected responding to it.

Generalization.   Pavlov found that conditioning resulted in salivation not only to the CS presented during training but also to other stimuli that were similar to it. In one experiment, Pavlov conditioned salivation to a tone of 1000 Hz.[*] After conditioning, the dogs salivated not only to the 1000-Hz tone but also to tones of 1100 Hz, 1200 Hz, and so on, with the greatest increase in salivation occurring to the tones most similar to the training stimulus (that is, 900 Hz and 1100 Hz). This phenomenon was called **generalization**, and to Pavlov it had clear adaptive advantages. In nature, we rarely if ever encounter exactly the same stimulus twice; even a human face is never viewed from exactly the same angle or in exactly the same light. It is crucial, therefore, that a response is not restricted to the precise stimulus encountered on conditioning trials but generalizes to similar stimuli.

---

[*] The pitch of a tone is determined by the frequency with which its basic sound pattern is repeated each second. Frequency is measured in units called hertz (Hz), where one Hz equals one cycle per second.

Discrimination.   In some situations, however, it may be very important *not* to respond in the same way to similar stimuli. The appropriate response that a subject may have to a mushroom, for example, may not be at all appropriate to a toadstool. To test whether his dogs could learn to distinguish, or discriminate, between similar stimuli if given sufficient exposure to them, Pavlov tried pairing a tone with food many hundreds of times, in the hope that salivation would increasingly come under the control of the precise tone that was being presented. Simple repetition of this kind, however, did not sharpen control significantly. Pavlov found that it was far more effective to use discrimination training in which conditioning trials with a positive stimulus (CS+) were alternated with presentations of a negative stimulus (CS−).

$$CS+ \longrightarrow food$$
$$CS- \longrightarrow$$

In a typical experiment, a 1000-Hz tone would be presented, followed by food, on half the trials; on the remaining trials, a 900-Hz tone would be presented without food. The typical results of such an experiment are shown in Figure 3.6. At first, the subjects responded to both stimuli, as responding conditioned to CS+ generalized to CS−. As training continued, responding was increasingly restricted to CS+. The subjects had learned to discriminate, or respond differentially to, the two stimuli.

Discrimination is the differential responding to two stimuli. As with many other learning terms, the term *discrimination* sometimes refers to the outcome (differential responding), sometimes to the procedure, and sometimes to the process assumed to underlie it.

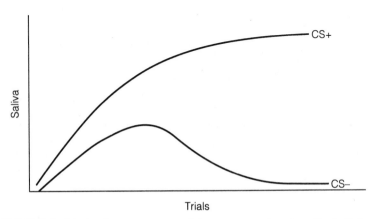

F I G U R E 3.6   Idealized representation of discrimination learning. On half the trials, a tone was followed by food (CS+); on the remaining trials, another tone was not followed by food (CS−).

3.2 THE NEED FOR CONTROL GROUPS

When they learned of Pavlov's research, Western psychologists also wanted to study classical conditioning. Did classical conditioning occur in humans? If so, was it confined to relatively minor responses such as salivation, or could it affect all aspects of our behavior?

An Example: Conditioning Fear

One of the first attempts to extend classical conditioning to other responses was carried out by John B. Watson, founder of the influential movement known as behaviorism. Watson argued that psychologists should be concerned with overt behavior rather than the hidden processes of the mind, and he argued for a greater concern with practical applications. Thus, in 1920, together with Rosalie Raynor, Watson attempted to study fear conditioning in a human infant.

Their subject's name was given in their published paper as Albert B., though he was later to be immortalized as Little Albert. Albert was normally a "stolid and unemotional" infant who almost never cried. As the first step in their experiment, Watson and Raynor presented Albert with a white rat and found that it elicited no signs of fear; Albert's only discernible reaction was an attempt to play with the animal. They then began conditioning trials in which every presentation of the white rat was followed by a loud noise that had previously been found to elicit strong fear. Almost immediately, Albert began to show signs of distress upon presentation of the rat, and these signs increased over succeeding trials. When they presented the rat on the eighth trial, they recorded Albert's behavior as follows:

> The instant the rat was shown the baby began to cry. Almost instantly he turned sharply to the left, fell over on left side, raised himself on all fours and began to crawl away so rapidly that he was caught with difficulty before reaching the edge of the table.
>
> (Watson & Raynor, 1920, p. 5)

This fear reaction also generalized to similar stimuli that, before conditioning, had been neutral (for example, a rabbit and a fur coat). Albert's fear reaction showed no signs of fading with time and was still present on a test trial given almost a month later. The experiment had to be terminated at this point because Albert's mother ceased working at the hospital where they had been testing him.

The results they obtained were very convincing: After only seven conditioning trials, Albert's reaction to the rat was converted from one of mild curiosity to one of apparent terror. But could the change in Albert's behavior really be attributed to classical conditioning? The answer depends on exactly what we mean by conditioning. The essential element in Pavlov's procedure seems to be that a stimulus acquires the capacity to elicit a response as a result of pairings with a second stimulus that already elicited it. Putting this same idea slightly more technically, we defined classical conditioning in Chapter 2 as an increase in the probability of a response to a CS as a result of pairings of that CS with a US. The loud noise used in Watson and Raynor's experiment certainly seemed to function as an unconditioned stimulus for fear; why, therefore, should we doubt whether Albert's fear of the rat was due to conditioning?

Alternative Explanations

The problem is that, although the observed fear response may have been due to pairings of the CS and US, the response could also be explained in other ways.

Sensitization.   One possible explanation is that Albert's fear increased simply because of the repeated presentations of the rat. This may seem very unlikely: If the rat did not elicit fear initially, why should continuing to present it repeatedly by itself endow it with the capacity to do so? The first point to note is that this explanation is possible even if it doesn't seem very likely. As we saw in Chapter 1, explanations that initially seemed wildly implausible sometimes turn out to be correct. In this case, moreover, we have already seen evidence that this explanation is far from implausible. In our discussion of the startle reflex in Chapter 1, we saw that reflexive responses to a stimulus can be sensitized with repeated presentations, especially if the CS is presented in an upsetting situation. If the rat did elicit a small amount of fear initially, it is entirely possible that it was simply the repeated presentations of the rat that increased Albert's fear, not the pairings of this stimulus with the loud noise.

Pseudoconditioning.   Psychology experiments must now adhere to a number of ethical standards, and adherence is generally monitored by an ethics committee at the institution where the research is carried out. By modern standards, it is doubtful whether an experiment such as Watson and Raynor's could now be carried out, because of the distress that Albert suffered. To allow us to explore further the methodological issues involved in assessing classical conditioning, however, let us suppose that we had available a procedure for measuring fear that did not actually produce fear! Armed with this procedure, suppose that we repeated the Watson and Raynor experiment but controlled for sensitization effects by using two groups of subjects: an experimental group that received pairings of the rat (CS) with the noise (US), and a control group that only received the CS. If Albert's fear was due solely to repeated presentations of the CS, the CS-only control group should show just as must fear as the conditioning group.

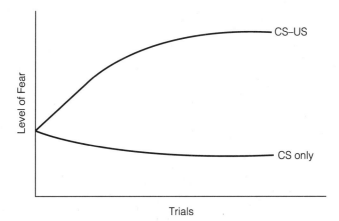

F I G U R E 3.7   Change in the level of fear displayed by two groups, one receiving pairings of the CS with a US, and the other receiving the CS by itself.

In all likelihood, the results of this experiment would resemble those shown in Figure 3.7: Rather than increasing over trials, fear levels in the control group would decrease. (When a stimulus is repeated, the response it elicits is generally much more likely to habituate than to become sensitized.) If we obtained this result, could we conclude that the increase in response in our experimental group was due to conditioning? The answer is still no: The increase may have been caused not by pairings of the CS with the US, but rather by presentations of the US by itself. In this case, repeated exposure to the loud noise might have made Albert more and more upset, so that almost any new stimulus might have produced fear.

Experimental evidence that presenting a US by itself really can affect responding to other stimuli comes from an experiment on eyelid conditioning by Kimble, Mann, and Dufort (1955). The experimental group received 60 pairings of a light with a puff of air to the eye. A control group received the identical treatment for the first 20 trials, but on trials 21–40 they received only the US. Finally, on trials 41–60 they again received paired presentations.

Trials	Experimental Group	Control Group
1–20	CS–US	CS–US
21–40	CS–US	US
41–60	CS–US	CS–US

How much improvement in responding to the CS should we expect during trials 21–40? The experimental group received 20 pairings of the CS

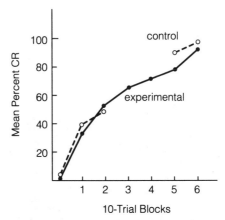

F I G U R E 3.8   Eyeblink conditioning. The experimental group received 60 pairings of a light with an air puff; the control group received CS–US pairings on trials 1–20 and 41–60 but only the air puff during the intervening interval. (Adapted from Kimble, Mann, & Dufort, 1955)

and US during this period, whereas the control group received only the US. If pairing is important, only the experimental group should have improved; if presentation of a US by itself can increase responding to a CS, then responding in the two groups should have been similar. As shown in Figure 3.8, the improvement in the two groups was not merely similar but almost identical. Thus, although the results of the experimental group on their own would have seemed impressive evidence for conditioning, the inclusion of the control group showed that this improvement was due solely to presentation of the US.

An increase in responding to a CS due to presentation of a US by itself is known as **pseudoconditioning** and is perhaps not as mysterious as it seems initially: It is not really surprising that subjects given repeated blasts of air to the eye should become jumpy enough that they blinked whenever any sudden stimulus was presented. (For another possible explanation of pseudoconditioning, see Wickens & Wickens, 1942.) Although pseudoconditioning is not usually as powerful as Kimble and associates found it to be, it is certainly possible that Albert's increased fear of the rat was due solely to repeated experiences of the loud noise, not to its pairings with the rat.

Interaction effects.   Suppose that with our newfound wisdom we again redesign our experiment, this time including a second control group that receives only the US by itself. (To assess conditioning in this group, we would introduce the CS by itself on a single test trial at the end of training.) Figure 3.9 shows the hypothetical results: Presentation of the US by itself increased fear

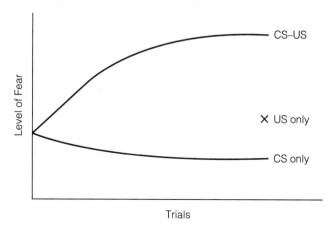

F I G U R E 3.9   Level of fear displayed by three groups—one given CS–US pairings, one given the CS by itself, and the third given the US by itself for the same number of trials followed by a single trial of the CS by itself.

on CS test trials, but not nearly as much as paired presentations of the CS and US. Now, at last, can we conclude that we have demonstrated conditioning?

The answer, frustratingly, is no. Although we have controlled for the *separate* effects of the CS by itself and the US by itself, we have not controlled for the possibility that, when presented concurrently, their combined effect may be greater than the sum of their individual effects. A nonadditive effect of this kind, when two variables are presented together, is known as an **interaction effect**. To clarify this concept, consider the following situation: Imagine yourself studying for an exam in a dingy hotel room. A dripping faucet in an adjacent room might bother you, but you might still be able to study; a flashing neon light outside your window might bother you, but again you might be able to ignore it. If both were going on simultaneously, however, their combined effects might drive you up the wall, in a way that you could not predict by considering the effects of each factor in isolation. In the same way, the combined effects of CS and US presentations might be much greater than the sum of their effects measured separately.

It is not enough, then, to control for the effects of the CS and US separately; we also need to control for any interaction between them. One simple procedure for doing this is to use an **unpaired control**—a control group in which the CS and the US are presented at widely separated times (Figure 3.10). Subjects in an unpaired control receive the same number of CS and US presentations as experimental subjects who receive normal conditioning trials, but these presentations are arranged so that the CS and US never occur together. If pairing of a CS and US produces an association, then the experi-

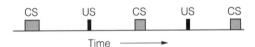

F I G U R E 3.10 The unpaired control procedure for classical conditioning. The CS and US are presented at widely separated time intervals.

mental group should respond more; if responding is due simply to the combined effects of receiving the CS and US separately, then responding in the two groups will be equal.

The analysis we have been pursuing may seem tedious or unimportant: What do the details of the control procedure matter, you may ask; what we want to know are the facts! As we saw in Chapter 1, however, it can be very difficult to determine what a fact is, because the facts for one generation have a nasty habit of becoming the laughable superstitions of the next generation. Indeed, as we shall see, more recent research has shown that the unpaired control also has important limitations as a control for assessing conditioning. For the moment, though, let us stop beating this not-quite-dead horse and accept that this control provides us with at least a rough tool for assessing conditioning. Can we now say whether fear can be classically conditioned?

3.3 THE GENERALITY OF CONDITIONING

With an acceptable procedure for assessing conditioning, we can now try to answer the question of what responses can be classically conditioned. To provide some structure for our discussion, we will begin by examining simpler responses, and only then turn to more complex responses such as emotions.

We can divide behavior into two broad classes, based on the subsystem of the nervous system involved in controlling the response. There are two semi-independent systems involved in transmitting impulses from the central nervous system to other parts of the body. The *skeletal nervous system* controls striped muscles, so called because their alternating bands of dark and light fibers give them a striated, or striped, appearance when examined under a microscope. Most of the muscles we think of when we hear the word *muscle*— biceps, triceps, deltoids, and so on—are in fact striped muscles, whose function is to adjust the position of the body in space. The *autonomic nervous system*, on the other hand, controls the smooth muscles and glands, both of which are involved in regulation of the internal environment. Smooth muscles, as you might imagine, have a uniform or smooth appearance under the microscope; they are responsible for movements within the body. Rhythmic contractions of the smooth muscles lining the gullet, for example, are responsible for the movement of food from the mouth to the stomach (contractions known as peristalsis); glands secrete chemical substances such as adrenalin and saliva.

The skeletal nervous system is thus responsible for coping with the external environment through bodily movement, whereas the autonomic nervous system regulates the internal milieu. The bodily movements controlled by the skeletal nervous system are called **skeletal responses**; the glandular and smooth muscle activities controlled by the autonomic nervous system are called **autonomic responses**. We will begin our exploration of what responses can be conditioned with autonomic responses; we will then look at skeletal responses and, finally, at more complex responses such as motives and emotions.

Autonomic Conditioning

We have already encountered evidence that at least one response controlled by the autonomic nervous system can be conditioned: salivation. For many years, however, it was unclear whether all autonomic responses, or only a limited subset of responses, could be conditioned. Soviet investigators reported successful conditioning of a wide range of autonomic responses—for example, urine formation in the kidney and insulin release by the pancreas. (See Bykov, 1957.) Psychologists in the West, however, had difficulty evaluating the Soviet claims because only brief summaries were available in translation and few Western psychologists had the surgical skills required to study autonomic responses directly.

Over the past two decades, researchers have developed a number of simple techniques that allow autonomic activity to be monitored indirectly, and research based on these techniques has confirmed the earlier Soviet reports. We cannot cover all this research, but will illustrate it with a few examples.

The GSR. When we encounter new or stressful situations, our bodies prepare for action through a complex set of responses known collectively as arousal. The adrenal gland secretes the hormone adrenalin, the heart rate increases, a change in blood pressure occurs, and so on. One component of arousal is perspiration, and we can measure this component by passing a very small electrical current through the skin and measuring the current that is transmitted. The skin's conductivity defines the *galvanic skin response*, or GSR, which is thus just a measure of perspiration: The more we perspire, the more readily our skin conducts an electric current. By measuring perspiration, therefore, the GSR gives us a simple index of a person's arousal.

Because it measures arousal, the GSR has been of considerable interest to psychologists. It can be used to assess concentration—the harder subjects concentrate, the more aroused they may become—and also the presence of emotions. The GSR is used as the main component of polygraph, or lie detector, tests: When people are lying, they tend to become aroused, so that by measuring the GSR we can obtain indirect evidence about whether someone is lying. (It is important to emphasize, however, that polygraph tests are very far from infallible. The fact that someone becomes aroused when asked an incriminating question does not necessarily mean that the person is lying; the person may just be embarrassed or frightened. See Podlesny & Raskin, 1977.)

The important point in the present context is that arousal, as measured by the GSR, is readily conditioned. If a person receives a mild electric shock, for example, arousal occurs; if this shock is preceded by a tone, the tone will also acquire the capacity to elicit the GSR. Champion and Jones (1961) have shown that this increase is genuinely due to classical conditioning: If the tone and shock are presented separately, in an unpaired control group, the GSR to the tone does not increase.

Blood glucose levels.   A central concept in understanding the activities of the autonomic nervous system is **homeostasis**, or the activities of the body that are directed to maintaining a stable internal environment. For example, we need to maintain the body's temperature at a constant level in order to survive; deviations in any direction, either up or down, can have lethal consequences. In a similar way, we act to maintain constant levels of water, energy, and so on. There is now evidence that many of the autonomic activities that regulate our internal environment can be conditioned.

One example involves the amount of glucose (a form of sugar) circulating in the blood. Siegel (1972) gave rats a number of injections of insulin, a hormone that decreases the level of glucose in the blood. Pavlov had hypothesized that the cues associated with the injection of a drug would act as conditioned stimuli, with the systemic effects of the drug then becoming conditioned to these cues. To test this hypothesis, Siegel gave his subjects a test injection of saline, a neutral fluid that normally has no effect. The saline injection did indeed elicit a strong conditioned response, but it was an *increase* in blood glucose rather than the decrease produced by the insulin. Appropriate controls showed that this result was due to the pairing of the injection with insulin.

Why was the conditioned response the opposite of the unconditioned response in this case, when in every other example of classical conditioning we have encountered the two responses were the same? Siegel (1978) has suggested that the answer could lie in the body's efforts to maintain a stable internal environment. When insulin is injected, it produces a fall in blood glucose below the optimal level; when the body senses this fall, it reacts by increasing glucose levels. It was this *compensatory response* that was conditioned, a system that may have evolved because by taking compensatory action in advance of a disturbance, the body can minimize the harmful effects of the disturbance.

An alternative explanation has been proposed by Eikelboom and Stewart (1982), who argue that the conditioned and unconditioned responses to insulin *are* the same; they appear to differ only because the unconditioned response has been incorrectly identified. Suppose, for example, that you accidentally cut your hand; would the bleeding that followed be an unconditioned response? They argue that it would not: Bleeding is a direct physical reaction to an opening in the skin, whereas an unconditioned response is a reflexive reaction that is mediated by the central nervous system. Similarly in the case of insulin, they suggest that insulin normally acts directly on the cells of the body to cause the removal of glucose from the blood, without any involvement of the central nervous system. However, when glucose levels then fall, this drop is detected by receptors in the brain, which then trigger an increase in blood glucose to compensate. The drop in glucose levels, in other words, is an unconditioned stimulus that produces an increase in glucose levels as an unconditioned response, and it is this increase that is then conditioned to the stimulus of the injection. If this argument is accepted, the conditioned and unconditioned reponses to insulin are both increases in blood glucose, with the common purpose of opposing the damaging effects of a shift from optimum levels.

Note that the issue here is not whether an increase in glucose levels can be conditioned—all sides agree that it can; the only issue is whether the unconditioned response is better understood as the initial decrease in glucose that follows an insulin injection, or the subsequent increase. (For an interpretation that combines the views of Siegel and of Eikelboom and Stewart, see Paletta & Wagner, 1986.) The question of whether conditioned and unconditioned responses are the same has potentially important theoretical implications, as we shall see in Chapter 5, but for our current purposes the important point is that glucose levels can be conditioned.

Pain sensitivity.   Siegel (1975) also investigated whether the effects of morphine could be conditioned. Morphine is one of the most effective painkillers, or analgesic drugs, that we have. (*Algesia* is derived from the Greek word meaning pain, and *an* means not; an analgesic drug is thus one that reduces pain.) With repeated administration, however, morphine loses its potency, a phenomenon known as *tolerance*. The reason for this loss of potency, Siegel suggested, could be classical conditioning. As far as a person in pain is concerned, any reduction in pain is highly desirable; but from the body's point of view, the morphine is interfering with the pain system which protects us by ensuring that we *do* react to harmful experiences by feeling pain. Thus, when an injection of morphine reduces pain (analgesia), the body responds with an increased sensitivity to pain, or *hyperalgesia*, so as to return sensitivity to its appropriate, homeostatic level. Siegel hypothesized that this compensatory, hyperalgesic reaction would be conditioned to the cues of being injected. Every time the morphine was administered, the conditioned hyperalgesic response would become stronger, and this would explain why the morphine loses its effectiveness: The analgesic effect of the morphine is being opposed by the conditioned hyperalgesic response.

To test this hypothesis, Siegel (1975) gave rats a series of morphine injections. If a compensatory reaction had been conditioned to the cues of being injected, then a test injection of saline should now cause an increase in the rats' sensitivity to pain, rather than decreasing it as morphine does. To measure pain sensitivity, Siegel used an ingeniously simple technique in which he placed the rats on a moderately hot metal plate and recorded the time until the rats licked their paws; the greater their pain sensitivity, the sooner they would lick their paws. Rats who had previously received morphine, he found, were more sensitive to pain following a saline test injection, and appropriate controls established that this was the result of conditioning.

Siegel found that this compensatory reaction was conditioned not only to the injection but also to the room in which the injection was given: Pain sensitivity was greater in the room where morphine had been administered than in other rooms. This effect, moreover, can be very powerful. Tiffany, Maude-Griffin and Drobes (1991) repeatedly injected rats with morphine in a distinctive environment. When they later tested pain sensitivity in that environment following an injection of morphine, they found that rats previously injected in that environment required six times as much morphine as control rats did to produce a set level of analgesia.

Siegel has suggested that the conditioning of compensatory reactions to environmental cues could also explain drug overdoses. Heroin, for example, will elicit compensatory reactions, and these responses become conditioned to the environment in which the heroin is normally injected. If an addict then takes heroin in a new setting, the conditioned compensatory reaction will be weaker and the effects of the heroin correspondingly magnified. In support of this hypothesis, Siegel (1984) interviewed survivors of heroin overdoses and found that 70 percent of the overdoses occurred when heroin was injected in an unfamiliar setting. Further evidence comes from a study by Siegel, Hinson, Krank, and McCully (1982) in which rats received daily injections of heroin to develop their tolerance and were then given a greatly increased dose in the test phase. Of the rats that were given the overdose in their same training environment, 32 percent died. If the overdose was administered in a different environment, however, 64 percent of the subjects succumbed. When drugs are administered repeatedly, conditioned compensatory reactions seem to play a vital role in determining how they affect us.

Nausea.   Recent research suggests that many of our autonomic responses to illness can also be classically conditioned. For example, when we become ill after eating spoiled food, the nausea that we experience may become conditioned to the taste of the food. In a study by Gustavson, Garcia, Hankins and Rusiniak (1974), coyotes were made ill after eating meat; the next time they were offered this meat, they all avoided it, and some vomited. This mechanism may also explain why cancer patients undergoing chemotherapy become ill before receiving treatment: The treatment itself induces nausea, and this nausea may then become conditioned to the hospital cues that preceded treatment. In the case of chemotherapy, as in the case of morphine, the conditioned response produces undesirable effects, but under normal conditions the conditioning of nausea to a food that makes us ill will help to ensure that we avoid a potentially dangerous food.

The immune system.   A related cause of illness is the invasion of the body by foreign substances called *antigens*; bacteria and viruses are examples. To protect ourselves from these invaders, the body's immune system will respond by producing *antibodies*—proteins that attack invading substances—and also by increasing the production of so-called killer cells, which destroy the body's own cells if they become infected and begin to malfunction. There is now evidence that both of these responses of the immune system, as well as others, can be classically conditioned.

In an experiment by MacQueen and Siegel (1989), for example, rats were given several pairings of a CS with a drug called cyclosporine, which suppresses the immune system and thereby interferes with the formation of antibodies. MacQueen and Siegel tested the hypothesis that the body would counter the suppressive effect of cyclosporine by increasing activity in the immune system, and that this compensatory response would be conditioned to the CS. They used a saccharin solution as the CS: Rats in the experimental group were injected with cyclosporine shortly after drinking the saccharin, whereas rats in an unpaired control group received the injection 24 hours later.

To test whether the saccharin had acquired the power to increase activity in the immune system, they injected the rats with a foreign substance (cells from a sheep) and measured the formation of antibodies in their blood. The rats were allowed to drink saccharin while the injection was taking effect. MacQueen and Seigel found significantly more antibodies in the experimental group than in the unpaired control, suggesting that the CS really was producing increased activity in the immune system.

Summary.   Research on drug effects and other autonomic responses has burgeoned in recent years, largely because of the pioneering work of Siegel and also of Ader and Cohen (1985). We cannot cover all of this research here, but among the responses that have been reported to be conditionable are the production of killer cells and the release of histamines, both activities controlled by the immune system, and compensatory responses that oppose the hypothermic effects of alcohol, the sedative effects of pentobarbital, and the anorexic effects of amphetamines. The autonomic system controls a bewildering array of responses, and it is beginning to look as if a very high proportion of these activities, perhaps all, can be classically conditioned.

Skeletal Conditioning

Conditioning is pervasive and powerful, insofar as autonomic responses are concerned. The list of skeletal responses that can be conditioned is not quite as impressive—in part because conditioning requires the existence of an unconditioned stimulus capable of eliciting the desired behavior, and the number of skeletal behaviors that can be elicited in this way is relatively small. Nevertheless, a significant number of skeletal responses can be conditioned—the eyeblink, the patellar or knee-jerk reflex, aggression, and so on—and in at least some of these cases the association formed is remarkably strong.

Autoshaping. A particularly interesting example was discovered almost by accident in the course of research into the effects of rewards. In order to study the effects of a reward on animal learning, it is typically necessary first to train the animal to perform some desired response, and this is done by shaping—first rewarding a response vaguely similar to the target behavior, then reinforcing a somewhat closer approximation, and so on. In research involving pigeons, for example, the birds typically are trained in a test cage that has a circular plastic disk, or key, mounted on one of its walls. To train the birds to peck the key, the experimenter first gives the birds food whenever they face the wall containing the key, then for moving their heads slightly toward the key, and so on.

This process can be laborious and time-consuming, and there was thus considerable interest when Brown and Jenkins (1968) announced the discovery of an automatic procedure for shaping key-pecking, which they called **autoshaping**. All the experimenter had to do was place the bird in a box and then collect it half an hour later; automatic programming equipment did the rest. Roughly once a minute, the key was illuminated for eight seconds, at the end of which the bird was given access to food for four seconds. Within two sessions, all 36 birds tested were pecking the key when it was illuminated.

At first, autoshaping was seen largely as a convenient practical tool, but it eventually struck people that something very strange was going on. There was no need for the birds to peck; they received food at the end of every trial regardless of their behavior. Nevertheless, the birds all soon responded vigorously on every trial. Did the birds just like pecking lighted keys, or was it conceivable that the pecking behavior elicited by the food was being conditioned to the preceding key light? Evidence for the conditioning interpretation was actually present in the original study, because Brown and Jenkins had included a condition in which the key light followed the food rather than preceding it. Only 2 out of 12 birds exposed to this condition began to peck the key. In other words, pigeons do not simply peck lighted keys; the response develops only when the key light and food are paired. (See also Jenkins & Moore, 1973.)

Sign tracking.   Brown and Jenkins specifically measured pecking at the key as the conditioned response, but subsequent research has made it clear that birds and other animals will engage in a variety of behaviors to bring themselves into contact with stimuli predicting food. If the bird is at the opposite end of the box when the light comes on, for example, it will come to the key to peck. Rats will also approach and contact a bar whose illumination is paired with food (Peterson, Ackil, Frommer, & Hearst, 1972). Pavlov (1941) also observed such behavior in his experiments: When a dog was removed from its harness after conditioning trials in which a light was paired with food, it would go over to the light and lick it!

In the natural environment, behavior of this kind would generally be adaptive, because the stimulus that most reliably precedes the ingestion of food generally *is* the food, or, more accurately, components of the food, such as its appearance or odor. There is thus adaptive value to tracking and making contact with any stimulus that reliably precedes food. For this reason, Hearst and Jenkins (1974) have suggested **sign tracking** as a generic term to cover autoshaping and similar situations in which animals approach and contact a stimulus that signals a US. Whichever term is used, this research suggests that classical conditioning can affect a very wide range of skeletal behaviors.

Conditioned Motivation

The skeletal and autonomic responses we have examined so far have all involved relatively discrete, easily specified responses such as salivation, blinking, and perspiration. In some cases, however, the conditioned response appears to be a more complex state, which, when aroused, has the capacity to motivate any of a wide range of responses.

Hunger.   To illustrate the distinction between a specific response and a motivational state, consider the following experiment by Weingarten (1983). Seven hungry rats were exposed to repeated pairings of a 4.5-minute tone with the presentation of food. Then, in a test phase, the rats were given continuous access to food so that they were sated. Nevertheless, when the tone was again presented, they immediately began to eat, consuming approximately 20 percent of their normal daily ration within a short period. A CS that had been paired with food, in other words, seemed to acquire the capacity to elicit hunger, so that the rats would eat whenever the CS was presented.

You may have experienced a comparable phenomenon in passing a bakery, where the smell of freshly baked bread suddenly made you feel hungry. The conditioned response in this case does not seem to be a single, well-defined response, but rather a broader motivational state that could lead to any of a number of behaviors directed toward satisfying it, such as buying the bread or hurrying home to eat a snack. (See also Zamble, 1967.)

There is growing evidence that classical conditioning plays a pervasive role in regulating eating. The first evidence for this role came from Pavlov, who suggested that we learn what foods are edible in part through conditioning. Puppies reared on milk did not salivate when shown solid food for the first time, suggesting that they did not recognize it as food. Only after the visual appearance of the food was paired several times with ingestion did the sight of the food begin to elicit salivation.

Conditioning may also influence our preferences for foods, as the positive or negative consequences that follow a food can become conditioned to it, and thereby alter its attractiveness. In an experiment by Capaldi, Campbell, Sheffer, and Bradford (1987), rats were given a flavored liquid and then, 30 minutes later, a meal. The greater the caloric value of the meal, the more the rats preferred that flavor in a later choice test. (See also Lucas & Timberlake, 1992.) Similarly, conditioning may teach us what not to eat: If a rat becomes ill after eating a food, it will refuse to eat it on subsequent occasions. (See the discussion of taste-aversion learning in Chapter 4.) Finally, conditioning can also induce satiety; Booth (1972) reported that stimuli paired with high-calorie meals reduced the duration of the rats' feeding.

These results suggest that conditioning can influence not only when we feel hungry but what foods we eat and when we stop eating them. Because of the considerable importance of conditioned or incentive motivation in directing behavior, we will look at two other examples: fear and sexual arousal.

Fear.   Before we can decide whether fear is conditionable, we need a way to measure it. In the case of human subjects, we could simply ask them how frightened they were, but people are not always aware of their fear, and even when they are they may not want to admit it. Thus, although introspective reports can provide some information, psychologists want a more objective method of measuring fear. One early solution for measuring fear in animals was to count feces: The more frightened a rat is, the more it will urinate and defecate. Feces counts, however, not only are unpleasant for the experimenter, but they have severe technical limitations. Although they give a good indication of a rat's initial fear level, there are distinct physiological limits to how long a rat will defecate. Thus, there are limits to the usefulness of this method for assessing long-term fear.

A far more satisfactory solution on all counts was devised by Estes and Skinner (1941) and is known as the **conditioned emotional response (CER)** procedure. It is based on the simple observation that frightened animals in a cage tend to freeze. By observing how long an animal remains immobile in the presence of a stimulus, therefore, we can gain a rough idea of how frightening that stimulus is. Estes and Skinner developed an ingeniously simple technique for measuring freezing automatically, without the experimenter having to be present. (As we shall see again in Chapter 6, Skinner was concerned throughout his career with finding the most efficient ways to run experiments.) Their technique was to give rats a task—bar-pressing for food—which they normally perform at a high rate. If a frightening stimulus is presented to the rats while they are responding, they will freeze, with the obvious result that their responding on the bar will be reduced. By counting the number of bar-presses made in the presence of a test stimulus, therefore, we obtain a simple and objective measure of the rats' fear.

In practice, a more useful index of fear is obtained by calculating a statistic known as a **suppression ratio**. If a tone is presented for three minutes, for example, we count the number of bar-presses that occur not only during the tone (B) but also during the preceding three minutes (A). The suppression ratio is then defined as:

$$\text{suppression ratio} = \frac{B}{A + B}$$

Suppose, for example, that a rat responded 50 times during the period before the tone was presented. If the tone was not frightening, the rat would continue to respond at roughly the same rate in its presence, so that it would also respond 50 times during period B. The suppression ratio would thus be:

$$\frac{B}{A + B} = \frac{50}{50 + 50} = 0.50$$

If, on the other hand, the tone elicited fear, the rat would freeze for as long as the tone was on, yielding a suppression ratio of:

$$\frac{B}{A + B} = \frac{0}{50 + 0} = 0$$

We thus have a somewhat unusual measure in which a lower score represents greater fear, with 0 representing the maximum measurable fear and 0.50 representing no fear.

Using the CER as a measure, a number of experiments have demonstrated that fear does become conditioned to stimuli that precede aversive events. To cite just one example, Annau and Kamin (1961) trained rats to press a bar to earn food, and then occasionally presented a three-minute noise followed by an electric shock. Different groups received shock intensities varying from 0.28 to 2.91 milliamps; the results are shown in Figure 3.11. The first

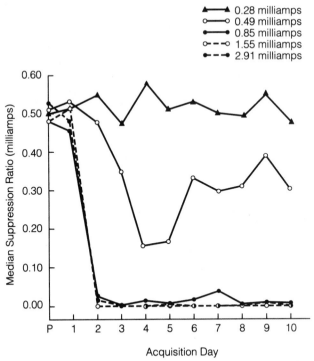

FIGURE 3.11   Acquisition of a conditioned emotional response (CER) over 10 days. Different groups received electrical shocks ranging in intensity from 0.28 milliamps to 2.91 milliamps. (Annau & Kamin, 1961)

time the noise was presented it had no effect; the rats simply carried on bar-pressing. The average suppression ratio for subjects that received a 0.28-milliamp shock remained at 0.50 on subsequent trials, suggesting little or no fear conditioning. For subjects receiving 0.49 milliamps, responding in the presence of the tone was suppressed initially but then recovered partially. A noise paired with a mild shock, in other words, induced fear at first; with continued exposure, though, subjects seemed to adapt to the shock and find it less frightening. When more severe shocks were used, however, there was little evidence of adaptation; responding was completely suppressed by the noise after only one pairing with shock and remained suppressed on all subsequent trials. Since the rats had been deprived of food for 23 hours before each session and thus, presumably, were quite hungry, their failure to work for food during the tone periods suggests a very high level of conditioned fear.

Sexual arousal.   The conditioning of sexual behavior was first reported in a study of Japanese quail by Farris (1967). Courtship in these birds normally involves a ritualized display by the male in which it circles the female while holding its body horizontal and strutting on its toes; eventually, the male begins to puff out its feathers and emit hoarse, vibrating calls. To see if this ritual could be conditioned, Farris placed male quail in a cage, sounded a buzzer for 10 seconds, and then opened a door, giving the male access to a receptive female. Within 15–20 pairings, all the males began to strut around the cage when the buzzer sounded, and within a few more trials they were puffing out their feathers and vibrating vigorously! Subjects in an unpaired control, on the other hand, showed no reaction to the buzzer. Similar findings have been reported in male rats (Zamble, Mitchell, & Findlay, 1986), including evidence that a distinctive odor paired with access to a receptive female will thereafter elicit the secretion of testosterone, a male hormone involved in controlling sexual behavior (Graham & Desjardins, 1980).

Evidence that classical conditioning may also play an important role in human sexual behavior comes from a study by Rachman and Hodgson (1968). The subjects were seven male volunteers, and the unconditioned stimuli used to produce sexual arousal were 40 slides of nude women. Each slide was preceded by a CS, a picture of knee-length, black, fur-lined boots. The picture of the boots was projected for 30 seconds, followed by 10 seconds of one of the nude slides. To assess sexual arousal, penile erection was measured by means of a rubber tube whose stretching could be monitored by an automatic recording system.

Initially, none of the subjects showed any sign of arousal to the boots. After only 30 pairings, however, strong arousal had been conditioned in five of the seven subjects, with an erection occurring every time the boots were presented. This response, moreover, generalized to similar stimuli: Three of the subjects also became aroused to brown fur boots, two to high-heeled black shoes, but none to low-heeled black shoes or sandals. At the conclusion of the experiment, sexual arousal to the boots was extinguished by repeatedly presenting the boots by themselves.

This experiment may arouse mixed feelings (it is almost sinister in some respects, hilarious in others), but its implications are potentially important. If sexual arousal is conditioned to the stimuli present when we become aroused, this conditioned arousal could influence what stimuli we then find exciting, and thus channel our sexual behavior. For example, conditioning of this kind could play an important role in the development of abnormal behaviors such as fetishes. In one case reported by McGuire, Carlisle, and Young (1965), a 17-year-old male saw through a window a girl dressed only in her underwear. Thereafter, he often masturbated while recalling this image and eventually developed a strong sexual obsession with female underwear, which he bought or stole. Whether all fetishes develop in this way, it would appear that classical conditioning can play a significant role in channeling sexual behavior.

Motivational interactions.   We have now seen that a stimulus paired with food may elicit not only a specific response such as salivation but also a more general state of hunger that can then motivate a wide range of behaviors directed toward obtaining food. Different stimuli may elicit different motives: Stimuli paired with food elicit hunger, stimuli paired with water elicit thirst, and so on. One important property of these motives is that they may be mutually inhibitory; that is, when one motive is aroused, it will tend to automatically inhibit other motives aroused at the same time.

The first evidence suggesting that motives can inhibit each other came from counterconditioning. As we saw earlier, Pavlov found that when a mild shock was paired with food, the shock ceased to elicit signs of fear and instead elicited salivation. One possible interpretation of this result is that salivation and manifestations of fear were incompatible at an overt level—one cannot physically salivate at the same time as, say, wincing—but this seems unlikely. A more plausible interpretation is that the pairing of the shock with food conditioned hunger to the shock, and this motive in turn inhibited the fear normally produced by the shock. As this motivational interpretation would suggest, Dickinson and Dearing (1979) found that pairing a shock with water caused the shock to lose its effectiveness as a punisher: It appeared as if the shock simply no longer elicited fear.

Just as hunger can inhibit fear, there is evidence that fear can inhibit hunger. You may have experienced this phenomenon for yourself: Imagine, for example, trying to eat just before taking an important exam. A similar phenomenon may be at work in the CER test we discussed earlier, in which presentation of a CS paired with shock will suppress responding to obtain food. One possible explanation is an incompatibility between overt responses: The CS elicits freezing, which prevents bar-pressing. An alternative possibility, however, is that the CS elicits fear, which in turn inhibits hunger; the reason the rats stop bar-pressing is that they have lost all interest in food. Other evidence supports the motivational interpretation. Suppose, for example, that rats are trained to press a bar to avoid shock, and that a tone that has previously been paired with shock is presented while they are bar-pressing. If the tone simply elicits freezing, then the rats should stop responding; but if the tone elicits fear, then their responding should increase, because this fear will make them even more anxious to avoid the shock. In fact, responding does increase (for example, Overmier, Bull, & Pack, 1971), suggesting that a CS paired with shock elicits not a simple response of freezing but a motivational state of fear, and that this fear may either increase or decrease responding, depending on the motive involved.

Most of the research on motivational inhibition has concentrated on the relationship between positive motives (such as hunger) and negative motives (such as fear), but there is also evidence that motives within these two broad categories can inhibit each other. When a rat is deprived of food, for example, its tendency to drink is reduced; conversely, thirst inhibits hunger (Toates, 1980; Ramachandran & Pearce, 1987). We do not know the full set of motives that inhibit one another, but it is clear that conditioning a motive to a stimulus can cause the inhibition of many other motives, presumably because in nature it is important that we concentrate on one goal at a time rather than shifting back and forth between conflicting motives. ("Should I look for food? Yes, but, well, I'm also thirsty, maybe I'll look for water, but . . .")

Expectations

We have seen evidence that a CS can elicit specific responses, such as salivation and blinking, and also more general motivational states. In addition, there is good reason to think that conditioned stimuli can elicit a state that corresponds to what we normally call an *expectation*. For example, suppose that a tone is paired with food. We have seen that the tone may elicit both salivation and hunger; in addition, it may elicit an expectation that a circular dish containing a mound of food is about to be presented. Suggestive evidence for the existence of some sort of expectation that food is about to be delivered comes from observations of subjects' behavior during conditioning experiments. We noted in our introduction to classical conditioning that dogs in a harness will often become restless when the CS is presented (presumably reflecting the conditioning of hunger), but they also begin to turn toward the tray where food is to be presented, as if they were expecting it (Zener, 1937).

Further evidence suggesting some sort of expectation comes from an experiment by Kruse, Overmier, Konz, and Rokke (1983) in which rats were trained in a box containing two levers. In the presence of one stimulus, pressing the left lever produced food pellets; in the presence of a second stimulus, it was pressing the right lever that was reinforced, this time by liquid sucrose. After the rats had learned to respond appropriately, the normal cue signaling which lever to press was no longer presented, and instead the rats received a third stimulus that had previously been paired with either food or sucrose. (See Figure 3.12.) If conditioning produces only a general increase in motivation ("I'm hungry"), we might expect the rats to respond more on both levers in order to obtain food, but there would be no reason for them to respond more on one of the levers then on the other. Suppose, however, that during conditioning trials the rats formed a specific expectation about what US would follow the CS. ("I'm about to receive food" or "I'm about to receive sucrose.") If they now received the food CS, this would elicit the expectation that food is available, and they should therefore respond more on the food lever. This was exactly what Kruse and associates found: The CS paired with food produced an increase in responding on the food lever, whereas the CS previously paired with sucrose produced greater responding on the sucrose lever.

These results suggest that a CS produces not just a motivational state, but also an expectation about the specific US that is to follow. In this case, the rats behaved as if they knew whether food or sucrose would follow; in an experiment by Capaldi, Hovancik, and Friedman (1976), they seemed to know

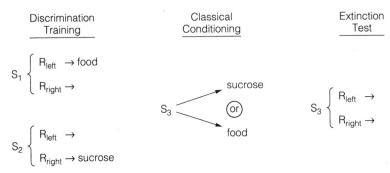

F I G U R E 3.12   The procedure used by Kruse, Overmier, Konz, and Rokke (1983). Subjects were trained to press the left lever to obtain food when stimulus S₁ was present, and to press the right lever to obtain sucrose when stimulus S₂ was present. During the classical conditioning phase, stimulus S₃ was paired with either food or sucrose. In the test phase, stimulus S₃ was presented to see which lever subjects would press; neither response was reinforced during this test phase.

whether a CS would be followed by one food pellet or five. Thus, rats seem to know not just that they are going to get food, but something about the nature of that food. We will return to this question of expectation in Chapter 5, where we will consider a very different interpretation, proposed by Pavlov, of what is learned. In the present context, the important point is simply that subjects seem to acquire *some* sort of knowledge about the specific US that will follow, whether or not it takes the form of a conscious expectation.

In the course of classical conditioning, therefore, at least three different kinds of responses may be conditioned: overt responses, such as salivation; motivational states, such as hunger; and some sort of expectation about the particular US that will follow. Figure 3.13 summarizes this situation. We have shown overt responses, motives, and expectations as alternative responses, but

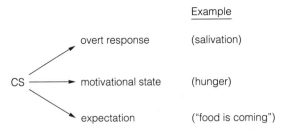

F I G U R E 3.13   Responses that can be learned during classical conditioning. We have shown these responses as alternatives, but two or even all three may be elicited simultaneously by the same CS. Yet another possibility is that the CS elicits one or two of these responses directly, with the others following only as an indirect consequence. For example, subjects might learn an expectation that food is coming, and this expectation might then lead to salivation and an increase in hunger.

another possibility is that it is really the expectation that is conditioned, and that this expectation then leads to both innately programmed internal responses ("When food is coming, start salivating") and motivational states that guide behavior toward the US ("Food is around; try to find it"). Another possibility, suggested by Wagner and Brandon (1989), is that emotional responses and expectations are conditioned simultaneously but independently. (See also Bombace, Brandon & Wagner, 1991.) We do not know very much about the relationships among these responses, but there is growing evidence that all three kinds of responses can be learned during classical conditioning.

3.4 SUMMARY

One of the characteristics of classical conditioning discovered by Pavlov was extinction: If a CS was presented by itself after conditioning, the conditioned response would gradually weaken, or extinguish. The excitatory connection between the CS and US was clearly still present, however, because responding to the CS spontaneously recovered with the passing of time. To explain the disappearance of responding during extinction, Pavlov postulated the formation of a new, inhibitory association that counterbalanced the excitatory connection. Support for this inhibitory process comes from the phenomenon of conditioned inhibition, in which a CS− occasionally accompanies the CS+, and the US is not presented on these compound trials. As a result, the inhibitory CS− acquires the capacity to block, or inhibit, responding to any CS+ that has been paired with that US, or even to reduce responding to the US itself.

Pavlov discovered another way to eliminate a conditioned response, which was to condition a new response to the CS that was incompatible with the old response; this procedure is called counterconditioning. If a mild shock is paired with food, for example, it will eventually cease to elicit any signs of fear, and instead the dog will simply salivate.

Another characteristic of conditioning discovered by Pavlov was generalization, in which the response conditioned to a CS would spread, or generalize, to similar stimuli. Generalization can be reduced, however, if subjects are given discrimination training in which a CS+ and a CS− are alternated, with only the CS+ followed by the US. At first, subjects tend to respond to both stimuli, but with continued training only the CS+ will elicit the response.

When psychologists in the West learned of Pavlov's research on salivation, they wanted to explore what other aspects of behavior could be conditioned, but it gradually became apparent that there were serious methodological problems in assessing conditioning. To determine whether a response is conditionable, it is not enough to pair a CS with a US and then see if the CS elicits the response. Any change could reflect sensitization (due to presentation of the CS by itself), pseudoconditioning (due to presentation of the US by itself), or an interaction between them. One way to control for these effects is to use an unpaired control group, in which the CS and US are presented separately.

Using this control, psychologists found that conditioning affects a wide range of skeletal and autonomic responses. Among the autonomic responses that can be conditioned are arousal (in the form of the GSR), blood glucose levels, sensitivity to pain, and activation of the body's immune system. The range of skeletal responses that can be classically conditioned is smaller, but one that has proven of particular importance for research purposes is key-pecking in pigeons, which can be autoshaped by pairing illumination of a key with the presentation of food.

In addition to these specific responses, conditioning can elicit more general motivational states. If a tone is paired with food, for example, the tone may come to elicit not only salivation but also hunger, which then can motivate a wide range of behaviors directed toward obtaining food. Among the motives that can be conditioned in this way are hunger, fear, and sexual arousal. Other evidence suggests that when one motive is aroused, it may inhibit others—hunger inhibits thirst, fear inhibits hunger, and so on. Through such mechanisms, conditioning can play a critical role in regulating motivation.

A third class of responses that can be conditioned are expectations, in which subjects learn about the precise properties of the US that is to follow the CS. When a tone is paired with food, for example, the tone may elicit a specific response of salivation, a general state of hunger, and also an expectation about the precise nature of the food that is to follow.

Far from being confined to salivation, then, conditioning is a remarkably general phenomenon, affecting responses ranging from blinking and urination to our most powerful emotions. In the words of Hilgard and Bower (1981, p. 58), "It would seem that almost anything that moves, squirts or wriggles could be conditioned." If we only knew the principles involved—that is, what factors determine the strength of conditioning—then we might be able to use conditioning to significantly alter human behavior. In Chapter 4 we will examine what we now know about these principles, and consider how successful psychologists have been in their attempts to apply them.

Selected Definitions

Extinction The disappearance of a conditioned response when a CS is presented by itself.

Spontaneous recovery An increase in the strength of an extinguished response after a period of time following the last extinction trial.

Conditioned inhibition A tendency for a stimulus to inhibit, or block, the response normally elicited by a CS. A number of different procedures can be used to establish a stimulus as a conditioned inhibitor, but generally the conditioned inhibitor signals that a US that normally would have occurred is not going to be presented. As a result, the conditioned inhibitor acquires the capacity to block the conditioned response normally elicited by the CS.

Counterconditioning A technique for eliminating a conditioned response that involves pairing a CS with another US to condition a new response. If the new response is incompatible with the old response, so that only one response can occur at a time, then the new response may replace the old one.

Generalization Responding to a test stimulus as a result of training with another stimulus. The response is said to have generalized from the training to the test stimulus.

Discrimination The differential responding to two stimuli. In classical conditioning, this may be achieved by discrimination training, in which one stimulus (CS+) is followed by a US but the second stimulus (CS−) is not.

Pseudoconditioning An increase in responding to a CS due to presentations of the US by itself.

Interaction effect An effect that may result when two variables are presented. Whenever the effect of two variables acting at the same time is different from the arithmetic sum of the effects of the two variables measured separately, an interaction effect is said to have occurred.

Unpaired control A control group in which the CS and the US are presented at widely separated times. An unpaired control is sometimes referred to as a random group.

Skeletal responses Bodily movements controlled by the skeletal nervous system.

Autonomic responses Glandular and smooth muscle activities controlled by the autonomic nervous system.

Homeostasis The attempts by the body to maintain a stable internal environment.

Autoshaping A procedure in which pigeons are trained to peck a key through pairings of illumination of that key with food.

Sign tracking The behavior of approaching and contacting a stimulus that has preceded an unconditioned stimulus such as food.

Conditioned emotional response (CER) A procedure for measuring fear based on the observation that frightened animals generally freeze. The stimulus to be tested is presented while subjects are responding to obtain a reward such as food. The reduction in their rate of responding to obtain food can be used as an indirect measure of their freezing, and thus of their fear.

Suppression ratio A statistical index used to measure the reduction in responding during a CER test. The index is B/(A + B), where B is the number of responses during the test stimulus and A is the number of responses during an equivalent period immediately prior to the test stimulus.

Review Questions

1. Why did Pavlov attribute extinction to an inhibitory process? What evidence supports his interpretation?

2. What is an unpaired control group? Why is it necessary?

3. What skeletal and autonomic behaviors can be classically conditioned? Why is the CR sometimes different from the UR?

4. What is the difference between an overt response and a motivational state? What evidence suggests that motivational states can be classically conditioned?

5. Describe the CER procedure and the use of suppression ratios to measure fear.

6. What evidence suggests that classical conditioning leads to the formation of expectations about the specific properties of the US that follows the CS?

C H A P T E R F O U R

Principles and Applications

Pavlov's discovery that salivation could be conditioned held out the promise that other behaviors, potentially much more important ones, could also be modified through conditioning. In this chapter we will review laboratory research on what factors determine the strength of conditioning and then look at some attempts to apply these principles in treating problems such as phobias and alcoholism.

4.1 THE LAWS OF ASSOCIATION

The British Associationists, sitting in their armchairs a few centuries ago, identified a number of laws of association, of which the most important were contiguity, frequency, and intensity. We will begin our survey of the principles of conditioning by considering the extent to which these laws have been supported by experimental research.

Contiguity

The most important principle of association was thought to be contiguity. The very concept of an association—a bond between two events that occur together—implicitly assumes that contiguity is necessary, and considerable effort has been devoted to exploring the role of contiguity in classical conditioning.

The CS–US sequence. As with most other aspects of conditioning, it was Pavlov who first investigated the role of contiguity in establishing a strong conditioned response. He experimented with four different temporal arrangements between the CS and the US. (See Figure 4.1.) In **delay conditioning**,

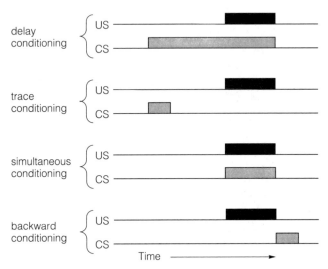

F I G U R E 4.1   Paradigms for four varieties of classical conditioning. The bars on the time line indicate periods during which a stimulus is presented. In simultaneous conditioning, for example, the US occurs at the same time and for the same duration as the CS.

once the CS came on, it remained on until the US was presented. In **trace conditioning**, the CS was terminated before the US began. As the British Associationists would have predicted, Pavlov found that conditioning was much stronger in the delay conditioning paradigm, where the CS and US were on at the same time.

The results obtained with the other two paradigms investigated by Pavlov, however, were not what the Associationists would have predicted. In **simultaneous conditioning**, the CS and the US came on simultaneously. According to Associationist views, conditioning should have been maximal, but in fact Pavlov found virtually no conditioning. Similarly, the CS and US were contiguous in **backward conditioning**, in which the US was presented first, before the CS, but again conditioning was poor. It appeared as if it was not enough for the CS and US to be contiguous: The CS had to precede the US for conditioning to occur.

Subsequent research has altered this conclusion: Simultaneous and backward conditioning *can* result in conditioning, provided that appropriate techniques are used to measure it. (See Rescorla, 1981.) For practical purposes, though, Pavlov's findings still provide the best guide: To obtain strong conditioning, the CS should precede the US and remain on until the US occurs.

The CS–US interval.   Western psychologists conducted a series of experiments to determine systematically how the strength of conditioning changed as the interval between the CS and US increased. In a typical study, Moeller (1954) looked at the effects of the CS–US interval on GSR conditioning. He used a trace conditioning paradigm in which a 100-millisecond burst of white noise was followed after a delay by a weak electric shock, with the interval between the onset of the CS and the onset of the US (the interstimulus interval, or ISI) set at either 250, 450, 1000, or 2500 milliseconds (ms). Moeller's results are illustrated in Figure 4.2, which shows that the strength of the conditioned response was greatest in the group with a 450-ms gap, and that little or no conditioning occurred at delays of 1000 and 2500 ms. Also, as Pavlov's experiments on simultaneous conditioning had suggested, Moeller found that conditioning became weaker as the CS–US interval became very short, and thus the onset of the CS and US came closer to being simultaneous. In other studies, the decrement at short delays has been even more pronounced (McAllister, 1953).

Whatever the reasons for the difficulty of simultaneous conditioning, the optimal interval for GSR conditioning is roughly one-half second (about 500 ms), with trace conditioning becoming impossible at around two seconds (2000 ms). (For further discussion, see Rescorla, 1982; Hawkins & Kandel, 1984.) Both the optimum interval and the maximum interval that will sustain conditioning vary somewhat for different responses, but as a general rule the shorter the interval between the CS and the US, the better the conditioning. (See Mackintosh, 1974.)

Testa (1975) has reported evidence that conditioning is also influenced by spatial contiguity. He exposed rats to a light followed by a blast of air and found that fear conditioning was strongest if both stimuli came from the same area of the box. This result makes good sense if we think of conditioning as a

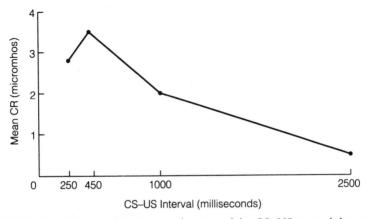

F I G U R E 4.2   GSR conditioning as a function of the CS–US interval during training. (Adapted from Moeller, 1954)

mechanism that has evolved to help us detect causes and react to them appropriately. If we suddenly experience pain, for example, it is vital that we accurately identify the source of that pain so that we can avoid it in the future. One good clue to an event's cause is temporal contiguity: If the pain is in your foot, for example, it is much more likely to have been caused by something you just stepped on than something you encountered an hour ago. Similarly, cause and effect are usually contiguous in space: Your foot pain is more likely to have been caused by something you stepped on, such as a snake, than by something overhead, such as a circling eagle. By making the likely cause of pain frightening, conditioning maximizes the chances that we will avoid the pain in the future.

Frequency

A second variable that the British Associationists thought determined the strength of an association between two events was the frequency of their pairing. Pavlov's research on salivary conditioning strongly supported this view (see Figure 2.6, p. 54), and so has subsequent research. In general, the strength of the conditioned response seems to increase most during the early trials of conditioning, with the rate of increase gradually declining as training continues, until performance eventually reaches a stable plateau, or **asymptote**.

Intensity

The third major principle proposed by the British Associationists was that the strength of any association would depend on the vividness or intensity of the stimuli involved; associations involving emotional or traumatic events, for example, would be remembered better. Again, controlled research on conditioning strongly supports this principle. In the Annau and Kamin experiment discussed earlier, for example, we saw that the amount of fear conditioned to a tone depended on the intensity of the shock used. There is also evidence that the intensity of the CS is of some importance, although this effect appears weaker. (See Grice, 1968.)

On the whole, then, the speculations of the British Associationists have been strongly confirmed by research under controlled conditions. Associative learning really does depend on contiguity, frequency, and intensity.

4.2 CONTINGENCY

Until 1966, all the available evidence converged on a coherent and satisfying picture of conditioning in which the foundation stone was contiguity: If two events are contiguous, then an association will be formed between them. The strength of this association might be modulated by other factors such as the intensity of the stimuli involved. Fundamentally, though, conditioning was considered a simple process in which associations were automatically formed between contiguous events. In that year, however, two landmark papers were published in *Psychonomic Science,* ironically a relatively obscure journal with a reputation for publishing competent but minor studies. These two papers posed a fundamental challenge to traditional views of the role of contiguity and unleashed an intellectual ferment—revolution would not be too strong a word—that continues to this day.

The Concept of Contingency

The first of these papers was the work of Robert Rescorla, a graduate student at the University of Pennsylvania. In his paper, Rescorla suggested that contiguity between two events was not sufficient for conditioning; something more was needed. Specifically, Rescorla suggested that a CS must not only be contiguous with a US but must also be an accurate predictor of the occurrence of the US. Suppose, for example, that we expose rats to a sequence of tones and shocks delivered according to one of the three arrangements diagramed in Figure 4.3. In all three cases the shocks are delivered at randomly chosen intervals, but the conditions differ in the timing of the tones. In *a,* the tones are also delivered at random, so the occurrence of a tone is of no value to the rat in predicting when the next shock is likely to occur; in *b,* a tone is presented just before each shock, so the tone is a highly accurate predictor; in *c,* an intermediate condition, shock is more likely when a tone has been presented but also occurs at other times.

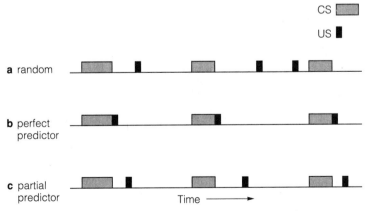

F I G U R E 4.3   Three CS–US contingencies: (a) The CS and the US are presented at random intervals. (b) The CS immediately precedes the US and is thus a perfect predictor of its occurrence. (c) The US tends to follow the CS but does not always do so.

A CS, then, can vary widely in its ability to predict a US, and it would be convenient if we had some mathematical measure of its predictive value. Indeed, several such measures are available, but we will focus on one measure termed a contingency. A **contingency** is a statistic derived from two probabilities: the probability that a US will occur in the presence of a CS—symbolized by p(US|CS)—and the probability that it will occur in the absence of the CS—p(US|no CS). By combining these two probabilities with the appropriate formula, it is possible to calculate a contingency coefficient that measures the extent to which the CS and US occur together.*

In situation *a*, for example, suppose that the probability of a shock during a one-minute tone is 0.10, and that its probability in the absence of the tone is also 0.10:

$$p(shock|tone) \quad = 0.10$$
$$p(shock|no\ tone) = 0.10$$

Since the likelihood of a shock is the same regardless of whether the tone is presented, the tone is of no predictive value, and the contingency in this case is zero.

In *b*, on the other hand, the shock always occurs when the tone is presented and never occurs when it is absent:

$$p(shock|tone) \quad = 1.0$$
$$p(shock|no\ tone) = 0$$

The tone is a perfect predictor of the shock's occurrence, and the calculated contingency is 1.0.

Let us turn finally to situation *c*. We have seen that a shock is more likely during the tone than in its absence, but we have also seen that the tone is not a perfect predictor. Let us assume the following probabilities:

$$p(shock|tone) \quad = 0.60$$
$$p(shock|no\ tone) = 0.20$$

Given these probabilities, the contingency would be 0.41.

A contingency, in other words, gives us a simple mathematical summary of the degree of relationship between two events. If two events occur at random

---

* In the examples that follow, we have used the correlation between the presence of the tone and the presence of the shock as a measure of the contingency between them. This situation can be represented as a 2 × 2 table in which the rows indicate the number of occasions when the CS was either present or absent and the columns indicate the occasions when the US was present or absent. The formula for calculating a correlation in a table of this kind can be found in most statistics texts.

with respect to one another, there is no contingency. But the greater the linkage between their occurrences, the greater their contingency, up to a maximum value of 1.0 when the two events always occur together. The greater the contingency between two events, the more useful one is as a predictor of the other.

You can check how well you understand all this by considering the following hypothetical situation: Suppose that you are a farmer who has just moved to a new county, and you need to be able to predict the probability of rain in order to decide whether to plant your corn. A salesperson for a weather forecasting company approaches you and tells you that the company has developed a new forecasting system that is far more accurate than any existing method. As proof, the salesperson shows you evidence that last year the company predicted rain on 100 days and it actually rained on 95 of those days. Should you buy the new forecasting service?

The answer, from the point of view of contingency, is no—or, at least, not necessarily. To determine the value of the company's predictions, you need to know not only the probability of rain when it was forecast, but also the probability when it was *not* forecast. Suppose, for example, that you had just moved to an area where it always rains on 95 days out of 100. Knowing the company's predictions would clearly be of very little aid in deciding whether rain was imminent. To evaluate the accuracy of any forecast or prediction, in other words, you need to consider not only how often the predicted event occurs when it is predicted but also how often it occurs when it is not predicted. If these probabilities are similar, then the prediction will not help you very much.

Contingency and Conditioning

A subject in a classical conditioning experiment faces a problem similar to that of the farmer who wants to predict rain. Consider, for example, a rat that suddenly becomes ill. If this illness were due to a food it had eaten earlier, it would obviously be advantageous for the rat to identify that food and avoid it in the future. In searching for a cue that could predict illness, however, the rat (like the farmer) might be seriously misled if it relied solely on contiguity. If a rat became ill after eating lima beans, for example, this would not necessarily mean that the lima beans had made the rat ill; if the rat became ill on days when it didn't eat lima beans as well as on days when it did, there would be no point to its avoiding lima beans in the future. In seeking to identify the true cause of an event, in other words, animals and humans would do better if they took into account the contingency between two events as well as their contiguity.

Figure 4.3b illustrates a typical conditioning experiment. The CS and US are contiguous in time, and because they always occur together, there is also a perfect contingency between them. This contingency had largely been ignored by previous psychologists, who instead focused their experimental efforts on the role of contiguity. The assumption that an association will be formed between contiguous events was, after all, at the heart of the Associationist tradition, so it was only natural to assume that conditioning, too, would depend solely on the contiguity of the CS and US. Rescorla, however, wondered whether animals might also take into account the degree of contingency between the two stimuli. What would happen, he asked, if a tone and shock were presented contiguously, as in most fear-conditioning experiments, but the shock was also presented in the absence of the tone, thereby eliminating their contingency?

Positive contingencies.   Although Rescorla's initial work on contingency was published in 1966, we will look first at the results of a later experiment reported in 1968. Figure 4.4 illustrates the design of this experiment. In the random group, rats received a series of tones and shocks delivered totally at random. Subjects in the contingency group received tones whenever their counterparts in the random group did, and they also received some—but not all—of the shocks delivered to subjects in the random group. Specifically, they received the shocks given to the random group while the tone was present but not when the tone was absent. Both groups thus received the same number of tones and the same number of pairings of the tone with the shock.

How should conditioning in the two groups compare? If conditioning depends simply on contiguity, then conditioning should be equal, since both

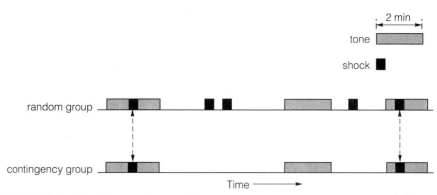

F I G U R E 4.4   The procedure used by Rescorla (1968). Note that a tone is indicated by a shaded bar and a shock is indicated by a solid bar. A solid bar inside a shaded bar indicates that the tone and the shock occurred simultaneously. In the random group, the tone and the shock were presented at random. In the contingency group, shock was presented only during the CS. As indicated by the broken lines, both groups received the same number of shocks in the presence of the CS.

had the same number of tone-shock pairings. If contingency also matters, however, then we should expect very different levels of conditioning in the two groups. In the contingency group, the tone is a good predictor of shock; in the random group, there is no contingency between them. Insofar as contingency is important, therefore, conditioning should be substantially weaker in the random group, despite their receiving exactly the same number of pairings of tone with shock. In accordance with this prediction, Rescorla found powerful conditioning in the contingency group: The rats totally stopped responding when the tone was presented in a CER test. But he found no conditioning whatsoever in the random group. In a second experiment, he varied the degree of contingency between the tone and shock by varying the probability of the shock in the tone's absence: He set the probability of shock in the presence of the tone at 0.40; he set the probability of shock in the absence of the tone at either 0, 0.10, 0.20, or 0.40. The more similar the probability of shock in the presence and absence of the tone, the weaker the contingency between them, and, as Figure 4.5 shows, the poorer the conditioning.

Negative contingencies.   Conditioning, then, depends on the degree of contingency between the CS and the US: The more likely the US is in the presence of the CS compared to its absence, the greater will be the conditioning. What would happen, though, if there were a *negative* contingency between the two stimuli—if, for example, a shock occurred in the absence of the tone but not in its presence? You may be able to anticipate the answer: The CS now signals a reduced likelihood of shock and, therefore, will reduce or inhibit fear. Evidence for this conclusion comes from Rescorla's original report (1966),

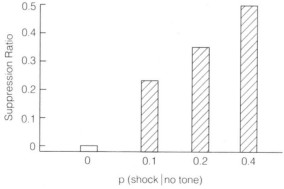

F I G U R E 4.5   Fear conditioning as a function of tone-shock contingency. The probability of shock in the presence of the tone was 0.4 in all groups, but the probability of shock in the absence of the tone varied from zero to 0.4. Note that a suppression ratio of zero indicates strong fear; a suppression ratio of 0.5 indicates no fear. (Based on data from Rescorla, 1968)

in which he compared groups exposed to either a positive, a negative, or a zero contingency between tone and shock.

Subjects in the zero-contingency, or random, group received 24 shocks and 24 tones, spaced randomly over a one-hour session. Subjects in the positive contingency group received the identical treatment, except that they received only those shocks that were programmed to occur within 30 seconds of the tone's onset. Finally, the negative contingency group received the same 24 tones but only the shocks that were not scheduled to occur within 30 seconds of a tone. Thus, in the positive contingency group, a shock was more likely when a tone had been presented, whereas in the negative contingency group it was less likely.

To measure conditioned fear, Rescorla presented the tone while his subjects were responding on a Sidman avoidance task in which they had to jump over a barrier in order to prevent the delivery of electric shocks. The shocks were programmed to occur every 10 seconds, but whenever the subject jumped over the barrier, all shocks scheduled for the following 30 seconds were canceled. Subjects trained on this task quickly learn to jump over the barrier to avoid the shock, and their rate of jumping provides a sensitive index of their fear: The greater their fear, the more frequently they jump over the barrier (Rescorla & LoLordo, 1965).

Rates of performing the avoidance response before and during the presen-

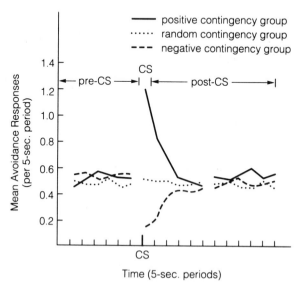

FIGURE 4.6   Rates of performing avoidance response before, during, and after the presentation of a five-second CS. During preceding conditioning trials, there was either a positive, a negative, or a zero (random) contingency between the CS and the shock. (Adapted from Rescorla, 1966)

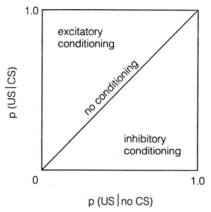

F I G U R E 4.7   A contingency space, showing all possible combinations of the probability of a US in the presence of a CS and in its absence.

tation of a tone are shown in Figure 4.6. In the positive contingency group, responding doubled when the tone was presented, suggesting that substantial fear conditioning had taken place. In the random group, the tone had no effect, whereas in the negative contingency group the tone actually reduced responding. Just as a positive contingency between a CS and a US produces excitatory conditioning, a negative contingency produces inhibitory conditioning. Combining these results, it appears as if a CS must predict some change in the likelihood of the US for conditioning to occur. If the CS predicts an increase in the likelihood of the US, then we find excitatory conditioning; if the CS predicts a reduced likelihood, then we find inhibitory conditioning.

The contingency space.   Figure 4.7 summarizes these conclusions in terms of a **contingency space,** in which each point represents a particular combination of the probability of the US in the presence of the CS and in the absence of the CS, and thus a particular contingency. When the probability of the US is greater in the presence of the CS than in its absence (all those points located above the diagonal line), then we obtain excitatory conditioning; when the probability in the presence of the CS is less than in its absence (all points below the diagonal line), then we obtain inhibitory conditioning; and when the probabilities are equal (the points along the diagonal line), we find no conditioning.

The fact that conditioning depends on the contingency between the CS and US is really just a fancy way of saying that conditioning depends on the extent to which the CS predicts the US. In one sense, this is hardly surprising. If a tone and shock occur at random, for example, so that the tone signals no increase in the likelihood of the shock, it is not surprising that the tone elicits no fear. When viewed from the traditional perspective of contiguity, however, these results are deeply disturbing. If an association is formed when a CS and US occur contiguously, why was no conditioning found in Rescorla's random group? The tone and shock were paired repeatedly, and we know that such pairings can produce very powerful fear conditioning. How could occasional presentations of the shock by itself have prevented fear being conditioned to this tone?

Attempts to answer this question have opened up a veritable Pandora's box, since the apparent simplicity of conditioning has been found to conceal an elaborate and intricate network of cognitive subprocesses. Because of the complexity of the processes involved, we will postpone answering this question until we can explore these processes more systematically (Chapters 4 and 10). Before leaving Rescorla's experiments, however, we will consider one other implication of his results, concerning the appropriate control group for conditioning.

The random control. Earlier, we suggested that to control for interaction effects we needed a group in which subjects received both CS and US, but unpaired. Specifically, we discussed the use of the unpaired control in which the CS and US are never presented together. In light of Rescorla's results, however, we can now see that an unpaired group actually represents a negative contingency between the CS and US: The US never occurs in the presence of the CS, but it does occur in its absence. The CS in the unpaired group will not be neutral but will actually inhibit responding. If we want a control group in which no conditioning of any kind occurs, therefore, the unpaired group is clearly not appropriate. Rescorla has suggested that we use a **random control**— a group for which the CS and US are presented completely at random rather than deliberately separated. The occasional pairings of the CS and US in this group may result in some conditioning, especially early in training (Kremer, 1971). However, if we present enough trials, the CS eventually becomes neutral, in the sense that it neither elicits nor inhibits the conditioned response (Keller, Ayres, & Mahoney, 1977).

It may seem that we have at long last found the ideal control group, but you may not be surprised to learn that the random control also has its problems. Seligman (1969) has argued that subjects exposed to a random contingency between tone and shock *do* learn: They learn that there is no correlation between the two events, and this knowledge may then affect their behavior in a variety of ways. Mackintosh (1973), for example, has shown that rats exposed to random presentations of a tone and shock have a difficult time learning to associate these events when they are later paired. It is as if the pretreatment phase teaches the rats that the two events are unrelated; as a result, they find it difficult to reverse this belief.

If what we are looking for is a control group in which no learning will occur, there probably is no such beast. As long as an organism is alive, learning of some kind about the environment is probably going to take place. We can control for the effects of contingency by using a random control, and we can control for the effects of contiguity by using an unpaired control. But there is no single procedure that will simultaneously control for all possible alternative explanations.

Over the years, then, we have seen a substantial shift in the control groups used in conditioning experiments. As we have seen, it is not possible to control for all possible variables, just those that seem most plausible. As our understanding of a phenomenon increases, however, our knowledge of which variables affect it, and thus need to be controlled, will also increase. In the case of conditioning, the discovery of pseudoconditioning and the importance of contingency both led to major changes in control group methodology. Scientific progress thus involves a peculiar paradox: In order to determine which variables are important, we need to be able to control for the effects of other potentially important variables, but to do so we must know what variables are important—which is precisely what we are trying to establish in the first place! Fortunately for the sake of researchers as well as students, the paradox is not absolute and can be overcome by painstaking effort. The task is not nearly so simple as it might at first appear, though.

4.3 PREPAREDNESS

The second seminal paper of 1966 was by Garcia and Koelling, and it again challenged the assumption that any two events that were contiguous would be associated. In particular, these researchers challenged the idea that it did not matter what stimulus was chosen as a CS. Pavlov had claimed, "Any natural phenomenon chosen at will may be converted into a conditioned stimulus . . . any visual stimulus, any desired sound, any odor, and the stimulation of any part of the skin" (1928, p. 86). Subsequent research almost universally supported Pavlov's position—that is, until the publication of Garcia and Koelling's paper.

Taste-Aversion Learning

Garcia and Koelling's experiment had its origins in naturalistic observations of animal behavior—in particular, of a phenomenon in rats called bait-shyness. Rats, it turns out, resist human efforts to exterminate them. When left poisoned bait, they tend to take only the smallest taste at first; then, if they survive, they never touch that food again. Classical conditioning might explain the rats' subsequent avoidance of the bait: Ingestion of the poisoned bait produces nausea, and this reaction becomes conditioned to the gustatory and olfactory cues that precede the nausea. On future occasions, the rats avoid that

food because the very odor or taste of the food makes them ill. This phenomenon is known as **taste-aversion learning**.

As attractive as this explanation is, it cannot account for one aspect of
the rats' behavior. Although the rats in Garcia and Koelling's experiment later
avoided the bait, they showed no reluctance to return to the place where they
had been poisoned, and to consume other foods there. If associations form
between any contiguous events, then we should expect place cues to be associated with illness as readily as taste and odor cues, but this did not appear to be
happening. Was it possible that the rats associated nausea with taste and odor,
but for some reason were unable to form similar associations involving visual
cues?

To test this hypothesis under controlled laboratory conditions, Garcia
and Koelling allowed rats to taste distinctly flavored water from a drinking tube
that was wired so that every lick produced not only water but a brief noise and
light flash. During exposure to this taste-noise-light compound, they received a
dose of radiation sufficient to induce gastrointestinal disturbance and nausea.
Then, on a test trial, the rats were exposed to each of the compound stimuli
separately, to determine which ones had become aversive. A lick then produced either the flavored water or plain water plus the noise-light compound.
Drinking was found to be severely depressed by the presence of the flavor but
was unaffected by the light and noise (Figure 4.8a). An aversion thus seemed
to be readily conditionable to gustatory cues, as suggested by naturalistic observations, but not at all to stimuli from the external environment. An alternative explanation, however, was possible: Perhaps the noise and light used were
simply too faint to be detected, so conditioning would not have been possible
no matter what unconditioned stimulus had been employed. To test this hypothesis, Garcia and Koelling repeated their experiment with the same compound CS, but with electric shock as the US instead of X rays. The results for
the suppression test are shown in Figure 4.8b, which illustrates that the audiovisual stimulus produced suppression of drinking and the taste stimulus had no
effect. We thus face this strange situation in which nausea cannot be conditioned to a noise, nor fear to a taste, even though each of these conditioned
stimuli is easily associated with the other US.

Subsequent research has established that it is possible to associate taste
with shock and noise with illness, but it is much more difficult, requiring many
more trials (for example, Best, Best, & Henggeler, 1977). Seligman (1970) has
coined the term **preparedness** to refer to the fact that we seem prepared to
associate some CS–US combinations more readily than others.[*] To the tra-

---

[*] The reality of the phenomenon of preparedness is undisputed, but there is still remarkably little
agreement as to what it should be called. Other terms for preparedness include *belongingness, relevance, selective association,* and *associative bias.*

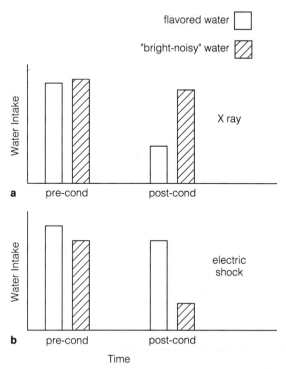

F I G U R E 4.8   Water intake before (pre) and after (post) conditioning: (a) when X rays were used as the US; (b) when shock was used as the US. The open bars represent intake of the flavored water; the solid bars represent intake of plain water when licking produced a noise and light. (Based on Garcia & Koelling, 1966)

ditional principles determining the strength of conditioning—contiguity, frequency, and intensity—we can thus add two more: contingency and preparedness.

Implications of Taste-Aversion Learning

Garcia and Koelling's experiment has proved to be one of the most influential studies on learning ever published. In part, this is because the phenomenon of taste-aversion learning is of considerable practical importance. It occurs not only in rats but in every other vertebrate species tested, and it undoubtedly plays an important role in regulating food preferences (Logue, 1988). In a study by Bernstein (1978), for example, cancer patients were given a distinctively flavored ice cream to eat one hour before undergoing chemotherapy, a treatment that induces nausea as a side effect, and the patients developed an aversion to the ice cream that preceded treatment. This process partly accounts for the substantial weight losses that accompany chemotherapy, since patients develop aversions to whatever foods they had eaten before treatment, and their diets thus become progressively more restricted. Similarly, Bernstein and Borson (1986) have suggested that taste-aversion learning may play a role in anorexia nervosa, a disorder in which patients develop an extreme resistance to eating and become emaciated. Many anorexics experience nausea and vomiting when they do eat; these aversive states may become conditioned to the foods that precede them, and this could further exacerbate the anorexic's reluctance to eat.

Taste-aversion learning, then, is an interesting phenomenon in its own right, but it also has important implications for how psychologists view learning, and, indeed, for psychology itself. Before we complete our discussion of Garcia and Koelling's work, therefore, we will look briefly at these implications.

The role of contiguity in associative learning.   According to the traditional view, all that matters in conditioning is contiguity: If two events are contiguous, then they will be associated. The evidence for preparedness, however, clearly shows that this is not the case. In the taste-aversion experiment, for example, noise was just as contiguous with illness as taste was, but this contiguity did not result in learning. Contiguity, therefore, is not sufficient for learning to take place. Other evidence, moreover, has shown that contiguity is not even necessary. In the Garcia and Koelling experiment, there was a delay of at least 20 minutes between the presentation of the taste and the animals' becoming ill; in a subsequent, memorable experiment by Etscorn and Stephens (1973), conditioning occurred despite a delay of 24 hours. Clearly, conditioning is not due simply to the linking of events that happen to occur contiguously: Some other process or processes must be involved. Garcia and Koelling's experiment thus contributed to a major theoretical shift in the way we view conditioning—from a simple process to one of considerable sophistication and complexity. We will examine this shift in greater detail in subsequent chapters.

The role of paradigms.   Garcia and Koelling's paper was published in *Psychonomic Science* not because they submitted it there first, but because the paper had been vehemently rejected by every major psychology journal to which they had sent it (Garcia, 1981). In part, these rejections may have reflected some genuine weaknesses in their paper, including ambiguities in the description of their procedure. (If you read accounts of their work in different texts, you will find significant differences in the descriptions of their procedure; the reason is simply that their own description was not clear, and different authors have interpreted it differently.) The fundamental reason for the paper's rejection, however, was that the reviewers simply did not believe their results. Reviewers felt that it just wasn't possible that a taste could be associated with illness and yet not be associated with an electric shock. Everyone knew (or, rather, believed) that the laws of conditioning were uniform for all responses.

This attitude might sound extraordinarily unscientific. In a fascinating and influential analysis of science entitled *The Structure of Scientific Revolutions,* however, Thomas Kuhn (1970) argues that the ignoring of evidence in this way is actually a common feature of science and in many ways is even healthy. Scientific research, he suggests, is guided by **paradigms**—sets of shared assumptions about the nature of the world and about what constitutes important and worthwhile problems. It is not possible to study everything; scientists have limited resources and must concentrate on problems that seem likely to yield productive answers. Our paradigms—fundamental, almost unconscious assumptions about what is important—guide these decisions.

If reported evidence contradicts a fundamental premise, the normal scientific reaction is to reject or discount the evidence. Skeptical scientists would claim, "The experiment could not have been properly carried out." In the overwhelming majority of cases, this rejection is probably justified. For example, if a physicist claimed that he could fly through the air unaided, by sheer willpower, other physicists would almost certainly be right to ignore the claim rather than spend time, money, and effort exploring this new phenomenon. Paradigms thus play a positive role by directing our attention to problems that are likely to be important. Faith in their ultimate correctness helps give scientists the courage to persevere in the face of failure. Recall, for example, Pavlov's building of a new laboratory when his early experiments were inconclusive. Sometimes, though, paradigms blind us to new evidence simply because this evidence contradicts older findings that have hardened into dogma.

The uniformity of associative learning.   From Pavlov's time, nearly all learning theorists have shared a fundamental assumption that the basic mechanisms of learning are the same across situations and species. When Pavlov began his research, he anticipated that some stimuli would be associated more easily with food than other stimuli, and in his early experiments he distinguished between "natural" stimuli, such as the sight and smell of food, and "artificial" stimuli, such as a light or buzzer. He eventually dropped this distinction, however, when it became clear that the results of his experiments with "natural" and "artificial" stimuli were indistinguishable. It did not matter what stimuli he used; the principles governing the formation of an association were always the same.

Garcia and Koelling's results clearly contradict this assumption: It *does* matter what CS is paired with what US; some CS–US combinations are learned much more easily than others. We will consider some of the implications of this finding in the next section, and again at greater length in Chapter 10; at this point, we simply note that associative learning is not the entirely general process that Pavlov and others imagined, capable of associating any events that happen to occur together. We seem to be innately predisposed to learn the relationships between some events more readily than others.

The Adaptive Value of Conditioning

Why is it that some associations are easier to learn than others? In trying to answer this question, it may be helpful to begin by standing back a bit and addressing the broader question of why classical conditioning exists at all.

The value of conditioning.   In discussing Pavlov's research, we referred repeatedly to his view that the process of conditioning has evolved because it helps animals to survive in their natural environments. One way of thinking about conditioning is as a means of identifying stimuli that cause or predict important events: If an animal knows where food is available, for example, or which of the other animals in its vicinity is likely to attack it, then it can use this information to guide appropriate action. This view was expressed with some eloquence by Culler (1938):

> [Without a signal] the animal would still be forced to wait in every case for the stimulus to arrive before beginning to meet it. The veil of the future would hang just before his eyes. Nature began long ago to push back the veil. Foresight proved to possess high survival-value, and conditioning is the means by which foresight is achieved.
>
> (Culler, 1938, p. 136)

Salivary conditioning provides one example of the advantages of foresight: If a dog knows when food is coming, it can begin to salivate beforehand, and this will allow it to consume the food more quickly—not a small advantage when predators or other hungry dogs are around. Similarly, if a rat learns to freeze whenever it hears an owl's wings, this freezing may enhance its chances of escaping detection and thus surviving.

In these examples, we can only speculate about the functional value of the conditioned response, but in some cases we have direct evidence. One example concerns the conditioning of sexual arousal. In an experiment by Zamble, Hadad, Mitchell, and Cutmore (1985), male rats were given access to a sexually receptive female. In one group, the female's appearance was preceded by a signal; in the other group, it was not. When the female's appearance was signaled, males initiated copulation more quickly and reached the point of ejaculation sooner. However unromantic such behavior may seem, a male that approaches a female faster is likely to have an advantage over competing suitors, and a male that finishes more quickly will have spent less time in a position where it is vulnerable to predators. The conditioning of sexual arousal will give this male a significant advantage in reproducing, thus ensuring that its genes—including those responsible for the conditioning of sexual arousal—will be passed on to a succeeding generation.

Another example comes from Hollis (1984), who studied the conditioning of aggression in a species of fish called the blue gourami. The males of this species establish territories, and then attack other males who intrude. Hollis gave her males conditioning trials in which the appearance of another male was reliable preceded by a light, and found that the aggressive behavior that was initially directed toward the intruder began to occur as soon as the light was presented. This could be seen as wasted effort—why engage in aggressive displays when no other male is around?—but Hollis found that if she now preceded test presentations of the intruder by the CS, the resident male was much more likely to win the ensuing fight. We do not yet know how the conditioning of aggression helped the resident to triumph: Perhaps hormones were released that ensured it was fully ready for battle, or perhaps the fact that it was already engaged in an aggressive display by the time its rival appeared helped to frighten that rival away. Whatever the mechanism, as the quotation from Culler would suggest, a forewarned fish proved to be a forearmed one.

The value of preparedness.   Returning now to the question of why some associations are learned more easily than others, this analysis suggests that it is likely to be because these associations are of greater value in the animal's natural environment. Consider, for example, a rat that became ill after eating rancid meat. If the only learning system it possessed was an all-purpose mechanism that associated all contiguous events, then it would have developed an aversion to all the stimuli present when it became ill. Insofar as this included the taste of the rancid meat, the aversion would have helped it to survive, but it would have been equally likely to develop an aversion to a bird that happened to be singing just when it became ill. If it thereafter ran for cover whenever it heard a singing bird, it would have been more likely to die of exhaustion than to prosper. The pressures of natural selection would thus favor rats that associated illness with preceding tastes, which were likely to have genuine predictive value, rather than potentially irrelevant lights or sounds.

This analysis is very speculative: We don't *know* that rats rely more on gustatory than visual cues to identify food, however plausible this may seem. However, this analysis does lead to an interesting prediction: that the cue which an animal will associate most readily with illness should be whatever cue it relies on to identify food in its natural environment, no matter what that cue is. Rats forage for food at night; they rely on taste and odor, rather than visual appearance, to identify their food. For rats, therefore, it makes sense that taste cues will be associated with illness more readily than visual cues. Birds, on the other hand, rely on visual cues to identify their food; according to an adaptive analysis, therefore, birds should be more likely to associate visual cues with illness. In accordance with this prediction, Wilcoxon, Dragoin, and Kral (1971) found that when quail were made ill following the ingestion of blue, sour water, they developed a stronger aversion to the color than to the taste. Thus, although the analysis presented in this section is very speculative, there is at least some reason to think it may be right.

4.4 BLOCKING

The 1960s were a difficult time for the principle of contiguity. First, Rescorla showed that temporal contiguity between a CS and a US was not sufficient to ensure conditioning; the CS must also be a good predictor of the US. Then Garcia and Koelling showed that even valid predictors are not always conditioned. In 1969, a third event undermined still further the traditional view of contiguity, and suggested an alternative analysis to replace it. This event was the publication of a paper by Leo Kamin.

The Phenomenon of Blocking

Kamin (1969) gave rats fear-conditioning trials in which two stimuli, a noise (N) and a light (L), were paired with an electric shock. The noise and the light came on together, remained on for three minutes, and were immediately followed by the shock. To assess conditioning to the light, Kamin used a CER test in which the light was presented while the rats pressed a bar to obtain food. The suppression ratio for the light was 0.05, indicating substantial fear conditioning. (Recall that a suppression ratio of 0.50 indicates no fear and zero indicates maximal fear.)

Kamin was interested primarily in a second group, though. The subjects in this second group received identical pairings of the noise-light compound with shock, but these compound trials were preceded by trials in which the noise by itself was paired with shock.

	Pretraining	Conditioning
blocking group:	N ⟶ shock	NL ⟶ shock
control group:		NL ⟶ shock

For subjects in the blocking group, therefore, the noise already elicited fear when the compound trials began. What effect should we expect this to have on conditioning to the light?

According to a contiguity analysis, we should expect strong conditioning to the light in both groups, because, in both, the light was repeatedly and contiguously paired with the shock. The results for the two groups, however, were very different. The suppression ratio in the control group was 0.05; the ratio for subjects given preliminary conditioning to the noise was 0.45, a statistic indistinguishable from the 0.50 level representing no fear. In other words, prior conditioning to the noise had blocked conditioning to the light. Kamin thus called this phenomenon, in which prior conditioning to one element of a compound prevents conditioning to the other element, **blocking**.

Kamin's Memory-Scan Hypothesis

Why should previous conditioning to one element of a compound block conditioning to the other? Kamin's explanation is intriguing. When an important event such as shock occurs, he said, animals search their memories to identify cues that could help to predict the event in the future. Imagine, for example, that a rat foraging for food in a forest is suddenly attacked by an owl. If it survives the attack, it will search its memory to identify cues that preceded the attack and thus help it avoid such an event in the future. If the rat had heard the beating of the owl's wings just before the attack, for example, then the next time it heard this sound it would dive for cover.

Kamin first assumed, then, that unconditioned stimuli trigger memory searches for predictive cues. He further assumed that such searches require effort. In taste-aversion conditioning, for example, we have seen that animals may develop an aversion to foods consumed up to 24 hours earlier, indicating that any memory search must cover events spread over at least this time period. Such a search would require considerable time and effort, and Kamin speculated that, to save energy, subjects would scan their memories only if the US were unexpected or surprising. If the US were expected, then by definition some cue predicting its occurrence must already have been available, so that no further search would be needed.

To see how this analysis can account for blocking, consider first the control group that received only the compound trials. The first shock would have been unexpected and would have triggered a memory search for the cause. Quiz) The rats would remember the preceding noise and light, and thus both cues would be associated with the shock.

Similarly in the blocking group, when the shock was presented in the preliminary phase, it would initially have been surprising and would have triggered a memory search in which the rats remembered the preceding noise and associated it with the shock. As this association was strengthened over trials, the rats would have learned to expect the shock. When the shock again followed the noise on the compound trials, therefore, the rats would not have been surprised; they would not have searched their memories for a cause, and thus would not have associated the preceding light with the shock.

At an empirical level, the phenomenon of blocking demonstrates that contiguous pairing of a CS with a US does not always result in conditioning. In particular, conditioning to a CS depends on the other stimuli present at the time. If another CS is present that has already been associated with the US, conditioning will not occur. According to Kamin, this is because conditioning involves an active search through memory for causes, and only an unexpected US will trigger this search.

May the Better Predictor Win

We will consider the validity of Kamin's explanation in later chapters, but there can be no question about the reality of blocking as an empirical phenomenon. Blocking thus adds to the growing evidence that contiguity is neither necessary nor sufficient for conditioning. The evidence that contiguity is not necessary is that taste and illness can be associated even with intervals between them of up to 24 hours. Conversely, contiguous pairings of a CS with a US do not always result in conditioning, so contiguity is shown to be insufficient for conditioning. Rescorla showed that the CS must also be a good predictor of the US: If a US is as likely to occur in the absence of a CS as in its presence, no conditioning occurs. Garcia and Koelling showed that conditioning also depended on the particular CS–US combination involved. Finally, blocking shows that conditioning will not occur if another stimulus that already predicts the US is present.

The fact that conditioning does not occur to any stimulus that happens to precede a US is fortunate, because the consequences otherwise could be quite catastrophic. Consider again the rat attacked by an owl. Developing a fear of the sound of the owl flying would undoubtedly help the rat survive, but what if it also became frightened of other stimuli present at the time, such as trees, grass, and other animals? If it ran for cover every time it saw a blade of grass, it probably would die of exhaustion.

It is crucial, then, that unconditioned stimuli not be associated with every stimulus that precedes them, and the conditioning system has evolved to ensure that this does not happen. Instead, conditioning seems to concentrate on stimuli that are good predictors of a US—either because, in the evolutionary history of the species, these stimuli have been more likely to be its cause (Garcia & Koelling, 1966) or because they are currently the best available predictors of its occurrence (Rescorla, 1966, and Kamin, 1969; see also Wagner, 1969). Conditioning, in other words, is a beautifully adaptive system that targets the cues most likely to be the true causes or predictors of important events. How this is achieved is one of the most important issues currently debated by learning theorists, and one to which we will return in Chapter 5.

4.5 APPLICATIONS OF CONDITIONING

In the course of this chapter, we have traced psychologists' efforts to unravel the mysteries of associative learning through experimental analysis of both animal and human behavior. By studying conditioning in the controlled environment of the laboratory, where extraneous stimuli could be rigorously excluded, Pavlov and his successors hoped to be able to tease apart the complex processes involved in the formation of associations. The problem of manipulating only one variable at a time proved more difficult than was perhaps anticipated. Over the years, though, scientists have made considerable progress, as evidenced by Pavlov's brilliant dissection of the excitatory and inhibitory processes underlying extinction, and by Rescorla's more recent demonstration of the role of contingency in conditioning. Having isolated some of the principles of association under the artificial conditions of the laboratory, can we now combine or synthesize them to predict behavior in more complex and volatile environments? Can we, in other words, apply these principles to help people living not in the highly simplified, one-stimulus-at-a-time conditions of a concrete laboratory in St. Petersburg, but amid the complexity and chaos of the real world?

Systematic Desensitization

The first speculations about the possiblity of applying classical conditioning principles to practical problems appeared in the study by Watson and Raynor (1920), discussed in Chapter 3, in which they conditioned "little Albert" to fear a rat by pairing the rat with presentations of a loud noise. At the end of their published report, they suggested that fear conditioning in children of the kind that they had demonstrated might explain many of the phobias and anxieties found in adults. They also offered a number of suggestions about how it might be possible to eliminate such fears—suggestions that were eventually to form the basis for most of the current therapies for phobias.

Peter and the rabbit.   One of Watson and Raynor's suggestions for eliminating fear was to associate the fear stimulus with a pleasurable experience, such as eating or sexual stimulation. The pleasant feelings elicited by these events would be incompatible with fear, they reasoned, so that if these reactions could be conditioned, then fear might be suppressed. This is, of course, the counterconditioning procedure originally described by Pavlov. The first human application of this counterconditioning strategy was in an experiment by Mary Cover Jones (1924). One of her subjects, a boy named Peter, was terrified of rabbits, and, following Watson and Raynor's suggestion, she resolved to introduce the rabbit while Peter was engaged in the pleasurable activity of eating. Obviously, she didn't want to introduce the rabbit too suddenly; if she had simply dropped the rabbit on Peter's lap while he was eating, it is unlikely that his fear would have diminished. So she introduced the rabbit only very gradually over a period of days, first keeping it at a distance and then moving it progressively closer to the boy's chair. The result was nothing short of spectacular, as Peter not only lost all fear of the rabbit but began to actively seek out opportunities to play with it.

Systematic desensitization therapy.   By 1924, then, both conditioning and elimination of fear had been demonstrated successfully with humans, but for reasons that are still obscure, there was little further research into this area for almost 30 years. The next significant development was not until the mid 1950s, when Joseph Wolpe reported on a therapy he had developed called **systematic desensitization.** Wolpe's technique was similar to that of Jones, except that his counterconditioning procedure used relaxation rather than eating as the response. In addition, instead of actually presenting the fear stimuli, he asked his patients to imagine the stimuli. A therapist using Wolpe's technique would ask patients to describe situations that frightened them and then would arrange these stimuli in a hierarchy based on their aversiveness. A patient who had a fear of snakes, for example, might find the idea of looking at a toy snake to be only somewhat threatening. Other stimuli involving snakes would then be arranged in ascending order according to their fearfulness, until the most frightening situation was reached—perhaps picking up a live snake. The therapist would train the patient in special techniques to encourage deep relaxation. (See Wolpe & Lazarus, 1966.) Typically, a patient would start with the lowest stimulus in the hierarchy and alternately visualize that frightening scene and then relax. Only when the patient reported complete relaxation while imagining that scene would the therapist ask the patient to visualize the next scene, and so on.

Wolpe reported remarkable success with this technique in eliminating phobias, and subsequent studies have largely confirmed his claims. In a study by Paul (1969), for example, students who had severe anxieties about public speaking were treated with systematic desensitization or insight-oriented psychotherapy (which focuses on identifying the cause of the phobia). When examined two years later, 85 percent of those given desensitization showed significant improvement relative to pretreatment levels, compared to 50 percent in a psychotherapy group and only 22 percent in an untreated control group.

Symptom substitution.   Despite this impressive evidence, Wolpe's claims were initially met with considerable skepticism, in large part because of his theoretical rationale. Wolpe believed that phobias and other neuroses were really learned behaviors, and he thought it should be possible to modify these behaviors by using the same conditioning principles that had generated them in the first place. Most practicing therapists, however, subscribed to a very different interpretation of neurosis, one originally developed by Sigmund Freud. Freud saw neuroses as only external manifestations of much more fundamental conflicts within the mind. The mind, Freud believed, is composed of three fundamental forces—the id, the ego, and the superego—and the goals of these forces are often in opposition. The intense conflicts that result from such opposition are very painful and are therefore suppressed in the unconscious; but they sometimes become too powerful to be contained in this way and may erupt in partially disguised, symbolic forms such as dreams or phobias. The important point in this interpretation is that phobias are only symptoms of underlying disturbances, much as yellow skin is only a symptom of jaundice rather than the disease itself. To treat only the external behavior, Freudians argued, was useless, since the underlying malaise would still be present, and the elimination of one symptom would only result in its replacement by another—an effect referred to as **symptom substitution.** Snakes, for example, were seen by Freud as a sexual symbol, and fear of snakes was thus a disguised, external manifestation of anxiety about sex. Freudians believed that even if systematic desensitization succeeded in eliminating a fear of snakes, the underlying fear of sex would still be present and would inevitably emerge in some other form, such as a facial tic.

The evidence to date, however, has not borne out the Freudians' prediction. Paul, for example, reexamined his patients two years after the conclusion of treatment and found no recurrence of the old symptoms or emergence of new ones. Indeed, in some cases the elimination of phobias has been found to lead to a general improvement in other areas of functioning such as marital relationships. At an empirical level, therefore, there can be little doubt that systematic desensitization is one of the most effective treatments for phobias currently available. (For a more extensive review, see Wilson, 1982.)

Is it really conditioning?   A more troublesome question from the point of view of learning theory is whether this success is really due to classical conditioning. For one thing, the stimuli employed are very different from those commonly used in the laboratory. The CS, for example, is an *imaginary* event rather than an event experienced directly. Also, the US involves verbal instructions to relax, which bear only a remote resemblance to unconditioned stimuli such as food and electric shock used in most conditioning experiments. Desensitization, in other words, relies heavily on cognitive processes such as imagery and language, and we still know very little about how these processes relate to those more commonly studied in conditioning. One suggestive piece of evidence, however, comes from an experiment by Barber and Hahn (1964), who found that directly experiencing a painful stimulus and simply imagining it produced very similar physiological signs of arousal. An actual event and its image, in other words, may to some extent be functionally equivalent, so that conditioning based on images may not be substantially different from conditioning based on conventional stimuli.

Even if we were to accept that the stimuli used in desensitization correspond to traditional conditioned and unconditioned stimuli, however, the success of the therapy need not be due to associative pairing. Relaxation training by itself may result in a general lessening of anxiety; perhaps the patient expects that the treatment will work because it appears so "scientific." (You may recall the discussion of subject expectations in Chapter 1.)

Some evidence that the success of the therapy genuinely depends on an associative process comes from a well-controlled experiment by Davison (1968). Using college students with an intense fear of snakes as subjects, Davison first measured their fear objectively by seeing how far they could advance through a 13-step test involving progressively greater contact with snakes, ranging from simply approaching a jar containing a snake to actually picking up the snake bare-handed and holding it for 30 seconds. The experimenter asked students in the desensitization group to imagine progressively more aversive scenes involving snakes while simultaneously engaging in deep relaxation exercises. The experimenter guided students in a second group through an identical relaxation procedure, except that the images they were asked to create concerned childhood events rather than snakes. Since childhood disturbances are widely thought to underlie phobias, subjects in this group should have expected to improve just as much as subjects in the first group, the only difference between them being whether relaxation was conditioned to snakes or to childhood memories. The experimenter asked students in a third group to imagine snakes but did not train the students in relaxation techniques. Students in a fourth group received no treatment. In effect, the first group received pairing of the CS (snakes) and the US (relaxation), whereas the second group received the US only, the third received the CS only, and the fourth received no treatment. When the students were later retested on the 13-step fear inventory, the desensitization subjects (group 1) were the only ones to show any significant improvement; they improved by an average of five steps.

These results suggest that the success of desensitization really does depend on an associative process of counterconditioning, but the area has remained controversial. Kazdin and Wilcoxon (1976), for example, have argued that experiments like Davison's did not adequately control for subject expectations, because the control treatment was not as plausible as desensitization. In studies in which the plausibility of the different treatments was equated, they argue, the results are not nearly so favorable to a conditioning interpretation. Mathews (1978), on the other hand, suggests that subject expectations have been found to play an important role only in studies using subjects with mild fears; true phobics are much less influenced by the therapist's confidence or expressions of reassurance. In studies using true phobics, desensitization has proven far more effective than the various controls. The relative importance of conditioning and expectations in the success of systematic desensitization remains to be resolved, but in empirical terms there can be little doubt that the therapy is effective.

Aversion Therapy

A second major application of conditioning principles has been **aversion therapy,** in which the goal is not to eliminate fear but rather to harness it to produce avoidance of a harmful situation. This principle is by no means new, with some of the most imaginative—and gruesome—applications stemming from ancient times. Pliny the Elder, for example, recommended a treatment for alcoholism that consisted of covertly putting the putrid body of a dead spider in the bottom of the alcoholic's tankard. When the drinker would innocently tip the contents into his mouth, the resulting revulsion and nausea supposedly would deter him from ever drinking again. A somewhat more modern example (technically, at any rate) involved the treatment of a 14-year-old boy who wanted to give up smoking (Raymond, 1964). The boy was given injections of apomorphine, a drug that produces intense nausea, and each injection was timed so that it would take effect while the boy was in the middle of smoking.

> On the first occasion he was given an injection of apomorphine 1/20g, and after seven minutes he was told to start smoking. At eleven minutes he became nauseated and vomited copiously. Four days later he came for the second treatment, and said that he still had the craving for cigarettes, but had not in fact smoked since the previous session because he felt nauseated when he tried to light one. . . . Two months later he left school and started working. He said he had "got a bit down" at work and wanted to "keep in with the others," so he had accepted a proffered cigarette. He immediately felt faint and hot, and was unable to smoke. It is now a year since his treatment, and his parents confirm that he no longer smokes.
>
> (Raymond, 1964, p. 290)

Although Raymond's results were highly impressive, subsequent results have been more mixed. Not all studies have obtained positive results, and even when the treatment has been effective initially, patients have often relapsed after treatment was discontinued. We do not fully understand the reasons for the variation in outcome, but one important factor now appears to be the unconditioned stimulus used. Raymond used apomorphine; because this is a highly dangerous drug, most follow-up studies have used electric shock instead. As we saw in our discussion of preparedness, however, stimuli such as the taste of alcohol or the odor of cigarette smoke are difficult to associate with shock, and this could account for the higher failure rate in these studies (Lamon, Wilson, & Leaf, 1977). Studies that have used CS–US combinations thought to be more readily associated—in the case of cigarette smoking, using hot, smoky air as the aversive stimulus—have reported considerable success (for example, Lichtenstein, Harris, Birchler, Wahl, & Schmahl, 1973; Wiens & Menustik, 1983).

As for the difficulty in maintaining treatment gains, this may be the result of discrimination learning. Subjects rapidly learn that whereas drinking alcohol in the clinical setting is followed by an electric shock, for example, drinking in their neighborhood bar or with friends has no such consequences. Rather than learning not to drink, they simply learn not to drink in the presence of the experimenter. More recent studies emphasize modifying contingencies in the natural environment, providing posttreatment "booster" sessions, and providing training in coping with temptation, and there is evidence to suggest that these approaches may be more effective (for example, Hall, Rugg, Tunstall, & Jones, 1984). In the case of alcoholism, for example, Boland, Mellor, and Revusky (1978) combined both of the strategies we have discussed by first pairing alcohol with lithium, a drug that induces nausea, and then giving follow-up treatments. Six months after treatment, they found that 50 percent of the chronic alcoholics in the treatment group were still abstinent, compared to only 12 percent of the controls. This is one of the most successful outcomes ever reported in the treatment of chronic alcoholics and provides some grounds for optimism for the future. (See also Nathan, 1985.)

Behavior Therapy

Both systematic desensitization and aversion therapy are examples of **behavior therapy**, which emphasizes the environmental determinants of behavior rather than the patient's mental state. On the assumption that our current and past environment determines how we think and feel and that these mental states then determine how we behave (Figure 4.9), traditional psychodynamic therapies emphasize changing patients' minds; they generally involve a therapist talking to patients, trying to give them greater insight into their problems. Behavior therapies, on the other hand, focus on an overt problem behavior and try to modify the behavior by altering the patient's environment.

We can further illustrate the difference between these approaches by considering their divergent attitudes toward *enuresis*, or bed-wetting. Freudians view enuresis as a symptom of an underlying psychological conflict, and they

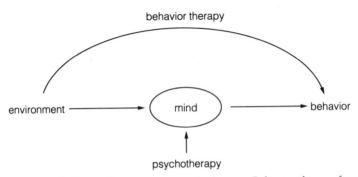

FIGURE 4.9   Behavior therapy versus psychotherapy. Behavior therapy focuses on the role of the environment in controlling behavior, whereas psychotherapy focuses on the role of the mind.

would attempt to treat it through extensive therapy sessions in which the child is helped to recognize the underlying conflict and come to terms with it. Behavior therapists, on the other hand, view bed-wetting simply as an undesirable response, and they would search for learning principles that might help to change the behavior.

The most effective treatment for enuresis, developed by Mowrer and Mowrer (1938), consists simply of a moisture detector wired to the child's bed in such a way that a buzzer will sound whenever the bed is wet. The rationale for this treatment is classical conditioning. The buzzer acts as an unconditioned stimulus to wake the child when he or she wets, and this waking response is hypothesized to become conditioned to the full-bladder cues that precede it. In the future, then, the child will wake up before he or she urinates. (For a discussion of alternative interpretations, see Doleys, 1977.)

This treatment has proved very effective, with average success rates of 75–80 percent across studies (Doleys, 1977). No symptom substitution occurred, and observations of the children following treatment suggested that they were "happier, less anxious, and more grown-up . . . with dramatic positive changes in self-image" (Baker, 1969, p. 49). Because relatively few controlled studies have been carried out on the effectiveness of psychotherapy for enuresis, it is difficult to make precise comparisons, but the available evidence suggests that conditioning-based approaches have a higher success rate and require substantially less treatment time (Doleys, 1977).

A Cognitive Analysis

The success of conditioning-based treatments for enuresis and phobias, and, less clearly, for alcoholism, suggests that behavioral treatments can be highly effective—sometimes far more so than psychodynamic therapies. This success, however, does not necessarily mean that behavior analysis is superior in all respects. In the case of phobias, for example, the behavior analysis assumes that phobias arise through a traumatic experience involving the phobic object—Albert would be a classic example. But interviews with phobic patients have not always supported this assumption. In one study by Goorney and O'Connor (1971), only one fourth of phobic patients interviewed could recall an aversive experience with the object they now feared. Some of the remaining subjects may have had such experiences and forgotten or repressed them, but in at least some of these cases the phobia may have been an indirect or symptomatic expression of some other problem, as the Freudians have long argued.

Support for this view comes from a case reported by Lazarus (1971) in which a patient came for treatment because of a phobia about bridges. Probing further, Lazarus discovered that the patient had never had any unpleasant experiences involving bridges, and that his phobia had appeared suddenly, soon after he had been offered a promotion at work—a job that he could reach only by crossing a bridge. The patient had deep fears over his ability to handle the work required by this promotion, and Lazarus eventually concluded that the fear of bridges had emerged as a more socially acceptable excuse for avoiding the promotion. Lazarus used desensitization to treat the patient's fears related to the promotion, and the patient's fear of bridges soon disappeared.

Lazarus's approach combines elements from behavioral and psychodynamic approaches: The therapist concentrated on the patient's concealed fears, rather than accepting the behavioral symptom at face value; but once the underlying source of the patient's anxiety was identified, the therapist used conditioning principles to help the patient overcome the anxiety. Reliance on conditioning in this instance, however, does not imply that conditioning and psychodynamic treatments are necessarily antithetical. There is no reason that therapists cannot try to alter the environmental contingencies controlling a problem behavior *and* try to give patients insight into their problems. These two approaches can be combined in many ways, in terms of both theories and treatments, and we do not yet know which will prove the most effective (Lazarus, 1981; Meichenbaum & Cameron, 1982). For our purposes, though, it is sufficient to note that an understanding of conditioning principles has already made a significant contribution to the development of more effective therapies and seems likely to continue to do so.

4.6 SUMMARY

Until 1966, almost 70 years of research on conditioning had supported an attractively simple model: An association is formed whenever two stimuli are contiguous, with the strength of the association depending on their temporal and spatial contiguity, their intensity, and the frequency of their pairing. In the period between 1966 and 1969, however, three papers were published that fundamentally challenged this view.

The first paper, by Rescorla (1966), showed that conditioning depended not only on the time separating the CS and US but also on their contingency—the extent to which two events occur together over time, as measured by the probability of a US in the presence of a CS and in its absence. If the probability of the US is greater in the presence of the CS than in its absence, then the CS signals that the US is more likely, and excitatory conditioning occurs; if the probability of the US is lower following the CS, then the CS signals that the US is less likely, and inhibitory conditioning occurs; if the probability of the US is the same in the presence of the CS as in its absence, then no conditioning occurs. Identical pairings of a CS and a US can thus increase, decrease, or have no effect on conditioning, depending on how often the US occurs in the absence of the CS.

The second seminal paper of 1966 was by Garcia and Koelling. They exposed rats to a compound stimulus composed of a taste, a noise, and a light, followed with a dose of radiation sufficient to induce illness. The rats developed a strong aversion to the taste but not to the light or the noise. When they changed the unconditioned stimulus from radiation to an electric shock, they obtained the opposite result: The rats avoided the light and noise but not the taste. The fact that the CS and US are contiguous, then, does not guarantee conditioning, because the rats were selectively prepared to associate some CS–US combinations more readily than others. The reason for the evolution of this selective mechanism is almost certainly its adaptive value. You are much more likely to survive if you avoid what you had eaten before you became ill; avoiding what you had seen or heard has less bearing on survival.

The third critical paper was published three years later by Leo Kamin (1969). Using rats as subjects, Kamin found that if fear had been previously conditioned to one element of a compound, it would block conditioning to the other element. Thus, if an experimenter paired a noise-light compound with electric shock, no fear would be conditioned to the light if the noise had previously been paired with a shock. The reason, Kamin suggested, was that unexpected unconditioned stimuli trigger a search through memory for cues that predict their occurrence. If a US is expected, however, then by definition an adequate predictor must already be present, so no further search is necessary. In the blocking experiment, previous conditioning to the noise established it as a reliable predictor of the shock, so no memory search was initiated on the compound trials and thus no association formed between the light and shock.

Each of these findings has a number of important implications, ranging from the appropriate control group for conditioning to how paradigms guide scientists' evaluation of evidence. But the most important implication concerns the roles of contiguity in learning. The traditional view—that an association would be formed whenever two stimuli were contiguous—is clearly wrong. Tone and shock were contiguous in Rescorla's experiment, but no conditioning occurred if the US also occurred in the absence of the CS. Light and illness were contiguous in Garcia and Koelling's experiment, but conditioning occurred exclusively to the taste. And light was contiguous with shock in Kamin's experiment, but no conditioning was found if the accompanying noise had previously been paired with shock. Contiguity does not ensure conditioning.

The common thread uniting these experiments is that conditioning does not occur equally to whatever stimuli happen to precede a US; conditioning occurs to those stimuli that are good predictors of the US. In the case of preparedness, the knowledge that tastes are better predictors of illness than noise seems to be innate. In contingency learning and blocking, however, we learn the best predictors through experience.

From the time that Pavlov's work on dogs became known, psychologists were intrigued by its possible implications for human behavior. Watson and Raynor (1920) showed that fear could be conditioned in young children, and they speculated that many adult fears might be acquired in this way. If fears were acquired through conditioning, they suggested, then it should also be possible to eliminate them through conditioning. One technique they advocated was counterconditioning, which eventually became the basis of systematic desensitization, a therapy in which phobics are asked to imagine progressively more frightening scenes while simultaneously relaxing. Systematic desensitization has proved to be one of the most effective therapies for treating phobics, although it is not yet clear exactly how much of its effectiveness is due to conditioning and how much to other factors such as subjects' belief that they will improve.

Another important application of conditioning principles is aversion therapy, in which undesirable habits are eliminated through pairing with painful stimuli. To treat alcoholism, for example, the drinking of alcohol is paired with a chemical agent that induces nausea. Aversion therapy has been found to be highly effective in the initial treatment of both alcoholism and cigarette smoking, but roughly half the patients return to drinking or smoking after treatment is discontinued. Research is now increasingly directed toward finding techniques for preventing relapses or treating them once they occur.

Systematic desensitization and aversion therapy are both examples of behavior therapy, which emphasizes environmental determinants of behavior rather than the patient's mental state. Many types of behavior therapy have undeniably been effective. Controversy continues, however, over whether this success should be attributed solely to classical conditioning. One challenge arises from studies on the origin of phobias. A conditioning analysis attributes a phobia to a traumatic experience with the feared object, but only about a quarter of phobic patients can recall such experiences. These findings have led some therapists to search for ways to combine behavioral, cognitive, and Freudian assumptions to explain and treat behavior. The optimal combination remains to be determined, but research on classical conditioning has already contributed significantly to the development of more effective therapies.

Selected Definitions

Delay conditioning   A technique that involves presenting the CS until the US is presented. Some definitions further restrict this term, confining it to situations in which there is also a long interval between CS onset and US onset.

Trace conditioning   A technique that involves presenting the CS and terminating it before presenting the US.

Simultaneous conditioning   A technique that involves presenting the CS and US at the same time.

Backward conditioning   A technique that involves presenting the US before presenting the CS.

Asymptote In mathematics, a stable value that a curve on a graph approaches but never quite reaches. As used in learning, it generally describes the level of performance at which improvement ceases, so that further training would produce no additional improvement.

Contingency A measure of the extent to which two events occur together, or co-vary, over time. A contingency coefficient is a mathematical statistic determined by two probabilities—the probability that a US will occur in the presence of a CS, and the probability that it will occur in the absence of the CS.

Contingency space A visual representation of all possible contingencies that shows the probability of the US both in the presence of the CS and in the absence of the CS.

Random control A control group in which the CS and US are presented completely at random rather than deliberately separated. A random control is also known as a truly random control, to distinguish it from the unpaired control group in which the CS and US are always kept separate.

Taste-aversion learning A phenomenon in which a subject learns to avoid the taste or odor of a particular food as a result of that food's association with illness.

Preparedness The tendency to associate some CS–US combinations more readily than others.

Paradigm A set of shared assumptions about the nature of the world and about what constitutes important and worthwhile problems.

Blocking A phenomenon in which prior conditioning to one element prevents conditioning to other elements of a compound.

Systematic desensitization A therapy technique based on counterconditioning. In this technique, a patient alternately visualizes fear-evoking stimuli and uses deep relaxation to eventually eliminate the fear.

Symptom substitution The replacement of one problem behavior (believed to be symptomatic of an underlying malaise) by another behavior that is equally undesirable.

Aversion therapy A procedure for eliminating an unwanted behavior by conditioning fear to stimuli associated with that behavior.

Behavior therapy A form of therapy that focuses on environmental determinants of behavior rather than on the patient's mental state.

Review Questions

1. How did Rescorla disentangle the roles of contiguity and contingency in conditioning?

2. What is a contingency space? What conditioning is likely to occur at different points within the space?

3. What is the purpose of the random and unpaired control groups? What are the arguments for and against using the random control as *the* control group for classical conditioning?

4. How did Garcia and Koelling show that the conditioning of a stronger aversion to a taste than to a light was not due simply to the greater salience of the taste as a conditioned stimulus?

5. What is Kuhn's concept of a paradigm? Do you think the advantages of scientific paradigms outweigh their disadvantages?

6. How might classical conditioning contribute to an animal's survival? Why might it be better *not* to associate a US with some stimuli that are contiguous with it?

7. How did Kamin account for blocking?

8. Is contiguity necessary or sufficient for conditioning? Explain.

9. How could the Pavlovian concepts of generalization and counterconditioning be used to account for the success of systematic desensitization?

10. Is the success of systematic desensitization really due to classical conditioning? Explain.

11. What are the differences between behavior therapy and psychodynamic approaches to therapy? What arguments support each approach?

CHAPTER FIVE

THEORIES OF CONDITIONING

Pavlov found that when a tone was paired with food, the tone would eventually begin to elicit salivation. To explain this result, he hypothesized that presentation of any stimulus activates a corresponding set of neurons in the brain, which he called a center. If the tone and food centers were active simultaneously, Pavlov said, an association would be formed between them. The next time the food was presented, excitation of the tone center would be transmitted to the food center, with the result that the dog would salivate as if food had been presented.

This explanation is attractively simple, but, over time, learning theorists have challenged its assumptions. This chapter explores some alternative theories that have been proposed. We will begin by concentrating on perhaps the most central issue in any theory of conditioning: the role of contiguity.

Pavlov had essentially followed the British Associationists in assuming that an association would be formed between any cortical centers that were active simultaneously, and thus between any stimuli that occurred contiguously. The evidence reviewed in Chapter 4 for contingency, preparedness, and blocking, however, makes it clear that this simply isn't so. In the case of contingency, for example, Rescorla showed that pairings of a tone with shock will not result in conditioning if the shock occurs with equal probability in the absence of the tone. The fact that a CS is contiguous with a US, then, does not always result in conditioning.

One way to explain the failure of conditioning in this situation is to assume that animals are capable of computing probabilities. The rats could have counted how many shocks occurred in the tone's absence, and also recorded how much time elapsed. Using these data, they could have determined the average probability of the shock in the tone's absence, and in a similar fashion computed the shock's probability in the tone's presence. When these probabilities turned out to be the same, they would realize that the tone signaled no increase in the likelihood of shock, and there would be no reason to be afraid.

It is not impossible that animals carry out the complex processes implicit in this account—measuring time, counting event frequencies, and computing probabilities. In 1972, however, two psychologists published a theory that offered a much simpler account. The theory was the work of Robert Rescorla and Allan Wagner, from Yale University, and it offered an account for almost every major aspect of conditioning—the occurrence of conditioning itself, extinction, blocking, the effects of contingency, and so on. And it achieved all this using only a single, simple equation!

The Rescorla-Wagner model has proved to be one of the most remarkable and influential models in psychology, and we therefore will begin our exploration of theories of conditioning by examining it in some detail. Before we begin, it may be worth noting that some sections of the exposition are difficult and may require careful rereading. This may seem to contradict the previous claim that the model is simple, but once you understand the model it really is simple. The catch is that it is stated in mathematical form, so you will have to master unfamiliar symbols and concepts before the model begins to make sense. Mastering this new terminology is not easy, but the potential reward is an insight into how a few simple assumptions may explain what seems to be a bewildering array of unrelated facts.

5.1 THE RESCORLA-WAGNER MODEL

The foundation of the Rescorla-Wagner model was Kamin's work on blocking. As we saw in Chapter 4, Kamin found that when a noise-light compound was followed by shock, no fear was conditioned to the light if the noise had previously been presented by itself with the shock. From the perspective of contiguity, this result was bewildering: Why, when the light was paired with a powerful electric shock, was fear not conditioned to it? Kamin explained the results in this way: For conditioning to occur, the unconditioned stimulus must be unexpected, or surprising. If a US is surprising, subjects search their memory for possible causes; if the US is expected, though, then an adequate predictor of its occurrence must already be available—hence no memory search occurs, and no learning takes place.

Learning and the Role of Expectations

For Kamin, then, the key to learning lay in the concept of surprise. In other words, learning depends to some extent on the discrepancy between what happens to us and what we expected to happen. If we expect a shock to occur, we do not learn; but if the same shock occurs unexpectedly, then it upsets us far more, and we search for an explanation. Thus, the same event may have very different effects, depending on our initial expectations.

Expectation is a very powerful psychological concept, with applications extending far beyond conditioning. Research on perception, for example, has shown that what we perceive is also strongly influenced by our expectations. In a representative experiment by Warren (1970), subjects were played a tape containing the sentence, "The state governors met with their respective legislatures convening in the capital city." The section of the tape containing the first *s* in *legislatures* had been cut out and replaced by the sound of someone coughing. It was impossible for anyone to hear the *s*, because it simply was not there. Yet, 19 out of 20 subjects nevertheless reported hearing every single part of the sentence distinctly. Even when they were told that one segment of the sentence had been removed, they still were unable to identify the segment. What we perceive depends to some extent, then, on what we expect to perceive.

Another example of the importance of expectations comes from research on aggression. It has long been known that one of the major causes of aggression is an unpleasant experience: If someone kicks you, for example, you are likely to kick back. However, some evidence suggests that it is not the aversive experiences that cause aggression, but rather aversive events that are unexpected. Davies (1962), for example, has suggested that political revolutions are most likely to occur not when social conditions are consistently bad (people seem to adapt to stable suffering), but rather when there is a period of increasing prosperity followed by a sudden downturn. The Russian Revolution broke out in 1917, not during the many centuries when Russian peasants lived as serfs, but when a dramatic increase in prosperity due to industrialization was reversed by war with Germany. Similarly, the French Revolution occurred when years of increasing prosperity were interrupted by crop failures and economic crisis. Apparently, it is not suffering that causes revolution, but suffering that follows a period in which more positive conditions are experienced. (See also Chapter 6 on contrast effects.)

The Model

In a wide range of contexts, then, our reactions to events are influenced powerfully by our expectations, and Kamin suggested that this principle also affects our reactions to a US. Rescorla and Wagner extended this fundamental insight of Kamin's. Kamin said that conditioning depended on whether the US was unexpected; Rescorla and Wagner subsequently proposed that the precise *amount* of conditioning depended on the extent of the subject's surprise. That is, surprise determines not only whether conditioning occurs, but how strongly it occurs. The more unexpected the US, the more conditioning occurs.

The learning curve. To enable researchers to predict the precise amount of conditioning, Rescorla and Wagner stated their model in mathematical form. They began by substituting the language of association for Kamin's cognitive terminology. When a CS and a US are paired, they said, an association would be formed between them, and they used the symbol V to represent the strength of this association. They assumed that if the CS–US pairings were repeated, the strength of the association would increase in roughly the manner shown in Figure 5.1a. One important point to note about this learning curve is that the increase in associative strength is not constant over trials. On the first trial, V increases by a substantial amount. Over successive trials, the increase in V on

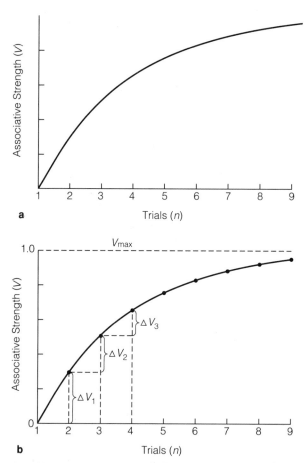

F I G U R E 5.1 How associative strength (V) increases over conditioning trials (n) according to the Rescorla-Wagner model: (a) a typical learning curve; (b) the same curve, showing the change in associative strength on each trial (ΔV) and the asymptotic value of associative strength (V_{max}).

each trial gets progressively smaller, until eventually V approaches a stable value.

Rescorla used the symbol ΔV to represent the change in associative strength on each trial (Δ, or delta, is the mathematical symbol for change). The change in associative strength produced by the first trial was ΔV_1, the change on trial 2 was ΔV_2, and so on. As we saw in Chapter 4, a stable value that a curve approaches but never quite reaches is called an *asymptote*, and we will use the symbol V_{max} to represent the asymptotic value of V (Figure 5.1b).

Quantifying surprise.   We can summarize the model to this point by saying that associative strength increases over trials until it reaches a stable maximum value; in mathematical symbols, V increases by ΔV on each trial until it approaches V_{max}. To predict the strength of association, then, we need a formula to predict ΔV. A number of formulas were possible; in choosing one, Rescorla and Wagner were guided by their assumption that the amount of conditioning depends on the amount of surprise. To quantify surprise, they focused on the relationship between V and V_{max}. At the beginning of conditioning, when V is much less than V_{max}, the subject will not expect the US and hence will be surprised when it occurs. As V increases over trials and approaches V_{max}, the occurrence of the US will be progressively less surprising. The difference between V and V_{max}, therefore, provides us with a useful index of surprise: The smaller the difference between V and V_{max}, the less surprising the occurrence of the US will be.

Figure 5.2 illustrates this point by focusing on two trials, one early on in conditioning and the other later. Early in conditioning (point 1), there will be a large difference between V and V_{max}, and substantial conditioning will occur.

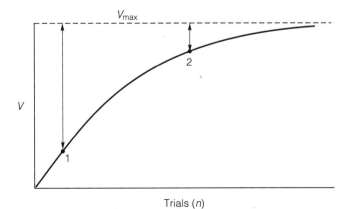

Trials (n)

F I G U R E 5.2   The relationship between V and V_{max} early and late in conditioning. Early in conditioning (point 1), the difference between V and V_{max} is great. Later (point 2), the difference is much less.

As conditioning proceeds, however (point 2), the difference between V and V_{max} will decrease, and the US will be less surprising. The notion that the amount of conditioning depends on the amount of surprise, therefore, can potentially be translated into mathematical form by saying that the amount of conditioning on any trial n (ΔV_n) will depend on the difference between V and V_{max}:

$$\Delta V_n \approx V_{max} - V_n$$

where

    V_n = the strength of the association at the beginning of trial n
    ΔV_n = the change in the strength of the association produced by trial n

Parameters.   In our presentation of the model to this point, we have talked as if the learning curve shown in Figure 5.1 is the one found in all conditioning curves, but this is not quite right. The overall shape of the curve—increasing over trials, but at a declining rate—is indeed uniform, or at least roughly so, but the asymptotic level of conditioning and the rate at which this asymptote is reached vary across experiments. In the Annau and Kamin (1961) experiment on fear conditioning, for example, intense shock produced much higher asymptotic levels of fear than milder shocks did (see Figure 3.11, p. 100).

Figure 5.3 illustrates the difference between the asymptote and the rate of conditioning, portraying a range of possible learning curves. In Figure 5.3a, the curves differ in asymptotic levels of conditioning but reach this level after the same number of trials; in Figure 5.3b, the curves reach the same asymptote but vary in the rate at which they get there.

If the growth in associative strength differs in different experiments, how can we use a single equation to predict these different outcomes? In mathematical formulas this is achieved through the use of constants called **parameters**. Suppose, for example, that we linked two variables, X and Y, by the equation

$$Y = cX$$

where c was a constant. If the value of the parameter c was set at 2 ($Y = 2X$), then the value of Y would increase twice as fast as the value of X; if the value of c was set at 3 ($Y = 3X$), Y would increase three times as fast. By varying the value of the parameter c, then, we can use the same basic equation to predict a range of different results.

To enable theorists to predict variations in the rate and asymptotic value of conditioning, Rescorla and Wagner used two parameters. To predict the asymptotic level of conditioning, they used V_{max}, and to take into account

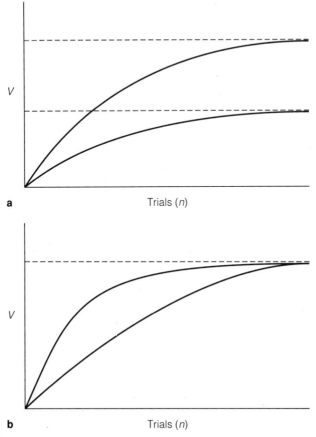

F I G U R E 5.3   Variations in the asymptote (broken line) and rate of conditioning:
(a) two learning curves that change at the same rate but approach different asymptotes;
(b) two curves that approach the same asymptote but at different rates.

different speeds of conditioning they introduced the parameter c. * The complete statement of the equation was thus:

$$\Delta V_n = c(V_{max} - V_n)$$

---

* The value of the parameter V_{max} was assumed to be determined solely by the US used, whereas
the value of c was determined by both the CS and the US. In fact, Rescorla and Wagner used two
different constants, α and β, to represent the effects of the CS and US, rather than the single
parameter c, and they also used the symbol λ to represent asymptotic conditioning rather than V_{max}.
We have altered the symbols in order to make the exposition of the model easier to follow. Should
you read the model in the original, you will find the equation stated as:

$$\Delta V_n = \alpha\beta(\lambda - V_n)$$

The value of c in our version of the equation must lie between 0 and 1.

5.2 THE RESCORLA-WAGNER MODEL: DERIVING PREDICTIONS

We now have an equation with which we can predict the precise change in associative strength on any trial. To test the model, therefore, it might seem that all we need to do is present a series of CS–US trials, calculate the predicted value of V for each trial, and see if these predictions are correct. This simple summary, however, hides a number of serious practical difficulties.

One problem is that V represents the strength of a *theoretical* association. We can see a dog salivate, but we cannot directly observe the association assumed to produce this behavior. If the strength of association was 15, for example, how many drops of saliva should we expect to see? Before we can test the model's predictions, we need rules relating associative strength to overt behavior.

Parameter Estimation

A second problem is that we need to know the values of c and V_{max} before we can predict V. V_{max}, for example, refers to the maximum strength of the association, but if we cannot observe an association, then we have no rational basis for deciding its maximum strength. If we paired a tone with 5 grams of food, for example, would the maximum strength of association be 1 unit or 5 or 77?

One solution is to try out a variety of values, chosen at random, and see which one leads to the most accurate prediction of behavior. If we found that setting V_{max} at 7 when the US is 5 grams resulted in highly accurate predictions, we could then use this value in further applications involving this US. Again, though, this solution is far more difficult in practice than it sounds. Suppose, for example, that after choosing a set of parameter values and selecting a rule for converting V into drops of saliva we found that our prediction was wrong. How could we locate the source of the error? It may have been in just one of the parameters or in all of them; it may not have been in the parameters at all but in the rule for translating V into behavior. In a complex model with many assumptions, it can be frustratingly difficult to identify the source of any error and thus to correct it.

In light of these difficulties, you may not be altogether surprised to learn that in the entire history of learning theory there has been only one sustained effort to develop a comprehensive mathematical model of the kind we have been discussing (Hull, 1943), and that after more than a decade of effort the researchers involved largely abandoned the effort. This failure convinced many learning theorists that mathematical models were more trouble than they were worth, and for almost 20 years there was little further interest. (For a notable exception, see Estes, 1959.) Rescorla and Wagner's work has rekindled interest, however, by showing that it is not necessary to know the exact values of a model's parameters in order to test it. Instead of estimating the real values of the parameters c and V_{max}, they derived predictions using totally arbitrary values.

The use of arbitrary values might seem pointless to you, but although this strategy precludes *quantitative* predictions, it turns out that the model can still make some very interesting *qualitative* predictions. That is, although the exact points on the learning curve depend on the values of c and V_{max} used in the equation, no matter which values are chosen, the equation always predicts a learning curve of the same general shape. Thus, although we cannot predict the exact number of drops of saliva, we can still make qualitative predictions as to whether salivation will increase or decrease, and, as we shall see, even simple statements of this kind can sometimes lead to surprising and interesting predictions.

To see how this can happen, we will first consider how the model ac-counts for relatively straightforward phenomena such as conditioning and ex-tinction. Then, once the basic operations of the model are a bit clearer, we will turn to some of its more striking predictions. To begin, though, let us take a look at how the model accounts for the basic shape of the learning curve during conditioning.

Conditioning

Suppose that we repeatedly paired a tone with food, as in the hypothetical experiment whose results are illustrated by the learning curve presented in Figure 5.1. To see what sort of results the model might predict in this situation, let us arbitrarily assume that the value of V_{max} appropriate to the amount of food we are using is 1.0, and the value of c is 0.30. How much learning should we then expect?

As shown in Table 5.1, associative strength at the beginning of trial 1 is assumed to be zero, so the amount of conditioning on that first trial would be:

$$\Delta V_1 = c(V_{max} - V_1) = 0.30(1.0 - 0) = 0.30$$

TABLE 5.1   Using the Rescorla-Wagner Model to Predict Conditioning

Trial	V_n	$\Delta V_n = c\,(V_{max} - V_n)$
1	0.00	$\Delta V_1 = 0.30\,(1 - 0.00) = 0.30$
2	0.30	$\Delta V_2 = 0.30\,(1 - 0.30) = 0.21$
3	0.51	$\Delta V_3 = 0.30\,(1 - 0.51) = 0.15$
4	0.66	$\Delta V_4 = 0.30\,(1 - 0.66) = 0.10$

At the beginning of trial 2, the strength of the association would thus be 0.30, and the change in associative strength produced by that trial would be:

$$\Delta V_2 = c(V_{max} - V_2) = 0.30(1.0 - 0.30) = 0.21$$

The predicted values for V on the next two trials are shown in the table. As you can see, they correspond exactly to the values plotted in Figure 5.1.

Our success in predicting these hypothetical data is perhaps not too surprising (especially when you consider that the calculations were done first and the graph simply plots these calculations), but it does indicate the capacity of the model to generate learning curves of the shape found in most conditioning experiments. The predicted shape of the curve is the same, moreover, regardless of what values of c and V_{max} are used. These parameters alter the height of the asymptote and the speed with which it is reached, but in all cases the basic shape of the curve remains the same. (You might find it useful to verify this for yourself by working through some calculations using other values. Note that c must have a value between 0 and 1.0.)

Extinction

What about other aspects of conditioning? For example, can the model explain decreases in responding as well as increases? Not only can it explain such changes, but it does so using exactly the same equation used to predict conditioning. The key to understanding how one equation can predict diametrically opposite results lies in V_{max}. We have said that V_{max} is the strength of the association that would be produced if a CS and US were paired repeatedly. In extinction, we know that the level of conditioning reached after extended training is zero. The value of V_{max} on any trial in which a US is not presented, therefore, must also be zero.

To see the implications of this, suppose that after the third conditioning trial in our previous example we began to present the CS by itself. On the first extinction trial, V would have an initial value of 0.66 (see Table 5.1), but as a result of nonreinforcement on that trial, its associative strength would be changed by:

$$\Delta V_1 = c(V_{max} - V_1) = 0.30(0 - 0.66) = -0.198$$

The strength of the association, in other words, would be decreased by approximately 0.20, and its new strength would be:

$$V_2 = 0.66 - 0.20 = 0.46$$

A second extinction trial would decrease its strength by a further -0.14, and so on, until eventually V would approach its asymptotic value of zero. (See

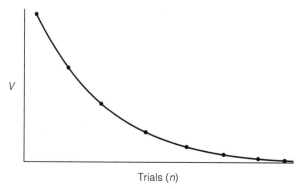

Trials (*n*)

F I G U R E 5.4   An example of extinction as predicted by the Rescorla-Wagner model.

Figure 5.4.) Using only a single equation, therefore, the model can predict extinction as well as conditioning.

Blocking

We can also use the model to explain blocking. Before doing so, however, we need to consider how conditioning is affected if two stimuli instead of just one are present on a trial.

Compound trials.   We said earlier that conditioning on any trial depends on how surprising the US is, which in turn depends on how much the subject expected the US to occur. Rescorla and Wagner assumed that if two conditioned stimuli, a and b, were presented together, the subject would take both stimuli into account in estimating the likelihood of the US. Specifically, they proposed that the association or expectation at the beginning of a trial would be the sum of the strengths of each of the stimuli present:

$$V_{ab} = V_a + V_b$$

Suppose, for example, that a and b had been paired separately with food and had associative strengths of 0.30 and 0.50, respectively. If the two stimuli were presented together, subjects would assume that food must *really* be likely. The associative strength of the compound would be:

$$V_{ab} = V_a + V_b = 0.30 + 0.50 = 0.80$$

In calculating unexpectedness, we need to take into account all the stimuli present. Thus, the amount of conditioning on a compound trial in which a and b occur together would be:

$$\Delta V_a = \Delta V_b = c(V_{max} - V_{ab})^*$$

where:

$$V_{ab} = V_a + V_b$$

Kamin's blocking experiment.   We can now explain the results of Kamin's blocking experiment. Recall that a noise was paired with shock for a number of trials, and then a noise-light compound was paired with shock. During the noise trials, the associative strength of the noise would have increased until it essentially reached asymptote. If we assume that V_{max} for the shock was 1.0, then by the end of conditioning,

$$V_{noise} = 1.0$$

If the noise were presented with the light, then their combined associative strength would be:

$$V_{nl} = V_{noise} + V_{light} = 1.0 + 0 = 1.0$$

The amount of conditioning to the light on this trial would therefore be:

$$\Delta V_{light} = c(V_{max} - V_{nl}) = 0.3(1.0 - 1.0) = 0.3(0) = 0$$

In other words, no conditioning would occur, which is exactly the result Kamin found.

This derivation illustrates again the fundamental principle that the amount of conditioning depends not simply on the US (in the model, the effect of the US is mediated by V_{max}), but also on what the subject expects (V). Suppose, for example, that a rat received a 10-volt electric shock. If it had not been expecting shock, this would cause a large increase in its fear; if it had expected precisely this shock, its fear would not change from the original expectation; and if it had been expecting a 20-volt shock, its fear would actually decrease. The same shock, in other words, could lead to either an

---

* In this example, and in all examples that follow, we have assumed that a and b are equally salient stimuli and that the values of c are the same for both. (Recall that c is determined by the CS as well as the US.) If a and b are not equally salient, a different value of c will be needed for each, and the amount learned on a compound trial will be:

$$\Delta V_a = c_a(V_{max} - V_{ab})$$
$$\Delta V_b = c_b(V_{max} - V_{ab})$$

increase, a decrease, or no change in fear, depending on the rat's initial expectation.

Restated in the associative terminology of the model, whether conditioning will increase or decrease when a US is presented depends on the relationship between V and V_{max}. If V is less than V_{max}, as it is during conditioning, then the quantity $(V_{max} - V)$ is positive, and associative strength will increase (point 1 in Figure 5.5). If V is greater than V_{max}, as it is during extinction, then the quantity $(V_{max} - V)$ is negative, and associative strength will be reduced (point 2 in the figure). Finally, if conditioning is at asymptote, so $V = V_{max}$, then the quantity $(V_{max} - V)$ is zero, and there will be no change in associative strength (point 3). Exactly the same US, therefore, can produce either an increase, a decrease, or no change in conditioning, depending on the associative strength at the beginning of the trial.

5.3 EVALUATING THE RESCORLA-WAGNER MODEL

The Rescorla-Wagner model, then, is able to account for such basic conditioning phenomena as the occurrence of conditioning itself, extinction, and blocking, and it is able to do so using only a single basic equation. The model is in many respects an extraordinary achievement, but the real test of any model lies not so much in its ability to describe known phenomena as in the ability to predict new ones. To assess the model's success in this crucial respect, we will focus on one of its strangest and most counterintuitive predictions: In some circumstances, pairing a CS with a US will result not in conditioning but in extinction.

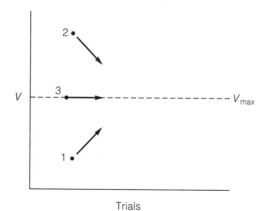

Trials

F I G U R E 5.5   The direction of learning as determined by the relationship between V and V_{max}. When V is less than V_{max} (point 1), associative strength increases. When V is greater than V_{max} (point 2), associative strength decreases. When V equals V_{max} (point 3), associative strength does not change.

New Predictions: Overexpectation

Suppose that we were to expose rats to a series of conditioning trials in which a tone and a light were separately paired with an intense shock:

$$\text{tone} \longrightarrow \text{shock}$$
$$\text{light} \longrightarrow \text{shock}$$

Then suppose that the tone and light were presented together on the next conditioning trial:

$$\text{tone} + \text{light} \longrightarrow \text{shock}$$

What effect should this have on fear of the tone? Since the tone is again being followed by an unpleasant shock, you might expect a further increase in fear, but, according to the Rescorla-Wagner model, the situation is not necessarily that simple. As we've already seen, the amount of conditioning in any situation depends not simply on the US but also on the associative strength at the beginning of the trial. Suppose, for example, that only a few trials were given before the compound trial, so fear levels to the two stimuli were only moderate:

$$V_a = V_b = 0.20$$

On the compound trial, V_{ab} would be 0.40, so that the change in associative strength on that trial would be:

$$\Delta V_a = \Delta V_b = c(V_{max} - V_{ab}) = 0.3(1.0 - 0.4) = 0.18$$

In accordance with common sense, in other words, the model predicts an increase in fear conditioning on this trial.

Now suppose that extensive conditioning to the tone and light took place before the first compound trial, with the result that:

$$V_a = V_b = 0.9$$

In this case, the associative strength of the compound would be 1.8, so that on the compound trial:

$$\Delta V_a = \Delta V_b = c(V_{max} - V_{ab}) = 0.3(1.0 - 1.8) = -0.24$$

Even though the compound is still being followed by a powerful electric shock, the model now predicts a *decrease* in fear levels!

This prediction was tested in an experiment by Rescorla (1970). In the first phase, rats were given extensive pairings of both a tone and a light with

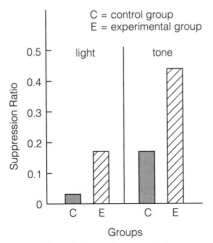

F I G U R E 5.6   Fear elicited by a light and a tone following simple conditioning or after additional conditioning trials in which the tone and light were presented jointly, followed by shock. (Based on data from Rescorla, 1970)

shock, so that fear conditioning to each would be essentially at asymptotic levels. An experimental group was then given 12 compound trials in which the tone and the light were presented together and followed by the same shock as in training; a control group received no further training. Finally, fear conditioning to the two stimuli was assessed by presenting them separately in a CER (conditioned emotional response) test. (See Chapter 3 for a discussion of the CER test.)

Figure 5.6 shows the results of this experiment. Let us look first at the results for the light: Note that responding was suppressed much more in the control group (suppression ratio of 0.03) than in the experimental group (suppression ratio of 0.17). The initial pairing of the light with shock, in other words, had resulted in strong fear conditioning, but the additional pairings in the experimental group actually reduced that fear. The effect on the tone was, if anything, even more dramatic, with the extra compound trials resulting in an even greater decrease in fear. Indeed, the tone no longer appeared to elicit any fear at all; the observed suppression ratio of 0.44 was virtually indistinguishable from the neutral point of 0.50. Extra pairings of the tone and light with shock not only did not increase fear, as common sense might predict, but actually reduced or even eliminated it! It is a bizarre result, but precisely what the model predicts. [*]

---

[*] The result is not nearly so strange when viewed from the perspective of the model, because the associative strength of the compound at the beginning of the extra-pairings phase was far greater than V_{max}. If the net fear level is greater than that justified by the shock that actually occurs, it is quite reasonable that subjects will react by reducing their level of fear.

The Implications for Contingency

In some circumstances, then, pairing a stimulus with shock may actively reduce fear of that stimulus. This finding provides us with the key to understanding another fundamental property of conditioning: the effects of contingency. In Chapter 4, we saw that if a CS and a US are presented noncontingently—that is, if the US occurs as often in the absence of the CS as in its presence—then no conditioning occurs. Why, though, does presenting the US by itself inter- fere with conditioning? According to the principle of contiguity, any event paired with a US should become associated with it, so that when the noncon- tingent group receives the CS and US together, conditioning should occur. How can presenting the US by itself interfere with the formation of this association?

The key to answering this question, according to Rescorla and Wagner, lies in recognizing that the US is not presented by itself. No stimulus ever occurs in a vacuum; there are always other stimuli present. For a rat in a fear- conditioning experiment, a given stimulus (a) may not be present during shock, but a variety of other cues will be present—visual cues from the walls, tactile cues from the floor, and so on. Some of these background cues (b) will be present uniformly throughout the session; they will be present when a is paired with the shock and also when shock occurs in the absence of a. A more realistic depiction of the actual course of events, then, is:

$$ab \longrightarrow US. . .b \longrightarrow US. . .ab \longrightarrow US. . .b \longrightarrow US$$

Given a sequence of such trials, how much conditioning should we ex- pect to occur with a and b? Intuitively, it is very difficult to say. This is one case in which a mathematical model has an advantage over a more intuitive formu- lation such as that of Kamin. Figure 5.7 shows the model's prediction.

Initially, conditioning occurs with both a and b, because both are paired with the shock. Eventually, though, conditioning reaches a point where, al- though V_a and V_b individually are less than V_{max}, their combined strength on a compound trial will exceed V_{max}. In such situations, as we have just seen, the shock will actually reduce fear associated with a and b. When b by itself is paired with the shock on the next trial, V_b will still be less than V_{max}, so $(V_{max} - V_b)$ will be positive and the associative strength of b will again increase. Over a series of such trials, the model predicts that the strength of b will alternately increase and then decrease, depending on whether a is also present, but that the net effect will be a long-term increase. Since a occurs only on compound trials, however, and since the combined associative strength of a and b on such trials always exceeds V_{max}, the model predicts that a will con- tinue to lose associative strength.

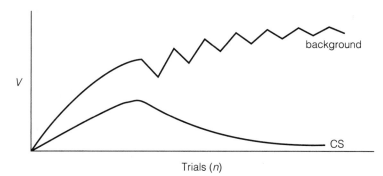

F I G U R E 5.7   Changes in associative strength predicted by the Rescorla-Wagner model when a CS and a US are presented noncontingently. It is predicted that the CS will not develop associative strength, but that strong background stimuli such as the test apparatus will develop associative strength.

Thus, the model predicts that when shock is presented noncontingently, fear will be strongly conditioned to the background cues but not to the CS. These predictions have been confirmed. Odling-Smee (1975) demonstrated that noncontingent shock results in much greater fear of the apparatus than does contingent shock; as we saw in Chapter 4, Rescorla (1966) demonstrated no fear of the nominal CS. Once confirmed, of course, this prediction makes good sense. The apparatus is a strong predictor of shock, because the rat receives shocks only when it is inside the apparatus. Therefore, the apparatus comes to elicit strong fear. The probability of shock when the CS appears, however, is no greater than in its absence, so the rat is quite right not to become more frightened when it is presented.

The seemingly mysterious effects of presenting a US noncontingently, then, can be accounted for if we consider each US presentation as a conditioning trial in which the US becomes associated with whatever stimuli are present at the time. Conditioning, in other words, *can* be explained in terms of contiguity, provided that we realize the following:

1. The strength of conditioning depends not just on the characteristics of the US but also on whether it was expected.

2. Conditioning occurs not just to the nominal CS but also to background cues that may be present.

With these assumptions, we can use the model to explain the effects of noncontingent pairings simply in terms of the associations that form between contiguous stimuli. The end result is impressively sophisticated: Subjects behave as if they are calculating complex probabilities. In fact, the actual mechanism may be surprisingly simple.

The Model's Limitations

We have examined in some detail one prediction of the model; other predictions have also been tested and, on the whole, have been strongly confirmed (for example, Blough, 1975). In some important respects, however, the model's predictions have proved incorrect, and we will look at two examples.

Configural learning.   According to the model, the associative strength of a compound is the sum of the strengths of its components. Suppose, for example, that two stimuli, a and b, were independently paired with a US so that each had an associative strength of 0.5. If the two were presented together, their combined associative strength would then be:

$$V_{ab} = V_a + V_b = 0.5 + 0.5 = 1.0$$

In other words, when two conditioned stimuli are presented together, the model predicts greater responding to the compound than to either of the elements on its own. As plausible as this prediction may seem, there are some situations in which responding to a compound is substantially *less* than to its components.

In one experiment demonstrating this point, Bellingham, Gillette-Bellingham, and Kehoe (1985) gave rats discrimination training that involved mixing conditioning trials. Trials in which a tone and a light were paired separately with food alternated with compound trials in which the tone and light were presented together without food:

$$
\begin{array}{ll}
\text{tone} & \longrightarrow \text{food} \\
\text{light} & \longrightarrow \text{food} \\
\text{tone-light} & \longrightarrow
\end{array}
$$

The rats learned to respond at a high rate to the tone and the light by themselves, responding on 90 percent of trials. When the tone and light were presented together, however, responding declined to only 30 percent. Clearly, the associative strength of the compound in this situation was not the sum of its components.

The rats behaved as if they understood that the tone and light on their own were signals for food but that, when presented together, they were not. In effect, they were responding to the compound as a unique stimulus or configuration, c, rather than as simply a + b. This phenomenon, in which subjects respond to a compound stimulus in a dramatically different way than they would respond to its elements presented separately, is known as **configural learning.** In Chapter 11, we will return to the question of how this is achieved, but clearly the model's "additive sum" rule is not always right. (See also Pearce & Wilson, 1991.)

Latent inhibition.   A second instance in which the predictions of the model have proved incorrect involves preexposure to a stimulus by itself before it is paired with a US. In an experiment by Lubow and Moore (1959), a group of sheep and goats were repeatedly shown a flashing light. The animals then received conditioning trials in which the same light was paired with shock. A control group received the identical conditioning trials but without preexposure to the light.

How should preexposure to the light affect subsequent conditioning? According to the Rescorla-Wagner model, when a light is presented by itself during preexposure, no conditioning will occur because no US is presented. In mathematical terms, V_{max} is always zero when no US is presented. If the light is initially neutral ($V = 0$), then:

$$\Delta V = c(V_{max} - V) = c(0 - 0) = 0$$

At the beginning of conditioning in Lubow and Moore's experiment, the light should have had no associative strength in either group, and learning in the two groups should have proceeded identically. Contrary to this prediction, Lubow and Moore found that conditioning was significantly slower in the group preexposed to the light, a phenomenon they termed **latent inhibition** because they believed that the CS becomes inhibitory during the preexposure phase. Subsequent evidence, though, has made it clear that the CS is neither excitatory nor inhibitory; it is simply difficult to condition. (See Reiss & Wagner, 1972.)

The most likely explanation for this phenomenon is that when a stimulus is repeatedly presented by itself, we learn to ignore it. If that stimulus is then paired with a US, we are slow to learn about this new relationship because we have previously learned that the stimulus is unimportant. (For more detailed accounts, see Mackintosh, 1975; Pearce & Hall, 1980.) As simple as this account may seem, the Rescorla-Wagner model does not incorporate any mechanism for learning to attend selectively to stimuli, and thus cannot predict the effect.

Evaluation

Using only a single equation (in essence, a simple comparison of V and V_{max}), the Rescorla-Wagner model can explain an astonishing range of facts about conditioning, including why conditioning, extinction, and blocking occur; why presentation of a US by itself interferes with conditioning; and so on. In addition, it makes a variety of counterintuitive predictions—for example, that a conditioning trial may reduce associative strength—and these predictions generally have been supported. The evidence for configural learning and latent inhibition, however, shows that the model cannot account for all aspects of

conditioning and thus needs to be modified. (See also DeVito & Fowler, 1986.)

One important weakness of the model lies in its treatment of the CS. Configural learning and latent inhibition indicate that subjects can learn to respond to compounds as integral units, rather than as independent elements, and can learn to increase or decrease attention to stimuli on the basis of their past predictive value. How the subject processes the CS, then, can play an important role in determining conditioning, and the Rescorla-Wagner model needs to incorporate assumptions about CS processing if it is to provide a comprehensive account of conditioning.

Learning theorists have offered a number of suggestions to improve the model. Rescorla (1976) and Wagner (1981) suggested relatively small changes that would allow the model to account for both latent inhibition and configural learning. (See also Sutton & Barto, 1981.) Schull (1979) and Pearce and Hall (1980) suggested potentially more substantial changes, and other theorists have suggested alternative models (for example, Gibbon & Balsam, 1981; Wagner & Brandon, 1989). It is not yet clear how these alternative accounts can best be integrated. However, the success the model has already achieved in explaining so many phenomena with only a few simple assumptions suggests that the model may prove to be a major landmark in the development of our understanding of learning.

5.4 WHAT IS LEARNED THROUGH CONDITIONING?

The Rescorla-Wagner model provides us with a powerful tool for predicting the strength of the association formed on any trial, but the model does not tell us about the nature of this association. When a tone is paired with food, for example, what exactly is it that the dog associates? Pavlov's view, as we have seen, was that the simultaneous activation of the tone and food centers of the brain results in the formation of a new associative pathway between them, so that whenever the tone is presented in the future, the excitation it produces will be transmitted to the food center, and then to the salivary glands via innate pathways. An alternative analysis, first proposed by Clark Hull (1943), is that when the tone is followed by salivation, an association forms between the tone and salivary centers so the tone will elicit salivation directly.

S–S or S–R?

Pavlov's formulation is sometimes referred to as an **S–S theory**, because it assumes that an association is formed between two stimuli, the CS and the US. (See Figure 5.8a.) Hull's view, on the other hand, is known as an **S–R theory**, because it postulates a direct link between the conditioned stimulus and the response. (See Figure 5.8b.) One way to test which theory is right is to alter the

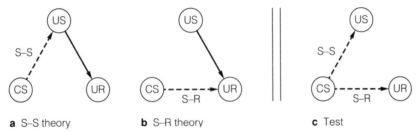

a S–S theory   **b** S–R theory   **c** Test

F I G U R E 5.8   Two versions of what a subject learns during conditioning: (a) The S–S theory holds that an association is formed between the CS and US centers in the brain; excitation is then transmitted from the US center to the UR center via an innate link. (b) The S–R theory holds that an association is formed directly between the CS and the UR. (c) If the link between the US and the UR centers were broken, S–S theory predicts that the CS would no longer elicit a response, whereas S–R theory predicts that it would.

value of the US after conditioning has occurred. Suppose, for example, that after pairing a tone with food we could induce a dog's aversion to that food, so that the dog no longer would eat it. According to Pavlov, presenting the tone leads to excitation of the food center, which is then transmitted to the salivary center. If the link between the food and salivary center is broken, the tone should no longer elicit salivation. (See Figure 5.8c.) According to S–R theory, on the other hand, conditioning results in a direct association between the tone and salivation. Subsequent devaluation of the food cannot alter this association, and thus the tone should continue to elicit salivation.

These predictions were tested in an experiment on rats by Holland and Straub (1979). During the conditioning phase, a 10-second noise was followed by the delivery of food pellets. The experimenters measured conditioning by the rats' general activity (such as movement around the cage) during the noise. After conditioning was established (the rats' activity doubled when the noise came on), subsequent trials made food unattractive by pairing it with the highly aversive experience of rotation at high speed. The rats were allowed to eat freely from a large dish of pellets for five minutes and were then placed in a cage mounted on a phonograph turntable inclined at 45 degrees and rotated at 120 revolutions per minute for 10 minutes. Finally, the noise was presented again one day later to see if it would still elicit activity.

If the rats had associated the noise with food (S–S theory), then devaluing the food should prevent the noise from eliciting activity. S–R theory, in contrast, predicted that the noise-activity association would still be intact and conditioned activity would be unaffected. In fact, Holland and Straub found a significant decrease in activity to the noise. This reduced activity, moreover, could not be attributed simply to the fact that the rats had been ill, because conditioned activity was unaffected in control subjects whose illness was not associated with food. It was the devaluation of the US that weakened the conditioned response.

Signal or Substitute?

The fact that a change in US value affects responding strongly implies that a representation of the US must form part of the causal chain linking the CS and the response. There are very different views, however, about the nature of this CS–US link. According to one of the earliest cognitive theorists of associative learning, Edward Tolman (1932), the link was in the form of an expectation: If a tone is followed by food, a dog will form an expectation that future tones will also be followed by food. Tolman was not very specific about how this expectation would then be translated into a conditioned response, but the general notion was that the dog would take whatever action was appropriate to prepare for the expected food. Thus, a dog would salivate when it expected food, because such anticipatory salivation would help it to digest the food more quickly and efficiently (see Hollis, 1982); a rabbit would blink when it expected a puff of air to its eye, because this blink would protect the eye.

Stimulus substitution. Pavlov's interpretation was very different. As we have seen, he believed that the CS and the US centers became linked so that activation of the CS center would automatically lead to activation of the US center. The CS would therefore elicit exactly the same behaviors as the US; essentially, it would *become* the US—hence the term **stimulus substitution**. For Tolman, the CS became a signal that food was coming (imagine the subject thinking, "Oh boy, I'm about to get food"); for Pavlov, it became a substitute for that food, eliciting identical responses (imagine the subject thinking, "Oh boy, what lovely food this is").

At first, Pavlov's substitution theory may seem so unlikely that it is barely worth discussing. A dog may not be a brilliant scholar, but surely it has enough sense to be able to distinguish a tone or a light from food! On closer examination, however, it is perhaps not as crazy as it sounds. First of all, the assumption that a dog knows that a light is not food begs the important question of how it knows. We tend to think that identifying food is trivially simple; everyone knows, for example, that apples are edible but pebbles are not. Babies, however, do *not* know this, and will often try to ingest objects that are emphatically not edible.

In many species, the young must actively learn to identify food, either by observing their parents or through their own experience. Birds, for example, have quite different pecking movements for eating food and drinking water, but when a newly hatched chick is presented with a drop of water for the first time, it initially attempts to eat it rather than drink it. After only one or two pecks, however, it abruptly changes to the more appropriate drinking response

(Hunt & Smith, 1967). What appears to happen is that the presence of water in the chick's beak triggers an innate recognition response. The chick associates this response with the visual cues that preceded ingestion, so that the sight of water will thereafter trigger appropriate drinking behavior.

For the dogs in Pavlov's experiments, therefore, the experience of a light followed by food could have triggered an innate mechanism identifying the light as food, so that it would then elicit salivation and all the other responses appropriate to food. But if the dog really believed the light was food, you may ask yourself, why doesn't it try to eat it? The answer is, it does! Pavlov found that when a dog is released from its harness after pairings of a light bulb with food, it eagerly runs over to the light bulb and licks it! The dogs didn't actually chew or swallow the bulb, but this may have been because the bulb's hardness inhibited the dog's swallowing reflexes.

In some studies in which the physical characteristics of the CS have been more appropriate, evidence has been reported that animals will try to ingest the CS. One example we have already encountered is autoshaping, in which a pigeon exposed to pairing of a circular key light with food will begin to peck the key. The existence of this phenomenon is very difficult to explain in terms of expectations: If the key light is simply a signal that food is imminent, why does the pigeon bother to peck it? If the lighted key has been identified as food, on the other hand, this pecking at the key becomes more understandable: The bird is trying to eat it.

Powerful support for this interpretation comes from a classic experiment by Jenkins and Moore (1973), who paired a lighted key with food in one group and with water in another. As we have already noted, a bird's responses to food and water are different. When given food, a pigeon pecks with its beak open; when given water, its beak is almost closed, and the pigeon uses its tongue to pump the water into its mouth. Also, a pigeon pecks water with its eyes open, but it pecks food with its eyes closed. (Food pecking is much more forceful, and the pigeon may close its eyes to protect them from ricocheting pebbles.) According to the substitution hypothesis, therefore, pigeons exposed to light-food pairings should try to eat the key with an open beak and closed eyes, whereas those exposed to light-water pairings should peck with a closed beak and open eyes. As Figure 5.9 shows, this was exactly what happened. The pigeons seemed to be trying to eat the key paired with food and to drink the key paired with water.

Further evidence of the power of the mechanism involved, and of its apparent irrationality, comes from another study by Jenkins (reported in Hearst & Jenkins, 1974), in which the key light was located along one wall of a six-foot-long box and the food source along another (Figure 5.10). The key light was occasionally presented for five seconds, followed by the raising of a grain magazine so that the grain was accessible for four seconds. Because of the layout of the box, if the pigeons approached the key and pecked it when the light

FIGURE 5.9 Typical responses of key-pecking following autoshaping trials. The photographs on the left show trials in which water was the US. The photographs on the right show trials in which food was the US. (Jenkins & Moore, 1973; photographs courtesy of Bruce Moore)

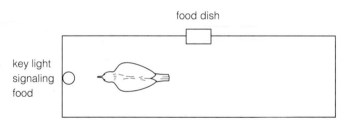

F I G U R E 5.10   Top view of the apparatus used by Jenkins to study autoshaping in pigeons. (Adapted from Domjan & Burkhard, 1986)

came on, they could not return to the food dispenser in time to obtain all the available food. Nevertheless, Jenkins found that his birds would run over to the light as soon as it came on, peck it, and then quickly hurry back to the food magazine. Because of the length of the box, they missed most or all of the food on the trials in which they pecked. Despite this, they continued to peck the key in session after session. (See also Williams & Williams, 1969.) Pecking the key seemed more important to the birds than eating.

Expectations.   Pavlov's substitution theory thus needs to be taken seriously: In many situations, animals do behave as if a CS paired with food really is food, and will persist in trying to eat the CS even if it costs them real food. On the other hand, there is also persuasive evidence to support Tolman's view that a CS acts as a signal that the US is coming. In Chapter 3, we discussed the fact that dogs in salivary conditioning experiments do not just salivate; they also turn toward the food tray and, if released from the harness, will approach the tray. Their behavior strongly suggests that they expect to find food there, and similar results have been obtained in other experiments. One example is the Jenkins experiment we just discussed, in which the CS light and the food magazine were located three feet apart. In general, the pigeons oriented toward the CS, but in some cases they approached the food dispenser instead.

Similar evidence comes from an experiment on rats by Timberlake, Wahl, and King (1982) in which a metal ball was rolled across the floor of a rat's cage shortly before food was made available. The results depended in part on the interval between the appearance of the ball and the presentation of food. With a short delay, as soon as the rats saw the ball they ran over to the pellet dispenser and waited there for food; with a longer delay, the rats picked up the rolling ball and chewed it. (See also Jenkins, Barrera, Ireland, & Woodside, 1978.) We thus have a distinctly confusing situation in which animals sometimes behave as if the CS is merely a signal that food is coming, but on other occasions behave as if the CS really is food.

A dual-brain hypothesis.   One way to resolve this conflict is to assume that both views are correct, and that the reason why the outcome varies is that classical conditioning actually involves two distinct learning systems—one based on signaling, and the other on substitution. Perhaps the first learning system to evolve was a relatively primitive one in which the CS was simply associated with the US, and thus elicited the same responses. In the course of time, a higher, cognition-based system appeared that involved active anticipation of the US, thus allowing subjects to select a wider range of preparatory responses than the innate ones. Insofar as both systems still coexist in vertebrates, this would explain why animals sometimes act as if the CS were a signal for food and at other times as if it actually were food.

Indirect evidence supporting this hypothesis comes from what is known about the evolution of the vertebrate brain. Studies of fossil records and of the brains of living species suggest that the vertebrate brain has changed enormously in the course of evolution. These changes, however, have consisted not so much in the disappearance of old structures—most of the primitive structures of an alligator or rat brain can still be easily recognized, almost unchanged, in that of a human—as in the elaboration of new structures. In particular, there has been a massive increase in the outer covering of the brain known as the *neocortex.* * The proportion of the brain devoted to neocortex in humans is 150 times greater, relative to body weight, than it is in the treeshrew-like mammals from which we are thought to have descended. The functions of this vastly expanded neocortex include cognitive processes such as thinking and language. The neocortex is also the center of awareness. (If the neocortex is damaged or anesthetized, a person loses consciousness.)

In the course of evolution, the anatomy of the central core of the brain has remained unchanged to a remarkable extent, with emerging cognitive functions concentrated in a massively expanded outer region. Insofar as the older core has retained its old functions as well as structure, a relatively primitive associative system might still be present in vertebrates along with a more advanced cognitive one.

There are some grounds, then, for suspecting that classical conditioning involves two systems: a relatively primitive one based on stimulus substitution, and a more cognitive one based on expectations. It must immediately be admitted, however, that this proposed synthesis is extremely vague. Consider the Timberlake, Wahl, and King experiment again. Why did the rats sometimes try to eat the metal ball but at other times run over to the food dispenser? Our two-process account gives us no basis for predicting when one system or the other will dominate. Thus, although a dual-brain account offers us a plausible framework for understanding conditioning, it is at present more of a promissory note for the future ("Here is the framework—details to be filled in

---

* The outer covering of the brain is called the *cortex.* Some form of cortex is present in most vertebrates, but it is expanded considerably in mammals, and the larger, newer section of the cortex is called the neocortex. In humans, most of the cortex consists of neocortex.

later") than a clearly defined theory. The picture the account paints for us is attractively simple, but we will have to await further evidence before we can decide if the portrait is accurate.

5.5 THE PROBLEM OF PERFORMANCE

Despite the apparent simplicity of classical conditioning—all that happens is a CS is followed by a US—we have seen that after nearly 100 years of research we are still not sure what a dog (or a human) learns in this situation. Whatever the answer may prove to be—whether the CS is a signal for the US or a substitute—we face a further problem: How is what is learned translated into performance?

The distinction between learning and performance is one that we will be encountering repeatedly; roughly, it is the difference between what we *know* and what we *do*. For example, you may have learned that studying is a good way to improve your grades, but this does not necessarily mean you spend all your time studying; how you use your knowledge will depend on many other factors, including your motivation to get a good grade and the attractions of the other activities that are available to you.

Though a dog's task in a classical conditioning experiment may seem very different, in some respects it faces similar problems in deciding what action to pursue. Suppose, for example, that a dog has learned that a 30-second tone is followed by food: What should it actually *do* with that knowledge? An expectancy account suggests that the dog should take "appropriate" action, but it doesn't give us any rules that would allow us to predict in advance what that appropriate action will be. Should the dog wait by the tray, or should it perhaps circle the area in order to keep watch for other dogs or predators that might try to steal the food when it arrives? And if it does decide to wait by the tray, should it go over to the tray as soon as the tone starts, or should it wait until 25 seconds have elapsed and the food is truly imminent? An expectancy analysis gives us no formal guidance as to what the dog should do, leaving us to rely on our intuitions.

The stimulus-substitution account, on the other hand, gives us a very clear rule for predicting the conditioned response: Since the CS is now the US, it should elicit the same responses as the US. In other words, the conditioned response should be identical to the unconditioned response.

Predicting the Conditioned Response

Autonomic responses. In the case of autonomic responses, the conditioned autonomic response does seem to be the same as the unconditioned response. The main exception we have encountered concerned reactions to drugs, where the CR often appeared to be opposite to the UR, but Eikelboom and Stewart

(1982) have provided a plausible account for this apparent discrepancy. (See Chapter 3.) On the evidence currently available, therefore, conditioned autonomic responses generally seem to be the same as the unconditioned responses, as a stimulus-substitution account predicts.

Skeletal responses.   The situation is considerably more complex in the case of skeletal responses. In many cases the conditioned skeletal response is the same as the unconditioned response—the eyeblink is a classic example—but in recent years evidence has been growing that these responses sometimes differ considerably. One example concerns electric shock. If a rat is placed in a cage and given shock through the floor, its unconditioned response to the shock is to jump and prance about the cage in an effort to escape it. If the shock is preceded by a tone, however, the rat's conditioned response to the tone is to freeze (Fanselow, 1989).

Another case in which the CR and UR are different comes from an autoshaping experiment by Wasserman (1973) that used heat as the unconditioned stimulus instead of food. Chicks were placed in a cool chamber, and occasional illuminations of a green key light (CS) were followed by activation of a heat lamp (US). The chicks' unconditioned response to the heat lamp was to extend their wings, but their response to the CS was to approach the key, peck it, and then snuggle up against it. Again, the conditioned response could hardly be described as identical to the unconditioned response.

A third example comes from an experiment by Holland (1977) in which rats were exposed to pairings of a tone with food. Holland found that his subjects began to jerk their heads each time the tone was presented, even though neither the tone nor the food elicited this response before they were paired. At least insofar as skeletal responses are concerned, therefore, there are many situations in which the CR and UR are not the same.

A Behavior-System Analysis

This evidence poses problems for both of the accounts of learning that we have looked at, because it means that neither can predict how a subject will behave after conditioning. The expectancy analysis offers us no guidance as to what to expect; the stimulus-substitution analysis offers us clear guidance, but the guidance is wrong. What now?

Fortunately, a number of theorists have converged on a very similar explanation for the evidence we have been reviewing (for example, Jenkins, Barrera, Ireland, & Woodside, 1978; Timberlake, 1984). In effect, this explanation emphasizes the role of motivation in determining the conditioned response. We saw in Chapter 3 that when a CS is paired with a US, one result is the conditioning of a motivational state. If the food is used as a US, for example, the CS paired with it will come to elicit hunger. Hunger will then elicit behaviors appropriate to *obtaining* food as well as consuming it. If you were a lion and saw an antelope in the distance, for example, you would not immediately begin to make chewing movements: You would need to stalk and kill the antelope before trying to eat it. Similarly in a classical conditioning situation, the CS will elicit behaviors directed toward obtaining the US as well as consuming it.

Behavior systems.   It may not at first be obvious how this insight can explain some of the peculiar conditioned responses we discussed earlier; to make the explanation clearer, we will begin by outlining a version developed by Timberlake (1984), which he called a behavior-system approach. The first assumption is that behavior is organized within relatively independent systems, with each system determining the initiation and sequencing of the behaviors that it controls. A rat, for example, must perform many activities to survive—finding food and water, avoiding predators, obtaining a mate—and each of these activities is controlled by a different **behavior system.**

Suppose, for example, that a rat is hungry. Provided that other motives are not even stronger, hunger will cause activation of the feeding system which, in turn, will activate alternative subsystems for obtaining food. Figure 5.11 presents a highly simplified outline of a possible feeding system, involving

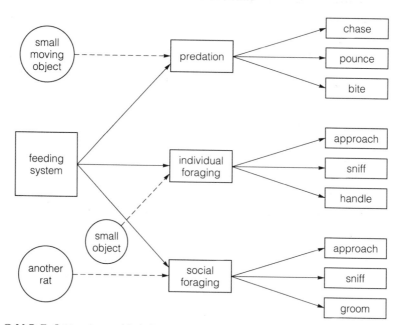

F I G U R E 5.11   A possible behavior system for feeding in rats. Hunger is assumed to prime a set of possible food-obtaining responses; a primed response will occur if its natural releasing stimulus is present.

only three subsystems; the actual feeding system is thought to be considerably more complex. (The account presented here is not Timberlake's, but a synthesis of systems proposed by Timberlake & Lucas, 1989, and Davey, 1989.) The example assumes that the rat can choose among three main strategies for obtaining food: chasing a live prey, foraging alone for foods such as wheat grains, or foraging together with other rats. (Rats are nocturnal animals that live in colonies, and they will often gather together into groups, engage in social behaviors such as grooming, and then go off together to search for food.) Which of these subsystems is activated will depend on the stimuli present at the time. If a small moving object is visible, this may activate the predatory system; a small object resembling a wheat grain may activate the foraging system; the presence of other rats may activate social foraging. Whichever system is activated, it will prime a further set of possible responses, such as chasing and biting; again, which of these primed responses actually occurs will depend on the stimuli that are present.

The stimuli that guide these responses are in some respects like Pavlovian unconditioned stimuli, in that they innately elicit certain responses; but whether an animal responds to the stimulus also depends on the animal's motivational state. If a lion has just fed, for example, then even the most succulent antelope will not elicit stalking behavior. Stimuli of this kind, which have the potential to release responses, rather than reliably eliciting them in every case, are sometimes referred to as *releasing stimuli* or *releasers*. (In the lion example, the antelope is a releaser for stalking behavior.) According to the behavior-system analysis, then, behavior is organized into a number of motivational systems. When a motivational system is aroused, it primes a set of potential responses. The presence of a releasing stimulus then triggers one of these primed responses.

The conditioned response. How does all this help us to understand the conditioned response? If a CS is paired with a US, we have seen that one result will be the conditioning of a motivational state. If a rat is exposed to pairings of a tone with food, for example, then the tone will come to elicit hunger. But what the rat does when it is hungry will depend on the stimuli that are present. In particular, behavior-system theorists have suggested that the response will depend on *whether the CS resembles a releaser for feeding behavior*. If the CS is a small moving object, for example, then it may resemble the releaser for predatory behavior, and the rat may chase the CS. On the other hand, if the CS is very small and stationary, it may look like the sort of grains that elicit foraging behavior, and the rat may approach and sniff it.

The assumption that the nature of the conditioned response will depend on whether the CS resembles a releaser allows us to account for many of the conditioned responses discussed earlier. Consider, for example, why a signal paired with shock causes a rat to freeze. A rat's defensive system includes a number of responses; one of the main determinants of which response will occur is how far away a potential predator is. (See Fanselow, 1989.) If a predator is distant, a rat will freeze in order to avoid detection; if the predator is close and attacks the rat, the rat will struggle to escape. For the rat, shock in an experiment is probably the equivalent of being attacked by a predator, and the shock thus elicits attempts to escape. However, if the shock is preceded by a warning signal, and if this signal is at least potentially similar to the properties of a predator seen at a distance (because of the importance of detecting predators, and their potential concealment, it seems a reasonable guess that in this case almost any stimulus may be accepted as a sign of a possible predator), then the rat will respond to the predator-at-a-distance stimulus by freezing.

Wasserman's experiment on autoshaping with heat as the US provides another illustration of how a behavior-system analysis can account for otherwise puzzling conditioned responses. In that experiment, the chicks' unconditioned response to the heat lamp was to spread their wings, but their conditioned response to the illuminated key was to peck the key and snuggle up to it. Hogan (1974) has pointed out that when chicks are cold, they peck at their mother's feathers to get her to open them, and then push up against her body and snuggle. The chicks' behavior toward the key, in other words, exactly matched the behavior they would normally direct toward a hen when seeking heat, presumably because the stimulus properties of the key resembled some aspect of the hen's appearance.

One prediction that follows from this analysis is that what response is conditioned in an experiment may depend on what CS is paired with the US: Different CSs may vary in what releasers they resemble, and thus may come to elicit different conditioned responses. Two experiments by Timberlake illustrate this point. In both experiments he used rats as subjects and food as the unconditioned stimulus, but he varied what stimulus preceded the food. In the Timberlake, Wahl, and King (1982) experiment described earlier, the CS was a metal ball rolling across the floor of the rat's cage; in an experiment by Timberlake and Grant (1975), the CS was the placing of another rat into the cage. When the CS was a rolling ball, the rats responded by chasing the ball, picking it up, and gnawing it. When the CS was another rat, they instead approached the rat, sniffed it, and engaged in social behaviors such as grooming. Those could just have been the normal social behaviors of rats, but these behaviors occurred at a far lower rate in a control group in which the rat's appearance was not paired with food. It was the pairing of the rat with food that made it elicit social behavior.

Why did exactly the same US produce such different behaviors in the two experiments? You may already be able to see how the different outcomes can be explained by a behavior-system analysis. The pairing of the CS with food meant that the CS would elicit hunger and thus activate the feeding system. The presence of a small moving object would elicit the predatory behaviors of chasing and gnawing, whereas the presence of another rat would activate the social foraging system, eliciting behaviors such as sniffing and grooming.

In summary, a behavior-system analysis says that behavior is jointly determined by the animal's motivational state and the releasing stimuli that are present. If a CS is paired with a US, the CS will arouse a motivational state; the response directed toward the CS will depend on whether it resembles a releaser for the relevant motivational system. In some respects, this account resembles Pavlov's view that the CS becomes the US: A pigeon in an autoshaping experiment really may be trying to eat the key. However, whether this happens will depend on how closely the CS resembles the innate releasers for eating behavior. In Timberlake's experiments, the rat would gnaw the metal ball as if it were food, but it did not try to eat the other rat: Because another rat was a releaser for very different feeding behaviors, it elicited a different conditioned response.

One problem with this account is that we do not know enough about the releasers that control an animal's behavior to be able to predict whether a CS such as light or a tone will resemble one of these releasers, and thus we cannot predict in advance what conditioned response will occur. In our account of Wasserman's chick experiment, for example, we suggested that the chicks snuggled up to the key because it resembled some aspect of a hen, but we have no independent evidence that this is so. * This problem is by no means insoluble—all we need is more research to identify releasers and measure their similarity to conditioned stimuli—but it does mean that although the behavior-system approach provides a framework for thinking about conditioning, it does not yet lead to many testable predictions. In the few cases where prediction has been possible, however, the results so far have been encouraging. (For a particularly impressive example, see Fanselow, 1989.)

Summary. We suggested in the preceding section that classical conditioning involves learning about the relationship between the CS and the US, and that this learning may take two forms: an association between the CS and US centers, so that presentation of the CS activates the US center, and an expectation that allows the subject to anticipate the exact properties of the US that is to follow. Whether the CS–US relationship is stored in the form of an

---

* You may find it hard to believe that a chick could confuse an illuminated plastic key with its mother, but research on animal behavior has shown that young animals often respond to very limited aspects of their parents' appearance. In a famous experiment by Tinbergen and Perdeck (1950), the authors investigated the behavior of young herring gulls, who peck at their parents' bills to get them to regurgitate food. They used a variety of models to determine what aspects of the parents' appearance elicited this pecking response, and they found that the model would elicit pecking even if it lacked a body, or even a head: All that was necessary was that it have an elongated shape with a red spot on it, so that in this one respect it resembled the bill of a real herring gull.

association, an expectation, or both, however, we need a set of performance rules to allow us to predict how this knowledge will be translated into performance.

In the case of autonomic responses, this performance rule may be very simple: The CS activates the US center, which in turn activates the autonomic responses to which it is innately linked. In the case of skeletal responses, however, a stimulus-substitution analysis does not work, because the conditioned and unconditioned responses often differ. To account for these differences, we have suggested that the CS activates a conditioned motivational state, which in turn primes a set of possible responses. Figure 5.12 summarizes this account. We have assumed that the CS will activate either an expectation or a direct connection to the US center; the US center will then activate a behavior system and thereby prime a preorganized set of skeletal and autonomic responses, though these will not occur unless the appropriate releasing stimuli are present.

It cannot be overemphasized that the summary presented in Figure 5.12 is *very* tentative. We know that following classical conditioning a CS may elicit a variety of different responses, including skeletal and autonomic responses, motivational states, and expectations. Whether all these various responses are tied together in the way illustrated in the figure, however, is far from established, and other ways of integrating the data are possible (for example, Timberlake & Lucas, 1989). Psychologists have made considerable progress in understanding what responses are learned in classical conditioning experiments, but we still know very little about how these responses are internally organized or linked.

5.6 IS CONDITIONING AUTOMATIC?

One reason for the initial interest in conditioning—and one reason the word *conditioning* has acquired ominous overtones, suggesting brainwashing and the

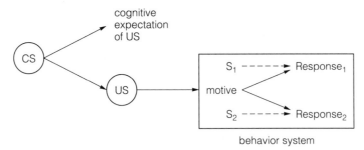

FIGURE 5.12 One possible version of how a conditioned stimulus affects behavior. The CS activates both an expectation that the US is coming and the US center; the US center then activates a behavior system, which primes a set of skeletal and autonomic responses. The primed responses will occur if appropriate releasing stimuli are present.

world of George Orwell's 1984—is that it seems a wholly automatic process, occurring without our awareness and even against our wishes. Pavlov rings a bell and the dog salivates; a dictator—or advertiser—says the critical word and the conditioned masses respond with instant fear or rapture. But is this image realistic? Can conditioning really occur without our awareness or against our will? We will try to answer these questions in this section, beginning with the role of awareness.

Conditioning Without Awareness

A number of experiments have examined whether conditioning can occur without awareness, and the results have generally suggested that it cannot. (See Brewer, 1974.) In a GSR conditioning experiment by Pendery and Maltzman (1977), for example, subjects were interviewed after the experiment was over to determine if they had been aware of the relationship between the CS and the US. (The CS had been embedded in another task so that it was not obvious.) As Figure 5.13 shows, although responding increased over trials in subjects who had been aware of the contingency, there was no sign of conditioning in unaware subjects. When awareness is assessed on a trial-by-trial basis, moreover, no conditioning is observed prior to the first trial on which awareness is reported (for example, Biferno & Dawson, 1977). There are thus strong grounds for believing that conditioning in humans occurs only when subjects are aware of the CS–US contingency.

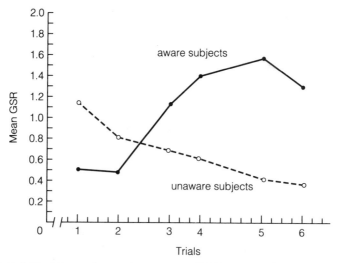

F I G U R E 5.13   Mean galvanic skin response (GSR) to a word paired with shock. The solid line represents the change in responses for subjects who were aware of the contingency. The broken line represents the change in responses for subjects who were not aware of the contingency. (Adapted from Pendery & Maltzman, 1977)

The dual-brain hypothesis discussed earlier, however, implies that a more primitive associative system may still be present in humans along with the more sophisticated cognitive system. The massive elaboration of the neocortex in humans suggests that the cognitive system will normally dominate responding, but if the influence of this cognitive system could somehow be reduced, we might expect to see conditioning controlled by the more primitive system in which learning occurs without awareness.

Eyeblink conditioning.   Direct evidence for this hypothesis comes from a series of experiments by Kenneth Spence (1966). Spence noted that extinction of eyeblink responses in animals is a very slow process, often requiring more than 500 trials, but that it is virtually instantaneous in humans, with the conditioned response disappearing after only one or two extinction trials. Spence believed that the slow extinction in animals was due to the response's being controlled by a more primitive associative system. In humans, the cognitive system plays a more dominant role: As soon as subjects realize that the CS is no longer being followed by the US, they immediately stop blinking. The fact that extinction is rapid, however, does not necessarily mean that the slow associative system is no longer present. Spence believed that this slower system remains active in humans, but that its output is being overridden by the dominant cognitive system. If the cognitive system could be eliminated, he argued, then extinction in humans would follow the same gradual time course observed in animals.

To test this hypothesis, Spence needed some way to eliminate the cognitive system. One simple solution would have been to remove the cortex surgically. Perhaps anticipating the difficulties that might have arisen in recruiting subjects, Spence devised an ingenious alternative. Rather than eliminating the cognitive system physically, he eliminated it functionally, by giving his subjects a demanding distraction task. If the task were sufficiently difficult, Spence reasoned, the processing capacity of the cognitive system would be fully absorbed, and any conditioning would be under the control of the associative system.

Spence, Homzie, and Rutledge (1964) used two groups of college students as subjects and gave both groups trials in which a tone was followed half a second later by an air puff. The experimental group was told that the purpose of the study was to examine the effects of distraction on problem solving. When a warning light came on, the subjects were supposed to push a button indicating which one of two lights they believed would be illuminated two seconds later. To distract them, it was further explained, irrelevant tones and air puffs would be presented during the two-second decision period. A control group received the same pairings of tone and air puff, but without the concurrent problem-solving task.

After 50 pairings of the tone and air puff, extinction was begun. Instead

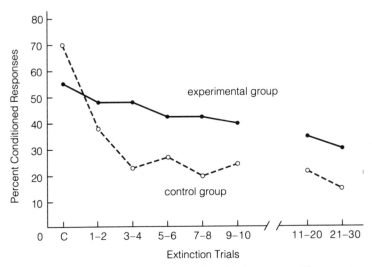

F I G U R E 5.14   Extinction of a conditioned eyeblink response. The experimental subjects were given a distraction task to prevent awareness of the change in contingency; control subjects were not. On the x-axis, C indicates responding at the end of the conditioning phase. (Spence, Homzie, & Rutledge, 1964)

of omitting the air puff, however, the experimenters lengthened the CS–US interval from 0.5 to 2.5 seconds. Previous research had shown that conditioned blinking would extinguish at this interval; by continuing to present the air puff, the experimenters hoped to draw the subjects' attention away from the change in CS–US contingency. The dual-brain hypothesis predicts that, with the cognitive system eliminated, blinking should extinguish gradually. As Figure 5.14 shows, this is what the experimenters found. Responding in the control group extinguished very quickly, dropping from around 70 percent to 25 percent in only three trials. Conditioned responding in the experimental group, however, declined much more gradually, and after 10 trials had fallen by only 14 percent. Postexperiment interviews confirmed that subjects in the experimental group had not been aware of the change in the CS–US interval during extinction, whereas almost all of the control subjects had noticed the change.

Thus, extinction was slow when subjects were not aware of the change in contingency but rapid when they were. The results are consistent with the view that conditioning in humans involves two distinct systems: an unconscious system in which associations change slowly, and a cognitive system in which awareness leads to abrupt changes in responding. As with all human studies, however, we can question the adequacy of the procedure used by Spence, Homzie, and Rutledge for assessing awareness. All but one of the subjects in the experimental group reported no awareness of the light-air puff contingency. Perhaps they really had been aware of this contingency at the time but, because it had seemed irrelevant to the main purpose of the experiment, had paid little attention to it and had forgotten about it by the time they were interviewed. (If this seems unlikely, see Fuhrer & Baer, 1980.) Or perhaps they did remember the contingency but sensed that the experimenters did not want to hear about it, and they wanted to convey what they believed the experimenters wanted. (See Orne, 1962.) If the cortex really could be eliminated physically, we could be considerably more confident that conditioning can occur without awareness.

Spinal conditioning.   As it happens, there is actually a study in which this condition has been satisfied. Ince, Brucker, and Alba (1978) reported an experiment involving a 40-year-old male whose spinal cord had been accidentally severed at the eighth thoracic vertebra. As a result, all sensory and motor pathways linking his brain with the lower half of his body had been severed, and he could not feel any sensation in this region. If conditioning could be achieved using stimuli presented to the lower half of his body, there would be no possibility of the brain's involvement. Thus, conditioning could not be due to conscious awareness of the CS–US contingency.

The experimenters' motivation was practical rather than theoretical. The patient's injury meant that he could not control the muscles in the lower half of his body, including those involved in urination. In order to provide him with at least some control over urination, the experimenters decided to try classical conditioning. If urination could be conditioned to a stimulus that the patient could control, they reasoned, then, indirectly, he would be able to control urination by presenting himself with this stimulus. They used a mild shock to the patient's thigh as the CS, and a more powerful shock to the abdomen as an unconditioned stimulus to elicit urination. (Because of the severing of the spinal cord, the patient could not feel either stimulus and thus suffered no pain.) The procedure was a resounding success; the CS came to elicit significant amounts of urination whenever it was presented. Since consciousness is generally thought to originate in the cortex, this result was almost certainly an instance in which conditioning occurred without awareness. (See also Siegel, 1970; Rabin & Rabin, 1984.)

Conditioning and advertising.   Such conditioning without awareness may play an important role in our daily lives. Certainly, much advertising is based on what seems to be a conditioning process. By pairing a product with highly positive stimuli, advertisers hope that our feelings about the positive stimuli will be transferred, without our awareness, to the target. A picture of an automobile, for example, may be accompanied by an attractive female, and a commercial for a political candidate may be set against a scenic background and accompanied by patriotic or other stirring music. There is at least some evidence, moreover, that such juxtapositions do result in the conditioning of emotional reactions to the target stimulus. In a study by Janis, Kaye, and Kirschner (1965), subjects who read a persuasive message while eating were significantly more likely to accept the positions advocated than subjects who read the identical articles while not eating. Gorn (1982) found that attractive music played during a commercial significantly increased preference for the product. And, as we discussed in Chapter 1, Smith and Engel (1968) found that the presence of an attractive woman standing next to an automobile powerfully influenced subjects' evaluation of that car. In both these studies, the authors interviewed their subjects at the completion of the experiments and found that almost all subjects denied that their rating of the product had been affected by the attractive stimulus that accompanied it. (For a review of other evidence in this area, see Schwarz, Bless, & Bohner, 1991.)

None of the evidence we have reviewed is conclusive on its own. The Ince, Brucker, and Alba study on spinal conditioning involved only a single subject; the Spence, Homzie, and Rutledge study may not have assessed awareness properly; and the effects of food or of an attractive woman on our attitudes are not necessarily due to classical conditioning. Considered together, however, the evidence suggests that conditioning can occur without awareness under some circumstances.

Involuntary Conditioning

A closely related question concerns involuntary responding. Insofar as conditioning is under the control of conscious processes, then responding should depend on the subject's conscious belief that a US is about to occur. Suppose, for example, that a subject is given GSR conditioning trials in which a CS is paired with a mild electric shock, and the subject is told that the shock no longer will be presented. To ensure that the subject believes the message, the shock electrodes are removed from the subject's arm. According to a cognitive analysis, if the subject genuinely believes that the shock no longer is going to occur, the GSR should disappear immediately, despite all the previous pairings.

This prediction has been supported in a number of studies: The GSR disappeared almost immediately when subjects were told that shock would no longer be presented (for example, Cook, Hodes, & Lang, 1986). The shocks used in these studies, however, have generally been quite mild. If a more powerful US were used, so the conditioned response was stronger, we might guess that the subject's conscious beliefs would be much less effective in controlling behavior.

One source of support for this prediction comes from studies on taste-aversion learning in which people have been found to develop strong aversions to foods eaten before they became ill, even when they are aware that the illness they experienced was caused by other factors, such as chemotherapy or a viral infection (Bernstein, 1978; Logue, 1988). Further evidence comes from a study by Campbell, Sanderson, and Laverty (1964) in which subjects were administered a curare-like drug that induces total muscular paralysis.* The paralysis lasted for roughly two minutes; a tone was presented just before its onset and remained on for its duration. This paralysis was a terrifying experience. Subjects could not breathe, and reported that they felt they were going to die. The authors anticipated that the fear elicited by this experience would become conditioned to the accompanying tone. To determine how long it would take to extinguish this fear, they gave their subjects 30 presentations of the tone by itself, but there was no sign of any extinction in the GSR. One week later, another 30 extinction trials were given, but, if any change could be discerned, the conditioned response became stronger rather than weaker. In all, some subjects received a total of 300 trials spread over several months, with no sign of any diminution in the conditioned response. This study raises serious ethical issues, but its results suggest that when a fear is sufficiently strong, our rational belief that there really is no danger may not be enough to overcome the fear.

One practical implication is that, although it may be worth reasoning with individuals who have mild fears, rational persuasion may be of little or no value when the fears involved are intense. If someone has a mild fear of flying, for example, it may be helpful to point out that the chances of dying are much lower when travelling in an airplane than in an automobile. For someone with a true phobia, however, such attempts at rational reassurance may be of no value. Only carefully structured experiences aimed at demonstrating that the situation is safe, as in systematic desensitization, may help.

Under some circumstances, then, conditioning does seem to be automatic. It can occur without awareness, and in some cases against our will. The popular image of involuntary brainwashing, however, is almost certainly exaggerated. As we have seen, in most cases subjects are aware of what is happening. Even in the case of advertising, where we sometimes seem unaware of how our emotions are being manipulated, there is evidence that the effects of this conditioning are neither as powerful nor as long-lasting as more reasoned presentations of logical arguments (Petty & Cacioppo, 1981). Human beings seem to be a funny mixture of rationality and emotionality, and both aspects need to be taken into account in predicting our behavior.

5.7 SUMMARY

Pavlov believed that when two areas of the brain are active simultaneously, an association is formed between them. Whenever a CS is paired with a US,

---

* Curare is an organic alkaloid drug extracted from various tropical plants and used in modern medicine. It was first discovered by South American Indians, who applied curare to the tips of their arrows for use in hunting game.

therefore, an association should be formed. But the evidence for blocking and the importance of contingencies contradict this view. Even if a CS is contiguous with a US, conditioning does not occur if the CS is not a good predictor of the US (that is, if they are not contingent) or if a better predictor is available (as in the case of blocking). The fact that conditioning becomes focused on stimuli that are good predictors of the US indicates that conditioning is a highly adaptive process, but it also poses a serious challenge for learning theorists: How do animals learn to identify the best predictor?

A surprising answer was provided in 1972 by Rescorla and Wagner, who proposed that the amount of conditioning on any trial is determined not simply by the US but by the subject's expectation that the US will occur. According to this model, the change in associative strength (ΔV) on any trial is determined by the relationship between the associative strength at the beginning of the trial (V) and the asymptotic strength that could be supported by the US (V_{max}):

$$\Delta V = c(V_{max} - V)$$

When two or more stimuli are present on a trial, the associative strength of the compound is the sum of the strengths of the elements:

$$V_{ab} = V_a + V_b$$

To derive quantitative predictions from the model, it is necessary to assign values to the parameters c and V_{max}. Rescorla and Wagner showed that even if the true values of these parameters are not known (that is, even if they are assigned arbitrary values), they can still make qualitative predictions about whether associative strength will increase or decrease. These qualitative predictions proved surprisingly powerful, and Rescorla and Wagner showed how the model could account for phenomena as diverse as conditioning, extinction, and blocking using only a single equation. The key to these predictions lies in the relationship between V and V_{max}: When V is less than V_{max}, $(V_{max} - V)$ is a positive number and associative strength is predicted to increase, resulting in conditioning; when V is greater than V_{max}, $(V_{max} - V)$ is negative and associative strength is reduced, resulting in extinction; when V equals V_{max} (as in blocking, in which one element of the compound has already been conditioned), then associative strength will not change.

According to the model, then, the same US may increase, decrease, or have no effect on conditioning, depending on whether current associative strength is less than, greater than, or equal to V_{max}. One prediction that follows from this analysis is that if two conditioned stimuli are paired separately with a US and then the compound is conditioned, the result will be a decrease in responding. Researchers have confirmed this and other counterintuitive predictions.

The last finding mentioned also allows us to explain what happens when a CS and a US are presented noncontingently. When the US is presented initially, conditioning occurs to whatever stimuli precede it, including the CS and whatever background cues may be present. Because the background cues are present on all US presentations and the CS only on some, conditioning is more rapid to the background cues; once the combined strength of the CS and the background cues is greater than V_{max}, associative strength is reduced on trials in which the CS is presented. The net result is that conditioning is eventually concentrated on the background cues, with the associative strength of the CS returning to zero. Presentations of the US by itself, in other words, do not prevent conditioning; rather, the associative strength of the CS increases initially but then is reduced as conditioning becomes focused on the background cues.

The model, then, can account for both blocking and contingency in terms of the formation of associations between stimuli that are contiguous, as long as the calculation of associative strength takes into account the existing strength of the stimuli paired with the US. Thus, although the end result of conditioning is impressively sophisticated, with responding concentrated on stimuli that are good predictors rather than just those that happen to precede the US, the underlying mechanism may be based on very simple associations.

As impressive as its achievements have been, the model cannot account for all aspects of conditioning. The evidence for configural learning shows that when stimuli are presented as a compound, responding is not always determined by the associative strengths of the elements, as the model assumes; subjects can learn to treat a compound as a unique stimulus, or configuration, and respond to it very differently than to either of its elements. Similarly, the phenomenon of latent inhibition suggests that subjects can learn to ignore stimuli that have proved to be of little significance in the past. Such evidence suggests that the Rescorla-Wagner model needs to be modified, but its success in accounting for so many aspects of conditioning in terms of only a few simple assumptions suggests that it will prove to be one of the major landmarks in the development of our understanding of learning.

The Rescorla-Wagner model has important implications for Pavlov's contention that an association is formed whenever two brain centers are active simultaneously. The model suggests that contiguity between a CS and a US is not sufficient to produce conditioning; it suggests that the US must also be unexpected.

A further challenge to Pavlov's explanation of conditioning concerns the identity of the associated events. Pavlov believed that during conditioning an association is formed between the CS and US centers (an S–S connection).

When the CS is presented on subsequent trials, activity in the CS center is transmitted to the US center and from there to the unconditioned response. An alternative possibility, however, is that the CS becomes directly connected with the unconditioned response during conditioning (an S–R connection).

One way of distinguishing between these alternatives is to break the connection between the US and UR following conditioning. If an S–S connection was formed between the CS and US, then breaking the connection between the US and UR should prevent the CS from eliciting the response. If the CS was directly associated with the response, however, then changes in the status of the US should have no effect. Tests of this prediction have supported the S–S analysis: Devaluation of the US following conditioning does affect responding to the CS.

Evidence that responding to the CS depends on the current value of the US suggests that Pavlov was right: Conditioning must involve some form of S–S connection. The precise form of this connection, however, remains uncertain. Pavlov assumed a simple association in which activity in a CS center would be transmitted to the US center and from there to the response. A CS would thus elicit exactly the same response as the US, so that, in effect, the CS becomes the US. There is evidence to support this prediction; in some experiments, animals have treated the CS exactly as they did the US. Dogs licked a light bulb paired with food, pigeons tried to drink a key paired with water, and so on. In some of these same experiments, however, animals also behaved as if they knew the US was coming—for example, moving toward the area where food was to be delivered. It is thus not clear whether the CS serves as a signal that the US is coming or becomes a substitute for it.

One way to account for this conflicting evidence is to assume that both the substitution theory and the signal theory are right. In the course of evolution, two distinct learning systems may have evolved—a relatively primitive one based on substitution, and a more sophisticated cognitive system based on expectations. Insofar as both systems still coexist, this would explain why animals (and humans) sometimes react to a CS as if it were the US and sometimes as if it were only a signal. This dual-brain hypothesis is seductive, in that it could account for much of the conflicting evidence. But it is also vague, since it gives us few guidelines about when we should expect one behavior and when we should expect the other.

Whether the CS is a signal, a substitute, or both, we need to be able to predict how subjects will use what they have learned to guide their performance. For many years, it appeared that subjects in a conditioning experiment had little problem in deciding what to do: They simply made the same response to the CS that they had previously made to the US. This still appears to be the case for autonomic responses, but in recent years it has become clear that conditioned and unconditioned skeletal responses are often very different. For example, a rat usually reacts to shock by exhibiting frantic activity, but its reaction to a signal predicting shock is often to freeze.

One way to accommodate such evidence is to assume that the conditioned response involves an attempt to obtain or avoid the US, whichever is appropriate. According to one version of this hypothesis, behavior is organized into systems, such as feeding and defense. When one of these motivational systems is activated, it primes a set of possible responses; which of these responses will occur depends on the releasing stimuli that are present. (An antelope, for example, will release a hungry lion's hunting behavior.) Motivational states can be conditioned, and the CS will then activate the appropriate behavior system; the specific response to the CS will depend partly on whether the CS resembles any of the relevant releasing stimuli. If a rat receives conditioning trials in which a metal ball is rolled across its cage just before it receives food, for example, the food presentations will condition hunger to the apparatus cues; the rat will then chase the ball because this small moving object resembles the releasing stimuli for its hunting behavior. This behavior-system analysis provides a plausible explanation for the results of many conditioning experiments, but our limited knowledge about the releasing stimuli that control animal behavior has meant that the model is not yet detailed enough to allow many testable predictions.

If we do possess two distinct learning systems, one plausible assumption is that learning in the more primitive system proceeds unconsciously, whereas learning in the cognitive system is based on awareness. If this is so, we might expect that conditioning occurs normally with awareness, since the cognitive system recognizes the relationship between the CS and US, but that learning without prior awareness can occur in situations in which the normally dominant cognitive system is either distracted or physically disabled. Some evidence supports both conclusions. Spence found that eyeblink conditioning occurred without awareness when subjects were suitably distracted. Similar results have been obtained with a subject who had spinal damage and who could not have detected either the CS or US.

A related issue concerns whether subjects' rational beliefs control their conditioned responses. In most cases, the answer seems to be yes, but in situations in which the conditioned response is very strong, there is evidence that subjects' rational beliefs or expectations no longer determine their responses. Within the dual-brain framework, this suggests that the cognitive system can normally override responding under the control of the more primitive system, but that when the associations within the latter system are very strong, the cognitive system may no longer be able to inhibit responding.

On the surface, classical conditioning is almost the simplest learning system that could be imagined—all we do is pair a CS with a US—but after nearly 100 years of research, we are still not entirely sure what animals or humans learn in this situation, nor how this learning is translated into performance. Pairing one event with another may indeed be simple, but the processes we use in deciding how to respond are not.

Selected Definitions

V The strength of the association that is formed when a CS and a US are paired.

Parameters Constant factors used in mathematical formulas. The value of a parameter is a fixed quantity, not a variable. By varying the values of parameters, researchers can use the same basic equation to predict a range of experimental results.

Configural learning When responding to a compound is sharply different from responding to its components presented separately, and this difference cannot be accounted for by adding the strengths of the components, subjects are said to be responding to the compound as a unique configuration.

Latent inhibition Presentations of a stimulus by itself which retard subsequent conditioning to that stimulus.

S–S theory The term applied to Pavlov's view of conditioning, which assumed that an association is formed between two stimuli, the CS and the US.

S–R theory A view of conditioning that, in contrast to Pavlov's view, assumes there is a direct link between the conditioned stimulus and the response.

Stimulus substitution Pavlov's interpretation of the process that occurs during conditioning. He believed that activation of the CS center of the brain would be transferred to the US center and would therefore elicit the same behaviors as the US. In his view, the CS essentially becomes the US.

Behavior system A regulatory system that links motivational states with innate stimulus-response units. The assumption is that a motivational state primes a set of possible responses, which are then triggered if the natural releasing stimulus is present.

Review Questions

1. What is the equation used by Rescorla and Wagner to predict learning? What does each symbol represent?

2. How is Kamin's concept of surprise incorporated within the Rescorla-Wagner model?

3. What effect does the choice of the parameters c and V_{max} have on the shape of the learning curve? How are the values of these parameters related to the CS and US used on a trial?

4. Why didn't Rescorla and Wagner try to determine the real values of the parameters c and V_{max}? What approach did they use instead, and what are the implications of this approach for deriving predictions from the model?

5. How can the same equation be used to predict both conditioning and extinction?

6. How does the model account for blocking?

7. There are two crucial tests of any theoretical model: Can it account for known phenomena, and can it accurately predict new ones? What is an example of the Rescorla-Wagner model's new predictions?

8. The Rescorla-Wagner model shows how a few simple assumptions can be used to account for seemingly complex behavior. How does the model's explanation of contingency illustrate this?

9. How do configural learning and latent inhibition show the model's limitations?

10. How might the model be used to account for conditioned inhibition?

11. Does classical conditioning involve the learning of S–S or S–R associations?

12. What was Pavlov's stimulus-substitution hypothesis? What is the evidence for this hypothesis?

13. What is the difference between signal and substitution accounts of conditioning? What evidence supports a signaling interpretation?

14. How does the dual-brain hypothesis attempt to account for the conflicting evidence on whether a CS functions as a signal or a substitute for the US?

15. What evidence suggests that the CR is not always the same as the UR? How would Timberlake's behavior-system analysis account for the cases in which these responses differ?

16. What evidence suggests that conditioning can occur without awareness?

17. What evidence suggests that subjects' conscious expectations do not always control their responding?

INSTRUMENTAL CONDITIONING

CHAPTER SIX

REINFORCEMENT

One of the most obvious ways to encourage a behavior is to reward it. Parents praise children's good behavior; companies pay salespeople bonuses for high output; universities promote productive researchers. There is nothing new or profound about the idea of using rewards to encourage behavior—the principle was probably known and used long before the discovery of fire.

If the principle of reward or reinforcement is so obvious, why is behavior often so hard to change? Why do parents find it so difficult to get their teenage children to clean their rooms? Or, to take a more immediately relevant example, why do students often find it so difficult to make themselves study? There are, after all, very powerful reinforcers for studying: in the short term, good course grades; in the longer term, a better job. Yet students often leave studying until the last minute, and sometimes don't even get around to it then. Similarly, smoking and overeating may take years off our lives, and people are often desperate to give up these habits; yet the habits persist. Why is behavior in these situations apparently so irrational, when reinforcers as potent as a good job and longer life have little effect? Clearly, the principle of reinforcement cannot be quite as simple as it sounds.

To understand why reinforcers seem to control behavior in some situations but not others, we will examine experimental research into the principles that determine the effectiveness of reinforcement. In Chapter 7 we will extend our survey to the principles of punishment. Then, in Chapter 8, we will examine some of the attempts that have been made to apply the principles discovered in the laboratory in real life, and what these attempts have revealed about both the strengths and weaknesses of reinforcement as a tool for altering behavior. We will begin, though, with a brief overview of some of the procedures that have been used to study reinforcement.

6.1 BASIC PROCEDURES

Thorndike devised the puzzle box to allow him to study reinforcement, but most subsequent research has been carried out using two other pieces of equipment: the maze and the Skinner box.

The Maze

At almost the same time as Thorndike was carrying out his research, W. S. Small at Clark University was using a maze to study learning in rats. The history of mazes goes back at least as far as the ancient Egyptians, and outdoor mazes became extremely popular in the eighteenth century. Outdoor mazes were constructed using tall hedges, and the game was to find one's way through the intricate network of connecting passages. Small reasoned that such mazes would provide an ideal apparatus for studying learning in rats, because many rats lived in complex underground burrows and thus should be equipped to solve such problems.

Small (1901) based his maze on a famous garden maze built at Hampton Court Palace in England; Figure 6.1a shows its layout. Small placed the rats at

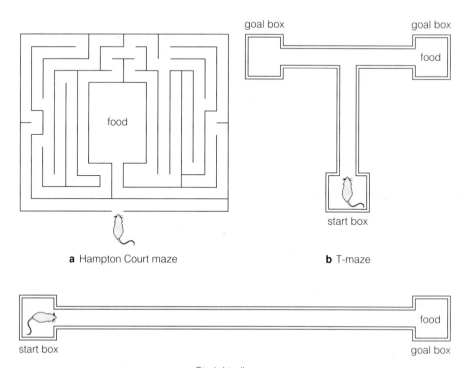

a Hampton Court maze

b T-maze

c Straight-alley maze

FIGURE 6.1   Three mazes for studying learning.

the entrance, observed how long it took them to find their way to the central section that contained food, and recorded how many errors (entries into blind alleys) they made in the process.

As research with mazes continued, it became clear that this problem was too complex for the learning processes involved to be easily analyzed, and researchers began to design progressively simpler mazes. One of the most popular mazes proved to be the *T-maze* shown in Figure 6.1b, in which the rat only had to learn a single turn. The subject was placed in the start box and allowed to run down a straight alley to a choice point, where it could turn either right or left. Both choices led to goal boxes, but only one contained food. Learning was measured by how many trials were needed for the rat to learn to choose the correct alley consistently.

Even the T-maze, however, proved undesirably complex for some purposes, and many experiments were carried out using the straight-alley maze (Figure 6.1c) referred to in previous chapters. All the rats had to do in this apparatus was run from the start box to the goal box, and learning was measured by the change in the animal's speed of running down the alley.

The Skinner Box

The culminating step in the trend toward simpler equipment to study reinforcement was taken by B. F. Skinner, who, along with Pavlov and Thorndike, has been one of the most influential figures in the study of associative learning. One of Skinner's early experiments involved training a rat to run down an eight-foot alley to obtain food. The procedure was tedious. Skinner had to place the rat at one end of the alley, wait for it to get to the other end, then pick it up and return it to the starting point for another run. He soon modified the apparatus so that once the rat reached the food, it could continue along another alley and return by itself to the starting point. Then, to save having to place food in the alley after every trial, Skinner introduced a sensing device so that the rat's weight in the section of the alley leading to the food caused the automatic dispensing of a food pellet. Finally, it struck Skinner that there was really no need for the alley: Instead of having the rat run down the alley as the response to be learned, why not place the rat in one place and give it some response that it could perform repeatedly there?

To achieve this, Skinner built four ventilated, soundproof chambers (note the similarity to Pavlov's fort), with a horizontal lever or bar in each, which the rat could press to obtain a food pellet (Figure 6.2). The device he built is known as a *Skinner box*. To ensure that the rats would eat the food pellet as soon as it was presented (and thus that the reinforcer would follow pressing the bar with as little delay as possible), Skinner first gave his rats *magazine training*, which consisted of presenting the food at periodic intervals. Because the sound of the food delivery was repeatedly followed by eating, the

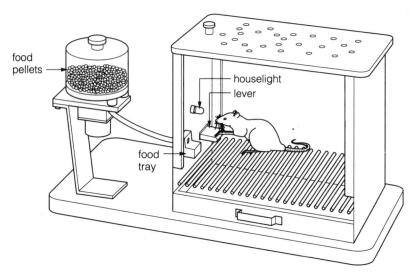

FIGURE 6.2   A Skinner box, or operant chamber. When the rat presses the lever, a food pellet is released from the dispenser behind the chamber into a tube that carries it to the food tray next to the lever. A light mounted above the food tray illuminates the chamber.

rats soon learned to approach the food magazine as soon as they heard the sound.

Shaping

At this stage, Skinner would introduce the lever into the cage and present food only when the rat pressed the bar. In his experiments, Skinner simply waited until this happened. Other experimenters subsequently speeded up the process by using the method of successive approximation, or **shaping**. To train a response that occurs only rarely, this technique begins by reinforcing whatever aspect of the subject's behavior is closest to the desired response. Once this behavior begins to occur more often, the experimenter withholds reinforcement until some closer approximation to the desired response occurs, and so on until the desired response has been established. In the case of bar-pressing, the experimenter might initially reinforce the rat for orienting itself to the bar, then for moving closer to it, then for rearing above it, and, finally, for pushing down on it.

In sum, the Skinner box offers significant advantages for studying learning. There is no need to place animals in the maze and then remove them after each trial; instead, the experimenter simply places the animal in the box and leaves it there. The animal can then respond repeatedly without further intervention by the experimenter, because delivery of the food and recording of the response all occur automatically.

Skinner called responses such as bar-pressing *operants*, because they operated upon the environment to change it. An **operant** is defined as a response that can be modified by its consequences. Bar-pressing in rats is a prototypical operant, whereas salivation is probably not an operant, because it probably cannot be reinforced. (See Chapter 9.) The term *operant level* refers to the initial rate at which an operant is performed before reinforcement is made contingent on it, and the Skinner box is often called an *operant chamber*. Finally, the procedure normally used in this chamber is referred to as a *free-operant procedure* because subjects are free to respond when and as often as they like, in contrast to a *discrete-trial procedure* used in a maze, or in Thorndike's original puzzle box, in which only one response can occur per trial.

6.2 PRIMARY, SECONDARY, AND SOCIAL REINFORCERS

Having reviewed techniques for studying reinforcement, we can now begin to examine the principles that determine whether reinforcement is effective. One of the most important steps in using reinforcement effectively is to identify potential reinforcers (as in the old recipe for elephant stew, the first step of which was to "catch an elephant"), and much early research on reinforcement was concentrated on this task.

Primary Reinforcers

One obvious set of candidates were stimuli that are needed for survival, such as food and water. It makes sense that such stimuli would become reinforcing in the course of evolution, because an animal that repeats a response that has led to food is likely to have a better chance of obtaining food in the future. Thus, the gene that established food as a reinforcer is likely to be transmitted to future generations. It therefore came as no surprise when early research demonstrated that stimuli such as food, water, and sex were all reinforcing.

In the early 1950s, however, evidence began to accumulate that not all reinforcers were necessary for survival, at least not in the simple physical sense that food is. In an experiment by Butler (1954), for example, monkeys were placed in an enclosed cage with two wooden panels, one painted yellow and the other blue. If a monkey pushed open the blue door, it was allowed to look out into the experimental room beyond for a period of 30 seconds. If it pushed against the yellow door, an opaque screen immediately came down, terminating the trial. Not only did the monkeys quickly solve this problem, learning to push only the blue door, regardless of the side on which it was presented, but they proved remarkably persistent in performing the response. In one experiment in which there was a trial once a minute—that is, a 30-second opportunity to look out into the room, followed by a 30-second blank interval—one subject responded on every single trial for nine hours without a break. A second subject responded for 11 hours, and a third for an extraordinary 19 consecutive hours. Visual access to the surrounding room was clearly not necessary for the monkeys' survival in any direct sense, but it proved a remarkably potent reinforcer. As Butler commented, "That monkeys would work as long and as persistently for food is highly unlikely."

Visual stimulation now appears to be only one example of a large set of events that Kish (1966) has referred to as *sensory reinforcers*. These are stimuli whose physical effects seem largely confined to the receptors and nerves involved in their detection and have no effect on general metabolism. Intuitively, their most important characteristic seems to be that they provide variety in our perceptual environment. Rats, for example, prefer to explore complex mazes with many turns rather than simple ones (Montgomery, 1954); humans confined in a dark room will push a button that turns on a panel of flashing lights, with the rate of button-pushing increasing as the pattern of lights becomes less predictable (Jones, Wilkinson, & Braden, 1961).

The reinforcers we have discussed to this point—food, water, and sensory stimulation—are effective essentially from birth. This point is most obvious in the case of food and water, but it is true in the case of sensory reinforcers as well. Siqueland and DeLucia (1969) found that sensory stimulation was reinforcing for infants as young as three weeks, who would increase their rate of sucking on a rubber nipple if this resulted in presentation of photographic slides. Reinforcers that require no special training to be effective are called **primary reinforcers.**

The Premack principle.   The evidence that sensory stimulation can be reinforcing suggests that reinforcers are not all physically necessary for survival. Is there any other characteristic, then, that is shared by reinforcers such as hamburgers, sex, and flashing lights? Perhaps the most useful integrating principle is that suggested by David Premack (1965, 1971). Premack argued that different experiences all have different values for us, and that these values can be inferred by observing the amount of time in which we engage in these activities when they are freely available. The common characteristic of reinforcers, said Premack, is that they are all high-probability activities. Is it possible, then, that *any* high-probability activity will reinforce any response that has a lower probability?

Suppose for example, that a group of children were given free access to a number of foods and found to prefer potatoes to spinach, but to strongly prefer ice cream to both of them. If high-probability responses reinforce lower-probability responses, then—as all mothers know—we should be able to use access to ice cream to reinforce eating spinach ("If you eat all of your vegetables, then you can have dessert"). However, we should also be able to use access to potatoes to reinforce eating spinach, albeit less effectively, because eating potatoes is also a higher-probability response. Furthermore, access to potatoes should *not* reinforce eating ice cream, because a less probable response should not reinforce a more probable one.

Premack tested these and other predictions, and found that most of them were supported. (See Premack, 1965.) <u>The suggestion that more probable responses will reinforce less probable responses thus became known as the</u> **Premack principle**. One of these predictions, however, turned out to be incorrect in at least some situations. In the previous example, the Premack principle says that eating potatoes will not reinforce eating ice cream, and this may seem obvious: What child would eat more ice cream in order to get potatoes? The answer turns out to be that they all will, provided that they genuinely like potatoes, and that eating ice cream is the only way they can obtain them. (For supporting evidence, see Eisenberger, Karpman, & Trattner, 1967; Allison, 1989.)

The response deprivation hypothesis.   To explain this finding, Timberlake and Allison (1974) suggested that when we are given a free choice among various activities, we have a preferred way of distributing our time among these activities. According to Timberlake and Allison's **response deprivation hypothesis**, if we are not allowed to perform a response at the level we prefer—if we are, in effect, deprived of the response—then access to this activity will be reinforcing. In our potato example, if you are unable to eat potatoes at your preferred level, then you will perform other responses in order to obtain potatoes, even if those other responses are themselves more valued, such as eating ice cream.[*]

The response deprivation hypothesis retains Premack's emphasis on activities as reinforcers. What determines the reinforcement value of an activity, however, is not whether it is more probable than the response to be reinforced, but rather whether the current level of the activity is below its optimum level. The further an activity is below its preferred level, the more reinforcing it will be; conversely, the more you prefer an activity, the more reinforcing it will be when you are deprived of it. <u>In this respect, the response deprivation hypothesis points to the same conclusion as the Premack principle: If you want to find a</u>

---

[*] However, you will not increase your consumption of ice cream sufficiently to obtain all the potatoes you would normally eat if this would require you to eat too much ice cream. According to Timberlake and Allison, we have a preferred or optimum way of allocating our time among competing activities—what they call a *bliss point*—and if we have to increase the time we spend on one activity in order to gain access to another, we will compromise on a level of performance that keeps both activities as close as possible to the behavioral bliss point.

good reinforcer, look for activities that people like to engage in when they have a free choice.

Although the Premack principle has had to be modified, it has contributed significantly to liberating psychologists from an overly narrow view of what events are reinforcing. Earlier theorists tended to sort events into rigidly defined categories, but Premack's work has suggested a much more fluid and relativistic interpretation: What is reinforcing varies from moment to moment and from individual to individual. Whatever someone voluntarily spends his or her time doing—whether it is pulling weeds, skydiving, or sitting by the fireside knitting—*that* is what is likely to be reinforcing for that person.

A childish application.   A particularly delightful application of this principle has been reported by Homme, deBaca, Devine, Steinhorst, and Rickert (1963). The subjects were unruly three-year-olds who repeatedly ignored their nursery school teacher's instructions and, instead, raced around the room screaming and pushing furniture. This kind of behavior can be wearing on even the most patient adults, but it is particularly hard to bear for those responsible for the children's safety. One common reaction of parents in such situations is to lose their tempers and punish the children in order to get them to do as they are told. Instead, Homme and his co-workers set out to reinforce good behavior through a judicious application of the Premack principle. They reinforced the children's behavior whenever the children sat and played quietly for a specified period of time, with the reinforcer being several minutes of uninterrupted running and screaming! Within only a few days, the children were obeying the teacher's instructions almost perfectly, so that "an observer, new on the scene, almost certainly would have assumed extensive aversive control was being used" (Homme et al., 1963). Later on, new and even better reinforcers were developed through continued observation of the children's behavior, including such decidedly unusual rewards as allowing the children to throw a plastic cup across the room, to kick a wastepaper basket, and, best of all, to push the teacher around the room in a swivel chair on rolling wheels!

The moral to this story is that it is a mistake to think of reinforcers in terms of a restricted list of "approved" stimuli. There is no magic list of reinforcers; the best way to determine what will be reinforcing for someone is to observe that person's behavior.

Secondary Reinforcers

In contrast to primary reinforcers, which are effective from birth, some of the most powerful reinforcers affecting our behavior are **secondary reinforcers,** which have acquired their reinforcing properties through experience. Money, for example, is not at first a very effective reinforcer; showering an infant with dollar bills is unlikely to have any discernible impact on its behavior. As we grow older, though, money becomes increasingly important; in some cases, it becomes an obsession. How, then, do secondary reinforcers, such as money or the word *good*, acquire their reinforcing properties?

Establishing a secondary reinforcer.   One of the first attempts to answer this question was by John B. Wolfe (1936), who examined whether the powerful effects of money in real life could be reproduced in the animal laboratory. Using six chimpanzees as subjects, Wolfe first trained them to place a token into a vending machine to obtain grapes. Once they had mastered this task, they were given a heavy lever to operate to obtain further tokens; Wolfe found that they would work as hard to operate the lever when the reward was tokens as when it was the grapes themselves. Furthermore, their behavior bore some striking similarities to that of humans with regard to money. In one experiment in which the chimpanzees were tested in pairs, Wolfe found that the dominant member of the pair sometimes would push aside its subordinate in order to gain access to the lever. If the subordinate had already amassed a pile of tokens, then the dominant one might simply take them away. In one of the pairs, however, the subordinate, Bula, developed an effective counterstrategy. She would turn toward her partner, Bimba, extend her hand palm up, and begin to whine. This apparent begging was invariably successful: As soon as she began to whine, Bimba would quickly hand her one of the tokens and would continue doing so until she stopped whining.

The reinforcing properties of the tokens in this study were not innate. Wolfe used tokens of different colors, and he found that if tokens of a particular color were no longer exchanged for grapes, the chimpanzees would quickly lose interest in them. Wolfe considered a number of explanations for why the tokens became reinforcing, one of which was that the reinforcing properties of the food had become classically conditioned to the tokens because of their temporal contiguity. If this explanation was correct, then the strength of a secondary reinforcer should depend on the same associative principles that determine conditioning: contiguity, frequency, intensity, and so on.

Empirical tests of this prediction have generally supported it, and the principles of classical conditioning and secondary reinforcement have proved to be very similar. (For reviews, see Wike, 1966; Fantino, 1977.) To establish the word *good* as a secondary reinforcer, for example, it should be paired with a primary reinforcer (such as candy) as closely and as often as possible. And, as in classical conditioning, it is important not to present a secondary reinforcer too often by itself. If you repeatedly say "good" to a child without any other reinforcing consequences following, the reinforcing properties of the word will extinguish (for example, Warren & Cairns, 1972).

Another important principle of secondary reinforcement, but one that has no direct parallel in classical conditioning, is that it is helpful to pair the secondary reinforcer with a variety of primary reinforcers rather than just one.

Suppose, for example, you wanted to establish a plastic token as a secondary reinforcer for children. If the token were paired only with candy, then the token might be attractive only at times when the children wanted candy. If it were paired with a variety of reinforcers, however—candy, ice cream, longer play periods, and so on—then it would be likely to be effective in a much wider range of circumstances. We shall consider some important applications of this principle in Chapter 8.

Signal or substitute?   In empirical terms, the process of establishing a secondary reinforcer is similar, if not identical, to that of classical conditioning. As in the case of conditioning, however, there is controversy over what is learned. According to the substitution view, if a teacher says "good" and then gives a child candy, the reinforcing properties of the candy are conditioned to the word *good*, and the child will feel a warm glow of pleasure whenever he or she hears the word. According to a signal analysis, however, we do not value the word *good* for its own sake, but consider it only a means to an end: We know that whoever is praising us is well disposed toward us and is thus likely to give us other reinforcers.

Which view is right? Do we value *good* as a reinforcer in its own right or as a means to an end? As in the case of conditioning itself, there is evidence for both interpretations (for example, Lieberman, 1972; Case, Fantino, & Wixted, 1985). As in conditioning, both views may be right. For example, we value money, a secondary reinforcer, partly because of what we can buy with it; but it also becomes an end in itself. There are many stories of elderly people who die in poverty and are then found to have had a fortune hidden under their mattresses; such stories may be dramatic examples of money becoming an end in itself rather than a means to an end.

Social Reinforcers

A third possible category of reinforcers (one not usually treated separately) is *social reinforcers*—stimuli whose reinforcing properties derive uniquely from the behavior of other members of the same species. In practice, the meaning of this term is clearer than its definition and includes such things as praise, affection, and even just attention.

One reason for treating social reinforcers separately is that they are a blend of both primary and secondary reinforcers. Poulson (1983) found that an adult's smile could reinforce behavior in infants as young as three months, suggesting that smiling may be innately reinforcing. But there is also considerable evidence that the power of social reinforcers can be altered by pairing them with other reinforcers. The reinforcing properties of the word *good*, for example, can be increased by following it with candy (Warren & Cairns,

1972). Thus, although social reinforcement may have an innate basis, experience also plays an important role.

Perhaps the stronger motivation for treating social reinforcers separately, however, is to emphasize their practical importance. Social reinforcers such as praise and attention are probably the reinforcers we encounter most often in our daily lives, and they play an important—and often underestimated—role in controlling our behavior.

One illustration of the power of social reinforcers comes from a study by Allen, Hart, Buell, Harris, and Wolf (1964). The subject was a four-year-old girl, Ann, who had just started nursery school. From the time of her arrival, she spent most of her time interacting with adults rather than playing with other children, and as time went on she developed a variety of behavioral problems. She complained frequently about skin abrasions that no one else could see; she spoke in a low voice that was very difficult to hear; and she spent increasing amounts of time standing by herself, pulling at her lower lip and fingering her cheek.

One possible analysis of Ann's behavior might have been that she was an insecure and unhappy child, and thus needed as much comfort and reassurance as possible to help her adjust to her new surroundings. In one crucial respect, however, the authors' analysis was very different. They noted that the common feature of all of Ann's problem behaviors was that they elicited adult attention. If she stood by herself, for example, a teacher was soon likely to come over to ask what was wrong. Because adult attention was reinforcing, the teachers might have been encouraging the very behaviors they were trying to eliminate. The authors' advice to the teachers, therefore, was to change the reinforcement contingencies by paying attention to Ann whenever she played with others but ignoring her when she stood alone.

Because the baseline, or operant level, of Ann's social play was so low, it was difficult for the teachers to reinforce it. They therefore shaped this behavior by paying attention to Ann initially for any approximation to social play—for example, just standing near other children—and gradually changed the requirement for reinforcement to talking or actually playing with other children. The reinforcer was social attention: A teacher would come over to Ann, smile, talk to her about what she was doing, and so on. The results are shown in Figure 6.3. Before treatment was instituted, Ann spent an average of only 10 percent of her time interacting with other children, but when adult attention was made contingent on such activity, it increased almost immediately to 60 percent.

One possibility is that this increase would have occurred even in the absence of social reinforcement; perhaps Ann was just adjusting to the school environment. To establish whether the change in her behavior had really been due to the altered reinforcement contingencies, the teachers were asked to revert to their earlier behavior of attending to Ann only when she was alone.

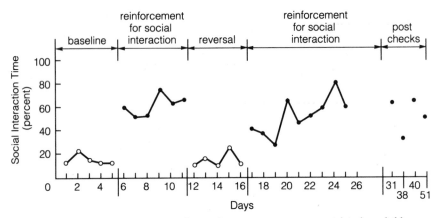

FIGURE 6.3   The percentage of time Ann spent interacting with other children at her preschool. (Adapted from Allen et al., 1964)

The result was an immediate return to isolated play; when the teachers again made attention contingent on social play, social behavior quickly reappeared. The frequency of reinforcement was then gradually reduced and eventually faded out altogether, but Ann's social play remained at a high level, perhaps because as her skills at playing with other children increased, this play provided its own source of reinforcement.

Social reinforcers can be very powerful: Even a small shift in adult attention—not money, not candy, but just attention—was sufficient to substantially alter Ann's behavior. Also, as often happens, the crucial role of social reinforcement in directing Ann's behavior was not at first appreciated. Actions such as paying attention to someone are such a common part of our lives that we take them for granted, but, as we shall see again in other applications, social reinforcement can play a very powerful role in controlling behavior.

6.3 DELAY OF REINFORCEMENT

Having identified a set of potential reinforcers, we now turn to the question of what determines whether they will be effective in strengthening behavior. One likely factor is the delay between the response and the reinforcer. The British Associationists believed that the contiguity between two events was the most important factor determining whether they would be associated; as we have seen, this belief was strongly confirmed in research on classical conditioning, in which delays of even one or two seconds were generally sufficient to impair learning or prevent it altogether. It thus seemed highly likely to early learning researchers that contiguity would prove equally critical in reinforcement. Their attempts to confirm this hypothesis in the laboratory, however, quickly ran into difficulties.

Does Delay Matter?

The early studies. In a study by Wolfe (1934), the experimenter tested rats in a T-maze with food always available in the goal box on one side. (This is known as a *spatial discrimination,* because the subject has to learn to go to a particular location in space.) Wolfe modified the apparatus by inserting delay boxes between the choice point and the goal boxes. By varying how long subjects were held in the delay box before the door to the goal box was opened, Wolfe could control precisely the delay between the rat's making a correct choice response and receiving food. Up to a point, his results confirmed the importance of contiguity: Lengthening the delay from 0 to 60 seconds in different groups led to a similar increase in the number of trials required for solution. Increasing the delay beyond 60 seconds, however, had little effect, and Wolfe found some evidence of learning even when food was delayed for 20 minutes.

If delays of even a few seconds normally prevented learning in classical conditioning, how did learning take place for Wolfe's rats when the correct response and food were separated by 20 minutes? Hull (1943) suggested that the answer might lie in secondary reinforcement. As soon as the rat was released from the delay box on the correct side, it received food; thus, the stimuli associated with this box—its color, odor, and so on—were contiguous with food. As a result, these stimuli could have become secondary reinforcers, and the next time the rat made the correct response and entered the delay box it would have received immediate reinforcement. According to Hull, then, the rat developed a preference for the correct side not because it realized that this response led to food, but because it produced immediate secondary reinforcement.

This explanation is highly counterintuitive. Would a rat really develop a preference for the correct side of a maze simply because it preferred the delay box on that side? To find out, Perkins (1947) repeated Wolfe's experiment but randomly interchanged the delay boxes between trials, so that both delay boxes were on the correct side on half the trials and thus both would become secondary reinforcers. Therefore, secondary reinforcers would follow incorrect as well as correct responses, which would mean that secondary reinforcement could not contribute to a preference for the correct side. According to Hull's analysis, the rats in this condition should no longer have had any reason to prefer the correct side. In accordance with this prediction, Perkins found that learning in this group was significantly slower than in a control group for which the delay boxes were not interchanged. However, although learning was slower, some learning did occur nevertheless, despite the fact that reinforcement following a correct response was delayed for 45 seconds. In a second experiment, Perkins varied the delay of reinforcement for groups with interchanged delay boxes and found that learning would occur with delays of up to 2 minutes.

In one respect these results support Hull's analysis: When secondary reinforcement was eliminated, the maximum delay at which learning was possible was reduced from 20 minutes to 2 minutes. The fact that learning occurred with a delay of up to 2 minutes, however, was still puzzling. If events must be contiguous to be associated, how could a response be associated with food that was presented 2 minutes later?

Spence's hypothesis.   A possible answer was provided by one of Hull's colleagues, Kenneth Spence (1947), who suggested that although Perkins had eliminated one source of secondary reinforcement, a second source still remained. To understand Spence's analysis, we must first outline a traditional scheme in psychology for classifying stimuli according to their point of origin.

Stimuli that originate outside the body, such as light and sound, are called *exteroceptive stimuli*; stimuli that have their origins within the body, such as hunger and fear, are called *interoceptive stimuli*. One particularly important subdivision of interoceptive stimuli are *proprioceptive stimuli*, which originate in muscular movement. Sensory receptors are located in all skeletal muscles, and these proprioceptors generate neural signals whenever the muscles contract. If you move your thumb, for example, you can feel its movement even with your eyes closed; this sensation is made possible by proprioceptive stimuli from the muscle.

At the time Spence wrote, neuroanatomical studies had established the existence of these receptors, but to this base of empirical evidence Spence added a crucial theoretical assumption. Whenever a muscle contracts, he said, a trace of the proprioceptive stimulus produced lingers on in the nervous system even after the movement is completed, with the intensity of this trace decaying gradually over time (Figure 6.4). If a flashbulb goes off while you are sitting in a dark room, for example, you will experience a bright afterimage that then fades. Spence hypothesized that a similar decaying trace would persist after physical movements. In Perkins's experiment, a rat's turn to the correct side would have produced a distinctive proprioceptive stimulus, and if its trace was still present when food arrived it would have acquired reinforcing properties. The next time the rat made the correct response, the proprioceptive stimuli produced would have provided immediate secondary reinforcement. In effect, the rat was now reinforcing itself for correct turns!

Spence's hypothesis also explained why learning was better in Wolfe's study than in Perkins's. As we saw earlier, the laws governing the establishment of a secondary reinforcer are essentially identical to those of classical conditioning. One of these principles, first established by Pavlov, is that conditioning depends not only on the time between the onset of a CS and a US, but on whether the CS remains present throughout the interval. Delay conditioning, in which the CS remains present until the US arrives, is substantially more effective than trace conditioning, in which the CS terminates beforehand. In

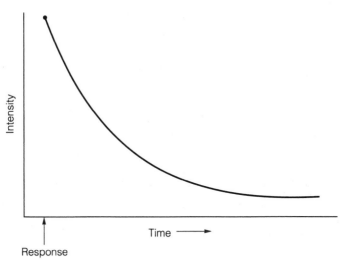

F I G U R E 6.4   Hypothetical curve of how the intensity of a proprioceptive trace decays over time.

Wolfe's experiment, the delay box was present throughout the delay interval; in Perkins's experiment, only a trace of the proprioceptive stimulus would have remained. According to a conditioning analysis, therefore, the delay box should become a stronger secondary reinforcer than the proprioceptive trace. Thus, learning in Wolfe's experiment should have been stronger than in Perkins's, as it was.

By assuming that proprioceptive stimuli could function as secondary reinforcers, Spence was able to provide a comprehensive—and rather neat—account for all the available experimental evidence. Moreover, although some details of his analysis were untestable (there was no direct evidence that movements gave rise to slowly decaying traces, much less that these traces then functioned as secondary reinforcers), the theory as a whole did lead to a testable prediction. For learning to occur, Spence said, some form of immediate reinforcement is required. If proprioceptive as well as exteroceptive secondary reinforcement could be eliminated, Spence argued, then even a brief delay in the presentation of food should seriously impair learning.

But how could proprioceptive secondary reinforcement be eliminated? As long as a response produces a proprioceptive stimulus, it is impossible to prevent a trace of this stimulus from being paired with food, and thus from functioning as a secondary reinforcer for future responses.

Grice's test.   A solution to this conundrum was soon provided in a brilliant experiment by one of Spence's students, G. Robert Grice (1948). Recognizing the impossibility of preventing secondary reinforcement of the correct response, Grice instead devised an ingenious procedure to control for its effects. In Chapter 1, we saw that the occurrence of some extraneous variables such as the passing of time cannot be physically prevented, but their role can nevertheless be disentangled through the use of an appropriate control group for comparison. In a similar fashion, Grice now set out to control for the effects of secondary reinforcement by comparing two responses. One, R_1, was followed by a secondary reinforcer (S^r), and then, after a delay, by food. The second response, R_2, produced the same secondary reinforcer but not the food:

$$R_1 \longrightarrow S^r \longrightarrow \text{food}$$
$$R_2 \longrightarrow S^r$$

Because the secondary reinforcer followed R_2 as well as R_1, it would strengthen both responses equally. Any difference in the strength of the two responses, therefore, could only be due to the food acting across the delay interval to strengthen R_1 directly.

The apparatus Grice used is shown, in overhead view, in Figure 6.5. At the entrance to the maze, the rats could enter either a black or a white alley. Whichever alley they chose, they then entered a delay box painted gray, and, after confinement for a set period, were released into the goal box. The positions of the black and white alleys were alternated randomly over trials: On half the trials, white was on the left; on the other half, white was on the right. Food was always available in the goal box following the white alley. Thus, in contrast to the spatial discrimination used by Wolfe and Perkins, in which food was contingent on the choice of a particular side, this was a *visual discrimination* in which reinforcement was contingent on the choice of a particular color, regardless of its location.

Because food was available equally often on both sides of the apparatus, turns to both left and right were followed by food. Proprioceptive stimuli from

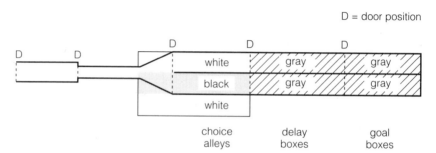

FIGURE 6.5   Overhead view of the visual discrimination maze used by Grice. The section containing the choice alleys could be moved so that the black alley was either to the rat's left or to its right. (Adapted from Grice, 1948)

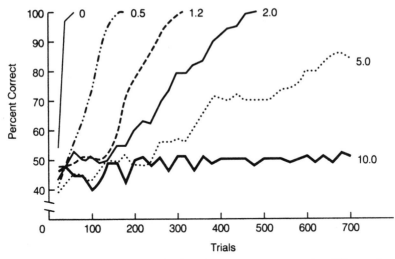

F I G U R E 6.6 Learning curves for Grice's six groups experiencing different time delays of reinforcement. (Grice, 1948)

both of these responses were thus paired with food; whether the rat made a correct or incorrect response on any trial, it would receive immediate proprioceptive secondary reinforcement. Similarly, because both delay boxes were followed by food, both would become secondary reinforcers. Thus, whether the rat chose the black alley or the white alley on any trial, it would receive the same amount of exteroceptive and proprioceptive secondary reinforcement. The only way it could learn the correct response would be by directly associating this response with the delayed food.

As Spence had predicted, even short delays of reinforcement now profoundly disrupted learning. Figure 6.6 shows the percentage of correct responses over trials for groups trained with different delays. The group with no delay learned the correct response quite rapidly, requiring an average of only 20 trials to reach a criterion of 90 percent correct. A group for whom reinforcement was delayed for half a second, however, required five times as many trials to reach the same criterion. Delays of 1 and 2 seconds impaired learning even more severely, and at 10 seconds learning proved virtually impossible: Three of the five subjects in this group showed no preference for the correct response even after 1440 trials! Just as Spence had predicted, when all sources of immediate reinforcement were effectively eliminated, then even small delays of reinforcement had catastrophic effects on learning. *

---

* If you have a sharp eye for experimental design, you may have realized that Grice did not, in fact, eliminate all possible sources of secondary reinforcement. If the color of the correct alley also gave rise to a persisting trace, then this color could have acted as a secondary reinforcer for the correct response. Indeed, this may be why Grice still obtained a small amount of learning with delays of up to 5 seconds.

The Role of Interference

Grice's results left little doubt about the importance of immediate reinforcement for learning. Less clear, however, was *why* immediate reinforcement was so critical. You might think that a 2-second gap between a correct response and reinforcement would not be all that harmful; yet, in Grice's experiment it clearly was. Why? One possible explanation was that the rat, with its very small brain (only about 0.003 the size of a human brain), has only a limited capacity for storing events, and unless food is delivered quickly, no trace of the preceding response will be left to be reinforced. In the years since Grice's experiment, however, it has become clear that this explanation is simply not tenable. In an experiment by Petrinovich and Bolles (1957), for example, rats were trained on an alternation problem in which the location of food in a T-maze was changed after every trial. If a turn to the right was reinforced on one trial, then only a turn to the left would produce food on the following trial, and so on. To respond correctly on any trial, therefore, the rat had to remember its response on the preceding trial. Petrinovich and Bolles found that their subjects could learn to respond correctly even when trials were separated by several hours. Similar results have since been reported with delays of up to 24 hours (Capaldi, 1971). Rats are clearly capable of recalling their behavior over periods far longer than a few seconds.

Why, then, did delaying reinforcement have such devastating consequences in Grice's experiment? The most likely explanation is now thought to be interference from other responses (Revusky, 1971; B. A. Williams, 1978). From the vantage point of the experimenter, it may seem obvious that food was contingent on entry into the white alley, but from the rat's perspective the situation was altogether more confusing. In the first place, there was no particular reason for the rat to believe that the food was contingent on its behavior at all. Perhaps the rat thought that the goal box contained food intermittently, in the same way that a tree produces nuts only in some seasons, with the availability of food in both cases being entirely independent of the rat's behavior. (See also Lawrence & Hommel, 1961.) Even if the rat suspected that food was response-contingent, there were any number of responses that could have been responsible. Perhaps it was one of the responses that followed entry into the alley (R_c)—sniffing in a corner, rearing, walking down one side, and so forth—or perhaps it was one of the many responses made before entering the alley that was responsible for the food. From the rat's perspective, food was preceded by an almost infinite string of responses:

$$R_{-4} \; R_{-3} \; R_{-2} \; R_{-1} \; R_c \; R_1 \; R_2 \; R_3 \longrightarrow food$$

There was no obvious basis for identifying which of these responses actually produced the food. Moreover, at any given moment the rat was performing not one response but many responses—not just entering the white alley, for example, but breathing at a certain rate, holding its head at a particular angle, and so on.

From the rat's point of view, then, the situation was not the simple one illustrated in Figure 6.7a, but more nearly that shown in Figure 6.7b. Any reinforcer would be preceded by literally thousands of responses—in the case of reinforcement in humans, a rich profusion of thumb twitches, stomach contractions, leg flexions, and eyeblinks. From this vast array, the subject must somehow extract the one response that actually produced the reinforcer. Viewed in this light, the wonder is that Grice's rats ever solved the problem at all!

Implications for Human Learning

The evidence we have been reviewing suggests that even brief delays in reinforcement can severely impair learning. All of the evidence, however, has come from rats, and you may be wondering whether brief delays would have nearly such serious consequences in humans. In many situations, the answer is no. Rewards often affect our behavior even when they have been delayed for hours or even days. In some of these cases, immediate secondary reinforcers such as praise are probably involved. Even if reinforcement is not delivered immediately (for example, if a child cleans her or his room when the parents are not present), the response and reinforcer may still be brought into temporal

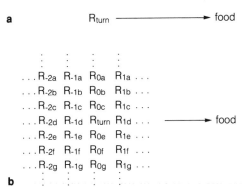

F I G U R E 6.7   A rat's task in a maze when reinforcement is delayed. (a) The experimenter's view: A turn to the right (R_{turn}) produces food. (b) The rat's view: The correct response is preceded by many responses (R_{-1}, R_{-2}, and so on) and followed by many responses (for example, R_1). Moreover, at any moment in time the rat is engaged in multiple behaviors (R_a, R_b, and so on). Thus, the correct response is only one of a vast array of responses that preceded food, and identifying which response produced the food is not simple.

contiguity through the medium of language: "I see you cleaned your room this morning; you can stay up late tonight as a reward."

The availability of language undoubtedly helps to mitigate the effects of long delays for humans, but it would be a mistake to conclude from this that delays in the presentation of reinforcers are therefore unimportant. Language does not always allow us to fully reinstate the response we wish to reinforce. If you are teaching someone to play tennis, for example, saying "That was a very good serve" after the game is over may be of little value, because the person will no longer be able to recall the serve in enough detail to be able to reproduce it. Even if the correct response is recalled fully, a delayed reinforcer may be a less effective incentive for changing behavior. If you offer a neighbor's child $10 to mow your lawn, for example, the child will probably be much more interested if you offer to pay as soon as the job is completed than a week later. In both cases the child knows that she or he will ultimately receive the same reinforcer, but an immediate reinforcer may nevertheless have greater appeal.

Rachlin and Green (1972) conducted on experiment that is analogous to the situation of the lawn-mowing child. Using pigeons as subjects, Rachlin and Green offered them a choice between pecking one key that produced 2 seconds' worth of grain immediately, and a second key that produced 4 seconds' worth after a 4-second delay:

$$R_1 \longrightarrow 2 \text{ seconds of food}$$
$$R_2 \xrightarrow{\hspace{4cm}} 4 \text{ seconds of food}$$

Even though the second response produced twice as much food, the birds preferred the immediate reinforcer on 95 percent of the trials.

The practical implications of this principle are nicely illustrated in a study by Phillips (1968). In order to improve procedures for treating juvenile delinquents, Phillips established a residential home for boys called Achievement Place. One problem shared by most delinquents is failure in school, which in turn reflects an almost total failure to do any assigned homework. As one component of the treatment program, therefore, Phillips set out to encourage homework completion through the use of reinforcers. Whenever an assignment was completed to an acceptable standard, the boys were allowed to stay up for one hour past their normal bedtime on weekends. This reward was known as "weekly time." The effect of this reward on the behavior of one boy, Tom, is shown in Figure 6.8. Over a 14-day period, Tom did not complete a single assignment.

One possible explanation for this failure was that the reinforcer being used was not sufficiently attractive; maybe Tom just didn't value being allowed to stay up late. Another possible explanation was the delay between completing an assignment during the week and being allowed to stay up on the weekend. To find out, Phillips used exactly the same reinforcer in the next phase of

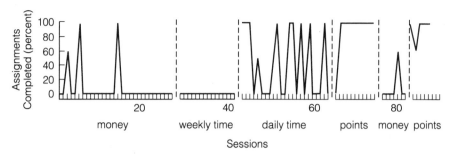

F I G U R E 6.8   Percentage of homework assignments completed by Tom under different reinforcement conditions. (Adapted from Phillips, 1968)

the study—one hour of late time for each correct assignment—but now allowed Tom to stay up on the night that an assignment was completed rather than waiting until the weekend. These results are also shown in Figure 6.8, in the section labeled "daily time." We can see that the percentage of homework assignments completed rose immediately from 0 to an average of 50 percent. Even though the same reinforcer was used in both conditions, its effectiveness varied dramatically depending on the delay in its presentation. Thus, although reinforcers can be effective after a delay, as a general rule they should be delivered as soon after a response as possible if they are to achieve their full potential. Failure to adhere to this principle may be one of the most important reasons that reinforcers are sometimes ineffective.

At the beginning of the chapter, we referred to the puzzle of why students have difficulty studying despite the potent rewards—good grades, a job that pays well—contingent on this behavior. One important reason is almost certainly the delay involved in reinforcement. The reinforcers for studying arrive only after very long delays, whereas those for alternative activities, such as going to a movie or a football game, are essentially immediate. The student who doesn't study may thus be behaving much like the pigeon in the Rachlin and Green study: Both may know that in the long term one response produces much more valuable consequences, but both are nevertheless unable to resist the temptation of immediate gratification. The moral to this section can thus be summarized very simply: For a reinforcer to be maximally effective, it should be presented as soon as possible after a response.

6.4 SCHEDULES OF REINFORCEMENT

Earlier, we discussed B. F. Skinner's passion for efficiency and how it led to the development of the Skinner box. Another of his timesaving innovations was a device for automatically producing graphs of an animal's behavior. The device, called a *cumulative recorder*, consists of a rotating drum with a pen resting above

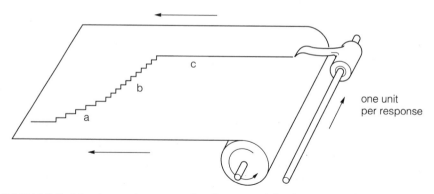

F I G U R E 6.9 A cumulative recorder. Rotation of the drum moves the paper to the left; a motor pulls the pen one step toward the top of the paper every time the subject makes a response.

it; the rotation of the drum moves a strip of paper under the pen, and the pen is moved one step along the drum every time the subject makes a response (Figure 6.9). If no response is made, the pen remains in the same position while the paper is moved beneath it, the result being a horizontal line. If the rat presses the bar, the pen moves one step vertically; the more often the animal responds, the higher the pen rises up the paper. The height of the pen at any point thus provides a measure of the total, or cumulative, responses emitted since the beginning of the session. Because the total number of responses emitted can never fall, a cumulative record can only rise or remain constant, and the angle at which the curve rises reflects the rate of the subject's responding.

The cumulative record in Figure 6.9 illustrates these points. At the beginning of the session, the subject responded at a steady rate of 10 responses per minute; this is shown as an ascending, stepped line (segment a). After 10 minutes, the subject's rate of responding doubled, and the stepped line rises more steeply (segment b). Finally, after 20 minutes, the subject stopped responding. Because the cumulative number of responses since the beginning of the session remains at 300 responses, the response curve is now horizontal (segment c).

Skinner now had a highly efficient technique for studying learning. Once he put an animal into the test chamber, he did not have to move it, give it food, or record its responses; it was all done automatically. His next important contribution arose by accident. He ran his experiments on weekends as well as during the week, and one Saturday he discovered that his supply of pellets would not last until Monday. Instead of reinforcing every bar-press as he had always done in the past, therefore, he decided to reinforce only one per minute. This had two gratifying consequences:

1. His supply of pellets lasted almost indefinitely.

2. The rats continued to respond and, after some initial perturbations, did so at a steady rate.

Over time, Skinner tried a number of different rules, or **reinforcement schedules**, for deciding which responses to reinforce, and he found that the choice of schedule had important consequences for how his animals responded. We will begin by defining some of the schedules he used and then look at their effects on behavior.

Ratio and Interval Schedules

The schedules. The simplest schedule is to reinforce a response every time it occurs. This schedule is known, not unreasonably, as a continuous reinforcement (CRF) schedule. In the real world, though, behavior is rarely reinforced so consistently. Children, for example, are not praised every time they tell the truth, and factory workers are not paid every time they tighten a screw. Instead, most behavior is reinforced on intermittent, or partial, reinforcement schedules.

Two types of partial reinforcement schedules have been studied most commonly: ratio schedules and interval schedules. In a **ratio schedule**, reinforcement depends on the number of responses that have been emitted. In piecework, for example, a worker's wages depend solely on the number of units completed, regardless of how long the job takes. In an **interval schedule**, on the other hand, it is the passage of time since the last reinforcement, rather than the number of responses, that determines whether the next response will be reinforced. Whether you find mail the next time you go to your mailbox, for example, will depend on how long it has been since the last time you found mail, not on how often you visited the mailbox in the interim. *

Further complicating matters, ratio and interval schedules can be subdivided according to whether the requirement for reinforcement is fixed or variable. In a *fixed interval (FI) schedule*, the interval that must elapse before a response can be reinforced is always the same, whereas in a *variable interval (VI) schedule* this interval is varied. In an FI 60-second schedule, for example, 60 seconds must always elapse following a reinforcement before a response can be reinforced again, whereas in a VI 60-second schedule, the interval might be as

---

* Note that reinforcement in an interval schedule still requires a response: You do not obtain your mail unless you go to the mailbox. The designation *interval* means that the availability of reinforcement is determined by the passage of time, but once reinforcement becomes available, a response is still required to obtain it.

short as 5 seconds or as long as 2 minutes. (The 60 seconds in the schedule's name refers to the average.) Ratio schedules are subdivided in a similar way. In a *fixed ratio (FR) schedule,* the number of responses required for reinforcement is always the same. In a *variable ratio (VR) schedule,* the number of responses required to obtain reinforcement varies across successive reinforcements. For example, FR 30 means that every 30th response will be reinforced; VR 30 means that an average of 30 responses (sometimes only 5 responses, sometimes 50, and so on) will be required for reinforcement. Figure 6.10 summarizes the four main types of intermittent, or partial, reinforcement schedules in terms of the requirement for reinforcement (interval or ratio) and whether it is fixed or variable.

Patterns of responding.   Learning the distinctions among the various schedules can be tedious, but each schedule has somewhat different effects on behavior, and these differences can be important. Figure 6.11 presents cumulative records illustrating the typical patterns of responding obtained under FI and FR schedules of reinforcement.

In an FI schedule (Figure 6.11a), reinforcement becomes available only after a fixed period of time has elapsed following the previous reinforcement; each short diagonal mark on the record indicates the occurrence of a reinforcer. We can see that immediately after reinforcement, subjects respond at a very low rate, but this rate steadily accelerates and reaches a peak just before the next reinforcement is due. Thus, subjects tend to respond in a cyclical

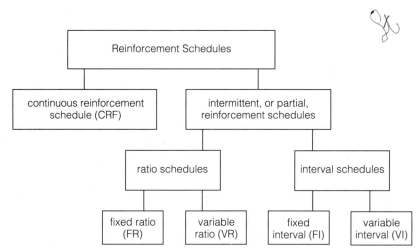

F I G U R E 6.10   Four main types of ratio and interval schedules. These are categorized according to whether the criterion for reinforcing a response is the passage of time or the number of previous responses, and whether this criterion is fixed or variable.

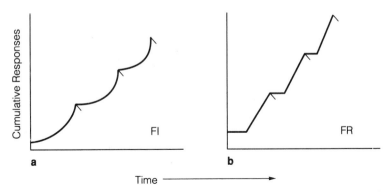

F I G U R E 6.11   Typical cumulative response records generated by two types of schedules: (a) fixed interval (FI); (b) fixed ratio (FR). The short diagonal marks indicate presentations of a reinforcer.

pattern. (For a review of evidence that this pattern is not always obtained, however, see Lowe, 1979.)

Because of its appearance when graphed, this positively accelerated response pattern is called an *FI scallop*, and it can have important implications for the practical use of FI schedules. For example, if you were a parent who wanted to encourage a daughter to study by praising this behavior, it would be a great mistake to visit her room only at regular, hourly intervals. If your praise were the main reinforcer for studying, it is likely that your daughter would be studying at regular, hourly intervals. Ironically, psychology professors (including those teaching learning) seem to make exactly this mistake by scheduling exams at predictable, fixed intervals, with the result that students' studying often takes the form of a classic FI scallop: a zero or very low rate of studying immediately after an exam, gradually rising to a frantic peak the night before the next exam!

Figure 6.11b shows the pattern of responding typically maintained by an FR schedule. Here, reinforcement is contingent on a fixed number of responses, and the result is generally "pause-and-run" behavior. The subject pauses for a while after reinforcement (the greater the response requirement, the longer the pause), and then switches to a steady rate of responding, which is maintained until the next reinforcement is earned. If the ratio requirement is too great, however, *ratio strain* may be observed: The subject will begin to respond, then pause, respond a bit more, pause again, and so on. If the schedule requirement is not reduced at this point, the subject may soon cease to respond altogether.

Finally, Figure 6.12 shows typical responding on VI and VR schedules. Because reinforcement can occur at any time on these schedules, subjects

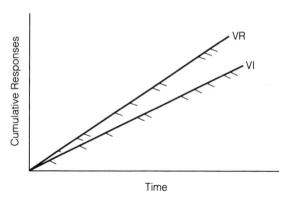

F I G U R E 6.12   Typical responding under variable ratio (VR) and variable interval (VI) schedules with the same average rates of reinforcement. As in Figure 6.11, the short diagonal marks indicate presentations of a reinforcer.

respond much more consistently over time; when the responses are plotted on a cumulative record, responding appears as a straight line.

The partial reinforcement effect.   One puzzling consequence of presenting reinforcement on a partial reinforcement schedule is what happens when reinforcement is discontinued—that is, during extinction. Suppose, for example, that two groups of rats are allowed to run down a straight alley 100 times, with one group finding food in the goal box on every trial (CRF), and the other only on every second trial (FR 2). If both groups are now extinguished, which group of rats would you expect to stop running sooner?

On the surface, the answer might appear to be simple. Reinforcement, as we all know, strengthens responding, and nonreinforcement weakens it. If one group is reinforced 100 times and another only 50, responding should obviously be weaker in the latter group. And if responding were weaker in this group, we should certainly expect that it would be easier to eliminate responding in this group. However, we would be wrong. Not only would responding in the partially reinforced group not be easier to extinguish, it would be harder, and the less often responding were reinforced, the harder it would be.

This effect was nicely demonstrated in an experiment with college students by Lewis and Duncan (1956). The students were given an opportunity to play a slot machine; they were told that they could play as long as they wanted, and that each time they won they would earn five cents. For their first eight plays, they were reinforced for between 0 and 100 percent of their responses; thereafter, no reinforcement was given. Figure 6.13 shows how long subjects continued to play the slot machine after reinforcement was discontinued: The lower the percentage of reinforcement during the initial phase, the longer subjects persisted in playing. The fact that partial reinforcement during train-

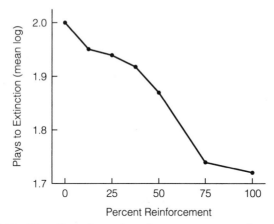

F I G U R E 6.13   The effect of partial reinforcement on responding during extinction. The lower the percentage of reinforcement college students received for playing a slot machine during training, the longer they persisted in playing during extinction. (Adapted from Lewis & Duncan, 1956)

ing increases responding during extinction is known as the **partial reinforcement effect (PRE)**.[*]

One way of explaining this initially surprising result is in terms of how subjects know that conditions have changed, and that it is no longer appropriate to continue responding. For subjects who have always been reinforced, the transition to extinction is obvious, and they are likely to quit responding quickly. For subjects who have become accustomed to nonreinforcement during training, the transition to extinction is less obvious, and they are likely to persist in the hope that they will eventually be reinforced. A real-life example of this phenomenon might be if you had a new car that always started instantly on cold mornings. If it suddenly failed one morning, you might try again a few times. Before long, though, you would probably give up and phone a service station. If, on the other hand, your car always gave you trouble, requiring many attempts before it started, it is likely that you would continue trying for much longer. We will look at a more sophisticated version of this account in the next chapter, and see how it can be used to make some surprising predictions.

Choosing a schedule. Having described the properties of the five schedules most often studied—CRF, FI, FR, VI, and VR—can we now say which one is

---

[*] In the Lewis and Duncan experiment, the no-reinforcement condition (0%) resulted in the highest levels of responding during extinction, but this is not usually the case. The persistent responding in this group was probably due to the wording of the instructions, which implied that *some* reinforcement would be given if subjects responded. When this reinforcement was not forthcoming following the first eight plays, subjects kept trying.

the best? The answer, you may not be surprised to hear, depends on how we define *best*. If your sole concern was that a response have a high probability of occurrence—that a child, for example, always tell the truth—then continuous reinforcement would have considerable attractions, because consistent rein- forcement induces a very strong preference for the reinforced response over possible alternatives. This schedule, however, also has serious disadvantages. One important problem is that continuous reinforcement is costly: In monetary terms, it costs whatever the value of the reinforcer is, but it also requires considerable time and effort of the person delivering the reinforcer to ensure that he or she is always present when the desired response occurs.

A second serious disadvantage of continuous reinforcement is the effect on responding during extinction. In most of the natural settings where we use reinforcement, there are likely to be many occasions on which a response occurs but we are not around to reinforce it. If responding has been established using continuous reinforcement, then as soon as reinforcement does not occur, the response will quickly extinguish. If the response has been established using partial reinforcement, however, it will be much more likely to persist long enough for you to have another chance to reinforce it. Where persistence in the face of nonreinforcement is important, therefore—and this is probably the case for most responses—an intermittent reinforcement schedule during train- ing is preferable to a continuous one. The greater the intermittency, moreover, the more persistent the behavior will be, so that the optimal strategy in most situations is to establish responding initially using continuous reinforcement but, once the behavior has been established, to gradually reduce the probability of reinforcement to the lowest level that will maintain a satisfactory response rate.

Given that you have decided on a partial reinforcement schedule, which one should you use? For most purposes, variable schedules are preferable to fixed ones, because the unpredictability of reinforcement generates much more consistent responding (and, incidentally, higher average rates). Our search for the "best" schedule, therefore, has narrowed to two candidates: VR and VI. Which one should you use?

The answer turns out to be a bit complicated. In one comparison of these schedules, Ferster and Skinner (1957) trained one pigeon to peck a key on a VR schedule. A second bird was tested at the same time, and whenever the first bird earned a reinforcement on the VR schedule, reinforcement was also made available to the second bird, who then had to peck its key only once to obtain it. Because the VR schedule for the first bird resulted in irregular intervals between the availability of reinforcement, the second bird was effectively on a VI schedule. Since the yoking procedure ensured that both birds received the same number of reinforcements, you might think that both would have re- sponded at roughly the same rate. In fact, the bird on the VR schedule re- sponded three times as often as the bird on the VI.

This result is surprising in some ways, but in other ways makes good intuitive sense. A VR schedule requires a high rate of responding to maximize reinforcement, whereas on a VI schedule a subject can respond at a low rate and still obtain almost as many reinforcements as if it responded furiously. It is not altogether surprising, therefore, that VR schedules generate higher response rates. (For a more technical analysis of the underlying mechanisms, see Peele, Casey, & Silberberg, 1984.) There is one circumstance, however, in which a VR schedule will generate *less* responding than an equivalent VI. We saw earlier that high ratio requirements sometimes produce ratio strain, with subjects eventually ceasing to respond. A VI schedule with comparably long intervals between reinforcement, however, can maintain a low but steady rate of responding indefinitely. If the ratio requirement is not excessive, then a VR schedule is the most effective way to generate high rates of responding. But if reinforcement is to be delivered only infrequently, then a VI schedule is more likely to sustain responding.

DRL and DRO Schedules

We have discussed only a few of the schedules of reinforcement that have been studied in the laboratory. Space considerations preclude coverage of all the others, but we will briefly mention two schedules that researchers encounter relatively frequently. (For a more thorough review, see Zeiler, 1977.) In a *differential reinforcement of low rate (DRL)* schedule, responses are reinforced only if they are separated by a minimum temporal interval. Suppose, for example, that a subject responds at the intervals shown in the following record:

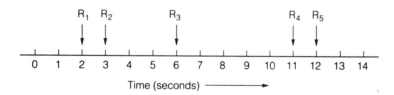

The time between successive responses is known as the *interresponse time*, or *IRT*, and is usually treated as a property of the terminal response; thus, a response may be said to have an IRT of one second, two seconds, and so on. In the record shown here, the second response (R_2) occurs one second after R_1 and thus has an IRT of one second; the third response (R_3) has an IRT of three seconds, and so forth. In a DRL schedule, a response is reinforced whenever its IRT exceeds the minimum value specified by the schedule. In a DRL two-second schedule, for example, a response would be reinforced only if it occurred at least two seconds after the response that preceded it. Using such a schedule in this example, R_3 and R_4 would be reinforced, but R_2 and R_5 would not. Because responses must be spaced a minimum distance apart in order to be reinforced, the DRL schedule encourages low rates of responding—hence its name.

If the goal is to eliminate responding rather than reduce it, a very useful alternative is a *differential reinforcement of other behavior* (DRO) schedule. In this schedule, reinforcement is contingent on a specified period's having elapsed without a single instance of the response in question. In a study by Lowitz and Suib (1978), for example, a DRO one-minute schedule was used to eliminate persistent thumbsucking in an eight-year-old girl. She was given a penny whenever 60 seconds passed without any instances of thumbsucking, and within five sessions the behavior had been eliminated entirely.

Concurrent Schedules

We have concentrated so far on the effects of reinforcement operating upon a single response in isolation. In real life, however, we rarely decide simply whether or not to make a particular response; instead, we choose a response from a number of possible alternatives, each with its own set of reinforcers. On a typical evening, for example, you might face the alternatives of going to the library to study, meeting your friends, or watching television. In situations such as this, in which you have to choose from among a variety of activities, each of which is reinforced, what determines your choice?

One way to study such choice behavior in the laboratory is by using a **concurrent schedule**. Subjects are provided with two responses they can make—two levers they can press, two buttons they can push—and each response is reinforced on an independent schedule. In a *conc* VI 30 VI 60 schedule, for example, a human subject might be reinforced for pushing one button on a VI 30-second schedule, while responses on the second button are reinforced on an independently run VI 60-second schedule.

Herrnstein (1961) has summarized the results of research using this paradigm in what he called the **matching law**. If you have several activities concurrently available to you, the matching law says that the percentage of your time that you allocate to one of those activities will match the percentage of your reinforcers that you obtain from participating in that activity.[*] Suppose, for example, that you were working on the *conc* VI 30 VI 60 schedule described previously. Initially, you would probably respond about equally on both buttons. Because of the way in which reinforcement is delivered on VI schedules, however, you would soon find yourself earning about twice as many reinforcers on the VI 30 button as on the VI 60 button. As a result, you would begin to shift your responding to the first button. Herrnstein's matching law predicts

---

[*] The matching law is normally stated in terms of rate of response rather than amount of time spent on an activity, but in most situations the two measures are equivalent (Baum & Rachlin, 1969).

that eventually you would end up responding exactly twice as often on the first button as on the second one. This prediction has been tested in a wide range of experiments, involving humans as well as rats and pigeons, and on the whole the results have strongly confirmed the matching law (Davison & McCarthy, 1988).

One nice illustration of the matching law comes from an experiment by Conger and Killeen (1974), in which groups of college students were asked to participate in a 30-minute discussion about drug abuse. The membership of the group was rigged so that the real subjects had confederates of the experimenter sitting on their left and right. As the conversation proceded, the confederates would occasionally reinforce the subject by praising his or her comments (for example, saying "That's a good point"). During the first 15 minutes of the experiment, 82 percent of the reinforcers that subjects received came from the confederate on their left; by the end of the 15 minutes, the subjects were spending 78 percent of their time conversing with that person. The reinforcement schedules were then changed, so that during the second 15-minute period subjects received only 38 percent of their reinforcements from the confederate on their left. By the end of the next 15-minute period, subjects were conversing with that same person only 29 percent of the time. In this case, the fit to the matching law was not exact, but considering how short the experimental period was, the precision with which subjects matched their behavior to the rate of reinforcement they were receiving was almost uncanny. We do seem to be exquisitely sensitive to the proportion of our reinforcers we receive from a given activity.

The predictions of the matching law are not always correct, but on the whole they are impressive. A separate, and heated, question is *why* subjects distribute their behavior in accordance with the matching law: What is the nature of the learning or decision mechanisms that underlie this behavior? This issue is beyond the scope of this text, but if you would like to learn more about some of the processes involved in choice and decision making, excellent reviews of various approaches to this problem are available in Rachlin, Logue, Gibbon, and Frankel (1986) and Payne and Bettman (1992).

A Criminally Successful Application

By now, your feelings about schedules may resemble those of the child whose review of a book about penguins began: "This book told me more about penguins than I wanted to know." Learning the technical distinctions among schedules is tedious and may appear pointless. As we suggested earlier, though, different schedules can have very different effects, and when used imaginatively, schedules can be a powerful tool for altering behavior.

In a striking demonstration of the importance of the schedule used, Kandel, Ayllon, and Roberts (1976) used reinforcement as part of a remedial high school education program in a Georgia state prison. The subjects were two inmates, one with a measured IQ of 65, the other with an IQ of 91. To reinforce studying, they were awarded points whenever they passed a test with a score of 80 percent or better, and these points could then be exchanged for a variety of reinforcers such as cigarettes, cookies, and extra visiting privileges. With 1000 points, for example, a convict could buy a radio as a present for his family.

The program produced significant progress, but not as much as the authors had hoped. One possible explanation was that the inmates simply were not bright enough to progress any faster. (With IQs of 65 and 91, it was perhaps remarkable that they had progressed as fast as they had.) Another possibility was that the reinforcement schedule did not provide sufficient incentive for the hard work required. To find out, the authors devised a new schedule in which the faster the inmates progressed, the more points they earned. If an inmate completed one grade level in a subject in 90 days, for example, he received 120 points; if he did it in only 4 days, he received 900 points; and if he did it in only 1 day he received 4700 points. The result was a quite staggering rate of progress. Under the old schedule, one of the convicts, Sanford, had completed ninth-grade English in three months—all things considered, not unimpressive. Under the new schedule, he completed tenth-, eleventh-, and part of twelfth-grade English in just one week. He often missed recreational periods and stayed up all night to work. As he remarked to one of the instructors, he wanted to "get when the gettin' was good." Over the five months of the program—standard reinforcement schedule as well as enriched—he advanced 4.6 years in high school arithmetic, 4.9 years in reading, and 6.6 years in language. In other words, he completed almost five years of high school in five months—roughly 12 times the normal rate. And Sanford was the one with an IQ of 65!

These results have at least two important implications. First, and most relevant to our current concern, they illustrate how powerfully the choice of reinforcement schedule can determine the effectiveness of reinforcement. More generally, they hint at how often we underestimate people's ability to learn and change. Knowing Sanford's criminal record and apparent IQ, few would have believed that he was capable of such progress. But under appropriate learning conditions, all of us—learning disabled as well as gifted, criminal as well as noncriminal—may be capable of far more learning than is commonly assumed. Too often, we blame failure on the learner: "Oh, he's too stupid." "She's just not trying." A much more productive reaction to failure may be to assume that our teaching methods are at fault and to search for better methods. We have now seen two examples in which a critical reexamination of teaching procedures led to dramatic improvements in learning—Phillip's change to immediate reinforcement at Achievement Place, and the Kandel group's imaginative use of a new reinforcement schedule—and we shall encounter others as we proceed. The department store motto notwithstanding, the customer is not *always* right; sometimes the student really is at fault. However, greater faith in human potential can sometimes pay handsome dividends.

6.5 MOTIVATION

Whether you respond to obtain a reinforcer depends not only on your knowing that the response will produce the reinforcer but also on your motivation to obtain it. Motivation, in turn, depends partly on deprivation and partly on the attractiveness of the reinforcer. How much you eat, for example, will depend not only on how hungry you are but also on how much you like the food. In this section we will examine how each of these factors influences the effectiveness of reinforcement, starting with deprivation.

Drive

The role of deprivation in reinforcement is nicely illustrated in an experiment by Clark (1958). In the first phase of Clark's study, rats were trained to press a bar to obtain food on a VI one-minute schedule. After all the rats had learned to bar-press, Clark arranged them into groups and deprived them of food for between 1 and 23 hours before running the next session. As shown in Figure 6.14, the longer the rats had been deprived, the faster they pressed the bar to obtain food. Studies have also shown that hungry rats will press the bar harder (Notterman & Mintz, 1965).

In addition to indicating the importance of deprivation in determining behavior, these results also suggest that we need to distinguish between learning and performance. The different response rates in the various groups could not have been due to differences in learning, because all the rats had had the identical training. The likelihood of the rats' performing this learned response, however, depended on how long they had been deprived of food. Performance thus depends on motivation as well as on learning.

Psychologists have proposed a number of theories about the mechanism through which motivation controls behavior. Hull (1943) proposed that deprivation induces an internal aversive state, which he called a *drive*, and that such drives increase the vigor of all behavior. There is some evidence that drives do have a general energizing effect. (For example, hunger or anxiety may make you generally restless or fidgety.) It has since become clear, though, that the main effect of a drive is to selectively increase behaviors likely to reduce the drive. (For a review, see Bolles, 1975.) If you are hungry, for example, you will be particularly likely to engage in behaviors that reduce hunger, such as going to the refrigerator or a nearby restaurant. As with the rats in the Clark study, the hungrier you are, the faster and more vigorously you are likely to carry out these responses.

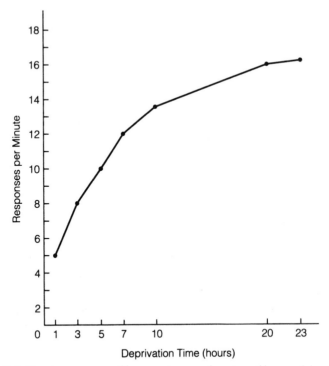

F I G U R E 6.14   Average rate of bar-pressing as a function of hours of deprivation. (Adapted from Clark, 1958)

In summary, performance depends on motivation as well as learning, and one determinant of motivation is deprivation level, or drive. Drives act to selectively increase responses that will reduce them, and they also increase the vigor with which these responses are performed.

Incentive

A second determinant of motivation is the attractiveness, or **incentive** value, of the reinforcer. Some reinforcers are more attractive to us, and we therefore work harder to obtain them. In one study illustrating this point, Crespi (1942) trained rats to run down a straight-alley maze to a goal box containing either 1, 16, or 256 pellets of food. The larger the amount of food presented, the more attractive the reinforcer should be as an incentive for running, and thus the faster the rats should have run down the alley to obtain it. As shown in the left-hand section of Figure 6.15, this was what Crespi found.

Learning or motivation?   Crespi's results demonstrate the importance of the amount of reinforcement as a determinant of performance, but they do not tell

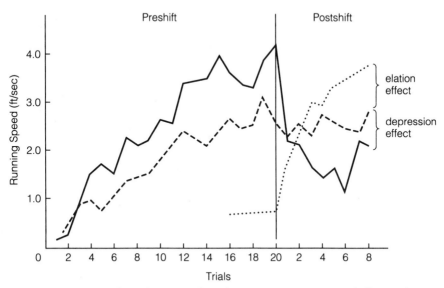

F I G U R E 6.15   Effect of amount of reinforcement on running speed. During the initial phase (left portion of the graph), groups received either 1, 16, or 256 pellets of food on each trial; all groups then received 16 pellets (shown on the right side of the graph). The group previously given 1 pellet ran faster than the group already accustomed to 16 pellets, resulting in an elation effect, or positive contrast. The group previously given 256 pellets ran slower than the group accustomed to 16 pellets, resulting in a depression effect, or negative contrast. (Adapted from Crespi, 1942)

us whether it affects learning or motivation. According to Thorndike, the effect is on learning. The Law of Effect states that satisfaction stamps in an association between the response and the situation in which it occurs, with greater satisfaction producing a stronger association. In the maze, greater amounts of food produce a stronger association between the cues of the maze and the response of running, so the cues more strongly elicit running.

Another possibility is that the amount of reinforcement affects motivation. According to the cognitive analysis of learning proposed by Tolman (1932), reinforcement leads to the formation of an expectation that food is available in the goal box. The rats then run to the goal box because they know that it contains food and are motivated to obtain it because they are hungry. According to Tolman's analysis, rats that find greater amounts of food in the goal box don't learn *better*, they learn *differently*; that is, they learn to expect a greater amount rather than a smaller amount, and it is this different expectation that motivates faster running.

According to Thorndike, then, larger reinforcers produce better learning of the response, whereas according to Tolman, they increase motivation. To find out which account was right, Crespi ran a second phase in which he gave all three groups 16 pellets of food. The right-hand section of Figure 6.15 shows the results of this second phase: The rats that shifted from 256 pellets to 16 pellets decreased their speed of running, whereas those that shifted from 1 pellet to 16 increased theirs.

The fact that running speed decreased in the group that shifted from 256 to 16 pellets has devastating implications for a learning interpretation. Although the amount of reinforcement was reduced, the rats in this group were nevertheless still receiving food in the goal box; according to the Law of Effect, associative strength should have continued to increase. Running speed, therefore, should either have increased or, if already at asymptote, have remained stable. The fact that it fell suggests that the primary effect of amount of reinforcement was on motivation rather than on learning. This does not necessarily imply that amount of reinforcement has no effect on learning. Indeed, most learning theorists would now probably agree that amount of reinforcement does affect learning, but that the effect is on what is learned rather than on how well it is learned. In the acquisition phase of the Crespi study, the rats in the 16- and 256-pellet groups may have learned equally quickly that there was food in the goal box; but whereas the rats in one group learned to expect 256 pellets, the rats in the other group learned to expect 16 pellets. Similarly, when amount of reinforcement was changed in the test phase, this would have affected learning about what was in the goal box. In the words of Logan and Wagner:

> If a rat's speed of running decreases over a series of trials after its reward has been reduced, it is unreasonable to conclude that the current trials have caused the animal to know less about the runway or about the appropriateness of running. Common sense says that the animal simply learned that he would receive a smaller reward as a consequence of the running.

(Logan & Wagner, 1965, p. 43)

In this study, then, the amount of reinforcement had some effect on learning, in the sense that the amount presented is itself one of the things a subject learns, but its main effect was on motivation. In assessing motivation, then, we need to take into account the attractiveness of the reinforcer (incentive) as well as the length of deprivation (drive). These two factors contribute independently to motivation, as shown by the fact that Crespi's rats were all deprived of food equally but nevertheless ran at different speeds depending on the amount of food available. To use a carrot-and-stick analogy, deprivation functions as a stick to drive us forward, and the reinforcer functions as a carrot to attract us; we need to take both into account in predicting how hard someone will work to obtain a reinforcer.

Contrast effects.   Crespi's results also have some important practical implications. Look again at Figure 6.15. You will see that the group that shifted from 1 to 16 pellets not only reached the level of those given 16 pellets throughout, but significantly exceeded it. Crespi called this overshoot an *elation effect*, implying that it was caused by the subject's euphoria at receiving more food than it had expected. Conversely, running speed in the 256/16 group not only fell to the level of the group trained throughout on 16 pellets but dropped significantly below it, a phenomenon Crespi labeled the *depression effect*.

The terms *elation* and *depression* imply emotional effects that should disappear as subjects become accustomed to the new levels of reinforcement. In some cases, however, the effects seem enduring. (For a review, see Flaherty, 1982.) Psychologists have thus come to prefer the more neutral terminology of **contrast effects** to describe these phenomena, emphasizing that the effect of any reinforcer depends on how it contrasts with reinforcers experienced previously. Crespi's elation effect is now called **positive contrast**, and the depression effect is called **negative contrast**.

The existence of contrast effects means that in choosing a reinforcer we need to take into account the reinforcers a subject has received in the past. If you own a car and a color television, the promise of a bicycle as a reward may not be very exciting, but if you grew up in poverty in Asia, it may seem priceless. A corollary of this principle is that, with extended exposure, large rewards may progressively lose their effectiveness. A heroin addict, for example, needs ever larger fixes to generate the same high. Similarly, a child accustomed to large rewards may need ever greater incentives to produce the same level of satisfaction. This may explain the age-old parental complaint, "Kids today just don't appreciate the value of money. Why, when *I* was a kid . . .." When standards of living improve, people become accustomed to the new levels; what was once a powerful reinforcer may now have little effect.

Learning and Motivation

In discussing amount of reinforcement, we suggested that its main effect was on motivation rather than on learning. The learned response in Crespi's study, however, was simply running down an alley; where more difficult tasks are involved, there is some evidence that motivation affects learning as well as performance. In an experiment by Broadhurst (1957), rats were trained on a visual discrimination in a Y-maze. The maze was flooded with water, but a platform located in one arm of the Y allowed the rats to escape. The position of the platform was shifted randomly over trials, but its current location was always signaled by the illumination of the arms; the brighter of the two arms always contained the platform. To determine the effects of motivation on learning, Broadhurst varied how long the rats were held underwater before being allowed to swim through the maze; the confinement period ranged from zero to eight seconds. In addition, he examined the role of problem difficulty by

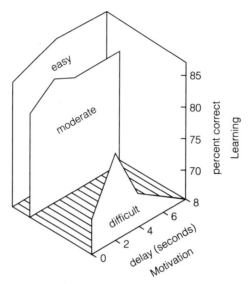

F I G U R E 6.16   Results of a visual discrimination experiment to determine the effects of motivation on learning. The percentage of correct responses on a discrimination learning task was affected by both motivation and problem difficulty. (Broadhurst, 1957)

varying the relative brightness of the alleys in different groups. For the easiest problem, the correct alley was 300 times brighter than the incorrect one, whereas for the most difficult problem the illumination ratio was only 15 to 1.

The results for the different groups are shown in Figure 6.16, which plots in three-dimensional form the percentage of correct responses over the first 100 trials as a function of both drive level and problem difficulty. In all three cases, drive level did influence the speed of learning, but the optimal level of motivation varied with the difficulty of the problem. On the easy problem, drive seemed to enhance learning uniformly: The longer that subjects were deprived of air, the fewer errors they made while learning. On the difficult problem, on the other hand, the fastest learning occurred with deprivations of only two seconds; increases in deprivation beyond this value resulted in a substantial decrease in learning.

Broadhurst's results suggest that motivation does affect learning rate, but that the relationship is a complex one. With relatively simple problems, increasing motivation enhances learning, but on more difficult problems high motivation may actually be harmful. This inverse relationship between task difficulty and optimum motivation—the more difficult the problem, the lower the optimum level of motivation—has been observed in a number of other studies (for example, Bregman & McAllister, 1982; Hochauser & Fowler, 1975). The phenomenon is known as the **Yerkes-Dodson law,** named for the two psychologists who first discovered it.

The reasons that high motivation interferes with the learning of difficult tasks are not fully understood, but one plausible explanation involves the effect of motivation on attention (Easterbrook, 1959). According to this hypothesis, attention becomes more highly focused when we are aroused; we concentrate more intensely on only a few stimuli while effectively ignoring all others. For simple problems, in which the relevant cues are obvious, focused attention is likely to facilitate learning. For problems in which the important cues are more subtle, however, a subject that focuses attention too narrowly may miss the critical cues and thus take much longer to solve the problem. (For experimental support, see Telegdy & Cohen, 1971; Geen, 1985.)

Suppose that you are a parent who wants to encourage your child to study. The Yerkes-Dodson law suggests that a larger reinforcer is likely to aid learning if the task is an easy one, but that it may impair performance if the task is difficult. This prediction was tested in an experiment by Suedfeld and Landon (1970), in which subjects were offered rewards ranging from nothing to $7.50 for the successful completion of a task. If the task was a relatively simple one (memorizing a list of names), then increasing the reward was beneficial up to a point; increases in the reward beyond this value impaired learning. If the task was more complex (suggesting as many uses as possible for an object shown in a line drawing), then any reward impaired performance, with larger rewards leading to progressively poorer performance. (See also J. T. Spence, 1970; McGraw & McCullers, 1979.)

Thus, although high motivation generally enhances learning and performance, it is important to recognize that this is not always the case. In particular, high motivation seems more likely to be disruptive when the task is a difficult one, though it must be said that our understanding of what constitutes a difficult task is still disappointingly primitive. In terms of subjective mental effort, for example, it is far from clear why memorizing a list of names is in any way easier than suggesting uses for an object. Our ability to predict in advance the situations in which large rewards will be counterproductive is thus still limited. All we can really say is that particular caution is advisable in cases where the task may be difficult. This state of affairs is far from satisfactory, and the relationship between the difficulty of a task and the optimum motivational level is clearly an area in which further research is needed.

6.6 STIMULUS CONTROL

We have assumed that whenever someone presents a reinforcer it strengthens whatever response preceded it. If you were given $100 every time you spent one hour studying, for example, it seems a safe bet that this would increase your studying time. This view of reinforcement, however, can be misleading, as revealed in the following, classic experiment by Guttman and Kalish (1956).

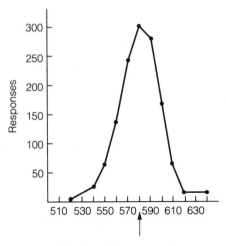

Wavelength (nanometers)

F I G U R E 6.17   Generalization of responding to colors of different wavelengths. The pigeons' pecking was reinforced during training only in the presence of the 580-nm stimulus (indicated by the arrow). (Adapted from Guttman & Kalish, 1956)

The Concept of Stimulus Control

Guttman and Kalish used pigeons as subjects in their experiment, first training them to peck at a circular plastic disk, or key. The key was mounted on one wall of a Skinner box, and pecking was reinforced on a VI schedule with food from a grain magazine located below the key. Each training session lasted 30 minutes, and the key was illuminated throughout with a yellowish-orange light of 580 nanometers (nm).[*]

To find out what the birds had learned, Guttman and Kalish then ran a test session in which the color of the key was varied. Sometimes it was green (550 nm), sometimes red (640 nm), and so on, with each light presented for 30 seconds at a time. The birds responded vigorously whenever the key was illuminated with the training stimulus (580 nm), but responding fell off sharply when the test wavelengths diverged from this value. In other groups, the color of the key during training was either 530, 550, or 600 nm. In each case, the pigeons responded best during the test phase to the color present during reinforcement. Figure 6.17 displays the data for the group trained with 580 nm. Contrary to our earlier response-strengthening hypothesis, reinforcement did not result in a general tendency to peck the key, but rather to peck the particular stimulus that had been present during reinforcement. Subsequent

---

[*] A nanometer is a measure of a light's wavelength, which determines its color.

experiments have extended this finding, showing that even seemingly irrelevant features of the training situation, such as the appearance of the walls or the texture of the floor, may also acquire control over responding. (See Balsam & Tomie, 1985.)

These results illustrate the phenomenon of **stimulus control**, in which the likelihood of a response varies according to the stimuli present at the time. The tendency to respond to the training stimulus may generalize to similar stimuli—a phenomenon known as **generalization**—and the progressive decline in responding as the test conditions diverge from those during training is known as a *generalization gradient*.

As Thorndike recognized, therefore, we need to remember that reinforcement does not strengthen a response universally, but rather increases its likelihood to the stimuli present when it is reinforced. This principle, however, needs one further qualification: Although responding may come under the control of some of the stimuli present during reinforcement, it may not be controlled by all of them. In a study by Jenkins and Harrison (1960), pigeons were trained to peck a key using a procedure almost identical to that in Guttman and Kalish's experiment. The stimulus present throughout training, however, was a 1000-Hz tone rather than a color. When Jenkins and Harrison varied the frequency of the tone during generalization testing, they found that it exerted no control over the response: The birds pecked at the same rate regardless of what tone was present.

This result was puzzling. Since the tone was present during reinforcement in exactly the same way as the light had been, why did the light come to control responding but not the tone? One obvious explanation is that birds do not hear tones, but this is not so. We will return to this question shortly, but for now we will simply note that only some of the stimuli present during reinforcement may acquire control over the response. We can thus reformulate the principle of reinforcement as follows: When a response is reinforced, some subset of the stimuli present may acquire control over it, so that the response will become more likely when these stimuli, or others similar to them, are present.

Encouraging Generalization

The fact that a reinforced response is most likely to occur in the situation in which it was reinforced has important practical implications. Suppose, for example, that a little girl admitted stealing a friend's toy and that her mother praised her for her honesty. The mother may have meant to encourage a general tendency to be honest, but the effect might be to increase honesty only when a toy is involved, or when the mother is present. (See Rincover & Koegel, 1975.) How, then, can we reduce stimulus control to ensure that a reinforced response will generalize widely across situations? The answer, in brief, is to provide training in a variety of settings. To encourage honesty, for example, we would need to reinforce it in different situations—in different places, with different people, and so forth.

At first, this requirement might seem discouraging; people encounter an almost infinite variety of situations in real life, and we could hardly reinforce behavior in all of them. Fortunately, it is not necessary to do so: As long as reinforcement is provided in more than one setting, the reinforced behavior will often generalize quite widely.

In a study by Stokes, Baer, and Jackson (1974), for example, retarded children in a state institution were trained to greet people by waving. The experimenter first prompted the desired response by demonstrating it and, if necessary, physically guiding the children's arms through the movement. This response was then reinforced by the experimenter's smiling, saying hello, and serving candies to the children. After the children had learned to greet the experimenter reliably with a wave, generalization of this response was measured by observing the percentage of occasions on which other members of staff were greeted with a wave.

Figure 6.18 presents the experimental results for a boy named Bruce. Before training was instituted, Bruce's operant level of greeting staff members was virtually zero. Following the training phase, there was an initial increase in this behavior, but then it fell rapidly. A second training phase was therefore instituted, but with a different staff member acting as the trainer. The result, as

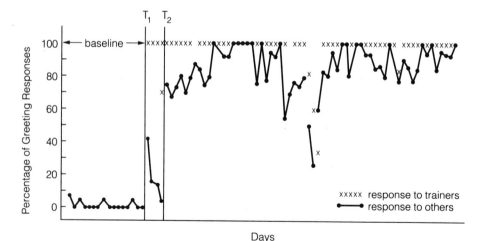

FIGURE 6.18   Generalization of greeting behavior. The percentage of social encounters in which Bruce greeted the other person is shown over successive days. Training was given by one experimenter at the point marked T_1 and then by a second experimenter at T_2. Greetings directed to the trainers and to others are plotted separately. (Adapted from Stokes, Baer, & Jackson, 1974)

shown in the last panel of the figure, was that greeting behavior now generalized widely, with Bruce greeting more than 20 members of staff whenever he encountered them, regardless of where in the hospital (or even in the city) the encounter took place. This behavior was maintained for more than six months, even though the only reinforcement was the natural one provided by having people return the greeting and smile. Thus, by having more than one trainer (as in this experiment) or by giving training in more than one setting, it is possible to increase substantially the likelihood that a desired response will generalize.

Encouraging Discrimination

Sometimes, the practical problem may be quite the opposite: Rather than wanting a response to generalize widely, we may want it to be confined to the training situation or, even more narrowly, to only one of the stimuli present during training—a phenomenon known as **discrimination**. Suppose, for example, that you praised a child who crossed the street when the light was green. You would not want the response to be controlled by all the stimuli present, so that the child would cross only when certain weather conditions were present or when the same car was parked nearby. You would want the child to learn to cross the street only when the light was green. To establish or sharpen control by just one element of the training situation, we can use **discrimination training**, in which behavior is reinforced in the presence of the desired stimulus (S+) but not in the presence of other stimuli (S−).

Let's go back now to the Jenkins and Harrison (1960) experiment on key-pecking in the presence of a tone, which was found to exert no control over the response. (See the S+ only gradient in Figure 6.19.) The experimenters then used discrimination training to establish the tone as a *discriminative stimulus*—a stimulus that signals availability of reinforcement, and thereby comes to control when responding occurs. They alternated 30-second periods in which the tone was on with periods in which it was off. Key-pecking was reinforced on a VI 20-second schedule when the tone (S+) was present, but not when it was absent (S−):

$$S+: R \longrightarrow food$$
$$S-: R \longrightarrow$$

The results for the subsequent generalization test are shown in Figure 6.19: Responding was greatest when the S+ was present, but it fell off sharply as the frequency of the test tone departed from 1000 Hz. By giving subjects discrimination training in which a response is reinforced only in the presence of a particular stimulus, therefore, we can train subjects to respond only in its presence.

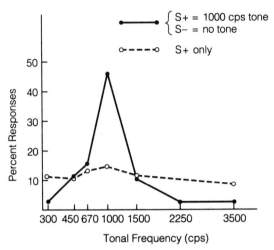

F I G U R E 6.19   Generalization gradients along a tone dimension. Following training with a single tone throughout, the generalization gradient is flat; following discrimination training, the gradient is steep. (Adapted from Jenkins & Harrison, 1960)

This finding provides a possible solution to the puzzle of why key color in the Guttman and Kalish experiment acquired control over pecking, whereas the tone in the Jenkins and Harrison experiment did not. When the birds pecked at the key, their behavior was reinforced; when they pecked at the surrounding wall, their behavior was not reinforced. The pigeons thus received implicit discrimination training in which responding was reinforced in the presence of the color but not in its absence. The color, therefore, would have acquired control over their pecking. In the Jenkins and Harrison experiment, on the other hand, the birds never had a chance to experience nonreinforcement in the absence of the tone; they couldn't, because the tone was always present. The tone thus failed to acquire stimulus control. (For supporting evidence, see Heinemann & Rudolph, 1963.)

Let us summarize these findings. Some subset of the stimuli present during reinforcement generally will acquire control over the response, so that the response will be particularly likely to occur when those stimuli are present. Such control can be enhanced by providing discrimination training, in which the response is reinforced only when a discriminative stimulus is present. Conversely, generalization of a response can be encouraged by reinforcing the response in a variety of contexts, with training in even two or three different settings sometimes being sufficient to ensure widespread generalization. (For more extensive discussion of the processes that underlie the development of stimulus control, see Chapter 12.)

6.7 A Preliminary Application

To illustrate how the principles we have been discussing can be applied in real life, we will look at a case reported by Wolf, Risley, and Mees (1964). The subject was a boy named Dicky. Until he was nine months old, Dicky's behavior was normal, but then he developed cataracts in both eyes, which in turn led to a series of aberrant behaviors. He had difficulty falling asleep, for example, and would cry unless his parents remained by his bedside until he was asleep. Similarly, in other situations in which he didn't get what he wanted, he would have violent tantrums in which he would bang his head, slap his face, and pull his hair. After one of these tantrums, his mother commented that "he was a mess, all black and blue and bleeding" (Wolf, Risley, & Mees, 1964, p. 305).

Dicky's Glasses

Dicky underwent an eye operation for his cataracts, and his parents were told that he had to wear corrective glasses if his vision was to recover. Despite strenuous efforts, however, they could not get Dicky to wear the glasses. When Dicky was three years old, he was diagnosed as schizophrenic and was admitted to a mental hospital for children. The staff there again tried to get Dicky to wear his glasses, but again without success. After six months of failure, Dicky's ophthalmologist warned that unless he began to wear his glasses within the next six months, he would lose his vision permanently.

At this point, the hospital staff sought the assistance of Wolf, Risley, and Mees. They decided to teach Dicky to wear the glasses using the principles of reinforcement that had been identified in experiments with animals. First, recognizing the importance of immediate reinforcement, they repeatedly paired the noise of a clicker with presentations of candy, so that the noise would become a secondary reinforcer that could then be presented the instant Dicky responded appropriately. Then, since the desired response was one that, to put it mildly, occurred infrequently, they decided to use the technique of shaping, which had originally been developed to train rats to press bars. A shaping program was planned in which Dicky would be reinforced—immediately with the clicker, followed as soon as possible by food—first, simply for picking up the glasses, then for holding them for progressively longer periods, then for moving them toward his head, and so on.

When the authors instituted this program, the result was almost total failure. Although Dicky would hold the glasses, he would not wear them properly on his head. If you had been one of the psychologists involved, what would you have done at this point? One reasonable response would have been to give up, on the grounds that Dicky was simply too psychotic to be treated. The authors, however, believed that reinforcement can work with any individual, no matter how disabled or disturbed; if reinforcement did not work, they believed, then the fault must lie in the way it was being used, rather than in the subject. Specifically, they speculated that the reason Dicky wasn't working to obtain the reinforcer may have been that the incentive value of the reinforcer was not great enough.

To obtain a more effective reinforcer, therefore, the experimenters made bites of meals contingent on appropriate behavior. Dicky still responded poorly at breakfast, and again at lunch. But a third session was given at 2:00 P.M., when Dicky was hungrier, and the shaping program then worked beautifully! Dicky was trained to put his glasses on, and then to wear them for longer and longer periods. His eyesight was saved, and over the years a similar training program was used to alter other aspects of his behavior. He learned to talk, to play with other children, and, eventually, to read and write. By the time he was 13, his measured IQ had increased from 50 to 110, and he was enrolled in a class for normal children (Nedelman & Sulzbacher, 1972).

The Importance of Gradual Change

The circumstances of Dicky's case are particularly dramatic, but shaping can be a powerful and useful tool in a wide range of more mundane situations. Consider, for example, the problem of teaching children to swim. You may have had the experience, at a swimming pool or beach, of watching a father trying to train his child to swim. At first, the father may cheerfully encourage the child: "Come on, there's no danger, Daddy will hold you." Then, as the child continues to resist, the father becomes increasingly impatient and the encouragements increasingly grim: "Don't be such a baby; come here right now!" The child ends up terrified, the parent in a rage.

A more fruitful approach in situations such as this, where a response is difficult to establish, is to shape it gradually. Professional programs for teaching swimming are modeled very closely on the principles we have been discussing. The key is to proceed gradually, asking children to advance at each stage only as much as they feel comfortable. At first, they may be asked to sit by the side of the pool, with only their legs in the water, then to practice kicking in the water while holding onto the side, then while holding onto a board, then with inflated water wings on their arms to support them. Finally, the air pressure in the wings may be reduced, until the child is swimming with no support. At each step, the advance is only a small one, and, with encouragement and social reinforcement, almost all children learn quickly.

The general principle underlying shaping is that when a task is difficult, begin with a simpler situation and move only gradually to the more complex one. This principle can be applied very widely. In the case of delayed reinforcement, for example, we have seen that delays of even a few seconds may prevent learning. If at first reinforcement is given immediately, however, and the delay then lengthened gradually, behavior may eventually be maintained despite delays of minutes or even hours. Similarly, in schedules of reinforcement, abruptly imposing a requirement of 500 responses for reinforcement may result in equally abrupt extinction of the response. If the requirement is introduced gradually, however—first requiring 1 response, then 2, 5, 10, and so on— behavior can be maintained even with quite substantial ratio requirements.

This principle of moving only gradually from the simple to the complex is also applicable to discrimination learning. When discrimination is very difficult—for example, when teaching a child with no musical experience to discriminate an oboe from a bassoon—learning may be much more rapid if we start with an easy discrimination and move gradually to the more difficult one. One application of this approach was reported by Sidman and Stoddard (1967), who wanted to teach a group of retarded boys to discriminate a circle from an ellipse. The experimenters used a screen divided into nine sections to present the stimuli. The center section was blank, one of the other sections contained a circle, and each of the other sections contained an ellipse. If the children pushed the section containing the circle, a chime sounded and they were given candy. If they made an error, they were asked to keep responding until they succeeded. This is known as a *correction procedure*. Once a correct response had been made, a new configuration was presented, with the position of the circle altered to ensure that the children attended to the shape of the circle rather than to its position in the configuration.

For one group, the same basic problem—one circle and seven ellipses— was presented on every trial. For a second group, a fading procedure was used in which the first problem presented was a very simple one: Only the section containing the circle was illuminated; all the other sections were black (Figure 6.20a). Once the children had learned to push the circle, the brightness of the other sections was gradually increased. In the next phase, the ellipses were introduced, but initially they were presented in faint outline. The outlines were then made progressively more distinct (Figure 6.20b), until finally training was being given on the same problem as the first group had received throughout.

For one group, then, all training was given on the problem that ultimately had to be mastered, whereas a second group started with a much simpler problem whose difficulty was increased only gradually. In the first group, only 1 of the 9 boys managed to solve the problem even after 180 attempts; in the fading group, however, 7 out of 10 succeeded, requiring an average of only 20 trials. This outcome does not imply that shaping or fading should always be used. If a problem is simple, obviously there is no need to start with a simpler one. When a problem is difficult, however, starting with a simpler problem can save both teacher and learner much time and aggravation.

In real life, this can be a difficult principle to hold onto. It is easy to become angry and blame the learner for being lazy or stupid. If reinforcement

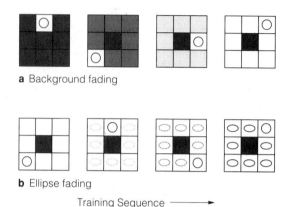

a Background fading

b Ellipse fading

Training Sequence ⟶

F I G U R E 6.20   Some of the steps used in Sidman and Stoddard's fading program: (a) The brightness of the background squares was gradually increased, thereby diminishing the difference between the correct stimulus (the circle) and the other alternatives. (b) The outline of the ellipses on the other squares was then gradually made more distinct. (Adapted from Sidman & Stoddard, 1967)

isn't working, however, it is worth considering carefully whether the principles we have reviewed in this chapter have been applied properly. The effectiveness of a reinforcer depends on the amount of reinforcement, the delay, and the schedule used; on the deprivation conditions and the stimuli present; and on the difficulty of the problem, which can sometimes be eased through shaping or fading. When these principles are applied properly, reinforcement can be a potent tool for changing behavior.

6.8 SUMMARY

The fact that children (and students, and college professors) so rarely do what we want them to do suggests that the principles of reinforcement may not be as obvious as they seem. Research suggests that one factor determining whether reinforcement will be effective is the reinforcer used; some events are more reinforcing that others. Premack suggested that the effectiveness of a reinforcer can be predicted by observing how much time subjects devote to this activity when it is freely available. In general, high-probability activities are very effective reinforcers. Because activities differ in their probability from moment to moment and from individual to individual, the Premack principle suggests a much more fluid and relativistic approach to identifying reinforcers than more traditional views.

In addition to primary reinforcers that require no training, learned or secondary reinforcers can also be very potent. Secondary reinforcers such as money acquire their reinforcing properties through pairing with primary reinforcers; in general, the principles involved are the same as those in classical conditioning.

An important determinant of the effectiveness of any reinforcer is how long it is delayed following a response. Studies with animals suggest that reinforcement of some kind—primary or secondary—must occur almost immediately if a response is to be strengthened, with delays of even a few seconds leading to a dramatic decrease in learning. In humans, the availability of language can help to bridge the gap symbolically between a response and a delayed reinforcer. Delay remains a crucial factor, however, and failure to deliver reinforcement quickly enough may be one of the most important reasons that reinforcement sometimes seems ineffective.

Another important determinant of a reinforcer's effectiveness is the schedule on which it is presented. Skinner experimented with a number of partial reinforcement schedules and found that each had somewhat different effects on the rate and pattern of responding. To generate a high rate of responding, continuous reinforcement is less effective than partial reinforcement—especially variable ratio and interval schedules, in which the reinforced response cannot easily be predicted. Another advantage of partial reinforcement schedules is that they encourage more persistent responding during periods when reinforcement is not available: When subjects are accustomed to being reinforced only occasionally during training, they are more likely to persist in the face of nonreinforcement during extinction.

In choice situations, where we have to choose among several activities each of which is reinforced, research has shown that the amount of time we allocate to any of these activities matches the proportion of the available reinforcers we have obtained by this activity. This matching law has proven useful in predicting behavior in a wide range of situations.

Whether subjects respond to obtain a reinforcer depends not only on learning, but also on motivation. Motivation, in turn, depends on how long the subject has been deprived of the reinforcer. Deprivation is assumed to generate an aversive internal drive, which then selectively energizes behavior to reduce it. Another determinant of motivation is the incentive value of the reinforcer, although incentive value depends in part on the subject's previous experience with other reinforcers. Although the main effect of motivation is on performance, motivation may also affect learning. The Yerkes-Dodson law says that the optimum level of motivation for learning depends on the difficulty of the task. For simple tasks, high motivation is helpful; on more difficult tasks, strong motivation can narrow attention in a way that interferes with learning. In general, then, using a powerful reinforcer is likely to enhance learning and performance. When a task is difficult, though, the use of large incentives can actually be counterproductive.

The effects of reinforcement also depend on the situation in which the reinforcer is given. Reinforcement does not result in a uniform increase in the probability of a response; rather, a subset of the stimuli present when a response is reinforced tends to acquire control over it, so that the response becomes more likely in the presence of these and similar stimuli. In situations in which it is desirable that a response occur widely, it is important that training occur in a variety of settings. Fortunately, the number of such settings need not be very great; in some cases, training in just two situations is sufficient to produce wide generalization. Conversely, when it is desirable that a response occur in only one situation, stimulus control can be enhanced by discrimination training in which the response is reinforced in that situation but not in others.

A final principle, and one that is too often ignored, involves introducing difficult tasks or contingencies gradually. When a response is difficult to learn, it may be possible to shape it by first reinforcing a simpler response, and only gradually requiring closer approximations to the target behavior. Similarly, if it is difficult to maintain behavior with a particular delay or schedule, the problem can sometimes be circumvented by starting with more powerful reinforcement contingencies—reinforcing every response immediately—and then gradually moving toward the more difficult contingencies.

When reinforcement is used in accordance with all of these principles, it can be substantially more powerful than our everyday experience might suggest. The examples discussed in this chapter include a schizophrenic child who wouldn't wear his glasses, an uneducated prison inmate with a measured IQ of 65, and teenage delinquents who would not do their homework. In all of these cases, months or even years of effort produced no change in behavior. The appropriate use of reinforcement, however, produced substantial changes in behavior almost immediately.

Selected Definitions

Shaping A technique for training responses that are initially unlikely to occur. The first step is to reinforce whatever aspect of an individual's behavior is closest to the desired response. As this behavior begins to occur more often, the trainer withholds reinforcement until some closer approximation to the desired response occurs, and so on.

Operant A response that can be modified by its consequences.

Reinforcer An event that increases the probability of a response when presented after it. A **primary reinforcer** is a reinforcer that requires no special training to be effective; a primary reinforcer will thus be effective for all members of a species from birth. A **secondary reinforcer** is a stimulus that acquires its reinforcing properties through experience. In most cases, secondary reinforcers are established by pairing a stimulus with a primary reinforcer.

Premack principle A basic law that states that the opportunity to perform a response can be used to reinforce any other response whose probability of occurrence is lower.

Response deprivation hypothesis This says that whether an activity will serve as a reinforcer depends on whether the current level of the activity is below its preferred level. Suppose, for example, that a subject is given free access to two responses, R_1 and R_2, and that the time spent in these activities during this baseline phase is measured. If the subject is then required to perform R_1 in order to gain access to R_2, then R_1 will increase only if the level of R_2 during this test phase would otherwise fall below its baseline level.

Reinforcement schedules Rules that determine when a response will be reinforced. In a **ratio schedule**, reinforcement depends on the number of responses that have been emitted. In an **interval schedule**, whether a response is reinforced depends on how much time has elapsed since the last reinforcement.

Partial reinforcement effect (PRE) The higher the proportion of responses that are not reinforced during training, the more persistent responding is during extinction.

Concurrent schedule Two schedules that are used to reinforce two responses that can be made at the same time; the reinforcement schedule for one response operates independently of the reinforcement schedule for the other response.

Matching law In essence, the matching law states that when you have a choice among several activities, the percentage of your time that you devote to one of these activities will match the percentage of the available reinforcers that you have gained from this activity. A more formal statement would be that if the rate at which two responses are performed is represented by $Resp_A$ and $Resp_B$, and the rate of reinforcement obtained by these two activities is represented by $Reinf_A$ and $Reinf_B$, then:

$$\frac{Resp_A}{Resp_A + Resp_B} = \frac{Reinf_A}{Reinf_A + Reinf_B}$$

Incentive The motivational properties of a reinforcer. The incentive value of a reinforcer is determined partly by its nature (ice cream, for example, is generally more desirable than cod liver oil) and partly by its quantity.

Contrast effect A change in a reinforcer's effectiveness due to prior experience with other reinforcers. An increase in a reinforcer's effectiveness due to previous experience with less valued reinforcers is called **positive contrast**; a decrease in a reinforcer's effectiveness due to previous experience with more valued reinforcers is called **negative contrast**.

Yerkes-Dodson law An inverse relationship between task difficulty and optimum motivation: the more difficult the problem, the lower the optimum motivation.

Stimulus control A phenomenon in which the likelihood of a response varies according to the stimuli present at the time. A response is under stimulus control if its probability of occurrence differs in the presence of different stimuli.

Generalization Responding to one stimulus due to training involving some other stimulus. In most cases, the amount of generalization depends on the similarity of the training and test stimuli.

Discrimination Differential responding to two stimuli. In **discrimination training**, differential responding to two stimuli is encouraged by presenting both stimuli but reinforcing responding only in the presence of one.

      Discrimination and generalization are two sides of the same coin, and both can be defined in terms of the generalization gradient obtained after training with one stimulus. Insofar as subjects respond to a test stimulus, this defines generalization; insofar as the generalized response is weaker than that to the training stimulus, this defines discrimination. Terrace (1966) has argued for the replacement of both terms by that of *stimulus control*. The steeper the overall shape of the generalization gradient, the more the response is under stimulus control.

Review Questions

1. Define the following terms: T-maze, Skinner box, magazine training, operant level, free-operant and discrete-trial procedures, sensory reinforcers, social reinforcers, spatial and visual discriminations, proprioceptive stimuli, cumulative record, partial reinforcement, FI scallop, ratio strain, IRT, drive, and generalization gradient.

2. How does the response deprivation hypothesis differ from the Premack principle?

3. How did Spence account for the discrepant results of early experiments on delayed reinforcement? How did Grice test Spence's explanation?

4. Why do even short delays of reinforcement have such devastating effects on learning in animals? Why are delays still sometimes harmful in humans, despite the availability of language to bridge the temporal gap between response and reinforcer?

5. Define the following schedules: CRF, FI, VI, FR, VR, DRL, DRO. What are the characteristic effects of these schedules on the rate and pattern of responding? If your goal were to produce persistent responding, which one of these schedules should you use?

6. Why does the Crespi experiment suggest that the amount of reinforcement influences motivation rather than learning? How can this result be reconciled with the result obtained by Suedfeld and Landon?

7. What does the Yerkes-Dodson law imply about the use of large incentives to encourage students to get good grades?

8. What can be done to increase or decrease stimulus control?

9. How can the principle of gradual change be applied to training a response, establishing a discrimination, and introducing delayed and intermittent reinforcement?

10. Every vertical mark on the "response" line in the record below represents a response. If response 1 has just been reinforced, what other responses will be reinforced if the schedule is:

   a. FI 60 seconds?
   b. VI 60 seconds, with the first two intervals being 30 and 60 seconds?
   c. FR 3?*

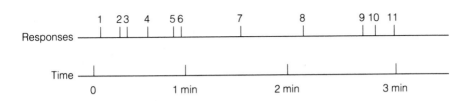

C H A P T E R   S E V E N

RESPONSE SUPPRESSION

Of several responses made to the same situation . . . those which are accompanied or closely followed by discomfort to the animal will, other things being equal, have their connection with the situation weakened, so that, when it recurs, they will be less likely to occur.

(Edward L. Thorndike, *Animal Intelligence*, 1911, p. 244)

We are gradually discovering—at an untold cost in human suffering—that in the long run punishment doesn't reduce the probability that an act will occur.

(B. F. Skinner, *Walden Two*, 1948b)

7.1 PUNISHMENT

Punishment is one of society's oldest techniques for controlling behavior, and also one of its most controversial. Does it really work? If we spank a child for disobeying an order or send an adult to prison for stealing, will the treatment really be effective? Or are we only building up a reservoir of hostility and bitterness that will lead to even more antisocial behavior in the future?

Methodological Issues

Punishment can be defined in learning theory terms as a reduction in the likelihood of a response due to the presentation of an aversive stimulus or, in the case of **negative punishment**, due to the removal of a reinforcing stimulus. Spanking a child is an example of punishment; taking away the child's allowance is an example of negative punishment. Neither punishment nor negative punishment should be confused with **negative reinforcement**, which is defined as an *increase* in the probability of a response due to the removal of an aversive stimulus. (The behavior of taking aspirin, for example, is negatively reinforced by the termination of pain.)

Observation versus experiment.   There has been no lack of debate over the effectiveness of punishment, but rarely can either side produce unequivocal evidence to support its position. This is perhaps not surprising. How, after all, can we evaluate the long-term effects of punishment? Let's use spanking as an example: It might seem easy enough to compare the behavior of children who are spanked with those who are not, but in practice such data are often difficult to interpret. In a study by Eron, Walder, Toigo, and Lefkowitz (1963), for example, parents of 451 schoolchildren were interviewed to find out what kinds of punishment they used in different situations. If their children were rude, for example, they were asked whether they would say, "Young men (ladies) don't do that sort of thing," or "Get on that chair and don't move until you apologize," or would spank the child until he or she cried. The researchers found that the harsher the punishment chosen by the parents, the more likely the children were to be aggressive at school. Punishing aggression, in other words, seemed to increase the frequency of this behavior rather than reduce it.

As we shall see later, there is some support for this conclusion, but this study nevertheless poses serious problems of interpretation. First of all, even though the parents said they would have used a certain form of punishment, this does not necessarily mean that they would actually have done so. And even if they did, we cannot be sure that it was their use of this punishment that made their children aggressive. Might not some other aspects of the parents' behavior—a lack of love or concern, for example—have produced both the punitiveness and the aggression? Or perhaps the causal relationship is reversed: Perhaps the children's persistent aggression and disobedience, produced by other causes, progressively forced the parents to use punishments of ever-increasing severity. The fact that punishment and aggression are correlated, in other words, does not necessarily mean that punishment has caused the aggression. Thus, although studies based on questionnaires or on more direct forms of observation may be an important source of hypotheses about causal relationships, it is difficult to reach unequivocal conclusions by observing behavior in a complex social environment.

Animals versus humans.   The obvious alternative is experimentation under the controlled conditions of the laboratory. In the case of punishment, though, this raises serious problems. For obvious reasons, psychologists are extremely reluctant to use severe punishment in studies that involve human subjects. If punishment is to be studied in the laboratory, therefore, we must either use very mild punishments, such as verbal rebukes, or else employ animals as our subjects.

Each of these alternatives has its drawbacks. It is certainly useful to know how a child will react to being told "No, that's wrong" by a stranger, but this may not be a reliable guide to the effects of being spanked by an enraged parent. So, what are the drawbacks to using animals as experimental subjects? As we have already seen, there are many similarities in the laws of learning across different species; by no stretch of the imagination, however, could a human being be described simply as a very large rat.

In trying to determine the effects of severe punishment, then, is it better to extrapolate from the effects of mild punishment in humans or severe punishment in animals? In practice, psychologists have resolved this dilemma by using both approaches; in the course of this chapter we will look at the results obtained with each, and at the extent to which they have contributed to a unified picture of the effects of punishment. We will begin by examining the effects of punishment on the punished response and consider whether punishment really produces long-term suppression of behavior. We will first look at the results of experiments using animals and then consider the extent to which the principles of punishment found in animals also apply to humans. Finally, we will consider the effects of punishment on other behavior; that is, even in situations in which punishment does suppress the punished response, might it have side effects that would make its use inadvisable?

Punishment in Animals

By studying punishment under controlled conditions, we have argued, it should be considerably easier to determine its effects. Even in the confines of the animal laboratory, however, these effects have proved controversial. The early evidence was largely negative, suggesting that punishment had little or no effect on behavior. Thus, although Thorndike had accorded punishment equal status with reinforcement in his first statement of the Law of Effect, his own research subsequently convinced him that punishment led to no permanent reduction in behavior. Similarly, B. F. Skinner (1938) was persuaded by the results of his research with rats that the effects of punishment were at best only temporary. In one of these experiments, a group of rats was first trained to press a bar in order to obtain food, then presentations of the food were discontinued. This is known as an **extinction** procedure; the typical result is a gradual decrease in responding, until subjects eventually stop responding altogether. To evaluate the effects of punishment, Skinner divided his subjects into two groups during the extinction phase, with subjects in one of the groups being punished every time they pressed the bar during the first 10 minutes of extinction. The punishment consisted of a slap on the rat's paw.

Figure 7.1 shows the cumulative number of responses made during extinction. Initially, the punishment contingency appeared highly effective; subjects stopped responding for as long as it was in effect. After the punishment period ended, however, they gradually began to respond again, until by the end of the second session they had emitted the same total number of responses during extinction as the control subjects who had never been punished. Punishment, in other words, seemed to suppress responding only temporarily, leading Skinner and others to conclude that it was an ineffective and undesirable technique for changing behavior.

This conclusion, however, was based on very little evidence. Because of their reluctance to inflict pain, most experimenters either avoided punishment altogether or chose relatively mild stimuli as their punishers. As we have mentioned, Skinner used a slap on the paw to punish his rats, and Thorndike's conclusions were based on experiments with humans using the word "wrong" as the aversive event. Only in the past few decades have experiments using more intense punishers been reported in any number, and the effect has been to reverse dramatically the earlier negative conclusions: At least insofar as the white rat is concerned, there is now compelling evidence that punishment can produce powerful and enduring suppression of behavior. Boe and Church (1967), for example, repeated Skinner's bar-pressing experiment but used electric shock as the punishing event rather than a slap on the paw. To evaluate the importance of punishment severity, they varied the intensity of the shock for different groups from 0 to 220 volts.

With mild intensities of shock, their results resembled Skinner's, as Figure 7.2 shows. The brief period of shock at the end of training produced little

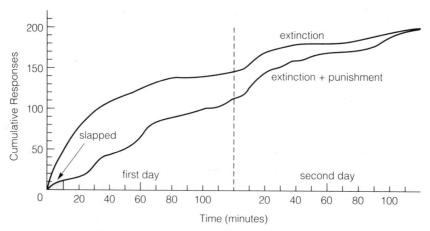

F I G U R E 7.1   The effect of punishment on responding during extinction. Bar-presses during the first 10 minutes of extinction were punished in the extinction + punishment group but not in the extinction group; the figure plots the cumulative number of responses during extinction. (Skinner, 1938)

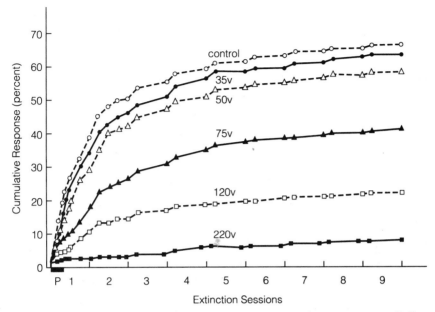

F I G U R E 7.2   The effect of shock intensity on responses during extinction. Different groups received shocks ranging in intensity from 0 volts (the control group) to 220 volts during a 15-minute period at the beginning of extinction, marked *P* on the x-axis. The measure of responding was the cumulative number of responses during extinction, expressed as a percentage of responding during the last session of training. In the 220-volt group, for example, the total number of responses during extinction was less than 10 percent of responses during the final session of reinforcement. (Boe & Church, 1967)

enduring reduction in the number of responses emitted during extinction. As the intensity of the shock was increased, however, the effect on subsequent responding became increasingly pronounced, until, in the 220-volt group, responding was not only suppressed during the punishment period but showed virtually no signs of recovery over nine subsequent sessions. If the punishment used is of sufficient severity, in other words, even a brief period of punishment may result in profound and enduring suppression of behavior.*

Intensity.   One important determinant of a punishment's effectiveness, then, is the intensity of the punisher used. This might at first seem to imply that when punishment is used, the intensity of the punishment should be as strong

---

* Although the shock used in this study was undoubtedly aversive, it was not as intense as you might think. The aversiveness of a shock depends on the amount of current passing through the body rather than the shock voltage; under the conditions of this study, the shocks were intense but not physically harmful.

as possible, but there are obvious objections to this conclusion: Punishment, after all, is painful, and it is clearly undesirable to inflict more pain than absolutely necessary. (As we shall see in the following section, intense punishment is objectionable on practical as well as ethical grounds.) On the other hand, if the punishment used is too mild, it may be ineffective, and the problem may not be remedied easily by then switching to a stronger punishment. In a study by Azrin, Holz, and Hake (1963), for example, pigeons were punished with electric shock for pecking a key that also produced food. When the intensity of the shock was set at 80 volts, responding was totally suppressed. When the voltage was initially set at 60 volts, however, it had little effect, and when its intensity was then increased in gradual steps, subjects continued to respond even when the voltage reached 300 volts. In other words, if punishment intensity is set at low levels initially and then increased only gradually, it may prove ineffective, presumably because subjects adapt to the gradually increasing intensity. The optimum level of punishment is thus the minimum level that is actually effective in suppressing the punished response, but choosing that level is a skill that perhaps can be acquired only through experience.

Delay.   A second important factor determining the effectiveness of punishment is the delay between the response and the punisher. In an experiment by Solomon, Turner, and Lessac (1968), dogs were offered a choice between two foods, one highly preferred and the other less so. The foods were presented in two dishes, located on either side of the experimenter's chair. If the dogs approached the dish that contained the less preferred food, they were allowed to eat freely; but if they began to eat the preferred food, the experimenter would hit them on the snout with a rolled-up newspaper. The delay interval between the moment when the dogs started eating and the time they were punished was either 0, 5, or 15 seconds for different groups.

Regardless of which delay was used, all the subjects learned quickly, requiring an average of only three or four punishments before avoiding the preferred food entirely. In order to determine the extent to which these punishments had resulted in an enduring change in behavior, the dogs were deprived of food and exposed to a daily series of 10-minute temptation trials. During these tests, the hungry dogs were returned to the room in which they had previously been trained, but with the experimenter now absent; one food dish contained 500 grams of the preferred food, and another dish contained only 20 grams of the nonpreferred food. The question was, how long would the hungry dogs be able to resist the temptation of eating the preferred food under these circumstances?

For the group that was punished with a 15-second delay during training, the answer was about three minutes. The dogs that had been punished after a delay of 5 seconds, however, resisted eating for eight days, whereas those that had been punished immediately went without eating for two weeks. A delay of only a few seconds in punishing a response, therefore, may have profound implications for the effectiveness of punishment—in this case, resisting eating for three minutes versus two weeks.

Schedule.   The effects of punishment also depend critically on the schedule used. In the Azrin, Holz, and Hake (1963) experiment referred to earlier, for example, pigeons were first trained to peck a key to obtain food; then shock was also made contingent on pecking, while the reinforcement contingency remained in effect. The schedule on which the shock was presented varied from FR 1 (every response punished) to FR 1000 (only one response in 1000 punished). Punishment of every response resulted in total suppression of pecking, but as the probability of punishment was reduced, responding was much less affected. As common sense would suggest, for punishment to be effective it should be delivered as immediately and consistently as possible.

Stimulus control.   Another important factor in determining the effectiveness of punishment is the similarity between the conditions during training and testing. If the dogs in Solomon's study had been tested in the training room with the experimenter still present, for example, it seems likely that they would have resisted eating even longer, whereas if they had been tested in a totally different room, without any experimenter and with different dishes, they would probably have given in to temptation far sooner.

Support for this prediction comes from an experiment by Honig and Slivka (1964), who looked at the effects of punishment on key-pecking in pigeons. During preliminary training, a plastic key was illuminated with one of seven alternating colors, varying in wavelength from 490 to 610 nanometers (nm), and pecking was reinforced in the presence of each. When the rate of pecking to each color was roughly equal, Honig and Slivka began to selectively punish responding in the presence of the 550-nm stimulus by presenting an electric shock whenever this color was pecked.

The results of this selective punishment are illustrated in Figure 7.3, which shows the rate of responding to each stimulus recorded over nine days of punishment training. Punishment of responding to the 550-nm stimulus was highly effective from the outset, because the birds almost immediately stopped responding whenever this color appeared on the key. The extent to which responding was suppressed in the presence of the other colors, however, depended on their similarity to the punished stimulus. Responding to the 530- and 570-nm stimuli, for example, was also strongly suppressed, but as the test stimuli became increasingly dissimilar to the punished stimulus, the amount of suppression decreased. Moreover, as training continued and the birds learned that punishment occurred only in the presence of the 550-nm wavelength, their rate of responding to the nonpunished wavelengths progressively increased. In other words, if punishment is delivered in one situation, its effects

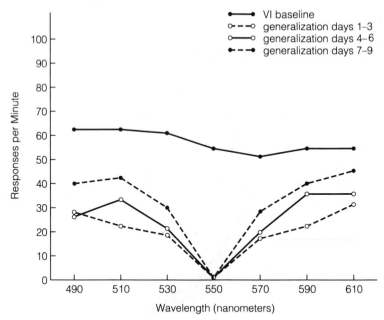

F I G U R E 7.3   Generalization of a punished response. During the baseline condition, key-pecking was reinforced in the presence of each of seven different colors. The remaining curves show the changes in responding to each of these colors following the introduction of punishment in the presence of the 550-nm stimulus. (Honig & Slivka, 1964)

may at first generalize, but if subjects repeatedly find that responding in other situations is safe, then responding may eventually be suppressed only in the setting in which it is actually punished.

One important implication of this finding is that if you want to eliminate a response entirely it may not be sufficient to punish it in only one situation. Suppose, for example, that you wanted to train young children not to play in the street. Ideally, an explanation of the dangers involved would be sufficient, but if this failed you might then find it necessary to punish the children every time you caught them playing in the street. If the children were punished only when you were nearby, however, they might very well learn a discrimination: If a parent is nearby, playing in the street is dangerous; if a parent is not nearby, then it's perfectly safe! To ensure that behavior is suppressed more generally, you would need to ensure that it was punished in different streets, by different adults, and, if possible, when no adult was present at all, so that the children would learn that playing in *any* street is dangerous, regardless of whether anyone appears to be watching.

The Honig and Slivka study, then, suggests some of the practical difficulties that may arise in trying to use punishment effectively in the natural environment. Like the Boe and Church experiment and the Solomon, Turner, and Lessac experiment, it also illustrates the potential power of this procedure: Only a small number of shocks was necessary to eliminate responding in the presence of the 550-nm wavelength, and once responding to this stimulus was reduced, it remained at very low levels for at least the nine days during which responding was measured.

Insofar as animal behavior is concerned, then, there can now be little doubt that punishment, used appropriately, can produce profound and enduring suppression of behavior. There are some fascinating exceptions to this rule—situations in which, far from reducing responding, punishment may paradoxically strengthen it (for example, Fowler & Wischner, 1969; Morse & Kelleher, 1977). In general, though, punishment does seem to be effective in suppressing behavior in animals.

Punishment in Humans

Similarities between animal and human reactions.   Are the effects of intense punishment on humans the same as those observed on animals? For obvious reasons, the data on this point are limited, but what evidence we do have suggests a number of similarities. In a clinical study reported by Bucher and Lovaas (1968), for example, electric shock was used to treat self-destructive behavior in autistic children. Autism is a psychiatric disorder in which children become totally isolated from their social environment, having neither verbal nor physical contact with other human beings. Typically, autistic children spend their day rocking back and forth and fondling themselves, sometimes engaging in bizarre and highly stereotyped gestures. One of the most horrifying manifestations of this syndrome is self-destructive behavior, in which children may repeatedly and viciously attack their own bodies. In the case of a seven-year-old boy named John, the resultant physical damage was so serious that he had to be hospitalized and kept in complete physical restraint 24 hours a day. "When removed from restraint he would immediately hit his head against the crib, beat his head with his fists, and scream. . . . He was so unmanageable that he had to be fed in full restraints; he would not take food otherwise. His head was covered with scar tissue, and his ears were swollen and bleeding" (Bucher & Lovaas, 1968, p. 86).

Because of the risk of permanent physical damage resulting from continued confinement, it was vital that some way be found to eliminate this behavior as quickly as possible. One technique that had previously been found to be effective consisted of ignoring the self-injurious behavior (thereby eliminating adult attention as a possible source of reinforcement) and simultaneously rewarding incompatible behaviors such as hand-clapping or singing songs. Because of the particular circumstances involved, however, this approach was not feasible, and Bucher and Lovaas decided instead to use punishment. This might at first seem to be a bizarre choice of treatment, since John's behavior suggested that, if anything, he enjoyed being hurt. Nevertheless, once a day John was taken to a special room where his restraints were removed, and he was given an immediate electric shock every time he hit himself. The results are shown in Figure 7.4, which plots the number of self-destructive responses observed during successive treatment sessions. During the first 15 baseline sessions, the experimenters did not administer punishment, and John hit himself an average of almost 250 times during each session. When punishment was introduced in session 16, however, this behavior disappeared almost immediately.

To determine the extent to which self-injurious behavior would be suppressed in other situations, different experimenters were present in the test room on different days. Only the first experimenter ever punished hitting, and whenever this experimenter was present, self-destructive behavior remained at very low levels. When the other experimenters were present, however, there was a perceptible increase in its frequency (though still far below baseline levels), and as testing continued it began to rise alarmingly. As with the pigeons in the Honig and Slivka experiment, John seemed to be learning that punishment occurred only in a particular situation, and, as a result, suppressed his self-destructive behavior only in that situation. During session 30, therefore, experimenter 3 was also instructed to use punishment whenever John hit himself, and thereafter there were no further recurrences of this behavior,

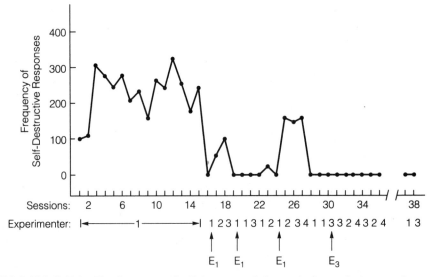

FIGURE 7.4   The frequency of self-destructive behavior before and after punishment. The experimenter present during each session is indicated; shock was administered by experimenter 1 (E_1) or experimenter 3 (E_3) during the sessions marked by an arrow. (Adapted from Bucher & Lovaas, 1968)

regardless of which experimenter was present in the room. Using a total of only 12 shocks, Bucher and Lovaas were able to completely eliminate a response that had occurred previously at a rate of several thousand times a day for more than five years. Similar results were obtained with the other children treated.

The role of language.   The work of Bucher and Lovaas suggests that the effects of punishment on humans may be very similar to the effects on animals. As we have argued previously, however, the fact that the principles of animal and human learning are sometimes similar does not necessarily mean that they are identical. In particular, it would be very strange indeed if the unique cognitive and linguistic capacities of humans did not play some role in determining their reactions to punishment.

This point is neatly illustrated in an experiment by Aronfreed (1968), who studied the effects of delayed punishment using a procedure very similar to that devised by Solomon. Instead of offering dogs a choice of food dishes, Aronfreed asked schoolchildren to choose one of two toys, and then to describe the chosen toy to the experimenter. One of the toys was highly attractive, the other much less so. If they selected the unattractive toy, the children were allowed to describe it, but if they chose the attractive toy the experimenter would punish them by saying "No" and taking away a candy from a pile they had been given previously. For some of the children, this punishment took place as soon as they began to reach for the attractive toy, but for others it was delayed for either 2, 6, or 12 seconds. This procedure was then repeated for each of 10 different pairs of toys, with choices of the attractive member of each pair always being punished.

As in Solomon's study, the delay of punishment had little apparent effect on initial learning; virtually all the children learned to avoid the attractive toy after only two or three punishments. Again as in Solomon's study, however, the effect of the delay interval proved more dramatic when behavior was measured in the experimenter's absence. During this testing phase, just as the experimenter finished laying out a new pair of toys, he would explain that he had suddenly remembered something he needed to do elsewhere and would leave the child alone with the toys for 10 minutes. Of those children who had been punished immediately during training, only half made any attempt to play with the attractive toy, and the majority of these children waited at least five minutes before doing so. Of the children whose punishment had been delayed for even six seconds during training, however, almost all transgressed during the temptation period, and most did so within less than a minute of the experimenter's departure. Thus, delays of even a few seconds seemed to reduce substantially the effectiveness of punishment.

Up to this point, the effects of punishment found by Aronfreed using children are almost uncannily similar to those found by Solomon using dogs. Some of the children in Aronfreed's delayed punishment condition, however, not only were punished when they picked up an attractive toy but also were given an explanation for why they should not do so. This toy was difficult to tell about, they were told, and was therefore only for older children. The children in this group were subsequently found to be significantly more likely to resist temptation than those not given an explanation. Similar findings have been reported from field studies in which parents have been interviewed to determine what sorts of punishment they used. In a study by Sears, Maccoby, and Levin (1957), for example, mothers who made extensive use of reasoning reported punishment to be far more effective than those who reported using punishment alone.

Why should the addition of just a few words of explanation make punishment so much more effective? One possibility is that an explanation may help to clarify what behavior is actually being punished. If a child were punished in the evening for something he did that morning, for example, in the absence of some explanation he would clearly have considerable difficulty connecting these events. The effectiveness of the explanation in Aronfreed's situation, however, may have involved a second factor: providing justification for the punishment. The children were not only being told which behavior to avoid (playing with the attractive toy), but why (because it was only appropriate for older children). If the explanation helped the children to perceive the punishment as fair, it may have reduced their resentment and thus increased their willingness to cooperate.

Evidence that both clarification and justification were important in Aronfreed's situation comes from a later study by Cheyne (1969). Using a similar situation, Cheyne punished one group of children by saying "That's bad" when they chose a certain toy. With a second group of children, he told them explicitly which response was forbidden: "That's bad, you shouldn't play with that toy." As expected, the clarification group deviated significantly less in a later temptation situation, suggesting that the effectiveness of delayed punishment does depend on how clearly the punished response is identified. The least deviation of all, however, occurred in a third group of children, who were told not only which response was forbidden but why: "That toy belongs to someone else." If a punishment is perceived as fair or reasonable, in other words, it may be considerably more effective.

A Theoretical Analysis

One question of interest to psychologists has been why punishment suppresses behavior. There is evidence that the effects of punishment depend on emotion as well as on reason. In Aronfreed's study, for example, we saw that a delayed punishment was significantly more effective when accompanied by an explanation. Even when an explanation was provided, however, the delayed punishment still was not as effective as an immediate one. One possible interpretation of this result is that suppression of a response depends not just on knowledge of the consequences—"If I touch this toy, I will be punished"—but also on the amount of fear elicited.

If a child has a hand slapped just as he or she reaches into a cookie jar, the contiguity between these events may result in conditioning of fear to the proprioceptive cues produced by the reaching response. The next time the child approaches the jar, therefore, this response will elicit fear, and this fear may then inhibit the response. (For a more detailed analysis, see the section on avoidance in Chapter 9.) If there is a delay between the response and punishment, however, less fear will be conditioned. Thus, even though the child may still know that he or she will be punished for responding, there will be less fear present to prevent the child from doing so.

As children grow older and their cognitive capacities increase, there may be a shift in the balance between cognitive and emotional factors, with cognition becoming progressively more important. In the Cheyne study cited earlier, children were told not to play with a certain toy because "That toy belongs to someone else." This added instruction increased obedience in third-grade children, but it had no effect on those in kindergarten. In other words, as children grow older, their behavior seems to come increasingly under the control of generalized moral codes or rules. Thus, although physical punishment may sometimes be necessary to establish these rules with younger children, it may be increasingly possible to rely on verbal appeals to these ethical codes, rather than on the direct elicitation of fear, as the children grow older.

We have not been able to cover fully even those variables whose importance is now recognized, and there is much about punishment that we do not yet understand. (More detailed coverage is available in Walters & Grusec, 1977, and Axelrod & Apsche, 1983.) On the basis of current evidence, however, punishment seems to be most effective when it is immediate, firm, consistent, delivered in a variety of settings, and accompanied by a clear (and fair) explanation. Used under these conditions, there seems little doubt that punishment can be a powerful and effective technique for suppressing behavior.

7.2 SIDE EFFECTS OF PUNISHMENT

Insofar as we confine our attention to the effects of punishment on the response being punished, the evidence reviewed in the preceding section points unequivocally to the effectiveness of punishment. But does this necessarily mean that we should use it? In addition to suppressing the response being punished, punishment might produce damaging side effects so that, on balance, punishment might do more harm than good.

A Traumatic Example of Punishment

An experiment by Masserman and Pechtel (1953) suggests that the possibility of side effects needs to be taken seriously. Masserman and Pechtel used rhesus and spider monkeys as subjects. In the first phase of the experiment, the monkeys were trained to press a switch to obtain food. Once this response had been learned, the experimenters began to punish the monkeys as soon as they reached into a food pod to obtain the reinforcer they had earned. Specifically, just as the monkey's hand entered the food pod, the experimenters would insert a toy snake into the pod though a curtain on the other side. On the surface, this punishment may sound innocuous; but to a monkey reared in the wild, the sight of a snake is often terrifying. As soon as the subjects in this experiment saw the snake, they jumped up and ran screaming to the opposite end of the enclosure, where they would then crouch in terror, trembling and defecating. After only two to five punishments, they completely stopped approaching the food pod and refused to eat even when given free food in other areas of the test cage.

In a sense, then, punishment in this situation might be said to have been highly effective, because it led to the immediate and total suppression of the punished response. It also resulted, however, in some unanticipated side effects. First of all, the effects of the punishment generalized far beyond the test cage in which it was actually administered. Thus, even though eating was punished only in the test cage, eating patterns elsewhere in the laboratory were also profoundly disturbed, as subjects either avoided food altogether, even refusing to go near it, or else frantically crammed any material at hand into their mouths, stuffing their cheeks with straw, or gulping entire bananas at a single swallow. The net result was that, despite specially enriched diets, their body weights soon fell by 15–25 percent.

The effects of being punished, moreover, extended far beyond the monkey's eating. Sexual behavior, for example, was also profoundly disturbed:

> The neurotic male monkeys showed almost complete cessation of heterosexual interest; whereas the females initiated homosexual behavior that persisted even during nonestrual periods. . . . Auto-eroticism became so extreme in one male vervet monkey that, in a period of over ten months, he devoted a major portion of [his day] to fondling his penis and swallowing semen sucked from its glans.
>
> (Masserman & Pechtel, 1953, p. 261)

Similar disturbances were observed in other social relationships, as the monkeys who had been punished became submissive to even the smallest and weakest members of the colony who had not been treated. Many also began to develop classic neurotic symptoms. Almost all, for example, developed respiratory disturbances, including severe asthmatic attacks that would last for hours at a time, and many also developed facial and muscular tics. In addition, two vervet monkeys showed clear signs of hallucination, picking up and chewing nonexistent food particles while simultaneously ignoring real food placed before them. As the neuroses progressed, each subject seemed to withdraw further and further into its own private world:

> *Thus, the Rhesus and Spiders would sit for hours with head down or stare at the wall behind the apparatus, moving only slightly in response even to major stimuli such as turning on flood lights or starting the motion picture camera. . . . This reached an extreme in the two Spiders which, for a period of five months, assumed a cataleptoid immobility so pronounced that every morning—the time of their original experiential traumata—the animals were almost completely indifferent to all stimuli and could be scooped up unprotesting on the blade of a shovel.*

(Masserman & Pechtel, 1953, pp. 260–261)

Clearly, the effects of punishment are not always this devastating: Millions of children have been spanked by their parents without becoming permanently neurotic. Nevertheless, these results do warn us in dramatic fashion that severe punishment can have consequences extending far beyond the response nominally being punished. And, although effects of this magnitude may appear only when punishments of exceptional severity are used, there is reason to think that even much milder forms of punishment may sometimes have harmful consequences.

Fear

The problem is that aversive stimuli may have a variety of effects. One such effect may be to suppress the preceding response, but another is to elicit emotions such as fear and anxiety, and these emotions may then be classically conditioned to the stimuli that accompany the punishment. Suppose, for example, that a young student was publicly criticized by his or her teacher for poor performance. For some children, such criticism might act as a spur to greater effort, but for others the consequences might be less benign. If schoolwork were repeatedly associated with failure and punishment, studying might eventually become a source of fear rather than pleasure, so that the child would begin to avoid studying (and school) whenever possible. In one experimental analogue of this situation, J. A. Martin (1977) gave six-year-old boys a series of tasks to perform. On some tasks, the boys were praised when they worked; on others, they were reprimanded when they did not work; on a third set of tasks, they were ignored regardless of their behavior. The boys spent more time working on the tasks for which inattention produced reprimands. However, when they were given an opportunity to perform the tasks when the experimenter was not present, they never chose the tasks that had been associated with reprimands.

Even in cases in which children do work harder when they are punished, the punishment of mistakes can lead to a deterioration in performance rather than an improvement. In our discussion of the Yerkes-Dodson law, we noted that increases in motivation may result in a narrowing of attention, so that on complex tasks highly motivated subjects may actually do worse (for example, Zaffy & Bruning, 1966). If children are punished for doing poorly, therefore, in their anxiety to improve they may actually do worse, at least on complex tasks that require careful attention.

Interfering with attention.   Evidence for the occurrence of such effects is still largely anecdotal, but some experimental support comes from a study by Cheyne, Goyeche, and Walters (1969). Using a situation similar to that developed by Aronfreed, they asked children to select one of two toys. If the children selected the wrong toy, a buzzer was sounded; the intensity of the buzzer was 0, 88, or 104 decibels (db) for different groups of children. In addition, half the children were then given a verbal explanation of what they had done wrong. To measure the effectiveness of the punishment, the experimenters observed how much time the children spent playing with the forbidden toy during a subsequent temptation test. If no explanation was given, more intense punishment produced greater obedience (Figure 7.5). For children who received an explanation, however, the 104-db buzzer produced less obedience than the weaker buzzer.

On the surface, this result is bizarre: Why should an intense punishment be less effective than a mild one? If fear leads to a narrowing of attention, however, then the anxiety aroused by the 104-db buzzer might have interfered with the children's ability to listen to the explanation that followed. Supporting evidence for this interpretation comes from comparing the behavior of the children who received an explanation with the behavior of those who did not. Adding an explanation increased obedience for children in the 0- and 88-db groups but had no perceptible effect on children who received the 104-db buzzer. The children in this group, in other words, behaved exactly as if they had not heard what the experimenter was saying.

A vicious circle.   Thus, although more intense punishments may be more effective on the whole, in at least some situations the fear they elicit is counterproductive. In particular, we need to be especially careful about the use of punishment in school, where one of the primary goals is to encourage the learning of complex cognitive skills. If a child is punished for doing poorly in school (as opposed to misbehaving), the resultant anxiety may make him or her even more likely to fail the next time; if the teacher then becomes even angrier ("You're not trying!"), the child becomes even more anxious, hence more

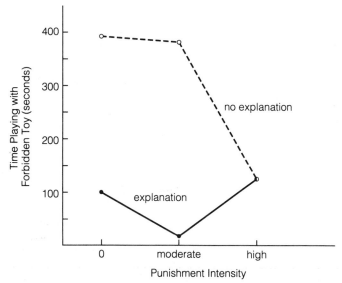

F I G U R E 7.5   The effect of punishment intensity and explanations on a child's obedience to instructions. Intense punishment produced greater obedience than moderate punishment in children not given an explanation, but intense punishment was less effective for children who did receive an explanation. (Based on data from Cheyne, Goyeche, & Walters, 1969)

likely to fail, and so on in a vicious circle. Eventually, if the child fails often enough, she or he may learn to not even try, even though the child may have the ability to do well if she or he were to try (Dweck & Licht, 1980; see also the discussion of learned helplessness in Chapter 13).

It is important to emphasize that effects of this kind are by no means inevitable. Children differ widely in their reactions to anxiety: For some, a particular punishment may be incapacitating; for others, the same punishment may be an incentive to greater effort. The available evidence, however, suggests that the possibility of harmful side effects is one that needs to be taken seriously.

Aggression

Pain-elicited aggression.   Another possible consequence of presenting an aversive stimulus is that it may elicit aggression. This effect is known as *pain-elicited aggression*. In a study by Ulrich and Azrin (1962), pairs of rats from the same litter were placed in a test cage and given electric shocks through the floor of the cage. The authors reported that the rats responded to the shocks by rearing up on their hind legs and beginning to push each other. If the shocks were very intense, and continued long enough, the rats would begin to bite each other.

In subsequent experiments, Ulrich and his colleagues reported similar results with virtually every species tested, including species as diverse as cats, raccoons, monkeys, and alligators. In other words, it appeared as if the tendency to attack when hurt is one of the most powerful and universal of all animal instincts.

Subsequent research has challenged some aspects of Ulrich's findings, particularly in the case of the rat. Blanchard, Blanchard, and Takahashi (1977) presented evidence that much of the rats' observed behavior was actually defensive rather than aggressive—rearing is part of rats' defensive behavior, to protect themselves against attacks on more vulnerable areas of their body. At present, therefore, it is not clear whether aggression in the form of physical attack should be regarded as a common behavior, or as one that occurs only in fairly extreme circumstances. Some research on humans, however, suggests that we too may have at least some tendency to become aggressive when we are hurt. In one experiment by Berkowitz, Cochrane, and Embree (1979), university women were asked to act as teachers and either reinforce or punish a partner who was engaged in a learning task. Some of the "teachers" had one of their hands in a tank of cold water; others had one of their hands in a tank of warm water. Women whose hands were in cold water were significantly more likely to be punitive toward their partners than women whose hands were in warm water.

Modeled aggression.   There is also evidence that the use of punishment may serve as a model for aggressive behavior. Children, after all, are highly imitative, particularly when the model is important or influential in their lives (Flanders, 1968). If a parent frequently uses physical force to control a child, therefore, it seems not unlikely that the child might learn to imitate this behavior. In an early study on imitation by Bandura, Ross, and Ross (1963), nursery school children were exposed to an adult model who punched and kicked a large inflated doll. When the children were later left alone with the doll, they proved significantly more likely to attack the doll than were children in control groups who had not seen the model do so.

You might argue that the measure of aggression used was highly artificial: Does the fact that a child is more likely to attack a doll really tell us anything about the likelihood that the child will punch a friend? A field study by Leyens, Camino, Parke, and Berkowitz (1975) suggests that this phenomenon may be disturbingly general. In their study, adolescents at a Belgian residential center for juvenile delinquents were exposed for two weeks to one of two sets of recreational films; one set emphasized physical violence, including films such as *Bonnie and Clyde* and *The Dirty Dozen*. To determine the effect of these films, the experimenters recorded the frequency of aggressive behavior during morning and evening play periods. (*Aggression* was defined as "physical contact of sufficient intensity to potentially inflict pain on the victim" and included hitting, slapping, choking, and kicking.) The result was that the adolescents exposed to the violent films became significantly more likely to attack one another, with the frequency of such attacks almost tripling from the first to the second week of the treatment period. Adolescents exposed to the nonviolent films, on the other hand, showed a significant decrease in aggression over the same period.

If exposure to violence on film could have such a substantial effect after just one or two weeks, it seems at least possible that repeated exposure to violence from a model as influential as a parent might play a major role in determining a child's aggressiveness. In accordance with this prediction, children who are severely punished by their parents have been found to be far more likely to be physically aggressive toward their peers (Eron et al., 1963) and to have a much greater chance of becoming juvenile delinquents (Glueck & Glueck, 1950). As discussed earlier, we must exercise considerable caution in interpreting correlational data of this kind, but the evidence from pain-elicited aggression studies in animals and correlational studies in humans is consistent in pointing to a strong link between punishment and aggression.

Evaluating Punishment

There is considerable evidence, then, that punishment may play a powerful role in eliciting fear and aggression. Again, this does not mean that every child who is spanked will become a frightened neurotic or a sadistic criminal. Children differ widely in their reactions to punishment, and the likelihood of side effects may depend on factors such as the severity of the punishment, the nature of the punished response, and the social context in which the punishment is embedded. In studies in which severe electric shock has been used to alter autistic behavior, no apparent harm has been observed (Risley, 1968), and others have reported beneficial side effects (Lovaas, Schaeffer, & Simmons, 1965). Nevertheless, the evidence reviewed in this section suggests that the risk of harmful side effects is a real one and needs to be taken seriously. (See Figure 7.6.)

Overall, then, the literature on punishment would seem to support two diametrically opposed conclusions: that punishment *should* be used, because it can be highly effective in suppressing undesirable behavior, and that it *should not* be used, because it can produce side effects that are highly undesirable. What should we conclude from this confusing situation?

In some situations, there may be no practical alternative to the use of physical or strong verbal punishment. If a young child is playing with matches, for example, the only way to ensure that he or she immediately stops doing so may be through the use of physical punishment. As a child grows older,

F I G U R E 7.6   The problems of punishment. (Drawing by Ziegler; © 1991. The New Yorker Magazine, Inc.)

however, and more amenable to techniques based on reasoning, it should be possible to place increasing emphasis on verbal disapproval rather than on physical force. Insofar as physical punishment continues to be necessary, the wisest course would seem to be to use the minimum force necessary for the punishment to be effective.

In many situations, however, it may be possible to avoid the use of punishment. In particular, rather than trying to punish children when they are bad, it may be preferable to reinforce behavior when they are good. A study by Madsen, Becker, Thomas, Koser, and Plager (1970) compared the effectiveness of reinforcement and punishment in getting first-grade children to stay in their seats. In the first phase of the study, observers in the classroom recorded how often the children got out of their seats at times when they shouldn't over a six-day period. The teachers were then asked to punish the children for standing by ordering the children to sit down whenever they got up. As you might expect, the immediate effect of this command was for the children to sit down, so that from the teacher's point of view the command might have appeared highly effective. When the frequency of inappropriate standing was measured over the course of the entire day, however, the introduction of punishment was found to produce an overall *increase* in standing. (See Figure

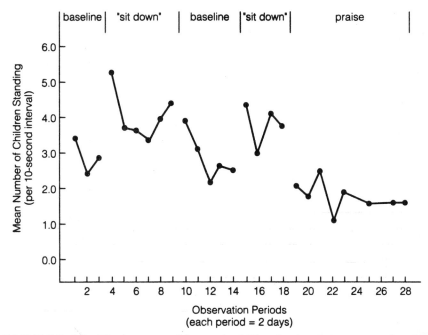

F I G U R E 7.7. The frequency of first-grade children leaving their seats as a function of the teacher's reaction. (Adapted from Madsen, Becker, Thomas, Koser, & Plager, 1970)

7.7.) The fact that the teacher paid attention to the children when they stood up, in other words, seemed to be more reinforcing for them than the teacher's disapproval was punishing. After repeating the baseline and punishment phases to establish the reliability of this result, Madsen and associates then asked the teacher to stop punishing standing and instead to reinforce incompatible behavior: They asked the teacher to praise the children or smile at them whenever they were sitting down and working. As Figure 7.7 shows, this proved highly effective: For the first time, the frequency of standing fell significantly below its baseline level.

The use of reinforcement in this way may require considerable effort and imagination. It is far easier to yell at children when they are being bad than to think, "I wonder how I could reinforce good behavior instead?" In addition, such reinforcement may not always be effective. The available evidence, however, suggests that the effort involved may be well worthwhile: Not only may reinforcement be more effective than punishment in eliminating the target behavior, but it also may do so at much less cost to the child's long-term social and emotional development.

7.3 EXTINCTION

One reason that children persist in certain forms of undesirable behavior is that they are strongly reinforced for doing so. Stealing, for example, may be reinforced not only by the obvious material benefits it brings but also by the respect and admiration it elicits from peers. In trying to eliminate such behavior, therefore, one possible alternative to punishment is simply to withhold the reinforcers that have been maintaining the behavior. In the case of stealing, this could be very difficult: How do you ensure that stealing will never be successful, or that a child's friends will never admire it? In situations in which the sources of reinforcement can be controlled, however, this technique can be surprisingly powerful.

A Practical Application of Extinction

In one case reported by C. D. Williams (1959), the subject was a two-year-old boy who had been seriously ill for the first year and a half of his life. Even after he recovered physically, however, he continued to demand special attention and throw tantrums whenever he did not get his way. On going to bed, for example, he insisted that both his parents stay with him until he was asleep, and if either of them left the room—or even tried to read—he would cry bitterly until they returned to the room and resumed giving him attention. Since falling asleep typically required from 30 minutes to two hours, his demands became a considerable strain on his parents, and they consulted Williams for advice.

One analysis of the boy's behavior might have been that he had suffered severe psychological trauma as a result of his earlier illness, and now needed all the love and attention he could get. Williams, however, felt that he had simply become used to receiving attention during his illness, and that his tantrum behavior was now being maintained by the attention it produced. To eliminate this behavior, therefore, Williams recommended that the parents simply ignore any crying that took place after they put the child to bed. On the first night, the child screamed and raged for 45 minutes before finally falling asleep (Figure 7.8, solid line). The parents did not go in, however, and on the following night he didn't cry at all. Crying reappeared briefly on a few subsequent nights, but within a week it had disappeared completely.

One week later, the boy's aunt baby-sat for him so his parents could have a night out. When she put him to sleep, he again began to cry, and she went in to him. As shown in Figure 7.8 (broken line), this single reinforcement was enough to trigger another massive burst of crying on the following night, but the parents again refused to go in, and within a week the crying had disappeared again, this time permanently. Simply by ignoring his tantrums, therefore, his parents were able to eliminate this behavior within a matter of days,

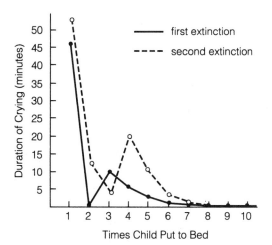

F I G U R E 7.8   Extinction of a child's tantrum behavior. (C. D. Williams, 1959)

and follow-up observations two years later suggested that he had become a friendly and outgoing child, with no sign of any harmful aftereffects.

Extinction as Punishment

Extinction, or nonreinforcement of a previously reinforced response, obviously works. But it has long posed a theoretical puzzle: Nonreinforcement simply means that a response is followed by nothing, and why should nothing weaken a previously well-learned response? As in the case of punishment, one possible explanation could be couched in terms of rational decision making: Once subjects learn that responding no longer produces a reinforcer, they rationally decide to stop responding, because the reinforcer had been their only motive for responding. If we watch an angry monkey screeching at a bar that has suddenly stopped producing food, however, or a man kicking a vending machine in which he has just lost 50 cents, their behavior doesn't look as if it is guided by rational calculations of the optimal strategy, but by frustration and anger. Whatever rational processes may be involved in extinction, in other words, there appears to be a strong emotional component that also needs to be considered.

Indeed, it is possible to explain the effects of extinction entirely in terms of emotion. In Chapter 6, we saw that the effectiveness of a reinforcer depends to some extent on a subject's prior experience with other reinforcers. In Crespi's experiment on rats running down an alley, for example, exposing a rat to 256 food pellets substantially reduced the incentive value of smaller amounts, such as 16 pellets.

Suppose, now, that we also regard nonreward as an event, with an incen-

F I G U R E 7.9   An incentive scale, plotting negative, positive, and neutral events on a continuum. This scale is for a hypothetical experiment using rats as subjects.

tive value of zero. We could then plot all possible events on a single continuum of incentive value, ranging from positive events such as food to negative events such as electric shock, with neutral events such as nonreward in the middle. (See Figure 7.9.) If experience with an attractive incentive reduces the incentive value of all lesser incentives, then exposure to 256 pellets should reduce the incentive value not only of 16 pellets but also of 0 pellets. If nonreward starts with an incentive value of zero, however, any reduction can only mean that its incentive value becomes negative, so it would effectively be aversive. Nonreward after reinforcement, in other words, would effectively be a form of punishment!

Rather than viewing extinction as a rational process in which subjects cease to respond because such responding is a waste of effort, we can interpret extinction as a form of punishment in which the aversive event is the discontinuation of an expected reinforcer. Of course, this interpretation is not necessarily incompatible with a rational interpretation (reason and emotion could both play important roles), but the punishment interpretation does lead to a number of interesting predictions: If extinction is a form of punishment, then it should have the same side effects, albeit in a somewhat milder form.

Extinction-induced aggression.   Just as electric shock elicits aggression, for example, we should expect extinction to do the same. This prediction was tested by Azrin, Hutchinson, and Hake (1966), using pigeons. They placed two birds in a cage, one free to move around and the other (the target bird) immobilized in a stocklike apparatus, with a key mounted on one wall. Pecks on this key during the baseline phase had no effect. Then, during the experimental phase, pecks made by the free bird were alternately reinforced and extinguished. The reinforcement periods were signaled by a tone, and the pigeon soon learned to respond steadily whenever the tone was on. Whenever an extinction period began, however, the free pigeon would immediately turn away from the key and begin to attack the target bird. These attacks, moreover, were not mere feints; they "consisted of strong pecks at the throat and head of the target bird, especially around the eyes. The feathers of the target bird were often pulled out and the skin bruised" (Azrin, Hutchinson, & Hake, 1966, p. 204). The ferocity of these attacks gradually diminished over several minutes, but each new extinction period would bring a renewed burst of aggression. The absence of reinforcement during the baseline period, on the other hand, did not produce any such aggression. As predicted by a contrast analysis, in other words, nonreinforcement by itself appears to be quite neutral; it is only when contrasted with reinforcement that it becomes aversive.

Nation and Cooney (1982) report evidence suggesting similar effects in humans. They gave college students a task in which they had to move a rod in a certain direction; successful responses automatically produced a reinforcer. Subjects were told that a loud noise would sometimes be played during the experiment, and that they could turn the noise off either by pressing a button or hitting a pad—the latter response required considerably more force. During the training phase, subjects preferred to turn the noise off by pushing the button, but when extinction began, and they found that they were no longer receiving reinforcement, subjects began to hit the pad instead. The force with which they hit the pad, moreover, increased dramatically during the early stages of extinction, then gradually fell back. The measure of aggression used here is an indirect one, but subjects' behavior certainly suggested some element of anger or frustration.

The frustration effect.   Further evidence for the frustrating nature of extinction comes from a study by Amsel and Roussel (1952). They hypothesized that frustration was an aversive drive, so that, like hunger and other drives, it should produce an increase in the vigor of behavior known as the **frustration effect.** To test this proposition, they trained rats in a double-alley apparatus in which there were two goal boxes, located in the middle and at the end of a long runway (Figure 7.10). During initial training, food was available in both goal boxes. During the test phase, however, food was absent from the first goal box on half the trials. During the test, then, subjects ran down the alley to the first goal box, where they found food half the time, and then after a brief delay ran on to the second goal box in which food was always present. According to Amsel and Roussel, the omission of reinforcement in the first goal box should have produced frustration, and this motivational state should have acted as a drive to energize subsequent behavior. The rats, in other words, should have run down the second alley faster on trials in which they were frustrated, and the results supported this prediction. Furthermore, as in the case of aggression, it has been shown that it is not nonreinforcement per se that produces frustra-

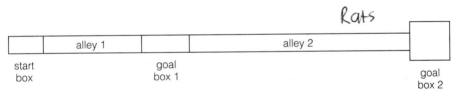

F I G U R E 7.10   An overhead view of the double-alley apparatus used in the Amsel and Roussel (1952) frustration experiment.

tion, but nonreinforcement following a response that was previously reinforced (Wagner, 1959).

Research on schedules of reinforcement has revealed behaviors that may also reflect a frustration effect. If subjects are trained on an FI schedule in which, say, reinforcement is delivered once every five minutes, then, as we saw in the preceding chapter, they eventually learn to respond at a low rate early in the interval and to respond increasingly more rapidly as the moment for reinforcement approaches. If they are given the opportunity to perform other responses while they are waiting for reinforcement, however, they will sometimes engage in what seem to be bizarre behaviors. If rats are given food as a reinforcer, for example, Falk (1961) reported that they would drink massive amounts of water during the waiting period—in certain conditions, up to half their body weight in just a few hours. Falk called this behavior *schedule-induced polydipsia,* and a number of other schedule-induced behaviors have been observed, including *pica,* in which rats and monkeys will ingest wood shavings while they wait (Roper, Edwards, & Crossland, 1983). Also, while rats will normally not drink alcohol, they will drink excessive amounts when trained on interval schedules (Gilbert, 1974). And humans seem to engage in similar behaviors, eating, biting their nails, or smoking cigarettes as they wait (for example, Cantor & Wilson, 1984).

In all these cases, the behaviors occur at levels far above their norm, and they are concentrated during the period following one reinforcement, when the wait until the next reinforcement is longest. Bolles (1979) has suggested that all of these behaviors may be reflections of frustration induced by having to wait for reinforcement in a situation in which there is nothing they can do to hasten its delivery. There are strong grounds, then, for supposing that nonreinforcement in a situation in which it is anticipated is aversive, and thus that extinction is a form of punishment, albeit a generally milder form.

One practical implication is that the use of extinction to eliminate undesirable behaviors may generate the same side effects as punishment, including anger and aggression. One example comes from a study by Herbert, Pinkston, Hayden, Sajwaj, Pinkston, Cordua, and Jackson (1973), in which the mothers of six deviant children were instructed to ignore their children when they misbehaved, in order to prevent misbehavior being reinforced by attention. This technique has been very effective in many studies, but when the children in this group found that they were no longer receiving attention, they became furious: Four of the six children assaulted their mothers, and one kicked out a window of the room in which training was being given! Thus while extinction is normally a relatively mild form of punishment, it can produce powerful side effects in some circumstances. (This frustration effect could also explain why the boy in the Williams study cried so long the first night that his parents ignored his tantrums.)

7.4 THE PARTIAL REINFORCEMENT EFFECT

In our discussion of the partial reinforcement effect (PRE) in the preceding chapter, we saw that when responding is reinforced only occasionally during training, subjects persist in responding during extinction far longer than if every response is reinforced during training. If rats are trained to run down a straight alley to obtain food, for example, a group that is reinforced on only 50 percent of the trials during training will run longer when food is no longer presented in the goal box than a group that is reinforced on every trial. In situations like this, it looks as if nonreinforcement during training is actually strengthening the response, a very peculiar result indeed. In this section, we will examine in more detail why this occurs.

The Discrimination Hypothesis

The key to understanding the partial reinforcement effect may lie in a careful analysis of the stimuli present at the time of reinforcement. As we saw in our earlier discussion of stimulus control (Chapter 6), responses do not occur in a vacuum: Stimuli are always present, and a subset of these stimuli acquires control over the reinforced response. According to the **discrimination hypothesis**, the level of responding in any situation is determined by the similarity of the stimuli present to those that prevailed during training. Suppose, for example, that a rat were trained to run down a black alley to obtain food. If the alley were again black during extinction, the rat clearly would be more likely to respond than if the color were suddenly changed to white. The amount of responding in extinction, therefore, should depend on the similarity of the stimuli present during extinction to those present during training.

Now suppose that nonreinforcement were a detectable event in the same way as a black alley. For a subject trained under partial reinforcement, the stimulus of nonreinforcement would be present during both training and extinction, so at least in this respect the two conditions would be highly similar. For a subject reinforced continuously during training, on the other hand, the sudden omission of reinforcement during extinction would mark a radical departure from the conditions during training, so it should now be much less likely to respond. The partial reinforcement effect could thus be due to the fact that nonreinforcement during training increases the similarity between training and extinction, and thus enhances the likelihood that subjects will continue to respond during extinction as they did during training.

Capaldi's Sequential Model

By emphasizing the role of the stimuli present during training, the discrimination hypothesis provides a simple but flexible framework for analyzing the PRE.

A number of theories based on this framework have been proposed (for example, Sheffield, 1949; Amsel, 1962), of which perhaps the most impressive in terms of its ability to predict behavior over a wide range of settings has been that of E. J. Capaldi (1967, 1971).

In its broad outlines, Capaldi's analysis is the same as the one already sketched: Responding during extinction is assumed to depend on the similarity of the stimuli present during training and extinction, and nonreward is assumed to be an event with stimulus properties. Capaldi suggests, for example, that when a rat is placed in a maze, the cues of the maze will remind it of its previous experiences there, in much the same way that the sight of a doctor's office might remind you of your last visit. When returned to the maze at the beginning of an extinction trial, therefore, the rat would remember its failure to find food there on the previous trial, and this memory would form part of the stimulus complex that would determine how it responded. The likelihood of a response would thus depend on the degree to which this memory stimulus (nonreinforcement)—symbolized by Capaldi as S^N—had previously been associated with responding.

Memory as a stimulus.   To understand Capaldi's analysis, imagine an experiment in which three groups of rats were trained to run down an alley for food, with each group receiving two reinforced trials. Suppose, however, that the groups received their reinforcements on different schedules: CRF, fixed ratio 2, and fixed ratio 3. If we symbolize a trial ending in reinforcement by R, and one ending in nonreinforcement by N, then the sequence of trials during training for each group would be:

$$\text{CRF: R R}$$
$$\text{FR 2: N R N R}$$
$$\text{FR 3: N N R N N R}$$

Which of these groups would Capaldi's analysis predict to respond most during extinction? The answer would depend on the strength of the association established between S^N and responding during training. For the CRF group, the strength of this association would be zero, since nonreinforcement—and hence S^N—never occurred during training, and thus could not be associated with running. For the group trained on FR 2, on the other hand, S^N would have been associated with running. During training, each reinforced trial was preceded by a nonreinforced trial; these subjects, on being placed in the maze at the beginning of a reinforced trial, would have recalled not being reinforced on the previous trial. If we further assume that reinforcement produces an association between the preceding response and whatever stimuli are present, then the association between the memory stimulus S^N and running down the alley would be strengthened on each reinforced trial. When S^N was encountered in extinction, therefore, this group would be more likely to respond than the group trained on CRF, because the memory of nonreinforcement would have become associated with the response of running.

N–R transitions. During extinction, then, responding in the FR 2 group would be stronger than in the control group. To understand Capaldi's predictions about responding in the FR 3 group, though, we need to introduce two further elements of his model. Capaldi assumed that the strength of the association between S^N and responding depended on how often a nonreinforced trial was followed by a reinforced one, a sequence he called an **N–R transition.** In the sequence N R N R, for example, there are two N–R transitions (N–R N–R), so the association between S^N and responding would be strengthened twice. Clearly, the more of these transitions there are during training, the more the association between S^N and responding will be strengthened, and hence the more responding should occur during extinction.

N length. A second factor that needs to be considered in predicting responding in the FR 3 group is what Capaldi called **N length.** He assumed that animals can remember the outcome not only of the immediately preceding trial but also of earlier trials. A sequence of four nonreinforced trials might produce one memory (S^N_4), whereas a sequence of eight nonreinforced trials might produce a very different memory (S^N_8). The memories that become associated with responding during training, then, depend on how many nonreinforced trials precede each reinforced one. In our FR 2 group, for example, the N length during training would have been one ($N R N R$), whereas in the FR 3 group it would have been two ($N N R N N R$). The memory associated with responding during training, therefore, would have been S^N_1 in the FR 2 group and S^N_2 in the FR 3 group.

Putting it all together. What are the implications of this analysis for responding during extinction? The first point to note is that if subjects remember the outcomes of more than one trial, then each extinction trial begins with a different memory: On trial 2, subjects remember one nonreward trial (S^N_1), on trial 3 they remember two (S^N_2), and so on. In order to predict responding on a particular trial, therefore, we need to know the extent to which the memory stimulus present on this trial has previously been associated with responding. On the fifth extinction trial, for example, the subject will recall a run of four nonreinforced trials in a row; in order to predict responding on this trial, we need to know how strongly S^N_4 was associated with responding during training.

Since a run of four nonreinforcements never occurred during training in either of the partial reinforcement groups, S^N_4 would not have been directly associated with responding in either. Insofar as the memory of four nonreinforcements is similar to that of one or two, however, responding might generalize from these memories to S^N_4. For the FR 2 group, the memory associated with responding during training is S^N_1; insofar as S^N_4 is similar to S^N_1—that is, insofar as the memory of four consecutive nonreinforcements resembles the memory of one nonreinforcement—then responding will generalize to this extinction trial. Note, however, that the stimulus conditions on the fifth extinction trial will be more familiar for subjects in the FR 3 group than those in the FR 2 group, because the memory of four nonreinforcements will be more similar to the memory of two nonreinforcements than the memory of one. The same situation, moreover, will prevail on each of the succeeding extinction trials, because a run of two nonreinforcements during training will always be more like a long run of nonreinforcement during extinction than will a run of only a single trial. (For a graphic representation of this situation, see Figure 7.11.) When N length is taken into account, therefore, Capaldi's model predicts—correctly, as we saw in Chapter 5—that longer runs of nonreinforcement during training will lead to more persistent responding during extinction.

New predictions. Capaldi's model might at first seem a very complicated way of saying what the discrimination hypothesis expresses far more simply, but, by stating his assumptions more precisely, Capaldi has been able to predict behavior over a very wide range of situations. In some cases, these predictions have been fairly commonplace, adding little to what could have been achieved through common sense; in other cases, his predictions have not simply gone

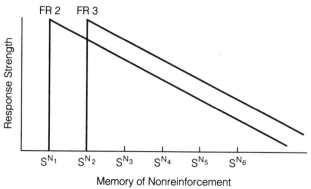

Memory of Nonreinforcement

F I G U R E 7.11   Schematic representation of generalization between memories of nonreinforcement. For a group trained on an FR 2 schedule, the memory of a single nonreinforcement (S^{N_1}) would be associated with reinforcement, and the tendency to respond to this memory would generalize to similar memories. For a group trained on an FR 3 schedule of reinforcement, the memory of two nonreinforced trials (S^{N_2}) would be present on reinforced trials and thus become associated with responding. For any longer sequence of nonreinforcement, the memory of two nonreinforcements would be more similar than the memory of only one nonreinforcement; thus, the generalized tendency to respond would always be greater in the group trained on the FR 3 schedule.

beyond common sense but have strongly contradicted it. To take just one example, suppose that two groups of rats were trained to run down a straight alley for food, with three trials a day arranged according to the following sequence:

Group I: R N R
Group II: R R N

If we analyzed this situation in terms of the discrimination hypothesis, we might argue that both groups should respond equally during extinction, because both received the same number of N and R trials, arranged in what seems a similarly haphazard sequence. According to Capaldi's analysis, however, the results in the two cases should be very different. In the first group, nonreinforcement on the second trial precedes reinforcement on the third, so that S^N will be associated with responding on this trial. In the second group, however, the nonreinforced trial is not followed by reinforcement; S^N, therefore, will not be present on a reinforced trial, and hence should not become associated with responding. For all intents and purposes, therefore, this final N trial might just as well not have taken place: Subjects in this group not only should respond less during extinction than subjects in the first group, but they should respond just as if they had been reinforced continuously throughout.

This prediction has now been tested in a number of experiments (for example, Mackintosh & Little, 1970; Spivey & Hess, 1968), and in every case the results have supported Capaldi's analysis. In one particularly striking experiment by Capaldi and Kassover (1970), one group received three times as many nonreinforcements during training as another, but when these trials were presented at the end of each daily sequence—so that they were never followed by reinforcement—they proved to have absolutely no effect on responding during extinction. It is not simply the experience of nonreinforcement during training that produces the PRE, then, but the particular sequence of nonreinforcement followed by reinforcement—hence Capaldi's naming of his theory the *sequential model*.

Capaldi has reported a wide range of other experiments testing his model, and on the whole these have provided impressive support. (See also Leonard, 1969.) Some problems remain, however. For example, Capaldi has not yet fully specified the properties of the memory system involved, nor the rules governing generalization from one experimental situation to another. Also, other models of the PRE have also been proposed (for example, Amsel, 1972; Wong, 1978; Daly & Daly, 1982), and it is not yet clear how the useful features of these alternative models can best be integrated. Nevertheless, Capaldi's model has enjoyed substantial success, and it illustrates how seemingly mysterious phenomena such as the PRE can sometimes be explained through a careful analysis of the stimuli present. More generally, it suggests again, as did the

Rescorla-Wagner model earlier, the surprising power of even a few simple assumptions to predict behavior, provided that these assumptions are stated clearly. The principles of learning sometimes seem little more than common sense: It is hardly surprising, for example, that reinforcement strengthens behavior, or that responding is more likely in a situation in which training is given. When these principles are combined in a clear and explicit model, however, they can lead to predictions that go beyond—and sometimes even contradict—anything suggested by intuition or common sense.

7.5 SUMMARY

One obvious technique for eliminating behavior is punishment, but punishment has been and remains intensely controversial. Early research suggested that punishment had only a temporary effect on behavior, but more recent research has reversed this conclusion. When punishment is immediate, firm, accompanied by a clear (and fair) explanation, and when it occurs in a variety of settings, it can be a very powerful tool for eliminating undesirable behavior.

Evidence of the effectiveness of punishment, however, has not ended the controversy over its use, because the positive effects on the punished response must be weighed against the danger of harmful side effects. One problem is that the presentation of an aversive stimulus elicits fear, and this fear may be classically conditioned to the stimuli that precede punishment. For example, although punishment of poor schoolwork may act as an incentive to try harder, its long-term effects may be less benign. Strong emotions tend to narrow attention, so that a child who is punished for poor schoolwork may actually do worse. This may lead to a vicious circle in which failure increases anxiety, which then leads to still more failure, until the child eventually learns to stop trying and perhaps even to avoid school altogether.

A second undesirable consequence of punishment is a tendency toward increased aggression. Aversive stimuli directly elicit aggression; even if this aggression is not expressed immediately, there is a danger that it will later be directed at the individual administering the punishment or else displaced onto other, less powerful targets. Also, an adult's use of punishment may provide a model for a child that the use of physical force is an appropriate technique for getting what he or she wants. These dangers, it must be emphasized, are still largely speculative, but observational evidence also suggests a strong correlation between the use of severe punishment and antisocial behaviors such as aggression.

It is not easy to weigh the immediate advantages of punishment in eliminating undesirable behavior against the possibility of harmful side effects, but punishment is certainly not an enjoyable experience; when less aversive alternatives are available, they seem clearly preferable. Rather than punishing bad behavior, it may be possible to reinforce good behavior instead, and classroom studies suggest that this technique can be very effective. (Chapter 8 discusses this topic in detail.) When punishment is necessary—to suppress self-injurious behavior, for example—the best advice seems to be to use the minimal force necessary for the punishment to be effective.

Another alternative to punishing a response is to extinguish it by withholding the reinforcers that maintain it. One theory of extinction is that it is itself a form of punishment, as nonreinforcement of a previously reinforced response induces an aversive state of frustration. If so, extinction is, in general, a relatively mild form of punishment, and one that is very effective, provided that the reinforcer in question can be withheld successfully.

One aspect of extinction that has attracted considerable interest is the partial reinforcement effect, in which partial reinforcement during training produces greater responding during extinction than does continuous reinforcement. This effect is puzzling in some respects: It seems that more frequent reinforcement should produce a stronger response, and hence greater resistance to extinction. But the paradox can be resolved if we take into account the stimulus context. The discrimination hypothesis suggests that responding during extinction depends on the similarity of the stimuli present during extinction to the stimuli present during training. Insofar as nonreinforcement is regarded as a discriminable stimulus, subjects that experience nonreinforcement during training will be reinforced for responding in the presence of this stimulus and, hence, will be more likely to continue responding when they again encounter nonreinforcement during extinction.

One of the most successful applications of this approach has been the sequential model of E. J. Capaldi. Capaldi assumes that the memory of previous nonreinforcements is an important part of the stimulus complex that determines responding during extinction. If a rat is trained to run a maze under partial reinforcement, for example, the rat will recall, on reinforcement trials, previous experiences of nonreinforcement; if the rat nevertheless runs down the alley and is reinforced, the memory of nonreinforcement will become associated with the response of running. When the rat again encounters nonreinforcement during extinction, this stimulus will continue to elicit running.

The precise amount of running during extinction will depend on the strength of the association formed during training between memories of nonreinforcement and running, and on the similarity of these memories to those present during extinction. The strength of the association between nonreinforcement and running is determined by the number of times nonreinforced trials preceded reinforced ones (N–R transitions); the similarity of training and testing is determined by how many nonreinforced trials preceded a reinforced one during training (N length). The longer the N length and the more N–R transitions, the more subjects will respond during extinction.

By taking into account the stimuli present during training, and, in particular, by treating memories of nonreinforcement as an important element of the stimulus complex, Capaldi has been able to explain the partial reinforcement effect and generate some new and counterintuitive predictions. These predictions generally have been well supported. As with the Rescorla-Wagner model, this success shows the potential power of simple assumptions to explain seemingly complex behavior, provided that the assumptions are stated with sufficient clarity and precision.

Selected Definitions

Punishment A decrease in the likelihood of a response due to the presentation of an aversive stimulus or, in the case of **negative punishment**, the removal of a reinforcing stimulus.

Neither punishment nor negative punishment should be confused with **negative reinforcement**, which is defined as an increase in the probability of a response due to the removal of an aversive stimulus. Reinforcement—including negative reinforcement—always involves the strengthening of a response, and punishment always involves its weakening. Reinforcement is called positive when the effect is due to the presentation of a stimulus; it is called negative when a stimulus is removed.

Extinction Nonreinforcement of a previously reinforced response. The typical result of the extinction procedure is a gradual decrease in responding.

Frustration effect An increase in the vigor of the behavior that immediately follows nonreinforcement of a previously reinforced response.

Discrimination hypothesis A theory that attempts to explain the partial reinforcement effect. It states that the level of responding in any situation is determined by the similarity of the stimuli present to those that prevailed during training.

N–R transition A sequence in which a nonreinforced trial (N) is followed by a reinforced trial (R). According to Capaldi's sequential model, the more times a nonreinforced trial is followed by a reinforced trial, the more the reinforced response will be associated with the memory of nonreinforcement (S^N). The experience of nonreinforcement during extinction will then be more likely to elicit the response that was reinforced during training.

N length The number of nonreinforced trials that precede each reinforced one. (For example, in an FR 3 group, the N length would be two.) The greater the N length during training, the more conditions during training will resemble those during extinction. The response reinforced during training will then be more likely to be repeated during extinction.

Review Questions

1. Define *pain-elicited aggression* and S^N.

2. What are the advantages and disadvantages of using animal experiments to study punishment?

3. What determines whether punishment is effective?

4. To what extent are the principles of punishment the same in animals and humans?

5. Why do explanations enhance the effectiveness of punishment?

6. Extinction and punishment could both be explained as examples of rational decision making in which subjects decide how to respond on the basis of the consequences they expect to follow. What evidence points to an important role of emotion in both these procedures?

7. What are the possible harmful effects of punishment?

8. What is your own conclusion about whether punishment should be used, and, if so, when? What are some possible alternatives to punishment for eliminating undesirable behavior?

9. What is the partial reinforcement effect? How does the discrimination hypothesis account for it?

10. How does Capaldi's sequential model account for the PRE?

11. In what ways are the Capaldi and Rescorla-Wagner models similar?

APPLICATIONS

In the introduction to Chapter 6, we considered the paradox that the principles of reinforcement appear so simple, yet in real life behavior is often remarkably difficult to change. One explanation, we suggested, was that the principles of reinforcement may not be as simple as they first appear; in the course of that chapter, we reviewed evidence consistent with that view. Even brief delays of reinforcement, for example, have far more severe effects on learning than is commonly realized, and our understanding of phenomena such as motivation and stimulus control is still limited. Therefore, we could readily account for our difficulty in using reinforcement effectively by the fact that we have an incomplete understanding of the principles governing its use.

There is, however, another possibility. Even in those cases in which we do understand the principles of reinforcement, it may appear ineffective because we fail to apply the principles in a coherent and systematic way. That is, we may already know enough to use reinforcement effectively, if only we would apply that knowledge systematically. This, at any rate, was the belief of a number of influential learning psychologists and has led to a major effort over the past two decades, under the rubric of **behavior modification**, to apply the principles of reinforcement developed in the animal laboratory to practical problems of human behavior. In this chapter we will review some of these programs, considering the extent to which they have been successful, and, insofar as they have failed, what these failures can tell us about the remaining gaps in our knowledge. We will begin by looking at some of the attempts that have been made to apply the principles of reinforcement to education.

8.1 Reinforcement in the Classroom

Reinforcement principles have been applied to a wide range of educational problems and institutional settings. We will focus our attention in this section on examples involving schoolchildren, teenage delinquents, and university students.

Classroom Behavior

One of the most difficult problems for any teacher is children who are severely disruptive in class. By talking, moving around, and so on, they not only fail to learn themselves but also seriously interfere with the work of those around them. To test a reinforcement-based program for dealing with this problem, Hall, Lund, and Jackson (1968) went to a school in a severely deprived urban area. They asked the teachers and principal to identify the children in the school whose behavior posed the most serious problems. One child, a third-grade boy named Robbie, had been in trouble ever since he entered the school. He had received repeated scoldings, been sent to the principal, and even been spanked—all to no avail. A classroom observer found that Robbie spent only 25 percent of his time on assigned tasks, the remainder of the time being devoted to activities such as talking, snapping rubber bands, drinking milk very slowly and then playing with the carton, and so on. His teacher often urged him to work; indeed, 55 percent of her contacts with Robbie occurred at times when he was not working.

If you were the teacher in charge of the class, what would you do? One natural reaction would be to punish him, but this had already been tried repeatedly without success. The experimenters' analysis was that the teacher was actually encouraging Robbie's misbehavior by giving him attention when he misbehaved. As we saw in our discussion of social reinforcement, attention from others, even when that attention comes in the form of scolding, can be reinforcing. The experimenters therefore recommended that the teacher use attention to reinforce appropriate behavior. They asked her to ignore Robbie whenever he misbehaved. When he behaved appropriately for one minute, however, she was to come over and praise him, making comments such as, "Very nice, Robbie, you've been working very well."

The results are shown in Figure 8.1. When reinforcement was introduced, there was an immediate increase in the proportion of time Robbie spent studying. When the teacher returned to the baseline condition—that is, scolding inappropriate behavior—studying fell; it improved again, however, when reinforcement was reinstated. This improvement, moreover, proved durable: Observations made 14 weeks after the training program had ended revealed that Robbie was still spending 79 percent of his time working, compared to only 25 percent during the baseline phase. Not surprisingly, this change in the

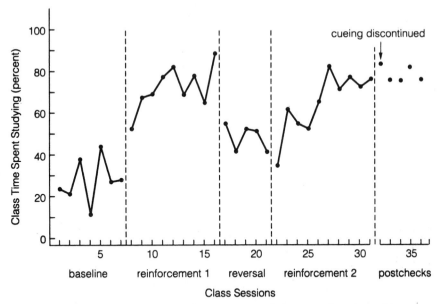

F I G U R E 8.1   Effect of praise on the proportion of class time the subject devoted to studying. (Hall, Lund, & Jackson, 1968)

amount of time spent working also led to a substantial improvement in the quality of Robbie's work. On spelling tests, for example, his performance improved from 57 percent to 97 percent.

This improvement was not achieved without effort. To ensure that Robbie would be reinforced immediately when he studied, his behavior had to be monitored constantly. To help the teacher, the classroom observer signaled surreptitiously whenever the criterion for reinforcement was met. In the early stages of the program, therefore, considerable effort was needed to implement it, but in the long term the improvement in Robbie's behavior meant that he required substantially less of the teacher's attention, and this behavior was maintained when cueing was discontinued. The experimenters obtained similar results with the other children studied. Thus, even a seemingly trivial reinforcer—just a little bit of praise and attention—produced remarkable changes in the behavior of the most severely disruptive children in the school, provided that this reinforcement was both immediate and consistent.

Teaching Sports

Allison and Ayllon (1980) reported an application of reinforcement to a different type of teaching problem. The subjects were university students in a physical education course. The normal teaching technique consisted of an explanation of the required behavior—for example, how to serve when playing tennis—after which the instructor modeled the behavior, then the students carried out the behavior themselves, and the instructor gave verbal feedback on the students' success. The training program was fairly standard, but a good one, with lots of explanation and demonstration. Progress, however, was very slow. Figure 8.2 plots the results for a student named Greg: On only a single occasion did he manage to serve correctly, and there was no evidence of improvement even after 150 trials.

In an effort to improve learning, the experimenter made a number of changes in the teaching procedure; at the heart of these changes was the principle of immediate reinforcement. Students were again asked to execute the required stroke; if they did so correctly, the instructor immediately praised them. If they made an error, however, the instructor blew a whistle and told them to freeze. The instructor gave a verbal explanation of the students' mistakes while the students were stationary; then the instructor modeled the correct position and asked the students to assume it. The freezing served several purposes. First, it provided immediate feedback following an error, eliminating the delay of waiting until students finished their serve. Second, having students move from the wrong position to the correct position allowed them to compare directly the resulting sensations; in future, the sensory feedback from the correct position could act as a source of immediate secondary reinforcement. Finally, the requirement to freeze may also have served as an immediate punishment for the actions involved in serving incorrectly.

As shown in Figure 8.2, this seemingly small change in the immediacy of feedback resulted in dramatic improvement in the quality of Greg's tennis serve. Similar improvements were observed in other students in the class, and also in other sports such as football and gymnastics. One implication of these results is that if a student is not doing well, it may not help very much to leave the student alone to practice over and over again—each time practicing incorrectly. To improve at any task—whether learning a sport or a foreign language, or developing social relationships—we need feedback on the success of our

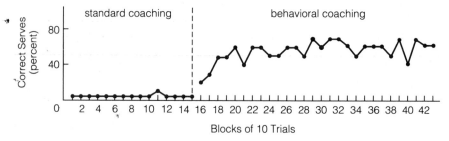

F I G U R E 8.2   Subject's improvement in tennis serving under standard and behavioral coaching. (Adapted from Allison & Ayllon, 1980)

efforts, and this feedback should be immediate and frequent if it is to be maximally effective. Providing such feedback may initially be very time-consuming for a teacher, but close monitoring of a student's behavior may require less teaching time in the long run because of the rapid improvement that results.

The Token Economy

The preceding studies support the view that failures of reinforcement may be due to the reinforcement's being used in a perfunctory, haphazard way. When reinforcement is used more systematically, and, in particular, when it is immediate and consistent, then even relatively small changes in reinforcement—a pat on the back, or providing exam results immediately instead of days or weeks later—can produce dramatic changes in behavior.

It would be misleading, however, to imply that applications of reinforcement principles are always this effective. Consider, for example, the "reinforce good behavior, ignore bad behavior" strategy used by Hall, Lund, and Jackson. In many of the studies that used this method, the results were similar to those reported by Hall's group; in others, though, students whose disruptive behavior was ignored have really gone haywire, finally forcing premature cancellation of the program (for example, O'Leary, Becker, Evans, & Saudargas, 1969).

In some of these failures, the problem was that the teachers did not implement the system properly. In the Hall, Lund, and Jackson study, for example, the technique was successful in six of the seven classes in which it was tried. In the one case where it failed, the experimenters found that the teacher had been unable to ignore bad behavior and had continued to become angry and to scold the student whenever he was disobedient.

In other cases, the problem may have been that the social reinforcers used were not effective reinforcers for the students concerned. As we noted in Chapter 6, social reinforcers gain or lose their effectiveness in part through one's experience with the reinforcer; for some children, social reinforcers such as praise and attention are not effective (at any rate, not from their teachers). Where praise fails, a possible alternative is the token economy, in which points or tokens are established as secondary reinforcers through pairings with a variety of more potent reinforcers. If children behave appropriately in class, for example, they are immediately given points that can later be exchanged for backup reinforcers such as candy. The advantages of using tokens as reinforcers are:

1. Because they are easily dispensed, they can be delivered immediately after the child makes a response.

2. Because they are exchangeable for a wide variety of backup reinforcers, they are always likely to be attractive. Even if a child does not want candy

at a particular moment, the token may still be desirable because it can also be exchanged for other reinforcers such as toys.

One example of a token economy that we have already encountered is the study by Phillips (1968), in which juvenile delinquents were treated in a residential center called Achievement Place. The boys were given points for appropriate behavior, and these points could be exchanged for reinforcers such as snacks, money, permission to go into town, and so forth. When permission to stay up late was used to reinforce completion of homework assignments, the average percentage completed was 50 percent; when points were made contingent on completion, this percentage rose to 100 percent. (See Figure 6.8, p. 215.) Success of this kind has been reported in a number of studies. (For a review, see Kazdin, 1977.) As we shall see, token economies need to be used with some caution; nevertheless, they provide a potentially useful alternative for situations in which conventional reinforcers such as praise prove ineffective.

8.2 THE PROBLEM OF MAINTAINING BEHAVIOR

When psychologists first attempted to apply the principles of reinforcement to problem behaviors, there was considerable doubt that they would succeed. Could the behavior of delinquents, much less of retarded children or psychotics, really be altered just by reinforcing them for appropriate behavior? Over the years, it has become clear that the answer is yes: Provided that reinforcement is used in a coherent and systematic way, it can be effective in settings as diverse as elementary schools and universities, prisons and psychiatric wards. It is now well established that behavior can be altered by reinforcement; it is much less clear whether these changes can be maintained once the reinforcement program is terminated.

Consider, for example, the token economy used in Achievement Place. Look again at Figure 6.8 (p. 215). Note that when points were made contingent on Tom's completion of homework, the percentage of assignments completed rose to 100 percent; when points were eventually discontinued, however, the percentage of completions fell back to zero. If you think about it, you'll realize that Tom's behavior is hardly surprising. When he received a reward he valued for studying, he studied; when this reward was discontinued, he stopped studying. After all, why should anyone persist in a behavior if it no longer produces reinforcement?

The implicit assumption in the programs we have been reviewing is that there are sources of reinforcement in the natural environment that will maintain the desired behavior if only it can be established initially. A delinquent may need external incentives to learn to read, for example, but once the behavior is established, the inherent pleasure available from reading books, newspapers, and so on should maintain the behavior. In some cases, though, it may take time for these natural reinforcers to develop; if the reinforcement program is to be effective, then, it may be necessary to ensure that the reinforced behavior will continue long enough for the natural reinforcers to assume control.

Several of the principles reviewed in the previous chapter can be used to encourage the persistence of behavior long enough for these natural reinforcers to assume control. One such technique is intermittent reinforcement. As we noted in Chapter 6, the greater the intermittency of reinforcement during training, the longer behavior will persist after reinforcement is terminated. In most reinforcement programs, therefore, continuous reinforcement is used to establish a behavior initially, but the frequency of reinforcement is progressively reduced as training continues.

Another technique for maximizing the persistence of behavior is to reinforce it in a variety of settings. According to the principle of stimulus control, reinforcement strengthens behavior most in the particular setting in which training is given. By reinforcing behavior in a variety of settings, however, we can increase the likelihood that it will generalize widely, and thus not extinguish the instant there is a change in conditions (for example, on leaving the classroom in which training was given).

A third potentially useful technique involves fading out the reinforcement program gradually, rather than terminating it abruptly. In our discussion of shaping, we saw that a response established in the presence of one stimulus is more likely to persist if that stimulus is faded out gradually rather than removed abruptly, and this principle also applies to more complex situations such as a reinforcement program. In a study by Hall, Axelrod, Tyler, Grief, Jones, and Robertson (1972), for example, the experimenters were students in a university course on behavior modification. These students carried out projects in their own homes using the principles studied in the course. One such project involved a boy named Jerry, who had started wearing an orthodontic device when he was eight years old. Jerry was supposed to wear the device for 12 hours a day. In practice, though, he wore it for only a few hours a day because he hated it. After eight years, four dentists, and $3300 in bills, Jerry's condition was essentially unchanged.

As a first step toward altering this behavior, Jerry's mother began to keep careful records of how often he wore the device, so she could accurately assess the effects of any treatment. During this baseline period, Jerry wore the device only 25 percent of the time. (See Figure 8.3.) To increase this percentage, his mother first tried social reinforcement. She did not reprimand her son when he failed to wear the device, but she praised him when he did. This social reinforcement produced a substantial increase in the desired behavior—he wore the device 36 percent of the time—but for practical purposes the increase was

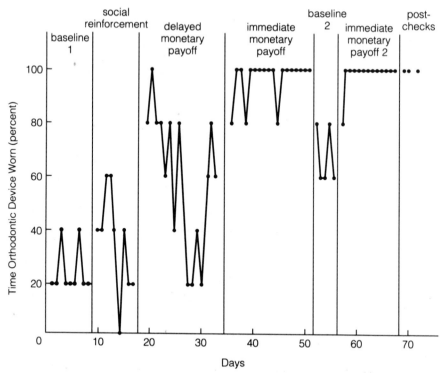

F I G U R E 8.3 Effects of three different reinforcement techniques: social reinforcement in the form of praise; money with a delayed payoff; and money with an immediate payoff. The reinforced behavior was the wearing of an orthodontic device. (Hall et al., 1972)

not sufficient. In the next phase, therefore, his mother tried a more powerful reinforcer: money. Whenever Jerry was wearing the device when his mother checked, he received 25 cents; whenever he was not, he lost 25 cents. His mother paid him at the end of each month, and the amount of time Jerry spent wearing the device increased to 60 percent. To increase it still further, his mother changed to immediate reinforcement—Jerry received payment immediately after each inspection—and the amount of wearing time now rose to 95 percent! As we have seen again and again (and again . . .), a reinforcer presented after a delay is generally far less effective than the same reinforcer given immediately.

At this point, the reinforcement program was discontinued, and the amount of time Jerry spent wearing the device immediately declined to 64 percent. This still represented a substantial improvement over the original figure of 25 percent, but the change was still not sufficient to cure Jerry's dental problems. The immediate reinforcement condition was therefore reinstituted, and Jerry returned to wearing the device reliably (the percentage this time was 99 percent). Instead of terminating the program abruptly, his mother now faded it out gradually. The frequency with which Jerry's behavior was checked was gradually reduced from five times a day to only once every two weeks, and the behavior was now maintained. Eight months later, Jerry's dentist told him that he had made great progress and no longer needed to wear the device. By using reinforcement and then fading it out gradually, Jerry's mother was able to establish and maintain a behavior that years of scolding and nagging had proved powerless to influence.

8.3 HARMFUL EFFECTS OF REINFORCEMENT

The material reviewed in the previous sections testifies to the beneficial effects that reinforcement can have when used properly. When encouraged to use reinforcement more frequently, however, parents and teachers sometimes react with suspicion, especially when the proposed reinforcer is a material one such as tokens or money. In this section, we will consider some of the reasons for this suspicion and the extent to which it may be justified.

Moral Objections

Bribery. One common objection to the use of reinforcement is that it seems to be a form of bribery. Why should a child be offered money or other rewards to mow the lawn or do other chores? Many people believe it is their duty to do those tasks. They might see a material inducement as nothing more than a bribe.

This view has some appeal: There is something disturbing about offering a reward to get someone to do something they should be doing anyway. However, we need to consider this issue in the context of available alternatives. There is no problem if children accept responsibility, but what alternatives are available if they do not? We could admonish them to do their duty, or threaten them with punishment if they disobey, and these strategies may be appropriate in some circumstances. In at least some situations, however, these disciplinary techniques are ineffective as well as unpleasant. Consider the examples we have already seen: Robbie's teachers tried punishment to eliminate his misbehavior without success, and eight years of reprimands had no effect on getting Jerry to wear his orthodontic device. In both cases, however, the introduction of reinforcement led to a rapid and substantial improvement in behavior, which was then maintained even after reinforcement was discontinued. These examples do not prove that reinforcement is always preferable to punishment, but they do suggest that reinforcement may be more effective than traditional forms of discipline in at least some circumstances, and may avoid harmful side effects that sometimes come with punishment. (See Chapter 7.) O'Leary, Poulos, and Devine (1972) discuss other issues concerning the relationship between reinforcement and bribery.

Greed.   A second objection to the use of rewards—particularly material rewards—is that they promote greed. If children were offered $20 for cleaning their rooms, in this view, they would soon begin demanding money for doing other chores too, rather than accepting the chores as a necessary aspect of cooperative living. In fact, we have already encountered indirect evidence that material reinforcers have this effect. In Chapter 6, we saw that extended exposure to a particular reinforcer devalues lesser reinforcers: A rat that had run down an alley to obtain 64 food pellets would not work nearly as hard to obtain 16 pellets as it would have before exposure to 64 pellets. In other words, it looked very much as if the rat had become greedy! To avoid this problem, most reinforcement programs begin by using relatively mild reinforcers such as social praise, turning to material reinforcers only if praise proves ineffective.

Undermining Intrinsic Motivation

A further objection to the use of reinforcers is that they may devalue the activity on which they are contingent. One view is that a person should be directed toward a certain behavior by **intrinsic motivation**—motivation that comes from the activity itself rather than any consequences that might follow it. In the words of A. S. Neil, a Scottish educator who founded an influential school known as Summerhill:

> The danger in rewarding a child is not as extreme as that of punishing him, but the undermining of the child's morale through the giving of rewards is more subtle. Rewards are superfluous and negative. To offer a prize for doing a deed is tantamount to declaring that the deed is not worth doing for its own sake. . . . A reward should, for the most part, be subjective: self-satisfaction for the work accomplished.
>
> (Neil, 1960, pp. 162–163)

In practice, it is sometimes difficult to distinguish precisely intrinsic and extrinsic reinforcers. Take, for example, the activity of eating. Should eating be considered intrinsically motivated because the pleasure derives from eating itself, or is the food an extrinsic reinforcer? In theory, however, the distinction seems reasonably clear: intrinsically motivated behaviors are those that are relatively independent of external or arbitrary reinforcers.

Gold stars and children's drawings.   Powerful support for Neil's view comes from a study by Lepper, Greene, and Nisbett (1973). The purpose of their experiment was to investigate the effects of reinforcement on children's behavior in drawing pictures. In the first phase, the spontaneous level of drawing was determined by providing a nursery class with free access to felt-tip markers and paper and observing how much time they spent in drawing during a three-hour period. One week later, the children were told that there was a visitor who would like to see what kinds of pictures children draw with markers. A reward group was told that they would receive a Good Player award—consisting of a card with a gold star, a red ribbon, and their names inscribed—if they drew a picture. A control group was also asked to draw a picture, but no reward was mentioned.

To test the effects of the reward, markers were again made available in the nursery one to two weeks later. Children in the control group spent almost exactly the same amount of time drawing as they had during the baseline phase, but the children who had been rewarded spent only half as much time.

The aversiveness of being controlled.   Why should reinforcing children for drawing reduce interest in this activity? A number of explanations have been proposed in addition to Neil's (for example, Lepper, Greene, & Nisbett, 1973; Reiss & Sushinsky, 1975), but a consensus seems to be emerging that the key lies in the children's perception of being controlled (Lepper, 1981; Deci & Ryan, 1980). When a reinforcer is made contingent on an activity, children may perceive that they are engaging in this task not because of its inherent interest but rather to obtain something that the experimenter would otherwise not give them. This sense of being controlled or manipulated is aversive and could be responsible for the children's loss of interest in the activity.

Intriguing evidence for what could be a parallel effect in rhesus monkeys has recently been reported by Washburn, Hopkins, and Rumbaugh (1991). The monkeys had already been trained to perform five computer-controlled games—for example, using a joystick to cause a "laser light" to hit a moving target on a computer screen. Successful performance was reinforced with fruit-flavored food pellets. In one condition, subjects were allowed to choose which game they played; in a second condition, the order in which games were played was decided by the experimenters. (The order was matched to the one chosen by the subject in the previous session.) Washburn and associates found that when the monkeys were allowed to choose the games, their performance was significantly better than when the same games were assigned by the experimenter. These results almost exactly duplicate one aspect of children's performance on the drawing task: When reward was made contingent on drawing, children not only became less likely to draw pictures in a free-play situation, but the quality of the drawing that they did produce was judged by independent raters to be significantly lower (Lepper, Greene, & Nisbett, 1973).

These studies all suggest that a feeling of being controlled can undermine intrinsic interest in a task. Thus, whether reinforcement will have a damaging effect may depend on whether recipients perceive it as an attempt to control their behavior. In one test of this hypothesis, Ryan (1982) gave students a number of interesting puzzles to solve. In one group, the experimenter said "Good" whenever the students solved a puzzle; in a second group, the experimenter said "Good, you're doing as you should." As predicted by the control hypothesis, subsequent interest in the task was significantly lower in the second group. The more we feel controlled, the less becomes our interest in the task we are being forced to perform.

Evaluating Reinforcement

When is reinforcement harmful?   If reinforcement reduces long-term interest in an activity, why was it so effective in the studies reviewed earlier in this chapter, in which changes in behavior were maintained even after reinforcement was discontinued? Clearly, reinforcement does not always reduce interest; the outcome must somehow depend on the particular circumstances in which it is used. One obvious difference between the Lepper group study and earlier applications is that the activities reinforced in most of the earlier studies were not all that exciting to begin with. Robbie, for example, hardly derived pleasure from studying, nor did Jerry enjoy wearing his orthodontic device. In contrast, the Lepper study involved reinforcing a very attractive activity— drawing pictures. Perhaps reinforcement reduces interest only when intrinsic interest is high to begin with.

Support for this hypothesis comes from Lepper, Greene, and Nisbett's data. During the baseline phase, most of the children spent considerable time drawing; for these children, as we have seen, reinforcement significantly reduced interest. Some children, however, showed little interest in drawing initially, and these children became more interested in drawing following the reward. In practical terms, if a child hates lawn mowing, there is probably little danger that his or her interest will be reduced by the offer of a reinforcer; in fact, the pleasure derived from earning money and feeling grown-up may actually enhance interest. However, for those children who already enjoy mowing lawns—a rare and much prized species—the offer of a reward might well prove counterproductive.

This lawn-mowing example hints at another factor that may determine whether reinforcement will undermine or enhance intrinsic interest. This factor involves the ability of the reward to encourage feelings of competence. In a study by Enzle and Ross (1978), university students were offered $1.50 for working on difficult puzzles. In one group, the reward was promised simply for participating in the experiment; in a second group, it was contingent on achieving a level of competence well above average (this level was not specified in advance, but all the subjects in this group were told that they had reached this level). As in earlier studies in this area, subjects who were reinforced simply for participation showed significantly less interest in the task after the experiment was over, but subjects reinforced for their skill showed greater interest. When reinforcement implies a greater level of competence, the pleasure we experience seems to enhance our enjoyment of the task: "This is something I'm good at; what fun!" It is important to remember, however, that this effect is likely to emerge only in situations in which people do not feel controlled. When there is strong pressure to do well, even a reward for achievement may not compensate for the aversive experience of being controlled or pressured.

Reinforcement, then, is unlikely to reduce interest in a task if the task is unattractive or, if the task is interesting, if the reinforcer is presented in a way that encourages feelings of competence and is not seen as manipulative. If, for example, you wanted to encourage children to practice the piano, it would probably be better to praise them for practicing rather than offering a material reward (praise seems less likely to be perceived as a mechanism of control), and to make this praise contingent on competence ("That sounds lovely; you've really improved") rather than on obedience ("That's wonderful; you've practiced for an hour just as you were supposed to").

The principle of minimal force.   Despite the sometimes spectacular success of applied reinforcement programs such as token economies, parents and teachers are often resistant to the use of reinforcement, and it is now clear that at least some of their concerns are justified. Rewards can encourage greed and lead to a sense of being controlled, which will reduce long-term interest in the reinforced activity. Finally, there is one more problem, which we touched on in Chapter 6. Reinforcement may increase motivation, and when a task is difficult, this heightened motivation can paradoxically impair performance.

These difficulties do not mean that we should never use reinforcement. When a task is unattractive, reinforcement may be a far more pleasant—and effective—technique than alternatives such as threats or admonitions to be good. To minimize the problem of harmful side effects, however, current evidence suggests that when reinforcement is used it is best to follow what might be called the principle of minimal force—that is, to use the least powerful reinforcer that is likely to be effective. (See Lepper, 1981.) In general, it is best to start with relatively mild reinforcers such as praise, turning to material reinforcers only if praise proves ineffective. Whatever the reinforcer chosen, it should be administered in such a way that it encourages feelings of competence rather than mere obedience.

No one likes to be manipulated or controlled, and the more reinforcement is perceived as part of a caring relationship, the more likely it is to be effective. One technique that may be helpful in this respect is a **behavioral contract,** in which the parties involved agree on what behaviors they want to be changed and the consequences that will follow. In a family setting, for example, parents and children could first discuss what behaviors they wanted from each other. The parents, for example, might want the children to clean their rooms; the children might want their parents to stop nagging them. They would also agree on what reinforcers or punishers would be used to encourage compliance. Such contracts may reduce feelings of being controlled, since both parties are reciprocally exerting control over each other. Whatever the reason, though, preliminary results suggest that behavioral contracts can be a very effective treatment for family problems. (See Kirschenbaum & Flanery, 1983.)

8.4 ALTERNATIVES TO REINFORCEMENT: MODELING

The evidence just reviewed suggests that reinforcement can be counterproductive in some situations, particularly when the behavior to be encouraged already possesses some attractiveness. Is there any other way of encouraging such behaviors?

Modeling

One potential alternative is **observational learning**, or **modeling**. Evidence from animal studies suggests that one of the most important ways in which animals learn what foods are edible, or what predators to avoid, is by observing the behavior of their parents or peers. For example, some species of birds respond to predators by "mobbing" them—flying toward them in groups while emitting distinctive calls. Curio, Ernst, and Vieth (1978) showed that blackbirds who observed other blackbirds mobbing a target would then themselves mob the target, even though the target was initially neutral. Similarly, rhesus monkeys learn how to behave toward snakes by observing the behavior of other monkeys. Cook, Mineka, Wolkenstein, and Laitsch (1985) found that lab-reared monkeys, who have no fear of snakes, became intensely frightened of snakes if they observed other monkeys behaving fearfully toward snakes. Conversely, monkeys who saw another monkey behaving calmly with snakes were significantly less likely to later become afraid of snakes (Mineka & Cook, 1986).

Anecdotal evidence suggests that human behavior is also strongly influenced by the behavior of those around us—our parents' religion, our friends' drinking or smoking habits, the fashions worn by Hollywood stars, and so on. Laboratory experiments have confirmed this. Garlington and Dericco (1977), for example, assessed the influence of peers on college student drinking. Subjects were told that they were participating in a study of normal drinking patterns and were asked to drink in pairs in a simulated tavern. One member of each pair was a confederate of the experimenter, and for the first few sessions the confederate matched his rate of drinking to that of the real subject. In subsequent phases, however, he sharply increased or decreased his own rate of drinking. The effects on one subject are shown in Figure 8.4. With remarkable precision, the subject matched his rate of drinking to that of the model.

Researchers have found that models also influence altruistic or helping behavior. People in a shopping center, for example, have been found to be far more likely to make a donation to the Salvation Army if they see someone else make a donation. Similarly, motorists are more likely to stop and help someone change a flat tire if they have just seen someone else receiving help a quarter of a mile earlier (Bryan & Test, 1967).

Modeling in the Treatment of Phobias

One of the most vivid illustrations of the power of models—and of how that power can be harnessed constructively—comes from a study by Bandura, Blanchard, and Ritter (1969). The subjects were adults with an intense fear of snakes—so intense that they could not engage in normal outdoor activities such as gardening and hiking. After testing the subjects to measure their fear,

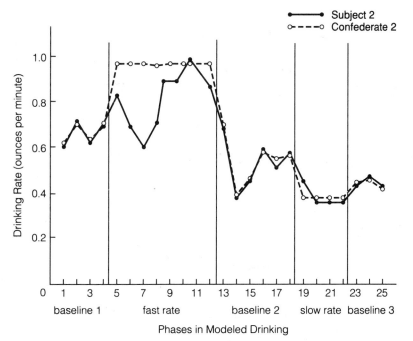

F I G U R E 8.4   The influence of a model on the rate of drinking alcoholic beverages. Initially, a confederate of the experimenter matched his own rate of drinking to that of the subject, but at two points he sharply increased and then decreased his own rate of drinking. (Adapted from Garlington & Dericco, 1977)

the experimenters arranged the subjects in four groups. A control group received no treatment, a second group received systematic desensitization, and a third group was shown a film of children and adults handling snakes without any signs of fear. The final group was exposed to a combination of live modeling and participation. They were first taken to a room with a one-way mirror, through which they watched the model handling a live, four-foot king snake for 15 minutes. They were then invited into the room and encouraged to gradually move closer to the snake. Then, while the model held the snake securely by head and tail, the subjects were invited to touch the snake with their gloved hand. If they were unable to do this, they placed their hand on top of the model's, and then gradually slid their hand down the model's until they were directly touching the snake. With the model always demonstrating the required behavior first, they then moved through a series of progressively more difficult behaviors.

To assess the subjects' fear levels after treatment, the experimenters again administered the objective test, which involved a 29-step sequence of progressively more frightening actions. In the first stage, subjects were simply asked to approach the glass cage containing the snake; the final step involved holding the snake in their laps and allowing it to move around them while they kept their hands at their sides. The results are shown in Figure 8.5. Although the control subjects showed little change, the systematic desensitization and film model groups both improved substantially, from a test score of about 10 to a test score of about 17. The group exposed to live modeling with participation, however, showed the most spectacular improvement of all, with an average score of 27.

The experimenters made a separate analysis of the percentage of subjects who reached point 29—that is, who allowed the snake to crawl over them and didn't move. None of the controls reached this level, compared with 25 percent of the systematic desensitization group, 33 percent of the modeling group, and an extraordinary 92 percent of the live modeling group. Seeing a live model holding a snake without fear thus produced an almost unbelievable reduction in fear; after only two hours of training, most subjects overcame what had previously been an intense, highly debilitating phobia. A follow-up study one month later revealed that this improvement was maintained in virtually all subjects, with many now engaging in outdoor recreational activities that previously had been barred to them. An additional study by Blanchard (1969) suggested that approximately 60 percent of the improvement was due to the use of a live model, with the remaining 40 percent accounted for by the subjects' active participation.

In addition to highlighting one of the most effective therapies ever reported, the Bandura, Blanchard, and Ritter study provides powerful evidence for the extent to which behavior can be influenced by seeing how others behave in similar situations. If you wanted to encourage some behavior, there-

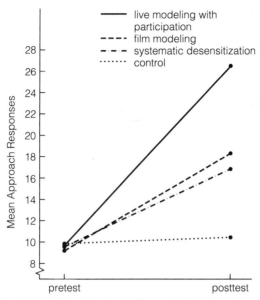

FIGURE 8.5   Phobics' fear of snakes before and after three forms of therapy. Fear
was assessed by progress through a progressively more frightening set of interactions
with a four-foot king snake; the higher the score, the less the subject's fear. (Bandura,
Blanchard, & Ritter, 1969)

fore, one alternative to reinforcing it would be to engage in the behavior
yourself. If you wanted to encourage a child to practice the piano, for example,
you could practice the piano yourself or, better still, practice it with the child.
In this way, the child would receive not only a model of the importance you
attach to piano playing but also the social reinforcement derived from doing it
together. Once the behavior is sufficiently established to supply its own intrinsic reinforcement, modeling can be faded gradually.

Determinants of Imitation

People, of course, do not imitate every behavior they see. We see scores of
people every day engaging in hundreds of behaviors, and we could not begin to
imitate all of these behaviors. What, then, determines whether we imitate a
particular behavior?

Characteristics of the model.   One factor in determining whether we imitate
a behavior involves the characteristics of the model. In one amusing example,
Lefkowitz, Blake, and Mouton (1955) observed what happened if a confederate
of the experimenter crossed a street against a red light. If the model was dressed
in a freshly pressed suit and tie, 14 percent of the pedestrians observing the

model followed; if the same model was dressed in scuffed shoes, soiled trousers, and a blue denim shirt, only 0.007 percent followed. The social status of the model is clearly one important factor in determining imitation; this is one reason that breakfast cereal manufacturers hire famous athletes to promote their products.

Another characteristic of models that influences our tendency to imitate them is their warmth or friendliness. In a study by Mischel and Grusec (1966), nursery school children were asked to accompany the experimenter to a room to play with toys. With one group, the experimenter played with the children in a warm and friendly way. With the second group, she ignored the children, saying that she had work to do. After playing for 20 minutes, the children in both groups were invited to play a cash register game with the experimenter, during which she engaged in a number of distinctive behaviors, such as saying "Bop" whenever she hit a key and marching around the table saying "March, march, march. . . ." She then said she had to leave for a few minutes and observed the children through a one-way mirror to see whether they imitated her distinctive behaviors. Children toward whom the model had previously been friendly were found to be far more likely to imitate her behaviors than the children toward whom she had been distant.

A third significant characteristic of models is their power—the extent to which they control resources we value. In the Mischel and Grusec experiment just described, half the children were told that the model was going to be their future teacher, and half were told that she was just a visitor. Those who believed that she was going to be their teacher were significantly more likely to imitate her behavior, even though this imitation served no apparent purpose, since, as far as they knew, no one was watching them. Summarizing this evidence, then, it appears that the more we like or admire models and the greater their power, the more we tend to imitate them. (For more comprehensive reviews, see Flanders, 1968; Rosenthal & Bandura, 1978.)

Consequences of the model's behavior.   Another factor influencing imitation involves the consequences that follow the modeled behavior. In a study by Bandura (1965), for example, nursery school children watched a film in which an adult model encountered an adult-size, inflatable plastic doll. The model ordered the doll to get out of his way and, when the doll failed to comply, punched it on the nose. For some of the children, this scene was followed by another adult's congratulating the model and giving him candy and soda. A second group, by contrast, saw the model upbraided as a bully and hit with a rolled-up magazine. To find out if the children would imitate the model's behavior, they were taken to a room containing a number of toys including the inflatable plastic doll; those children who had seen the model's violence reinforced proved far more likely to imitate his aggressive behavior than those who had seen him punished. Children, in other words, behave entirely sensibly: If a behavior produces positive consequences for others, they are more likely to try it themselves than if they see the behavior evoke punishment.

8.5 ALTERNATIVES TO REINFORCEMENT: SELF-CONTROL

Greatest weakness of Rf [handwritten margin note]

We have seen that the greatest weakness of reinforcement programs lies not in establishing behaviors initially, but rather in maintaining them when the program is discontinued. If no reinforcement is provided, the response may simply extinguish, and, in cases where the reinforcement program was seen as overly controlling, interest in the task may actually be less than it was originally.

A potential solution to both of these problems (lack of reinforcement from others and resentment of control) is to encourage **self-control**—that is, training people to control their own behavior rather than relying on reinforcement from external sources. The concept of self-control might at first seem to contradict the assumption of lawfulness, which we discussed in Chapter 1: If the environment controls behavior, you might ask, how can people be said to control their own behavior? B. F. Skinner suggested a solution to this apparent paradox (1953). He argued that behavior was indeed controlled by the environment, but that an individual's behavior could alter that environment and in this way change the probability of future behavior. Suppose, for example, that a man wanted to lose weight but had difficulty resisting candy bars. One strategy he could employ would be to remove any candy from his house every morning, so that if he felt hungry in the evening he might be deterred from eating by the effort required to obtain more candy. His behavior in removing candy (the controlling response) would alter the probability of eating the candy later (the controlled response), but both behaviors would still be lawfully determined by the past and present environment. *

Self-control, then, can be viewed as a set of behaviors that alter the probability of future behaviors. (For different interpretations of self-control, see M. L. Hoffman, 1983; Kohlberg, 1976.) A variety of techniques for enhancing self-control have been studied by psychologists. We shall look at three of them: stimulus control, distraction, and self-reinforcement.

---

* You may wonder why the dieter in our example should be any more successful at removing candy in the morning than he is at not eating it later. If he does not have the willpower or self-control to resist eating, why should he be any better at carrying out his intention to remove the candy? The answer, according to Rachlin (1974), lies in the different reinforcement contingencies affecting the two behaviors. Although the reinforcement for dieting is delayed—weight loss may only become obvious after days or weeks of dieting—the reinforcement for eating is immediate. When faced with a choice between eating and not eating, therefore, the immediately reinforced behavior of eating may prove stronger. The situation in the morning, however, is different. The reinforcement for removing candy from the house is still delayed, but so too is the reinforcement for leaving the candy in the house (it won't be eaten until the evening). The balance between these reinforcers, therefore, is not tilted so strongly in the direction of eating the candy, so the diet-appropriate behavior has a better chance of predominating.

Techniques of Self-Control

Stimulus control.   In our discussion of the principles of reinforcement, we saw that stimuli present when a response is reinforced acquire control over that response. Thus, if our goal is to eliminate maladaptive behaviors, one strategy might be to restrict those behaviors to a very limited range of situations so that they will not become associated with other stimuli.

Bootzin (1972) used this principle in developing a self-control treatment for insomnia. Patients with insomnia typically toss and turn for hours before falling asleep, worrying all the while about problems that arose during the day. If we assume that worrying about a problem is in some respects reinforcing, then, according to a stimulus control analysis, the bed would become associated with worrying, and the very act of going to bed on subsequent nights would tend to elicit this behavior. Bootzin's advice to his client, therefore, was to ensure that the stimulus of being in bed would be associated only with sleeping and not with worrying. Bootzin advised the client to go to bed when he felt tired and not to engage in any other activity, such as reading or watching television, while in bed. If he could not sleep, he was to get up and not return to bed until he again felt sleepy. The goal was that the stimulus of being in bed would become uniquely associated with sleeping. The technique proved highly effective: The client reported within two weeks that he was falling asleep quickly every night and sleeping soundly. Subsequent studies with larger samples have confirmed the effectiveness of this technique. (See Bootzin & Nicassio, 1978.)

Distraction.   Another useful self-control technique is distraction. When faced with a painful or unpleasant task, a useful strategy can be to distract yourself from its aversive aspects by concentrating on positive thoughts or images. In an experimental test of this approach by Kanfer and Seidner (1973), subjects were asked to keep their hands in a bucket of ice water for as long as they could stand it. A control group, given no special instructions, kept their hands in the ice water for an average of 57 seconds. Those in another group were shown slides of holiday scenes to distract them, and they endured the pain of the ice water for almost twice as long (99 seconds). Best of all, however, was a third group who were allowed to control the slides themselves; this group endured the pain almost three times as long (149 seconds). Distraction, in other words, increased tolerance of pain, and the greatest increase occurred in the situation in which subjects controlled the distracting stimuli. Together with other evidence (e.g., Glass, Singer, & Friedman, 1969), these results suggest that subjects who believe themselves in control can tolerate aversive situations much better than those who perceive themselves as helpless.

Distraction can also be useful in coping with situations in which reinforcement is delayed. Walter Mischel and his colleagues have investigated the ability of children to tolerate delay of gratification by giving them a task in which they can have a less preferred reinforcer immediately (for example, a marshmallow) or a preferred reinforcer (for example, a pretzel) if they are willing to wait for a specified interval. In one experiment by Mischel, Ebbesen, and Zeiss (1972), children who were given no special instructions endured the delay for an average of less than 30 seconds before opting for the immediately available reinforcer. Children who were encouraged to spend the delay interval thinking of something that was fun to do, on the other hand, waited 12 minutes. (For a review of related research, see Mischel & Mischel, 1977.)

Self-reinforcement. One of the main reasons that reinforcement is sometimes ineffective is that the delay between response and reinforcer is too long. Consider, for example, the behavior of studying. There are a number of powerful reinforcers for studying—good grades, parental approval, improved career prospects, and so on—but these reinforcers are delayed for weeks, months, or even years. To take a wildly hypothetical example, consider a college student who has to choose between reading a psychology text and going out on a date. The reinforcement for the date is relatively immediate; the reinforcement for studying is delayed days or weeks. From a reinforcement perspective, it is hardly surprising that many students have difficulty studying under these conditions.

When the environment does not provide immediate reinforcement for a behavior, one possible strategy is for individuals to reinforce themselves. This may at first sound implausible (can you really reinforce your own behavior?), but some evidence suggests that it is possible and can be effective. In one of the first studies on self-reinforcement, Bandura and Perloff (1967) invited children to turn a toy wheel. Children in the control group received no reinforcement for playing, but those in a self-reinforcement group were given a supply of tokens and told to take as many as they wanted whenever they turned the wheel a specified number of times. At the end of the experiment, they were told, the tokens would be exchanged for prizes, and the more tokens they had, the better the prizes they would receive. To encourage them to feel free to take as many tokens as they wished, the experimenter left the room while they played the game. An external reinforcement group was also included; these children received tokens automatically when they turned the wheel, with the number of tokens set at a level to match that of the children in the self-reinforcement group.

As you might expect, the children who were given tokens for turning the wheel did so significantly more than those in the unreinforced control group. Perhaps more surprisingly, however, so too did the children in the self-reinforcement group. Indeed, these children turned the wheel as often as those reinforced by the experimenter. Self-reinforcement, in other words, was just as effective as reinforcement from an external agent, and in some subsequent studies self-reinforcement has actually been more effective (for example, Jackson & Van Zoost, 1972).

The Development of Self-Control

Bandura and Perloff's results suggest that people can successfully reinforce their own behavior, but you may find yourself feeling skeptical. Since the tokens were freely available and the children could take as many as they wanted without the experimenter knowing, why didn't they just take the tokens they wanted without increasing their rate of playing?

A reinforcement analysis.   The concept of self-reinforcement is a strange one; it is almost as if one part of a person is reinforcing another for good behavior. Popular accounts of self-control in terms of willpower have the same flavor: In this view, one component of the mind, the will, forces other components to do its bidding. Skinner's analysis offers us a different perspective for interpreting this situation. Self-control, according to Skinner, is simply a behavior like any other, and it thus will be performed insofar as it is itself reinforced. Children, for example, may learn to reinforce themselves—perhaps with candy or, more likely, with praise ("I've been such a good girl")—because such behavior is itself reinforced by others. When children praise themselves appropriately, they may in turn be praised by others. (Tommy: "I did a good job cleaning my room, didn't I, Mommy?" Mother: "Yes, Tommy, you did it beautifully.") If the children cheat, they will be reprimanded eventually. If we get enough appropriate feedback, we may eventually learn to praise ourselves only when such praise is merited.

With regard to the Bandura and Perloff study, this analysis implies that the children reinforced themselves appropriately—that is, they reinforced themselves only when they had genuinely reached the set criterion—because they had learned in the past that accurate self-reinforcement was itself likely to be reinforced. There is little evidence to tell us whether self-reinforcement is actually learned in this way, but a study by Drabman, Spitalnik, and O'Leary (1973) suggests that it could be. The subjects were 10-year-old boys in a class for children with academic and emotional problems. Eight of the most disruptive boys in the class were selected for special training, and a token economy was established in which the boys were given points on a five-point scale for good behavior and for completing assignments; at the end of each lesson, the points could be exchanged for cakes, candies, or pennies.

The program was highly effective: The frequency of disruptive behavior fell by two-thirds, and the average number of assignments completed rose from 83 to 130. It was not possible, however, to maintain the token economy indefinitely. What, then, could be done to ensure that the gains would be sustained once the program was withdrawn?

Since a teacher could not always be available to provide reinforcement, Drabman and his colleagues decided to train the children to reinforce themselves. At the end of each lesson, the boys were to award themselves points on the basis of how they had behaved, with these points then being exchanged for other reinforcers in the usual way. To ensure that the boys would reinforce themselves appropriately, they instituted a training program in which the boys were initially reinforced by the teacher for accurate self-reinforcement. Once this behavior had been learned, the frequency of checking by the teacher was progressively reduced.

Specifically, the teacher monitored the boys' behavior during the self-reinforcement phase, and at the end of each lesson the boys' self-ratings were compared with the teacher's ratings. If the boys' ratings were within one point of the teacher's, they received the points they had given themselves; if the ratings matched accurately, the boys also received a bonus point; but if they had deviated from the teacher's ratings by more than a point, they received no points. To reduce the likelihood that the checking would be seen as a form of control, the experimenters explained that being selected for checking was a privilege, because only those boys who were checked would have the chance to earn bonus points.

Over days, the proportion of boys selected for checking was gradually reduced, until all the boys were receiving whatever points they had awarded themselves without any formal checking. On days when their self-ratings exactly matched the teacher's, though, the teacher strongly praised them.

The results are shown in Figure 8.6. During the final phase, in which they received whatever points they had awarded themselves, their behavior was not only maintained at the levels achieved when the teacher controlled reinforcement, but, if anything, actually exceeded those levels. This final phase continued for only 12 days, so we cannot be certain how long this behavior would have been maintained. However, the results of a subsequent study by Wood and Flynn (1978) are encouraging. In this study, 13-year-old delinquents in a program based on Achievement Place were trained to clean their rooms to an extremely high standard. (For example, their shoes not only had to be put away in a closet but had to be placed neatly next to each other.) The room's cleanliness was judged on a 15-point scale. Before training was instituted, the boys averaged only 3.4 points; after training in self-reinforcement, this rose to 13 points. The use of points was then discontinued, so that the boys received no reinforcement for cleaning their rooms other than occasional praise, but the high standard of cleanliness established during the self-reinforcement program was nevertheless maintained without decrement over 60 days. These results support the view that self-reinforcement is a behavior that can itself be reinforced and that, once learned, can be effective in maintaining other behaviors.

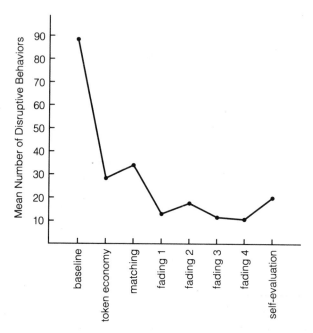

F I G U R E 8.6   Mean number of disruptive behaviors in successive phases of a self-control program. (Adapted from Drabman, Spitalnik, & O'Leary, 1973)

Self-control and modeling.   We can view self-control, then, as a behavior, or a set of behaviors, that can be learned. Just as other behaviors can be learned through modeling as well as through reinforcement, we might expect modeling to play an important role in the development of self-control also.

In one test of this hypothesis, Mischel and Liebert (1966) gave children an opportunity to watch someone model self-reinforcement. The experimenters asked the children to help a toy manufacturer test a new game, a three-foot bowling alley. They gave the children a bowl of tokens and told them that the more tokens they obtained, the better the prize they would receive at the end of the experiment. The children then began to play the game along with a model, who at various times said, "That's a good score. That deserves a chip," and thereupon took one.

For half the children, the model adopted a stringent criterion for self-reinforcement, taking a token only when she had obtained a score of 20. In the lenient condition, by contrast, the model took a chip whenever she obtained 15 or 20. Finally, the experimenter left, telling the children to continue to play and to take tokens as often as they wished.

The children in the two groups matched with superb accuracy the standards previously exhibited by the model, with the subjects in the high-criterion group in particular never taking a token for a score of less than 20. Thus, even though the children had been encouraged to take tokens whenever they wished, and even though they believed themselves to be unobserved, they adhered to the standards of the model. The powerful influence of the model in this situation suggests that "practice what you preach" may be good advice for all those who wish to influence the behavior of others (or are in the position, however unwillingly, of influencing the behavior of others).

Improving Your Studying

To summarize some of the self-control principles we have been discussing, we will conclude by considering how you can use self-control principles to increase the amount of time you spend studying. According to several successful programs (for example, Goldiamond, 1965; Fox, 1966), your first step should be to find a quiet spot where you can work with minimal disturbance—for example, an isolated desk in a library. Begin by setting yourself a modest target for how long you will study, and then reinforce yourself (self-reinforcement) when you reach your target (the reinforcer could be coffee, a break with friends, or even just a notation on a special record card—an accurate record of progress can be a surprisingly powerful reinforcer). Then, over days, gradually increase your target (shaping).

For this strategy to work, it is important to choose an effective reinforcer. Some evidence suggests that a public declaration of both your goals and your progress—for example, posting a graph of your studying time where your friends can see it and thus encourage you—may also be important. (See Hayes, Rosenfarb, Wulfert, Munt, Korn, & Zettle, 1985.) Also, you need to set goals that are realistically attainable. If you are very poor at concentrating, you may need to set your initial goal at only 15 minutes, or even 5 minutes, and then increase your target gradually.

To maximize the probability that your desk will become a cue for studying and not for other behaviors, ensure that studying is the only activity you engage in while there. If you feel an uncontrollable urge to daydream or have a snack, leave immediately, and return only when you feel able to resume concentrating on your work (stimulus control). These are by no means the only useful techniques for improving studying habits. (For some other techniques, see Fox, 1966; Weinstein & Meyer, 1986.) However, if you do want to improve your studying, you may find this approach a helpful component of a broader program based on careful reading, underlining, reviewing what you have read as soon as you finish a section, and other basic study skills.

8.6 SUMMARY

Over the past few chapters, we have reviewed a wide range of material on the practical applications of reinforcement—to disruptive and schizophrenic children, to convicts, even to university students—and there can be little doubt of its potential effectiveness. Sometimes, even seemingly minor changes, such as praising youngsters when they are good instead of scolding them when they are bad, can produce dramatic changes in behavior, provided that this reinforcement is immediate and consistent. Psychologists have assumed that once the desired behaviors are established, reinforcers in the natural environment will then serve to maintain them.

In many cases, this assumption is justified. Once a child has learned to read, for example, the pleasure derived from this activity will serve to maintain it without any need for support or encouragement from others. In other cases, however—such as a delinquent trying to study or an alcoholic trying to abstain from drinking—the naturally available reinforcers may not be sufficient. One of the most difficult questions now facing researchers is how to encourage the long-term maintenance of behavior following termination of a reinforcement program.

One strategy is to provide more time for the natural reinforcers to assume control, by ensuring that the learned behaviors do not immediately extinguish. To this end, the schedule of reinforcement used during training can be reduced, behavior can be reinforced in a variety of settings, and, finally, the entire reinforcement program can be faded gradually rather than terminated abruptly. As we saw in the case of Jerry, who eventually learned to wear his orthodontic device without supervision, this fading strategy can be very effective.

In other situations, though, reinforcement may have harmful side effects that make its use undesirable. Opinions differ about whether some uses of reinforcement should be considered bribery, but there is little doubt that the use of material reinforcers can encourage greed and undermine intrinsic motivation. To minimize the likelihood of these outcomes, the principle of "minimal force" should always be applied: Use the mildest reinforcer that is likely to be effective (generally, this will be praise), and, whenever possible, use reinforcement in a way that encourages feelings of competence and skill rather than mere obedience. A parent or teacher who reinforces children for sitting quietly or for doing as they "should" may succeed initially, but at a long-term cost to the children's pride and intrinsic motivation.

One possible alternative to reinforcement of desired behavior is modeling. We are all influenced by the behavior of those around us, and the evidence reviewed in this chapter suggests that models who are liked or admired can play a powerful role in shaping behavior. If a child—or anyone else, for that matter—is not behaving as you wish, one useful question to consider is whether you are behaving as you wish!

A second alternative to reinforcement is self-control. The phenomenon of self-control is not well understood; we do not know, for example, why some individuals seem to find it easy to control their own behavior, whereas others rely much more heavily on support or supervision from others. In this chapter, we have focused on B. F. Skinner's approach, which interprets self-control as a set of controlling responses that alter the environment in order to change the probability of subsequent responses. This is by no means the only possible interpretation of self-control, but it has the advantage of suggesting that self-control can be learned rather than being a form of willpower that you either have or do not have. Research on self-control techniques such as stimulus control, distraction, and self-reinforcement have supported this analysis by showing that individuals can learn to increase their self-control substantially. The reason that some individuals exhibit better self-control than others may not be their superior willpower, but simply that they have learned the appropriate behaviors better.

Here are two final thoughts. In Chapter 1, we discussed the assumption that animal and human behavior is similar in important respects, so that research in the animal laboratory might someday make important contributions to our understanding of human behavior. We have since encountered considerable support for this assumption. The importance of immediate reinforcement, the usefulness of gradual shaping, and the role of motivation in impairing as well as enhancing learning—all of these principles were discovered initially in experiments on animals, and all have proved of real value in practical programs to use reinforcement more effectively.

It is also important, however, to recognize the limitations of animal research and the ways in which research with humans has revealed principles not suggested by work with animals. One example is the finding that reinforcement can reduce intrinsic motivation, as when children reinforced for drawing a picture become less likely to do so outside the experimental situation. One implication of this research is that the effect of reinforcement may depend on the recipient's perception of the motivation of the giver. If reinforcement is seen as a means of control for the benefit of the controller, then it is less likely to be effective. Similarly, we saw that the effectiveness of punishment depends on whether it is accompanied by a clear and fair explanation. If we perceive punishment as fair, we are more likely to cooperate in future with the person who has punished us. A third example comes from research on modeling, which has shown that the extent to which we imitate the behavior of a model depends on whether we perceive the model as friendly. The common theme in all these examples is that reinforcement does not occur in a vacuum: It is often embedded within a complex social relationship, and its effectiveness may depend not just on the physical characteristics of the reinforcer but on the recipient's perception of the motive underlying its presentation. If a child feels that a reinforcer is being used as an expression of caring, the effect may be very different than if it is perceived as a means of exacting obedience ("If you sit quietly, you can have a candy").

In sum, reinforcement can be highly effective and is generally more fun for all concerned than alternatives such as reprimands or punishment. It is not a panacea for all problems, though, and, above all, it is not simple: You will not get very far by popping candy into people's mouths whenever they do what you want. Reinforcement is part of a complex social relationship, and we are only beginning to understand the nature of such relationships and how they determine the effects of reinforcement. Laboratory research has significantly increased our ability to use reinforcement effectively, but the application of these principles needs to proceed with some caution and even some humility.

Selected Definitions

Behavior modification An approach that conceptualizes human problems in terms of behaviors rather than mental states and then uses learning principles to change these behaviors. In some cases, the term *behavior therapy* is used interchangeably with *behavior modification*.

Token economy A systematic procedure for reinforcing behavior in which tokens are made contingent on the performance of desired behaviors; the tokens can later be exchanged for backup reinforcers such as candy. In early applications in mental hospitals, access to the backup reinforcers was restricted so that they could be obtained only with tokens; this was the basis for the term *economy*.

Intrinsic motivation Motivation to perform an activity that derives from the activity itself, rather than from any consequences that might follow the activity.

Behavioral contract An agreement by both parties (for example, a parent and a child) on the behavior they want to change and the consequences that will follow the behavior change.

Observational learning The learning of new behaviors by observing the behavior of others. The individual exhibiting the behavior is called a model, and observational learning is sometimes referred to as *imitation* (which emphasizes the behavior of the observer) or **modeling** (which emphasizes the behavior of the model).

Self-control According to Skinner, the performing of one response in order to alter the probability of some subsequent response.

Review Questions

1. The principle of "minimal force" suggests starting with relatively mild reinforcers such as praise, whenever possible. Can social reinforcers such as praise really modify difficult behaviors? If they fail, what other reinforcers can be used?

2. What can be done to increase the likelihood that behaviors will persist long enough after a reinforcement program is terminated to allow natural reinforcers to acquire control?

3. What are the potentially harmful effects of reinforcement? In what situations are these most likely to occur?

4. What alternatives are there to reinforcement for encouraging behavior?

5. What determines whether we imitate the behavior of a model?

6. What are some of the techniques by which people control their own behavior? How can they be applied to studying?

7. Self-control is often attributed to willpower, which is seen as a unitary trait that people either have or don't. How does Skinner explain self-control? How does his account differ from that of willpower? What does each definition have to say about variability in self-control? In other words, should a person who shows strong self-control in one situation (for example, giving up smoking) also have above-average self-control in other situations (for example, studying)?

8. Insofar as self-reinforcement is effective, how can we explain why people adhere to this regimen rather than taking the available reinforcers whenever they want?

CHAPTER NINE

314

THEORIES OF REINFORCEMENT

The Law of Effect Revisited

In Chapter 8 we concentrated on practical questions concerning the use of reinforcement; we turn now to theoretical issues. We will start by taking a more detailed look at Thorndike's belief that reinforcement acts to automatically stamp in an association between the situation and the response. We will examine whether the mechanism of reinforcement is as automatic as Thorndike supposed, and, what may sound like a very strange question, whether reinforcement really affects learning at all. We will then address one of the thorniest problems for reinforcement theorists, which is to explain avoidance learning. (If we manage to successfully avoid an event, nothing happens, but how can nothing reinforce our behavior?) Finally, we will look at the relationship between reinforcement and classical conditioning, and consider whether they are different processes or two aspects of the same process.

This may sound like a ragbag of largely unrelated questions, but they all address the fundamental question of what happens when a reinforcer is presented. Though the questions may sound very different, we will discover a considerable degree of similarity in the answers.

9.1 IS REINFORCEMENT AUTOMATIC?

One of the most important characteristics of reinforcement, according to Thorndike, was that it functioned automatically, without any need for conscious deliberation:

> [A reward] does not pick out the "right" or "essential" or "useful" connection by any mystical or logical potency. It is, on the contrary, as natural in its action as a falling stone. . . . It will strengthen connections which are wrong, irrelevant or useless, provided that they are close enough to the satisfier.

> (Thorndike, 1935, p. 39)

Is Contiguity Sufficient?

Superstition.   One implication of Thorndike's claim that reinforcement acts automatically, then, is that it should strengthen whatever behavior happens to precede it. Striking support for this view came from an experiment by B. F. Skinner (1948a). Using pigeons as subjects, Skinner placed them in a box and gave them grain to eat once every 15 seconds. The birds did not have to perform any response to obtain this food; the grain was presented every 15 seconds regardless of their behavior. Most of the birds nevertheless developed highly stereotyped behaviors, which they repeated over and over during the interval between reinforcements. One turned around in circles repeatedly, another brushed its head along the floor, a third tossed its head as if lifting an invisible bar, and so on.

The explanation for these strange behaviors, Skinner suggested, lay in the automatic nature of reinforcement. When the food was first presented, it would have strengthened whatever behavior the bird happened to be engaged in at the time. As a result, the bird would have been more likely to repeat this response, and if one of these repetitions happened to coincide with the next presentation of food, it would have been strengthened still further, and so on. This process, in which the accidental conjunction of a response and a reinforcer results in strengthening of the response, is called *adventitious reinforcement*. Not all of the repeated responses would have been followed by reinforcement, of course, and on some occasions food might have followed another response and strengthened it instead. In the end, however, Skinner found that six of his eight birds acquired highly stereotyped responses, even though these behaviors played no role in producing food. Skinner called these response patterns **superstitions** and suggested that a similar process might underlie the emergence of superstitious behavior in humans.

Doubts about Skinner's interpretation of superstition, however, were raised subsequently in a paper by Staddon and Simmelhag (1971). Using a procedure similar to Skinner's, they also found that subjects developed idiosyncratic patterns of behavior during the early stages of the interval between reinforcers. (They called these early responses *interim behaviors*.) They found, however, that as the time for reinforcement approached, all the birds began to behave in the same way, orienting toward the wall containing the grain magazine and pecking at it. The uniformity of this terminal behavior suggested that it could not have been due to adventitious reinforcement, since this would have produced different behaviors in each bird. Staddon and Simmelhag attributed this behavior instead to classical conditioning: Food elicited the bird's approach to the grain magazine and its pecking, and this behavior became conditioned to the time at which the food was delivered. As for the more idiosyncratic interim behaviors, Staddon and Simmelhag argued that these behaviors could not be due to adventitious reinforcement either, because the terminal behaviors intervened between the interim behaviors and reinforcement, and thus would have prevented their strengthening.

The reasons for the discrepancy between Skinner's results, in which idiosyncratic behaviors were observed throughout the interval, and Staddon and Simmelhag's, are not yet clear. (For some interesting speculations, see Eldridge, Pear, Torgrud, & Evers, 1988.) However, there have been enough replications of Skinner's findings to suggest that reinforcers *can* strengthen whatever behaviors happen to precede them, whether or not they always do so.

Particularly interesting evidence has come from a recent study by Ono (1987), in which the subjects were humans. Ono had his subjects sit at a table that contained three levers and a counter. He instructed the subjects to obtain as many points as they could and then exposed them to a fixed-time schedule in which a point was added to the counter every 30 seconds. Ono found, as had Skinner, that his subjects began to develop idiosyncratic behaviors, even though no response was necessary to obtain points. One subject, for example, developed a pattern of pulling a lever several times in succession and then holding it. He had just performed this sequence at the moment when he first received reinforcement, and as he repeated this pattern and continued to obtain reinforcement, the behavior became firmly established.

Considered as a whole, the literature on superstition suggests that reinforcers do tend to strengthen whatever behaviors happen to precede them, although other factors, such as classical conditioning and the interval between reinforcers, are important in determining whether a stable superstition develops. (If the interval between reinforcers is too long, the behavior initially strengthened may extinguish before the arrival of the next reinforcer.) In particular, Ono's results suggest that superstitions in humans may also be due to adventitious reinforcement, because behaviors that happen to precede a desirable outcome are strengthened. The gambler who breathes on his dice before rolling them, and the basketball coach who always wears her "lucky" socks on the night of a big game, may have acquired these superstitions in exactly the same way as Skinner's pigeons.

Contiguity versus contingency.   Even more dramatic evidence for the power of reinforcers to strengthen whatever behavior precedes them comes from a line of research initiated by G. V. Thomas (1981). Whereas in Skinner's experiment responses had no effect on reinforcement, Thomas arranged matters so that the response to be learned actually reduced the probability of reinforcement.

Thomas placed rats in a Skinner box and gave them one pellet of food every 20 seconds. As in Skinner's study, the food was free; that is, the rats did not have to perform any response to obtain it. However, a bar was also present in the box, and if the rat pressed the bar during any 20-second interval, it would immediately receive the food pellet that had been scheduled for the end of that interval. However, this response also canceled the pellet scheduled to occur after the following 20-second interval. Suppose, for example, that a rat pressed the lever 5 seconds into the session. It would immediately receive the pellet of food that had been scheduled to occur at 20 seconds, but it would lose the pellet scheduled for 40 seconds. If it responded again at, say, 42 seconds, it would immediately receive the pellet scheduled for 60 seconds but lose the pellet scheduled for 80 seconds. Thus, if a rat did not press the bar at all, it would receive food every 20 seconds, but if it responded regularly, food would be presented only once every 40 seconds.

In effect, Thomas was pitting the effects of contiguity against those of contingency. The response of pressing the lever was sometimes followed immediately by food (contiguity), but in the end this response reduced the probability of food. Thus, whereas in Skinner's experiment there was no contingency between responding and food, in Thomas's there was actually a negative contingency: The probability of food following a response was less than its probability in the absence of a response.

Despite this negative contingency, Thomas's rats learned to respond at a relatively high rate, and they continued to do so for many sessions. Figure 9.1 shows the results for a typical subject. The rat did not respond at all during the

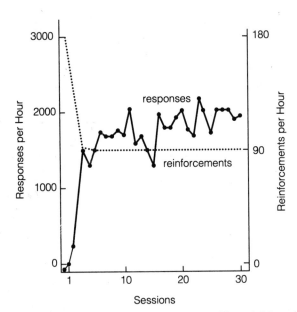

FIGURE 9.1   Pitting contiguity against contingency. The solid line shows a rat's rate of bar-pressing. This response sometimes produced food immediately, but it reduced the overall rate of reinforcement. The dotted line shows the overall rate of reinforcement. (Thomas, 1981)

first two sessions, but once it began to do so, its response rate increased rapidly to approximately 2000 per hour. This high rate of responding halved its rate of reinforcement from about 180 to 90 reinforcements per hour; despite this, it continued to respond for 30 sessions.

Implications for human behavior. In effect, the rats were misled by the contiguity between bar-pressing and obtaining food, and they inferred a causal relationship, even though their behavior actually reduced the amount of food they obtained. You might be tempted to think that this is yet more evidence for the stupidity of animals and assume that humans would never behave so foolishly, but Wasserman and Neunaber (1986) have reported that people placed in similar situations behave almost identically. Their experimental design was essentially the same as Thomas's, except that they used college students as subjects. The students were told that they would earn points whenever a light came on, and that pressing or not pressing a telegraph key might increase the number of light flashes. For subjects in the control group, the light came on at fixed intervals, regardless of whether they responded. However, for subjects in the experimental group, the procedure was identical to that in Thomas's experiment: The first response in an interval moved forward the light flash that had been scheduled for the end of the interval, but canceled the light flash in the following interval.

Figure 9.2 shows how responding changed over successive intervals. Subjects in the experimental group responded far more than those in the control group, even though by doing so they received fewer points. When asked at the end of the experiment to describe the relationship between pressing the key and obtaining light flashes, they reported that responding somewhat increased the frequency of flashes.

These results suggest that humans as well as animals may be misled at times by the contiguity of a response and reinforcer and may infer a causal relationship where none exists. If so, one question that naturally arises is why the effects of contiguity outweigh those of contingency in the case of reinforcement, whereas the opposite seems true in classical conditioning. (See Chapter 4.) Part of the answer may be that reinforcement encourages a kind of self-fulfilling prophecy. Suppose that someone experiences an accidental conjunction of a response and reinforcer and, as a result, repeats that behavior—for example, a coach who starts wearing blue socks after a dramatic victory in which he wore blue socks. If he wears blue socks to every game, he will have no opportunity to learn that games are won even in the absence of blue socks. And if he cannot compare the probability of winning in the presence and absence of blue socks, he will have no basis for altering this behavior. In classical conditioning, on the other hand, it is the experimenter who controls when the CS and US are presented, and thus can ensure that subjects are exposed to both of the important probabilities.

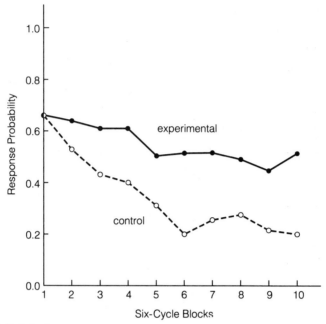

F I G U R E 9.2   Pitting contiguity against contingency in humans. Subjects were instructed to make a light flash as often as they could. For subjects in the control group, their responses had no effect on the preprogrammed rate of light flashes. For subjects in the experimental group, responses sometimes produced an immediate light flash but reduced the total number of flashes. (Based on Wasserman & Neunaber, 1986)

Reinforcement Without Awareness

The "uh-huh" effect.   Perhaps a more direct test of the claim that reinforcement acts automatically is that it should strengthen behavior even when subjects are unaware of the reinforcement contingency. One test of this prediction was reported by Greenspoon (1955). Using college students as subjects, he gave them 25 minutes to say all the words they could think of. Whenever the word was a plural noun, the experimenter reinforced it by saying "mmm-hmm." The result was a significant increase in the frequency of these words over the course of the session, but postexperiment interviews revealed no awareness that the experimenter had been reinforcing these words.

This experiment and similar ones suggested that reinforcement can occur without awareness, but researchers soon began to raise questions about the techniques used to assess awareness in these studies. Typically, subjects were asked only a few brief questions, and these questions were sometimes very general (for example, "Were you aware of the purpose of the experiment?"). Thus, subjects might have been aware of the reinforcement contingency but didn't mention it because they did not realize the experimenter was asking about it. (The questions were deliberately vague because the experimenters did not want to suggest the correct hypothesis to subjects who might previously have been unaware of it.)

In one attempt to overcome this problem, DeNike and Spielberger (1963) used the same reinforcement procedure as Greenspoon, but then interviewed subjects much more extensively afterward, with successive questions becoming progressively more specific in probing awareness of the reinforcement contingency. Figure 9.3 shows how the frequency of plural nouns changed over the course of the session. The frequency increased substantially with subjects who were later found to have been aware of the reinforcement contingency, but no learning occurred in unaware subjects.

Although the results of other experiments using the Greenspoon task have varied somewhat, in general it appears that when awareness is rigorously assessed, subjects do not learn unless they are aware of the reinforcement contingency. (See Spielberger & DeNike, 1966.) One possible interpretation of this outcome is that reinforcement never occurs without awareness, but an alternative possibility is that the Greenspoon task may not be a suitable procedure for demonstrating such learning. The problem is that if you are participat-

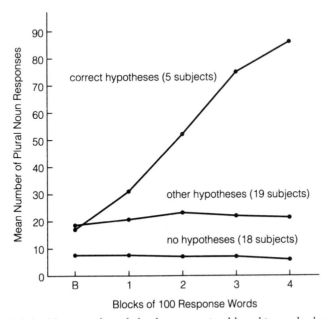

F I G U R E 9.3   Mean number of plural nouns emitted by subjects who later reported either awareness that reinforcement was contingent on plural nouns, other hypotheses about reinforcement, or no hypotheses. Reinforcement was not presented during the baseline period (B). (DeNike & Spielberger, 1963)

ing in an experiment and the experimenter repeatedly nods or says "uh-huh" for no apparent reason, you are likely to wonder what is going on and search for explanations of the experimenter's behavior. Saltz (1971) has suggested that the act of generating and testing alternative hypotheses may interfere with the automatic operation of reinforcement, perhaps because the brain's learning capacity is limited, so that cognitive resources devoted to hypothesis testing interfere with other forms of learning. Subjects who do not test the correct hypothesis, therefore, will not learn.

Surreptitious reinforcement.   If this analysis is correct, we should be more likely to find reinforcement without awareness in tasks in which the reinforcer used is not likely to arouse suspicion. In one such study by Hefferline, Keenan, and Harford (1959), subjects were told that they were participating in a study of the effects of stress on body tension. Electrodes were attached to their bodies to assess muscular tension, and the effect of stress was evaluated by randomly alternating periods of soothing music and a harsh noise. In reality, however, the duration of the noise was not random: The noise was terminated whenever the subjects contracted a very small muscle within their left thumb—a response so small that it could not be observed visually and could be detected only by an electrode mounted above the muscle. Over the course of the session, there was a dramatic increase in contractions of the muscle. When interviewed afterward, however, all the subjects "still believed that they had been passive victims with respect to the onset and duration of the noise, and all seemed astounded to learn that they themselves had been in control" (p. 1339). In a subsequent experiment, Hefferline and Keenan (1961) extended this result by showing that they could differentially reinforce subjects for contractions of particular magnitudes, so that subjects could learn to precisely control a muscle whose activity they could not detect.

Further evidence for reinforcement without awareness comes from an ingenious experiment by Rosenfeld and Baer (1969). On the surface, their procedure was very similar to that of Greenspoon, except that the response chosen for reinforcement was more subtle. Subjects were told that they were participating in a study of social attitudes and were asked questions about topics such as the Vietnam conflict. The interviewer—a graduate student recruited by the authors to carry out the study—was told to observe the subjects to see if they engaged in any distinctive mannerisms and then to reinforce one of these behaviors by nodding his head whenever the behavior occurred.

The first subject was observed to rub his chin occasionally as he talked, so the interviewer, in consultation with the authors, set out to reinforce this behavior. In fact, however, the "subject" was actually a confederate of the experimenter: He pretended to be naive, but he had been briefed in advance about what would happen and was instructed to rub his chin whenever the interviewer said "yeah." In other words, the interviewer was trying to reinforce the "subject" for chin rubbing, but, unbeknown to him, the "subject" was actually using the desired outcome of chin rubbing to reinforce the interviewer for saying "yeah."

The frequency with which the interviewer said "yeah" over the course of the experiment is shown in Figure 9.4. During the baseline phase, the "subject" rubbed his chin at random intervals, regardless of the interviewer's behavior. When chin rubbing was then made contingent on the interviewer's saying "yeah," the frequency of this verbal behavior increased substantially; when reinforcement was discontinued, it returned to low levels. In subsequent sessions, the frequency of "yeah" again increased when reinforced, but not when reinforcement was made contingent on a different verbal behavior ("mm-hmm"). Chin rubbing was thus clearly effective in reinforcing the response on which it was contingent, but the "experimenter" was totally unaware that his own behavior was being reinforced. When eventually told what had happened, his reaction was one of stunned incredulity. (The procedure, incidentally, is neatly summarized in the title of Rosenfeld and Baer's 1969 report: "Unnoticed Verbal Conditioning of an Aware Experimenter by a More Aware Subject: The Double-Agent Effect.")

Evaluating Automatic Reinforcement

In summary, there is still some controversy over Thorndike's claims about reinforcement; however, at least under some conditions, reinforcement seems to operate in the automatic fashion he suggested. It can strengthen whatever

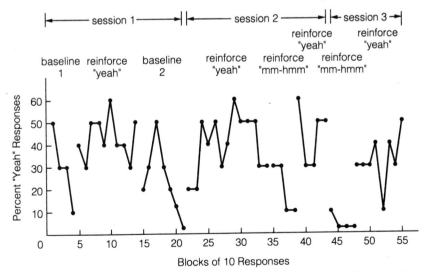

F I G U R E 9.4 The effect of a desired outcome (the interviewee's rubbing his chin) on the interviewer's saying "yeah." During different phases of the experiment, the interviewee rubbed his chin at random (baselines), after the interviewer said "yeah," or after he said "mm-hmm." (Rosenfeld & Baer, 1969)

response precedes it, even if this response is irrelevant or even counterproductive (Skinner, 1948a; Thomas, 1981); and it can be effective even if subjects are not aware of the reinforcement contingency.

Automatic reinforcement of this kind could play an important role in determining our behavior. Suppose, for example, that you were a Democrat but all your friends were Republicans; suppose, further, that they were obviously pleased and supportive whenever you referred positively to Republican politicians. Might social reinforcement of this kind lead you to shift your political beliefs, even if you were not consciously seeking to gain your friends' approval? An experiment by Scott (1959) suggests that it might. He staged a series of debates in which participants were told that winners would be selected on the basis of their style of presentation. (In fact, they were selected randomly.) Those who won the debate became significantly more likely to believe the positions they had advocated than those who had lost. Thus, even though approval was explicitly made contingent on style of presentation rather than content, those reinforced for stating a position became more likely to believe it.

As in the case of classical conditioning, it is important to remember that in most situations subjects are aware of the reinforcement contingencies affecting them. (For a particularly robust statement of this view, see Brewer, 1974.) If learning sometimes does occur without awareness, such learning is almost certainly the exception rather than the rule.

9.2 IS REINFORCEMENT NECESSARY FOR LEARNING?

According to the Law of Effect, a reward stamps in an association between the preceding stimulus and a response. The brain, in this view, is something like a coin-operated photocopier: Just as you have to put money in the machine to get it to produce a copy, so you have to supply a reinforcer to activate the brain's copying mechanism and get it to form an association.

A very different view of learning was proposed by cognitive theorists such as Tolman (1932, 1948). They argued that as we interact with the world around us, we are constantly noticing features of our environment and storing information about them. Reinforcement, in their view, does not cause learning; rather, the occurrence of a reinforcer is simply one of the many things we learn about, and we then use this knowledge in deciding our behavior. If the brain is to be compared to any machine, in the cognitive view, then a more appropriate metaphor would be a powerful computer that carries out a complex sequence of operations on the information fed into it. The presentation of a reinforcer is simply one more bit of information, one more fact about the environment, to be used in calculating the optimal response.

Learning Without Reinforcement

These two perspectives lead to very different predictions. According to the Law of Effect, learning should occur only if a reinforcer is presented, whereas the cognitive analysis suggests that learning should occur without reinforcement.

Latent learning.   One early test of these opposing views was reported by Tolman and Honzik (1930a). They trained two groups of rats to run through a complex maze with 14 choice points, but only one group was given food when they reached the goal box. If reinforcement is necessary for learning, then only the subjects in the reinforced group (R) should have learned the correct path to the goal box, and this was what Tolman and Honzik found: Whereas the number of errors made by the reinforced group steadily decreased, the performance of the nonreinforced group (N) improved only slightly. The failure of the nonreinforced subjects to *perform* the correct response, however, did not necessarily prove that they had not *learned* it. Perhaps they had learned the correct path to the goal box just as well as the reinforced subjects had, but did not choose this path because they had no incentive to do so.

To find out, Tolman and Honzik ran a third group (NR), which was not reinforced on the first 10 days but was reinforced thereafter. If these subjects had learned the correct path to the goal box during the nonreinforced trials, then they should begin to take it as soon as they realized that the goal box contained food. If reinforcement was necessary for learning, on the other hand, then learning should occur for the first time on trial 11, and their performance should then improve at the same gradual rate shown by the reinforced subjects at the beginning of the experiment. A cognitive analysis thus predicted immediate improvement after the introduction of food, whereas reinforcement theory predicted gradual learning.

As shown in Figure 9.5, it was the cognitive analysis that was supported: The performance of the switched subjects instantly matched that of the subjects who had already had 10 trials of reward. It thus appeared as if the rats had learned the correct path to the goal box during the nonreinforced trials, but that this learning had remained unused, or latent, until the introduction of a reinforcer provided an incentive for using it. This phenomenon is known as **latent learning.**

Perceptual learning.   A second example of learning in the absence of reinforcement comes from experiments on **perceptual learning**, in which subjects' ability to discriminate between stimuli improves as a result of simple exposure. In an experiment by Gibson, Walk, Pick, and Tighe (1958), for example, rats reared with a metal triangle mounted on the walls of their cage were subsequently much better at solving a discrimination problem in which they had to

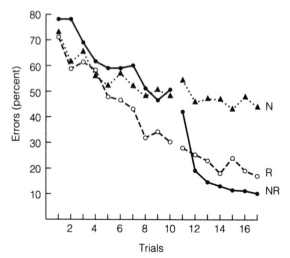

FIGURE 9.5   Latent learning. Group R was given food in the goal box on every trial, group N was never given food, and group NR was given food starting on trial 11. (Adapted from Tolman & Honzik, 1930a)

discriminate this triangle from another shape. Similarly, human subjects in psychophysical experiments rapidly improved in their ability to hear a very weak tone or to discriminate between similar lights, even if given no feedback about the accuracy of their performance (Gibson, 1969). You may have experienced similar improvements in your ability to recognize different musical instruments or different wines or beers. At first, all the stimuli sounded or tasted much the same, but with experience they became increasingly distinct, until eventually you may have found it difficult to understand how you could ever have confused them.

The common thread uniting these examples is that mere exposure to a stimulus, whether a triangle or a trombone, may be sufficient to produce learning about its characteristics, in the absence of any external reinforcement. The phrase "mere exposure" probably needs qualification, however, because evidence from human studies suggests a more active process of stimulus exploration than mere exposure might imply. In an experiment by DeRivera (1959), naval cadets were given a set of 10 fingerprints to examine during the pretraining phase and were then asked to learn an association between each fingerprint and a digit. Subjects who had been asked to look for differences among the fingerprints during preexposure performed better during the test phase than did subjects who had been asked to look for common features. It is not simply exposure to stimuli that matters, in other words: How subjects attend to the stimuli—and, in particular, whether they actively search for distinguishing features—will influence whether they improve at discriminating them.

Perceptual learning, then, involves a more active process on the part of the subject than the phrase "mere exposure" might imply. In the present context, however, the important point is that in perceptual learning, as in latent learning, and also sensory preconditioning (Chapter 2), reinforcement is not necessary for learning to occur: Simple exposure to stimuli sometimes leads ✳ to substantial learning about their properties and relationships.

The Role of the Reinforcer

The fact that reinforcement is not necessary for learning does not necessarily mean that it has no effect on learning. In experiments on latent learning, for example, performance in the experimental group does not always immediately improve to the level of the group rewarded throughout, and one possibility is that the rewarded group had learned somewhat more during the initial phase. (For further evidence that reinforcement can enhance learning about preceding events, see White & Milner, 1992.)

Whether or not a reinforcer affects learning about the events that precede it, we know that the introduction of a reinforcer does affect performance. The rats in Tolman and Honzik's experiment did not need reinforcement to learn the correct path to the goal box, but the introduction of food clearly influenced their decision to take that path. How, then, does reinforcement influence performance?

Information. Whereas the Law of Effect assumes that a reinforcer affects learning about preceding events, a cognitive analysis suggests that a reinforcer is an event that is itself learned about. If we obtain food after making a response, for example, then we learn that this response is one way of obtaining food, and we can use this information to obtain food in the future. Returning to our earlier computer analogy, the brain's task, like the computer's, is to process or analyze information. The brain must first perceive or *code* the stimulus input, and then memorize or *store* it until it is needed. (See also Chapter 12.) What response is then made will be determined by *decision processes* in which the stored information is analyzed to determine the optimal response. A reinforcer, in this view, is an event that is stored in exactly the same way as other events; it differs from other events not because it affects learning, but because we use information about its occurrence to plan future responses.

An experiment by Buchwald (1967) nicely illustrates this cognitive, or informational, perspective. He trained human subjects on a paired-associate learning task in which they were given a list of 40 words, one at a time, and had to respond to each word by saying either "7" or "9." If they made the correct response, the experimenter immediately said "Right," whereas if they made an incorrect response he said "Wrong." The results of the experiment were hardly surprising: The frequency of correct responses increased over repetitions of the list.

Thorndike's explanation for results of this kind was that "Right" was a reinforcer, so that its presentation strengthened the association between the word and the correct digit. "Wrong," on the other hand, was aversive, so that its presentation weakened the preceding association. Buchwald's analysis was very different. According to Buchwald, the word "Right" does not facilitate learning at all, but is itself an event that must be remembered. Confronted by the stimulus "cat," for example, the subject might respond with the number "3," and then be told "Right" by the experimenter. In order to be correct on the next trial, he would have to remember both the response he had made and its outcome: He could make an error if he forgot his response *or* if he remembered the response but could not recall whether or not it had been correct. Being told "Right," in this interpretation, had no effect on learning; instead, it was itself something that had to be remembered, and whose recall determines performance—in this case, whether the subject decided to repeat the response.

To distinguish between the learning and performance interpretations, Buchwald introduced a condition in which the outcome of a particular trial was not revealed until the *following* trial. That is, when each word was presented again on the following trial, Buchwald would tell subjects whether their response on the preceding trial had been correct before asking them to respond. According to the Law of Effect, delaying reinforcement in this way should severely impair learning of the word-digit associations, but Buchwald predicted that it would actually enhance performance! According to his analysis, subjects could make errors if they forgot either the response or its outcome; by delaying the outcome, therefore, he eliminated one possible source of error. Because subjects in the delayed condition needed to remember only their response, their performance should be facilitated relative to control subjects who had to remember both their response and its outcome. This prediction was confirmed: Performance was significantly better when the trial outcome was delayed. (See also Buchwald, 1969.) "Right" or "Wrong," then, seemed to provide information that guided subjects' performance, but did not directly affect their memory for preceding events. (For further analysis of the role of reinforcers in learning, see Chapter 12.)

Motivation.   Insofar as reinforcement is simply a source of information, we might assume that subjects use this information rationally to determine their behavior. If you know that studying is the best way to obtain a good grade, for example, then you might use this information to calculate how much of your time to allocate to studying. (This decision, of course, would also depend on the other alternatives available to you, and on the value you attach to each of them.) Similarly, a cognitive analysis suggests that a rat will learn that pressing a bar produces food and will use this information rationally in deciding whether to press the bar.

Some evidence, however, suggests that the decision-making process is not always as rational as this simple informational model would seem to imply. For example, Meltzer and Brahlek (1968) trained rats to press a bar on an FI 3-minute schedule of reinforcement, and found that subjects who received a larger amount of food pressed the lever faster. This might at first seem entirely sensible—of course, we respond more when a more attractive incentive is available—but because of the fixed-interval schedule used, a higher rate of response had minimal effect on how soon the rats received food: The subjects in both groups received food approximately once every 3 minutes no matter how fast they responded. The higher rate of response in this instance thus looks more like an effect of excitement than a rational calculation of optimal behavior.

We have encountered evidence for emotional effects such as this a number of times in previous chapters. In our discussion of amount of reinforcement, for example, we discussed the experiment by Crespi (1942) in which he trained rats to run down an alley to a goal box containing food. A group that was originally trained with 1 pellet of the food in the goal box and then switched to 16 pellets ran down the alley much faster than rats that received 16 pellets throughout, a result that looked much more like an emotional reaction than a rational response. (See also Zamble, 1967.) We encountered further evidence for emotional or motivational effects in our discussion of extinction, where we saw that animals often react to the omission of an expected reinforcer with what looks very much like frustration. Pigeons that are no longer reinforced for pecking a key do not simply decide that there is no longer any point in making this response; instead, they viciously attack another pigeon (Azrin, Hutchinson, & Hake, 1966). Similarly, college students who are no longer being reinforced prefer to hit a pad to turn off a loud noise rather than press a button as they had previously. This frustration effect may also explain why people often hit and kick malfunctioning vending machines with a force that is perhaps not entirely attributable to a rational belief that jarring the mechanism might release the desired soft drink or candy bar.

In all of these cases, it looks as if the consequence that follows a response does not simply give the subject information, but also produces a state of excitement or emotion that can affect the vigor of subsequent responding. Our understanding of such motivational effects is still fairly primitive, but one influential analysis was proposed by Hull (1952) and Spence (1956). They suggested that the presentation of a reinforcer leads to the conditioning of a motivational state, which they called **incentive motivation**. There are thus two sources of motivation: drive, which is determined by how long a subject has been deprived of the reinforcer; and incentive motivation, which is determined by the attractiveness of the reinforcer. Together, drive and incentive motivation determine the total motivation to obtain a reinforcer, and this, in turn, affects both the choice of a response (when we are hungry, we are more like to engage in behaviors that lead to food) and the intensity or vigor of that response (we work harder to obtain large rewards than small ones).

As noted earlier, our understanding of exactly how motivation influences response selection and vigor is far from complete. (For two sharply contrasting accounts, see Bindra, 1972, and Mackintosh, 1983.) For our present purposes, the main point is simply that reinforcers influence motivation as well as providing information, and that these motivational effects are not always as rational as an informational account might imply.

9.3 AVOIDANCE

One of the most difficult puzzles for reinforcement theorists concerns avoidance learning. An **avoidance response** is one that postpones or prevents an unpleasant event. An **escape response** is one that terminates an unpleasant stimulus.

On the face of it, learning to avoid unpleasant events is quite straightforward. In a typical avoidance experiment, a rat is trained in a shuttle box with a hurdle in the middle (Figure 9.6). A tone is presented for 10 seconds, followed by an electric shock delivered through the floor of the cage. If the rat jumps over the hurdle while the shock is on, the shock is immediately terminated. If

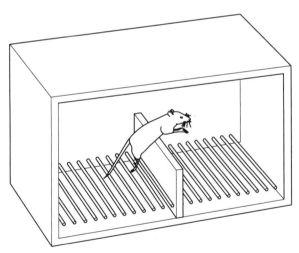

F I G U R E 9.6 A typical shuttle box used for avoidance training. Electric shock is delivered through the grid floor, but the shock can be avoided if the rat shuttles from one side of the box to the other by jumping over the barrier.

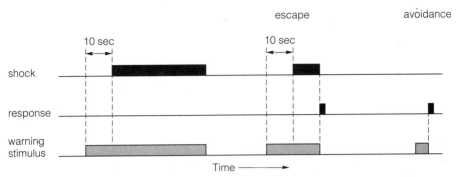

F I G U R E 9.7   Diagram of a signaled avoidance procedure. Shock is typically pre-sented following a 10-second warning stimulus. If the subject makes no response, the shock terminates after a fixed period; if the subject responds during the shock, both the warning stimulus and the shock are immediately terminated; if the subject responds be-fore the shock, the warning stimulus is terminated and the forthcoming shock is can-celed.

the rat jumps before the shock comes on, then the tone is turned off and the scheduled shock is canceled; this is even better, from the rat's point of view. Thus, depending on when the rat jumps over the barrier, it can either escape from the shock once it is on or avoid it altogether. The procedure is called **signaled avoidance**, because the experimenter provides a signal to indicate when the shock is imminent. Figure 9.7 diagrams the procedure.

Typical performance for one subject on this task (in this case, a dog) is shown in Figure 9.8. For the first seven trials, the dog's response latency was greater than 10 seconds, so it received a shock on every trial. It avoided shock on trial 8, however, and continued to do so on every trial thereafter.

In some respects, this result is hardly surprising: If an animal can avoid an unpleasant shock by jumping over a barrier, then of course it will do so. For reinforcement theorists, however, this learning posed a serious dilemma, be-cause the consequence of a successful avoidance response was that absolutely nothing happened. How could *nothing* act to reinforce behavior?

Two-Factor Theory

An ingenious solution to this problem was proposed by O. Hobart Mowrer (1947), whose explanation has become known as **two-factor theory**. Accord-ing to Mowrer, the pairing of tone and shock results in conditioning of fear to the tone. When the rat eventually jumps over the hurdle and terminates the tone, therefore, its level of fear is reduced. And, since fear is aversive, the termination of this aversive state reinforces jumping. Thus, the rat jumps over

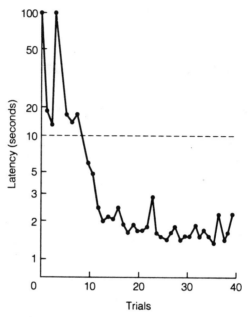

F I G U R E 9.8　Avoidance learning of a typical dog. Shock was initiated 10 seconds after the onset of the warning stimulus, so responses that had a latency of less than 10 seconds avoided shock. (Adapted from Solomon & Wynne, 1953)

the barrier not because it wants to avoid shock, but in order to escape from the warning stimulus. According to this theory, then, avoidance learning depends on two processes: classical conditioning of fear to the tone, and reinforcement of the avoidance response by termination of the tone.

The motivational role of fear.　This analysis has a number of testable implications. The first derives from the assumption that fear provides the motive for avoidance behavior. In Chapter 6, we saw that motives such as hunger and thirst increase the vigor of responses that reduce them. If fear provides the motive for avoidance behavior, therefore, then increasing subjects' fear should increase the speed of their avoidance responding.

In one test of this prediction, Rescorla and LoLordo (1965) trained dogs using a procedure known as **Sidman avoidance**. No warning stimulus is used in this procedure, and shock is programmed to occur at fixed time intervals (the shock–shock interval). If the subject makes an avoidance response, however, the next programmed shock is postponed for a fixed period (the response–shock interval). In Rescorla and LoLordo's experiment, shocks were programmed to occur every 10 seconds, but every time the dogs jumped over the hurdle in the shuttle box they ensured a shock-free period of 30 seconds. By

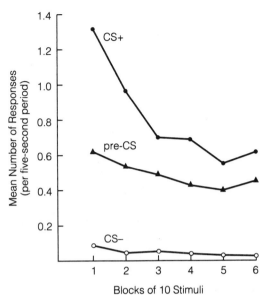

F I G U R E 9.9   The effect of presenting a conditioned stimulus on ongoing avoidance responding. Dogs responding on a Sidman avoidance task received a stimulus previously paired with either the presence of shock (CS+) or its absence (CS−). The pre-CS curve shows responding prior to presentation of the test stimulus. (Rescorla & LoLordo, 1965)

jumping at least once every 30 seconds, therefore, the dogs could ensure that they would never receive a shock.*

Once the dogs learned the avoidance response, Rescorla and Lolordo confined them to one half of the shuttle box and gave them discriminative fear conditioning trials in which one tone (CS+) was followed by shock, but a second tone (CS−) was not. Sidman avoidance training was then resumed, and once the dogs were again responding reliably, CS+ and CS− were occasionally presented for five seconds at a time. Figure 9.9 shows that when CS+ was presented the rate of jumping immediately doubled despite the fact that the dogs were already responding at a rate that avoided shock (the pre-CS curve). When CS− was presented, on the other hand, the rate of responding fell to almost zero. As predicted by two-factor theory, therefore, conditioned fear

---

* Two-factor theory accounts for responding under Sidman avoidance by assuming that temporal cues play the role of the warning stimulus in signaled avoidance: As the time for shock approaches, fear increases, and the avoidance response reduces fear because this response is always followed by a shock-free period. One way of conceptualizing this analysis is in terms of two hypothetical stimuli, S_1 and S_2. The passing of a fixed amount of time, S_1, is followed by shock, whereas the feedback produced by the avoidance response, S_2, is not. Fear, therefore, is conditioned more strongly to S_1 than to S_2, and thus the occurrence of the response produces a transition to a lower level of fear.

exerted powerful control over the rate of responding. (See also Overmier & Lawry, 1979.)

Escape from fear is reinforcing.   Mowrer's second assumption was that avoidance responses are reinforced by escape from the warning stimulus. To test whether termination of the warning stimulus on its own is really reinforcing, Brown and Jacobs (1949) gave rats conditioning trials in which a light-tone compound was paired with shock; the rats could not avoid the shock. A control group received the same light-tone compound but no shock. Then, in the test phase, the rats were placed in a test box and the light-tone compound was presented. If the rats jumped over the barrier, the compound was immediately terminated.

As shown in Figure 9.10, the latency of the jumping response declined substantially in the experimental subjects, as they scrambled across the hurdle to escape from the warning stimulus. Escape from a stimulus paired with shock clearly is reinforcing. (See also McAllister & McAllister, 1992.)

There is thus considerable support for the two assumptions at the heart of two-factor theory: that conditioned fear motivates avoidance responding, and that termination of this fear reinforces it. Despite these successes, however,

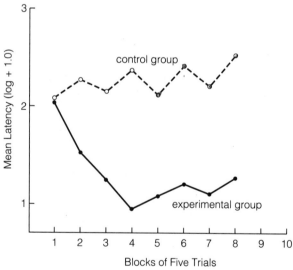

FIGURE 9.10   The reinforcing properties of escape from a warning stimulus. Rats in a shuttle box were given a tone-light compound that they could terminate by jumping over a hurdle; the graph shows the change in the mean latency of the escape response over trials. For subjects in the experimental group, the compound had previously been paired with shock; for subjects in the control group, the compound had been presented without shock. (Adapted from Brown & Jacobs, 1949)

other evidence has been reported that poses some problems for two-factor theory. We will examine this evidence in the following sections.

The Response Problem

One problem arose when psychologists tried to train rats to avoid shock by performing responses other than running in an alley. The most embarrassing of these problems arose when experimenters tried to train bar-pressing as an avoidance response. In previous chapters we have seen that rats are very good at pressing bars to obtain food, and we have now seen that they learn very rapidly to jump over a hurdle or run down an alley to avoid shock. So, bar-pressing is an easily learned response, and avoidance of shock is a very powerful reinforcer. You might think, therefore, that it would be very easy to train rats to press a bar in order to avoid shock. Certainly most learning psychologists thought so, but it gradually became clear that this optimism was misplaced. Whereas rats need an average of only six trials to learn to run down an alley to avoid shock, they need hundreds of trials to learn to press a bar to avoid shock, and many never do. (For a review, see Bolles, 1970.)

Since pressing the bar turns off the warning stimulus in exactly the same way as running down an alley, two-factor theory says that pressing the bar should produce a substantial reduction in the rat's fear, and hence should be easily learned. Why, then, do rats fare so badly on this simple task?

Bolles's SSDR model.   Bolles (1970) offered a possible explanation. He began by arguing that two-factor theory was based on a fundamental misinterpretation of the role of avoidance learning in an animal's life, illustrating his point with a fable:

> Once upon a time there was a little animal who ran around in the forest. One day while he was running around, our hero was suddenly attacked by a predator. He was hurt and, of course, frightened, but he was lucky and managed to escape. . . . Some time later our furry friend was again running around in the forest . . . when suddenly . . . he heard or saw or smelled some stimulus which on the earlier occasion had preceded the attack by the predator. Now on this occasion our friend became frightened, he immediately took flight as he had on the previous occasion, and quickly got safely back home. . . . I propose that this familiar fable . . . is utter nonsense. No owl hoots or whistles 5 seconds before pouncing on a mouse. . . . Nor will the owl give the mouse enough trials for the necessary learning to occur.
>
> (Bolles, 1970, p. 32)

If an animal is to survive, Bolles argued, it needs innately programmed responses to dangerous situations. Because each species has somewhat different behaviors for coping with danger, Bolles called these responses **species-specific defense reactions (SSDRs)**. He suggested that rats have three main defensive reactions—broadly, freezing, flight, or fight—and that which of these responses will occur depends on the rat's environment at the time it is frightened. If the rat is in a confined space in which escape is impossible, it is likely to freeze; if it is in an open field, it is more likely to run for cover. (See also Grossen & Kelley, 1972.)

Applying this analysis to laboratory research on avoidance learning, Bolles has argued that most of the responses that occur in these experiments are innate SSDRs. Insofar as rats do learn an avoidance response, Bolles has proposed several ways in which the presence of SSDRs might influence this learning. We will concentrate here on the simplest of these possibilities, which is that the ease of learning an avoidance response will depend on its compatibility with the SSDR elicited by the experimental situation. In an alley, the rat's SSDR will be to run, and it thus very easy to train this response; indeed, Bolles (1989) suggests that training a rat to run in this situation is rather like teaching a child to sneeze if you stick a feather in his nose. A Skinner box, on the other hand, is a confined space, and here the rat's SSDR will be to freeze; if a rat is freezing, it will clearly be very hard for it to learn to press a bar.

This competing-response version of how SSDRs interfere with learning, however, has run into problems. For example, Bolles has suggested that the reason why rats quickly learn to run down alleys to avoid shock is that running is the rat's SSDR in environments like alleys. Fanselow and Lester (1988), however, have reviewed extensive evidence that when rats are given unavoidable shocks in an alley, their conditioned response on future trials is not to run but to freeze. (They suggest that freezing is a more adaptive response to dangerous situations for a rat, in part because it minimizes the chances of a predator's detecting them.) If freezing is the rat's SSDR in alleys as well as in Skinner boxes, then it is not clear why this freezing does not interfere with learning to run just as much as with learning to press a bar.

The competing-response analysis also has problems in explaining some of the other avoidance responses that rats have difficulty learning. For example, rats are not good at learning to avoid shock by standing on their hind legs or turning, even though these responses occur at a moderately high level during each session. Again, therefore, the difficulty rats have in learning these responses cannot readily be attributed to SSDRs' preventing performance of the responses. Thus, although it is now clear that rats do have powerful SSDRs in dangerous situations, the details of how these SSDRs interact with the response to be learned remain unclear.

Stimulus change. If freezing is not the reason—or, at any rate, not the sole reason—why rats have difficulty in learning to press a bar to avoid shock, what is? A potentially important clue comes from the fact that all of the avoidance responses that rats have difficulty learning—standing, turning, and bar-press-ing—share the characteristic that they leave the rat in the situation where it became frightened. In a Skinner box, for example, if a rat presses the bar it still finds itself in exactly the same situation it was in before it responded, whereas in a straight alley running allows it to escape from the situation. Why, then, is it so important for the rat to get away from the situation where it first became frightened?

A slightly modified or extended version of two-factor theory provides one possible answer. Two-factor theory assumes that avoidance responding is rein-forced if the stimuli that follow the response elicit less fear than the stimuli that precede it. If most of the stimuli that are present following a response are the same as the stimuli that preceded it, then levels of fear will not be reduced very much, and learning will be impaired. Thus, the reason that rats have difficulty learning to press a bar to avoid shock could simply be that the stimuli present following a response are almost exactly the same as those that were present before, and responding thus produces very little reduction in fear.

If responding produced a greater change in the stimulus situation, accord-ing to this analysis, then rats would find it easier to learn that the stimuli that are present following the response are not paired with shock, and learning would be enhanced. This prediction has been confirmed. In an experiment by D'Amato, Fazzaro, and Etkin (1968), for example, a noise was presented every time the experimental subjects pressed the bar; these rats learned to press the bar much faster than control subjects who did not receive the noise. An even better way to change the stimulus environment, of course, would be to allow the rat to escape from the Skinner box after pressing the bar, and Crawford and Masterson (1978) tested whether this would enhance avoidance learning even more. When their subjects pressed the bar, they not only avoided shock but opened a door that allowed them to leave the Skinner box. In this situation, learning to press the bar proved to be very rapid. (See also Modaresi, 1990.)

Rats can learn to press a bar to avoid shock, therefore, provided that the response produces a substantial change in the rat's stimulus environment. This result is consistent with two-factor theory's assumption that avoidance re-sponding is reinforced by a reduction in fear, as long as we recognize that the stimuli that precede and follow the response must be clearly discriminable if fear levels are to be reduced substantially.

Two-factor theory, then, may be able to account for at least some of the variation in the ease of learning different avoidance responses. Note, however, that this account is a very speculative one. To explain the difficulty of learning to press a bar, we have suggested that bar-pressing does not produce as much change in the rat's environment as moving to a different section of the appa-ratus. This may be so, but each bar-press is nevertheless followed by termina-tion of the warning stimulus, which is typically a bright light or loud noise. Even if this represents less change than movement to another part of the environment, we might still expect *some* difference in the amount of fear conditioned to "box cues + warning stimulus" and "box cues alone," and thus that subjects would eventually learn to press the bar, albeit more slowly. For two-factor theory's explanation to be more convincing, its assumptions about conditioning to different elements of the environment need to be spelled out more clearly, so that we can predict in advance which responses will produce sufficient fear reduction for learning to occur and which will not. As we shall see in Chapter 12, this problem is not unique to two-factor theory, but it will be difficult to evaluate the theory's account of variations in response learning until we have a better understanding of how conditioning is distributed among the elements of a complex stimulus environment.

In summary, one of the major puzzles in the field of avoidance learning is why some avoidance responses are much harder to learn than others. One reason seems to be that animals have innate SSDRs to dangerous situations which constrain what other responses will occur, although the details of this interaction are not yet well understood. A second factor seems to be the nature of the stimulus change produced by the response—the greater the change, the more easily the response is learned—a finding that is readily interpreted in terms of fear reduction. As with Bolles's SSDR model, however, two-factor theory provides a conceptual framework, rather than a detailed theory, for approaching the response problem. Thus, although psychologists have made progress in understanding why some avoidance responses are easier to learn than others, the problem has not yet been solved.

The Case of the Nonchalant Jumper

A further problem for two-factor theory has come from evidence that fear and avoidance responding are not linked as firmly as the theory suggests. According to the theory, fear provides the motive for avoidance responding; but once the response is well learned, subjects respond without apparent fear. For example, when dogs are first trained in a shuttle box, they urinate and defecate when the warning stimulus is presented; but as training continues, these signs of fear disappear, until eventually subjects jump over the barrier with apparent nonchalance (for example, Solomon & Wynne, 1953).

Appearances, of course, can be deceptive, but more objective measures of fear point to the same conclusion. Kamin, Brimer, and Black (1963) trained four groups of rats on an avoidance task until they had avoided shock on either 1, 3, 9, or 27 consecutive trials. They then tested fear levels by presenting the CS in a conditioned emotional response (CER) test. The suppression ratio after 9 trials was substantially lower than after 1 or 3 trials, indicating an increase in fear (Figure 9.11). By the 27th trial, however, presentation of the tone produced almost no suppression, confirming the anecdotal impression that fear disappears as the avoidance response becomes well established.

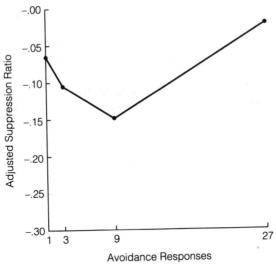

FIGURE 9.11   The fear elicited by a CS at different stages of avoidance training. Fear was measured using a CER test, which was administered before avoidance training and then again after subjects had made either 1, 3, 9, or 27 consecutive avoidance responses. The pretest suppression score was subtracted from the final score to show how much the fear elicited by the tone had changed as a result of avoidance training, and it is this adjusted suppression score that is shown. The more fear increased during training, the more negative the score. (Adapted from Kamin, Brimer, & Black, 1963)

This reduction in fear is not, in itself, damaging to two-factor theory; after all, once the avoidance response was learned, shock was no longer presented. According to the theory, however, the virtual disappearance of fear should be accompanied by a dramatic decline in avoidance responding, and this simply does not happen. If you look back at Figure 9.8, you will see that once the subject avoided shock on trial 8, it received no further shocks, but its response latencies nevertheless continued to improve, at first rapidly and then more slowly. Although all signs of fear had disappeared, there was no decline in avoidance.

This point is made even more dramatic in a study of avoidance learning by Solomon, Kamin, and Wynne (1953). In the first phase, dogs were trained to jump over a barrier to avoid shock, and were then given extinction trials in which no shock was presented. Since the warning stimulus was no longer followed by shock, fear should have extinguished, and thus (according to two-factor theory) avoidance responding should have stopped. The dogs, however, continued to respond for 200 trials without any sign of slackening, and one persisted for 650 trials—until the experimenters gave up. It is possible, of course, that the dogs would eventually have stopped responding had training continued long enough, but according to two-factor theory there should have been at least some extinction of fear, and thus some slowing down in the latency of the avoidance response to the warning signal. Quite the contrary, responding actually became faster during extinction and continued to show signs of improvement for 200 trials.

A Cognitive Analysis

Despite its success, then, two-factor theory has serious difficulty in accounting for the persistence of avoidance responding after fear has disappeared. (For a defense of the theory, see Levis, 1989.) An alternative, cognitive explanation has been proposed by Seligman and Johnston (1973). Building on the work of earlier cognitive theorists such as Tolman, Seligman and Johnston proposed that avoidance responding is based not on fear, but on the subject's expectation that this response will avoid shock. During the initial training trials, when the warning stimulus is repeatedly followed by shock, it is assumed that subjects form an expectation that shock will occur whenever this stimulus is presented. When the animal finally jumps over the barrier and avoids the shock, it forms a new expectation—that shock does not occur if the response is made. The next time the warning stimulus is presented, the animal recalls both expectations—shock if it doesn't jump, no shock if it does—and since the outcome of no shock is clearly preferable, it performs the response that will produce this outcome.

One important point to note about this analysis is that fear plays almost no role: The subject jumps not because it is frightened, but because it prefers the outcome of no shock and, therefore, executes the response that will produce it. Seligman and Johnston do assume that fear is classically conditioned and that this fear plays an important role in directing the animal's initial reactions; they believe, however, that once the required avoidance response is performed successfully and the animal learns that this response will avoid shock, its behavior thereafter is based solely on this expectation.

The nonchalant jumper revisited. Because of the small role allocated to fear in this theory, it can readily account for the evidence that was so embarrassing for two-factor theory. First, regarding the disappearance of fear during training, the theory assumes that once the avoidance response is learned, and thus the warning stimulus is no longer followed by shock, the fear conditioned to this stimulus will extinguish. The dog will continue to jump, however, because it still expects shock to occur if it doesn't, and it prefers to avoid this outcome. The situation is analogous to that of pedestrians at a traffic light: If they don't cross, it is not because they are frightened but because they know that if they were to cross they might be run over. It is this knowledge that restrains them, not any active sense of fear.

Regarding the difficulty of extinguishing avoidance behavior, this too follows directly from a cognitive analysis. The theory assumes that avoidance depends on two expectations: In the absence of a response, shock will occur; if a response is made, shock will not occur. On the first extinction trial, the dog holds both these expectations and therefore responds. When it does not receive a shock, its expectation that responding will not be followed by shock is confirmed, and it therefore continues to jump. With each new trial, this expectation receives further confirmation, so, if anything, the dog's tendency to jump is strengthened—exactly the result that Solomon's group found.

Flooding.   According to this cognitive analysis, the only way to extinguish an avoidance response is to alter the expectations on which it is based. In normal extinction, the animal keeps jumping because it expects shock if it does not jump, and because it keeps responding it never gets to test this expectation. If it could somehow be prevented from jumping, however, it would discover that this expectation was no longer correct and, hence, would stop responding. In one test of this prediction, Katzev and Berman (1974) trained rats to avoid shock in a shuttle box and then gave them 50 extinction trials during which shock was no longer presented. The CS was presented as always, and subjects in the normal extinction group were allowed to jump over the barrier to terminate it. Subjects in the response prevention, or **flooding**, group, however, had a barrier placed above the hurdle so they could no longer jump over it, although they still received the CS at the same time and for the same duration as subjects in the normal extinction group. Both groups thus received identical exposure to the CS; according to two-factor analysis, fear, and therefore avoidance, should have extinguished equally in both. When subsequently tested with the barrier removed, however, the two groups responded very differently: Subjects given normal extinction still responded on 59 percent of the test trials, whereas those prevented from responding responded on only 32 percent of test trials. As predicted by a cognitive analysis, response prevention, or flooding, does lead to rapid extinction of avoidance responding. (See also Mineka, 1979.)

Fearful problems.   Seligman and Johnston's cognitive theory, then, not only can account for the evidence that proved so difficult for two-factor theory but can also generate accurate predictions of its own. Unfortunately, its strength is also its weakness: The fact that fear plays a minor role in the theory allows it to explain the independence of avoidance and fear; for the same reason, it has difficulty explaining evidence that fear does influence avoidance. The Rescorla and LoLordo experiment described earlier provides one example of this problem, but the theory's difficulties emerge in even sharper focus in an experiment by Grossen, Kostansek, and Bolles (1969).

These experimenters trained rats to jump over a barrier to avoid shock, and then presented them with a tone that had previously been paired with food. What effect should the tone's presentation have on avoidance responding? According to two-factor theory, it should reduce responding. As we saw in Chapter 3, stimuli paired with food come to elicit a conditioned motivational. state of hunger, and, since motives such as hunger and fear are mutually inhibitory, hunger reduces fear. According to two-factor theory, therefore, presentation of the tone should reduce fear and therefore reduce avoidance responding.

According to Seligman and Johnston's cognitive analysis, on the other hand, the noise should have no effect. The tone might lead subjects to expect food, but the rats also know that they will receive a painful shock if they do not respond. Since no shock is preferable to shock, they should continue to respond. As predicted by two-factor theory, however, presentation of the tone produced a significant decrease in avoidance responding. A cognitive analysis based solely on expectations has considerable difficulty explaining this result. Similarly, it has difficulty explaining the parallel result in the CER procedure, in which a stimulus paired with shock in a classical-conditioning paradigm suppresses responding for food. Both results make much more sense if we assume that responding is based not simply on rational expectations but on emotions.

Synthesis: Information and Motivation

Two-factor theory views avoidance responding as a means of escaping from fear. This analysis is supported by evidence that stimuli that increase fear also increase avoidance, and that the termination of such stimuli is reinforcing; however, the theory cannot explain why avoidance persists so strongly after fear has disappeared. A cognitive analysis can account for this evidence, because it attributes avoidance to a rational decision to avoid unpleasant consequences rather than attributing avoidance to fear, but for this very reason it has difficulty explaining instances in which fear does influence behavior.

One obvious solution is to assume that both theories are correct—that avoidance behavior is based on both rational expectations and fear. This information/motivation approach to avoidance is very similar to the account we proposed in the preceding section for reinforcement involving the presentation of food. In both cases, one effect of reinforcement seems to be to provide information that allows the formation of an expectation: A rat can learn that pressing a bar produces food or reduces the probability of shock. However, a purely informational analysis cannot fully account for behavior in either situation; we also need to take into account motivational effects that are not necessarily rational: Rats that are excited by the prospect of food or the fear of shock may press a lever much more often than rational considerations would suggest. To develop a comprehensive theory of behavior, therefore, we need to consider the effects of both information and motivation. In the case of avoidance, learning theorists have made good progress in identifying the role of each element on its own, but much work remains to be done before we understand how these elements interact to jointly determine behavior.

9.4 REINFORCEMENT AND CONDITIONING: ONE PROCESS OR TWO?

We have examined reinforcement in some detail in this chapter, trying to understand the learning processes that are involved. Similarly, in Chapter 5 we examined the learning processes involved in classical conditioning. We turn now to the relationship between these two forms of learning, and consider whether the processes involved are the same or different.

Before tackling this issue, it may be helpful to review the distinction between the two forms. In a typical experiment on classical conditioning, food is presented following a stimulus, regardless of the subject's response: Pavlov's dogs received food following a tone, whether or not they salivated. In reinforcement, on the other hand, the reinforcer follows a response, and it is the stimulus that is (usually) irrelevant: Thorndike's cats were given food whenever they escaped from the puzzle box, regardless of what noises or other stimuli were present at the time.

The procedures followed in experiments on classical conditioning and reinforcement are thus clearly different. The fact that the *procedures* differ, however, does not necessarily mean that the learning *processes* involved are also different. As we noted in Chapter 2, processes are internal events that lead to visible consequences, and the fact that procedures or overt behaviors differ does not necessarily mean that the underlying processes also differ. Consider a falling apple and the movement of the sun through the sky. On the surface, these appear to be very different phenomena, involving different objects and different forms of movement, but Newton was able to show that the underlying process, gravity, was the same in both cases. The fact that two forms of learning involve different procedures thus does not necessarily imply that they involve different processes.

How, then, can we decide whether reinforcement and conditioning involve the same process? Ultimately, the answer will probably come from our theories of the two forms of learning: If it turns out that exactly the same theory can account for both phenomena, in the same way that Newton's theory of gravity accounted for the movement of all objects, then this would be strong evidence that the underlying processes are the same. At present, however, no such unifying theory is available. Although psychologists have made considerable progress in accounting for some aspects of both reinforcement and classical conditioning (for example, the Rescorla-Wagner model and Capaldi's model of the PRE), we do not yet have a theory that can fully account for all aspects of either form of learning, much less for both.

In the absence of a comprehensive theory, another approach is to examine the similarities between the two forms of learning. If the same process were involved in both, then we should expect important similarities in the observable characteristics of learning in the two situations. To help us decide whether reinforcement and classical conditioning involve one process or two, therefore, we will examine their similarity along three dimensions and try to answer the following questions: Do they involve the same contingencies? Do they affect the same responses? Do they obey the same laws?

Contingencies

In an experiment on classical conditioning, a CS is followed by a US, but the strength of conditioning depends not simply on whether these stimuli occur together but on whether there is a correlation between them. If the US is sometimes presented in the absence of the CS, then, as Rescorla (1966) showed, conditioning is impaired. We can also express the importance of the CS–US correlation by saying that the US must be *contingent* on the CS; that is, it must occur more often following the CS than it occurs in its absence. Similarly, in experiments on reinforcement we arrange a contingency between a response and a reinforcer, so that the reinforcer is more likely to occur following the response than at other times. Classical conditioning and reinforcement thus differ in the contingency arranged by the experimenter: In classical conditioning, food or some other stimulus (S*) is contingent on a stimulus, and in reinforcement it is contingent on a response:

$$\text{classical conditioning: } S \longrightarrow S^*$$
$$\text{reinforcement: } R \longrightarrow S^*$$

In terms of contingencies, therefore, it might seem obvious that classical conditioning and reinforcement do involve different contingencies. Alas, the matter is not so simple. The problem is that virtually every experiment on classical conditioning and reinforcement involves *both* contingencies. Consider first a simple salivary conditioning experiment in which a tone is followed by food. From the experimenter's perspective, the food is contingent only on the tone, not on whether the dog salivates. Nevertheless, even though the experimenter does not arrange a reinforcement contingency *deliberately*, one could be present implicitly. Suppose that food tastes better when it is preceded by salivation—quite a reasonable supposition. If so, the amount of reinforcement will be greater on trials in which the dog salivates than on trials in which it does not, and this implicit reinforcement contingency could account for any increase in salivation.

Parallel problems arise in experiments on reinforcement. Consider a typical reinforcement experiment in which a pigeon is given food every time it

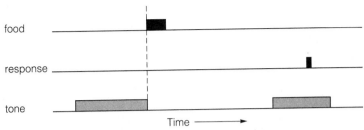

F I G U R E 9.12   Diagram of Sheffield's omission procedure. Food normally followed a tone but was omitted on any trial in which the dog salivated (response).

pecks a key. You might think that this behavior was clearly due to the R–S* contingency between pecking and food, but there is also an implicit S–S* contingency here, in that the bird will have looked at the illuminated key (in the course of pecking it) immediately before it receives food. In our discussion of autoshaping (Chapter 3), we saw that pigeons will peck an illuminated key that reliably precedes the presentation of food, and thus it is at least possible that the pecking that emerges in a typical reinforcement experiment is actually due to this implicit S–S* contingency, rather than the R–S* reinforcement contingency arranged by the experiment.

We need to distinguish, then, between the contingency arranged by the experimenter and the contingency that is *actually* controlling the subject's behavior. Because S–S* contingencies are potentially present in experiments on reinforcement as well as classical conditioning, these S–S* contingencies could be responsible for learning in both cases. Equally, however, since R–S* contingencies are also potentially present in both situations, it could be reinforcement that is responsible for both. We will examine each of these possibilities, starting with reinforcement.†

Is classical conditioning due to reinforcement?   We have seen that classically conditioned responses such as salivation could be due either to the CS–US contingencies arranged by the experimenter or to the reinforcement contingencies that are present implicitly. To separate these possibilities, F. D. Sheffield (1965) devised a very clever technique, which he called the omission procedure. He gave dogs standard salivary conditioning trials in which a tone was followed by food; on any trial in which the dog salivated, however, the food scheduled for the end of the trial was canceled or omitted (Figure 9.12). Salivation was thus never followed by food, so that any increase in salivation

---

† To simplify our exposition, we will sometimes use the term *conditioning* as a shorthand for *classical conditioning*; to avoid confusion, though, it is important to remember that in other contexts the term *conditioning* can refer to instrumental as well as classical conditioning.

could not be due to reinforcement. Because food continued to be presented on trials when the dog didn't salivate, however, food was still more likely following the tone than it was in the tone's absence. A conditioning analysis thus predicted that the dogs should still salivate to at least some extent, and this is what Sheffield found. One dog, Vicki, salivated on approximately half the trials and continued to do so for 800 trials, despite the fact that this salivation was costing her food. Salivation thus could not have been due solely to reinforcement; by a process of elimination, the S–S* contingency between tone and food must have played at least some role.

Is reinforcement due to classical conditioning? Is it possible, then, that all learning is actually due to classical conditioning? In experiments in which a reinforcer is made contingent on some response, S–S* contingencies inevitably will also be present implicitly, and it could be these S–S* contingencies that are responsible for learning.

In Chapter 3, we discussed the phenomenon of sign tracking, in which rats learn to approach stimuli that have been paired with food. When a rat presses a bar or a pigeon pecks a key to obtain food, contact with the bar or key will immediately precede the delivery of food, with the result that sign tracking could lead subjects to approach or contact these manipulanda on future trials. There is evidence that sign tracking of this kind does influence responding in many reinforcement experiments (for example, Peterson, Ackil, Frommer, & Hearst, 1972), but S–S* contingencies cannot account for all of the effects of reinforcement. In particular, classical conditioning may play a powerful role in experiments in which the reinforced response involves movement toward or away from a particular stimulus, but a classical conditioning explanation is much less plausible when the reinforced response is less clearly oriented toward a discrete stimulus. For example, it is easy to reinforce a dog for lifting its leg, but it is very difficult to account for such learning in terms of the dog's trying to approach a stimulus that was previously correlated with food (Wahlsten & Cole, 1972; see also Bolles, Holtz, Dunn, & Hill, 1980; Davey, Oakley, & Cleland, 1981). Thus, just as we cannot account for classical conditioning solely in terms of reinforcement, we cannot explain reinforcement solely in terms of conditioning. Classical conditioning and reinforcement do involve different contingencies.

Responses

If conditioning and reinforcement were manifestations of a single learning process, we should expect the behaviors that can be established by each method to be similar. There is evidence, however, that this is not so, as the set of responses that can be classically conditioned differs from the set that can be reinforced. We will look first at the responses that can be classically condi-

tioned and then at the responses that can be modified by their consequences—
or, in Skinner's terminology, operants.

Conditioned responses.   As we saw in Chapter 3, most if not all responses
controlled by the autonomic nervous system—salivation and GSR are examples—can be classically conditioned. In addition, a wide range of behaviors
controlled by the skeletal nervous system can be conditioned, including key-
pecking in pigeons and blinking in humans. However, the proportion of skeletal responses that can be conditioned appears to be considerably smaller than
the proportion of autonomic responses. Moreover, it is possible to argue that
even these skeletal responses should not all be regarded as truly conditioned
responses. In previous sections, we have repeatedly encountered the suggestion
that stimuli paired with food and shock come to elicit motivational states, and
that these conditioned or incentive motives then prime a range of innate
responses. The response that actually occurs depends on the stimuli that are
present at the time: A frightened rat may freeze or run, a hungry rat may chase
prey or forage for seeds, and so on. If this analysis is correct, then it is possible
to argue that only the motivational state is conditioned; the skeletal responses
that follow are simply innate reactions to whatever releasing stimuli happen to
be present.

A human analogy may clarify this argument. Suppose that you lived in a
house with a butler and he rang the dinner bell every night before you ate; as a
result, you would eventually begin to feel hungry any time you heard the dinner
bell. If you now heard a similar bell while you were walking in town, you might
go to the nearest restaurant to buy a hamburger, but the true conditioned
response in this instance would be your feeling of hunger, not your walking into
a MacDonald's or Burger King.

Whether or not this argument is accepted, it appears that most, if not all,
autonomic responses can be conditioned, but that the proportion of skeletal
responses that can be conditioned is much smaller.

Operant responses.   We have encountered evidence that reinforcement is
effective with a very wide range of skeletal responses. (For some qualifications
of this view, see Chapter 10.) If we turn to autonomic responses, it is much less
clear whether these responses can be reinforced. In a review of the literature
published in 1961, Kimble concluded that it was not possible to reinforce
autonomic responses—a conclusion based on only two studies! The reason he
cited so few studies, however, was that only a couple existed. This, in turn, was
because attempts to demonstrate reinforcement of autonomic responses face
some formidable methodological problems.

Suppose, for example, that we wanted to know whether we could reinforce activity of the heart, a smooth muscle controlled by the autonomic

nervous system. To find out, we could attach recording electrodes to a rat and then give it food pellets whenever its heart rate increased. We might well find an increase in heart rate, but would this prove that heart rate had been reinforced? An equally plausible explanation might be that heart rate increased because the rat was running around its cage or breathing rapidly, and that it was this skeletal response that was then reinforced, with changes in heart rate emerging only as an indirect by-product. Similar opportunities for skeletal mediation would exist for almost any autonomic response because of the complex interrelationships between the two systems.

In order to demonstrate conclusively reinforcement of autonomic behavior, then, we would have to eliminate the possibility of skeletal mediation by somehow blocking skeletal responses while not interfering with autonomic ones. This may sound impossible, but, as it happens, psychologists have long known of a drug possessing exactly these properties. Curare is a potentially fatal poison that functions by selectively blocking the transmission of electrical signals from nerves to skeletal muscles, thus paralyzing all skeletal muscles while leaving autonomic activity intact. The use of this drug, however, poses a number of major technical problems—among them, how to keep subjects alive (breathing is impossible when the chest muscles are paralyzed) and how to reinforce subjects (a paralyzed rat is, on the whole, in a poor position to eat, drink, or be merry).

These problems were eventually overcome in a brilliant series of experiments by Neal Miller and Leo DiCara. They used modern surgical techniques such as artificial respiration to keep their curarized subjects alive, and ICS (electrical stimulation of the brain) as a reinforcer. (Tiny electrical currents delivered to certain areas of the brain have been found to be remarkably powerful reinforcers; rats will press a bar as often as twice a second for 24 hours to obtain such stimulation.) Miller and DiCara (1967) made ICS contingent on an increase in heart rate in one group of curarized rats, and, to ensure that ICS was not simply eliciting this increase, made the same reinforcer contingent on a decrease in heart rate in a second group. Heart rate in both groups changed in the appropriate direction, increasing or decreasing by as much as 25 percent. In other situations, Miller and his colleagues were able to modify autonomic behavior with exquisite precision, in one case training their subjects to increase blood flow in only one ear (DiCara & Miller, 1968).

Unfortunately, these results have proven difficult to replicate, even by the original experimenters. In one of the more poignant graphs ever published in a psychology article, Miller and Dworkin (1974) plotted the magnitude of the effect obtained in the laboratory as a function of the year of publication: The result was a steadily decreasing line, with the magnitude eventually approaching zero.

Whether autonomic responses can be reinforced, then, is not clear. Success has been reported in a number of studies with humans (Miller, 1985), but it is very difficult to rule out the possibility of skeletal mediation in these studies. In animal studies, where this possibility has been eliminated, learning has proved elusive. On the question of whether autonomic behavior can be reinforced, therefore, the wisest verdict at the present time may be one borrowed from the Scottish legal system: Not proven.

In summary, there do seem to be substantial differences between the behaviors that can be classically conditioned and those that can be reinforced. In the case of classical conditioning, we can condition most if not all autonomic responses, but only a subset of skeletal responses. In the case of reinforcement, on the other hand, it is skeletal responses that are easy to reinforce and autonomic responses that are difficult, perhaps impossible. It appears that classical conditioning is more effective with autonomic responses, and reinforcement with skeletal responses.

Principles

After wading through some of the conceptual confusions of the preceding sections, you may be relieved to hear that you are now, at last, on firm ground. The answer to the question of whether the principles of conditioning and reinforcement are similar is: Yes. In almost every respect, the principles that have been found to determine the strength of conditioning have their counterpart in reinforcement, and vice versa. The strength of a conditioned response depends on the contiguity, frequency, and intensity of the events to be associated, and, in exactly the same way, the strength of a reinforced response depends on contiguity (delay of reinforcement), frequency (schedule of reinforcement), and intensity (amount of reinforcement). Similarly, eliminating the contingency between a response and a reinforcer by also presenting the reinforcer noncontingently disrupts reinforcement in exactly the same way as it does conditioning (for example, Hammond, 1980).

If we go beyond the laws of association to look at other characteristics of learning in conditioning and reinforcement experiments, the list of similarities grows. In both, subjects learn to discriminate between stimuli that signal different consequences. (See also Ross & LoLordo, 1987.) In addition, responding trained to one stimulus will generalize to similar ones, and a partial reinforcement schedule during training increases responding during extinction. So great are the similarities, the more interesting question has become not whether the two forms of learning are similar but whether there are any respects in which they differ. At one time, it appeared as if the effects of partial reinforcement schedules on responding in extinction might provide such a difference, but even this is now in doubt. (See Gibbon, Farrell, Locurto, Duncan, & Terrace, 1980.) The characteristics of learning in classical conditioning and reinforcement experiments are similar to a remarkable degree, if not identical.

One Process?

What, then, shall we conclude about whether reinforcement and classical conditioning involve one process or two? They clearly involve different contingencies, and they also differ in the responses that they can strengthen, both of which suggest that different processes are involved. On the other hand, the extraordinary similarity in their associative principles points to exactly the opposite conclusion. How can we reconcile this conflicting evidence?

An E_1–E_2 associative system.   The simplest way to account for the similarity of the learning principles is to assume that classical conditioning and reinforcement are both based on a common system for detecting relationships between events. It is perhaps easier to understand how this could have come about if we consider the evolutionary pressures that are thought to have shaped the development of learning systems. (The following discussion is indebted in a number of respects to Dickinson, 1980.)

To survive in the world, animals must be able to predict where and when important events are going to occur: They must know which parts of their environment contain food, when a predator is nearby, which foods will make them ill, and so on. Some of this knowledge can be innately built in, but some of it needs to be learned, and to acquire this knowledge animals may have evolved a single learning system for detecting relationships between events. That is, if some event E_1 reliably precedes an important event E_2, animals possess a learning system that will detect the fact that these events tend to occur together:

$$E_1 \longrightarrow E_2$$

In the case of reinforcement, the relationship is between a response and a stimulus (an R–S^* association), while in the case of classical conditioning the relationship is between two stimuli (an S–S^* relationship), but the same learning system for detecting the co-occurrence of events may be involved in both cases.

The existence of a common learning system would explain why the principles of learning observed in classical conditioning and reinforcement are virtually identical. In classical conditioning, for example, a delay between the CS and US makes learning harder; similarly, in reinforcement, a delay between the response and the reinforcer impairs learning. The reason for this parallel could be that the same learning system is involved in both cases, and that this system is less likely to identify two events as being related if they occur at widely separated times.

If classical conditioning and reinforcement are products of the same associative system, however, then why is reinforcement much more effective with skeletal responses than with autonomic responses, whereas the reverse is the case for classical conditioning? If the same associative mechanism is at work in both cases, why do the two forms of learning differ in what responses they can most easily influence?

R–S* associations.   Let us consider reinforcement first. We have suggested that reinforcement leads to the formation of an R–S* association between the response and the reinforcer that follows it. If so, why is it so much harder to reinforce autonomic responses than skeletal responses?

One possibility is that autonomic responses are less salient or obvious than skeletal responses, and therefore harder to detect. If you are not aware of having made a response, it will be very hard to learn that this response is followed by some other event. (For an argument along these lines, see Mackintosh, 1983.) On the other hand, Hefferline's demonstrations that subjects can be reinforced for tiny movements of their thumb muscle cast some doubt upon this salience or stimulus-feedback hypothesis: An undetectable muscular contraction would not seem to produce much more stimulus feedback than an autonomic response such as salivation, yet it appears to be easier to learn. If small movements really can be learned, and if autonomic responses really cannot, then it seems unlikely that the detectability of the response is the crucial difference.

Another possibility is that the difficulty of associating autonomic responses with reinforcers may be another instance of preparedness. In discussing taste-aversion learning, we suggested that rats may have difficulty associating visual and auditory cues with food because the formation of such associations could actually be harmful. In nature, an auditory stimulus is extremely unlikely to have a causal relationship with gastrointestinal illness, so that developing an aversion to a sound that just happened to precede illness would probably be counterproductive. Similarly, it is highly unlikely that autonomic responses such as an increase in activity in the pancreas would have any causal relationship to finding food in the external world. As a result, our learning system may have evolved in such a way that it simply will not associate autonomic responses with external reinforcers; by not strengthening preceding autonomic responses every time an external reinforcer is presented, the learning system avoids potential disastrous turbulence in an internal environment that needs to be kept as constant as possible.

S–S* associations.   In the case of classical conditioning, we need to explain why it is autonomic responses that are easier to learn. The first important point to note is that in classical conditioning a response is not learned directly: It is an S–S* association that is learned, not an R–S* association. (See Chapter 5.) Thus, whereas in the case of reinforcement it as least potentially possible to strengthen any response that precedes the reinforcer, in classical conditioning the response will be determined by the performance rules that govern how the S–S* associations are translated into behavior.

In Chapter 5 we outlined one possible interpretation of how S–S* learning is translated into performance. We suggested that classical conditioning involves two distinct learning systems: a relatively primitive system that simply associates the CS and US centers, and a cognitive system that leads to the formation of expectations about what US will occur. We further suggested that activation of the US center within the more primitive system would lead to activation of a motivational system, which would in turn prime a set of skeletal and autonomic responses. If the food center were activated, for example, this would prime the salivary glands and also those skeletal responses that are innately programmed for obtaining food. (See Figure 5.12, p. 179, for a summary of this hypothetical system.)

As we emphasized in Chapter 5, our understanding of the performance rules governing classical conditioning is still very rudimentary, and the details of the system outlined above should not be regarded with undue reverence. The important point in the present context is simply that the responses that occur in classical conditioning are largely determined by innately wired connections within the brain. According to this analysis, the reason that the range of skeletal responses that can be conditioned is smaller than the set of autonomic responses is that only a relatively small number of skeletal responses are prewired for any one motivational system. If you present food, then classical conditioning will affect at best only the skeletal responses that are prewired for obtaining food; if you present electric shock, then at best you will get only the skeletal responses that are primed for avoiding predators. The net result is that the range of autonomic behaviors that can be classically conditioned will be as wide as the range of autonomic responses that can be elicited by an unconditioned stimulus—that is, probably all of them—while the range of skeletal responses that can be classically conditioned will be much smaller.

Conclusion

We have suggested that classical conditioning and reinforcement may both be products of a single system for detecting relationships among events. This common system would explain why the principles of learning observed in experiments on classical conditioning and reinforcement are virtually identical. As to why the procedures affect different responses, we have suggested that in the case of reinforcement, subjects learn R–S* associations or relationships, and that there may be limits to what autonomic responses can be associated with external reinforcers such as food. In the case of classical conditioning, we have suggested that the limitation may lie in the innate rules for translating S–S* associations into performance: S–S* associations can potentially activate any autonomic response, but the motivational state that is conditioned to a CS will prime only a limited set of skeletal responses.

Thus, there are plausible grounds for supposing that both classical conditioning and reinforcement are based on a common learning system, but if so, we need much more information about how the output of this system is translated into performance. This may prove one of the key areas for future research. (For a review of the problem and possible solutions, see Dickinson, 1980; Rescorla & Holland, 1982; Balsam & Tomie, 1985.)

9.5 SUMMARY

Thorndike believed that a reinforcer would automatically strengthen whatever behavior preceded it, a claim strongly supported by Skinner's work on superstition. Skinner gave pigeons free food every 15 seconds and, even though no behavior was required to obtain the food, found that each bird developed idiosyncratic patterns of behavior, presumably because food strengthened whatever response happened to precede it. Indeed, Thomas (1981) has shown that rats will learn a response that precedes food even when this response actually cuts the rate of food delivery by half. Finally, research with human subjects has shown that reinforcement can strengthen subtle responses without the subjects' being aware that they are being reinforced. In all these cases, there is conflicting evidence—some experimenters, for example, have had difficulty replicating Skinner's superstition experiment—but on balance it appears that reinforcers do automatically strengthen behavior in at least some circumstances.

A second implication of Thorndike's belief that reinforcers stamp in an association between the preceding stimulus and response is that reinforcers directly cause learning. An alternative view, proposed by cognitive theorists such as Tolman, is that we are constantly learning about the world around us, and that reinforcement is not necessary for learning to occur. Experiments on latent learning have supported this view: Rats that are not given food following a trip through a maze learn just as much about the layout of the maze as do rats that are reinforced. Further evidence that reinforcement is not necessary for learning comes from the phenomenon of perceptual learning, in which our ability to discriminate between stimuli such as faces and wines improves simply through continued exposure to these stimuli. These results suggest that the main effect of reinforcement is not on learning but on performance: In the case of the rat in the maze, reinforcement does not teach it what path leads to the goal box, but rather influences its decision to take that path.

One way in which reinforcement influences performance is by providing information about which response is correct. A reinforcer, from this perspective, is simply an event that enters into an association, rather than one that influences other associations. Once we have learned that pressing a button turns on a radio, or that doing our homework earns praise, we can then use this information in deciding how to behave in the future. A purely informational interpretation of reinforcement, however, would imply that behavior is entirely rational, and we know that this is not so. A rat that is given a large amount of food for pressing a lever may become excited and press the lever much faster than is actually necessary; the omission of food can produce frustration and aggression. Reinforcement thus seems to affect motivation as well as providing information, and we need to take both into account in order to predict behavior.

The difficulty of doing this is illustrated by research on avoidance learning. In a typical avoidance experiment, rats are given a tone followed 10 seconds later by shock; if they jump over a barrier before the 10 seconds have elapsed, the warning signal is terminated and the shock delivery canceled. To explain learning in this situation, Mowrer proposed a two-factor theory in which the classical conditioning of fear provided the basis for the reinforcement of the avoidance response. Specifically, pairing of the tone with shock would condition fear to the tone, and termination of the tone would reduce this fear and thereby reinforce jumping.

The importance of fear is shown in studies in which a previously conditioned stimulus is presented while subjects are responding on an avoidance task: Stimuli that elicit fear increase responding, whereas stimuli that inhibit fear reduce responding. Similarly, the reinforcing properties of fear reduction are shown in studies in which rats learn to jump over a barrier in order to turn off a stimulus previously associated with shock.

One challenge to two-factor theory has come from evidence that some responses are much harder to learn than others, even though they all terminate the warning stimulus and, therefore, should be reinforced equally by fear reduction. To account for this variability, Bolles has proposed that animals have a set of innate, species-specific defense reactions (SSDRs) to fear, and that responses that are incompatible with these SSDRs are very difficult to learn. The details of how SSDRs such as freezing interfere with responses such as bar-pressing, however, are not yet well understood. A second factor in the difficulty of training bar-pressing as an avoidance response may be that it produces relatively little change in the rat's environment and, as a result, does not reduce conditioned fear levels sufficiently to reinforce the bar-press. If so, two-factor theory may be able to account for some of the variation in the ease of learning different avoidance responses, but the theory will still have to be modified to accord a greater role to innate SSDRs as determinants of performance.

A further challenge to two-factor theory comes from evidence that avoidance responding is not as dependent on fear as the theory suggests. Once subjects learn to avoid shock, they no longer show signs of fear when they respond. According to two-factor theory, this should lead to a marked reduction in avoidance responding, but subjects continue to respond vigorously; even when shock is discontinued, responding may persist for hundreds of trials without weakening. Thus, although fear plays a major role in avoidance behavior, fear does not seem to be necessary for a response to occur.

To account for the persistence of avoidance responding in the absence of fear, Seligman and Johnston (1973) have proposed a cognitive analysis in which responding is based not on fear, but on the rational belief that the response will reduce the likelihood of shock. According to their account, subjects in avoidance experiments learn that shock occurs following a warning stimulus, but does not occur if they respond; because they prefer not to receive a shock, they respond. The persistence of avoidance responding in extinction follows naturally from this analysis: Animals jump because they expect this response to be followed by no shock, and extinction trials simply confirm this expectation. For avoidance responding to extinguish, according to this analysis, subjects must have an opportunity to learn that shock no longer occurs if they do not respond, and experiments in which responding is prevented during extinction (flooding) have confirmed this prediction.

A cognitive analysis, then, can explain the persistence of avoidance responding after fear has extinguished, but it has difficulty accounting for experiments in which fear does influence avoidance responding. One obvious resolution is to assume that two-factor theory and cognitive accounts are both right, with avoidance responding being controlled by a mixture of fear (and the SSDRs this fear elicits) and the rational expectation that responding will avoid shock. If so, this literature suggests the same conclusion as the literature on other forms of reinforcement: Both expectations and emotions seem to play a role in directing performance, and we need to take both into account in predicting behavior.

The final topic covered in this chapter—the relationship between classical conditioning and reinforcement—suggests that we may now know more about the mechanisms of learning than about how this learning is translated into performance. Reinforcement and classical conditioning are extraordinarily similar in their basic principles, which suggests that they involve the same learning mechanism, but neither form of learning is able to account for the other: $R–S^*$ and $S–S^*$ contingencies have different effects on behavior, and the effects of one cannot be reduced to the other. Another way to account for their similarity is to assume that both rely on a common system for detecting relationships between events. If event E_1 is followed by another event E_2, then whether E_1 is a stimulus, as in the case of classical conditioning, or a response, as in the case of instrumental conditioning, the same learning mechanism may be involved in detecting the $E_1–E_2$ relationship.

Any analysis that claims that reinforcement and classical conditioning are based on the same learning process needs to be able to explain why classical conditioning influences autonomic responses more than skeletal responses, whereas the reverse is true for reinforcement—indeed, there is some doubt whether it is possible to reinforce autonomic responses at all. In the case of reinforcement, the greater difficulty of reinforcing autonomic responses may be an instance of preparedness: The learning system may have evolved so as to ensure that autonomic responses cannot be associated with reinforcers, because changes in autonomic behavior consequent on the delivery of external reinforcers might seriously interfere with the body's homeostatic mechanisms. In the case of classical conditioning, the fact that only a relatively small subset of skeletal responses can be conditioned may be a reflection of the performance rules for translating learned S–S* associations into behavior. When a US center is activated, it in turn activates a motivational or behavior system which primes only those skeletal responses that have been innately programmed for dealing with that US. The result is that classical conditioning affects only a subset of possible skeletal responses.

By considering the role of preparedness in reinforcement and of innately organized behavior systems in classical conditioning, therefore, we can potentially explain why these forms of learning affect different responses, even though they involve a common associative system. However, this explanation is highly speculative, as there is very little evidence available for assessing its validity. Thus, although there are plausible grounds for believing that there is one basic system for detecting relationships between events, we still know very little about how we use information about these relationships in deciding what response to make.

Selected Definitions

Superstition A response acquired as a result of its accidental contiguity with a reinforcer.

Latent learning Learning that occurs during nonreinforced trials but remains unused until the introduction of a reinforcer provides an incentive for using it.

Perceptual learning An improvement in a subject's ability to discriminate between stimuli as a result of exposure to those stimuli.

Incentive motivation A motivational state elicited by a stimulus as a result of classical conditioning. If a stimulus is paired with food, for example, the stimulus is assumed to elicit a motivational state that will affect responding in the same way that hunger does, influencing both the choice of responses and the vigor with which they are performed.

Avoidance response A response that postpones or prevents an aversive event.

Escape response A response that terminates an aversive stimulus that is already present.

Signaled avoidance An avoidance-training procedure in which a warning stimulus is followed by an aversive event such as shock; the shock is not presented if the subject responds before the shock is scheduled to occur.

Two-factor theory A theory proposed by O. Hobart Mowrer to explain avoidance learning. According to this theory, avoidance learning depends on classical conditioning of fear to a warning stimulus and reinforcement of the avoidance response by termination of this stimulus.

Sidman avoidance An avoidance procedure developed by Murray Sidman that does not employ a warning stimulus. An aversive event such as shock is scheduled to occur at fixed time intervals (the shock–shock interval); if the subject makes the required avoidance response at any time during this interval, the next programmed shock is postponed for a fixed period (the response–shock interval).

Species-specific defense reactions (SSDRs) Innate responses elicited by stimuli that signal danger. The reaction of a mouse to the approach of a cat, for example, is likely to be very different from the reaction of a pigeon in the same situation—hence the term *species-specific*.

Flooding A technique for overcoming conditioned fear by presenting the fear-evoking stimulus in a situation in which the subject cannot escape from the stimulus.

Omission procedure A technique developed by Sheffield for determining whether conditioned responses are really due to classical conditioning or to reinforcement contingencies implicit in the conditioning procedure. In an omission procedure, the US is omitted on any trial during which there is a response. Because responses are never followed by reinforcement, any increase in responding cannot be due to reinforcement.

Review Questions

1. In what ways does the Law of Effect imply that reinforcement is automatic?

2. Are contiguous pairings of a response and a reinforcer sufficient to produce learning?

3. Do humans learn superstitions in the same way as pigeons? Why don't people eventually realize that these superstitions are incorrect?

4. Can reinforcement affect people's behavior without their realizing it? How might the conflicting evidence in this area be explained?

5. What is meant by a learning process? On what basis can we decide whether two instances of learning involve the same learning process?

6. Do reinforcement and conditioning involve the same contingency?

7. What responses can be learned through classical conditioning? What responses can be learned through reinforcement?

8. Do conditioning and reinforcement involve the same learning process? How could the distinction between learning and performance be used to explain the conflicting evidence?

9. How does Mowrer's two-factor theory account for avoidance learning? What evidence supports this theory? What evidence opposes it?

10. How does Seligman and Johnston's cognitive analysis account for avoidance learning? What evidence supports it, and what evidence opposes it?

11. Depending on their compatibility, classically conditioned responses can either facilitate or interfere with the learning or performance of reinforced responses. Describe each of these four interactions, using the examples given in this chapter.

THEORETICAL PROCESSES IN ASSOCIATIVE LEARNING

CHAPTER TEN

LEARNING IN AN
EVOLUTIONARY CONTEXT

In preceding chapters we have treated classical conditioning and reinforcement as if they were entirely general processes whose effects were the same in all species. In discussing the principles of classical conditioning, for example, we based our conclusions on experiments involving, among other things, salivation in dogs, nausea in rats, and key-pecking in pigeons. The implicit assumption was that the principles of classical conditioning were everywhere the same; regardless of the response or the species, the same basic process was at work.

This assumption is critical to attempts to apply the results of animal research to human behavior: Unless the principles of learning are fundamentally similar, there is little reason to think that studies of salivation in dogs or bar-pressing in rats will have much relevance to humans. But is this assumption correct? Are the fundamental principles of learning really the same in all animal species?

10.1 THE GENERAL PROCESS VIEW

Early research strongly supported the view that the principles of learning were identical in all species—or, more accurately, in all vertebrates, which were the species normally studied. In Pavlov's research on classical conditioning, for example, he found that it did not matter what stimulus he used as a US: whether he presented dogs with food to elicit salivation or a mild electric shock to elicit leg flexion, the principles of conditioning were exactly the same. Similarly, it did not matter what stimulus he used as a CS: "Any natural phenomenon chosen at will may be converted into a conditioned stimulus . . . any visual stimulus, any desired sound, any odor, and the stimulation of any part of the skin" (Pavlov, 1928, p. 86). Regardless of the particular stimuli chosen as the CS and the US, the principles governing the formation of an association were identical.

Thorndike found exactly the same pattern in his experiments on reinforcement. As we noted in Chapter 2, Thorndike varied what response his cats had to make to escape from the puzzle box, but he found the same pattern of trial-and-error learning in every case. Similarly, he experimented with different species—chicks, dogs, monkeys, and so on—but again the pattern of behavior was the same. It was this uniformity that led him to express his conclusions in the form of a universal Law of Effect.

Skinner, in his later experiments on reinforcement, observed the same uniformity. Skinner found that not all forms of behavior could be reinforced; he referred to those responses that could be modified by their consequences as operants. If a response had been shown to be an operant in one situation, however—that is, it could be strengthened by making a reinforcer contingent on it—he found that it could also be modified by other reinforcers, and that the principles were the same in each case: "The general topography of operant behavior is not important, because most if not all specific operants are conditioned. I suggest that the dynamic properties of operant behavior may be studied with a single reflex" (Skinner, 1938, pp. 45–46).

As one example of this uniformity, Skinner and his colleagues found that reinforcement schedules had virtually identical effects regardless of the response or the species. In one of his papers, Skinner (1956) presented a figure showing the effects of a mixture of FI and FR schedules on rats, pigeons, and monkeys (see Figure 10.1), and challenged his readers to say which results came from which species:

> Pigeon, rat, monkey, which is which? It doesn't matter. Of course, these three species have behavioral repertories which are as different as their anatomies. But once you have allowed for differences in the ways in which they make contact with the environment . . . what remains of their behavior shows astonishingly similar properties.
>
> (Skinner, 1956, p. 230)

It was this uniformity that led Skinner to title his most important work The Behavior of Organisms, even though almost all of the reported research was on bar-pressing in white rats!

In both classical conditioning and reinforcement, then, it did not seem to matter what events were being associated: One association was formed as easily as another. Moreover, as we saw in the preceding chapter, the principles of classical conditioning and reinforcement are remarkably similar, suggesting that the same associative process might be responsible for both. If we combine all these observations, one obvious possibility is that there is only one learning

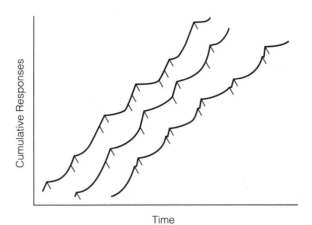

F I G U R E 10.1   Cumulative response records of responding in a pigeon, a rat, and a monkey. All three subjects were trained on a multiple FI FR, a schedule in which responding is reinforced on an FI schedule in the presence of one stimulus and on an FR schedule in the presence of a second stimulus. Despite the differences in the responses required, the reinforcers, and the species, the patterns of responding in the three subjects were remarkably uniform. (Adapted from Skinner, 1956)

system responsible for the formation of associations, and that this same system is always involved, regardless of the events being associated or the species.

Seligman (1970) has called this the **general process view**, and it can be stated somewhat more formally as follows:

1. *A general system.*   Whenever an association is formed between two events, E_1 and E_2, the same learning process or system is responsible. In particular, it does not matter whether E_1 is a stimulus, as in the case of classical conditioning, or a response, as in the case of reinforcement: The same underlying associative mechanism is responsible for both. [*]

2. *Interchangeability of events.*   One property of this associative mechanism is that it is indifferent to the events being associated. In the case of

---

[*] This version of the general process view is broader than Seligman's, as he did not explicitly assume that classical conditioning and reinforcement were a single process. Early learning theorists differed on this point: Some, such as Hull (1943), believed that there was a single process; others, such as Mowrer (1947), argued for a two-factor theory that assumed that classical conditioning and reinforcement were different processes. For a review, see Rescorla and Solomon (1967).

Another important point on which learning theorists were divided was whether learning was stored in the form of relatively simple associations, or more complex expectations. (See discussions in Chapters 5 and 11.) We will be using the term *association* in this chapter solely as a form of shorthand, to indicate that *some* learning about the association or relationship between E_1 and E_2 has occurred; we intend no implication as to whether this is stored in the form of an association or an expectation.

classical conditioning, any stimulus that is an adequate CS (that is, sufficiently salient to be capable of being associated with at least one US) can be associated with any US. Similarly, in the case of reinforcement, any operant response (that is, any response capable of being modified by at least one reinforcer) can be strengthened by any reinforcer. Stated more generally, any member of the E_1 category can be associated with any member of the E_2 category. (Seligman called this the premise of *equipotentiality*.)

3. *Generality across species.*   Associative learning in all vertebrate species is based on the same associative mechanism or system. [*]

As we have seen, early research provided considerable support for these assumptions, and as this evidence accumulated the general process view gradually became one of those fundamental beliefs that everyone takes for granted—an unchallengeable foundation stone of learning theory. If this assumption went largely unquestioned within learning theory, however, it was to come under increasing assault from workers outside this tradition. In the course of this chapter, we will be looking at some of these challenges and their possible implications.

In reading this material, you may find it helpful to bear in mind two extreme possibilities concerning the form learning takes in different species. At one extreme lies the general process view, with its assumption that seemingly different forms of learning are really manifestations of a fundamental mechanism that is always and everywhere the same. At the other extreme lies what might be called the multiprocess or "Let 1000 flowers bloom" view, which assumes that every species has evolved its own, unique forms of learning and that, because they have evolved independently, there is unlikely to be much relationship between them.

These extremes help to define a continuum of possibilities concerning the relationships between different forms of learning, from a single associative mechanism at one end to a myriad of unrelated forms at the other. In the remainder of this chapter, we will be considering where along this continuum reality lies.

10.2 AN EVOLUTIONARY PERSPECTIVE

One of the first challenges to the assumption that learning was uniform came from *ethologists*—behavioral biologists who study animal behavior under natu-

---

[*] Vertebrates are animals that possess a hard backbone to support their bodies, in contrast to invertebrate species, such as jellyfish and insects, which either have no hard structures or else have a hard outer shell. There are five main classes of vertebrates: fish, amphibians, reptiles, birds, and mammals.

ralistic conditions. Heavily influenced by Darwin's theory of evolution, ethologists take as their task not simply observing animal behavior, but trying to understand why it has evolved in the way that it has. Why is it, for example, that male bluebirds of paradise—birds with brilliantly colored turquoise and purple feathers—court females by hanging upside down from a branch and flapping their wings? What in the history of the species could have led them to adopt such seemingly bizarre behavior?

This concern with how behavior evolved has made ethologists very sensitive to differences in the way species behave. To understand their views, we will start by reviewing the main principles of evolution. We will then examine how this evolutionary perspective led them to a very different impression of learning than that of Pavlov, Thorndike, and Skinner.

Principles of Evolution

The concept of evolution was not invented by Charles Darwin, but he was undoubtedly its most brilliant and influential advocate. In *The Origin of Species*, he proposed that species were not created simultaneously, but rather evolved gradually over many thousands of years from common ancestors.

Natural selection.   To explain how this evolution occurred, he started from the observable fact that members of species vary, and suggested that some of these variants would make their possessors more likely to survive. Mice, for example, vary in their speed of running, and those that are faster are likely to be better at escaping from predators. Suppose, then, that at some point in mouse history, one mouse had the capacity to run faster than its peers. If so, it would have been likely to live longer and, crucially, to have more children. If we further suppose that whatever property make this mouse faster was heritable—that is, that its offspring would also generally be faster because of something they inherited from this parent—then these fast sons and daughters would also have been more likely to survive and reproduce, and so on, so that the proportion of fast individuals in the mouse population would gradually have increased.

The process by which environmental conditions (in this case, the presence of predators) selects out individuals who are fitter is known as **natural selection.** For natural selection to be effective, however, the adaptive characteristic must be one that can be passed on to succeeding generations. The mechanism of transmission is now known to be a *gene*, a gigantic string of complex molecules. Many genes are linked together to form still longer units called *chromosomes*, and these chromosomes are present in the nucleus of every cell in our bodies. In organisms that reproduce sexually, half of each parent's set of genes is transmitted to the offspring (the male cells carrying the half-set are sperm, the female carriers are eggs). Once an egg is fertilized, and thus the full number of chromosomes restored, the genes present in every cell act to control the chemical processes within that cell, and by this means ultimately control every aspect of the developing organism, from hair color to brain size.

Applying our knowledge of genes to evolution, we can rephrase our earlier explanation to say that if one mouse develops a gene that results in stronger muscles and hence faster running, it will be likely to live longer and have more offspring, so that over a number of generations this gene will come to be present in an ever larger proportion of the mouse population. Over time, then, mice will run faster, and as changes of this kind gradually accumulate, they may eventually result in a group of mice sufficiently different from their ancestors as to constitute a new species.

Adaptive value.   A crucial assumption in this analysis is that new traits will emerge only if they have some **adaptive value**—that is, if animals possessing the new trait are in some sense better adapted to their environment, and thus more likely to reproduce and pass on this trait. In deciding whether some trait has adaptive value, we need to consider not simply the trait by itself but how well it fits the species to its particular environment. In our mouse example, we suggested that faster mice would be more likely to survive, but this is not necessarily so. Suppose, for example, that the genetic mutation we have been considering produced larger muscles, and it was these larger muscles that enabled the mice to run faster. Being faster would undoubtedly help them evade predators, but their larger muscles would also mean that these mice weighed more and required more food to survive. If the environment provided sufficient food, the new gene would indeed have advantages, but in a harsher environment the costs might outweigh the benefits, and the gene would not be disseminated.

Niches.   In assessing adaptive value, then, we need to consider carefully the environment of the species concerned. We tend to think of the world as a fairly uniform environment, perhaps subdivided into a few major regions such as earth, air, and water, but evolutionary theorists have found it more useful to conceptualize the world as composed of millions of local habitats known as *niches.*

Consider, for example, a tree in a forest. It might at first seem to provide a uniform environment for its inhabitants, so that we should expect to find the same species of birds living on all its branches, but this is not so. For one thing, lower branches receive less light than upper ones, and as a result they support different forms of lichen and insects; also, upper branches are accessible to predators such as eagles in a way that lower branches are not. The net result is that a number of different species of birds may inhabit different levels of a single tree, each specialized to take advantage of the properties of its unique niche. In evaluating the adaptive value of a behavior, then, we need to take into account the features of the species' particular niche.

Summarizing our account, the theory of evolution suggests that natural selection will lead to the reproductive success of individuals that are better adapted to their local environment, and that over time this will result in a gradual change in the properties of species. One result is that natural selection will tend to lead to the divergence of species, as each species becomes increasingly specialized to exploit the potential of its local environment, or niche.

Learning and Evolution

This evolutionary perspective has potentially important implications for the development of learning in different species. On the one hand, the fact that all vertebrates are descended from a common ancestor suggests that there should be important similarities in their behavior. Consider, for example, the biological process of respiration. All mammalian species face a common problem of extracting oxygen from air, and this common problem has led to a common solution: The principles of respiration are fundamentally the same across mammalian species. Similarly, all vertebrates share a common environment in terms of causality: The cause of an event is always something that precedes it, and almost always something that precedes it closely. When an animal is injured, for example, the injury is likely to have been caused by something that happened just before the injury occurred. Thus, if at some point in evolutionary history a species developed a learning system that identified the stimuli that preceded injury—a system such as classical conditioning—it would not be surprising if this system were retained by all the species that descended from it. Thus, although we might expect some minor divergences in learning, as in respiration, the fundamental principles should remain the same. (See also Revusky, 1985.)

On the other hand, we must recognize that evolution involves not just the existence of common ancestors but descent from them, as species have been diverging from their ancestors over a period of many thousands of years. Thus, just as the physical structure of species change as they become increasingly adapted to their local environments—birds developed wings, fish developed fins—so, too, we might expect divergences in learning mechanisms, as each species became increasingly adapted to the unique requirements of its niche. (See, for example, Gould, 1986a.)

An evolutionary perspective, then, suggests that similar environments may lead to similar behaviors, but it also alerts us to the possibility that seemingly similar environments can nevertheless differ in important respects, and that these differences can lead to the evolution of different behaviors. It is difficult to predict in advance whether the similarities of two environments are more important than their differences, and thus whether or not we should expect similar learning mechanisms. Because of ethologists' evolutionary perspective, however, they were more sensitive than psychologists to the possibility of differences, and in observing animals in their natural habitats they discovered that learning did differ in significant respects. We will focus here on two examples involving birds: imprinting and song learning.

Imprinting. The first major challenge to the view that learning was the same in all vertebrates came from an Austrian ethologist, Konrad Lorenz. Earlier zoologists had noticed that precocial birds—species such as ducks and chickens that are able to walk as soon as they are born—will follow the first moving object they see after they hatch. Normally, this is their mother, with the happy result that families stay together when the mother goes off in search for food. If the first moving object a chick sees is a human being, however, it will instead become attached to that person, and will follow the person wherever he or she goes. If the chick is later reunited with its mother, it will show no interest, but instead hurry off after the person on whom it has imprinted, or even another human that happens to walk by.

These observations suggest that chicks have to learn to recognize their species, and that they do so by becoming attached to the first moving object they see. Lorenz called this development of a social attachment **imprinting**, and he suggested that imprinting differed from other forms of learning in several major respects.

First, whereas forms of learning such as classical conditioning can occur at any time in an animal's life, Lorenz said that imprinting would occur only during the first hours after hatching, which he called the **critical period**. If a duckling, for example, was not given an opportunity to imprint on its mother during its first few days, then it would never do so.

A second unique characteristic of imprinting, according to Lorenz, was that it was *irreversible*. "The process, once accomplished, is totally irreversible. . . . This absolute rigidity is something we never find in behavior acquired by associative learning, which can be unlearned or changed, at least to a certain extent" (Lorenz, 1937, p. 264). One consequence of this permanent attachment was that when the bird became an adult it would direct its sexual behavior either to the original imprinting stimulus or to one similar to it. In jackdaws, for example, adult males offer potential mates choice morsels of food as a way of courting them. Lorenz (1952) imprinted a male jackdaw on him when it was young, and found that when it reached sexual maturity it attempted to seduce him by offering him worms that it had thoughtfully predigested. When Lorenz refused this generous offer by keeping his mouth closed, the jackdaw instead deposited the worms in the nearest opening, his ear!

It appeared, then, that imprinting was unique in several respects: It occurred only in some species, it occurred only during a very brief critical period, and it was irreversible. Lorenz's evidence for these claims, however, came largely from naturalistic observations, and other ethologists and psychologists set out to test his claims under laboratory conditions, where alternative interpretations could be controlled for. In a typical experiment, a newly hatched duckling was placed in an apparatus like that shown in Figure 10.2: The stimulus on which it was to be imprinted was slowly rotated along the raised platform, and the duckling was allowed to follow behind it.

Laboratory research confirmed some of Lorenz's claims. For example, Lorenz believed that the crucial requirement for imprinting to take place was that the stimulus be moving, and experiments strongly confirmed this: Ducklings would imprint even to a milk bottle, provided that it was moving. Other experiments, however, revealed that imprinting was not as sharply differentiated from other forms of learning as he had supposed. The critical period, for example, is not as clearly defined as Lorenz's naturalistic observations had suggested, but can occur over a significantly longer period under some circumstances. (See, for example, R. T. Brown, 1975.) As a result, the critical period is now usually referred to as the **sensitive period**, to emphasize that imprinting is more likely to occur during this period, but is not necessarily limited to it.

Also, imprinting is not totally irreversible. In an experiment by Salzen and Meyer (1968), chicks were exposed to a colored ball for three days, at which point they showed typical attachment behavior—for example, preferring it to a second colored ball. Exposure to the second ball for a further three-day period, however, resulted in a reversal of this preference. Similarly, Guiton (1966) found that chicks that were exposed to a moving yellow glove when young later attempted to copulate with the glove in preference to a stuffed female chicken; if they were then allowed to live with other chickens rather than remaining in isolation, however, they developed a preference for the

F I G U R E 10.2   An apparatus for studying imprinting. (Adapted from Hess, 1959)

chicken model. Clearly, the preferences established during early life can be modified by later experience, and thus are not as rigid as Lorenz had supposed.

If experimental studies led to qualifications of the conclusions Lorenz had drawn from his naturalistic observations, they nevertheless supported the view of ethologists that different species may evolve specialized forms of learning to cope with the requirements of their unique environments. Imprinting, for example, is found only in precocial species, whose young are mobile from the moment of their hatching. In these species, young birds that can quickly learn to identify their parents will obviously be better able to follow them and thus survive; in species that spend their early lives in nests, there is no advantage to the young in learning to identify their parents, and in these species imprinting does not occur.

Imprinting contradicts the general process view not only because it is present only in some species, but also because, when it is present, the process is much more selective than a simple associative account would suggest. The general process view assumes that the nature of the stimulus does not matter, but although imprinting *can* occur to a wide range of moving stimuli, it is far stronger if the moving stimulus resembles the parent: Ducklings, for example, imprint better if the model resembles the parent visually and if it emits a sound resembling the normal duck call. (For a review, see Bateson, 1991.)

Contrary to the general process view, then, imprinting occurs only in some species and, when it does occur, occurs more readily to some stimuli than others. Rather than possessing a totally indiscriminate learning system, capable of learning about all stimuli equally, birds seem biologically predisposed to imprint on certain stimuli—stimuli that, not surprisingly, will maximize the chances that they will learn to follow their own mothers and not other adults or other species.

Song learning.   A second respect in which learning in birds reflects strong biological predispositions concerns the acquisition of songs. In some species, the ability to produce the species-typical song is innate, but in others, parts of the song are learned by listening to adults sing. If a white-crowned sparrow is exposed to a recording of an adult's song while young, for example, it will reproduce that song when it reaches sexual maturity. (See Marler, 1991, for a review.)

Song learning has been found to possess many of the same properties as imprinting; indeed, song learning can be thought of as a form of imprinting in which young birds learn to identify the song of their species rather than its visual appearance. As with imprinting, learning seems to be most likely to occur during a sensitive period early in the bird's life. A white-crowned sparrow will reproduce a song if the song is played during the first 10 to 50 days of its life, but not if the song is played later.

Also, once a song is learned, this learning is hard to reverse. The white-crowned sparrow again provides an illustration: If exposed to one song during the sensitive period and a second song afterwards, the second song has no effect (Marler, 1967).

A third similarity between song learning and imprinting is that in both cases learning is guided by genetic predispositions. Although some species will learn virtually any song to which they are exposed, in most species there are strong predispositions to learn songs that closely resemble the characteristic song of the species. If young song sparrows and swamp sparrows are exposed to recordings of either their own song or that of the other species, learning occurs much more quickly if the song they hear is their own (Marler & Richards, 1989). The birds behave as if they possessed a template or model of the ideal form, and the ease of learning is proportional to how closely the song fits this ideal. "It is as if the bird were a musician programmed to learn a single piece of Baroque music: Such an individual would be immune to the charms of Brahms or the Beatles, but would fixate instantly on anything by Bach or Vivaldi" (Staddon, 1983, p. 400).

Before leaving song learning, it may be worth pointing out some tantalizing parallels between song learning in birds and language learning in children. Just as birds are particularly likely to reproduce sounds that are characteristic of their species' song, human infants are more likely to attend to the sounds that are characteristic of human speech (Eimas, 1984). Also, once a bird has been exposed to a song, it will learn to imitate it by a trial-and-error process in which it produces a semi-random sequence of sounds, listens to itself, and then gradually modifies its song to make it resemble more closely the song to which it was exposed. Birds begin to produce these first approximations at a set age, even if they have been deafened just before this age and thus cannot modify the song they are producing. Similarly, human infants begin to babble at a particular age, and even naturally deaf children begin to babble at this age. It may be that language learning in humans builds on some of the same instinctive patterns that are present in song learning. (See Gould, 1986a.)

The adaptive value of learning.   In both song learning and imprinting, species differ in whether they exhibit this learning, and where it does occur, there are often strong predispositions to learn about particular stimuli. In both cases, moreover, the form of learning observed in a particular species seems to reflect the adaptive value of this learning. In the case of imprinting, we have seen that it occurs in precocial birds, for whom the ability to recognize one's parents is critical for survival, but not in tree-nesting birds, for whom recognition of the parent would have no value. Similarly, whether or not birds learn their songs seems to reflect the adaptive value of such learning. One example concerns *brood parasites*—birds that lay their eggs in the nests of other species, thereby tricking these other species into rearing their young (cuckoos are a notorious example). If young male cuckoos were to learn the song of the birds that reared them, when they became adult they would be at a serious disadvantage in attracting the attention of female cuckoos, with potentially disastrous consequences for the propagation of their genes. As an adaptive value analysis would predict, no brood parasite species learns to sing; they rely instead on innate songs. *

A common feature of both imprinting and song learning, then, is that both occur only in species for which such learning would have adaptive value. This also appears to be true of many other forms of learning in birds. For example, most birds do not learn to recognize their eggs, even though they see and handle them many times each day. Where there is an advantage to egg recognition—for example, in species whose nesting sites are closely packed together, so that there is a real danger of nests' and eggs' being confused—then the capacity for recognition is much more likely to be found. Similarly, birds that nest in trees have no need to recognize their young immediately after hatching, and in general cannot do so. However, these parents do begin to recognize their young when they fledge, or develop the feathers necessary for leaving the nest—precisely the moment when such recognition would have some value. (See Gould, 1986a.) In at least some circumstances, therefore, the capacity for learning does not seem to be a default option that is always present; rather, learning occurs only in those situations in which it is likely to be of value. It may be that the importance for birds of being light enough to fly means that they cannot afford to develop or maintain the larger brain size that would be required to learn about the appearance of their eggs or of their progeny—unless, that is, this learning capacity has unequivocal adaptive value.

Summary. The evidence on imprinting and song learning suggests that the strong form of the general process view—that learning is always and everywhere the same—is simply not tenable. Learning does take different forms in different species, and these forms reflect the requirements of each species' unique niche. However, the fact that learning in different species differs in some respects does not imply that it differs in all respects; imprinting, for example, is not as sharply differentiated from other forms of learning as the early evidence for critical periods and irreversibility seemed to suggest. We will examine the similarities among different forms of learning more systematically

---

* You might wonder why any birds learn to sing; why don't they all rely on innate songs? The answer is not clear, but one possibility is that where there are local "dialects," so that all the birds in an area share common elements to their song, birds will be easily able to discriminate local birds from birds that have flown in from elsewhere. This, in turn, may help the birds to direct aggression in defense of territories against the newcomers, who are likely to be less closely related genetically and thus, if allowed to remain in the area and mate, would pose a greater threat to the survival of the residents' genes. For a fuller explanation of why animals might have a greater interest in the survival of relatives, see *The Selfish Gene* by Richard Dawkins (1989).

in Section 10.4, and consider the extent to which different varieties of learning may nevertheless share common mechanisms; for now, the critical point is that there are far more differences than early learning theorists realized.

10.3 THE CHALLENGE WITHIN: ARE CLASSICAL CONDITIONING AND REINFORCEMENT UNIFORM PROCESSES?

The evidence for specialized forms of learning such as imprinting and song learning posed a serious challenge to the assumption of uniformity. At first, however, psychologists largely ignored this evidence. One reason was that the early evidence was largely observational, and, from Thorndike on, learning theorists have been deeply suspicious of purely observational evidence. In the case of imprinting, this suspicion proved to have some justification, as later experimental evidence did blur the sharp distinctions between imprinting and associative learning originally claimed by Lorenz.

A further reason why learning theorists paid little attention to the developing literature on imprinting was that it seemed to have little applicability to the central concern of these theorists, which was associative learning. Even if some species did develop specialized forms of learning, this did not necessarily mean that the mechanisms of associative learning in these species were different. Two species might differ in whether they were capable of imprinting, for example, but the effects of reinforcement in the two species might nevertheless be identical. And, as we have seen, decades of research on learning had consistently shown that the principles of classical conditioning and reinforcement were universal. Gradually, however, challenges to the general process view began to appear even within its associative heartland, and it is to this evidence that we now turn.

Classical Conditioning

Taste-aversion learning.   The most influential challenge arose from the work of John Garcia on taste-aversion learning. As we saw in Chapter 4, rats made ill after eating develop a strong aversion to the taste of the food they just ate, but not to its appearance. Garcia and Koelling (1966) showed that rats were differentially prepared to associate tastes with illness, and conversely, to associate auditory and visual cues with electric shock.

These results posed a fundamental challenge to the general process view. The strong form of this hypothesis states that there is a universal associative mechanism that will associate any two events that are paired: Whatever the nature of the CS and US, as long as they occur in temporal contiguity, they will be associated. Garcia and Koelling's findings make it clear that this is not so: Animals are selectively prepared to associate some events more easily than others.

Gut defense versus skin defense.   Garcia's challenge to the general process view, however, was even broader. He argued that classical conditioning involves at least two quite different subsystems: a gut-defense system, whose purpose is to protect animals from poisonous food, and a skin-defense system designed to protect them from predators (Garcia, Brett, & Rusiniak, 1989). These systems, he suggested, had evolved independently and, because of their different functions, had evolved quite different properties. Specifically, taste-aversion learning, which was a manifestation of the gut-defense system, differed from previously studied forms such as fear and eyeblink conditioning (which are involved in skin defense) in at least three ways:

1. *The stimuli that can be conditioned.*   As we have seen, Garcia and Koelling found strong conditioning to tastes, but not to noise or light, when they used illness as their US. When shock was the US, the results were reversed, with strong conditioning to audiovisual stimuli but none to tastes.

2. *The rapidity of conditioning.*   Whereas most forms of conditioning are relatively slow—eyeblink conditioning, for example, can take hundreds of trials—taste-aversion conditioning is generally very rapid, with powerful conditioning observed after only one or two trials.

3. *The CS–US interval.*   Where conditioning involves external stimuli, we have seen that temporal contiguity between the CS and US is critical. In fear conditioning, for example, no conditioning is found with delays of more than a few minutes, and in eyeblink conditioning no learning occurs with delays of even a few seconds. In taste-aversion conditioning, on the other hand, conditioning has been found even with a delay of several hours. (For a review, see Domjan, 1980.)

Such differences are bewildering if we assume a single associative mechanism, but they make far more sense if we assume that different subsystems evolved in response to particular needs. Consider first the case of fear conditioning. In nature, if you experience a sudden blow, it is almost certainly related to events that closely preceded it—for example, seeing an eagle circling in the sky, or hearing the sudden rush of its wings. There would be strong adaptive advantages, therefore, to developing a fear of the stimuli that immediately preceded attack. Becoming frightened of a robin seen two hours earlier, on the other hand, would not only be of little value but would probably be harmful, as avoiding this irrelevant stimulus would interfere with crucial activities such as searching for food.

The situation is very different in the case of illness. Here, the interval between eating a poisonous food and becoming ill is often several hours, so that a system that produced an aversion to distant events would have considerable value, especially if, as Garcia and Koelling found, conditioning is focused on foods eaten earlier, rather than, say, sounds that were heard. The differences between fear and taste-aversion conditioning, in other words, become readily explicable if we assume learning systems that evolved separately to cope with different problems.

On the other hand, there are also substantial similarities between conditioning in the two cases. First, the same basic conditioning phenomena are found in both: extinction, generalization, blocking, and so on. Also, even in the three areas in which differences have been observed most clearly—preparedness, frequency of pairings, and contiguity—these differences may be more of degree than of kind. Thus, although tastes can be associated more easily with illness, and visual stimuli with shock, it is nevertheless possible for reverse associations to be made. Visual stimuli, for example, can be associated with illness; it just takes more pairings. (See, for example, Braveman, 1977.)

Similarly, taste-aversion conditioning is not always faster than other forms of classical conditioning: Fear conditioning can also occur very quickly (recall our discussion of traumatic conditioning in section 5.6), and taste-aversion learning can be slow in some circumstances.

Finally, although the longest interval at which conditioning will take place is clearly greater in taste-aversion conditioning, contiguity remains important even here: Just as in other forms of conditioning, there is a maximum interval at which conditioning is still possible, and within this range shorter intervals produce better conditioning than longer intervals. (See Figure 10.3.)

In summary, the work of Garcia and others has made it clear that taste-aversion learning differs in a number of respects from traditionally studied forms of learning, such as fear and eyeblink conditioning. (For evidence of further differences, see LoLordo & Droungas, 1989.) However, there are also substantial similarities in the forms of learning observed, and where there are differences they often appear quantitative rather than qualitative. This pattern leads rather temptingly to the conclusion that the fundamental mechanism may be similar, albeit modified in the course of evolution to cope with the requirements of different situations and different species. We will again postpone a systematic evaluation of the case for a common mechanism until the concluding section; for now, the crucial point is that the strong version of the general process view is not tenable for classical conditioning any more than it was for imprinting.

Reinforcement: The Misbehavior of Organisms

What, then, of reinforcement? Can the assumption of an invariant learning process be defended any better in this domain? As we have seen, early research suggested that the mechanism of reinforcement was universal. Thorndike, for example, tested his cats in a variety of puzzle boxes, requiring a variety of

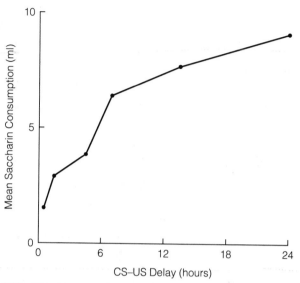

FIGURE 10.3   Taste-aversion learning as a function of the delay between drinking saccharin and becoming ill. The measure of learning is the amount of saccharin consumed during a test following the conditioning phase. (Adapted from Andrews & Braveman, 1975)

responses for escape, and he also tested a wide range of species. In every case, reinforcement was effective, and learning followed the same pattern—a gradual improvement over trials. Later research strongly supported the assumption of uniformity: Whether you reinforced bar-presses in rats, key-pecks in pigeons, or button-pushes in humans, the fundamental principles of reinforcement seemed to be the same.

Every once in a while, though, puzzling reports appeared of cases in which reinforcement did not work, or at any rate was far less effective than usual. Indeed, the first hint of this problem came in Thorndike's own research.

Unlickable cats.   In one of his experiments, Thorndike placed cats in a bare box; all they had to do to escape was to lick or scratch themselves. Given the frequency with which cats normally perform these responses, this should have been the simplest problem to solve, but, strangely, it proved the most difficult. Even after the cats had learned the required response, moreover, Thorndike observed

> *a noticeable tendency . . . to diminish the act until it becomes a mere vestige of a lick or scratch. . . . The licking degenerates into a mere quick turn of the head with one or two motions up and down with tongue extended. Instead of a hearty scratch, the cat waves its paw up and down rapidly for an instant. Moreover, if*

sometimes you do not let the cat out after this feeble reaction, it does not at once repeat the movement, as it would do if it depressed a thumbpiece, for instance, without success in getting the door open.

(Thorndike, 1911, p. 64)

Puzzling monkeys.   Another peculiar result was reported in 1950 by Harlow, Harlow, and Meyer. They presented monkeys with the puzzle illustrated in Figure 10.4. The monkeys were not reinforced for opening the puzzle; it was simply placed in their cage and left there. All of the monkeys nevertheless spent much time playing with it, and most eventually reached the point where they could open the puzzle within 20 seconds of its being placed in their cage. At this point, the experimenters placed a raisin under the hasp of the puzzle while the monkeys were watching, then put the puzzle back in their cage. You might think that the monkeys would now open the puzzle even more quickly than usual; instead, their performance deteriorated drastically, and three of the four monkeys now failed in their efforts to open the puzzle, even when allowed five minutes. Far from strengthening the response, reinforcement seemed to weaken it.

Miserly raccoons.   A third case in which reinforcement proved ineffective— and, in some ways, the strangest case of all—was reported by Keller Breland and Marion Breland in a delightful paper entitled "The Misbehavior of Organisms" (1961). After training as experimental psychologists at Harvard, the Brelands left academic psychology to start a company that trained animals to perform for commercial exhibitions. Everything went beautifully at first: They were able to use the principles of reinforcement developed in the laboratory to train species as diverse as cockatoos, pigs, reindeer, and whales. As time passed, however, they encountered more and more instances in which their subjects stubbornly refused to behave themselves.

In one project intended to illustrate the virtues of saving money, for

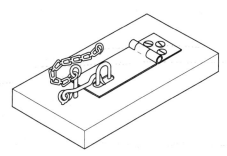

F I G U R E 10.4   Puzzle used by the monkeys in Harlow, Harlow, and Meyer's (1950) reinforcement experiment.

example, they reinforced a raccoon with food first for picking up a coin and then for carrying the coin across its cage and depositing it in a piggy bank. At first everything went smoothly, but as training progressed, the raccoon became increasingly reluctant to release the coin. It would begin to put it into the bank, but then pull it back and rub it back and forth between its paws in a distressingly miserly fashion. This rubbing behavior was never reinforced—quite the contrary, the longer the raccoon rubbed the coin, the longer it had to wait to receive food—but the amount of time spent rubbing nevertheless continued to increase, until eventually the planned exhibit had to be abandoned. This failure, moreover, was not an isolated instance. The Brelands encountered cows that would not learn to kick, chickens that grabbed plastic capsules and pounded them up and down on the floor instead of pecking them, whales that swallowed beach balls they were supposed to be working with, and so on. In all these cases, the Law of Effect just didn't seem to be working.

Why Does Reinforcement Fail?

For many years, these failures and others like them were largely ignored: In most cases reinforcement was highly effective, so the occasional failure was easily dismissed as an aberration. With the publication of John Garcia's work on taste-aversion conditioning, however, the climate changed. Until then, most psychologists had enthusiastically accepted the assumption that the fundamental mechanisms of associative learning were universal. Garcia's research, however, demonstrated that taste-aversion conditioning was not the same as, say, eyeblink conditioning: Strong taste aversions could be conditioned in just a single trial, even with a delay between ingestion and illness of several hours. If the ease of conditioning could vary so greatly depending on the CS and US involved, then the notion that responses might also vary in their reinforceability suddenly didn't seem so unthinkable, and the failures that had been ignored for so long became a focus of considerable interest to experimenters.

The resulting research has not entirely resolved the question of why some responses are so much harder to reinforce than others, but it has identified a number of factors that may be important. We will concentrate here on two: inflexible reflexes and competition from conditioned responses. (For a review of other factors, see Domjan, 1983.)

Inflexible reflexes.   Consider first Thorndike's difficulties in reinforcing licking and scratching. One possible explanation is suggested by the most obvious characteristic that these responses share: They are both reflexive behaviors, normally elicited by an unconditioned stimulus. One possibility, then, is that behaviors that are normally reflexive, or involuntary, may be more difficult to reinforce than other responses. In accordance with this analysis, research has shown that a number of other reflexive responses, such as face washing in golden hamsters and yawning in dogs, are also difficult to reinforce (Shettle-worth, 1983; Konorski, 1967). Not all the evidence is favorable (for example, Konorski, 1967), but it does currently seem as if the reflexive nature of licking and scratching could be one reason that they are hard to reinforce. (For other reasons, see Pearce, Colwill, & Hall, 1978; Iversen, Ragnarsdottir, & Randrup, 1984.)

If reflexive responses do prove to be more difficult to reinforce, this could plausibly be viewed as another example of the role of preparedness in learning. In Chapter 9 we noted that autonomic responses are very difficult to reinforce, and we suggested that one reason could be that reinforcement of autonomic responses would be maladaptive. If every time we received a reinforcer it strengthened all the autonomic responses that happened to be in progress at the time, the result could be disastrous. The evidence on licking and scratching raises the possibility that all reflexive responses may be hard to reinforce, skeletal as well as autonomic, because these responses are unlikely to have a genuine causal connection to the reinforcer. If a lion or other cat obtains food, for example, its success might reflect the efficiency of its stalking behavior, but it would be unlikely to be due to reflexive behaviors such as yawning or scratching. Natural selection, therefore, may have modified the reinforcement system to ensure that it does not strengthen reflexive behaviors, because these are responses that have evolved to cope with very specific problems such as a lack of oxygen, rather than as all-purpose behaviors capable of serving any of a variety of needs.

Competition from conditioned responses.   What may be a more important factor in cases where reinforcement fails is our old friend classical conditioning. We saw in Chapter 5 that stimuli paired with food may activate an animal's feeding system, which primes innately programmed behaviors for procuring and consuming food. Many of the failures of reinforcement we have discussed may be the result of competition between these conditioned responses and the response that the experimenter was trying to reinforce.

One example is the Brelands' study, in which a raccoon had difficulty learning to deposit a token in a piggy bank. Because the tokens were repeatedly paired with food in the early stages of training, and, critically, because the token's size and appearance may have resembled that of a raccoon's normal food, the raccoon may have learned to regard the token as food. Since raccoons wash or rub prospective food before eating it, its bizarre rubbing behavior may have been simply an attempt to prepare the coin for eating, and its refusal to deposit the coin in the bank an understandable reluctance to throw away its food.

Response interference might also explain the difficulty Harlow's monkeys had in opening the puzzle when it contained food. To open the puzzle, the monkeys had to release the restraining devices in a fixed sequence, first pulling out the pin, then releasing the hook, and finally opening the hasp. Before the experimenters introduced food, the monkeys almost always opened the pin first. When the raisin was introduced, however, they began instead by literally attacking the hasp under which the raisin had been placed. An obvious explanation is that the food's presence elicited innately prepared responses designed to obtain it, and that it was the frenzied execution of these responses that interfered with the learned response.

Support for this interference analysis comes from a study by Chapuis, Thinus-Blanc, and Poucet (1983), in which they trained dogs to approach a section of an open field that contained food. A barrier was then placed between the release point and the food (Figure 10.5), so that the dogs had to choose one of two new routes. One route deviated by only a small angle from the original route, but, because of the layout of the barrier, actually involved a much longer journey (path A); the second route required the dogs to move away from the food initially but nevertheless provided a shorter path to the food (path B). Before each test trial, the dogs were given walks along both paths to familiarize them with the distances involved. When the barrier was opaque, the dogs had a significant preference for the shorter route, but when the barrier was made of open mesh, so that the food was visible, preference for the shorter route fell to chance. It was as if the dogs became so excited at the prospect of receiving food that they could not resist the urge to take the "direct" path, even though the familiarization walks had shown them that it took longer. The sight of food may elicit an intense motivational state that overpowers more "rational" considerations.

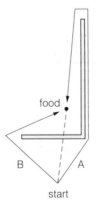

FIGURE 10.5 Overhead map of a detour problem. Dogs were released from the start point to obtain food located behind a barrier. The most direct path (shown by the broken line) was blocked by the barrier; path A started off at a closer angle to the direct path than path B but was longer. (Adapted from Chapuis, Thinus-Blanc, & Poucet, 1983)

In summary, much of the difficulty in reinforcing certain responses may be due to competition from classically conditioned responses.

Summary. Research on classical conditioning has shown that the ease of conditioning depends on the stimuli being associated. If a taste is paired with illness, for example, conditioning is faster, and occurs over a longer delay, than if a tone is paired with shock. Similarly in the case of reinforcement, some responses are much more difficult to reinforce than others, and this appears to depend in part on the response (reflexive responses appear harder to reinforce than voluntary responses) and in part on the combination of response and reinforcer used. It is easy to train rats to press a bar to obtain food, for example, but much more difficult to train them to press a bar to avoid shock. (See Chapter 9.) This difficulty, in turn, seems to be due largely to competition from classically conditioned responses. Whenever a reinforcer is presented, it is likely to condition responses to the stimuli that are present as well as reinforce whatever behavior preceded it, and these two processes sometimes strengthen behaviors that are incompatible. If the classically conditioned response is stronger, it may prevent the emergence of the reinforced response in the first place, or, as in the case of the Brelands' raccoon, the CR may eventually take the place of the reinforced response.

Together, these results make it clear that associative learning is not general in the sense that any combination of events E_1 and E_2 will be associated as easily as any other combination. In classical conditioning and reinforcement, as in imprinting and song learning, animals seem prepared, or predisposed, to acquire some kinds of knowledge more readily than others, and this predisposition seems to reflect the greater value of this knowledge in the animals' natural environment.

10.4 VARIATIONS ON A THEME

The general process view says that a single mechanism underlies all forms of associative learning. At this point, it may be worth reviewing the various assumptions that make up this hypothesis:

1. *A general system.*   All associative learning is due to a single system.

2. *Interchangeability of events.*   Any member of the E_1 class can be associated with any member of the E_2 class.

3. *Generality across species.*   This same mechanism underpins associative learning in all vertebrate species.

4. *All learning is associative learning.*   A further possible assumption, though one we have not previously spelled out, is that this one associative mech-

anism is responsible not just for associative learning, but for learning of every kind, because all learning ultimately relies on the formation of associations. (Recall Pavlov's statement that all education and training are ultimately based on the establishment of new nervous connections.)

The evidence we have reviewed in this chapter makes it clear that at least some of these assumptions are wrong. The assumption of event interchangeability, for example, is clearly violated by the fact that a flashing light, which is a perfectly adequate CS in some contexts, is very difficult to associate with illness, and, conversely, that a taste is very difficult to associate with shock. Similarly, the evidence on imprinting contradicts the assumption that learning is the same in all vertebrates: Although precocial birds develop an attachment to the first moving object they see, other birds do not. The mechanisms of learning in these species clearly cannot be identical.

On the other hand, when learning does occur, its characteristics are often very similar. In the case of taste-aversion learning and fear conditioning, for example, we have seen that the differences between these forms are more of degree than of kind: In both, conditioning depends on the contiguity of the CS and US, the number of pairings, the intensity of the US, and so on. Similarly, although imprinting differs from other forms of associative learning in that it occurs during a relatively brief period of life and is hard to reverse, these differences are again more of degree than of kind: For example, although imprinting is harder to reverse than most forms of conditioning, some strongly conditioned responses such as intense fear are also very hard to overcome.

An Adaptationist Perspective

One obvious way to integrate the evidence for both similarities and differences is to assume that the *basic* mechanisms of learning are similar across species, but that these basic mechanisms have been modified in the course of evolution to cope with the specialized requirements of different environments. For example, stimuli that predict damage to the skin, such as the appearance of a predator, usually occur immediately before the injury, whereas stimuli that predict gastrointestinal upsets, such as eating rotten food, are experienced many minutes or hours earlier. The result, as we have seen, is that taste aversions can be conditioned over far longer periods than fear. The fact that the two forms of conditioning share so many other properties, however, suggests that the two systems are still largely the same in other respects.

The idea that learning is basically a general process, but one that has often been modified in the course of evolution to cope with the demands of particular situations, has been called the **adaptationist approach** (for example, Beecher, 1988). According to this view, there are two powerful reasons why the mechanisms of learning are likely to be similar across species. The first is that the biological mechanisms underlying learning are not newly created in every species: Every species inherits genetic material from its ancestors, and this will inevitably lead to similarities in the mechanisms used by species descended from a relatively recent ancestor. Of course, if these species face different environments, the mechanisms they have inherited may be gradually modified and therefore diverge. The second important factor promoting similarity, however, is that, as far as learning is concerned, the broad outlines of the problems faced by different species are remarkably similar. For all species, causes precede effects, and in most instances there is close temporal contiguity between the two. It is thus hard to imagine a species in which the ability to identify the stimuli that immediately preceded an important event would not be advantageous. Similarly, it is hard to imagine a species for which it would not be advantageous to repeat responses that have consistently led to positive outcomes such as food, and to suppress responses that have consistently led to negative outcomes such as injury. It thus would not be surprising if once species evolved learning mechanisms for classical and instrumental conditioning, these mechanisms were retained by their descendants largely unaltered.

On the other hand, as we have seen repeatedly, there are differences as well as similarities in the environmental problems faced by different species. The adaptationist approach thus assumes that while the broad outline of any learning system will be largely constant, within this framework there may be significant modifications to the details so as to make the system more sensitive to the particular information needed for each species' survival. If so, the issue is not whether we should expect similarities or differences in learning in different species—there will inevitably be both—but rather to what extent the properties of the core system have been preserved as it has been modified to cope with special problems.

In one sense, the answer to this question does not matter much: The extent to which a common system has been preserved is simply a matter for empirical inquiry, and one that need no longer be a focus of great theoretical debate. Learning theorists, however, have long been attracted to the idea that learning could be explained in terms of a small number of basic principles, for much the same reason that physicists have searched for a small number of unifying principles such as gravity and electromagnetism. For all scientists, there is something elegant and attractive about being able to explain superficially unrelated phenomena in terms of a single, simple process. (Indeed, if scientists did not prefer a simple, orderly view of the universe to a complex and chaotic one, they probably would not have become scientists in the first place!) This preference for simpler explanations is expressed in the scientific principle of **parsimony**, which states that if alternative explanations can account for a phenomenon equally well, the simpler explanation—the one that makes the fewest assumptions—is preferred. In particular, if two phenomena can be explained equally well by assuming that they involve a single process or two separate processes, the single-process explanation is always to be preferred.

In the context of learning, the principle of parsimony has led psychologists to postulate as few basic mechanisms of learning as they can get away with. Of course, the fact that we might *like* different instances of learning to be manifestations of a common process does not guarantee that they will be, and in this chapter we have seen that learning is not identical in all situations. If the evidence forces us to assume different processes, however, the principle of parsimony still encourages us to hope that these processes differ as minimally as possible.

In the remainder of this chapter, therefore, we will consider how far we can push the claim that the basic mechanisms of learning are similar. We will look first at how well a uniform associative process can account for the cases in which classical conditioning and reinforcement fail, and then at whether this process can also explain imprinting and song learning. Note, though, that the claim to be considered is no longer whether all learning is identical: The evidence reviewed in this chapter has made it clear that the characteristics of learning differ in different situations, and thus that the processes underlying this learning almost certainly differ as well. The question to be considered now is not whether the underlying processes are identical, but how far we can push the view that they are similar.

Classical Conditioning and Reinforcement Reconsidered

In Chapter 9, we saw that the principles of classical conditioning and reinforcement were remarkably similar, and on this basis we suggested that a single event-correlation detection system might be responsible for learning in both cases. Similarly, in examining variations within each of the two paradigms in this chapter, we saw that where differences did exist—for example, in the classical conditioning of taste aversions and fear—the divergent forms still shared many similarities.

On the basis of this evidence, we have suggested that although the associative system has been modified in the course of evolution to cope with special problems, the modified forms are still similar in most respects. It is possible to argue, however, that the different forms of conditioning are even more similar than this review has suggested, and that most instances of classical conditioning and reinforcement really are the outcome of a single, invariant process.

The case for a single associative system is strongest in the realm of reinforcement. Earlier in this chapter we reviewed a number of cases in which reinforcement was ineffective, and we suggested that these failures were due largely to two factors: Reflexive responses are difficult to reinforce, and competition from classically conditioned responses may sometimes interfere with performance of the reinforced responses. Both of these explanations, we will argue, are compatible with the existence of a single reinforcement process.

Consider first the possibility that reflexive responses such as scratching and licking are harder to associate with subsequent events than voluntary responses. If so, this would indeed mean that the associative system involved is not entirely general, in the sense that some E_1–E_2 associations are harder to form than others. However, this would not contradict the interchangeability-of-events assumption, because this already assumes that only some responses—those Skinner called operants—can be modified by their consequences. The assumption, in other words, is not that *all* responses can be reinforced, but rather that if a response is an operant—that is, if it can be modified by at least one reinforcer—then it can be strengthened by any reinforcer. If reflexive responses cannot easily be reinforced, this would not contradict the interchangeability assumption, but simply expand the class of excluded responses: Whereas this class was once thought to cover only autonomic responses, it would have to be expanded to all reflexive responses, skeletal as well as autonomic.

The same logic applies even more forcefully to the second explanation we considered for failures of reinforcement—namely, competition from classically conditioned responses. In discussing the difficulties the Brelands' raccoon had in depositing a coin in a piggy bank, for example, we attributed the problem to classical conditioning of food properties to the coin, which caused the raccoon to hold and rub the coin rather than release it. If so, the problem was not that the raccoon could not learn the response-reinforcer relationship; quite the contrary, we have clear evidence that it did, because it did deposit the coin initially. The difficulty was not in *learning* the correct response but rather in *performing* it, because rubbing and releasing the coin were incompatible. The fact that the classically conditioned response ultimately became dominant does not change the fact that the reinforced response was also learned, and there is no reason to suppose that the reinforcement mechanism involved was any different from that in, say, a rat's learning to press a bar.

As far as reinforcement is concerned, then, most if not all of the instances in which reinforcement has failed are compatible with the existence of a single mechanism responsible for all learning. This claim for a universal mechanism runs into greater difficulty in the case of classical conditioning, where taste-aversion learning does seem to differ in a number of respects from other instances of conditioning. Even if these differences are more quantitative than qualitative, implying that the underlying mechanisms are basically similar, it is nevertheless clear that these mechanisms are not identical. Looking at classical conditioning and reinforcement as a whole, however, a surprisingly strong case can be made that both rely on the same associative mechanism, and that the properties of this process are very similar in most instances.

An Associative Analysis of Imprinting

What, then, of the more sweeping, even imperial, claim that *all* learning is associative? Could imprinting and song learning be due to the same associative processes as classical conditioning and reinforcement?

The perhaps surprising answer is yes. If we focus on imprinting as a test case, there is evidence that associative processes may play a central role in at least two aspects of imprinting—namely, how the duckling learns to recognize the model, and why it then follows this model wherever the model goes.

The role of perceptual learning.   How does a duckling manage to remember the first moving object it sees? The answer we will consider is that this may be an example of the much broader phenomenon of perceptual learning, in which simple exposure to stimuli increases our ability to discriminate them from other, potentially similar stimuli. (See Chapter 9.) For many years, psychologists had little idea of how perceptual learning occurs, but McLaren, Kaye, and Mackintosh (1989) have recently proposed a theory of perceptual learning that suggests it is based on several associative processes. We will focus here on only one of their suggestions: that perceptual learning is based on the formation of associations between the elements of a stimulus.

One key assumption of their model is that any stimulus—a wine, say, or a moving duck—consists of many stimulus elements, and that when we experience these elements in close temporal proximity we form associations between them. (See also Rescorla & Durlach, 1981.) With extended exposure to a song, for example, a bird will associate each of the song's notes with those that follow, so that eventually hearing only the first few notes will allow the bird to recall all those that follow. (You may notice the similarity of this account to the British Associationist account, in Chapter 2, of how we memorize passages such as the Lord's Prayer.)

One reason that exposure to a stimulus helps us to recognize it later, then, is that repeated exposure allows us to link its elements into a coherent unit, thereby producing a more accurate image or representation of the stimulus in our brains. As a result, exposure to even a small proportion of the elements—for example, hearing only a snatch of a song, or catching only a brief glimpse of a retreating duck—will summon up the entire representation, and this fuller representation will make it easier for us to discriminate the stimulus from otherwise similar stimuli. (For further analysis of how multiple associations may be formed among the elements of a compound, see the discussions of a neoassociative model of memory in Chapter 12 and of neural networks in Chapter 13.) When a duckling first glimpses its mother, then, the process of perceptual learning may be what allows it to form an accurate representation of its mother's features, and this perceptual learning may be based on fairly simple associative mechanisms. This still leaves us with the problem, though, of why the duckling chooses to follow its mother.

The role of classical conditioning.   One explanation for why ducklings and other precocial birds develop an attachment to the first moving object they see could be classical conditioning (for example, Hoffman, 1978). To understand this analysis, however, it may be helpful first to recall our discussion of autoshaping, in which pigeons learn to peck a key whose illumination is followed by food. (See Chapter 3.) To explain this pecking, we suggested that the pigeons associated the key light with food, and because the visual characteristics of the key also resembled the birds' natural food, they came to regard the key as food. The reason that the birds pecked the key, therefore, was that they were trying to eat it. (See also Jenkins & Moore, 1973.) More broadly, we considered the possibility that stimuli that are associated with a US come to activate innately programmed behavior systems which then direct behavior appropriate to that US (Timberlake & Lucas, 1989). As a further example, we noted that chicks exposed to water for the first time try to eat it rather than drink it, but that after a few experiences of ingesting the water they learn to recognize the visual cues as properties of water, and thereafter direct appropriate drinking movements toward them.

Exactly the same classical conditioning process could be at work in imprinting. When a duckling sees a moving object, one or more properties of this object (for example, the fact that it is moving) might trigger an innate perceptual analysis that identifies this object as the parent. The stimuli present at the time (for example, the other characteristics of the moving model, such as its shape and color) would then be associated with the parent, so that these stimuli would henceforth elicit the behaviors appropriate to a parent—in the case of a duckling, attempts to follow that parent wherever it goes. Thus, just as a chick learns to identify the stimuli that accompany drinking as water, the duckling learns to identify the stimuli that accompany a moving object as its parent, and both stimuli then trigger the appropriate innate responses.

This conditioning account of imprinting is by no means perfect. Whereas it is easy to extinguish most conditioned responses by presenting the CS by itself, we have seen that the attachment formed through imprinting is very difficult to alter, and it certainly does not seem to disappear simply through repeated exposure to the CS—the duckling will happily follow the model for many weeks. At present, therefore, it is difficult to accept classical conditioning as a complete account of imprinting, but it does look as if the two phenomena may involve similar processes.

Implications

In summary, it is clear that at least some of the assumptions of the general process view are wrong: The events that can be associated are not interchangeable, and learning in different species differs in significant respects. Nevertheless, the substantial similarities in most cases support the view that a common process or processes may be at work.

As to the nature of these processes, this is a question that we will be examining in considerable detail in subsequent chapters, but we can anticipate that analysis here by suggesting that a process such as classical conditioning may be based on a number of subprocesses. For example, the subject must attend to the CS when it is presented, it must then recall that CS when the US is presented, and, finally, it must form an association between their cortical representations. Classical conditioning, in other words, is not a unitary process, but may itself be based on a number of subprocesses, or building blocks. If so, the conclusion suggested by the material in this chapter is not that various forms of learning, such as classical conditioning and reinforcement, are identical, but rather that they all involve a number of component processes, such as memory and attention, and that the properties of these building blocks may be similar if not identical in most instances. (For a similar analysis, see Hollis, ten Cate, & Bateson, 1991.)

In this view, we can think of the different forms of learning as a set of houses designed by evolution. The houses differ not only in their main types (colonial versus ranch, or reinforcement versus classical conditioning), but also in the appearance of the houses within each class: Two ranch houses (taste-aversion learning and fear conditioning) may share the same basic design, but nevertheless differ in details such as color and size (speed of conditioning and maximum delay). The general process view claimed that all of these houses were identical; the adaptationist approach acknowledges that they differ, and attributes these differences to the need to adapt each house to the features of the local environment, such as the steepness of the hill on which the house is built. The particular version of this approach that we are now proposing is that, despite the differences in appearance of these houses, evolution may have used a relatively small set of building blocks in constructing them, and that the properties of these blocks (core processes such as memory, attention, and association) may have remained substantially unchanged.

Finally, before leaving this topic, it may be worth noting that many ethologists as well as psychologists have been moving toward some form of the adaptive learning hypothesis, which, while acknowledging significant differences in learning in different species, views these differences as variations on a common theme. (See, for example, Gould, 1986a; Bateson, 1991.) Not all psychologists or ethologists agree (for example, Johnston, 1981), but especially in light of the yawning gap that once existed between the psychological and ethological traditions, this convergence is encouraging. Psychologists have learned much from ethologists' studies of animals in their natural habitats, and ethologists have also shown increasing appreciation of the value of experiments under controlled conditions in illuminating behaviors first observed in the wild (for example, Krebs, 1991; Marler, 1991).

10.5 SUMMARY

Early research on learning by Pavlov, Thorndike, Skinner, and others suggested that the principles of learning were identical in different situations and different species. This, in turn, suggested that all of these forms of learning might be based on the same basic process—a view we have called the general process view. According to this hypothesis, whenever an association is formed between two events, E_1 and E_2, the same associative mechanism is involved (a general system). Furthermore, this system is assumed to be largely indifferent to the particular events being associated, so that any member of the E_1 category can be associated with any member of the E_2 category (interchangeability of events). Finally, associative learning in different species is assumed to be based on the same associative mechanisms (generality across species).

The first major challenge to this view came from ethologists—biologists who studied animal behavior largely through observations under natural conditions, rather than experiments in the laboratory. Their approach to animal behavior was strongly influenced by Darwin's theory of evolution, which suggested that all existing species have evolved from common ancestors. The main principle of evolution was natural selection, in which animals that were better suited to their environments were more likely to survive and reproduce, and thus pass on their genes to succeeding generations. Over time, natural selection would lead to a gradual change in the characteristics of each species, with a trend toward divergence as each species became more specialized to exploit the potential of its particular environment, or niche.

Insofar as species are closely related, and also face similar environments, an evolutionary perspective suggests that we should expect substantial similarities in learning. However, this perspective also alerts us to the possibility that environments that seem similar can differ in subtle but important ways, and thus that we should expect differences in learning as well as similarities. Observations of birds by ethologists such as Konrad Lorenz pointed to precisely such differences. He observed in some species of birds a phenomenon, which he called imprinting, in which the birds would develop a strong attachment to the first moving object they saw and follow this object wherever it went. Imprinting differs from other forms of associative learning in that it occurs largely during an early period of the bird's life, called the sensitive period, and once the attachment has developed it is difficult to reverse.

Another form of learning observed by ethologists was song learning, in which the young of some species of birds learn to imitate the songs of adults. Song learning is similar to imprinting in that it occurs during a sensitive period, is hard to reverse, and is strongly guided by genetic predispositions to certain stimuli (for example, birds are much more likely to imitate songs that resemble the natural songs of their species). In both imprinting and song learning, whether learning occurs in a species seems to reflect the adaptive value of the learning for that species: Learning is found in species where it would be useful, but not in species where it would not. The implication is that evolution has produced learning systems that are not entirely general, capable of associating any events that occur contiguously, but rather more focused systems that are geared to detecting the particular information that would help the species to survive. It is interesting to reflect on whether the human ability to learn might be constrained in similar ways.

The evidence on imprinting and song learning made it clear that learning is not entirely uniform; subsequent research on classical conditioning and reinforcement showed that here, too, learning is not as uniform as it once appeared. John Garcia showed that rats can associate tastes with illness and visual cues with shock, but they have great difficulty in associating either CS with the other US. The assumption of interchangeability was clearly wrong. Moreover, taste-aversion learning differed from conditioning involving other responses, such as fear, in aspects such as speed of conditioning and maximum delay interval at which conditioning could be obtained—differences that suggested that the associative mechanisms underlying these different forms must differ.

Research on reinforcement suggested a similar conclusion: A reinforcer that was effective for one response might be entirely ineffective for another response. The Brelands, for example, found that they could train a raccoon to deposit a coin in a piggy bank, but that it developed a disconcerting tendency to hold onto the coin and rub it instead of depositing it. Other cases in which reinforcement appeared ineffective included cats that could not learn to lick themselves, and monkeys that lost their ability to open puzzles when reinforced for doing so. It currently appears as if two main factors are responsible for these failures: involuntary or reflexive responses may be hard to reinforce, and classically conditioned responses may interfere with performance of the response that has been reinforced.

This evidence makes it clear that learning does differ in different situations (for example, not all CSs can be associated with all USs) and in different species (imprinting occurs in some species but not others). However, learning in these situations is also similar in many respects. Thus, although taste-aversion learning and fear conditioning differ in their quantitative properties, such as the maximum CS–US interval that will sustain conditioning, they nevertheless obey the same general principles. One way to integrate the evidence for similarities as well as differences is to assume that the basic mechanisms of learning are quite general across species, but that the details are modified in the course of evolution to allow species to adapt to the unique problems that each faces. This adaptationist approach suggests that there will be differences in learning in different situations and species, but that these differences can be understood as variations on a common theme.

We could, logically, have concluded our discussion at this point, but the scientific principle of parsimony drives psychologists to explain learning in terms of as few basic processes as they can get away with. We went on, therefore, to consider the possibility of an even stronger case for similarities in learning. We noted that the evidence that reinforcement is ineffective for some responses is entirely compatible with the claim that a single associative mechanism underlies all forms of conditioning. Furthermore, imprinting and song learning may also be products of associative processes. In the case of imprinting, a duckling's ability to recognize the stimulus to which it has been imprinted may be an instance of the much broader phenomenon of perceptual learning; perceptual learning, in turn, may be based on the formation of associations between the elements of a stimulus, allowing a fuller and more accurate representation. The explanation for why the duckling then follows this stimulus could be classical conditioning: Some elements of the stimulus, such as the fact that it is moving, may trigger an identification of the stimulus as the duckling's parent, and the other characteristics of the stimulus are then associated with the parental US. These characteristics then elicit the behavior appropriate to the parent—namely, following it. In sum, imprinting, song learning, classical conditioning, and reinforcement may all rely on a common core of associative processes.

This evidence suggests that a synthesis of the views of learning psychologists such as Pavlov and Thorndike and ethologists such as Lorenz may be emerging. The ethologists have clearly been supported in their belief that learning differs in different species, but there are also substantial similarities, and recent evidence suggests that very similar associative mechanisms may be involved. If different forms of learning, such as reinforcement and imprinting, are metaphorically pictured as houses, evolution may have constructed an impressive variety of houses by combining the same basic building blocks (associative mechanisms) in different ways.

Selected Definitions

General process view In its strongest form, this view says that a single, universal mechanism is responsible for learning in all situations and all species. The mechanism is normally assumed to be an associative one: An association is formed between any two events that occur together, regardless of the nature of the events.

Natural selection A description of the environmental contingencies that ensure that individuals who are fitter are more likely to survive and reproduce.

Adaptive value A trait is said to have adaptive value if it helps individuals adapt to their environment, making them more likely to survive and reproduce.

Imprinting The development by an animal of a strong social attachment, normally to its mother, during the early period of its life. A broader definition is that imprinting is the process by which some species learn to recognize other members of their species during this early period.

Critical period A short, sharply defined period during the first few days of a bird's life during which Lorenz believed that imprinting could occur. Later evidence has suggested that the period during which imprinting can occur is both longer and less clearly defined than Lorenz supposed; as a result, the period during which imprinting is most likely to occur is now called the **sensitive period**.

Adaptationist approach The idea that learning has evolved to help animals adapt to the unique requirements of their niches. In current usage, adaptationist positions seem to assume that the principles of learning are generally similar in different situations and species, but that variations on these common principles occur because of the different niches species occupy.

Parsimony The scientific principle that when different explanations of a phenomenon are equally consistent with the available evidence, we should prefer the simplest of the available explanations. The simplest explanation is the one that makes the fewest assumptions, or postulates the fewest processes, in order to explain a set of observations.

Review Questions

1. What is the general process view? What evidence supports it?

2. How does the theory of evolution account for the development of species?

3. According to an evolutionary perspective, under what circumstances should we expect learning in two species to be similar? Under what circumstances should it be different?

4. In what respects are imprinting and song learning similar?

5. In what respects did Lorenz believe imprinting to be unique? Was he right?

6. How would an evolutionary analysis explain why some forms of learning are found in some species but not in others?

7. Why does the evidence on taste-aversion learning pose a challenge to the general process view?

8. What evidence challenges the view that a reinforcer can strengthen any response that precedes it? How can this evidence be explained?

9. How does the evidence cited in this chapter provide further support for the view that motivational processes can sometimes lead to behavior that appears irrational? Can you imagine other contexts in which the same motivational processes might be highly adaptive?

10. What is the adaptationist view? How can the evidence that the effects of reinforcement and classical conditioning vary across situations be reconciled with the claim that there is basically a single learning system?

11. How could a single, universal associative system account for the existence of imprinting?

12. In what respects have psychologists and ethologists converged on a common view of how learning varies across situations and species?

CHAPTER ELEVEN

WHAT IS LEARNED?

Associative Versus Cognitive Theories of Learning

A hungry cat is placed in a box with a dish of food located just outside the box. At first, the cat struggles frantically, biting and clawing at the walls of the box in a frenzied effort to reach the food. Eventually, in the course of its struggles, it strikes against a latch and the door to the box opens, allowing it to escape and eat the food. Over subsequent trials, the time period between placing the cat in the box and the cat's striking the latch gradually decreases, until eventually the cat begins to run directly to the latch and paw it immediately on being placed in the cage. Why? What has the cat learned to produce such a radical transformation in its behavior?

At first, the answer to this question might appear so simple that it is hardly worth discussing. In fact, however, the related issues of what the cat learns, and how it learns it, have proved to be among the most complex and difficult in all of psychology, and it will require the whole of the rest of this book to set forth even the tentative outlines of a possible solution. In this chapter, we will focus on the first of these questions: What is learned when a response is reinforced? In reviewing the history of research on this question, we will try to understand why such a simple question has proved so extraordinarily difficult to answer. Then, after reviewing current views of what is learned, we will turn in Chapters 12 and 13 to consider how it is learned.

11.1 S–R THEORY

One obvious answer to the question of what the cat learned is an expectation: "If I press the latch, the door will open." According to this interpretation, learning in animals is essentially a rational process, so when the cat is first put into the box it immediately tries to figure out how to reach the food. Once it finds the appropriate response—in this case, pushing the latch—the next time it is placed in the box it recalls its earlier success and, being hungry, deliberately repeats the response in order to obtain the food. Now this explanation is not quite as simple as it may sound; some fairly complex memory and reasoning processes are implicitly assumed. (For example, having opened the door once, the cat must figure out what movements will produce the same outcome the next time; if this seems easy, try to imagine building a robot capable of turning a door handle no matter which direction the robot approached the door from.) Nevertheless, this explanation does provide a plausible account of the cat's behavior.

The Development of S–R Theory

Thorndike's associative analysis.   Thorndike, who first carried out the experiment we have been describing, considered an explanation along the lines described above, but closer analysis of his subjects' behavior led him to reject it. First of all, when a cat was initially placed in the puzzle box, there was no obvious indication of rational deliberation, of the cat's coolly looking the situation over in an effort to plan its escape. Instead, there was immediate frenzied activity. Thorndike observed: "It tries to squeeze through any opening; it claws and bites at the bars or wire; it thrusts its paw through any opening and claws at everything it reaches" (Thorndike, 1911, p. 35). Eventually, after 8 or 10 minutes of such scrambling about, the cat might accidentally contact the release mechanism and escape.

If the cat formed a rational appreciation of the situation, we might expect it to repeat this response immediately on subsequent trials:

> If there were in these animals any power of inference, however rudimentary, however sporadic, however dim, there should have appeared among the multitude some cases when an animal, seeing through the situation, knows the proper act, does it, and from then on does it immediately upon being confronted with the situation. There ought, that is, to be a sudden vertical descent in the time-curve.
>
> (Thorndike, 1911, p. 73)

In all the scores of animals Thorndike tested, however, not once did he observe sudden and enduring improvement of this kind. In most instances, improvement over trials was a slow, gradual affair. (See Figure 2.9, p. 60, for some representative records.) Latencies did sometimes drop sharply after an early success, but after a series of such successes there would often be an equally sharp increase in latency. Indeed, two cats, after performing the escape response successfully a number of times—six times in one case, eight in the other—abruptly ceased to perform it at all, and even when left in the box as long as 20 minutes, never again managed to get out.

To Thorndike, this gradual improvement in performance, with its occasional reversals and failures, did not at all resemble the behavior of a rational animal fully aware of the relationship between the latch and the door:

> *The gradual slope of the time-curve . . . shows the absence of reasoning. They represent the wearing smooth of a path in the brain, not the decisions of a rational consciousness.*
>
> (Thorndike, 1911, p. 74)

As we saw in Chapter 2, Thorndike proposed that when the cat managed to escape and eat the food, the resultant pleasure stamped in an association between the impulse to make the response and the sense impressions that accompanied it. The more the response was rewarded, the stronger this association would become until, eventually, as soon as the cat was placed in the box, the sensations aroused would automatically elicit an impulse to perform the response. Rather than appealing to complex reasoning processes to explain the cat's behavior, in other words, Thorndike argued that it could be explained solely in terms of the stamping in of simple associations.

This associative analysis of learning was a significant departure from earlier accounts in terms of reasoning. Success, argued Thorndike, would automatically strengthen whatever behavior preceded it, and over a series of trials, an animal's behavior would become increasingly adaptive and efficient. Thus, problem solving need not imply rational behavior; in at least some instances, it could be explained entirely in terms of simple associations. Thorndike did not claim that all learning was due to such associations, but he did suggest that they played a far more pervasive role in learning—in humans as well as animals—than had previously been recognized.

Watson's behaviorism.   Although Thorndike's analysis differed markedly from earlier cognitive accounts, in one respect it was still not sufficiently radical for early behaviorists such as John B. Watson (1913). The difficulty, from Watson's point of view, was that Thorndike still assumed that associations were formed between sensations and impulses—mental events inside the animal's head. The stamping in of an association, moreover, was attributed to the feelings of pleasure that followed it. But how could anyone know what sensations or feelings were going on inside an animal's head? A cat may view the world with the greatest discernment and sardonic amusement, or its mind may be a complete blank, devoid of all but the most primitive sensations; how can anyone possibly know which of these views is correct? And what value is there in explaining an animal's behavior in terms of its mental states if there is no way of evaluating the truth of such explanations?

The essence of the scientific method—the quality that distinguishes it from other intellectual pursuits such as literary criticism or philosophy—is that scientific debates are settled not by opinion, no matter how widely held or plausible, but by objective evidence. It is the ability to agree on basic facts that allows science to progress from one question to another without becoming bogged down in endless haggling. The only way to avoid such sterile controversies in psychology, according to Watson, was to totally exclude all references to the mind. All that we can see of an animal is its behavior, so it is this behavior on which we must focus. Watson realized that explanations phrased solely in terms of behavior might seem pale and colorless when compared to the vivid world of the mind, with its loves and lusts, terrors and anxieties, but he argued that such explanations of behavior would have the important advantage of being testable, thus allowing inadequate explanations to be discarded, and progress to be made.

Injunctions to avoid all references to the mind were painful enough to bear in the case of animal behavior; but Watson went further and argued that exactly the same prohibition should apply to explanations of human behavior. The problem is fundamentally the same: We can observe other people's behavior—smiling when given good news, frowning when given bad news—but we cannot directly feel their emotions, however strongly we may empathize, nor can we ever directly observe their thoughts. It might seem that this difficulty could be circumvented simply by asking subjects to describe their thoughts and feelings, but Watson argued that the history of introspective research had clearly demonstrated the futility of this strategy. We have already discussed in Chapter 1 some of the problems to which Watson was referring—the inaccessibility of the unconscious, and the inability of introspectionists to agree even when the processes under study were ostensibly conscious—but this point is so important (and counterintuitive) that it may be worth considering one further illustration of the difficulties.

One of the most influential of the early behaviorists was Clark Hull of Yale. In a classic study of concept learning (Hull, 1920), he showed subjects a set of 12 characters from the Chinese alphabet and asked them to memorize the name of each (the names used were actually nonsense syllables such as *li*, *ta*, *na*, and so on). After the subjects had successfully learned the names of the first set of characters, they were asked to learn the names of a second set, then a third, and so on. Each set was made up of completely new characters, but the 12 names used were always the same. As far as the subjects knew, the assignment of names to particular characters was random, but in fact all characters sharing the same name also shared a unique common feature; all characters named *na*, for example, had embedded in them a shape resembling a *p*. (See Figure 11.1.) As each new list was presented, Hull found that subjects became faster and faster at learning the names of the new characters, until after a few lists some subjects could give the correct name for a new character the very first time they saw it. When asked how they knew, however, many reported having no idea;

Name	Common Element	Set 1	Set 2	Set 3	Set 4	Set 5	Set 6

FIGURE 11.1 Some of the materials used by Hull to study concept learning. Characters in different lists that were assigned the same name also shared a common element or concept embedded within them; the common element is shown at the left. (Adapted from Hull, 1920)

not only were they unable to describe the common feature, but they didn't even know there was one. These subjects managed to solve the problem, in other words, without any conscious awareness of having done so.

S–R theory.   The strong implication of this and other experiments was that many of the processes involved in learning were unconscious, so that, at best, introspection could provide only an incomplete and fragmented account of the process. Given such difficulties in observing mental processes, behaviorists argued that learning should be described solely in terms of changes in visible behavior, which could be observed objectively. Thus, although Hull and Watson welcomed Thorndike's emphasis on the importance of simple associations, they rejected the assumption that these were formed between mental events. When Thorndike spoke of a sense impression or sensation, therefore, they substituted the visible object in the environment that gave rise to it—the stimulus. And when he spoke of mental impulses to respond, they substituted the muscular movements that resulted—the response. Learning, therefore, consisted of the formation of associations between stimuli and responses—or, as they eventually came to be known, S–R associations.

S–R theory, then, was the natural, perhaps inevitable, outgrowth of two fundamental beliefs: (1) Associationism—a belief that learning is due to fundamentally simple associations; and (2) **behaviorism**—a belief that, because the mind cannot be observed directly, psychological explanations must be couched in terms of visible, overt behavior.

A Cognitive Rejoinder

Cognitive psychologists vigorously rejected both of these assumptions. Learn-ing, they said, was far too complex and subtle to be explained by simple associations. As for the suggestion that psychologists should ignore what a person thinks or feels, a vivid rejoinder came from William McDougall, an eminent social psychologist and contemporary of Watson's. In the course of an entertaining and sometimes caustic debate with Watson, staged in 1929, he asked his listeners to imagine the following scene:

> I come into the hall and see a man on the platform scraping the guts of a cat with hairs from the tail of a horse; and, sitting silently in attitudes of rapt attention, are a thousand persons who presently break out into wild applause. How will the Behaviorist explain these strange incidents: How explain the fact that vibra-tions emitted by the cat-gut stimulate all the thousand into absolute silence and quiescence; and the further fact that the cessation of the stimulus seems to be a stimulus to the most frantic activity? Common sense and psychology agree in accepting the explanation that the audience heard the music with keen pleasure and vented their gratitude and admiration for the artist in shouts and hand clappings. But the Behaviorist knows nothing of pleasure and pain, of admira-tion and gratitude. He has relegated all such "metaphysical entities" to the dust heap, and must seek some other explanation. Let us leave him seeking it. The search will keep him harmlessly occupied for some centuries to come.

(Watson & McDougall, 1929, pp. 68–69)

The Issue

Clearly, agreement between the two camps was less than complete. It's impor-tant to note, however, that the argument was not so much over the mind's existence—with the possible exception of Watson himself, most behaviorists fully accepted its reality—as over whether mental states should play any role in the scientific explanation of behavior. According to the behaviorists, the im-possibility of observing mental states meant that any explanation that referred to such states would be untestable: Each theorist would insist on the validity of his or her own interpretation, and progress would be impossible.

It would be far better, argued Watson and other behaviorists, to explain behavior in terms of the hereditary and environmental variables that give rise to it. If someone becomes a murderer, for example, we should focus on the experiences that led to this behavior—for example, abandonment or harsh and vindictive punishment during childhood. Only by identifying these environ-mental causes can we prevent the recurrence of such behavior in the future. Psychologists such as McDougall, on the other hand, argued that people's thoughts and feelings play a crucial role in determining their behavior, and that to ignore mental states simply because they are sometimes difficult to observe would be folly, not unlike an ostrich hiding its head in the sand to avoid having to face an awkward reality.

Applying their analyses to learning, behaviorists argued that learning should be explained in terms of S–R associations, whereas cognitive psychologists argued that learning was due to the formation of new expectations. Each view, as we have seen, could muster plausible arguments in its favor; in the following sections, we will consider how well their arguments have stood up to experimental tests.

11.2 A Test: Learning Without Responding

Theorists on both sides agreed that the issue should be settled not by polemics but by evidence. What was needed was a learning situation in which the two views of learning would lead to different predictions about behavior; by observing which behavior occurred, it should then be possible to settle once and for all which view was correct. In practice, the search for "crucial" experiments was to prove far more difficult, and far more protracted, than any of the protagonists originally envisaged, and it is not possible for us to trace all the twists and turns in the ensuing debate. (A comprehensive review is available in Goldstein, Krantz, & Rains, 1965.) To illustrate the nature of the argument, however, we will focus on one of the issues that proved most decisive—that of learning without responding.

The potential importance of this issue was first identified by Thorndike. In an article published in 1946, entitled simply "Expectation," he compared the S–R and cognitive views of learning and suggested a simple way of distinguishing them. According to the S–R view, a reward stamps in whatever muscular response precedes it (or, more accurately, an association between that response and the stimuli present at the time). According to cognitive theorists, on the other hand, learning is fundamentally a perceptual process in which subjects perceive the relationships between events. In the case of a cat in a puzzle box, this view suggests that the cat will learn a general expectation that depressing the latch will open the door, rather than a specific set of muscular movements.

These two views have very different implications for what should be learned in a situation in which no response is made. If what is learned is a muscular response, then if no response is made, no learning should occur. According to cognitive theorists, however, it is not the response itself that is crucial, but the opportunity to perceive appropriate relationships among events. Provided the experimental situation allows these relationships to be perceived, learning should still be possible.

Rats in a Cart

Stated in this abstract form, the differences between the two positions may not be clear, but we can illustrate them more concretely using an experiment by McNamara, Long, and Wike (1956). Two groups of rats were placed in a simple T-maze in which food was available in the goal box on the right. One group of rats was allowed to run through the maze by themselves, but in the second group, the rats were carried through in a wire basket pushed by the experimenter. The sequence of trips to the left and right goal boxes matched exactly the sequence for the first group: When a subject in the first group freely turned to the right and received food, its yoked partner was carried to the same goal box and fed; when the first subject went to the left and found nothing, so did the other. The subjects in the two groups thus received exactly the same sequence of turns and reinforcements; the only difference was that in one group the rats ran through the maze by themselves, and in the other they were carried.

Following training, both groups were given nonreinforced test trials in which they were placed in the start box and allowed to run freely through the maze. (The experimenters withheld food to ensure that no further learning occurred during testing.) According to an S–R analysis, because subjects in the basket group never performed the correct response during training, this response would not have been associated with the cues of the maze. According to a cognitive analysis, however, these subjects would have had just as much opportunity to observe the appropriate relationship (that food is in the goal box on the right, not on the left) as those in the control group, and so should have learned equally.

This was exactly the result obtained: The preference for the correct side was virtually identical in the two groups (64 percent versus 66 percent). The fact that the turning response was not made clearly did not prevent its being learned. Learning, therefore, must involve something more than just the stamping in of particular movements.

Latent Extinction

Further evidence for learning without responding comes from the phenomenon of *latent extinction*, in which the response of running through a maze is extinguished simply by placing the animal in the goal box without food. In the first experiment to demonstrate this phenomenon, Seward and Levy (1949) trained rats to run down a straight alley to obtain food. Then, during the latent extinction phase, subjects in the experimental group were placed directly into the goal box, now empty, while those in the control group were left undisturbed in their home cages. Finally, both groups were given normal extinction trials in which they were again allowed to run down the alley but did not receive food.

According to a cognitive analysis, placement in the empty goal box during latent extinction should have reduced the rats' expectation of finding food there. When the rats were returned to the start box for the normal extinction trials, therefore, they would be less likely to run. S–R theorists, however, argued that an S–R association can be weakened only if the response actually occurs and is then not reinforced. Since the rats did not run down the alley during the latent extinction phase, the association between the alley cues and the running response should still be intact, because in the rats' experience running down the alley had always been followed by food. If running is simply elicited by the cues of the start box, rats in the latent extinction group should continue to run, whereas if running is controlled by an expectation of receiving food in the goal box, running should now be less likely.

Again, the experiment supported the cognitive prediction: Subjects given latent extinction trials ran significantly more slowly during extinction, a difference that was apparent even on the first trial. As in the McNamara, Long, and Wike experiment, substantial learning had occurred on trials in which no visible response had been made.

Further evidence for learning without responding has come from a number of sources. One that we have already encountered in our discussion of classical conditioning is the phenomenon of sensory preconditioning, in which the pairing of two neutral stimuli such as a tone and a light produces an association between them (Chapter 2). The key point in the present context is that neither stimulus elicits any overt response, so that, according to an S–R analysis, no learning should occur.

Similarly, studies of observational learning have shown that subjects can learn a response simply by observing other subjects perform it. Miyadi (1964) reports a study in which scientists left wheat grains on the beach for a group of Japanese macaque monkeys to eat. Separating the wheat from the sand was a laborious task for the monkeys; then one monkey, a young female named Imo, hit upon the brilliant technique of throwing the grain into a nearby stream: The heavier sand sank, leaving the wheat grains floating on the surface where they could be skimmed easily. One by one, the other members of the group picked up this technique by watching Imo perform it. (Interestingly, it was only the younger monkeys that adopted this and other new techniques; the older monkeys always proved too conservative.)

Together, these phenomena leave no doubt that animals can acquire new habits simply by observing the world around them. If learning is to be characterized in terms of the formation of associations, therefore, it is clear that these associations must sometimes involve covert events inside the organism that cannot be directly observed.

11.3 Neobehaviorism

Behaviorism arose out of a growing revulsion against the seemingly endless bickering of the introspectionists, with each observer studying his or her own private world and no two observers able to agree. The solution, as Watson saw it, was to eliminate all references to mental states from psychology, allowing as scientific data only those overt behaviors that could be observed objectively. The evidence for learning without responding, however, showed that learning could not be described solely in terms of visible behavior. This created a painful dilemma for behaviorists: Could S–R theory be salvaged? Or did its failure in this instance require a repudiation of behaviorism and concomitant return to introspection, with all its faults?

In fact, there was little thought of repudiation, and the history of science would provide few precedents for an abrupt reversal of this kind. Any theory is built on a complex network of assumptions, and although an incorrect prediction may mean that one of these assumptions is wrong, it hardly invalidates the entire set. Put less charitably, none of us likes to admit to being totally wrong—a small oversight, perhaps, but surely not a total failure! The practical problem confronting S–R theorists, then, was not so much whether to abandon their theory as how to modify it to account for learning without responding while doing the least damage to the theory's basic structure.

Hull's Contribution

Intervening variables.   The answer was provided by Clark Hull, and it was breathtaking in its simplicity: If we must assume covert behaviors, he said, let these behaviors have exactly the same properties as overt ones. Covert activities should be viewed as muscular responses, obeying exactly the same behavioral laws (laws of reinforcement, extinction, generalization, and so forth) as their overt counterparts. Rather than abandoning an S–R analysis, in other words, Hull proposed that it be extended to cover covert responses as well as overt ones.

But how could a behaviorist assume invisible responses? The very essence of behaviorism lay in its insistence on studying only those behaviors that can be observed objectively, and by no stretch of the imagination could invisible muscle twitches be said to meet this criterion. Hull's response, in essence, was that a blanket refusal to countenance unobservable events was based on a misreading of the practice in other sciences. Although it was true that all sciences insisted that disputes could be settled only by objectively observable evidence, this did not mean that hypothetical or invisible states could not be allowed at a theoretical level. Newton's theory of gravity, for example, assumed a force that was totally invisible, but it specified the precise effects this force should have on objects such as falling apples and orbiting planets, and it was these predictions that made the theory testable. As long as a hypothetical state meets this criterion of leading to testable predictions, there is no scientific reason for not allowing it. Applying this analysis to psychology, Hull argued that there could be no objection to assuming that some unobservable event (X) intervened between a stimulus and response,

$$S \longrightarrow X \longrightarrow R$$

provided that the relationships between S and X and between X and R were specified clearly enough to allow the unambiguous derivation of predictions. Hull called this hypothetical event X an **intervening variable**.

Hull viewed internal events as covert responses that would have exactly the same properties, and that would obey the same laws, as their overt counterparts. Thus, by applying the laws of learning already known from overt behavior, it would be possible to predict not only when a covert response would occur, but what its consequences would be for behavior.

Hull's approach, which eventually came to be known as **neobehaviorism**, thus modified behaviorism's rejection of internal states but retained its emphasis on simple associations as the building blocks of learning.* If learning is still fundamentally associative, however, how could Hull account for phenomena such as latent extinction? Here, you will recall, placing rats in an empty goal box led to a significant reduction in speed of running on subsequent trials. The effect is easily understandable in terms of expectations: Placement in the empty goal had reduced the rat's expectation of finding food there. But the effect is not easily understandable in terms of S–R associations. If latent extinction cannot be explained by associations involving an overt response, how could the postulation of a covert response with exactly the same properties help?

The r_g–s_g mechanism. The answer is not immediately obvious, but in a series of ingenious papers, Hull (1943, 1952) showed how this approach could be applied to a variety of phenomena that, on the surface, provided irrefutable evidence against S–R theory. The heart of Hull's approach was a covert response that he symbolized as r_g. To understand his explanation, we first need to understand this term. Consider a simple learning problem in which a rat is trained to run down a straight alley to a goal box containing food. Once it reaches the goal box, the food elicits eating, a goal response symbolized by Hull as R_G. Hull assumed that any response elicited by an unconditioned stimulus would become classically conditioned to the cues that preceded it. In this

---

* Neobehaviorism shares with older forms of behaviorism the belief that the primary data of psychology must come from objective observations of overt behavior. Neobehaviorism differs from these older forms in allowing the postulation of unobservable events at a theoretical level, provided that the theory leads to testable predictions about overt behavior.

situation, therefore, eating would become conditioned to the cues present on entering the goal box, so components of the eating response—chewing, salivating, and so on—would eventually occur as soon as the rat reached the goal, even before it actually received food (Figure 11.2). Since this chewing would precede food, and since, like any conditioned response, the conditioned chewing would be less vigorous than the full-blown response elicited by food itself, Hull called it a **fractional anticipatory goal response (r_g)**.

Hull assumed that some fractional component of eating would be conditioned to the situational cues in any situation in which food is presented. Furthermore, like any other muscular response, this conditioned eating behavior was assumed to produce proprioceptive feedback. (When you move your arm, for example, receptors located in the muscles of your arm allow you to feel the contractions involved; similar proprioceptive feedback is thought to be produced by all muscular activity.) Hull assumed that the rat's chewing response would produce a proprioceptive stimulus, which he symbolized by s_g. One important point to note about this r_g–s_g unit is that it is hypothetical: Although it may well be possible to measure it in many situations (see Deaux & Patten, 1964), the theory's validity does not depend on such direct observations. Just as Newton assumed that a gravitational force would be present between any two bodies, so Hull assumed that r_g would be conditioned whenever reinforcement was presented. In both cases, the critical test of the theory is not whether the hypothetical entity can be observed directly, but whether the assumption of its existence leads to accurate prediction of other events.

Explaining Latent Extinction

How, then, does the assumption that the rat is invisibly chewing allow us to explain latent extinction? A paper by Moltz (1957) showed how Hull's general strategy could be applied to this phenomenon, and we will trace how Moltz's analysis could be applied to the Seward and Levy experiment discussed earlier.

In the first stage of this experiment, you will recall, rats were trained to run down a straight alley to a goal box containing food. According to Hull's modified version of S–R theory, the presentation of food in the goal box should

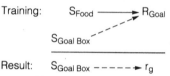

FIGURE 11.2   Classical conditioning as seen by Hull (1943). Food or other unconditioned stimuli presented in the goal box would elicit an unconditioned goal response, R_G, which would be conditioned to the cues of the goal box, S_{GB}. Hull called the conditioned form of the response a fractional anticipatory goal response, symbolized r_g.

have two effects. First, according to the principle of reinforcement, it should stamp in an association between the response of running and the stimuli present at the time (the color of the start box walls, the texture of its floor, and so on). Second, according to the principle of classical conditioning, food should elicit eating, a fractional component of which would be conditioned to the cues of the goal box (Figure 11.3). Once conditioned to the goal box, moreover, this response should generalize to similar stimuli, including the start box, because the start and goal boxes were virtually identical in appearance (the same shape, size, color, and so on).

When the rat was placed in the start box for the start of the next trial,

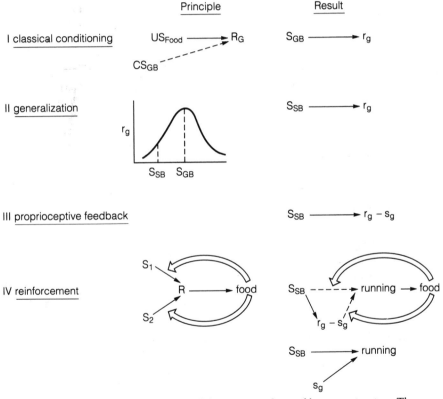

F I G U R E 11.3   An r_g–s_g analysis of the training phase of latent extinction. The presentation of food in the goal box would result in the classical conditioning of r_g to the goal box cues. This response would generalize to the start box, S_{SB}, and would produce a proprioceptive stimulus, s_g, whenever it occurred. The next time the rat ran down the alley to the goal box, reinforcement would stamp in a connection between the running response and the stimuli present at the time, including the start box and s_g. The general principle of learning applied to each stage of the analysis is shown at the left; its specific consequence in a latent extinction experiment is shown at the right.

therefore, the start box cues would elicit r_g, with this response in turn producing the proprioceptive stimulus s_g. When the rat ran down the alley, s_g would thus be one of the stimuli present as it ran. Because reinforcement was assumed to stamp in an association between the response that preceded it and whatever stimuli were present at the time, the presentation of food in the goal box would stamp in an association between running and s_g, as well as between running and external cues such as the color of the start box. On succeeding trials, the association between s_g and running would continue to be strengthened, so that by the end of training, whenever s_g occurred it would elicit a tendency to run.

Consider, now, what would happen on latent extinction trials if the rat were placed in the goal box without food. According to the Pavlovian principle of extinction, presentation of a conditioned stimulus by itself will extinguish any response previously conditioned to it. When food is not presented in the goal box, therefore, the eating response previously conditioned to that goal box (r_g) should extinguish (Figure 11.4). If r_g is not elicited by the goal box,

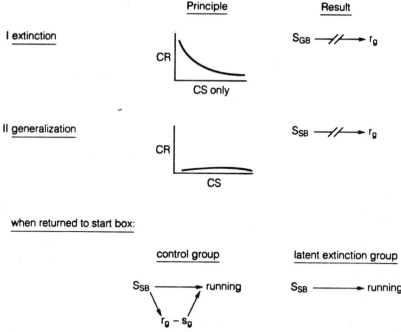

FIGURE 11.4   An r_g–s_g analysis of the latent extinction phase. Direct placements in the goal box without food would lead to the extinction of the previously conditioned response, r_g. If the goal box, S_{GB}, no longer elicited r_g, this response could no longer generalize to other stimuli. When the rats were returned to the start box for testing, therefore, r_g would not occur and therefore would not produce s_g. Thus, whereas subjects in the control group would still have two cues eliciting running, those in the latent extinction group would have only one.

moreover, it will no longer generalize to similar stimuli. When the rat is returned to the start box during the subsequent extinction phase, therefore, the cues of the start box will no longer elicit r_g, and since this response doesn't occur it will not produce the proprioceptive stimulus s_g. One of the stimuli that previously elicited running will thus no longer be present, so that, according to S–R theory, this response should be less likely to occur. And this, of course, was exactly what happened.

The phenomenon of latent extinction, then, can be explained purely in terms of S–R associations, without assuming that the rat has any expectation of what lies ahead in the goal box. On first reading, Moltz's explanation may seem inordinately complex, but each step, considered individually, is actually quite simple, involving only such familiar principles of learning as reinforcement, conditioning, generalization, and so forth. Thus, by appropriate combination of simple building blocks, Moltz was able to account for behavior of apparently considerable complexity.

The fact that S–R theory can account for latent extinction, of course, doesn't necessarily mean that its explanation is the right one; a cognitive analysis, after all, can also explain this behavior. When two theories can both account for the existing evidence, we need to invoke a more demanding criterion to separate them: We need to determine which theory is better at correctly predicting new phenomena. In the case of S–R theory, researchers have tested a number of its predictions; we will examine a test of one of the most remarkable (and thoroughly counterintuitive) of these predictions.

A Prediction: The Case of the Masochistic Rats

In a study by Fowler and Miller (1963), rats were once again trained to run down a straight alley to a goal box containing food. In this study, however, as soon as the subjects in the experimental group reached the food, they were given a brief electric shock before being allowed to consume it. For some subjects, the shock was delivered to their hind paws; for others, it was delivered to their forepaws; control subjects received no shock at all. From a cognitive perspective, we would expect the rats in both of the shock conditions to run down the alley much more slowly than the controls: If you know you're going to receive a painful shock as soon as you reach your goal, you're hardly likely to be eager to get there.

Up to a point, an S–R analysis points to the same conclusion: Thorndike's Law of Effect says that punishment will weaken an S–R association, just as reinforcement will strengthen it. According to Hull's revision of S–R theory, however, in predicting the effects of shock we also need to take into account the unconditioned responses it elicits, and these responses would be very different for shocks delivered to the forepaws and the hind paws. Specifically, whereas shocks to the hind paws elicit a tendency to jump forward, thus

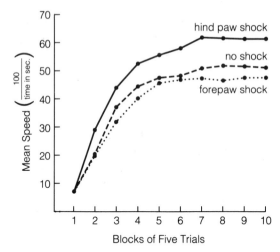

F I G U R E 11.5   Mean speeds of rats running down an alley to a goal box containing food. When the rats reached the goal box, they received either a shock to the forepaws, a shock to the hind paws, or no shock, depending on the group to which they belonged. (Adapted from Fowler & Miller, 1963)

moving away from the source of the shock, shocks to the forepaws elicit a tendency to recoil. Rats in the forepaw group would thus move backward when shocked in the goal, and this unconditioned response would become conditioned to the goal box cues, and, through generalization, should then occur throughout the alley. When returned to the apparatus for subsequent trials, therefore, the alley cues would elicit a tendency to move backward, which would interfere with the reinforced response of running. Rats in the hind paw group, on the other hand, would jump forward when shocked, so generalization of this response to the start box should result in an increase in the speed of running. Hull's version of S–R theory thus leads to the curious prediction that under some circumstances punishment should actually strengthen the punished response!

This prediction was supported: Rats in the hind paw group actually ran faster to reach the goal box than did subjects that had not been shocked at all (Figure 11.5). Furthermore, rats that received a 75-volt shock to their hind paws ran faster than those that received only a 60-volt shock, exactly as if they *liked* being shocked and couldn't wait to obtain it. From the standpoint of a cognitive analysis, this result is quite bizarre: If rats think ahead to what is going to happen in the goal box, surely those expecting a shock should run more slowly. But these results are exactly what an S–R analysis would lead us to expect. [*] Thus, although Hull's modification of S–R theory is in many ways

---

[*] As noted previously, shock in the goal box should have two effects in the hind paw group: punishing the preceding response of running, but also eliciting this behavior as an unconditioned re-

counterintuitive—it denies that a rat running down an alley knows why it is doing so, and instead insists on describing its behavior in terms of habits elicited automatically by the environment—in at least some situations animals appear to behave in just the simpleminded way that Hull's theory predicts.

11.4 A Cognitive Analysis

Hull's neobehaviorist approach represented a major liberalization of S–R theory, as for the first time the existence (and importance) of covert processes inside the organism was acknowledged. The notion that these internal processes involved nothing more than miniature muscle twitches, however, was still totally unacceptable to cognitive theorists such as Edward C. Tolman.

Tolman's Expectations

When Tolman observed a rat running down a maze, he did not see the blind repetition of a previously stamped-in habit, but the flexible and purposeful behavior of an animal trying to reach a goal. Comparing his views with those of Hull, he wrote:

> *We agree with the other school that the rat in running a maze is exposed to stimuli and is finally led as a result of these stimuli to the responses which actually occur. We feel, however, that the intervening brain processes are more complicated, more patterned and often, pragmatically speaking, more autonomous than do the stimulus-response psychologists.*
>
> (Tolman, 1948, p. 192)

Like Hull, however, Tolman distrusted introspection as a scientific tool. Tolman was thus the first of what would now be called **cognitive behaviorists**: While stressing the importance of cognitive processes, such as expectations and attention, in guiding behavior, he believed that these states could not be observed directly, but rather must be inferred from overt behavior. If we can't see what's going on in a rat's mind, though, how can we tell whether or not it has an expectation?

Docility.   One criterion suggested by Tolman for inferring the presence of an expectation was the flexibility, or **docility**, of behavior. Suppose, for example, that a rat is reinforced for running down an alley. If all it has learned is an S–R association, then we might expect it to repeat mechanically whatever move-

---

sponse. It is difficult to predict in advance which of these effects will be stronger. What is noteworthy is that an S–R analysis can predict that shock will increase running, whereas a cognitive analysis cannot.

ments it made on the first trial on all subsequent trials. If it has learned a general expectation that food is at the end of the alley, however, then we might expect it to respond flexibly by selecting whatever movements will get it there most efficiently.

One example of docility comes from an experiment by Macfarlane (1930). In the first phase, rats were trained to run through a partially flooded complex maze in order to reach a goal box containing food. Then, after the correct sequence of left and right turns had been well learned, the water level of the maze was increased so that running was no longer possible. If the rats had only learned a particular set of muscular movements during training, they should no longer have been able to find the correct path to the goal, because with the maze flooded these particular movements were no longer possible. In fact, Macfarlane found that his rats simply swam down the correct paths instead of running, without any errors. To Tolman, these results indicated that during training the rats had learned not a particular set of movements, but rather a general expectation that food was available in the goal box, and were flexibly choosing whatever movements would be most effective in getting them there.

Disruption.   A second criterion suggested by Tolman for identifying expectations was **disruption** of behavior when an expectation was not met. In Macfarlane's experiment, for example, there was an abrupt change in the rats' behavior when they were exposed to the new water levels for the first time. Instead of moving quickly through the maze, as on earlier trials, they "halted, sniffed, stood upright, tested the strength of the wire mesh about them and *then*—traveled down the correct alley. The entire run, for the most part, was made in this hesitant manner" (Macfarlane, 1930, p. 285). It looked, in other words, exactly as if they had previously formed an expectation about what water level to expect, and when this expectation was not met, began to actively search and explore the altered environment.

Even more striking evidence of disruption comes from an experiment by Tinklepaugh (1928) in which monkeys were trained to reach under one of two cups to retrieve a reward that they had earlier seen the experimenter place there. On some trials, the reward was a banana; on others, it was a piece of lettuce—a food that monkeys consider less desirable but will normally eat readily. On special test trials, after baiting the cup with a banana, Tinklepaugh would reach under the cup while the monkey wasn't looking and replace the banana with lettuce. Tinklepaugh reports the monkey's typical reaction when he told it to "come get the food":

> She jumps down from the chair, rushes to the proper container and picks it up. She extends her hand to seize the food. But her hand drops to the floor without touching it. She looks at the lettuce but (unless very hungry) does not touch it.

*She looks around the cup and behind the board. She stands up and looks under
and around her. She picks the cup up and examines it thoroughly inside and out.
She has on occasion turned toward observers present in the room and shrieked at
them in apparent anger. After several seconds spent searching, she gives a
glance towards the other cup, which she has been taught not to look into, and
then walks off to a nearby window. The lettuce is left untouched on the floor.*

(Tinklepaugh, 1928, p. 224)

Observations of this kind may not *prove* that the monkey expected a banana,
but it is very, very difficult to conceive of an alternative explanation.

Reinforcer Devaluation

One possible reaction to the Tinklepaugh experiment on the part of an S–R
theorist might be to concede that monkeys form expectations but to argue that
"lower" species such as rats learn only associations. Recent evidence, however,
suggests that even this fallback position may not be tenable. The most convincing evidence that rats, too, form expectations comes from experiments
using a reinforcer-devaluation procedure very similar to that used in studies of
classical conditioning (Chapter 5). The basic procedure is to train a rat to press
a bar to obtain food and then to make the food aversive by pairing it with an
aversive stimulus. If the rat had learned an S–R association during training,
subsequent devaluation of the reinforcer should have no effect: The stimuli of
the Skinner box, for example, should still automatically elicit bar-pressing. If
the rat had learned to expect food, however, then when this food became
unattractive, the rat should no longer respond to obtain it.

One of the first experiments to use this procedure was reported by Adams
and Dickinson (1981), but we will focus on a more sophisticated variant
developed by Colwill and Rescorla (1985). In the first phase, Colwill and
Rescorla trained rats to make two responses (pressing a lever and pulling a
chain) to obtain two different reinforcers (sucrose or food pellets). For example, one group learned to press a bar to obtain sucrose and to pull a chain to
obtain food pellets. One of these reinforcers was then paired with a mild dose of
a toxin, lithium chloride, until the rats would no longer consume it. There
were thus two main groups: one in which sucrose was devalued, and a second in
which food pellets were devalued. Finally, the rats were again allowed access to
the lever and chain, and responding was measured during an extinction test in
which neither reinforcer was presented.

Figure 11.6 shows the extinction data for responses that had previously
been reinforced with sucrose. Because no responses were reinforced during the
extinction test, there was a significant decrease in responding as testing progressed. More important, performance depended on which reinforcer had been
associated with illness. Rats for whom sucrose had been devalued responded

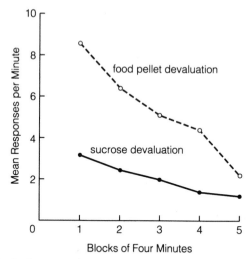

F I G U R E 11.6   Performance during extinction of a response that previously produced sucrose, following the conditioning of an aversion to either sucrose or food pellets.
(Adapted from Colwill & Rescorla, 1985)

significantly less to obtain sucrose than did rats for whom food pellets had been
devalued. The almost inescapable implication is that the rats knew which
reinforcer each response produced, so that when sucrose was devalued they
ceased to make the response that produced it.

11.5 SYNTHESIS

In reviewing the conflict between S–R and cognitive theories, we have seen
persuasive evidence for both views. S–R theorists, for example, could point to
the gradual learning that occurred with Thorndike's cats, and to the behavior
of the rats in Fowler and Miller's experiment, in which shock increased the
rats' running to get to the goal box, a behavior that hardly seemed to reflect a
keen awareness of consequences. On the other hand, the flexibility of behavior
in Macfarlane's rat-swimming experiment and the striking reactions of Tinklepaugh's monkeys provided equally strong support for a cognitive account. We
could continue to cite evidence supporting each side. (For persuasive evidence
supporting an S–R analysis, see Powell & Perkins, 1957; Morgan, 1974.
Equally impressive support for a cognitive interpretation is available in Hulse,
Fowler, & Honig, 1978; Premack & Woodruff, 1978.) But the fundamental
dilemma would remain the same: There is a considerable body of evidence on
both sides, making it very difficult to decide which is correct. Why should this
be so? Why, after decades of effort and literally hundreds of experiments

devoted to evaluating the two theories, is it still so difficult to say which one is right?

Why Was the Theoretical Debate So Difficult to Resolve?

Theoretical convergence.   One reason the debate was so difficult to resolve is that, over time, the assumptions of the two camps became increasingly similar, making it harder and harder to separate them experimentally. At first, the gulf between them was very wide: S–R theorists refused to allow any internal processes, and cognitive theorists concentrated on them to the exclusion of virtually everything else. As experimental evidence accumulated, however, there was a gradual convergence of the two positions, as theorists on both sides adjusted their views to accommodate the new evidence. The evidence for phenomena such as learning without responding led Hull to accept the importance of internal states, and the demonstrated inadequacies of introspection led Tolman to accept the behaviorist position that these internal states could not be observed directly. Both sides, therefore, agreed that statements about internal states must be regarded as theoretical hypotheses, and the validity of these hypotheses judged not by introspection but by the accuracy of the predictions to which they led.

The specific content of the proposed theories certainly sounded very different, but, in practice, Hull's r_g served many of the anticipatory functions of an expectation, occurring in the same sort of situations and playing a similar function in directing behavior. Regarding latent extinction, for example, Tolman said that a rat finding food in the goal box would develop an expectation, and Hull said it would develop an r_g; both agreed that on subsequent trials this expectation (r_g) would be aroused as soon as the rat was placed in the start box, and would remain present as it ran down the alley. Placements in the empty goal box during the latent extinction phase would then weaken this expectation (r_g). When the rat was returned to the start box for extinction trials, the expectation (r_g) would no longer be present, leading to slower running. Furthermore, both theorists agreed that the strength of the expectation (r_g) would depend on such variables as the frequency of reinforcement during training and the number of placements in the empty goal box during latent extinction. These similarities do not mean that the two accounts were identical in all respects; they were not. But they do help to explain why psychologists have had such difficulty devising experiments that would clearly separate them.

Theoretical ambiguity.   One problem in evaluating the claims of S–R and cognitive theory, then, is that the two theories are far more similar structurally than the differences in their terminology might suggest. A second, even more serious obstacle has been the vagueness with which each theory was formulated. As we have seen, a crucial requirement for testing any theory involving an intervening variable X is that this variable be clearly and unambiguously tied to antecedent stimuli (S) and consequent responses (R), so that the behavior to be expected in any situation can be clearly predicted:

$$ S \longrightarrow X \longrightarrow R $$

Unfortunately, neither Hull nor Tolman ever really succeeded in meeting this criterion.

In Tolman's case, although he certainly intended to provide clear definitions of what he meant by an expectation, in practice his definitions often turned out to be frustratingly vague. Consider again, for example, McNamara, Long, and Wike's experiment in which one group of rats was pushed through a maze in a basket while a second group was allowed to walk through normally. One possible prediction based on a cognitive analysis was that the subjects in the cart group would learn as well as the controls, because both groups would have the same number of reinforced and nonreinforced trials, and thus an equal opportunity to learn which goal box contained food. On the other hand, cognitive theorists could have predicted with equal plausibility that these rats would learn nothing about which side was correct, but only that if they sat quietly in the basket they would sometimes be rewarded with food! An expectation analysis simply doesn't tell us which outcome to expect: The crucial link between S and X is not specified, so we don't know which of the possible expectations would actually be learned in a given situation.

A similar ambiguity prevails at the link between a subject's expectation and its actual behavior. Tolman tells us that if an expectancy is not met, we should expect some kind of disruption—but *what* disruption? If a monkey finds a lettuce leaf instead of an expected banana, will it shriek and throw the lettuce away, or merely gaze at the experimenter mournfully and eat the lettuce anyway? To simply say that subjects learn expectations does not go very far toward helping us to predict what effect a particular expectation will have on actual behavior. This problem was neatly captured in a famous gibe by Guthrie (1952), who accused Tolman of leaving his subjects "buried in thought" at the choice point.

In Tolman's theorizing, then, an expectation is not clearly tied either to the environmental conditions that produce it or to the behavior that follows, so that any predictions were much more the products of Tolman's intuitions—"Now what would I do if I were in that situation?"—than of any clearly stated set of rules. If cognitive theorizing was plagued by vagueness, however, S–R theory was not without its own share of ambiguity. As we have already seen, the main virtue in treating internal events as if they are covert muscle twitches is that their occurrence can then be predicted objectively using the same laws of behavior known to govern overt responses. But what if all these rules are not known? Or if those principles that are known sometimes predict opposite effects? Unless all the laws of overt behavior are known, we cannot hope to predict covert behavior unambiguously, and the sad truth is that these laws are not fully known even in outline form, much less in the quantitative detail required to predict what will happen when different principles conflict. In Fowler and Miller's punishment experiment, for example, we saw that an S–R analysis could equally predict faster or slower running in subjects shocked on their hind legs; equally ambiguous predictions can be derived in the case of latent extinction. (See Gleitman, Nachmias, & Neisser, 1954.) On the surface, S–R theory may appear considerably more precise and objective than cognitive theory, but in practice its predictions often depend just as much on theorists' intuitions as do the predictions derived from cognitive theories. (For a more detailed—and devastating—critique of Hullian theory along these lines, see Koch, 1954.)

A two-format hypothesis.   Given the similarity of the two theories, and the ambiguity with which each was formulated, it is perhaps less surprising that psychologists have had so much difficulty determining which one is right. There is, however, still a third possible explanation that, if correct, would readily account for the difficulty in establishing which theory is correct: Perhaps they both are.

Throughout this chapter we have implicitly assumed that there could only be one kind of learning, but there is no logical reason why there could not be two. Perhaps, as we suggested in our analysis of classical conditioning, a relatively primitive associative system evolved first, but with the development of the neocortex a more sophisticated system evolved that allowed the anticipation of consequences. Each system could have important advantages, with the associative system allowing rapid and automatic responses in simple or dangerous situations, and the cognitive system allowing sophisticated planning in situations in which time permits consideration of alternative plans of actions and their consequences. Whatever their precise functions, the existence of the two systems would obviously explain why behavior appears so flexible and intentional in some situations, yet so rigid and mechanical in others.

Indeed, there is evidence that the two processes not only may coexist in the same organism but, in some cases, may even influence the same behavior simultaneously. In describing the results of the Colwill and Rescorla experiment, we noted that pairing of sucrose with illness resulted in a significant decrease in responding for sucrose. If you look back at Figure 11.6, however, you will see that although responding in the sucrose-devaluation group declined substantially, the rats in this group still did respond initially. Thus, despite the fact that the food had become highly aversive, to the point where the rats would not eat it, they nevertheless responded to obtain it; in some of the other experiments reported by Colwill and Rescorla (1986), this responding was quite substantial. One plausible explanation is that an S–R association was formed during training as well as an expectation, so that the experimental cues continued to automatically elicit responding, even though at another level the rats knew that they did not want the food for which they were responding. (See also Morgan, 1974.)

Whether or not associations and expectations can influence performance simultaneously, the hypothesis that animals can learn both has a number of attractions—not the least of which is that it would allow us to account for all the conflicting evidence on S–R versus cognitive learning virtually at a stroke. We will henceforth refer to this idea—that learning can take the form of either associations or expectations—as the *two-format hypothesis*.

Habits and Awareness in Human Behavior

One way of stating the hypothesis we have been considering is that knowledge can be stored in the brain in two distinct forms, forms that perhaps have developed independently in the course of evolution. The first is as an S–R habit, in which the occurrence of a stimulus automatically elicits a response without any anticipation of the consequences. In the other, knowledge is stored in the form of an expectation that can be recalled as needed to plan behavior. All the evidence we have considered so far for this distinction comes from animals, but research on human learning and memory has suggested similar distinctions.

Controlled versus automatic processing.   One simple example suggesting the role of both habits and expectations in human behavior is the learning of motor skills such as driving a car. At first, learners have to pay close attention to what they are doing, frantically monitoring every wheel movement and trying to anticipate what will have to be done next. With practice, however, these movements become increasingly smooth and automatic, until eventually the learner can drive without thinking about it and can even carry on a conversation at the same time.

Similar automation occurs in perceptual learning. Suppose, for example, that you were presented with a sheet of paper containing a long list of randomly chosen letters, and your task was to identify each instance of the letter A. Research by Schneider and Shiffrin (1977) using a related (though more demanding) task suggests that you would respond relatively slowly at first, and that you would have to concentrate in a way that would leave you little time to carry out other tasks simultaneously. With practice, however, you would improve substantially, until eventually you could carry out the task automatically, without any interference with your performance on simultaneous tasks. (For a particularly dramatic demonstration along these lines, see Hirst, Spelke, Reaves, Caharack, & Neisser, 1980.)

To explain perceptual and motor learning of this kind, Shiffrin and Schneider (1977) have proposed that there are two fundamentally different kinds of cognitive processes in the brain. **Controlled processes** correspond roughly to what we normally mean by *attention*: largely conscious processes of limited capacity, so that only one task can be carried out at a time. In **automatic processes**, on the other hand, a stimulus elicits a response, or one set of neurons activates another set, automatically, meaning that the occurrence of the first almost invariably activates the second. Automatic processes presumably do not require attention, so a very large number of automatic processes can occur simultaneously without interfering with one another or with tasks that require controlled processing. In the letter-identification task, subjects initially must use controlled processes to identify the letter A; with sufficient practice, strong connections or associations are formed between the perceptual and response units involved (that is, between seeing the letter A and announcing it). When these connections become sufficiently strong, the process occurs automatically, at great speed and without conscious attention.

The Shiffrin and Schneider model emphasizes the processes involved, but the end result is that in some situations a stimulus will elicit a response automatically, whereas in others responding will be slower and will require conscious attention. This view clearly has strong similarities to the distinction in animal learning between automatic S–R habits and cognitive expectations.

Procedural versus declarative memories.   Further evidence that knowledge may be stored within the brain in two different forms has come from studies of amnesia. Individuals who suffer certain forms of brain damage develop an *anterograde amnesia*, which means that they can remember experiences predating their injury but cannot form new memories. One example comes from the most intensively studied patient with this condition, identified in the literature as H. M. When told that his uncle had died, he experienced intense grief, but he shortly forgot about it and thereafter often asked when his uncle would come to visit. Each time he was told that his uncle was dead his reaction was one of surprise, and his grief as intense as on the first occasion (Milner, 1966).

Similarly, when H. M. was given daily training on a mirror drawing task, in which he had to trace over a drawing that he could see only through a mirror, he was unable to remember each day ever having performed the task previously; despite this, his performance improved over days (Milner, 1962). Although he could not consciously remember his earlier experiences, they had clearly left some kind of residue within his memory.

Evidence of this kind has suggested to many cognitive theorists that experience may be stored within the brain in two different forms, variously referred to by different theorists as *procedural* versus *declarative*, *skills* versus *conscious recollection, implicit* versus *explicit,* and so on. (For a review, see Squire, 1987.) The various theories are not identical, but their common theme is that some aspects of experience are coded in a procedural or habitual form, in which one event automatically activates another without conscious involvement, whereas other events are stored in a more autobiographical form to which subjects can gain conscious access. Thus, H. M. retained the ability to form **procedural memories,** so that experience with the mirror drawing task resulted in strengthening of the associations necessary for improved perceptual-motor coordination; as a result of his injury, though, he could no longer form (or perhaps retrieve) **declarative memories,** and thus could not recollect or "declare" the experiences that produced this improvement. Again, this distinction between unconscious habits and conscious recollections bears obvious similarities to the distinction between S–R habits and cognitive expectations.

It is by no means certain that the various distinctions we have been discussing—S–R associations versus expectations, controlled versus automatic processing, procedural versus declarative memories—all refer to the same events, or even that any of them are correct. They could all be convenient dichotomies created by theorists and may not reflect any psychological reality. The fact that theorists from so many different areas of investigation have converged on similar distinctions, however, does encourage the belief that they may be tapping some fundamental property of the brain's operations, and to this extent supports the hypothesis that associative learning can take two forms: automatic S–R associations, and more complex and forward-looking expectations.

The New Consensus

It can be difficult to estimate the size of a theoretical bandwagon—if you are on a wagon gathering speed, it is hard to get a clear view of those standing quietly outside, watching the wagon go by—but there can be no doubt that the "two-format" bandwagon has become very densely populated in recent years, with many of the most creative and influential learning theorists now on board (for example, Bolles, 1972; Mackintosh & Dickinson, 1979; Rescorla, 1987). After decades of theoretical warfare, it is almost as if a truce has been declared, with both sides agreeing that the other had a good case after all, and everyone going away amicably together for drinks and a barbecue.

This emerging consensus is highly gratifying. It suggests that years of theoretical battles have not been in vain, and it also clarifies why the war was so hard for each side to win. But it would be a mistake to conclude that all the issues have been resolved. Several important ones remain, and we will briefly consider three.

Remaining differences.   The consensus among the warring parties is not quite total. Although there is now impressive agreement about fundamental concepts, there remain differences in terminology. For example, Rescorla (1987), who describes himself as an "unreconstructed associationist," still prefers to use the language of associations in describing learning; thus, instead of talking of *expectations,* he uses the term *response–reinforcer association.*

In some respects, the distinction is purely linguistic, because what Rescorla means by a response–reinforcer, or R–S*, association seems almost identical to what Tolman meant by an expectation—a link between a response and a reinforcer that allows subjects to anticipate what will occur. A case can be made, however, that the choice of terms to describe this unit, whether associative or cognitive, has potentially important implications.

The advantage of the term *association* is that its meaning is more clearly defined: Two events are associated when one elicits or activates the other. Thus, the term avoids some of the excess (and ambiguous) theoretical baggage that the term *expectation* brings with it from its use in everyday discourse. On the other hand, for precisely this reason the term *expectation* may be preferable, because its richer (albeit ambiguous) meanings allow it to explain behavior that a strictly associative account has considerable difficulty with. Thus, in Chapters 12 and 13 we will discuss evidence that seems to require a more complex or hierarchical view of what is learned than may be possible in a purely associative account. For the moment, however, let us not disturb the prevailing mood of peace with calls to further battle; in most respects, associative and cognitive theorists seem to have converged on remarkably similar accounts of learning.

The specificity problem. We have seen that one of the fundamental problems in the controversy over what is learned was that neither theory was stated clearly enough, so that it was difficult to predict in advance which association or which expectation would be learned in any situation. Simply declaring that both sides were right does not eliminate this problem. For example, to predict what will happen in the cart experiment, we need to know precisely what expectation or R–S* association the rat will form while sitting in the cart; current theories do not allow this degree of precision. Similarly, we need to know precisely what S–R association will be formed, and how the S–R and R–S* associations will combine to determine behavior; again, no theory currently allows this. This lack of precision means that no matter what the outcome of any experiment—whether a rat behaves with impeccable rationality or blind stupidity—a two-format theorist could blithely conclude, "Oh yes, just what I expected, an association or expectation."

In a real sense, the two-format analysis we have been sketching is not a theory at all, but only an orientation or framework that can be used to organize existing evidence. The development of such a framework is not something to be dismissed lightly, but before it can turn into a genuine theory it needs to be made much more specific. Rather than saying that animals can learn associations or expectations, we need to be able to predict which associations or which expectations will be learned in any situation. It is this problem of developing more specific predictions to which we will devote our attention in the following chapter.

The performance problem.   One of the great strengths of S–R theory was that once we knew what had been learned in any situation—that is, what stimulus had become associated with what response—there was no ambiguity in predicting behavior: The subject would perform whatever response had become associated. Unfortunately, an expectancy or R–S* analysis is not so straightforward. Even if we know what a rat (or a monkey, or a human) expects in any situation, this does not necessarily allow us to predict what it will do.

When learning is analyzed in terms of expectations, it can be difficult to see the problem, because we automatically bring to bear our intuitions concerning what behavior should occur given a certain set of expectations. It is perhaps easier to see the severity of the problem if the analysis is stated in terms of R–S* associations rather than expectations. (Both approaches face identical problems in this area.) Suppose that a rat is trained in a Skinner box to press a bar to obtain food, and as a result forms an association between bar-pressing and food. The next time it is placed in the Skinner box, what will it do? It is all well and good to say that it has learned an association between pressing the bar and food, but all this means is that when it presses the bar it will expect food to follow. How does this expectation lead to its pressing the bar in the first place?

The short answer is that it doesn't; the R–S* association must be supplemented with other mechanisms or assumptions before it can be translated into behavior. It might seem that it should be easy to suggest such rules, but the progress that learning theorists have made in this area so far has been severely limited. (For a review, see Mackintosh, 1983.) We desperately need to rescue the rat "buried in thought" at the choice point by providing it with decision or performance rules for translating its thoughts into behavior. This may prove the next great challenge for learning research.

11.6 SUMMARY

When we observe a well-trained rat running down an alley to a goal box containing food, it is natural to assume that the rat is doing so because it knows that food is there and wants to obtain it. S–R theorists, however, rejected this account on two grounds:

1. We cannot know what a rat is thinking, so an explanation that refers to its expectations is untestable.

2. Behavior that seems to involve complex cognitive processes can often be explained in terms of simpler associations.

Together, these assumptions led to S–R theory—the assumption that reinforcement produces an association between environmental stimuli and the successful response. Thorndike's observations of learning in animals—its slow, erratic course and the rigidity with which a successful response was blindly repeated—provided strong initial support for this analysis.

Evidence for learning in situations in which subjects simply observed the environment, without making any active response, convinced neobehaviorists such as Clark Hull that learning could not be described solely in terms of visible behavior: We had to assume some kind of internal processes. Hull, however, continued to interpret learning in terms of simple associations; the only change was that hypothetical covert responses were to be allowed as well as visible overt ones. Tolman, on the other hand, believed subjects learned expectations that allowed them to anticipate the consequences of their behavior and to respond flexibly in selecting the most suitable behavior if a previously successful behavioral path were blocked. Both Hull and Tolman agreed, however, that the processes of learning could not be determined by introspection, because too much of the brain's functioning is simply inaccessible. The question of whether we learn associations or expectations, therefore, could only be settled by seeing which view led to more accurate predictions of behavior.

Over the years, both sides were able to amass considerable evidence in support of their interpretations, making a simple resolution of the controversy exceedingly difficult. One reason for the difficulty in deciding between the two theories was that structurally they were far more similar than the differences in their terminology suggested. A second, even more important factor was the ambiguity of both theories. A crucial requirement for testing any theory is that it make clear and unambiguous predictions, but neither side was ever able to state its position with sufficient precision to allow this. Still a third reason that it has been so difficult to establish which theory is right, however, could be that both are right. The first learning system to have evolved may have been of the fundamentally simple kind described by S–R theory, in which stimuli automatically elicit a response without any anticipation of the goal. In vertebrates, however, this may have been supplemented by a more sophisticated cognitive system involving the acquisition of abstract knowledge, or expectations.

Both kinds of learning have advantages, and there is evidence in humans that we can alternate between the two systems. In learning to drive a car, for example, at first you have to pay constant attention to what you are doing, but, with practice, these movements become increasingly automatic, until eventually you can drive without thinking about it. Carrying out a behavior automatically sometimes causes trouble (always going home by the same route, for example, even on a day when you had meant to take a different route to go shopping), but transferring control to a simpler system that can execute behavior automatically leaves the more flexible cognitive system free to cope with new demands. (See also Schneider & Shiffrin, 1977.) If the automatic component of this system can be equated with the associative system described by S–R theorists, then human learning may indeed be a blend of associative habits and cognitive expectations.

The belief that experiences can be stored in the brain in two forms, as associations and as expectations, has attracted considerable support in recent years, but important problems remain. One of these is what might be called the performance problem: Given that an animal or human has formed an expectation, how is that expectation translated into behavior? Knowing that a student expects to fail an exam unless he or she works harder does not tell us what the student will do in that situation; the student might work harder, get drunk, talk to the instructor, or drop out. Even in much simpler situations such as classical conditioning, we have seen that learning theorists still have great difficulty predicting in advance what behavior will emerge when a subject expects food or shock. We need explicitly stated decision or performance rules to allow us to predict the behavior to which an expectation will lead.

A further difficulty concerns the need for greater specificity in predicting what associations or expectations will be learned in the first place. On both practical and theoretical grounds, it is vital that theories be stated precisely enough to allow the unambiguous derivation of predictions. Unfortunately, current theories do not approach this state. Rather than just saying that subjects can learn associations or expectations, we need to be able to predict *which* association or *which* expectation will be formed in any situation. It is this problem of developing more specific predictions to which we will devote our attention in Chapters 12 and 13.

Selected Definitions

S–R theory A theory that assumes that learning involves the formation of associations between environmental stimuli and the responses made in their presence.

Behaviorism A difficult term to define because behaviorists come grouped in a number of different schools, and their views diverge on many issues. A common theme is a distrust of introspection as a tool for scientific investigation, and a consequent emphasis on explaining behavior in terms of environmental causes rather than mental states.

  Within this broad framework, behaviorists disagree about the precise role that should be accorded the mind within psychology. *Methodological behaviorists* believe that psychology should study only events that can be observed objectively—that is, about which independent observers can agree. Because the mind cannot be observed objectively, methodological behaviorists oppose any use of mental concepts within psychology.

  Skinner, on the other hand, is a *radical behaviorist:* He has no objection to studying the mind, but does not believe that overt behavior should be attributed to mental states. The ultimate cause of behavior, he argues, lies in the environment (and genetics), and behavior must be explained in terms of these environmental determinants if psychology is to be of practical value.

Neobehaviorism is a variant of behaviorism whose adherents are willing to accept internal or mental states at a theoretical level as intervening variables, provided that the theory is stated clearly enough to allow the derivation of predictions about overt behavior. The validity of the theory is then determined solely by the accuracy of its predictions about overt behavior, not by how well it accords with introspective knowledge.

Cognitive behaviorists share with neobehaviorists a willingness to accept mental states at a theoretical level—indeed, it was Tolman who first introduced the concept of an intervening variable (see Hull, 1943)—but differ in the kinds of intervening variables they employ. Whereas neobehaviorists view internal events as covert responses that obey the same laws as their overt counterparts, cognitive behaviorists postulate internal processes that correspond much more closely with those suggested by conscious experience: expectations, memory, attention, and so on.

Intervening variable A variable used in a theory to represent a hypothetical internal state. This state is elicited by a stimulus and helps to determine the eventual response; it thus intervenes between the stimulus and the response.

Fractional anticipatory goal response (r$_g$) The term used by Hull to describe a conditioned response. For example, if a rat receives food in the goal box of a maze, the salivation elicited by food will be conditioned to the sight of the goal box. Because the rat will then begin to salivate as soon as it approaches the goal box, Hull called the conditioned response an *anticipatory* goal response. And because conditioned responses are invariably weaker than the original unconditioned response, he called it a *fractional* goal response.

Docility Flexibility in choosing a new response when a previously used behavior is not effective. Tolman regarded this flexibility as evidence for the presence of an expectation. Suppose, for example, that a rat's path to the goal box in a maze was blocked by a barrier and the rat responded by climbing over the barrier. This flexibility suggests that the rat had not learned a fixed set of muscular movements, but rather had formed an expectation that there was food in the goal box; the rat then chose whatever response would get it to the goal box.

Disruption A term used by Tolman to describe the disturbance of behavior that is observed when an expected outcome is not obtained.

Automatic processes and **controlled processes** Two categories of cognitive processes proposed by Shiffrin and Schneider. An automatic process is one that occurs rapidly, without any need for attention. Because conscious attention is not required, a large number of automatic processes can be carried out simultaneously. A controlled process is a cognitive process that does require attention. Controlled processes are relatively slow, and only a limited number can be carried out at one time. With practice, however, controlled processes can become automatic.

Declarative memories and **procedural memories** Two forms in which experiences are stored in memory, as suggested by a number of theorists. Declarative memories are stored in a form to which subjects can gain conscious access—in other words, conscious recollections. Procedural memories are stored in a procedural, or habitual, form in which one event automatically activates another, without conscious involvement. Declarative memories provide the basis for recall of autobiographical experiences and facts; procedural memories provide the basis for skills and habits.

Review Questions

1. Define the following terms: latent extinction, observational learning, reinforcer devaluation, and the two-format hypothesis.

2. How did Thorndike and Watson contribute to the development of S–R theory?

3. What was the central disagreement between early cognitive and behavioral learning theorists?

4. What is the evidence that learning can occur without an overt response being made? Why was this evidence regarded as a critical test of S–R and cognitive theories of learning?

5. How did Hull, as a behaviorist, justify talking about internal events?

6. What is latent extinction? How can Hull's r_g–s_g mechanism be used to account for it?

7. Why did Tolman reject Hull's neobehaviorism? How did he suggest we might assess the presence of an expectation? What evidence supports his claim that animals learn expectations?

8. Why was it so difficult to decide whether S–R or cognitive theories of learning are correct?

9. What evidence suggests that learning involves both associations and expectations?

10. How has the associative account of learning evolved from Thorndike to Hull to Rescorla? In what ways has it changed, and in what ways has it remained the same?

11. One version of the two-format hypothesis is an evolutionary one that assumes that an associative system evolved first and was later supplemented by a cognitive one. What might this imply about the relationship between learning in rats, in monkeys, and in humans?

12. Current theories about expectations face two serious problems (though not, we hope, insurmountable ones). What are these problems?

CHAPTER TWELVE

HOW IS IT LEARNED?

An Information-Processing Model

We began our analysis of associative learning in Chapter 2 by imagining a dog alone in an empty room, the silence periodically broken by a bell and then food. As training continued, we suggested, the dog would begin to salivate when the bell was presented. In Chapter 5, we reviewed evidence consistent with two very different explanations for this change in behavior: that the bell became a substitute for food, or that it served as a signal that food was imminent. Similarly, in Chapter 11 we discussed evidence for two kinds of learning produced by reinforcement: an S–R association in which the stimuli present during reinforcement would automatically elicit the response, or an expectation that this response would produce food. In both classical and instrumental conditioning, in other words, there is evidence to suggest two kinds of learning—one based on relatively simple associations, the other on expectations. To put it another way, a stimulus may either activate behavior automatically, or it may provide information that subjects use to plan their next response.

As we have stressed repeatedly, this distinction is a speculative one: It is by no means certain that there really are two distinct forms of learning or, if there are, whether their properties correspond neatly to those of associations and expectations. In this chapter, however, we will no longer be concerned with the structure of what is learned—whether it is an association or expectation—but rather with the details of its contents: Given that an association or an expectation is formed, *which* association or *which* expectation will it be?

To give this question a more concrete focus, consider again the dog in our salivary conditioning experiment. When the bell is followed by the food, what determines what the dog will learn? The first important point to emphasize is that this task is not simple. Because the bell and food are separated by only a few seconds, it may seem obvious that the two are related, but this is because we know about the relationship in advance. From the point of view of the dog, the situation is far more confusing. There are literally thousands of stimuli impinging on the dog every second—a myriad of lights, sounds, odors, and so on—and any of these stimuli could potentially be a reliable predictor of food. Animals, moreover, learn not only about stimuli that precede a US immediately but also about events that occurred minutes or even hours earlier. Rats, for example, will develop an aversion to food eaten up to 24 hours before they become ill. (See Chapter 4.) If we recognize that conditioning can occur to stimuli over such an extended period, then we can see that the situation confronting a dog in a conditioning experiment is that food is preceded not by a single CS but rather by a vast array of simultaneous and successive sights, sounds, movements, and so on (Figure 6.7). What determines which members of this vast sea of events will become associated with the food?

One important factor will be the stimuli that received attention when they originally occurred. If a stimulus is not attended to, it is unlikely to be associated with any subsequent event. Assuming that subjects do attend to a stimulus, a second important factor in learning will be whether they recall it when they later receive food. In order to predict what is learned, therefore, we need to take into account the processes of memory and attention, which help to determine the result. We will therefore begin our exploration of the processes underlying associative learning by reviewing the principles of memory and attention. In particular, we will start by examining the theoretical framework that has guided much of the research on memory in recent years—that of *information processing*. We will then examine a broadly accepted or "consensual" model of memory in somewhat more detail. Finally, we will consider the extent to which this memory model can help us understand associative learning.

Before we begin, though, we need to offer a brief word concerning the range of material covered in this chapter. We are going to mix together, almost randomly, material from classical conditioning and reinforcement, and from studies involving associations and others involving expectations. This does not mean that the information-processing principles involved are identical in all these cases, but this chapter will emphasize those features that we believe to be shared. (See also Revusky, 1977.)

In a similar spirit, we will move back and forth between research on humans and animals, although the rationale here is somewhat more complex. In essence, we will assume that the fundamental principles of associative learning are the same or at least similar in all vertebrate species, although in humans conscious awareness and reasoning may play a substantially greater role in modulating the output of the associative system. Because our main concern is with the principles of associative learning, we will focus on research involving animals—experiments in which the subject's thinking and reasoning are presumed to play a lesser role. In cases where research on humans seems illuminating, however, we will also consider this research.

To sum up, in this chapter and the following one, we will proceed as if there is only a single associative learning system, and that its underlying principles are fundamentally the same whether we are dealing with classical conditioning or reinforcement, rats or humans. This assumption is almost certainly an oversimplification, and as our understanding of associative learning increases, it should become possible to make much finer distinctions. In the present state of our knowledge, however, this "single process" approach will provide us with a useful starting point for analyzing how associations or expectations are formed. *

12.1 THE CONCEPT OF INFORMATION PROCESSING

Over the past two decades, most of the research on memory has been guided by a theoretical perspective or framework known as information processing. This approach had its origins in the development of computer technology in the late 1940s, and it may help to understand the rationale behind it if we first consider briefly the properties of modern computers.

The Computer Analogy

In essence, a computer is a machine that can perform only a few very simple operations. To add the numbers 5 and 3, for example, a computer first stores the numbers in separate cells in its electronic memory, along with instructions, or a "program," that tells it how to add them. Using these instructions, the computer then retrieves from its memory these two numbers (5 and 3), and transfers them to a central processing unit (CPU) where they are added together. The computer then transfers the sum obtained to another memory cell and stores it there. Finally, it conveys the result to us by printing it on paper or displaying it on a screen.

This summary is something of an oversimplification. The steps outlined above would be broken down into tens or hundreds of separate operations. But it does accurately convey the way in which computers solve problems by breaking them down into a series of small steps. Each of these steps considered by itself (for example, adding 3 and 5) is extremely simple, but by performing the steps at almost unimaginable speed, the computer can solve problems of staggering complexity. As this ability of computers to solve problems became

---

* To simplify the exposition, we will not keep repeating "association or expectation," or "reinforcement or conditioning," but in each case we will use just one of these terms. In light of what has just been said, however, it should be clear, for example, that the use of the term *association* in this chapter is intended simply as a shorthand and does not imply any prejudgment of whether learning in a particular situation involves an association or an expectation.

clear in the 1940s and early 1950s, psychologists became increasingly fascinated by the mechanisms involved. If computers could solve complex problems by breaking them down into simpler steps, was it possible that human thinking might be based on the same strategy?

Many psychologists were initially skeptical: Could the rather elementary operations of a computer really provide a meaningful analogy to the richness and complexity of human thought? Computers, after all, could solve problems only if given extremely detailed, step-by-step instructions for doing so, and even with such instructions could only solve problems requiring rote, repetitive calculations. In essence, they seemed to be little more than glorified calculating machines. Over time, however, it became clear that these limitations were not as serious as they initially appeared. It turned out, for example, that computers could be programmed to "learn" from experience: Given the broad outlines of a problem, they could try out different strategies for solving the problem and then use whatever strategy proved most effective in solving future problems. Furthermore, we found that computers need not be confined to rote calculations; they can be programmed to use the same kinds of flexible, goal-oriented strategies used by humans, and in many areas can use them more effectively. Thus, computers have already beaten human world champions at games such as checkers, and it probably will not be long before they can also do so at chess.

Successes such as these do not prove that people and computers solve problems in identical ways, but they do suggest that the simple, sequential processing methods used by computers may perform many if not all of the tasks now carried out by the human brain. As a result, there has been considerable interest in computers among psychologists, and the concepts and terminology of computer programming have had a tremendous impact on theories of human memory and thought.

The Information-Processing Perspective

There has been widespread acceptance of the analytical framework of information processing that views problem solving as a sequence of simple operations, in each of which the information output of the preceding stage (for example, the sum 8 from our earlier example of 5 + 3) is subject to one further process or modification (that is, storage in a memory cell). This sequential analysis has aspects in common with both the cognitive and associative approaches discussed in the preceding chapter. It is most obviously similar to the cognitive approach in its emphasis on understanding internal processes, but in some respects it also strongly resembles associative theories. Consider, for example, the following quote from Newell and Simon, two of the most influential of the early information-processing theorists:

It looks more and more as if problem solving is accomplished through complex structures of familiar simple elements. The growing proof is that we can simulate problem solving in a number of situations using no more than these simple elements as the building blocks of our programs.

(Newell & Simon, 1963, p. 402)

This belief in the possibility of synthesizing complex behaviors from simple building blocks should be familiar, because it is virtually identical to that expressed by S–R theorists such as Clark Hull, and also manifested in later associative theories such as the Rescorla-Wagner model. Information processing thus combines the cognitive emphasis on internal processes with the associative belief that these processes are fundamentally simple, and its ability to synthesize these approaches has almost certainly been a major factor in the growth in its popularity. (See also Hintzman, 1978.)

Coding, Storage, and Retrieval

We have seen that the information-processing approach views memory and other cognitive processes as a sequence of relatively simple operations or processes. Regarding exactly what these subprocesses might be in the case of memory, information-processing theorists have used as their starting point the three stages a computer goes through in remembering material: coding the input, storing it, and then retrieving it when it is needed.

When information is presented to a computer, the first thing it does is transform, or code, that input into a form that it can process. This is known as **coding**. In the addition problem discussed earlier, for example, we might have typed in the numbers to be added, using the computer keyboard. For the computer to be able to use this information, it would first have to convert, or code, the information in the form of a series of electrical signals. These signals are then stored in electromagnetic cells located in the computer's memory. (The occurrence of a particular electrical impulse, for example, would be stored by magnetizing a particular memory cell.) This process is known as **storage**. Finally, when the stored information is needed for some purpose such as addition, it is retrieved from its location in memory and copied into the computer's central processing unit, where any required arithmetic operations can be carried out. This is known as **retrieval**.

Similarly, memory in animals and humans can be understood as the sequential coding, storage, and retrieval of information. Most of our understanding of these three processes has come from studies of human memory and, in particular, of verbal learning—how people memorize verbal material such as word lists and stories. In the next section, therefore, we will review what we have learned about these three stages in human memory. Then, in the sections that follow, we will consider the extent to which these principles can help us understand what is learned in associative learning.

12.2 AN INFORMATION-PROCESSING MODEL OF HUMAN MEMORY

Before we begin our analysis of how information is processed in human memory, a word of warning is in order: The literature on memory and attention is vast and would be difficult to summarize adequately in an entire book, much less a single section. The review that follows, therefore, is highly selective and will present only those principles that are most obviously and directly relevant to associative learning. For this reason, we will not be discussing the role of organization in memory (for example, the fact that an organized story is easier to remember than a random set of words or facts), even though organization plays a crucial role in memory and may well play an important role in associative learning. Finally, for the material that is covered, we will present only one interpretation of the available evidence. It is important to bear in mind that other views are possible; more detailed discussion of some other views can be found in excellent texts by Baddeley (1990), Anderson (1990), and Parkin (1987).

To provide a concrete focus for the discussion that follows, imagine that a stranger came up to you in the street and, without saying a word, handed you a piece of paper containing the single word *log*. What would determine whether you were later able to recall this word?

Coding

Sensory coding. The first requirement for remembering any stimulus is to identify it correctly when it occurs. In our example, you would first have to recognize the printed symbol as being the word *log*. Neurophysiological evidence suggests that the first stage in identifying a visual stimulus—in information-processing terminology, assigning it a code—is to break it down into its component features. At the earliest stage in visual processing, a receptor in the eye might be sensitive to the presence of light at only a single point on the retina (Figure 12.1). At the next level, the output of several receptors might converge on a single cell in such a way that this higher-order cell would be activated only if retinal receptors oriented in a horizontal line were stimulated; another second-order cell might be sensitive to the presence of a vertical line, and so on. The output of these "feature detector" cells is then passed on to cells higher up in the visual system that respond only to specific combinations of features. At each successive level, more and more complex combinations are required to produce a response, until cells of quite extraordinary specificity are reached. In the visual cortex of monkeys, for example, scientists have found a

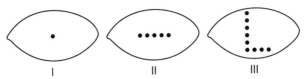

F I G U R E 12.1.   Hypothetical receptor fields at successive stages of visual processing. The oval shapes represent the retina; each small circle represents a single receptor within the retina. At the first level of processing (I), a neuron might fire in response to stimulation of one receptor at the retina; at the second level (II), a neuron might fire only if a set of receptors aligned in a horizontal line were stimulated; at the third level (III), a neuron might fire only in response to two lines arranged in an L-shape, and so on.

cell that is uniquely sensitive not simply to the sight of a monkey's paw but to a paw oriented in an upward direction (Gross, Bender, & Rocha-Miranda, 1969). Although no comparable neurophysiological evidence is available for the human visual system, it is believed that equivalent cells exist within the human brain to detect the written word *log*. (See also Lindsay & Norman, 1977.)

The role of context in coding.   Neurophysiological studies, then, suggest that we recognize stimulus patterns by first breaking them down into their component features and then recombining these features. On the whole, this feature analysis model has been strongly supported by psychological studies of perception, but in one important respect it has proved misleading. The neurophysiological evidence implies that perception is an essentially infallible process in which sequential analysis of features leads slowly but inevitably to accurate identification of the stimulus. This may be so in some cases, but in others we cannot detect enough features to identify the stimulus; the object may be partially obscured, we may glimpse it only briefly, and so forth. In situations like these, we must rely on the context in which the stimulus occurs to help us infer or guess what it might be.

This point is neatly illustrated in an experiment by Warren (1970), described in Chapter 5, in which subjects were played a tape containing the sentence "The state governors met with their respective legislatures convening in the capital city." The section of the tape containing the first s in *legislatures* had been cut out and replaced by the sound of someone coughing. Although it was physically impossible for anyone to hear the s, 19 out of 20 subjects nevertheless reported hearing every single part of the sentence distinctly. Even when they were told that one segment of the sentence had been removed, they still were unable to identify the segment. Even when few features of a stimulus are available to us, therefore—in this extreme case, no features—we may still perceive the stimulus by using contextual information and past experience to reconstruct what it must have been.

Perception, therefore, is not simply a process of copying the external world, but of interpreting it on the basis of whatever information is available. We extract as many features as circumstances (and our limited processing capacity) allow, and we use this fragmentary information to construct a model of the world outside us, in much the same way that physicists use the limited observations they can make of the real world to construct models of atoms and molecules.

In coding a stimulus, then, we combine information about its features and its context to identify it. The final step in this coding process may be the activation of a single neuron or set of neurons called a *node*. (Activating the preexisting node for *log* constitutes identification of this word.) We shall see in Chapter 13 that other theories of information coding within the brain are possible—in particular, that it is the pattern of activation across a very large network of neurons that codes information, rather than the activation of a single unit. For now, though, we will adopt the nodal terminology.

Short-term memory.   Given that a stimulus has been identified and a node activated, how long will activity in this node continue? Early experiments on human memory showed that people could recall word lists sometimes hours or even days later, but the subjects in these studies were free to keep thinking about the words during the retention interval, so the observed recall was, potentially, the fruit of extended practice. To find out how long material could be remembered without such practice, Peterson and Peterson (1959) gave subjects a consonant trigram (for example, CHJ) and then, after a delay of between 3 and 18 seconds, asked them to recall it. To prevent subjects' practicing the trigram during the retention interval, they had to count backward by threes from a designated number.

On the surface, the task was almost ridiculously easy: The subjects were being asked to remember a simple trigram for only a few seconds. However, as Figure 12.2 shows, the task proved to be exceedingly difficult. After only 3 seconds, 20 percent of the subjects could no longer recall the trigram; within 15 seconds, nearly all the subjects had forgotten it. Simply recognizing a word is not enough to ensure that it will be remembered: Unless subjects are allowed to continue working on or processing the code they have formed, it will decay and become inaccessible within a matter of seconds.

Long-term memory.   If material is forgotten within seconds, one obvious question is how we manage to form permanent or long-term memories. The answer, according to a memory model proposed by Shiffrin and Schneider (1977), is that **long-term memory (LTM)** depends on the formation of associations between the nodes that are active in **short-term memory (STM)**. In our *log* example, for you to be able to recall later the word that had been written on the paper, it would not be sufficient for it to have activated the *log* node in your

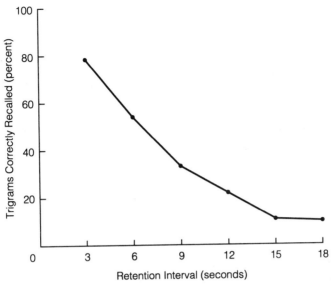

FIGURE 12.2   The percentage of consonant trigrams correctly recalled after retention intervals of between 3 and 18 seconds. (Peterson & Peterson, 1959)

brain; it would be just one more coding of a word that you would have heard thousands of times in your life, indistinguishable from all the others. To remember the particular occurrence, *log* would have to be associated with the context in which it occurred: the presence of the stranger, the place, the time of day, and so on. Only with the coding of such word-context associations would you be able to distinguish this experience of the word from all its predecessors.

To remember the word *log*, then, you would have to associate this word with the contextual cues that accompanied it—or, in neural terms, form associations between the nodes that were simultaneously active in short-term memory. Shiffrin and Schneider argue, however, that associations can be formed between nodes only during the time in which they are active. This time is limited by the fact that nodal activity decays rapidly, but subjects can get around this limitation by repetition or **rehearsal** of the word they want to remember: Every time the subject repeats the word, activity in the node is reinitiated, thus extending the time available for forming new associations. (A common example is repeating a telephone number during the interval between looking it up and actually dialing: By continually repeating the number, we keep the node in an active state, thereby preventing its decay.) The formation of long-term memories thus depends on rehearsing material in short-term memory so that it remains active long enough to allow the formation of new associations. (The term *rehearsal* was originally confined to repetition of verbal material, but it is now used more generally to refer to the maintenance of a neural center in an active state.)

Attention.   One of the central assumptions of information-processing theories is that the brain's capacity to process information is limited in important respects. Thus, although the brain contains billions of neurons, of which countless millions may be active at any given moment, some of the brain's operations are limited in the sense that only one or a small number can be carried out simultaneously. Such limitations in processing capacity are referred to as **attention.**

Rehearsal is one of the processes that is limited in this way: We can only rehearse or attend to a limited number of items in short-term memory at one time. To experience this limitation for yourself, repeat the following number after reading it only once:

683

You probably found it easy, but now try the following:

74095682153

The problem with repeating the longer number is that codes must be rehearsed periodically if they are to remain in an active state, but we can rehearse only a small number of codes at a time. Indeed, according to Shiffrin and Schneider, we can rehearse only a single code at a time; to remember more items than that we must rehearse them sequentially. With the number 683, for example, you rehearse the 6 first, then the 8, then the 3. After finishing the 3, you can return to the 6, and repeat the entire sequence as often as necessary. If the list of digits to be remembered is too long, however, then the first digit will have faded from memory before you can return to rehearse it. It is rather like the plate-spinning act in a circus, where the juggler runs from one plate to the next, giving each a reviving spin (rehearsal) as he goes. Each new spin returns the plate to its original state of activity, but if the juggler tries to maintain too many plates at once, the first plate will already have fallen to the table by the time he reaches the last one. In the case of memory, the number of items that can be kept active simultaneously is known as the *memory span*; for most people, it seems to be around seven items.

If several items are presented together repeatedly, their nodes may be associated together to form a new, higher-level node. The letter sequence *aksolptzvbgw*, for example, is much harder to recall than the sequence *constitution*; the reason is that we have experienced the sequence *constitution* so often that we have associated its elements together to form a new, single code. The process of associating codes together to form a single code is known as *chunking*;

the result is that a word such as *constitution* requires no more rehearsal to remember than a single letter such as *c*. Although chunking is of some help in overcoming the limited rehearsal capacity of short-term memory, we can still remember only a small fraction of the stimuli that are constantly inundating us. One of the most important determinants of memory, then, is how we allocate processing capacity or attention among the myriad of stimuli competing for it.

Storage

Given that a stimulus is successfully encoded and that we can remember it, say, one week later, you might think that we would then remember it forever, but this is clearly not the case. Why do we forget material after having successfully learned it? One obvious possibility is that memory traces decay with the passing of time. The ancient Greek philosopher Aristotle likened memory to a soft clay tablet: When an impression is first made, it is clear and vivid, but over time it becomes increasingly blurred, finally disappearing altogether. Similarly, the neural encoding of a stimulus might deteriorate over time, until it can no longer be deciphered.

As plausible as this explanation might sound, experimental research has provided only limited evidence for decay. In a classic study by Jenkins and Dallenbach (1924), for example, the experimenters gave subjects a list of nonsense syllables to memorize and then asked them to recall as many as they could after delays of up to eight hours. In one condition, the subjects spent the retention interval engaged in normal daily activities; in the other, they stayed in the laboratory and went to sleep. If forgetting is caused solely by the passing of time, then it should have been equal in both conditions, but, as Figure 12.3 shows, this was far from being the case. Subjects who were awake during the retention interval forgot much more than those who slept. The fact that subjects who slept did forget some of what they had learned could mean that time also causes forgetting, or it could have been the result of the subject's residual activity in the time before they fell asleep. Whatever the role of time may be, it is clear that forgetting is not caused solely by the passing of time: How subjects spend that time is critical.

Retroactive interference. In particular, it seems to be the formation of new memories during the time in which we are active that interferes with older memories. This **retroactive interference (RI)** of new memories with old ones is greatest when the memories involved are similar. In a study by Tulving and Psotka (1971), for example, subjects learned a list of words and were then asked to recall it 20 minutes later. Subjects who spent the retention interval working on an arithmetic reasoning task showed virtually no forgetting. Subjects who memorized new lists during the period, however, did forget, and the more lists they memorized, the more of the original list they forgot. Activity

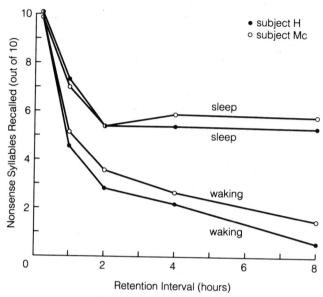

F I G U R E 12.3   The number of nonsense syllables recalled after intervals spent either awake or asleep. (Jenkins & Dallenbach, 1924)

itself, therefore, does not produce forgetting any more than time does: It is the encoding of new, similar material that seems to cause forgetting.

Proactive interference.   Memory for a word list may also be impaired by material learned previously. This phenomenon, termed **proactive interference (PI)**, was first identified in a classic paper by Underwood (1957), who analyzed published studies in which subjects had memorized a list until they could repeat it perfectly and were then tested for recall 24 hours later. The more lists that subjects had memorized before the experiment, the more of the target list they forgot over the 24 hours. It does not seem to matter very much, therefore, whether interfering material is learned before or after a target: The more similar material that resides in memory, the harder it is to recall a particular item.

In this respect, memory seems to be like a rapidly expanding library that receives books faster than it can catalog them. As the library continues to expand and the piles of uncataloged books grow ever higher, the task of searching through the piles to find a particular volume becomes greater and greater. The main cause of forgetting seems to be not the loss of material from storage but difficulties in locating or retrieving what is there.

Retrieval

What, then, determines our success in retrieving memories from storage? Aside from how well material is organized during original learning (memory's equivalent of a cataloging system), two factors seem to be particularly important in determining retrieval.

Retrieval cues. One factor is the similarity of the contextual cues present during retrieval to those present during coding. In discussing coding, we saw that a word or other stimulus is not coded in isolation: In order to establish permanent memories, associations are formed between the word to be remembered and contextual cues present at the time. If one of these cues is again present during retrieval, activation will spread from its node to all the others with which it is linked (Collins & Loftus, 1975). The more such cues are present—that is, the greater the similarity of training and test conditions—the more excitation will spread to the target node from the associated contextual nodes, and thus the greater the likelihood of the word's being recalled.

One illustration of the importance of retrieval cues that you may have experienced for yourself is passing someone in the street who seems very familiar but whom you can't quite place (a student in one of your classes or a teller at your bank, for example). A few days later you may see the person again but this time in more familiar surroundings, and you may recognize the person instantly. When you see people in the street, outside the context in which you previously encountered them, it is difficult to match a face with any existing memory trace, but when the contextual cues are restored, the appropriate node is reactivated instantly.

Some of the contextual cues that form part of the coding of an experience are surprisingly subtle. In a study by Smith (1979), for example, subjects memorized a word list and were then asked to recall it 20 minutes later. Subjects tested in the room in which they had originally studied the list recalled 33 percent more words than did subjects tested in a different room. Other seemingly unimportant cues such as your mood and physical condition can form part of the stored memory trace, and the presence of these "irrelevant" cues at recall can substantially improve memory. (See also Eich, 1980; Bower, 1981.)[*]

Cue overload. A second factor that influences retrieval is the number of different memories associated with a retrieval cue. We have suggested that when a node is activated, activation spreads to all the other nodes with which it is connected. The greater the number of these connections, however, the less excitation will flow to any one of them and, thus, the less likely it will be that a particular memory will be retrieved (Figure 12.4). If you've eaten in a restaurant only once, for example, returning to it may evoke vivid memories of

---

[*] Before you decide to do all your exam studying in the room in which you will be tested, we should add that contextual cues are much less important in the case of meaningful textual material, in which the coding of the semantic relationships between words is much more important than contextual associations in determining recall.

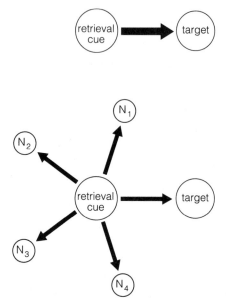

F I G U R E 12.4   The cue-overload hypothesis. If a retrieval cue node is associated with only one other node, it will stimulate that node strongly (symbolized by the thick arrow); the more nodes with which it is associated (represented by N_1, N_2, and so on), the less it will stimulate any one of them.

your earlier meal there. The more often you eat there, however, the more memories will become associated with the contextual cues of the restaurant, and the more difficult it will be for you to remember any particular meal: They all blur together. This phenomenon has been termed **cue overload** and seems to be one of the most important factors causing proactive and retroactive interference (Watkins & Watkins, 1976; Anderson, 1990).

The effectiveness of a retrieval cue, then, depends in part on how similar it is to the cues present during encoding and in part on how many other memories are associated with it. These principles do not by themselves provide a comprehensive account of forgetting; they require supplementation in a number of respects. (See, for example, Postman, Stark, & Fraser, 1968; E. Martin, 1971; Mandler, 1981.) But these principles probably do account for a good proportion of forgetting.

Summary

Let us summarize some of the points discussed so far. Whether we remember a stimulus such as the word *log* depends on whether we succeed in coding, storing, and retrieving it. In coding, we analyze a stimulus into its constituent features and then use these features together with contextual cues to infer what the original stimulus must have been. The final step in this sensory coding process seems to be activation of one or more cells in an integrated unit called a node. The nodes that are active simultaneously are collectively referred to as short-term memory; as implied by this term, activity in a node normally decays quite rapidly after the initiating stimulus is no longer present.

In order to form a permanent memory of a word, it must be associated with the contextual cues that accompany it; in neural terms, associations must be formed between the nodes that are active in short-term memory. The formation of a memory takes time, however, and to ensure that nodes remain active long enough for an association to be formed, subjects may repeat or rehearse the material they are trying to remember. Because our capacity to rehearse material is limited, the allocation of attention or rehearsal capacity to events is one of the crucial factors determining memory.

Once a code for an item has been successfully stored in memory, current theories suggest that it will remain there with little if any decay. Forgetting, according to these theories, is due not to the disappearance of items from storage but rather to difficulties in retrieving ones that are there. Retrieval is greatly facilitated if the contextual cues with which the word was associated during encoding are also present during retrieval: The more of these cues are present, the more activation will spread from their nodes to the target node, and thus the greater the likelihood of its reactivation. The effectiveness of a retrieval cue is diminished, however, if it is also associated with other memories. The more connections radiating out from a node, the less activation seems to flow through any one of them, and thus the less effective it will be as a retrieval cue.

12.3 STIMULUS CODING: RELATIONAL AND CONFIGURAL LEARNING

Having established a general framework for understanding memory, we will now consider how memory and attention can help us to understand associative learning. We will start in this section with research relevant to the coding of stimuli during associative learning; in subsequent sections we will examine the roles of retrieval and other processes.

S–R and Cognitive Theories of Coding

One of the earliest theories of stimulus encoding was proposed by S–R theorist Kenneth Spence (1936). As we saw earlier, the central tenet of S–R theory was that reinforcement stamps in associations between the reinforced response and whatever stimuli are present at the time. Regarding the nature of these stimuli, Spence proposed that any object or event could be regarded as a set of discrete elements and that each of these elements will form its own independent association with the reinforced response. Suppose, for example, that a rat was offered a choice between two cards, one of which always had food behind it. According to Spence, the various properties of this card—its color, size, shape, brightness—would each be associated independently with the reinforced response (Figure 12.5a).

Cognitive theorists rejected Spence's account on the grounds that it grossly oversimplified the role of perception in learning. Rather than directly associating the elements of a stimulus with a response, they argued, subjects would first transform or elaborate the raw sensory data in order to identify the objects in the real world that gave rise to them. It was only this transformed, or coded, stimulus—what Lawrence (1963) called the *stimulus as coded* (SAC)—that would be associated with the response (Figure 12.5b).

Transposition

As one example of such transformations, cognitive theorists said that subjects would search for relationships among stimuli. In our card example, suppose the positive card had an area of 200 square centimeters, and the negative one an area of 100 square centimeters. According to Spence, the size of the positive card (as well as its shape, brightness, and so on) would be associated directly with the approach response. According to cognitive theorists, on the other hand, subjects would first compare the two cards and encode the positive card in terms of its relative size. (If this seems unlikely, consider that the absolute size of any image on the retina is of little significance, since it will vary widely according to the object's distance. A 100-square-centimeter card may appear enormous at a distance of one inch, but it will appear miniscule at a distance of 100 yards.) Thus, whereas Spence believed that subjects would encode the positive stimulus as a card of 200 square centimeters, cognitive theorists said

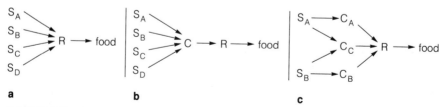

a   **b**   **c**

F I G U R E 12.5   Three theories of stimulus coding: (a) S–R theorists assumed that all elements of a stimulus would be associated independently with a reinforced response. (b) Cognitive theorists assumed that raw sensory input would be processed to produce a transformed or coded stimulus (C), and that it was this coded stimulus that would enter into any association. (c) Transposition and configural learning suggest that stimuli are coded in terms of both their independent properties and their relationships, and that any or all of these codes may then be associated with subsequent responses.

that subjects would learn to respond to the larger card. To put this another way, in cases where S–R theorists believed that subjects would code the absolute properties of any stimulus, regardless of what other stimuli were present, cognitive theorists believed that they would respond to the relational properties of the stimulus, as determined by its stimulus context.

Evidence for transposition.   To determine which of these analyses was correct, Austrian psychologist Wolfgang Kohler (1918/1939) trained two chimpanzees on a size discrimination activity involving 9 × 12 and 12 × 16 centimeter rectangles, with food placed behind the latter. After the chimpanzees had solved the problem, Kohler gave them test trials in which the formerly positive 12 × 16 centimeter rectangle was paired with a new rectangle measuring 15 × 20 centimeters (Figure 12.6). If the chimpanzees had coded the positive stimulus during training as a 12 × 16 centimeter card, they should continue to choose this card during the test phase; if they had learned to approach the larger card, they should prefer the 15 × 20 centimeter rectangle. In some respects, this is an extraordinary prediction—that after repeated reinforcement for approaching a particular card, subjects should ignore it and go to one they had never previously encountered—but this is exactly what Kohler found. The chimpanzees preferred the larger card on more than 90 percent of the test trials. This result, moreover, could not be attributed to any special intellectual capacities of chimpanzees, because Kohler obtained almost exactly the same results using baby chicks as subjects.

The most obvious explanation for the performance of Kohler's animals was that they had learned about the relationship between the cards during training, and that they based their responding during the test phase on this same relationship. Because they seemed to be transferring, or transposing, the relationship they had learned during training to the test problem, this phenomenon became known as **transposition**.

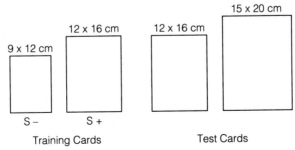

F I G U R E 12.6   Training and test cards used by Kohler (1918/1939). Food was located behind the 12 × 16 centimeter rectangle during training.

Spence's S–R model of transposition.   Transposition seemed to provide conclusive evidence that stimuli are coded in terms of their relationships. In a
brilliant paper published in 1937, however, Spence argued that transposition
could be explained in terms of simple associative principles, without invoking
complex perceptual processes. The first principle Spence appealed to was reinforcement: A response followed by a reinforcer will be associated with whatever
stimuli are present at the time. Spence's second principle was extinction: If a
response is not reinforced, an inhibitory connection will be established between the stimuli present and the response. The third principle was generalization: Both excitatory and inhibitory tendencies generalize to similar stimuli.

   To see how these three simple principles could account for transposition,
we will trace one of the hypothetical examples provided by Spence. Suppose,
he said, that subjects were trained on a size discrimination involving cards of
256 and 160 square centimeters, with food available behind the larger card
(hereafter referred to as 256+). As a result of reinforcement in the presence of
this stimulus, an excitatory connection would be formed between it and responding. Similarly, nonreinforcement of responding to 160− would result in
an inhibitory association between this stimulus and responding. Both of these
tendencies would generalize to similar stimuli, and although very little information about the shape of generalization gradients was available at the time
Spence wrote, he speculated that both excitatory and inhibitory generalization
gradients would have the concave form illustrated in Figure 12.7. (At the time
Spence wrote, only two experiments had ever been published on the generalization of excitation, and none on the generalization of inhibition.)

   The first point to notice about this graph (Figure 12.7) is that, because of
generalization, most stimuli would have both excitatory and inhibitory associa-

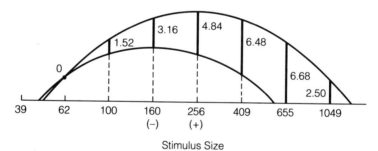

Stimulus Size

F I G U R E 12.7   Hypothetical generalization gradients proposed by Spence to account
for transposition. Reinforcement of choices of a 256-square-centimeter card would produce a positive generalization gradient around 256; nonreinforcement of a 160-square-
centimeter card would produce an inhibitory generalization gradient around 160. The net
associative strength of any stimulus would be the difference between the positive and
negative gradients; the numerical values for selected stimuli are indicated. (Adapted from
Spence, 1937)

tions with responding. There was no experimental evidence to suggest how these opposing tendencies would combine to determine responding, so Spence chose the simplest possible combination rule: that the net associative strength of any stimulus would be the sum of its positive and negative tendencies. If a stimulus had a generalized excitatory strength of +4.0 units, for example, and an inhibitory strength of -1.5 units, then its net associative strength would be:

$$4.0 + (-1.5) = +2.5$$

Assigning arbitrary values to the positive and negative stimuli used during training, Spence was then able to calculate how these tendencies would generalize to other stimuli and how these generalized values would combine to determine responding. This value for several representative stimuli is represented graphically in Figure 12.7 by the height of the line separating the excitatory and inhibitory gradients (that is, by the difference in their strengths) and is also given numerically. Looking at stimulus 256+, for example, we can see that its net strength after training would be 4.84 units, whereas that of stimulus 160− would be only 3.16. At the end of training, therefore, we should expect subjects to prefer 256+ to 160−, because its net associative strength would be greater. Notice, however, what would happen if subjects were presented with a choice between 256+ and the still larger stimulus of 409 square centimeters. Even though 409 had never been presented previously, its net associative strength would be greater than that of the 256+ stimulus, which was reinforced. By taking generalization into account, in other words, Spence was able to explain transposition without invoking any of the internal processing mechanisms postulated by cognitive theorists.

Testing the model.   As well as accounting for Kohler's data on transposition, Spence's model allows predictions about learning in many other situations. For example, the model can be applied not only to transposition experiments in which the training stimuli are presented simultaneously, but also to successive discrimination studies in which only one stimulus is present at a time. In an experiment on pigeons by Hanson (1959), for example, a key was illuminated alternately with lights of 550 and 590 nm, with pecking reinforced only in the presence of the 550-nm wavelength. The birds then received a series of non-reinforced presentations of other wavelengths in order to measure generalization.

According to Spence's analysis, during training an excitatory gradient should have been established around 550+ and an inhibitory gradient around 590−. If these gradients combined in the manner predicted by Spence, then peak responding during the test phase should have occurred not to 550+ but rather to some shorter wavelength, away from 590−. As shown in Figure 12.8, this **peak shift** is what Hanson found. In a control group trained only with

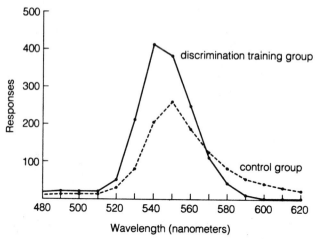

F I G U R E 12.8   Generalization gradients following training with only a 550-nm stimulus (control) or discrimination training between 550+ and 590– (discrimination). (Adapted from Hanson, 1959)

550+, peak responding during the generalization test was to the 550-nm wavelength, but in the discrimination training group the peak was shifted to 540 nm. Spence's model thus correctly predicted the almost bizarre finding that peak responding occurred not to the stimulus reinforced during training but to one displaced away from the negative stimulus (S–). [*]

The occurrence of peak shift, even under conditions in which S+ and S– were never present at the same time during training, provides strong support for Spence's assumption of interacting generalization gradients. (See also Honig, Boneau, Burstein, & Pennypacker, 1963.) Other evidence, however, suggests that although excitatory and inhibitory gradients do play an important role in discrimination learning, they cannot account for all of the evidence concerning transposition. A particularly neat illustration of this point

---

[*] One aspect of this study that was certainly not as Spence predicted was the height of the postdiscrimination gradient. Spence's generalization-of-inhibition analysis predicts that peak responding should shift from 550 nm to a shorter wavelength and that the level of responding to this wavelength should be less than in the control group. As shown in the graph, however, responding to 540 nm was substantially greater in the group given nonreinforced trials with 590–. The cause of this elevation is probably related to the phenomenon of amount contrast discussed in Chapter 6. Experience with a small amount of reinforcement, we saw then, enhances the effectiveness of larger amounts; in a similar fashion, it has been found that low rates of reinforcement may enhance the effectiveness of higher rates—a phenomenon known as *behavioral contrast*. In the group given discrimination training, nonreinforcement in the presence of 590 nm may have enhanced the effectiveness of reinforcement in the presence of 550 nm, thereby increasing responding. The final generalization gradient may thus be determined by an interaction among at least three processes: generalized excitation, generalized inhibition, and behavioral contrast.

comes from an experiment by Lawrence and DeRivera (1954), who trained rats on a brightness discrimination involving seven cards ranging in brightness from white (card 1) to black (card 7) in roughly equal steps. During training, the mid-gray card (card 4) was present on every trial, with one of the other cards mounted above it (Figure 12.9a). If the top card was light (card 1, 2, or 3), the rat was reinforced for going to the right; if it was dark (card 5, 6, or 7), the rat was reinforced for going to the left.

According to relational theory, the rats should have solved this problem on the basis of the relationship between the cards: If the top card was brighter, go right; if darker, go left. According to S–R theory, on the other hand, responding should be conditioned independently to each of the elements present on a reinforced trial. Turning to the right, therefore, should have become conditioned to cards 1, 2, and 3, since each would have been present on trials in which this response was reinforced. Similarly, cards 5, 6, and 7 should have become associated with a turn to the left. As for card 4, since it was present on trials in which turns to both right and left were reinforced, it should have become associated with both responses, and hence effectively neutral.

Since both theories predict successful learning, how can we decide which one is correct? Lawrence and DeRivera's solution was simple: They reversed the cards. Instead of presenting card 1 on top of card 4, for example, they presented 4 on top of 1 (Figure 12.9b). If subjects had solved the original problem on the basis of relationships, they should now reverse their responses, because the top card was now darker than the bottom one. If responding had been conditioned to each of the elements separately, on the other hand, subjects should continue to respond as they had during training, because card 4 would still be neutral and card 1 would still elicit a turn to the right. Unfortunately for S–R theory, more than 75 percent of the responses were reversed, indicating that the relationship between the cards was crucial in determining responding.

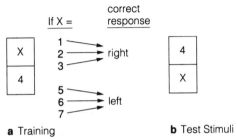

a Training **b** Test Stimuli

F I G U R E 12.9   Training and test stimuli used by Lawrence and DeRivera (1954). The cards varied in brightness between white (card 1) and black (card 7). The bottom card during training was always card 4. If the top card was 1, 2, or 3, a turn to the right was reinforced; if the top card was 5, 6, or 7, a turn to the left was reinforced.

Evaluating the model. Together with other evidence (see Hebert & Krantz, 1965), these results make it clear that subjects do sometimes code stimuli in terms of their relationship to each other. The fact that subjects can code relationships, however, does not mean that they always respond on this basis: There is considerable evidence that subjects also respond to the absolute properties of stimuli, and the current consensus is that subjects normally code both aspects of stimuli. In the Kohler experiment, for example, it is likely that the chimpanzees coded the correct card in terms of its absolute properties ("It is a 12 × 16 centimeter rectangle") as well as its relation to surrounding stimuli ("It is the larger rectangle"). According to this view, the property of the stimulus that will govern responding during testing depends on the precise characteristics of the test stimuli used, with transposition being observed with some test stimuli but absolute responding with others (Lane & Rabinowitz, 1979; Thomas, Mood, Morrison, & Wiertelak, 1991).

Configural Learning

Further evidence that stimuli are not always coded independently comes from experiments on **configural learning.** In one of the first experiments of this kind, Woodbury (1943) gave dogs trials with either a high-pitched buzzer (H), a low-pitched buzzer (L), or both together (HL). If the buzzers were presented on their own, responding on a lever was reinforced, but not if the buzzers were presented together:

$$H \; : R \longrightarrow food$$
$$L \; : R \longrightarrow food$$
$$HL : R \longrightarrow$$

The results for one of Woodbury's dogs, Chuck, are shown in Figure 12.10. When the buzzers were presented separately, Chuck responded on virtu-

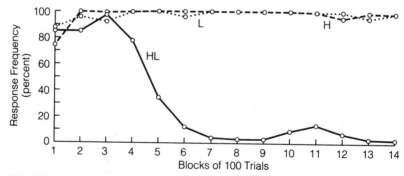

FIGURE 12.10 Configural learning. Presentations of high-pitched (H) and low-pitched (L) tones by themselves were reinforced, but the compound (HL) was not. (Adapted from Woodbury, 1943)

ally every trial. When they were presented in compound, at first Chuck also responded; as training continued, though, this response gradually extinguished. Thus, even though both elements of the compound elicited vigorous responding, when presented together there was no response.

This result is utterly mystifying if a compound is coded solely in terms of its constituent elements. If H elicits responding, and L elicits responding, then H and L together should also elicit responding. The result begins to make sense, however, if we assume that stimuli presented together may form a unique stimulus, or configuration, that is not like either of its components. If we relabel the HL compound as C to emphasize its unique qualities, then Woodbury's procedure can be represented as:

$$H : R \longrightarrow food$$
$$L : R \longrightarrow food$$
$$C : R \longrightarrow$$

Viewed in this light, it is hardly surprising that subjects eventually ceased to respond when the compound was presented.

The assumption that a compound is a totally unique stimulus, however, raises its own problems: If the HL compound bore no resemblance to its components (and this assumption is necessary to explain why responding to H and L did not generalize to HL), then why did the dogs continue to respond to the compound for hundreds of trials, even though responses on this trial were never reinforced? Rescorla suggested a possible solution. (There are those who believe that Rescorla is not a person, but a team of brilliant researchers working night and day who share the name.) According to Rescorla's "unique stimulus" hypothesis (Rescorla, 1973), an AB compound can be viewed as consisting of three stimuli: A, B, and a unique stimulus arising from their conjunction, which we will again label C. Thus, in Woodbury's experiment, H and L were paired with reinforcement, but the HLC compound was not. Applying the Rescorla-Wagner model to this situation, Rescorla (1973) was able to show that the compound would initially elicit responding because of the reinforcement given to H and L, but that with continued training C would become sufficiently inhibitory to block responding on the compound trials. This analysis can account for a wide range of experiments involving children (Zeaman & Hanley, 1983) as well as animals (Rescorla, 1973).

In summary, it is now clear that subjects do not process stimuli in total isolation. In the case of configural learning, the elements of a compound may be combined to form an integrated unit, with its own unique properties. (For a discussion of factors that encourage such perceptual integration, see Shepp, 1983; Rescorla, 1985b.) Similarly, the evidence for transposition indicates that subjects may actively compare contiguous stimuli and then store information about the relationship between them ("larger" or "brighter") as well as their absolute properties ("100 square centimeters" or "white"). In both cases, responding may be conditioned to the transformed or coded stimulus—the compound or the relationship—as well as to the separate elements. Thus, a more realistic view of coding is that shown in Figure 12.5c (p. 444). If two stimuli are presented together, each may receive its own code (C_A, C_B); in addition, information about their relationship may be stored in a third code (C_C); responding, then, may be conditioned to any or all of these codes.

12.4 STIMULUS CODING: ATTENTION

We have examined one of Spence's assumptions about encoding—that each stimulus is processed independently; we turn now to his second assumption—that all of the stimuli present when a response is reinforced will be associated with it. Spence assumed that if a large red triangle were reinforced, for example, all the features of this object would become associated with the correct response. Cognitive theorists, on the other hand, argued that the brain simply does not have the capacity to process all of the stimuli bombarding the senses, so that only some subset—those stimuli to which the subject attended—would be associated with any response. The issue was thus a very simple one: Do all stimuli present during reinforcement become associated with responding, or only a subset of those stimuli? But this simple issue proved remarkably difficult to answer. (For a review, see Mackintosh, 1965.) As in the case of transposition and latent extinction, many of the early skirmishes were won by S–R theory, but in the end it was the cognitive position that triumphed. It is now abundantly clear that the stimuli present during reinforcement do not all become associated with the response, so that some sort of selective mechanism must be taken into account.

Selective Attention

We will not try to unravel the intricate skein of argument that eventually led to this conclusion, but the central point is nicely illustrated in an experiment by Reynolds (1961). Using two pigeons as subjects, Reynolds trained them on a successive discrimination in which two stimuli were presented alternately for three minutes at a time. When the key was illuminated with the outline of a white triangle against a red background (S+), pecking was occasionally reinforced, but not when the stimulus was the outline of a white circle against a green background (S−). (See Figure 12.11a.) According to S–R theory, both components of S+ (the triangular shape and the red color) should have acquired control over pecking. According to an attentional analysis, on the other hand, only a subset of the stimuli present can be fully processed, and although this does not necessarily mean only one stimulus will receive attention—processing capacity is not necessarily that limited—it does leave open the

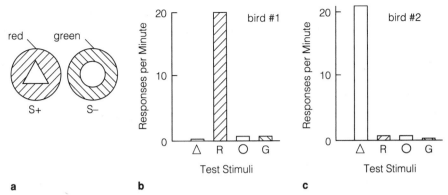

F I G U R E 12.11   Selective attention. During training, responses to a white triangle on a red background (S+) were reinforced; responses to a white circle on a green background (S−) were not. Test trials presented each element—triangle, red, circle, green—separately. Bird 1 responded to the color red, but not the triangle; bird 2 responded to the triangle, but not the color red. (Adapted from Reynolds, 1961)

possibility that Reynolds's birds would learn only about the triangle or only about the color red.

To test what the birds had learned, Reynolds simply presented the elements of each compound separately, illuminating the key with either the circle, the triangle, red, or green. Figure 12.11b shows the results for bird number 1. According to S–R theory, the red and triangle components should have elicited roughly equal responding, but this was not the case: The bird responded vigorously when the key was red, but ignored the triangle. The second bird, on the other hand, responded at a high rate when the triangle was present, but virtually not at all when the key was red (Figure 12.11c)! Both birds, in other words, learned about only one of the two stimuli present. This result illustrates the empirical phenomenon of **selective attention**, in which only a subset of the stimuli present comes to control responding.

Given that selection does occur, what determines which stimuli will be selected? In part, the determinants seem to be innate. Both monkeys and young children, for example, are significantly more likely to attend to the color of objects than to their shapes (Warren, 1954; Zeaman & Hanley, 1983). Experience, however, can lead to substantial changes in attentional preferences: We learn to attend to stimuli that have predictive value and ignore those that do not. In an experiment by Lubow and Moore (1959), for example, a flashing light was presented 10 times to a group of sheep and goats. When this same light was then paired with an electric shock, subjects who had received prior exposure to the light were conditioned significantly more slowly than untreated controls. Lubow and Moore called this phenomenon **latent inhibition** in the belief that presentations of the light on its own had endowed it with inhibitory properties, but subsequent research has made it clear that the light became neither excitatory nor inhibitory (for example, Reiss & Wagner, 1972). Rather, because the light had no significance during pretraining, the animals learned to ignore it, with the result that subsequent conditioning was impaired. (For a fuller analysis, see Mackintosh, 1983.)

A Perceptual Model of Attention

The dimensional model.   As the reality of selective attention became more clearly established in the late 1960s and early 1970s, researchers proposed a number of theoretical models to integrate the available information (for example, Zeaman & House, 1963; Sutherland & Mackintosh, 1971). Although these models differed in a number of respects, they also shared many features in common. Figure 12.12 presents a simplified outline of these common features. To help understand this figure, consider a situation in which a subject must choose between a red triangle and a green circle. The subject might attend to the shape of these objects, to their color, their size, and so on, but theories of selective attention assume that not all of these dimensions can be analyzed simultaneously. Paying attention to color can be thought of as a response, paying attention to shape as another response, and so on. Saying that attention is limited, therefore, is equivalent to saying that we can make only a limited number of analyzing or observing responses at one time. If a subject chooses to attend to the objects' colors, then chooses the red object and is reinforced, the model assumes that this reinforcement will strengthen not only the overt choice response but also the observing response that preceded it. Thus, in

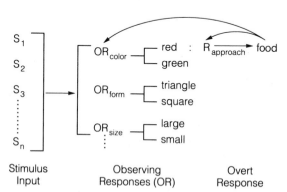

FIGURE 12.12   A dimensional model of attention. When presented with an object, subjects are assumed to analyze or observe only some of its dimensions. If the choice of a particular object is reinforced, this is assumed to strengthen not only the tendency to choose the particular stimulus analyzed (for example, red) but also to attend to the dimension on which it lies (color).

addition to acquiring a fetish for red objects, this subject should also develop a general tendency to attend to colors.

Dimensional models of attention, then, assume that subjects analyze stimuli in terms of dimensions, that they can process only a limited number of dimensions at any one time, and that reinforcement will strengthen not only overt behavior but also attention to particular dimensions. These models stimulated a flood of experiments to test their common assumptions and, where they differed, to establish which ones were superior. A full review of this literature is beyond the scope of this text, but we will consider two experimental paradigms that proved particularly informative: ED versus ID shifts, and blocking. (For coverage of other issues, see Mackintosh, 1975; Zeaman & House, 1979.)

ED versus ID shifts.   One key assumption of these models was that subjects learn to attend not to particular features of objects but to the dimensions along which these features lie. Thus, rather than attending specifically to red, subjects would attend to the dimension of color and analyze whatever colors were present. One way to test this prediction is to train subjects on one problem involving color and then on a second problem involving different colors. If they have learned a general tendency to attend to color while solving the first problem, they should be much better at solving the second problem than a control group not initially trained on color.

The most sophisticated design for achieving this objective involves a comparison of **intradimensional (ID) shifts** (in which the cues within the stimulus dimension change but the dimension remains the same) and **extradimensional (ED) shifts** (in which the relevant stimuli shift to a new dimension). We will illustrate this approach with a simplified outline of an experiment by Eimas (1966). In the first stage of this experiment, Eimas gave children discrimination training involving the pairs of objects shown in Figure 12.13a. For one group, color was the relevant dimension, and they were rewarded whenever they selected the red object in each pair. For a second group, the same stimuli were used, but form was the relevant dimension, and the children were reinforced for choosing the circle.

Then, to find out whether the children had learned to attend to particular stimuli or to dimensions, Eimas gave his subjects a second problem involving new shapes and colors (Figure 12.13b). For both groups, the basis of solution was color, with either blue or yellow being correct for different subgroups. For the group originally trained with color being relevant, this new problem involved an intradimensional (ID) shift: Although the cues within the color dimension had changed, color was still the relevant dimension. For the form group, on the other hand, the new problem represented an extradimensional (ED) shift: The relevant stimuli now lay along a different dimension.

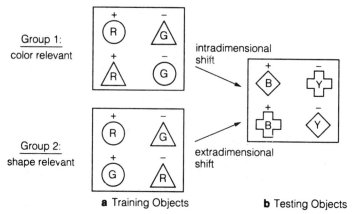

a Training Objects   **b** Testing Objects

F I G U R E 12.13   Representative stimuli used in intradimensional (ID) and extradimensional (ED) shifts. The shapes are colored either red (R), green (G), yellow (Y), or blue (B); the correct object in each pair is marked +, and the incorrect object is marked −. For subjects in the ID-shift group, the correct objects during both training and testing can be identified by their color; for subjects in the ED-shift group, the relevant dimension is shape during training but color during testing.

If subjects had learned to attend to specific stimuli during the first problem, the color pretraining group should do no better than the form pretraining group, because the colors they had learned to attend to during training were no longer present. According to a dimensional analysis, on the other hand, the color group learned to attend to color on the first problem, and thus should immediately attend to the correct dimension on the second problem. The form group, however, would start by attending to form rather than color, and thus should take longer to learn.

The results strongly supported the dimensional prediction: Subjects tested on the same dimension that had been relevant during pretraining learned significantly faster. Similar tests have been reported in experiments with animals (for example, Shepp & Schrier, 1969; Mackintosh & Little, 1969), and the results in all cases have confirmed that ID shifts are significantly easier than ED ones. The clear implication is that reinforcement for attention to a dimension in one problem increases the tendency to attend to that dimension in other situations. (See also Kemler & Shepp, 1971.)

Blocking: Attention as a Central Process

The results of studies of ED and ID shifts provided considerable support for dimensional models of attention, but the publication in 1969 of Kamin's work on blocking (Chapter 4) challenged one of the fundamental assumptions of existing theories of attention—namely, that selective attention was caused by a limitation in perceptual capacity, which meant that subjects could only process or attend to a small number of stimuli at any one time. Kamin, you may recall, gave two groups of rats fear-conditioning trials with a noise-light (NL) compound presented for three minutes, followed by an electric shock. One of the groups, however, received preliminary training in which the noise by itself was paired with shock:

	Pretraining	*Conditioning*
experimental group:	16 N ⟶ shock	8 NL ⟶ shock
control group:		8 NL ⟶ shock

When he later measured fear conditioning to the light, Kamin found strong conditioning in the control group but almost none in the group that was given preliminary pairings of the noise and shock. The earlier conditioning of fear to the noise seemed to block conditioning to the light when they were presented together.

Why should previous conditioning to one element of a compound block conditioning to the other element? One obvious explanation was provided by dimensional models of attention. During the pretraining trials in which the noise was paired with shock, the rats might have learned to attend to the noise, so that on the compound trials they would have been less likely to attend to the light and hence to associate it with shock.

We can explain blocking, then, if we assume that pretraining with the noise blocked attention to the light during the compound trials. Recall, however, that the noise and light were presented together for three minutes. Although a rat's processing capacity may be limited, it strains credulity to suppose that it could detect only a single stimulus in the course of three minutes! Moreover, Kamin was able to present empirical evidence that his rats had detected the light. Both the pretraining and conditioning trials had taken place during sessions in which the rats were also pressing a bar to obtain food, so Kamin could measure the suppressive effects of the stimuli on every conditioning trial. On the final trial during pretraining, the noise produced a suppression ratio of 0.02 (that is, strong conditioning). When the light was introduced on the next trial, however, the suppression ratio rose to 0.15. In other words, the rats clearly had detected the light, since introducing the light produced an immediate change in their behavior. If the rats attended to the light on this trial, though, why was fear not conditioned to it?

Kamin's memory-scan hypothesis.   Kamin's explanation, as we saw in Chapter 4, was that the occurrence of an important event such as electric shock would lead subjects to look back through their memories to identify possible causes or predictors of this event. This search, however, would require effort; to save time and energy, Kamin speculated, subjects would not scan their memories every time a US was presented, but only if the US was unexpected or surprising. If the US was expected, then, by definition, cues predicting its occurrence were already available, and no further search was necessary.

Let's apply this analysis to blocking. When the noise was followed by shock during pretraining, the occurrence of the shock would at first have been totally surprising, leading to an active search for stimuli that could have predicted it. Once subjects learned that the noise was always followed by shock, however, the shock's occurrence would no longer have been surprising and thus would no longer have triggered a memory search. By the end of pretraining, in other words, the occurrence of the shock no longer would have produced learning.

Testing the hypothesis. When the light was added to the noise on the compound trials, its introduction would have been a significant departure from the conditions during pretraining, so at first subjects might not have been certain that the shock would still follow. On the first compound trial, therefore, the shock might have engendered some degree of surprise and thus a small amount of conditioning. Once subjects realized that the noise was still a reliable predictor, however, the occurrence of the shock no longer would have been surprising. With the possible exception of the first trial, therefore, no memory search would have occurred on any of the compound trials, and hence no association would have been formed between the light and shock. Thus, whereas an attentional analysis attributes blocking in this case to a failure to attend to the light, Kamin argued that the rats were fully aware of the light but that, because the shock was not surprising, the rats made no attempt to form an association between the two events.

Could this hypothetical reconstruction of what was going on in the rat's mind really be correct? To find out, Kamin ran a third group, which, like the first experimental group, received 16 pretraining trials with a noise paired with shock, followed by 8 noise-light compound trials. At the conclusion of each three-minute noise-light presentation, the rats received an electric shock, as had all the earlier subjects, but then, after a five-second delay, they received a second shock:

$$16 \text{ N} \longrightarrow \text{shock } 8 \text{ NL} \longrightarrow \text{shock} \ldots \text{shock}$$

According to an attentional analysis, adding the second shock should have no effect. During pretraining, the rats would have learned to attend to the noise, so that when the light was introduced they would not process it. Adding a second shock should not change this result: If the rats did not notice the light, they would not be able to associate it with the second shock any more than with the first.

According to Kamin's surprise analysis, on the other hand, the introduction of this second shock should significantly alter the outcome. During pretraining, the rats would have learned that the noise was followed by a shock; on the compound trials, then, the rats would expect the occurrence of the first shock. The second shock, however, would come as a complete surprise, so the rats would search their memories for possible causes, notice the preceding light, and associate it with the shock. The presence of the second shock, in other words, should restore conditioning to the light. This was what Kamin found. When fear conditioning to the light was assessed in a CER test, suppression in the experimental group was just as great as in the control group not given pretraining (suppression ratios of 0.08 and 0.05, respectively). In other words, the rats apparently noticed the light, because when the light was followed by a surprising event, conditioning did occur.

Blocking in humans.   Further evidence that subjects really are aware of both elements of the compound has come from experiments on university students by Trabasso and Bower (1968). The overall design of their experiment was similar to that of Kamin's, except that the stimuli were strings of four letters (such as *MBKR*). The subjects' task was to read each string out loud and then decide whether it was an *alpha* or a *beta*, according to undisclosed criteria. The experimenter then told the subjects whether they had classified the string correctly.

Sixteen different strings were used, and the correct basis of classification was whether the second letter in the string was an *L* (alpha) or a *B* (beta). After subjects had learned to classify all the strings correctly, the stimulus set was changed so that all members of a category shared two features instead of just one. Specifically, the fourth letter of each string (*R* or *W*) now also predicted the classification. Finally, to determine if the subjects had learned anything about the fourth letter during this phase, the subjects were given test strings in which the second letter was blank (for example, *Z–KW*), so the string could be correctly classified only on the basis of the fourth letter. The results were virtually identical to Kamin's: Subjects given pretraining with one predictive feature failed to learn anything when a second predictive cue was introduced. Since the subjects had been required to read each letter out loud, they certainly "noticed" each letter, but, as in Kamin's study, they nevertheless failed to associate this stimulus with the outcome. The implication is that pretraining with one element of a compound blocks learning not because of a failure to detect the other element, but because it renders the outcome predictable; only if the outcome is unexpected or surprising will subjects search for predictive cues. (For some provocative qualifications on this conclusion, see Dickinson, Hall, & Mackintosh, 1976.)

Summary

Let us try to summarize the material in this section. Theorists such as Spence argued that all stimuli present during reinforcement are associated with the reinforced response, but experiments such as Reynolds's made it clear that some sort of selective mechanism must be postulated. Phenomena such as latent inhibition and ED versus ID shifts have further established that experience plays an important role in this selection process: Stimuli that have no predictive value come to be ignored, whereas those correlated with reinforcement receive greater attention. Selective attention, then, undoubtedly does occur, in the sense that we may learn more about some elements of a compound than others. Contrary to the implicit assumption of dimensional models of attention, however, selective attention is not necessarily due to a failure to perceive the stimuli: Both rats and university students failed to learn about stimuli whose presence they clearly noticed.

This does not mean that limited sensory capacity never plays a role in learning. When many stimuli are presented simultaneously and only limited time is available to process them, limitations in perceptual capacity may well play a significant role (Riley & Leith, 1976; but see also Lamb, 1991). In experiments such as Reynolds's and Kamin's, however, in which two stimuli are presented for three minutes at a time, it is simply not credible that subjects did not notice both stimuli (even if many psychologists believed precisely that!). In most real-life situations, it seems likely that ample time is available for stimuli to be detected, so that insofar as learning is selective, the selection must occur at some point following coding.

Logically, there are at least three possible reasons why a successfully coded stimulus might not be associated with a subsequent reinforcer:

1. The reinforcer does not initiate a memory search.

2. A search is initiated but does not retrieve the coded stimulus.

3. The stimulus is retrieved but nevertheless is not associated with the reinforcer.

In the following sections we will consider each of these possibilities.

12.5 THE ROLE OF THE REINFORCER: SURPRISE!

Given that a stimulus has been coded, what determines whether it will enter into an association with subsequent events? On this issue, as on many others, S–R and cognitive theorists adopted very different positions. According to S–R theorists such as Hull (1943), the critical condition determining whether learning will occur is reinforcement: If a reinforcer is presented, then learning will occur; otherwise, it will not. Whereas Kamin's work on blocking challenged the first assumption (that the presence of a reinforcer guarantees learning), it supported the second assumption—that learning would occur only under special circumstances. Indeed, blocking made the class of triggering events even more restrictive: Not just any reinforcer, but only unexpected ones, would be effective.

Cognitive theorists such as Tolman, on the other hand, argued that we are constantly exploring the world around us and learning about its features, whether or not we are reinforced for doing so. Cognitive theorists viewed learning not as a rare event triggered only under special conditions, but as a continuous process affecting every facet of daily life. In earlier chapters, moreover, we have already encountered considerable evidence supporting the cognitive view. In Chapter 2, for example, we discussed research on sensory preconditioning which showed that pairing stimuli such as a light and a tone was sufficient to establish an association between them, even though neither stimulus could plausibly be described as a reinforcer or "special event." Similarly, experiments on latent learning have shown that simple exposure to a maze was enough to allow rats to learn its layout, and experiments on perceptual learning have shown that subjects improve at discriminating stimuli such as faces or wines if simply exposed to them (Chapter 9). In all of these cases, reinforcement was not necessary for learning: Simple exposure to stimuli was sufficient to produce substantial learning about the relationships between them.

A Surprising Hypothesis

How can we reconcile these apparently contradictory conclusions? On the one hand, learning seems to be occurring all the time; on the other hand, blocking suggests that learning is a difficult process initiated only when an unexpected reinforcer is obtained. One possible resolution would be to accept the contention of reinforcement theorists that a special event of some kind is necessary for learning to occur, but to argue that this special event need not be a reinforcer: Perhaps any surprising event—a new room or an unexpected noise, as well as unpredicted food or shock—will trigger a search through memory for possible causes.

A mechanism of this sort might be of considerable survival value. A rat, for example, needs an accurate representation of its environment if it is to obtain food or escape from predators; similarly, it needs to explore new stimuli to determine their possible significance. According to this analysis, curiosity, far from killing the cat, is probably what kept it alive. Once a situation becomes familiar, however, there is no need to continue to explore it; thus, familiar stimuli will elicit neither exploratory behavior nor memory searches for predictive cues.

Marking

According to this surprise hypothesis, any salient and surprising stimulus should trigger a search for causes. Some support for this prediction comes from a series of experiments by Lieberman and Thomas (for example, Lieberman, McIntosh, & Thomas, 1979; Lieberman & Thomas, 1986; Thomas, Robertson, & Lieberman, 1987). In the first of these experiments, Lieberman, McIntosh, and Thomas trained rats in a modified T-maze in which turns to the right were rewarded with food after a one-minute delay, and turns to the left were not. As we saw in Chapter 6, even quite small delays in reinforcement typically have devastating effects on learning, and the rats in this experiment were no exception: They consistently failed to learn to turn right—unless, that is, they were picked up by the experimenter immediately after they made their choice response and then replaced in the maze and allowed to resume their journey! Subjects that were picked up in this way learned to enter the correct arm of the maze on an impressive 90 percent of trials, compared to only 50 percent for the unhandled controls.

Why should picking up animals after they make their choice responses enhance learning? One obvious possibility is that being handled is reinforcing, and that these rats were receiving immediate reinforcement every time they made the correct response. This explanation, however, doesn't work: The rats were picked up after incorrect choice responses as well as correct ones, so that any reinforcing properties of handling would have strengthened incorrect responses as much as correct ones. Why, then, did the handled rats learn?

A possible explanation lies in the surprise analysis presented above. When the rats were picked up, this must have been a rather startling event, and, as such, would have triggered a search through memory for possible causes. Since the last response made before being picked up was the choice response, the rats would have been particularly likely to identify this choice response as the cause of their misfortune. The experimenters suggested that the extra processing or attention paid to this response would have effectively marked it in the rat's memory so the rat would remember the response better. When the rats received food at the end of the trial, this food would have triggered another memory search for possible causes, and the handled rats would have been more likely to recall the marked choice response and associate it with food. Lieberman, McIntosh, and Thomas called this phenomenon **marking**.

Lieberman and his colleagues speculated that any salient and unexpected stimulus might enhance memory for the behavior that preceded it and, in a series of experiments, found evidence consistent with this analysis. For example, learning of the correct response was enhanced if followed not only by handling, but also by a brief light or noise. The effect also depended on the marker's occurring soon after the response to be learned; when there was a delay, some other response was more likely to precede the marker and thus to receive extra attention. The evidence for marking, then, is consistent with the view that any salient or novel stimulus may trigger learning about preceding events.

Note that the surprise hypothesis does not say that surprise is the *only* factor that determines whether learning will occur; the innate or learned importance of the stimuli concerned could also be important. Suppose, for example, that you were hit on the head by a feather or a baseball. The two events might be equally unexpected, but it would not be altogether surprising if the baseball attracted more attention and promoted a rather more vigorous search for antecedent causes. Reinforcement theory, in other words, is not totally wrong: Some events are undoubtedly more effective in producing learning than others. The class of events that will trigger a memory search, however, is far broader than reinforcers as conventionally defined.

12.6 RETRIEVAL

Suppose that a surprising event does occur and that it initiates a search for possible causes or predictors. What events are likely to be recalled? One possibility is that subjects will simply recall whatever events happen to be in their short-term memory at the time the surprising event occurs. We have seen, however, that rats develop aversions to foods eaten up to 24 hours before they became ill, and it is highly unlikely that the code for this food remained in active or short-term memory for the entire 24 hours. Almost certainly, therefore, subjects search memories in long-term as well as short-term storage—or, to use the terminology suggested by Lewis (1979), *inactive* as well as *active memory*. Given the enormous size of this storehouse, we now return rather more soberly to our original question: What determines which items will be retrieved?

Effects of Rehearsal on Memory

As we saw earlier, the likelihood that an event will be recalled depends on how much attention or rehearsal it received during coding: The more a word is rehearsed while in short-term memory, the better it will be remembered. (For distinctions between different kinds of rehearsal, however, see Cermak & Craik, 1979.) It may at first seem strange to think that animals might also be able to rehearse events in short-term memory—the very term *rehearsal* clearly implies repetition of words by saying them out loud or subvocally—but there is evidence that human subjects can also rehearse nonverbal material such as pictures (Watkins, Peynircioglu, & Burns, 1984). It is thus not altogether implausible that an animal's ability to remember an event might also depend on how much processing this event received during coding.

Stimulus duration.   Evidence that rehearsal during coding enhances memory in animals comes from an experiment by Grant (1976) on the effects of stimulus exposure time on memory. Grant hypothesized that the longer the duration of a stimulus, the more time subjects would have to process it, and the better they would remember it. To test this prediction, he used what has become one of the most popular techniques for studying short-term memory in animals, *delayed matching to sample (DMTS)*. In this procedure, the subject is shown one stimulus, called the sample, and then, after a delay, is offered a choice between that stimulus and another one. If the subject chooses the same stimulus as the sample (matching), it is rewarded. Performance on this task provides a simple index of how well the subject remembers the sample.

Grant used pigeons as subjects, and colors as sample and comparison stimuli. On a typical trial, the center key of a three-key array was illuminated with a red light, and then, after a delay, the side keys were illuminated with red and green lights (Figure 12.14). If the bird matched the sample by pecking the red side key, it was reinforced; if it pecked the green key, the trial terminated without reward. Grant varied the duration of the sample and also the interval between presentation of the sample and comparison stimuli. As shown in Figure 12.15, the longer that subjects had to remember the sample, the poorer their performance. The longer the sample had been presented, however, the better the subjects recalled it, suggesting that increased processing time leads to better memory.

Stimulus predictability.   Although Grant's study provides clear evidence for the importance of processing time, the processing in this case could have been determined solely by the continued presence of the external stimulus. There is no need to suppose that the pigeon could control or allocate its processing capacity as humans can. Stronger evidence for what might be called "internally

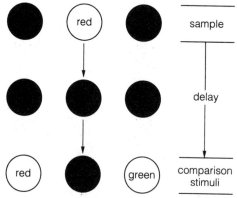

F I G U R E 12.14   Delayed matching to sample (DMTS) procedure. The sample is presented on the center key and then, after a delay during which the keys are dark, the same stimulus is presented on one of the side keys and an alternative on the other. Pecks to either side key terminate the trial; the pigeon is reinforced only if it has pecked the stimulus that matched the sample. In many DMTS experiments, including that of Grant (1976), the center key is initially white and the pigeon must peck it to produce the sample.

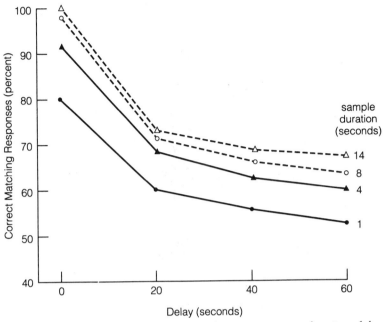

F I G U R E 12.15 Percentage of correct matching responses as a function of the duration of the sample and the delay between the sample and comparison stimuli. (Grant, 1976)

generated" rehearsal in animals (that is, processing not under the direct control of an external stimulus) comes from an experiment by Maki (1979).

The intuition underlying Maki's experiment was that the amount of attention paid to any stimulus would depend on how surprised subjects were by its occurrence: The more unexpected a stimulus is, the more attention it should attract, and the better it should be remembered. Maki tested this prediction using food as the stimulus to be remembered. Pigeons were first trained on a visual discrimination task in which they had to peck either a red key or a green key: If food was presented approximately 12 seconds before the trial began, then a peck to the red key was reinforced; otherwise, a peck to the green key was reinforced. In order to respond correctly, in other words, the birds had to remember whether the trial had been preceded by food.

To find out whether surprising events received greater processing, Maki then gave the birds separate training in which they were reinforced for pecking vertical lines (S+) but not horizontal ones (S−). Finally, the birds were returned to the red-green discrimination; now, though, presentations of food sometimes were preceded by the former S+ or S−. Since S− had never before been followed by food, the presentation of food following S− should have occasioned far more surprise than the same presentation following S+. The subjects should thus have paid more attention to the food on these trials and hence remembered it better. Performance on the following red-green presentations confirmed these expectations: The birds were significantly more likely to respond correctly on trials in which food was preceded by S− (72 percent) than S+ (54 percent). Surprising events, it appears, attract more attention and are better remembered. (See also Grant, Brewster, & Stierhoff, 1983.)

Neither of the studies cited can be accepted as conclusive evidence that rehearsal enhances memory, because rehearsal was not directly observed in either. Even in human subjects, the occurrence of rehearsal can only be inferred from verbal behavior ("Yes, I repeated that word four times") or its equivalent. Our conclusions concerning the role of rehearsal in animals, therefore, must be tentative, but it does appear as if the amount of rehearsal a stimulus receives during encoding strongly influences how well the subject will remember the stimulus.

Interference

One crucial determinant of whether we remember an event is how much time has elapsed since the event occurred: The more time has passed, the greater the likelihood of its being forgotten. As we saw earlier, however, research on verbal learning suggests that it is not time per se that causes forgetting, but rather the occurrence of interfering events during the retention interval. Although most of the evidence on interference has come from research on verbal learning, a number of similar studies have also been reported involving associative learning.

Interference in motor learning. Shea and Upton (1976) studied the role of interference in motor learning. In their study, they asked blindfolded subjects to move a handle 100 mm along a track and then 200 mm; 30 seconds later, they gave the subjects feedback regarding the distance by which they had missed the targets.

In tasks of this kind, in which the motor response is a simple one and subjects know in advance that they will have to remember it, subjects have little difficulty in learning, even when feedback is delayed for long periods. (In one remarkable experiment by Bilodeau and Bilodeau, 1958, feedback was delayed for seven days!) In accordance with this general finding, the performance of Shea and Upton's subjects improved significantly over trials, despite the delay in feedback (open circles in Figure 12.16). Subjects in an interference group, however, were asked to move the handle four more times during the delay interval while they waited for feedback, and performance in this group was substantially poorer (solid circles in figure). Forgetting in this experiment was thus due not to the passing of time per se but rather to the occurrence of a similar response during the retention interval.

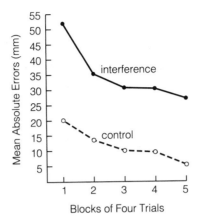

F I G U R E 12.16   The effect of interfering movements on motor learning. Blind-folded subjects had to move a handle first 100 mm and then 200 mm; 30 seconds later they were told how far they had deviated from the required distance. Subjects in the interference group were required to make additional movements during the delay interval; subjects in the control group were not required to do so. (Adapted from Shea & Upton, 1976)

Interference in classical conditioning.   A similar conclusion is suggested by an experiment on taste-aversion learning by Revusky (1971). He gave rats a saccharin-flavored solution to drink and then, one hour later, an injection of lithium chloride to make them ill. Fifteen minutes into the retention interval, he gave the rats in one group a vinegar solution to drink. Finally, after the rats had recovered from their illness, he assessed conditioning to the saccharin by allowing the rats free access to a saccharin solution for one hour.

If forgetting was due solely to the passing of time, conditioning to the saccharin should have been equal in the two groups, since, in both groups, one hour elapsed between the saccharin and the injection. The result, however, was that the vinegar group drank significantly more of the saccharin solution, indicating that the presence of the vinegar had interfered with conditioning to the saccharin. In a second experiment, Revusky found that tastes given before the CS also interfered with conditioning. The presence of other stimuli during conditioning, in other words, interferes with conditioning to the CS, and this is true whether the competing stimuli occur before or after the target. In retrieval terms, the formation of multiple memories in a situation somehow seems to make retrieval of any one of these memories more difficult.

Retrieval Cues

A third factor influencing retrieval is the similarity of the stimulus conditions during retrieval to those during coding. The more stimuli present during retrieval that were also present during coding, the better the chances are of retrieving the coded event.

One line of evidence supporting this proposition comes from experiments in which subjects are trained to perform a response and then tested under conditions that vary in their similarity to those during training. In one such experiment by Perkins and Weyant (1958), rats were first trained to run down a straight alley to obtain food and then given extinction trials. If the texture of the floor during extinction was the same as it had been during training (either rough or smooth, depending on the group), the rats ran significantly faster than if the floor texture had been altered. These results are consistent with a retrieval analysis that assumes that floor texture became associated with running during training, so that when these cues were again present during testing they reminded subjects of their experience during training and thus encouraged running. (See reviews by Spear, 1978, and Overton, 1985.)

This interpretation, however, must be viewed with great caution, because the results are also entirely consistent with a simple S–R analysis. Spence, for example, would hardly have been surprised by Perkins and Weyant's findings: If a particular floor texture is present during reinforcement, of course it will become associated with the reinforced response and thus increase the probability of this response's occurring if presented during extinction. In experiments involving responses that have already been learned, it is difficult to tell whether contextual cues such as floor texture act as retrieval cues (causing the subject to think "This is the maze in which I was once fed") or whether the contextual cues elicit the reinforced response directly.

One way to avoid this problem of interpretation is to investigate the role of retrieval cues during learning itself, before any associations have been formed. In one experiment illustrating this approach, Lett (1977) placed rats in a T-maze and then, as soon as they had made their choice responses, removed them from the maze and returned them to their home cages. They were held in their home cages for one minute and then given food if their choice response had been to the correct side. One group was fed in the home cage, but a second group was returned to the maze and fed in the start box.

According to a retrieval analysis, the stimuli present during retrieval should remind subjects of their earlier experience in the presence of these stimuli. The visual appearance, odor, and other characteristics of the maze should tend to remind the rats of their previous experience in the maze. The rats fed in the maze, then, should recall their last response in the maze and hence associate it with the food. For the rats fed in their home cage, on the other hand, the home cage cues should be less likely to provoke recall of events in the maze, and hence learning should be poorer. This was the result that Lett found: Rats fed in the maze were significantly better at learning to enter the correct arm of the maze.

The likelihood of retrieving a memory, then, depends on the similarity of conditions during retrieval to those during coding. The more stimuli present during retrieval that were also present during coding—even seemingly irrelevant stimuli such as the texture of the floor or the time of day—the greater is the likelihood that a memory will be retrieved. (See also Gordon, 1981.)

12.7 A NEOASSOCIATIVE MODEL OF LEARNING AND MEMORY

We have reviewed evidence that retrieval of a memory depends on at least three factors: how much attention an event receives during coding (rehearsal), what other events are coded in the same situation (interference), and the similarity between the stimuli present during retrieval and those present during encoding (retrieval cues). On the surface, these three variables may seem to be related only distantly, if at all, but it is possible to understand all of them in terms of a surprisingly simple model of brain functioning. The model to be presented does not come from any one source; it is a blend of a number of similar theories that have been proposed in recent years. (For similar approaches in human learning, see Collins & Loftus, 1975; Watkins, 1979; Anderson, 1984; in animal learning, Lett, 1979; Wagner, 1981.)

The Model

At the heart of the model lies the centuries-old principle of association. The core assumptions of the model are that when two areas of the brain are active simultaneously, an association is formed between them, and that if one of these areas is later reactivated, excitation will spread from it to the other—a phenomenon known as **spreading activation**. These two assumptions would hardly have been unfamiliar to Pavlov. The model may properly be called *neoassociative*, however, in the sense that it embeds these assumptions within a cognitive framework of memory and attention. (See also Anderson & Bower, 1973.) Briefly, the model's assumptions can be summarized as follows:

1. *Representation.* The occurrence of a stimulus or response will activate a corresponding representation, or neural center, in the brain.

2. *Short-term memory.* Once a center is activated, this activity normally will decay over time.

3. *Attention.* Activity in a center can be prolonged through attention, but the number of centers that can be maintained in an active state in short-term memory is limited. The amount of attention that will be paid to a

stimulus—that is, how strongly its center is activated—will depend on how salient and unexpected it is.

4. *Association.* Centers that are active simultaneously become associated. The greater the level of activity in two centers, and the longer they remain active together, the stronger the association will be.

5. *Spreading activation.* If a center is activated, this excitation will spread to other centers with which it is associated.

6. *Cue overload.* The more associations spread out from any center, the less of that center's activity will be transmitted through any one of them.

Explaining Basic Phenomena

To see how the model can be used to explain the phenomena reviewed in this chapter, consider a conditioning experiment in which a rat is placed in a Skinner box and exposed to pairings of a tone with shock. According to the model, the strength of the association formed between the tone and shock will depend on how long the tone center and the shock center are active simultaneously, and how active each center is during this time. Let us focus on the tone for a moment. The model tells us that the strength of conditioning will depend on how strongly the tone center is activated when the shock is presented. This activity can be generated in either of two ways: ongoing activity or spreading activation.

The first alternative, ongoing activity, means that the tone center is already in an active state at the time the shock is presented—perhaps because the tone is still present, or perhaps because it was sufficiently intense or unexpected that the activity it generated in the tone center has not yet decayed. Even if the tone center is no longer active at the time of shock onset, however, it can be reactivated by excitation spreading to it from other centers. Suppose, for example, that the Skinner box consists of three stimuli: black walls (S_1), a smooth floor (S_2), and a distinctive odor (S_3). Because all three of these cues were present during the tone, we can assume that their centers have all become associated with it. Since all three cues are also present during shock, excitation will spread from their centers to the associated tone center (T) and reactivate it (Figure 12.17a).

With this set of assumptions, we can now account for many of the phenomena considered in this chapter. We will consider three examples:

1. *The role of retrieval cues.* If any of the stimuli present during retrieval were associated with the tone during coding, then activation will spread from their centers to that of the tone. This mechanism would explain why, in Lett's (1977) experiment, feeding in the maze resulted in better learning than feeding in the home cage. The maze cues reactivated the

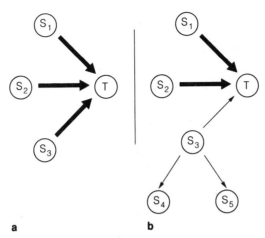

F I G U R E 12.17   A memory retrieval model: (a) The cortical centers for stimuli S_1, S_2, and S_3 become associated with a target memory T during learning. (b) If stimulus S_3 subsequently becomes associated with stimuli S_4 and S_5, then less activation will spread from S_3 to T. (The amount of excitation is represented by the width of the arrows.)

associated memory of running, so that activity in the response center was contiguous with that of the food center in short-term memory.

2. *Rehearsal.*   The more strongly a stimulus center is activated during coding, the more strongly it will be associated with the contextual cues present at the time, and the more likely it is to be reactivated by these cues during retrieval. The strength of activation during coding is assumed to depend, in turn, on how surprising the stimulus is: The more unexpected a stimulus is, the more attention will be paid to it. Thus, in the Maki (1979) experiment, food was better remembered when it was preceded by CS− than by CS+, because the presentation of food following CS− was more surprising.

3. *Interference.*   The cue overload assumption of the model states that the more associations spread out from a center, the less activity will be transmitted through any one of them. In our fear-conditioning example, suppose that the tone was followed by a clicking noise (S_4) and a flashing light (S_5), also presented in the black box. The black box center, S_3, would then be associated not only with T, as previously, but also with S_4 and S_5. The more associations with S_3, the less activation would spread from S_3 through any one of those associations. When shock was presented, therefore, activity in S_3 would be less likely to spread to T (Figure 12.17b). The model, in other words, explains why the occurrence of other events in the same context interferes with retrieval of a particular memory.

Testing the Neoassociative Model

With just a few simple assumptions, then, our model can account for much of the evidence reviewed in this chapter. Moreover, it makes a number of predictions. We will focus here on one concerning the role of attention in the formation of associations.

As we have seen, the model assumes that the strength of the association formed between two events depends on how long their representations are active simultaneously, but that there are limits to how many centers can be active at one time. Suppose, therefore, that following the presentation of a CS and a US, a third stimulus is presented: According to the model, any attention diverted to this new stimulus will reduce the attention given to the CS and US. Moreover, the amount of attention paid to this third stimulus will depend, as with any other stimulus, on how unexpected it is. Combining these assumptions, the model predicts that conditioning will be impaired if a CS and US are closely followed by a surprising event, because this surprising event will attract rehearsal capacity that would otherwise have strengthened the association between the CS and US.

This prediction was tested in a seminal experiment by Wagner, Rudy, and Whitlow (1973). Rabbits were given eyeblink-conditioning trials in which one stimulus, S+, was followed by a mild shock to the region of the eye, and another stimulus, S−, was presented on its own:

$$S+ \longrightarrow US$$
$$S- \longrightarrow$$

After the rabbits had learned to blink only to S+, they were given additional conditioning trials in which a new stimulus, X, was paired with the shock. For some subjects, these new conditioning trials were each followed after a 10-second delay by an unexpected event—either S+ presented without the shock or S− presented with the shock. For the remaining subjects, the pairings were in accord with earlier training—S+ followed by shock or S− without shock. According to the preceding analysis, subjects exposed to surprising posttrial episodes should have paid more attention to them, and, as a result, learning of the preceding CS–US association should be impaired. As shown in Figure 12.18, this was what Wagner's group found: Eyeblink conditioning was significantly slower in subjects for whom conditioning trials were followed by a surprising event.

In a second experiment, the experimenters varied the time interval between the CS–US pairing and the presentation of the unexpected posttrial episode. The more time that subjects are allowed to associate the CS and US, the less this association should be affected by a diversion of attention to other events; again, this was what Wagner's group found. As shown in Figure 12.19,

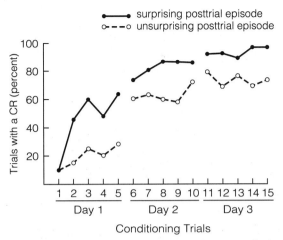

FIGURE 12.18 The effect on conditioning of stimuli presented after a trial. Each conditioning trial was followed 10 seconds later by either a surprising posttrial episode—for example, a previously established CS− followed by a US—or an unsurprising episode. (Adapted from Wagner, Rudy, & Whitlow, 1973)

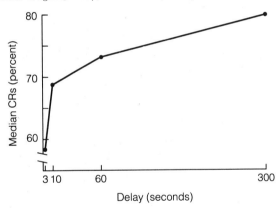

FIGURE 12.19 The impact of a surprising episode on conditioning as a function of the delay interval between the conditioning trial and the posttrial episode. (Adapted from Wagner, Rudy, & Whitlow, 1973)

the longer the delay between the conditioning trial and the posttrial unexpected event, the stronger conditioning was to the CS. These experiments thus provide strong support for the assumption that conditioning depends on how long two events are active simultaneously in memory: Because the number of items that can be kept in an active state at one time is limited, increased attention to one event may reduce learning about others. *

---

* You may wonder why presentation of a surprising US following a conditioning trial does not *enhance* conditioning by triggering a memory search that increases attention to the preceding CS and US. If so, you are quite right to wonder, because this is a possible prediction of our model. When

These results underscore once again the importance of surprise in learning. Surprising events receive more attention, and this may result not only in better memory for the event itself (Maki, 1979) but also in a memory search that enhances learning about preceding events (Kamin, 1969; Rescorla & Wagner, 1972; Lieberman, McIntosh, & Thomas, 1979). Because processing capacity is limited, however, enhanced attention to one event will inevitably mean less attention to others; as a result, events that are not identified as having caused the surprising event may suffer a loss of attention (Wagner, Rudy, & Whitlow, 1973).

The Model's Weaknesses

The model we have been considering has formidable strengths: Not only can it account for many of the known phenomena of information processing, but it also can predict new ones; indeed, much of the evidence treated in this chapter as "known" was actually generated partly in response to the demonstration by Wagner's group of the usefulness of the concepts of active memory and surprise. Before becoming too excited about the model's potential, however, we must consider its limitations.

A relatively minor one is that the model ignores coding. We saw earlier that subjects do not code stimuli in isolation, but rather use relationships among these stimuli to guide their coding. Our model ignores the details of this coding process and simply assumes that presentation of a stimulus will somehow activate a central representation. This problem could be handled by elaborating the model in more detail; more serious problems arise from evidence that challenges the model's existing assumptions. We will focus here on two such challenges: that associations are not formed between all simultaneously active representations, and, more broadly, that what is learned may not be an association at all.

Selective association.   The model assumes that all centers that are active at the same time become associated, and there is considerable evidence to support this assumption. In particular, it has been found that many of the contextual cues present during reinforcement—the texture of the floor, the time of day, the animal's hunger level—later act as effective retrieval cues. (For reviews of this evidence, see Spear, 1978, and Overton, 1985.) On the other hand, we

---

the second US is presented, it will attract attention to itself and thereby reduce attention to the preceding stimuli. However, if the earlier CS is still in short-term memory, the second US may itself become associated with this CS. In other words, the second US will interfere with conditioning by distracting attention from preceding events, but will also enhance conditioning via a direct association. To calculate the relative strength of these opposing processes would require that the model be stated in mathematical form; Wagner (1981) has proposed one such model, which predicts that the interference effect will predominate, as he found.

also have seen that the stimuli present during reinforcement do not all become associated with the response; recall, for example, Reynolds's pigeons, who learned about the shape or the color of a red triangle, but not about both.

The model attributes selective learning of this kind to limitations in processing capacity arising at one of two stages in learning:

1. *CS processing.* When many stimuli are present simultaneously, limitations in perceptual processing capacity may mean that only some of these stimuli succeed in activating their central representations; in the absence of such activation, no association will be formed.

2. *US processing.* The model assumes that an expected reinforcer will activate its center only weakly, so that again little or no learning will take place; it is through this assumption that the model accounts for blocking.

Selection can thus occur during the processing of both the CS and the US, and this allows the model to handle much of the evidence for selective learning. The model has difficulty, however, in explaining the fact that taste aversions can be conditioned to foods eaten hours before an animal becomes ill. Because it is highly unlikely that subjects retrieve every event that occurred over several hours, this result strongly implies a selective process in the retrieval search: When ill, we seem to be more likely to retrieve taste memories than, say, visual memories.

Once a taste is retrieved, moreover, it appears as if yet another selective process operates during the associative process itself. In the Garcia and Koelling (1966) experiment, for example, some subjects received a taste-noise-light compound followed immediately by either shock or irradiation (causing illness). The irradiated rats developed an aversion to the taste, but the shocked rats did not.

Why didn't the rats associate the taste with the shock? The model cannot argue that the rats did not attend to the taste, because when the taste was followed 15 minutes later by illness, other subjects had no difficulty associating the two experiences. Nor can it be argued that the rats did not attend to the shock, because an aversion was conditioned on these trials to the noise. Both the taste and the shock, therefore, must have activated their neural centers on these trials, so that, according to the model, a strong association should have been formed. The fact that it was not suggests that some selective mechanism must also have operated during the associative stage. We do not associate all active centers, as the model claims, but only some subset of the active centers. Associative learning, in other words, is apparently not nearly as promiscuous as our model implies: Selective mechanisms operate not only during the coding of stimuli but also during their retrieval and association.

Assuming that selection does occur during the associative stage, can we say anything about the principles involved? The perhaps embarrassing answer is that we can say too much: At least three theories have been proposed (Mackintosh, 1975; Pearce & Hall, 1980; Wagner, 1981), but their fundamental assumptions are almost diametrically opposed. The fact that they are so starkly different suggests that it should not be too long before a clever experimenter finds a way to determine which approach is best. For the moment, anyway, the principles governing which active centers will be associated are not well understood. (See also Mackintosh & Dickinson, 1979.)

Is any associative model adequate?   What may prove an even more fundamental problem for our model is its assumption that learning and memory can be explained entirely in terms of the formation of associations between contiguous events. One problem, which we reviewed at length in Chapter 11, is evidence for the flexibility and purposefulness of behavior. In Macfarlane's (1930) experiment, a rat that had learned to run through a maze readily switched to swimming when the maze was flooded. Even if we assume that the rats had learned a response-reinforcer association during training, and that the occurrence of the response would activate a representation of food, there is no mechanism within an associative account by which a central representation can flexibly select behaviors to achieve it. This flexibility or purposefulness of behavior seems better described in terms of a more abstract knowledge structure: The rat acquires the knowledge that food is located in a particular location and then selects whatever behavior seems best suited to reaching that goal.

A more recent illustration of the difficulties confronting a system in which the only permissible form of learning is an association—and one that comes, in a sense, from the heartland of the modern associative tradition—is the phenomenon of **occasion setting**. In an experiment by Rescorla (1985a), pigeons were trained in an autoshaping paradigm in which a five-second key light was followed by food on trials when the light was preceded by a noise, but not when it was presented on its own:

$$\text{noise} + \text{light} \longrightarrow \text{food}$$
$$\text{light} \longrightarrow$$

The noise, in other words, "set the occasion" for when the light would be followed by food, and the birds learned to behave appropriately, pecking the lighted key at a much higher rate on trials in which it had been preceded by the noise.

On the surface, this result poses few problems for an associative analysis. Because the noise and the light were both present on reinforced trials, both stimuli would have become associated with the food. On trials in which the noise and light were present together, therefore, the total activation reaching the food center would have been greater than on light-only trials, leading to a

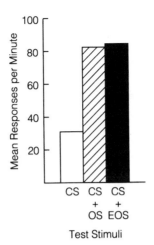

F I G U R E 12.20   The effect of extinction on the properties of an occasion-setting stimulus. The graph bars show the number of responses made to an autoshaped key light (CS) on its own, with an occasion setter (OS), or with an occasion setter that had been extinguished (EOS). (Adapted from Rescorla, 1985b)

stronger tendency to peck. * On the basis of other evidence, however, Rescorla doubted that the effectiveness of the noise was due to its association with food; to test this assumption, he now gave the birds 144 extinction trials in which the noise was presented on its own without food. Any association between the noise and food should have been eliminated after so many extinction trials, so that, according to an associative account, the noise should no longer have enhanced responding to the light.

For control purposes, Rescorla implemented this strategy with a design in which two different stimuli—a noise and a flashing houselight—were established as occasion setters (OSs) during the first phase of the experiment, and one of them was then presented on its own in extinction. The birds were then returned to the occasion-setting paradigm to see if the extinguished OS had lost its ability to enhance responding. As shown in Figure 12.20, this was not quite the result obtained: When the extinguished OS was presented, the birds responded almost three times as much as when the key light was presented by itself. Indeed, if anything, the extinguished OS was slightly more effective than the OS that had not been extinguished. The strength of the association between the OS and food was clearly not a very important factor in the capacity of the OS to increase responding.

---

* As noted earlier, the model provides no mechanism for translating activation of a US center into responding. For the purposes of the present argument, however, we are ignoring this problem and simply assuming that activation of a US center leads to an appropriate response.

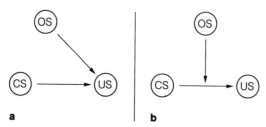

F I G U R E 12.21 Possible explanations for occasion setting: (a) The occasion setter becomes associated directly with the US. (b) The occasion setter enables or facilitates the transmission of excitation between the CS and US.

But if the OS did not increase responding because of its association with food, then why did it increase responding? Holland (1985) has proposed that occasion setters, rather than being directly associated with a US (Figure 12.21a), modulate or facilitate the association between the CS and US (Figure 12.21b). Let's return to the Rescorla experiment. According to this analysis, when the noise was presented, it facilitated the transmission of a signal between the key light and food centers; in the absence of such facilitation, the key light was less effective in activating the food center.

If this analysis is correct, then an associative account of occasion setting is still possible, but not one based solely on the formation of associations between active centers. (See also Ross & LoLordo, 1987.) Rather than learning a linear association between two centers, the birds apparently learned a three-term, hierarchical relationship in which a higher-order center (the OS) modulated the association between two lower centers. This result suggests that, even in the simplest learning situations, the principle of association through contiguity may not be adequate to account for learning. Again, the evidence points to the possibility of a more complex or hierarchical system; in the next chapter, we will examine more closely what the characteristics of this system might be.

12.8 SUMMARY

This has been a very long chapter, so we will first review briefly the main points. Our central concern has been to identify what determines the stimuli or responses that will be associated with a subsequent reinforcer. Adopting an information-processing framework, one determinant is how the stimulus is encoded. According to early theories of associative learning, all of the stimuli present at the time a response is reinforced become associated with it. Moreover, these theorists assumed that each of these stimuli forms its own association with the reinforced response, independent of what other stimuli are present at the time.

This analysis, it is now clear, was fundamentally flawed. The evidence for transposition established that stimuli are not coded independently: Subjects often notice relationships between stimuli ("This square is larger than that one") and may respond on the basis of these relationships rather than the absolute properties of the stimuli. Also, stimuli that occur together are sometimes coded as an integral compound, or configuration; again, responding may develop to the configuration ("Choose the red square") rather than to the elements of which it is composed.

Another important process during coding is attention to the stimulus, or rehearsal. The longer a stimulus is present, and the more unexpected its presentation, the more processing it receives, and the better it is remembered. Conversely, if a stimulus does not receive attention during encoding, it may not be remembered at all.

Early theories of attention took it for granted that attention was essentially a perceptual phenomenon: We cannot fully process all the stimuli impinging on our senses and, therefore, attend to or detect only a subset. Kamin's work on blocking, however, strongly challenged this assumption. In his experiments, a tone-light compound was present for three minutes, and it was difficult to believe that failure to learn about the light could have been due to a failure to detect it; in any case, Kamin presented evidence that his rats did detect both stimuli. Thus, although attention in a perceptual sense may play some role in learning, the most important limitations in processing capacity seem to arise at some stage following coding.

One possibility is that the reinforcer does not initiate a memory search. S–R theorists assumed that all reinforcers produce learning, but Kamin argued that searches through memory to identify predictive cues are difficult and thus are initiated only when the reinforcer is unexpected—that is, only when adequate predictors have not yet been identified. Evidence for latent and perceptual learning, on the other hand, suggests that we are constantly learning about the world around us, whether or not a reinforcer is presented. A possible reconciliation of these positions involves the assumption that learning is indeed limited, but that any salient and surprising stimulus will serve as a trigger—a surprising noise or a novel room, just as much as food or electric shock.

Given that a search is initiated, whether a particular stimulus is retrieved will depend on: (1) how strongly that stimulus was associated with contextual stimuli during coding; (2) the number of other events associated with these contextual stimuli; and (3) the number of contextual stimuli that are again present during retrieval.

The influence of these factors can be understood in terms of a neoassociative model, which assumes that presentation of a stimulus activates a neural representation or center in the brain, with the amount of activity depending on how salient or surprising the stimulus is. This activity is assumed to decay over time, but it may be prolonged through attention or rehearsal. Centers that are active at the same time become associated, so that, during retrieval, the presence of a contextual cue will produce activation of its own center, which will then spread to the centers with which it was associated during coding.

With some additional assumptions—for example, that the amount of excitation transmitted through any one pathway will depend on the total number of pathways emanating from a center—this model can account for much of the evidence on learning discussed in this chapter and can also generate some interesting predictions. One such prediction is that the formation of an association between two events will be impeded if the events are closely followed by a surprising event—a prediction supported in an influential series of experiments by Wagner, Rudy, and Whitlow (1973). The model is less successful, however, in its account of selection during learning. Selection could occur during coding, retrieval, or association (that is, a subject might not notice a stimulus initially, might fail to recall it, or might not relate it to the subsequent event), but the model in its present form provides little guidance concerning the principles governing selection at the associative and retrieval stages.

One noteworthy point concerns the relationship between the S–R model of learning, which we rejected earlier as essentially naive and simplistic, and the neoassociative model, which we have now hailed, albeit with some caution, as a promising framework. The two models share a common emphasis on the central role of associations: Learning is viewed as the formation of associations, and the crucial requirement for learning is that two events occur contiguously. The models differ considerably, however, in their assumptions concerning the nature of the events that are associated. S–R theorists worked within a behavioral framework in which they minimized speculation about internal processes. At first, the events to be associated were viewed as observable stimuli and responses; later, in Hull's neobehaviorist version, internal events were allowed, but they were assumed to be simple events having exactly the same properties as their external counterparts, and they were located in the periphery of the body rather than the brain. In trying to account for the effects of delayed reinforcement, for example, Spence assumed that responses would generate proprioceptive traces in the muscles, so that once these peripheral traces had decayed, learning no longer would be possible.

The neoassociative approach, on the other hand, is less wary of speculation about processes in the brain, and cognitive processes such as memory and attention are accorded a central role. Thus, although the model still assumes that events must be contiguous to be associated, it interprets these events as memories, so that subjects are capable of learning about relationships between events separated by hours or even days, provided that the appropriate memories are retrieved. In the same spirit, the model allows much more scope for complex processing of stimuli than its S–R predecessor: The stimulus as coded may be very different from the simple ray of light that initially fell on a receptor in the eye.

In one sense, then, our neoassociative model represents a considerable advance over earlier theories of associative learning, because it allocates a central role to cognitive processes such as memory and attention. On the other hand, it retains some of the weaknesses of earlier associative accounts. Although it allows for elaborate coding processes, it does not provide much in the way of detailed guidance about the way these processes work. Similarly, at the response end, the model is almost entirely silent regarding how the activation of a stimulus representation leads to behavior directed toward obtaining it. To paraphrase a criticism once made of S–R theory, the theory does a splendid job of accounting for the hyphen, but it is less successful in dealing with the stimulus and response units being associated. The model's success in accounting for a wide range of data with only a few assumptions, however, suggests that it could provide a foundation for future theorists to build on.

One final point of interest concerns the convergence in recent years between theories of animal and human learning. If you compare the concepts used in this chapter to explain associative learning in animals with those used to account for learning and memory in humans, you will find a very substantial overlap. To a remarkable extent, the same concepts are now being used to explain both sets of behavior. These concepts include the distinction between short- and long-term memory, the assumption that the capacity for active memory is limited but that this capacity can be extended through rehearsal, and the importance of interfering events and retrieval cues. In part, this similarity reflects the historical roots of human memory research in animal learning. Some of the early theories of human learning were derived from learning concepts developed through research on animals, and these concepts have remained influential. (For a historical survey, see Postman, 1985.)

In recent years, however, the direction of influence has been much more strongly from human to animal learning. The success of information-processing approaches in human research has helped to validate, and make acceptable, the use of cognitive concepts such as memory, attention, coding, and retrieval; animal-learning theorists using these concepts have been heavily influenced by the models developed by their human-learning colleagues. (See Wagner, 1981.) The fact that current theories of animal and human learning are often strikingly similar, therefore, does not necessarily prove that the underlying processes are equally similar: It could simply be that the theorists in the two camps have been busily borrowing each other's theories. If this convergence reflects a genuine similarity in underlying mechanisms, however, then animal learning may be far more cognitive—and human learning far more associative—than traditional views have suggested.

Selected Definitions

Coding, storage, and **retrieval** Terms originally used to distinguish different phases of a computer's operations, and now used in information-processing theories of human learning to distinguish analogous phases of the brain's operations. In computing, the term *coding* is used to describe transformation of the input to a computer into a form that can be processed (generally, electrical signals); *storage* refers to the storage of this transformed code in a memory cell; and *retrieval* refers to transferring the stored information from the computer's memory to the central processing unit where it can be used. In human memory, *coding* is the process by which an external stimulus is eventually assigned a neural representation or code within the brain; *storage* refers to the maintenance of these codes in long-term memory; and *retrieval* refers to recall of these memories.

Short-term memory (STM) and **long-term memory (LTM)** Memories that are retained only for relatively brief periods, on the order of seconds or minutes (short-term memory); and memories that are retained for longer periods (long-term memory). Current theories suggest that neurons are activated temporarily during the coding of a stimulus (short-term memory), and that associations are formed between the active neurons or nodes. If these associations are strong enough, then a permanent record of the experience will be retained (long-term memory).

Rehearsal A term originally confined to repetition of verbal material by saying it out loud or subvocally, but now used to refer to any maintenance of a neural center in an active state when the initiating stimulus is no longer present.

Attention Within associative learning, a term referring to the fact that only some of the stimuli present at a given moment influence our behavior. In this empirical usage, attention, or **selective attention**, is largely synonymous with our earlier definition of stimulus control.

Confusion may arise because the term *selective attention* is also used to refer to each of the following: (1) a *theory* of selective attention—namely, that selection is due to limitations in our perceptual processing capacity; (2) a *process* that maintains activity in a neural center (also called rehearsal) or selectively facilitates some other aspect of processing; (3) a *conscious experience*. When we say we are paying attention to what someone is saying, we mean in part that we are consciously aware of the person's words.

These meanings—an empirical relationship, a theory, a process, and a conscious experience—are very different, and it is often unclear which meaning is intended. The underlying theme shared by all these meanings is that we cannot do everything at once.

Proactive interference (PI) and **retroactive interference (RI)** Two types of memory interference. Memory theorists now believe that forgetting is due largely to difficulties in retrieving material that is stored in memory, and that this difficulty is caused by interference from other stored memories. *Proactive interfer-*

ence refers to interference from experiences that preceded the event to be remembered; *retroactive interference* refers to interference from experiences that follow the target event.

Cue overload A reduction in the effectiveness of a retrieval cue in activating an associated memory, due to the cue's association with other memories.

Transposition In a transposition experiment, subjects are trained to choose one of two stimuli and then are given a choice between a second set of stimuli. If they base their choices between the test stimuli on a relationship that was also present between the first pair (for example, that one card is larger than the other), they are said to have transferred, or transposed, the relationship from training to testing.

Peak shift A shift in the peak of a generalization gradient away from S−. If subjects are given a generalization test following reinforced training with a single stimulus, the peak of the generalization gradient will be located at the training stimulus. However, if subjects are given discrimination training involving two stimuli, the greatest responding during the generalization test occurs not to S+ (the stimulus reinforced during training) but to a stimulus further away from S− (the nonreinforced stimulus during training).

Configural learning Learning to respond to a compound stimulus in a manner entirely different than to its elements. Subjects behave as if they have learned to perceive the compound as a unique stimulus, or configuration, that is not like its components.

Latent inhibition Impairment in learning about the relationship between a stimulus and some consequence because of prior presentations of the stimulus by itself. Lubow and Moore, who discovered this phenomenon, believed that the stimulus acquired inhibitory properties when presented by itself, but subsequent research suggests that a stimulus presented by itself does not actively inhibit responding; rather, subjects learn to ignore the stimulus because it has no predictive value.

Extradimensional (ED) shift and **intradimensional (ID) shift** Test procedures for determining whether subjects who learn to discriminate between stimuli that differ along a dimension such as color acquire a general tendency to attend to that dimension. To answer this question, subjects are tested on a second discrimination involving new stimuli. In an intradimensional shift, the new stimuli differ along the same dimension that was relevant during training; in an extradimensional shift, the relevant stimuli shift to a new dimension. For example, suppose that subjects are trained to discriminate between a green object and a red object and are then required to solve a new discrimination involving either color or shape. If the subjects learn a general tendency to attend to color in the first problem, they should do better if the second problem also requires attention to color (an intradimensional shift) than if it requires attention to shape (an extradimensional shift).

Marking Enhanced memory for an experience due to the subsequent occurrence of a salient and unexpected event. The unexpected event is thought to trigger a search for causes that results in greater attention to preceding events.

Spreading activation Excitation that spreads from one activated area of the brain to another as a result of an earlier association formed between them.

Occasion setting A classical conditioning procedure in which a CS is followed by a US only on trials in which a third stimulus, the occasion setter, accompanies the CS. The third stimulus signals, or "sets the occasion," when the CS will be reinforced.

Review Questions

1. Define the following terms: node, memory span, stimulus as coded (SAC), behavioral contrast, active memory, inactive memory, retrieval cue, blocking, sensory preconditioning, and delayed matching to sample (DMTS).

2. What is the information-processing approach? How does it compare to earlier S–R and cognitive theories of learning?

3. Perception, or coding, is now viewed as a constructive rather than a reproductive process. What might this distinction mean? What evidence supports it?

4. What evidence suggests a need to distinguish between short- and long-term memory? What is the current view of how information is transferred from short- to long-term memory?

5. Once material has been coded and stored, why do we sometimes forget it?

6. What evidence suggests that stimuli are not always coded as independent elements?

7. S–R theorists opposed the postulation of internal processes; when such processes had to be invoked, they preferred the simplest possible mechanism that could account for the known facts. Cognitive theorists, by contrast, assumed that relatively complex internal processes would be required to explain learning. How does the history of transposition illustrate this conflict? How did Spence modify his original model to account for transposition? To what extent was his new model successful?

8. What evidence is there for selective attention? How does the dimensional model account for attention? What evidence supports this model?

9. Why does Kamin's research on blocking challenge the dimensional model? How did Kamin account for blocking? What evidence supports his interpretation?

10. Assuming that a stimulus is coded and stored in long-term memory, why might subjects fail to associate it with a subsequent reinforcer?

11. Reinforcement theorists argued that only the presentation of a reinforcer would trigger learning, whereas cognitive theorists viewed learning as a continuous process that required no special trigger. What evidence challenges the reinforcement view? What evidence challenges the cognitive view? How can the concept of surprise be used to synthesize the opposing positions?

12. How does the phenomenon of marking support the importance of memory and surprise in learning?

13. What method is often used to measure short-term memory in animals?

14. Assuming that a retrieval search is initiated, what factors determine whether a coded stimulus will be retrieved?

15. What is the neoassociative model of learning presented in this chapter? Why was it called *neoassociative*? How does the model account for the effects of rehearsal, retrieval cues, and interference?

16. What was the Wagner, Rudy, and Whitlow experiment? How does it provide a test of the neoassociative model?

17. The neoassociative model assumes that associations will be formed between all centers that are simultaneously active in short-term memory. In this sense, it is the old principle of association by contiguity transposed to a neural context. What evidence supports this assumption? What evidence contradicts it?

18. Why does the phenomenon of occasion setting challenge an associative account of learning?

19. Reinforcement is more effective if it is immediate and substantial. How might our neoassociative model account for these facts?

20. Do you believe that your brain has enough neurons to code all the material presented in this chapter?

CHAPTER THIRTEEN

Is Associative Learning
Simple or Complex?

To explain classical conditioning, Pavlov proposed a very simple theory: If stimuli such as a tone and food are presented together, each will activate a cortical center, and a new connection will be formed between these centers. If the tone is then presented by itself, activation will spread from its center through the new pathway to the food center, and from there to the salivary glands. Conditioning, in other words, could be understood in terms of the centuries-old assumption that associations are formed whenever two events occur contiguously.

In the 1960s, this assumption was challenged by three influential developments: Rescorla's demonstration of the importance of contingency, Garcia's discovery of the role of preparedness, and Kamin's work on blocking. In all three, a salient CS was contiguous with a powerful US, yet no conditioning occurred. It is possible that an entirely adequate explanation for this failure could have been formulated within the existing framework of associative learning; the Rescorla-Wagner model can be viewed as just such an answer. Other evidence, however, suggested that a more cognitive approach—one incorporating explicit assumptions about the cognitive processes underlying learning—might be more fruitful. The fact that subjects could learn relationships between events separated by several hours (Andrews & Braveman, 1975; Capaldi, 1971) pointed to the important role of memory in conditioning. Other evidence suggested the importance of selective attention (Reynolds, 1961; Eimas, 1966). Thus, by the end of the 1960s, converging evidence suggested that learning theorists needed to pay closer attention to the cognitive processes that shaped learning, and the success of a similar approach in explaining human learning gave powerful impetus to the cognitive bandwagon.

The bandwagon has not yet had time to roll very far, but in Chapter 12 we saw that the emerging model assumes a complex sequence of coding, storage, retrieval, and postretrieval processes. In one respect, however, this new information-processing analysis is remarkably similar to Pavlov's original account. Although the new approach assigns a key role to cognitive processes such as memory and attention, the assumption at its heart remains that associations will be formed between representations or cortical centers that are active at the same time. Thus, although a CS center may now be activated as a memory as well as by the physical presence of the CS, the fundamental process is still that active centers will become associated.

The venerable history of this assumption, and its success in assimilating new evidence, suggests that it should not be dismissed lightly. At several points, however, we have encountered evidence that challenges whether a purely associative account could ever be sufficient to account for learning. In Chapter 11, for example, we saw that if a maze is flooded so that a rat can no longer run to the goal box containing food, it will switch to swimming, even though the physical movements involved are very different (Macfarlane, 1930; Nissen, 1950). Tolman argued that this flexibility of behavior could not be accounted for in terms of simple associations and that a more complex cognitive structure, an expectation, was required.

In the examples we have considered to this point, the expectations involved have been relatively simple—"The water will be two inches high," or "The goal box contains food." In this chapter, we will turn to evidence that poses an even stronger challenge to an associative account by suggesting that even in the simplest learning situations animals may form expectations of sometimes remarkable complexity. Appropriately, we will begin our investigation of this claim with an ingenious experiment by Tolman.

13.1 COGNITIVE MAPS

Tolman believed that in some situations animals would learn expectations of considerable complexity. In particular, he suggested that animals exposed to a novel environment would form a maplike representation of that environment in the brain, indicating the location of different features of this environment and the paths linking them. Psychologists refer to this representation as a **cognitive map**.

Tolman's Cognitive Map Hypothesis

In one of the earliest experiments to test this hypothesis, Tolman and Honzik (1930b) trained rats in the maze illustrated in Figure 13.1. There were three possible paths from the start box to the goal box containing food, with path 1

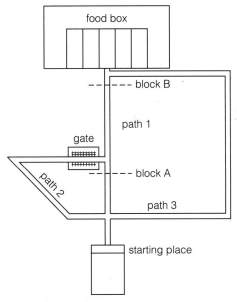

F I G U R E 13.1   Overhead view of the Tolman and Honzik rat maze. (Tolman & Honzik, 1930b)

being the shortest and path 3 the longest. At first, the rats were allowed to enter any path. Once they had acquired a preference for path 1, Tolman and Honzik blocked path 1 at point A. When the rats found that they could not proceed along path 1, they chose the next shortest path, path 2, on 91 percent of the test trials.

This result was readily explicable in terms of S–R theory as well as Tolman's cognitive map hypothesis. According to S–R theory, the sooner reinforcement is delivered following a response, the more effective it is in strengthening behavior. Because path 2 was shorter than path 3, entry into path 2 was followed by reinforcement more quickly, so that this response would have been strengthened more. According to Tolman, on the other hand, the rats chose path 2 because they had formed a cognitive map of the maze's layout and realized that path 2 was the shortest available path to the goal.

To separate these two explanations, Tolman and Honzik simply moved the block on path 1 from point A to point B. According to S–R theory, when the rats found that they could not get through path 1 and returned to the choice point, they should have made the next strongest response; that is, they should choose path 2. If the rats had a cognitive map, on the other hand, they would realize that the block at B also blocked access to the goal via path 2, and thus should now choose path 3, even though it was the longest path during training. Rather remarkably, this is exactly what the rats did: 93 percent of the rats chose path 3 on the first test trial.

But Is It Really a Map?

Tolman and Honzik's data suggested that rats not only could form cognitive maps but could use them with impressive efficiency to plot the optimal route through their environment. However, interest in cognitive maps faded over the years. In part, this was because subsequent evidence did not always unequivocally support a cognitive interpretation. An experiment by Kuo (1937), for example, found that the rats' ability to choose the optimum path was impaired if the width of the alleys was narrow, and it was not obvious why a rat's capacity to form a cognitive map should be affected by alley width. (For other anomalous results, see Young, Greenberg, Paton, & Jane, 1967; Deutsch & Clarkson, 1959.) There were thus genuine grounds for treating Tolman's claims cautiously, but the extent to which the evidence for cognitive maps was subsequently ignored is probably another reflection of the power of paradigms in guiding scientific research. (See Chapter 4.) The idea of cognitive maps simply did not fit with the then prevailing assumptions of behaviorism and S–R theory, and, as a result, researchers were not motivated to continue exploring this area. With the success of cognitive approaches to human learning in the 1960s and 1970s, however, interest in cognitive maps revived, and learning researchers again began to explore whether animals could really form such maps.

The Olton radial maze.   In an experiment published in 1976, David S. Olton of Johns Hopkins University introduced a new maze for studying learning, which has played an important role in the resurgence of interest in cognitive maps. The maze consists of eight arms radiating out from a central platform (Figure 13.2); at the beginning of each trial, food is placed at the end of each of these arms. The rats are allowed to enter the arms in whatever order they wish, and the trial continues until the rats have collected all the available food. The primary interest lies in how efficiently the rats perform—that is, how many times they make an error by reentering an arm they have already visited and that no longer contains food.

Olton and Samuelson (1976) found that, on average, rats chose the correct arm 7.9 times out of their first 8 choices—an almost perfect performance. Various controls established that this accurate performance was not based on "tricks" such as always turning in the same direction on leaving an arm or avoiding arms that contained residual odors from previous visits: The rats were genuinely remembering which arms they had visited. Less clear, however, was the basis for this memory. One possibility was that the rats had formed a true cognitive map in the Tolmanian sense; that is, they had a mental

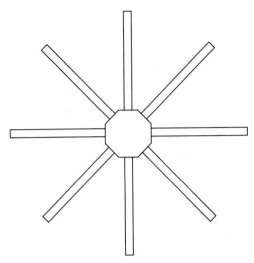

F I G U R E 13.2   Overhead view of the Olton radial maze. All eight arms of the maze are baited. The rat is placed on the center platform and allowed to enter the arms in whatever order it chooses. (Olton & Samuelson, 1976)

representation of the maze's layout and were, in effect, placing checks against arms they visited so they could avoid them in the future. There is a plausible alternative, however: Rather than having an overall conception of the maze's organization, the rats may have been responding on the basis of single cues in isolation. If a rat obtained food from a particular arm, for example, it could avoid that arm in the future by remembering a single property associated with that arm, such as a scratch on the floor at the entry to the arm, or a feature of the room located behind the arm. In other words, the rat could solve the problem by remembering eight discrete cues, without storing any information about the spatial relationship among these cues.

The Morris water maze.   A very simple procedure for distinguishing these alternatives was reported by Morris (1981). During the training phase, he placed rats in a circular tub of water, with a small platform within the tub to which the rats could swim to escape. The platform was located just under the surface of the water, so the rats could not see it directly. As a further precaution, Morris added milk to the water to make it opaque. Nevertheless, the rats quickly learned to swim directly to the platform as soon as they were released.

One possible explanation for this rapid learning was that the rats had formed a cognitive map showing the location of the platform relative to other points in the room. However, because the rats were always released from the same starting point at the edge of the tub, they could also have solved the problem by learning to swim toward a fixed landmark in the room such as a door. To find out which explanation was correct, Morris introduced test trials on which the rats were released from new starting points. If they had formed a map of the platform's location, they should still be able to swim directly to it. On the other hand, if they had been heading toward a single cue, they would now have had great difficulty, since this landmark would no longer be in line with the platform. As shown in Figure 13.3a, it was the cognitive map interpretation that was supported: The rats swam directly to the platform the first time they were released from the new positions.

It could still have been argued that some local cue was guiding the rats: Perhaps, despite all Morris's precautions, the platform really was visible, or vibrations through the water were providing cues about its location. To test this possibility, Morris gave a second group test trials in which he altered the position of the platform as well as the release point. If the rats could directly perceive the platform, they still would have swum directly toward it, but, as Figure 13.3b shows, they swam instead to where the platform had been during training and repeatedly circled this position before eventually moving off to explore other areas. The irresistible conclusion is that the rats were not responding on the basis of single cues, but were instead using a combination of cues from the surrounding environment to locate themselves and the platform so that they could take the most direct path between these two points. (See also Suzuki, Augerinos, & Black, 1980; Gould, 1986b.)

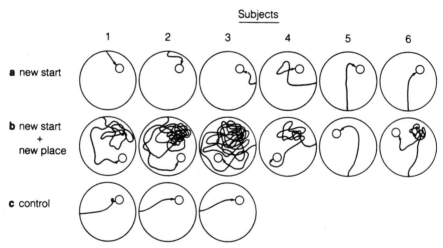

F I G U R E 13.3   Overhead view of the paths followed by rats in Morris's water maze on the first test trial. The location of the underwater platform is indicated by the small circle. During testing, the rats in the control group were released from the same starting point as during training; rats in the *new start* group were released from a new point; rats in the *new start + new platform* group were also released from a new point, but the position of the underwater platform was shifted. (Adapted from Morris, 1981)

Map Complexity

Although the issue is not finally settled (for alternative interpretations of some of the evidence presented here, see Pearce, 1987, and M. F. Brown, 1992), it now looks as if Tolman was right, and that animals do form cognitive maps of their environment. There is evidence, moreover, that animals form and use these maps with considerable skill.

Rats in a maze. Observations of rats in the Olton maze have revealed several impressive features of their performance. One is the sheer speed with which they make their choices. It is difficult to convey this in words, but observers who watch experienced rats performing in this maze are astonished by the rapidity with which choices are made. While the human observer is desperately trying to remember which arms the rat has already entered, the rat is busily scurrying into a new arm, selected apparently at random, efficiently avoiding arms already visited.

Another striking feature is the number of arms the rat can remember. In Olton's original maze, there were eight arms, and it is perhaps impressive enough that a rat can remember eight locations after only a single brief visit. However, a modified version of the maze designed by Roberts (1979) has 24 arms, and the rats in Roberts's experiment still attained a level of performance far above chance. The upper limit to rats' spatial memory is not yet known, but it is clearly substantial. (See also Phelps & Roberts, 1991.)

A third impressive feature of rats' spatial memory is its resistance to disruption. In an experiment by Beatty and Shavalia (1980a), rats were removed from the maze after making four choices and returned to their home cages for a delay interval before being allowed to complete their choices. After a four-hour delay, 90 percent of their choices were of arms not previously visited; even after a 12-hour delay, performance was still significantly above chance. In an even more demanding variant of this procedure, Beatty and Shavalia (1980b) transferred the rats to an identical maze in another room during the delay interval and allowed them to make another four choices. When tested four hours later, they still responded perfectly on both mazes, indicating that the rats could retain in memory, without any interference, maps of two almost identical mazes.

Clark's nutcrackers. As impressive as the performance of rats has been, perhaps the most remarkable example of animal memory discovered to date is that of the Clark's nutcracker. These birds live in alpine regions where little or no food is available in the long winters, so they harvest conifer seeds in the autumn and store them in underground caches. Scientists have estimated that, since each cache contains an average of only four seeds, a bird needs to recover a minimum of 2500 caches each winter if it is to survive. One explanation for the birds' success is that they actually remember 2500 different locations—a phenomenal memory load. A simpler and perhaps more plausible alternative is that the birds search for distinguishing cues—for example, signs of disturbance in the soil—to identify where seeds have been hidden.

To test these hypotheses, Vander Wall (1982) allowed two Clark's nut-crackers to hide seeds in a fenced-in enclosure that contained a soil and gravel floor and a number of landmarks such as rocks, shrubs, and logs. Several days later, he released these birds into the enclosure, along with two other birds that had not hidden seeds, releasing them one at a time to search for the hidden caches. If the birds relied solely on local visual or olfactory cues to identify caches, all four birds should have been equally successful in discovering the caches, but this was not the case. When the noncaching birds were released into the enclosure, they hopped along the surface and occasionally probed it with their beaks, but only about 10 percent of these probes uncovered a cache. In contrast, the birds who had hidden the seeds flew directly to the cache sites and obtained food on 70 percent of their probes. Moreover, each of these birds recovered almost exclusively their own caches: 52 of the 55 recoveries made by one bird were of its own caches, as were all 44 of the other bird's recoveries. The birds clearly were not searching at random; they remembered where they had hidden their seeds and flew directly to those sites.

To explore what cues the birds were using to guide their performance, Vander Wall covered the floor with a plastic sheet, leaving only a 1 × 2 meter oval area exposed, and provided eight large objects as landmarks, four in the left quadrant and four in the right quadrant (Figure 13.4). After the birds had hidden their seeds, the experimenter moved the four objects in the right area 20 centimeters further to the right; if the birds were using these objects as landmarks to guide their search, their probes in the right quadrant should be displaced 20 centimeters to the right. This was precisely the result obtained:

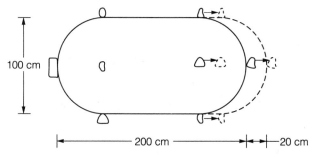

F I G U R E 13.4   Overhead view of the caching enclosure used by Vander Wall. The solid lines show the layout at the time the birds buried their food; the broken lines show the new positions of the objects and the right perimeter during the test trial. (Based on Vander Wall, 1982)

Probes in the left side of the enclosure occurred within an average of 1.3 centimeters of the caches, whereas those in the right side were displaced an average of 20.5 centimeters to the right. For objects located midway between the stable and shifted landmarks, moreover, the average displacement was 11 centimeters to the right; this suggested that the birds were using at least two objects, one to the left and one to the right, to guide their search, so that when these objects provided conflicting information, the birds split the difference between them. As was the case with rats, Clark's nutcrackers seem to form genuine cognitive maps, and Vander Wall's evidence suggests that these maps contain entries for up to 2500 items—and perhaps many more if landmarks are included.

13.2 RULE LEARNING

Another example of complex learning involves learning the rules governing the sequence in which events occur. In a sense, this whole book has been about rule learning, although the rules on which we have focused have involved relatively straightforward contingencies between two events—a CS and a US, or a response and a reinforcer. We have seen evidence that animals can learn relatively simple rules—"Pressing the bar produces food," and "The tone is followed by shock." There is evidence, however, that animals can also learn rules of substantially greater complexity. In this section, we will focus on two examples: learning set and learned helplessness.

Learning Set

One of the oldest controversies in psychology concerns whether learning in animals is a slow and gradual process based on associations, or a more intelligent process characterized by sudden insights. As we discussed in Chapter 2, Thorndike found that his animals learned to escape from a puzzle box only very slowly, and the gradual nature of this improvement led him to conclude that learning was the product of a gradual formation of associations rather than a sudden insight into the nature of the problem. Kohler (1927), however, argued that the physical arrangement of the puzzle box obscured the relationship between pressing the latch and the door's opening; when Kohler placed food outside a chimpanzee's cage beyond the animal's reach, he found that the chimp would suddenly solve the problem with what looked very much like a sudden flash of insight. In Thorndike's situation, therefore, learning was very gradual, whereas in Kohler's it appeared instantaneous.

A possible explanation for the difference in these results was eventually provided by Harlow's work on the formation of learning sets. He gave monkeys a series of problems in which they had to learn which of two objects concealed food. At first, learning was very slow: If a monkey obtained food on the first trial with a new pair of objects, its probability of choosing the correct object again on the next trial was only around 53 percent. Over a series of 312 problems, however, performance gradually improved, until eventually they were choosing the correct object 98 percent of the time after only a single trial. (See Figure 2.11, p. 68.) Harlow attributed this gradual improvement over trials to the development of a *learning set,* and suggested that the apparently insightful behavior of Kohler's chimpanzees might have been based on extensive past experience with sticks which had led to the formation of a similar learning set.

In at least some situations, then, intelligent, insightful behavior may be the fruit of extensive experience involving much more gradual learning, and this is almost certainly as true for humans as it is for animals. (Consider, for example, how many years it takes children to learn to walk and talk.) Our concern now, however, is not with the speed with which a learning set is formed, but rather with the mechanism underlying its acquisition. From the perspective of S–R theory, this improvement over problems is very difficult to explain. It is easy enough to understand why performance improves within a problem, where choice of the correct object is repeatedly reinforced; but how could reinforcement of the correct object in one problem lead to faster learning in a second problem involving an entirely different set of objects?

This improvement across problems becomes understandable, however, if we think of subjects as learning not only a specific response ("Choose the red square") but also a general strategy—characterized by Levine (1959) as *win-stay, lose-shift.* In a typical discrimination problem, the object that is correct on the first trial is also correct on subsequent trials. Therefore, if subjects are reinforced for choosing an object on the first trial, they will also be reinforced for choosing it on the next trial (win-stay). If subjects give the wrong response, on the other hand, they can obtain reward on the next trial by switching to the other object (lose-shift). Insofar as Harlow's monkeys had gradually learned this strategy over a series of problems, it would explain how they became able to instantly solve new problems they had never seen before.

If this analysis is correct, any training procedure that encourages the adoption of a win-stay, lose-shift strategy should produce the same one-trial learning eventually observed by Harlow. To test this prediction, Schusterman (1962) gave two groups of chimpanzees preliminary training designed to differentially encourage this strategy. For the *reversal* group, pretraining consisted of repeated reversals involving three pairs of objects. On the first problem, subjects were reinforced whenever they chose one member of the pair (A) but not the other (B). After they had mastered this problem, the reinforcement contingencies were reversed so that object B was now correct. Then, after this problem had been mastered in its turn, the reinforcement contingency was reversed yet again, and so on for a total of 700 trials. This reversal training was then continued for 200 trials with a second pair of objects, and a further 200 with a third pair. The second group was given training with the same three pairs of objects, except that for this *alternation* group the reinforcement contingencies were reversed on every trial: A was correct on the first trial, B on the second, A on the third, and so forth. Finally, both groups were shifted to a standard learning-set procedure that involved 180 problems in which the same object was correct on every trial.

Insofar as subjects learn only specific S–R associations, performance of the two groups should have been equal in the second phase, because they were exposed to the same stimuli during pretraining and each stimulus was reinforced on half the trials. If subjects had learned abstract strategies, on the other hand, we should expect a very different result, because the two kinds of pretraining would have encouraged opposite strategies. For the reversal group, the optimal strategy during training was to continue to choose the same object as long as it was reinforced, but then to switch to the other object as soon as it was not reinforced—that is, a win-stay, lose-shift strategy. For the alternation subjects, on the other hand, the optimal strategy was to abandon an object whenever it was reinforced but to stay with it whenever it was wrong—a win-shift, lose-stay strategy. When transferred to problems in which the same object was always correct, subjects in the reversal group should thus do very well, because they had already learned the appropriate win-stay strategy, whereas subjects in the alternation group should have great difficulty. As Figure 13.5 shows, this was the result, with the reversal subjects solving new problems significantly faster.

These results suggest that monkeys learn not only specific responses—"Choose the red square"—but also more general or abstract strategies—"Choose whatever object was correct on the preceding trial." (For a review of other evidence, see Medin, 1977.) The critical distinction lies in the bound-

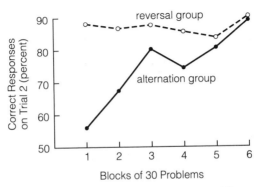

FIGURE 13.5 Learning-set performance in chimpanzees following reversal training or alternation training. (Based on Schusterman, 1962)

aries of the response class—whether it is narrowly identified with a particular set of stimuli or movements, or whether the class is defined in more general terms that can be transferred to new problems. In forming learning sets, monkeys seem to abstract the principles common to all the individual problems and then to apply this general strategy to new problems they have never seen before.

Learned Helplessness

Further evidence for the learning of general strategies comes from a now famous series of experiments by three graduate students at the University of Pennsylvania—Seligman, Maier, and Overmier. In their initial experiments, they trained dogs on an escape/avoidance task in a rectangular box with a shoulder-high barrier set in the center of the box. A 10-second warning light was occasionally presented, followed by a 50-second electric shock delivered through the floor of the cage. If the dog jumped over the barrier while the shock was on, the shock was immediately terminated; if it jumped before the shock was presented, the light was turned off and the scheduled shock canceled. Thus, the dogs could either escape the shock or avoid it altogether by jumping across the barrier when the light came on.

Seligman and Maier (1967) trained several groups on this procedure. One group of subjects was experimentally naive, but the second group was given preliminary training in which they were strapped into a harness and given 64 electric shocks. All of these shocks were inescapable: No matter what movements the dogs made, the intensity and duration of the shocks remained constant.

When placed in the test box, the naive dogs reacted by running about frantically until they eventually scrambled over the barrier and escaped the shock. After one or two experiences of this kind, the dogs began to escape more quickly, and, within a few trials, most were receiving little or no shock. (See the curve for the no-pretraining subjects in Figure 13.6.) The behavior of the dogs previously given inescapable shock, however, was very different. At first, they too ran about and howled when they received shock. After about 30 seconds, however, they typically lay down on the floor and stayed there, whining quietly, until the shock was terminated. In other words, it looked very much as if they had given up. For about two thirds of the subjects in this group, this picture of passive acquiescence continued on subsequent trials; they showed no signs of learning to escape or avoid the shock. (See the curve for the inescapable-shock subjects in Figure 13.6.)

There was, moreover, another puzzling feature of the behavior of these pretrained dogs. On most trials, as we have seen, they made little or no effort to escape, but occasionally one would jump over the barrier and thus terminate the shock. In naive dogs, a single success was usually enough to firmly establish

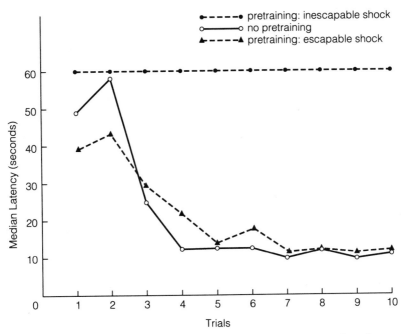

F I G U R E 13.6 Learned helplessness. Dogs were tested on an escape/avoidance task in which a warning signal was followed after 10 seconds by shock unless the dogs jumped over a barrier. Median response latencies are shown for subjects that received no pretraining, pretraining with shock they could escape, or previous shocks of identical duration that they could not escape. (Adapted from Maier, Seligman, & Solomon, 1969)

the jumping response, so that the dogs would repeat the response on all subsequent trials. But the dogs given inescapable shock during pretraining showed no sign of learning from a successful escape; on the trial following a successful escape, they immediately reverted to the pattern of passive acceptance shown earlier.

The learned helplessness hypothesis. Why did the dogs given inescapable shock not try to escape, or when they did escape, why did they fail to learn from this experience? Overmier and Seligman (1967) suggested that during pretraining these dogs had learned that they were helpless—that nothing they did would terminate the shock. When first shocked during the pretraining phase, they struggled vigorously, but as each successive attempt at escape failed, they gradually realized that there was nothing they could do. When they were transferred to the shuttle box, therefore, they made no effort to escape the shock, because they had learned that such efforts were futile. And on those occasions when they did manage to escape, they did not repeat the response, because such apparent successes during pretraining had always proved to be illusory. If on one pretraining trial a dog had lifted its right paw just as the shock was terminated, for example, it would have found that repeating this response on subsequent trials had no effect. When a jump over the barrier terminated shock during the test phase, therefore, this result would have been dismissed as just another coincidence.

According to Overmier and Seligman's **learned helplessness** hypothesis, during pretraining the dogs learned not simply that particular responses were ineffective but, more generally, that no response would alter the probability of being shocked—in the language of contingencies, that there was no contingency between their behavior and the shock. Another possible explanation for this failure to learn, however, was that it was due simply to exposure to intense shock. Perhaps these shocks resulted in conditioning of fear to the experimental environment, so that the dogs were immobilized by fear during testing (recall the CER paradigm); or perhaps, with repeated exposure, the dogs became habituated to the shock, so that it was no longer as aversive. The issue, in other words, was whether it was simply exposure to intense shock that impaired learning, or whether it was specifically the inescapability of this shock that was critical.

To find out, Seligman and Maier gave a third group pretraining with shock that was escapable. Subjects in this group were given electric shock while confined in a harness, but by pressing a panel with the nose or head, they could terminate the shock. These subjects were run in yoked pairs with subjects from the inescapable-shock group, so that whenever a subject in the escapable-shock group terminated the shock, shock was also terminated for its yoked partner in the inescapable-shock group. The subjects in the two groups thus received exactly the same amount of electric shocks, so that if it was exposure to shock that impaired learning, neither group should have learned to avoid shock in the test phase. As Figure 13.6 shows, however, subjects in the escapable-shock group not only learned, but did as well as naive subjects who had received no shock. As the learned helplessness hypothesis predicts, therefore, it is not shock per se that impairs learning, but the experience that this shock is uncontrollable.

The claim that animals can learn a general expectation of helplessness proved intensely controversial, in part because it was so contrary to the prevailing associative theories that defined learning in terms of associations between individual events. In learned helplessness, the experience of inescapable shock affected not only the responses that actually preceded it, such as struggling in the harness, but responses never previously made, such as jumping over a barrier. As in the case of learning set, subjects did not seem to be learning simply about individual responses, but rather to be abstracting general principles, or rules, that could be transferred to entirely new situations.

The controversy over this explanation still has not entirely abated, and there is evidence that other mechanisms may play an important role in the outcome. (For a review, see Maier & Jackson, 1979.) The best evidence currently available, however, suggests that animals in helplessness experiments do learn a general expectation that shock is independent of their behavior (Jackson, Alexander, & Maier, 1980; Maier, 1989).

Practical implications. In addition to its theoretical importance, the phenomenon of learned helplessness also has a number of important practical implications. For example, learned helplessness may be an important factor in the difficulty young children have with mathematics in school. Children who repeatedly fail at math may conclude that they are helpless and thus stop trying, even though they actually have the ability to do quite well. In an experimental analogue of this phenomenon, Dweck and Repucci (1973) had two teachers give fifth-grade children a series of problems. One of the teachers always gave the children solvable problems, and the other presented only unsolvable ones. When the second teacher finally gave the children some solvable problems, they failed to solve them, even though they had solved exactly the same problems earlier for the first teacher.

Seligman (1975) has suggested that feelings of helplessness may also lead to depression. People who experience a traumatic event—the loss of a job, a divorce, the death of a child—may come to believe that they are helpless to control either the original event or the trauma that follows, and this feeling of helplessness may be a key factor in inducing depression. There is some evidence that feelings of helplessness may have even more powerful effects. Visintainer, Volpicelli, and Seligman (1982) have reported that rats exposed to inescapable shock when young become significantly more vulnerable to cancer as adults. It is not known whether this mechanism also operates in humans, but experiences that might be expected to give rise to feelings of helplessness—the death of a spouse, or an elderly person's transfer to an institution—have been found to lead to a substantial increase in morbidity in the year following the trauma. (See Rowland, 1977.) We do not yet know whether the mechanism involved is the same as that in animal experiments, but perceptions of helplessness do seem to have powerful emotional consequences, and it would not be surprising if these had wide-ranging effects on the endocrine and immune systems.

13.3 Concept Learning

Yet another example of complex learning involves the learning of concepts. The term **concept** can be maddeningly difficult to define but generally refers to a set of objects or events that are bound together by common features or relationships. Triangles all have three sides; a square consists of four lines of equal length joined at right angles; and so forth. In these examples, it is possible to state the defining features of the concept with some precision.

Other, "fuzzy" concepts, however, are much more difficult to define. Consider the concept *dog*. A young child is shown a dog and told "dog"; the procedure is repeated with a second dog, and so on, until the child learns to say "dog" as soon as a new one is encountered. This achievement is so commonplace that we tend to take it for granted; but if we examine it more closely, we will find that it is quite remarkable. Different breeds of dog vary widely in their characteristics: Consider a dachshund, a Saint Bernard, a poodle, and a bulldog. What is it that unites these very different animals, yet distinguishes them from similar species such as a cat or a fox? It is very difficult to verbalize the boundaries of the concept, and yet children quickly and easily abstract the critical properties and use them almost without error. (See also Rosch, 1978.)

Concept Learning in Pigeons

The ability to form concepts is critical to language and thought and, thus, was long assumed to be unique to humans. Even if it had occurred to anyone to wonder whether animals, too, might be capable of forming concepts, there was no obvious way of answering this question. Suppose, for example, that you wanted to know whether a pigeon could form a complex concept such as *human being*. To find out if a child understands a concept such as *dog* is relatively simple: We can present pictures of different animals and ask whether each is a dog. A pigeon, however, cannot say "human being." How, then, can we determine whether it understands the concept?

In 1964, Herrnstein and Loveland provided an ingeniously simple solution to this problem by taking advantage of one response that pigeons can make with considerable ease and conviction: pecking. Using the standard techniques of instrumental or operant conditioning, they trained their birds to peck a key whenever they thought a human being was present. The experimenters projected a series of slides onto a screen, some containing a human being but others not. If the picture contained one or more people, pecks at the screen were occasionally reinforced with food. If pigeons are capable of forming the concept of human being, we should expect the birds to learn eventually to peck only when a human being was present in the picture.

To ensure that the birds were using a complex concept and not just relying on a simpler feature such as the presence of human flesh colors, Herrnstein and Loveland assembled a set of pictures that were matched in every possible respect except for the presence of a human:

> For any one session, approximately half the photographs contained at least one human being; the remainder contained no human beings—in the experimenter's best judgment. In no other systematic way did the two sets of slides appear to differ. Many slides contained human beings partly obscured by intervening objects: trees, automobiles, window frames, and so on. The people were distrib-

uted throughout the pictures: in the center or to one side or the other, near the top or the bottom, close up or distant. Some slides contained a single person; others contained groups of various sizes. The people themselves were clothed, semi-nude, or nude; adults or children; men or women; sitting, standing, or lying; black, white, or yellow. Lighting and coloration varied: some slides were dark, others light; some had either reddish or bluish tints, and so on.

(Herrnstein & Loveland, 1964, p. 239)

The results were straightforward: The birds quickly learned to peck more to positive stimuli than to negative ones. When presented with new stimuli that they had never seen previously, their average rate of pecking was 10 to 100 times faster if a human being was visible somewhere within the picture.

In subsequent experiments, Herrnstein and his colleagues have shown that pigeons are equally proficient at learning other concepts such as *tree*, *oak leaf*, and even *fish*. These concepts are learned, moreover, with quite astonishing speed. In one experiment (Herrnstein, 1979), the correct concept was *tree*. The positive and negative slides did not obviously differ in any respect other than the presence of a tree. Pigeons typically require from two to nine sessions to master relatively simple discriminations such as color (learning, for example, to peck a green key but not a red one). The birds in this experiment, however, learned to respond differentially to pictures containing trees after only a single session.

Is It Really Learning?

Given the rapidity of this learning, it is tempting to conclude that the birds were not really learning a concept at all, but rather using preexisting concepts that had become genetically ingrained through the course of evolution. Although this argument might apply to concepts such as *tree*, it is difficult to imagine what evolutionary pressures could have encouraged pigeons to develop an innate concept of *fish*. Definitive evidence that learning is involved comes from an experiment by Herrnstein, Loveland, and Cable (1976), in which pigeons learned to recognize a particular human being. The positive stimuli were pictures of this individual, and the negative stimuli were pictures of other people. Even though the pictures were closely matched in almost all respects (the negative pictures were taken in the same settings as the positive ones, and in some cases even involved people wearing the same clothing as the subject), the birds nevertheless had little difficulty learning to peck only when the subject was present. It seems safe to infer that the birds in this experiment were genuinely learning a new concept rather than tapping a preexisting one.

Once concept learning in pigeons is accepted as a reality, the existence of this capacity begins to look obvious. To mate successfully, for example, a pigeon needs to distinguish pigeons from doves (and male pigeons from female ones!). A pigeon also needs to discriminate acceptable foods from poisonous ones, cats from hedgehogs, and so forth. To survive, in other words, animals need to categorize objects appropriately in their environment, and it should not be surprising that they do so not on the basis of a single feature ("Any gray object is a pigeon") but by using a number of features that bear a particular relationship to one another (the head and feet of a pigeon, for example, must be at opposite ends of the body). It is perhaps less obvious that pigeons should have the ability to learn concepts, as opposed to using genetically programmed ones. However, if we consider evolutionary pressures (for example, the need for young birds and their mothers to learn to recognize each other), then it is not altogether surprising that animals can learn to identify complex stimuli and treat them as a unified conceptual class so that new exemplars are immediately categorized appropriately.

The fact that pigeons and other animals can learn concepts does not necessarily mean that their ability to do so is equal in all respects to that of humans; human concepts such as *justice* or *deceit* are almost certainly more complex than any concepts formed by pigeons. And even when pigeons and humans appear to categorize stimuli similarly, there may be subtle and not-so-subtle differences between the concepts that have actually been formed. In an experiment by Cerella (1980), for example, pigeons were taught to discriminate pictures of the cartoon character Charlie Brown from other characters in "Peanuts," such as Snoopy and Lucy. In the test phase, the experimenters presented transformed versions of the cartoon—for example, with Charlie Brown's head at the bottom of his body and his feet at the top. But the birds still responded as vigorously to these somewhat bizarre pictures as to the original training stimuli. The birds seemed to be responding to the features that make up Charlie Brown, but they clearly did not integrate these features into a perceptual whole in the same way that humans do. (See also Herrnstein, 1984.) To say that a rat or a pigeon can form concepts, then, is not the same as claiming that they are the intellectual peers of humans. Nevertheless, current evidence suggests that animals can form concepts of considerable complexity (Pepperberg, 1987; Vaughan, 1988; Wright, Cook, Rivera, Sands, & Delius, 1988). The human ability to form concepts of great abstractness is almost certainly a refinement of the simpler but still impressive ability of animals to detect uniformities or invariances in their environments.

13.4 Hypothesis Theory

When a response is reinforced, animals clearly do far more than just associate the response with the stimuli present. They may form detailed cognitive maps of their environment; they may learn general strategies for obtaining reinforcement (win-stay, lose-shift or learned helplessness); and they may compare current stimuli with those present during earlier reinforcements to identify common features (concept learning). Having acknowledged these achievements, can we now say anything about the learning processes that underlie them?

The Theory

One explanation for the way in which subjects solve complex problems is offered by *hypothesis theory* (Trabasso & Bower, 1968; Levine, 1975). According to this view, subjects approach any problem with a set of hypotheses about the solution, and they then proceed to test one hypothesis at a time. In the case of learning set, for example, Levine has suggested that monkeys begin training with a set of nine basic hypotheses concerning the likely solution (Levine, 1965). We have already considered one hypothesis—win-stay, lose-shift. A second hypothesis—win-shift, lose-stay—was also mentioned in connection with Schusterman's (1962) study of learning set in chimpanzees; it assumes that whatever object is correct on one trial will be incorrect on the following trial. (This is not as improbable as it may sound: In nature, if food is removed from a location, it is highly unlikely to reappear there seconds later.) Other hypotheses suggested by Levine include object and position preferences (always choosing the same object or position) and object alternation.

On each trial, subjects are assumed to select one of these hypotheses for testing and to base their response on it. If they are reinforced, this hypothesis is strengthened; if not, it is weakened. In Harlow's procedure, if a monkey adopts a position hypothesis, such as selecting the object on the right, it will be correct on 50 percent of the trials; if it selects win-stay, lose-shift, it will be reinforced on every trial. Over a series of trials, therefore, the win-stay hypothesis will become progressively stronger than the alternative hypotheses, thereby explaining the gradual improvement in trial 2 performance.

Levine (1971) has proposed a modified version of this model to account for concept learning in humans, the major difference between the two models being the speed of learning. In monkeys, reinforcement is assumed to result in only a small increase in the probability that a hypothesis will be selected; we assume that human subjects will always retain a hypothesis when it is correct. Levine's model assumes that:

1. Subjects start any problem with a set of hypotheses about the solution.

2. On each trial, subjects select one hypothesis for testing and base their response on this hypothesis.

3. If correct, they retain this hypothesis for testing on the following trial; if incorrect, they abandon it and select another hypothesis from those remaining in the set.

Predictions of Hypothesis Theory

This basic model can be elaborated in a variety of ways, but even in relatively simple form it leads to some interesting predictions. We will consider two of them here.

All-or-none learning.   The first prediction concerns the rapidity with which learning occurs. To illustrate this prediction, we will use a concept-learning experiment by Trabasso (1963) in which a picture of a flower was presented on every trial. The flowers differed in many dimensions, including type (tulip, daisy, and so on), color, and leaf shape. The subject's task was to decide which of two categories each picture belonged to. The correct classification was based on one of the flower's dimensions—for example, whether it was red or yellow—and subjects were told after each trial whether their response was correct.

How should we expect the probability of a correct response to change over trials? According to associative models of learning, reinforcement gradually strengthens an association between a response and the stimuli present. Therefore, as the response of saying "category A" is repeatedly reinforced on red trials, there should be a gradual increase in the probability that red will elicit this response. According to hypothesis theory, on the other hand, subjects test only a single hypothesis on each trial. As long as the subject's hypothesis is wrong—for example, that flowers with smooth leaves belong in category A—then responding will remain at chance (50 percent), because values of the irrelevant dimensions were assigned randomly. Once subjects select the correct hypothesis, however, they should respond correctly on all subsequent trials, because the model assumes that they will retain this hypothesis as long as it leads to reinforcement. In other words, subjects should start at 50 percent and stay there until they finally select the correct hypothesis, whereupon they should immediately respond at 100 percent. Thus, whereas associative learning models predict a gradual improvement over trials, hypothesis-testing models predict **all-or-none learning**, or **one-trial learning**.

To test this prediction, Trabasso examined each subject's data to determine the last trial on which an error occurred. Then, for each trial, he calculated the average performance of subjects who had not yet begun performing perfectly. According to hypothesis theory, subjects must have been using incorrect hypotheses on all trials preceding the last error. (Had they adopted the correct hypothesis, they would not have made any further errors.) Performance across these trials, therefore, should remain at chance. According to an incremental learning analysis, however, reinforcement for saying "A" on red trials should lead to a gradual strengthening of this response. The results are shown in Figure 13.7. Note that performance did not improve over trials, suggesting that reinforcement of the correct response had no effect as long as subjects were testing hypotheses about irrelevant dimensions.

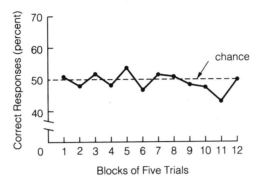

F I G U R E 13.7 Presolution performance during concept learning. The percentage of correct responses is shown for all trials prior to a subject's last error. (Adapted from Trabasso, 1963)

Nonlearning. A related prediction of the model concerns what happens when a subject's initial set of hypotheses does not contain the correct hypothesis. If the set is small—say, 5 to 10 hypotheses—subjects should soon realize that none of the hypotheses in this set is correct, and they may then generate a new set of hypotheses for testing. If the set is very large, however, they should continue to sample hypotheses from this incorrect set. If we now add the assumption that subjects learn only about the hypotheses they are testing, the theory predicts that subjects who start a problem with a very large set of hypotheses that does not include the solution should fail to solve it, no matter how simple the problem may be.

To test this prediction, Levine (1971) asked college students to select the letter A or B on every trial. If they said A, the experimenter told them that they were correct; if they said B, the experimenter told them that they were wrong. The problem was thus unbelievably simple: All subjects had to do was to learn to say A. Not surprisingly, subjects in a control group required an average of only three trials to solve it. To see what would happen if subjects did not include the correct solution in their hypothesis set, Levine gave a second group pretraining in which the correct letter on each trial was determined by a complex alternation sequence. The basis of solution for a typical problem was the sequence AABAAABABB, a sequence that was repeated over and over. If the subject did not solve the problem within 115 trials, the experimenter verbally explained the solution and then presented a new problem, again involving a complex alternation sequence. In all, subjects received six such problems during pretraining.

When transferred to the test problem, how should these subjects perform? Despite the utter simplicity of the problem, Levine predicted that subjects would find it unsolvable. On the first pretraining problem, subjects might begin by testing relatively simple hypotheses such as "A is always correct," but as simple hypotheses of this kind repeatedly proved inadequate, they would turn to more complex hypotheses. By the end of pretraining, Levine suggested, their hypothesis set would consist exclusively of such complex hypotheses. When transferred to the test problem, then, they would be unable to solve it, because their hypothesis set would not contain the simple hypothesis "A is correct."

The result was that 81 percent of the subjects failed to solve the problem, even when given 115 trials to do so. Indeed, there was no sign of any improvement in the performance of these subjects. On trials 91–100, for example, only 53 percent of their responses were correct, a figure statistically indistinguishable from chance. Thus, even though the response of saying A was reinforced every time it occurred, there was no increase in its probability. The implication is that reinforcement was not strengthening the overt response of saying A but rather whatever covert hypothesis gave rise to it.

Evaluating Hypothesis Theory

The evidence we have been reviewing supports the assumption that learning is based on the systematic testing of simple hypotheses drawn from a larger set. (For more detailed reviews of this literature, see Levine, 1975; Gholson, 1980.) Notwithstanding its success, hypothesis theory has two important weaknesses or limitations that we must also recognize.

First, it is unlikely that all learning is based on the testing of hypotheses. Whereas learning sometimes follows the all-or-none pattern predicted by the model, we have also encountered many instances in which learning has been very slow: cats struggling to escape from a puzzle box, humans learning to drive a car or to contract an invisibly small muscle in their thumb. It seems unlikely that learning in these situations is based on the systematic testing of hypotheses in the manner suggested by the theory. A more plausible conclusion is that learning may involve the testing of hypotheses in some situations, but that simpler, associative mechanisms are involved in others. (See also Kendler, 1979.)

A second weakness of the theory is that it provides us with little or no guidance concerning the origin of the subjects' hypotheses. Imagine, for example, that a subject starts a problem with 10 hypotheses; where do these hypotheses come from? One possibility is that subjects recall solutions that have proved successful in similar problems in the past. But this would not explain the ability of subjects to solve problems that are totally unfamiliar, as in the case of pigeons learning to recognize fish. If hypothesis testing is involved at all in such learning, then the pigeons must somehow use the outcomes of early trials to generate hypotheses about the solution. If the first four pictures all contain a human being or a three-toed sloth, for example, then subjects may notice this fact and adopt it as a hypothesis. If this analysis is correct, hypothesis models may be accurate as far as they go, but a full analysis of learning requires an understanding of how subjects detect features common to different stimuli or responses.

13.5 THE PROBLEM OF ABSTRACTION

We have reviewed evidence that even in relatively simple situations in which one response is reinforced or another punished, learning may be surprisingly complex. Rather than learning about the particular stimulus or response that preceded reinforcement, animals may combine this information with that from earlier trials in quite complex ways. A rat in a maze may not just learn to turn right; it may form a cognitive map of how all the sections of the maze are related. A monkey reinforced for choosing one object from each of a hundred pairs may not only learn about the particular objects that were reinforced but may also acquire a general strategy about continuing to choose whatever object was correct on the preceding trial until it is no longer reinforced. And pigeons reinforced for pecking at slides may not learn to peck at specific slides but may learn about the characteristics that all the correct pictures have in common.

In most of these cases, the animals tested seemed to be combining their experiences across a number of situations to detect or abstract shared features or common principles: "Food is always under the object reinforced on the previous trial." "No response I make will let me escape the shock." "There is a human being present in all the correct pictures." If we could understand this process of **abstraction,** we might have the key to all complex learning.

Prototypes and Exemplars

One useful clue to how abstraction occurs comes from an experiment by Posner and Keele (1968). In order to study how subjects derive new concepts they have never encountered previously, the experimenters created a series of artificial concepts by first generating a central or typical member of a concept and then creating other members of the concept by making small alterations in the original. Figure 13.8 shows the original members of three concepts, composed of an array of dots, together with other members of one of these categories created by randomly altering the positions of some of the dots.

In one experiment, Posner and Keele presented subjects with four pictures drawn from each of three categories. They did not show the picture of the original member of the concept, however. On each trial, the experimenter asked the subjects to tell which category each picture had been drawn from, and then gave the subject the correct answer. Posner and Keele found that their subjects learned the concepts reasonably quickly; when shown new examples, or *exemplars*, of each concept, moreover, they were able to classify them correctly the first time they were presented.

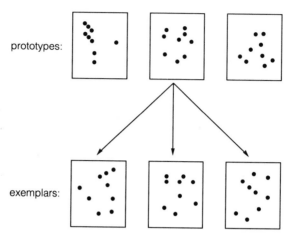

F I G U R E 13.8   Dot patterns used by Posner and Keele (1968) to study concept learning. Three of the prototypes used to generate instances of the concepts are shown at the top; three instances, or exemplars, derived from one of these prototypes by randomly moving some dots are shown at the bottom. (Adapted from Posner, 1973)

How did the subjects classify the new pictures? One possibility, now called *exemplar theory*, is that the subjects simply compared the new pictures to their memories of similar pictures they had seen previously. Thus, if a new picture closely resembled a pattern that they had learned belonged to category 2, then they would also classify the new picture in category 2. Categorization, in other words, was based on comparison of new stimuli with existing exemplars, or, in the language of earlier chapters, on generalization of the correct response from the training stimuli to the test stimuli. (See also Astley & Wasserman, 1992.)

An alternative theory is that during training subjects compared the stimuli that belonged to a concept and abstracted the shared features. Specifically, subjects might have combined exemplars of a concept to form a composite or average, which Posner and Keele called a *prototype*. Our prototype of a dog, for example, will have four legs and a tail because almost all dogs have these features, but its size may be an average based on the dogs we have encountered. (See also Rosch, 1978.) We will call this alternative theory, in which subjects learn concepts by abstracting prototypes, *prototype theory*.

Testing Prototype Theory

To determine whether classification of test stimuli was based on comparisons with individual exemplars or averaged prototypes, Posner and Keele ran a new experiment in which they presented a new set of test stimuli after training. Some of these had already been presented during training, but others were new exemplars of each category, including the original, or prototype, used to generate the concept.

The question of interest was whether the new stimuli would differ in the ease with which subjects classified them. If subjects classified new pictures by comparing them to exemplars already in memory, the new exemplars and the prototype should have been equally difficult to classify, because the exemplars had been carefully chosen to ensure that their similarity to each of the pictures presented during training was the same as that of the prototype. For example, if the original prototype and one of the training stimuli had 80 percent of their dots in the same position, then the new exemplar was chosen so that it too would have 80 percent of its dots in the same position as the training stimulus.

If subjects had averaged stimuli together during training to form prototypes, however, this averaged prototype obviously would be very similar to the prototype used by the experimenters to generate the concept in the first place. According to prototype theory, therefore, the subjects should have found the original prototype easier to classify than the new exemplars, because it would be much more similar to their own prototype. This was the result: Subjects made classification errors on 38 percent of the new exemplars but only 15 percent of the prototypes.

Further support for prototype theory comes from a similar experiment by Franks and Bransford (1971), in which subjects were asked if they had seen any of the test stimuli before. The striking result was that subjects were more likely to report recognizing the prototypes, which had never been presented, than the training stimuli, which they had actually seen. These results suggest that subjects had created prototypes during training, and that repeated processing of these prototypes on successive trials had made them more familiar than the training stimuli from which they had been derived.

This evidence strongly supports a prototype interpretation of concept learning, but other studies have also provided support for an exemplar interpretation (for example, Hintzman, 1986; Nosofsky, 1991; Astley & Wasserman, 1992). It is thus not yet clear whether concept learning involves simple comparison to stored exemplars or a more active process of abstraction. One possibility is that both theories may be right—that new instances of a concept are categorized by comparison both to an abstracted prototype and to specific exemplars previously encountered ("Hmm, that looks a lot like a bigger version of my neighbor's dachsund"). If so, then to understand complex learning, we may need a system that not only combines information to form a prototype but also preserves the individual experiences on which the prototype was based.

13.6 THE NEURAL NETWORK SOLUTION
(TO ASSOCIATION, ABSTRACTION,
AND EVERYTHING . . .)

As it happens, a number of models that satisfy this criterion have been proposed, but we will concentrate in this section on only one. (For reviews of other models, see Estes, 1986; Medin, 1989.) This approach is so new that no agreed-upon name has yet emerged, but the model has already had an explosive impact among scientists interested in the operations of the brain, including psychologists, neurophysiologists, computer scientists, and even physicists. One important reason for their excitement is that the new approach suggests what may be an optimal design for organizing electrical circuits to process information—a design that may already be the basis for the brain's organization and that could form the basis for a new generation of massively powerful computers. Within psychology, the significance of this new approach is that it offers an explanation not only for sophisticated cognitive processes such as abstraction, but also for most of the evidence on conditioning reviewed in the previous chapters. And it achieves all this using what is essentially a single, simple principle.

Among the terms that have been suggested to describe this new approach are *connectionist, parallel and distributed processing* (*PDP*), and *neural network*. We will use the term *neural network*, because it conveys a clearer sense of the model's fundamental assumptions.

Brains and Computers

Parallel processing.   At the heart of this new approach is a belief that psychological models should be based as closely as possible on the known properties of the brain. To understand this view, it may be helpful to begin by contrasting it with the computer or information-processing metaphor that has dominated cognitive psychology for the past two decades. As we saw in Chapter 12, the basic structure of a digital computer consists of a central processing unit (CPU) and a memory store: The CPU retrieves items from memory, carries out a sequence of operations such as addition and subtraction, and then transfers the result back to memory. The computer is capable of carrying out only very simple operations, but by performing them in an appropriate sequence and at extraordinarily high speeds—more than a million operations in a single second—it can solve highly complex problems.

The brain, however, is organized very differently. For one thing, there is no obvious distinction in the brain between the processing of information and its storage; there is only one unit, the neuron, that must somehow carry out both functions. As we saw in Chapter 2, when a neuron is stimulated, it produces an electrical impulse which is transmitted along the long part of the cell called the axon. When this impulse arrives at the axon terminal, it causes the release of neurotransmitter chemicals which move across the synaptic gap to the next neuron in the chain; the arrival of these neurotransmitters causes the second neuron to produce an electrical impulse, and so on. The brain consists of an almost unimaginably large number of such neurons—more than 10,000,000,000—organized in densely interconnected networks called **neural networks**. A single neuron may receive inputs from up to 50,000 other neu-

F I G U R E 13.9   Drawing of cortical neurons, illustrating the dense network of interconnections. (le Roy Conel, 1963)

rons. Figure 13.9 shows a small section of the brain, with some of the connections between the neurons. The complexity of the interconnections is
apparent.

In contrast to most computers, then, which carry out only a single operation at a time, the brain contains a vast array of neurons of which many
millions or even billions are active at a given moment. In the terminology of
electrical circuitry, the brain is a massively parallel system in which an enormous number of circuits operate simultaneously. Unlike most computers, then,
the brain is characterized by **parallel processing**.

This difference in architecture has important implications for function:
The structure of the brain allows it to easily solve problems that computers find
difficult, if not impossible. For example, most people find it easy to read other
people's handwriting, but this trivial skill is beyond the power of most current
computers. Neural network theorists believe that the computer has thus been a
partially misleading model for the functioning of the brain, and that psychological models should be based instead on the architecture of the brain—that is,
they should incorporate neuronlike units that can assume only a limited range
of firing states, and that are interconnected in dense networks.

Learning in a neural network.   How might learning occur in a neural network
of the kind we have described? Our knowledge of neural physiology is still
incomplete, but the outlines of the answer are becoming clear: Learning is
mediated by changes at the synapse, which result in more efficient transmission
of electrical impulses between neurons. In particular, Byrne (1985) has pro-

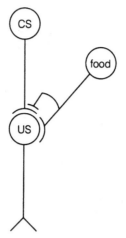

F I G U R E 13.10   A neuronal model of classical conditioning. In this simplified representation, a CS neuron is connected to a US neuron, and a food neuron is connected to both.

posed that the crucial change may be in the capacity of neurons to produce neurotransmitters.

Figure 13.10 illustrates how Byrne's proposal can be applied in the case of classical conditioning. A CS neuron is connected to a US neuron; in addition, there is a sensory neuron stimulated by food, which has connections to both the CS and US neurons. Suppose that initially the synaptic connection between the CS and US neurons is a weak one, in the sense that electrical activity in the CS results in the release of only a small quantity of neurotransmitters and thus fails to activate the US neuron. If food is now presented, electrical activity in the food neuron will cause the release of neurotransmitters at the synapses with both the CS and US neurons. If this neurotransmitter arrives at the CS neuron at a time when it is already active, chemical changes will be triggered that result in a permanent increase in the capacity of the CS neuron to produce neurotransmitters. The next time the CS is presented, the arrival of an electrical impulse at the synapse will cause the release of more neurotransmitters and thus will be more likely to activate the US neuron. Simultaneous activity in the CS and food neurons, in other words, would strengthen the CS–US connection, as classical conditioning requires.

Other models of how the connections between neurons are strengthened have also been proposed (for example, Hawkins & Kandel, 1984), but for our purposes the precise physiological mechanism is not important. The key assumption is simply that neurons that are active at the same time will have their connections strengthened.

A Neural Network Model

In outline, neural network models are surprisingly simple, and we have already covered their two main assumptions:

1. *Neural networks.* There is a network of neurons, with every neuron in the network connected to every other neuron.

2. *Learning.* If two neurons within the network are active at the same time, the connection between them will be strengthened, so that in future activity in one neuron will be more likely to produce activity in the other neuron.

In essence, these two assumptions are virtually identical to those made by Pavlov almost 100 years ago: When two cortical centers are active simultaneously, the connection between them will be strengthened. Neural network models, however, incorporate two changes in Pavlov's ideas, which have far-reaching implications for their ability to predict behavior. First, they assume that the networks involved are quite massive, so that associations will be formed simultaneously among very large numbers of active neurons. Second, they provide a mathematical formula that allows us to calculate exactly how much each of these connections will be strengthened. Together, these assumptions allow us to make predictions about the brain's functioning in a way that goes far beyond anything Pavlov ever attempted or could have attempted: The number of equations involved can be solved only by means of modern computers.

The delta rule. One of the crucial decisions in creating a neural network model, then, is choosing the formula to use in calculating how connections are strengthened. A number of formulas or rules have been suggested, but one of the most influential has been the *delta rule.*

To understand this rule, consider the arrangement of neurons shown in Figure 13.11, which is a slightly expanded version of the arrangement shown in Figure 13.10. The neurons labeled CS and US are assumed to be part of a much larger neural network, and each also receives input from sensory neurons located outside the network. Specifically, the presentation of a tone induces activity in a sensory receptor, which triggers electrical activity in the Tone neuron. This activity is then transmitted to the CS neuron in the brain. Similarly, the presentation of food triggers activity in taste receptors in the mouth, inducing activity in a Food neuron, and this activity is transmitted to a cortical US. If the tone and food are presented together, the CS and US neurons will be activated simultaneously and, according to the model, the connection between them will be strengthened.

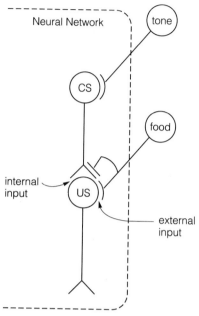

FIGURE 13.11   Illustration of the delta rule. If a CS and US neuron within a network are stimulated at the same time by sensory neurons from outside the network, the CS–US connection will be strengthened. The delta rule assumes that the degree of strengthening is determined by the difference between the internal input to the US neuron (from the CS) and the external input (from food).

We will call the excitation transmitted between the CS and US neurons in our example the *internal input*—that is, the input from within the network—and the excitation transmitted between the Food and US neurons the *external input*. The delta rule states that the strengthening of the connection between the CS and US neurons is determined by the relationship between the internal and external inputs. Ignoring some of the complexities of the actual formula, the delta rule in essence states that the change in the internal connection (ΔI) will be proportional to the difference between the internal and external inputs to the target neuron. Thus,

$$\Delta I = c \text{ (external input } - \text{ internal input)}$$

where c is some constant. If the internal input is less than the external input, the internal connection will be strengthened so that, in future, the internal input will match the external input more closely. In effect, the delta rule acts to match the input from within the neural network to that coming from outside it.

To illustrate this in concrete terms, suppose that there is a strong connection between the Food and US neurons, so that the presentation of food initially produces a rate of firing in the US neuron of 10 impulses per second. Suppose that the connection between the CS and US neurons is much weaker, so that activity in the CS neuron elicits a rate of firing in the US neuron of only 1 impulse per second. The CS, in other words, is much less effective than the Food neuron in stimulating the US neuron. If we ignore for the moment the constant in the delta rule, the difference between the external and internal inputs would be

$$\Delta I = (10 - 1) = 9$$

As a result, the internal connection between the CS and US neurons would be substantially strengthened.

Suppose that the next time the CS was presented, this stronger connection meant that the CS neuron elicited firing in the US neuron of, say, 5 impulses per second instead of only 1. The difference between the external and internal inputs would then be only

$$\Delta I = (10 - 5) = 5$$

On this trial, therefore, the CS–US connection would not be strengthened as much. Over a series of conditioning trials, the strength of the CS–US connection would continue to be adjusted toward that of the Food–US connection, but at a progressively slower rate. Once the internal and external inputs matched, additional pairings would have no further effect. In this way, the delta rule acts to match the strength of the internal input from the network to that of an external source.

The Rescorla-Wagner model.   Does any of this seem familiar? As you may have realized already, the delta rule achieves at the neural level exactly what the Rescorla-Wagner model achieves at the associative or behavioral level. The delta rule adjusts a neural connection so that it will match a value determined by input from outside the network; similarly, the Rescorla-Wagner model adjusts the strength of the CS–US association so that it will match an external value determined by the US used.

Indeed, not only is the logic of the two approaches the same, it turns out the formulas used are mathematically identical (see Sutton & Barto, 1981), even though they were developed entirely independently. (The delta rule was developed by Widrow & Hoff, 1960, for use in designing optimal electrical circuits.) The fact that workers in different areas have independently converged on the same rule may just be coincidence. But it could also be an indication that this rule is an optimal solution to the problem of how to modify electrical circuits to make them more adaptive—a solution that not only has been discovered by engineers for the design of electrical circuits, but also has emerged in the course of evolution as the basis for the operation of the brain's neural circuits.

Explaining Abstraction

In one sense, then, neural network models are little more than the Rescorla-Wagner model applied not just to two neurons but to many thousands of neurons in a vast network. How, then, does all of this help us to understand the problem of abstraction with which we began?

Forming a prototype.   Consider again a child learning the concept *dog*. No two dogs are identical—dachshunds, poodles, and bulldogs all differ greatly—but somehow the child abstracts the features in common. McClelland and Rumelhart (1985) have shown how a neural network presented with many instances of *dog* could similarly abstract a prototype and then use this prototype to classify new examples. In a real network in the brain, many tens of thousands of neurons would be involved, but to simplify their calculations McClelland and Rumelhart assumed a much smaller system. To follow their analysis, suppose that the visual system contains only 16 receptors, with each one responding to a single feature. Eight of these receptors respond to features that are characteristic of dogs, and we will label each of these features with the symbol D. Receptor D_1, for example, might detect the presence of a tail, receptor D_2 the presence of four legs, and so on. The other eight receptors, which we will label N_1, N_2, and so on, are sensitive to features that are not normally characteristic of dogs (for example, purple skin). Each of these receptors is connected to one of the units in a 16-unit network within the brain (Figure 13.12). Thus, if the child sees an animal with a tail, unit D_1 in the network will be activated; if the animal has four legs, unit D_2 will be activated; and so on.

McClelland and Rumelhart assumed that a prototypical dog would have all of the typical features of a dog—that is, $D_1D_2D_3D_4D_5D_6D_7D_8$. Real dogs, of course, do not have all the features of the prototype: Some have longer legs, some have shorter tails, and so on. McClelland and Rumelhart therefore also created individual dogs by randomly varying some of the features of the prototype. For example, one dog might have been assigned the features $D_1D_3D_4D_5D_6D_8N_1N_7$. This dog would share six of the eight features of the prototype but would have two unusual features, just as a dachshund is unusual in having very short legs. Another dog might have the features $D_2D_3D_5D_6D_7D_8N_3N_4$, a third $D_1D_2D_4D_6D_7D_8N_2N_4$, and so on. McClelland and Rumelhart created a total of 50 individual dogs in this way, and then

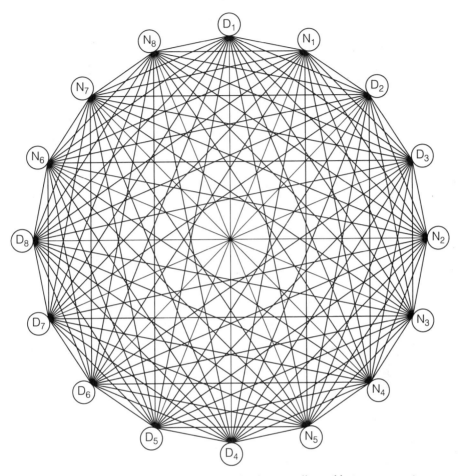

F I G U R E 13.12 A 16-unit neural network, showing all possible interconnections. Each circle represents a single neuron in the network.

"presented" the dogs to the network by assuming that the appropriate units of the net would be activated when each dog was presented. After each presentation, they used the delta rule to calculate alterations in the connections among the active units in the network.

Suppose, for example, that the first dog to be presented possessed the features $D_1D_3D_5D_6D_7D_8N_3N_5$. Because the D_1 and D_3 units in the network would be activated simultaneously, the connection between them would be strengthened in exactly the same way as in our earlier conditioning example. (The connection from D_1 to D_3 provides the internal input to D_3; the connection from the sensory receptor that detected the D_3 feature provides the external input.) Similarly, the connection from D_1 to D_5 would be strengthened, and so on.

McClelland and Rumelhart presented the network with a total of 50 dogs, adjusting the strength of the connections as necessary after each presentation. The result is shown in Figure 13.13, in which lines are drawn only between those features that have become strongly connected. The figure is actually a considerable simplification of the outcome. For example, it shows only connections involving the features of the prototype. (Because nonproto-

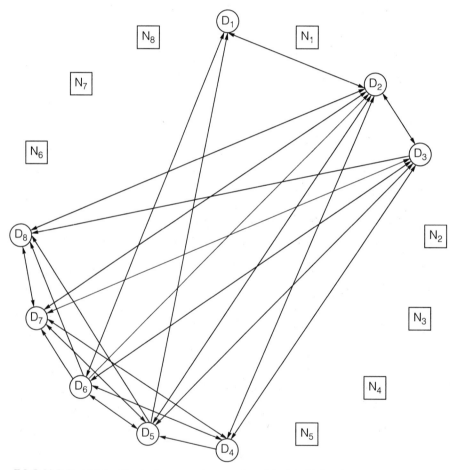

F I G U R E 13.13   Network connections predicted by McClelland and Rumelhart following 50 presentations of exemplars of the concept *dog*. The eight features possessed by the prototype are indicated by circles; nonprototype features are indicated by squares. Only strong connections involving the prototypical features are shown, but it is clear that these features have become strongly interconnected. (Based on data from McClelland & Rumelhart, 1985)

type features often occurred together, these features also tended to become associated with one another.) Nevertheless, the crucial result stands out clearly: Excitatory connections were formed between the features that were most typical of the category, so that activation of any subset of these features would spread to the others. Thus, the presentation of a new dog, even if it did not possess all the features of the prototype, would activate the entire prototype and thus lead to whatever behavior was appropriate to the prototype—calling it a dog, petting it, and so on.

Using a prototype. To illustrate how prototypes might be used to guide behavior, McClelland and Rumelhart ran a second experiment in which they presented the network with stimuli derived from three prototypes: one of a dog, another of a cat, and a third of a bagel. Because the visual features of cats and dogs are similar, six of the eight features of the dog and cat prototypes were made the same. To help assess the network's ability to categorize these stimuli, another eight features were added to the network to represent the category names—*cat, dog,* or *bagel.* (The network now contained a total of 24 features, 16 of which could be used to represent the visual properties of each object and 8 to represent each category name.) After the experimenters presented the network with 50 instances drawn from each of the three categories, they presented test stimuli consisting of only the name of the category or a visual pattern drawn from it. For every visual pattern presented, the network responded by activating the appropriate category name, and for every name, it activated the appropriate visual prototype. In effect, when presented with the word *dog,* the network responded with an image of this animal; when presented with a picture of a dog, the network recalled its name. The response to cats and bagels was similarly accurate.

The fact that a subset of a prototype's features can activate the entire set has a number of important implications. First, it means that the model will respond appropriately to an incomplete or distorted version of a familiar stimulus. If part of a dog is obscured by a tree, for example, the presence of the remaining features may still be sufficient to activate the prototype and thus produce recognition. Similarly, the model will be able to categorize stimuli it has never seen before: As long as enough features of the prototype are present, the entire prototype will be activated, even though the particular combination of features involved may be novel. Finally, the network can preserve information about individual dogs as well as the prototype. In one of their experiments, McClelland and Rumelhart gave the network experience with two particular dogs—one named Rover, the other Fido—as well as other dogs that were simply called *dog.* When given the name *dog,* the network activated the visual prototype for dog, but when told *Rover* or *Fido,* it produced the specific features of these two dogs. In other words, the network satisfies all the criteria for a model of abstraction specified in the previous section: It not only stores information about specific instances of a category but also abstracts the category prototype, and it can use this prototype to accurately categorize stimuli it has never previously encountered.

And Everything . . .

In the brief time that neural network models have been in existence, they have proved able to account for a wide range of phenomena in classical conditioning, in some cases far better than the Rescorla-Wagner model. (See Sutton & Barto, 1981; Gluck & Thompson, 1987; Kehoe, 1988.) They also have accounted for a wide range of phenomena in the very different domain of concept learning. (See McClelland & Rumelhart, 1986; Gluck & Bower, 1988; Kruschke, 1992.) If this were all these models could do, it would be remarkable enough, but there is evidence to suggest that they may be able to do much more. One example is their ability to account for many of the classic findings about associative memory. How is it, for example, that when presented with fragmentary information about an item stored in memory ("What is the Russian word for teapot? It begins with the letter S.") we can retrieve the item from the vast amount of information stored in our brains? The neural network solution is simple: Presentation of some features of a target memory will reactivate the other features with which they had been associated.

At a still higher level, there is evidence that neural networks may be able to account for many aspects of language and thought. An important problem in psycholinguistics, for example, concerns how children learn the rules governing the past tense of verbs. The most common method of forming the past tense of a verb in English is to add the letters *ed* to the end of the present tense form (jump–jumped, open–opened, and so on). However, many verbs follow different patterns (run–ran, send–sent, and so on). At first, children learn the correct form for all the verbs they know, but then, as their vocabulary grows, they begin to use the *ed* form for all verbs, even ones for which it is inappropriate (*runned*, *sended*, and so on), and for which they previously used the correct form. Finally, they return to using the correct form for all verbs. As complex as this developmental sequence is, Rumelhart and McClelland (1986) have shown that a neural network analysis predicts not only the sequence but also some of its finer details, including which forms are most likely to be confused. In a particularly striking demonstration of the power of networks, Sejnowski and Rosenberg (1987) have actually constructed a demonstration network that, when given examples of English words together with their pronunciation, can learn to read—in the sense that, when given the letters of an English word it has never previously encountered, it can pronounce that word correctly using a voice synthesizer. Given the extraordinary variability of English spelling rules—George Bernard Shaw once pointed out that, on the basis of how its components were sometimes pronounced, the made-up word *ghoti* could be pronounced "fish"—this is a considerable feat.

A Preliminary Evaluation

The evidence we have reviewed suggests that neural network models may be able to account for some of the most sophisticated aspects of human thought, including our ability to learn concepts and languages, and do so on the basis of a learning mechanism almost identical to that observed in slugs, a primitive creature with a brain of only a few hundred neurons. (See Gelperin, 1986.)

If the fundamental mechanism of the brain is the same in humans as in slugs, you may wonder, why are humans so much more intelligent? One difference lies in the sheer size of the networks involved: A network with millions of neurons can carry out computations and store data to a degree far beyond that of much smaller networks.

In addition, there are almost certainly critical differences in the organization of the networks. We have emphasized the role of parallel processing—many neurons operating at once—but we must also consider **sequential processing**, in which information processed in one subsystem is passed on to a second subsystem, and so on. Thus, although McClelland and Rumelhart assumed that a feature would be represented by a single neuron in the network, in reality the identification of features is in itself a massive undertaking, requiring many thousands or millions of neurons spread over a number of processing stages. In other words, before reaching our "prototype" network, visual input will already have undergone extensive processing; similarly, extensive processing will almost certainly follow this stage—for example, in combining concepts into sentences, plans of action, and so forth.

Neural networks, then, are not quite as simple as our initial discussion implied, and neural network models must eventually be made far more complex to account for sequential as well as parallel processing. Such complexity should not surprise us; it would be astonishing if a model of a system containing billions of neurons were not complex. What is far more remarkable is that the fundamental mechanism upon which the entire system is based appears to be genuinely simple, and that even small networks of randomly interconnected neurons are very powerful.

A possible objection to the approach we have been outlining is that it is too mechanistic: Instead of dealing with thoughts, images, and emotions, we seem to be lost in a sea of neurons. The difference in the two accounts is perhaps akin to the anecdote about a swan swimming in a lake: seen from above, all cool grace and elegance, but underneath the surface, paddling away furiously. The two views are not contradictory; they simply describe different levels of analysis. A neural account does not deny the reality of thoughts or emotions any more than an analysis of atomic structure denies the reality of thunderstorms or planets. An understanding of what is going on beneath the surface, however, can enhance our ability to understand and influence events at the higher level.

13.7 ASSOCIATIVE LEARNING AND COGNITION

In a sense, this whole text has been about the tension between two views of learning. Pavlov believed that education and training "are really nothing more than the results of an establishment of new nervous connections" (Pavlov, 1927, p. 26), and that an understanding of how associations are formed during conditioning would inevitably lead to an understanding of all learned behavior. Cognitive theorists such as Tolman, on the other hand, argued that learning was far too complex, too goal oriented, to be explained in terms of simple associations: Something more complicated, more like an expectation or a cognitive map, was required.

The history of learning theory can be seen as a series of swings between these two views, with cognitive theorists providing seemingly decisive evidence against associative accounts, only to have associative theorists show how, with a relatively minor adjustment, their theories could account for the new evidence after all. Thus, when latent extinction seemed to show that animals could anticipate the consequences of their actions, Hull showed how this behavior could be explained if S–R theory was broadened to include associations between covert events as well as overt ones. Similarly, Rescorla's demonstration that contiguity is not sufficient for conditioning—the CS and US must also be contingent—seemed at first to require that animals be capable of calculating complex probabilities of events over time. Eventually, however, Rescorla and Wagner showed how this behavior too could be understood in terms of associations, provided that the associative strength of all the stimuli present during conditioning was taken into account. And now, almost before learning theorists have had time to assimilate the evidence that animal learning is far more complex than had been supposed, with animals having the capacity to learn concepts and strategies and develop cognitive maps, an explanation of these behaviors in fundamentally associative terms has already been proposed by neural network theorists and others (for example, Astley & Wasserman, 1992; Couvillon & Bitterman, 1992).

In Chapter 11, we considered one possible reconciliation of the two viewpoints—that both might be right, with learning involving relatively simple associations in some situations but more complex expectations in others. Then, in Chapter 12, we considered some of the cognitive processes that contribute to shaping the two outcomes, including how events are coded and retrieved. The material reviewed in this chapter can be interpreted as providing a number of amendments to this emerging model of learning, summarized in Figure 13.14.

First, at the level of outcomes, it may be useful to categorize learning not only in terms of relatively simple forms such as associations and expectations, but also in terms of more complex structures such as cognitive maps, rules, and concepts. It is still not clear whether these are truly distinct forms of learning or variants of a single basic process, but in our present state of ignorance it is perhaps worth listing them separately, if only to emphasize the breadth and variety of learning.

A second amendment to our model is the inclusion of abstraction among the cognitive processes that shape learning. The crucial role of abstraction in the learning of complex concepts and rules is probably clear by now, but abstraction may be equally important in even the simplest forms of learning. Consider, for example, a rat learning to press a bar to obtain food. We tend to think of this as a relatively trivial accomplishment, but from the perspective of the rat it certainly is not. On one occasion it presses the bar with 10 grams of force with its right paw while holding its head at an angle of 45 degrees and breathing rapidly; on another occasion, it presses with 12 grams of force with its left paw while holding its head at 60 degrees and raising its tail; and so on. We know that the requirement for reinforcement is simply how far the bar travels, but the rat does not: It must abstract the critical feature from experiences that have varied widely over many dimensions. Even seemingly simple learning situations thus require the same cognitive processes of memory, attention, and abstraction required by more obviously demanding tasks such as problem solving and language learning. This does not mean that all forms of learning are equivalent in complexity—learning to press a bar is undoubtedly easier than coming to terms with Einstein's theory of relativity or the Rescorla-

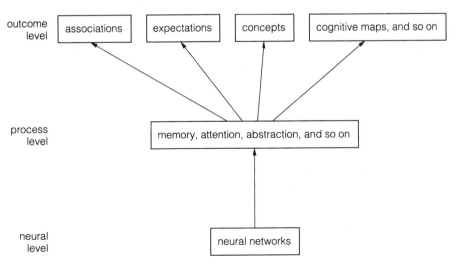

F I G U R E 13.14 A three-level analysis of associative learning.

Wagner model—but the difference in the skills required may be less dramatic than the terms *associative* and *cognitive* tend to imply. Associative learning may be simpler, but this does not mean that it is simple.

Still a third change to our conception of learning, and the one that in the end may prove the most important, is the introduction of a third level of analysis based on interactions at the neural level. The fundamental unit of analysis at this third level consists of associations between neurons, and neural network models are thus closely related to earlier associative accounts such as Pavlov's and Hull's. Indeed, if these models are able to explain concept learning and language acquisition as they claim to (that is, if the claims can be supported), they would provide striking confirmation for Pavlov's claim that an understanding of conditioning would ultimately lead to an understanding of all learned behavior. (Recall that the central principle of these network models, the delta rule, is essentially a restatement of the Rescorla-Wagner model of classical conditioning.)

In other respects, however, these models are much closer in spirit to cognitive analyses of learning than to S–R theory. S–R theorists argued that behavior should be analyzed in terms of simple, observable events such as stimuli and responses. Neural network models, however, accept the crucial role of internal processes in determining how we respond to a stimulus. Rather than denying cognitive processes such as memory, attention, or abstraction, network theorists make them a central focus of their investigations but then try to account for these cognitive processes in terms of more primitive interactions at a neural level. In terms of our earlier swan analogy, network theorists do not deny that swans swim gracefully; instead, they try to explain how they do it.

Neural network models, then, represent a new and richer version of our earlier attempt to reconcile associative and cognitive approaches to learning. As in that earlier synthesis, network models accept the reality of both associations and expectations at a behavioral level, and they also accept the importance of cognitive processes such as memory and attention in shaping those outcomes. They suggest, however, that these processes can themselves be understood at a more primitive level, with the fundamental principle being the association. It is too soon to say whether these models will succeed, but their solid grounding in the known structure of the brain gives them an inherent plausibility. If they do succeed, the emergence of these models may someday be seen as the single most important step in the evolution of psychology.

13.8 SUMMARY

When we introduced the topic of reinforcement, we implied that the learning involved was relatively simple: A rat in a maze learns to turn to the right; a pigeon in a Skinner box learns to peck a key. Reinforcement, as Thorndike had claimed, seemed to simply stamp in whatever movement preceded it. The evidence reviewed in this chapter, however, suggests that learning is far more complex than this. A rat in a maze does not just learn to turn to the right: It forms a cognitive map of its environment, a map that it can then use with remarkable efficiency to plan routes and remember locations it has already visited. Similarly, a pigeon reinforced for pecking a picture does not just learn to peck but may code the stimulus in terms of concepts such as *tree* or *human*. Even in the simplest conditioning situations, in other words, cognitive processes such as memory, attention, and abstraction play a critical role in determining what is learned.

Psychologists are not yet in agreement about the best way of accounting for the complex learning that they sometimes observe. One approach views complex learning as fundamentally different in kind from associative learning (for example, Kendler, 1979). Hypothesis theories, for example, assume that subjects facing difficult problems formulate hypotheses about the solution and then test these hypotheses one at a time. This analysis predicts all-or-none learning rather than the gradual improvement assumed by associative theories, and this prediction has been confirmed in a number of experiments.

The dividing line between hypothesis testing and associative learning, however, is not always clear. Hypotheses are beliefs or expectations about what outcome will follow a particular response. Simple conditioning situations may also involve expectations, and these may also be altered rapidly, as in the case of rats that acquire a strong aversion to a poisoned food after only a single experience. It is thus not yet clear whether complex learning involves fundamentally different principles from "simple" conditioning, or whether they differ only in degree.

An alternative approach to the relationship between these two processes is to assume that both occur at a behavioral level—in some situations we may learn relatively simple associations, whereas in others we may learn more complex cognitive maps or strategies—but that they are the product of a common set of underlying processes. In Chapter 12 we discussed some of the coding and retrieval principles that might shape both kinds of learning, and in this chapter we introduced a still deeper level of analysis in terms of neurons and their interconnections. Neural network models assume that learning involves the formation of associations between neurons organized in vast networks, and there is preliminary evidence that these models may be able to account for phenomena ranging from classical conditioning to language acquisition.

It is perhaps a matter of taste whether these models are described as fundamentally associative or cognitive in spirit. The fundamental unit of learning is unmistakably associative, but the complexity of these networks allows them to carry out precisely the complex processing described by cognitive theorists. Whichever description is preferred, neural network models attempt to account for much of behavior in terms of a small set of simple principles. If they succeed, these models will have provided us with an insight into the fundamental mechanisms of the human mind.

Selected Definitions

Cognitive map A mental representation of the spatial layout of an environment, indicating the location of different features of the environment and the paths linking them.

Learned helplessness An impairment in learning to escape or avoid an aversive stimulus such as shock, due to previous experiences in which the subject could not control the shock. Seligman, Maier, and Overmier attribute this impairment to a learned belief by subjects that they are helpless to alter the shock's probability.

Concept Generally, a set of objects or events bound together by common features or relationships.

All-or-none learning or **one-trial learning** A change in a single trial from responding at chance levels on a problem to responding correctly on all trials. Hypothesis theory attributes one-trial learning to the use of hypotheses: As long as subjects base their responses on incorrect hypotheses, they will respond at chance; but once they adopt the correct hypothesis, they will be correct on every trial. One-trial learning is also found in situations in which hypothesis testing is unlikely; taste-aversion conditioning is an example.

Abstraction A process whereby a subject combines experiences across a number of situations to detect or abstract the common features or principles.

Neural networks Densely interconnected sets of neurons in the brain. The neurons within a network can operate simultaneously and can influence one another's activity.

Parallel processing In the brain, any processes that occur simultaneously. Many of the brain's processes operate in parallel, and neural network theorists believe that this is an important factor in the brain's ability to solve problems, such as reading handwriting, that even the most powerful of modern computers cannot solve. Computers usually rely on **sequential processing**, in which only one operation is carried out at a time.

Review Questions

1. Define the following terms: insight; exemplar; synapse; delta rule; and win-stay, lose-shift.

2. What evidence did Tolman and Honzik provide for the existence of cognitive maps? Why did interest in cognitive maps fade? Why was interest revived after 1970?

3. Why was Olton and Samuelson's work not accepted as conclusive evidence for cognitive maps in animals? How did Morris's research help to resolve this issue?

4. What evidence suggests that animals' capacity to form and use maps is quite impressive?

5. The rapidity with which learning occurs has long been regarded as crucial evidence for distinguishing between associative and cognitive theories of learning. What was Thorndike's argument, and why did Kohler reject it? How could the phenomenon of learning set be used to explain the discrepant results of associative and cognitive theories? How does hypothesis theory account for the gradual formation of learning sets?

6. What was the evidence that originally gave rise to the concepts of learning set and learned helplessness? What evidence suggests that these phenomena are due to the formation of general rules or strategies?

7. What is a concept? What evidence suggests that animals can learn concepts?

8. What is hypothesis theory? What evidence supports it? What are its limitations?

9. Evidence that learning is sometimes gradual and sometimes all-or-none might be taken as support for the two-format hypothesis introduced in Chapter 11—that is, a distinction between associative or habit learning and expectancy learning. Is associative learning always gradual? Is expectancy learning always rapid?

10. How do prototype and exemplar theories account for concept learning? What evidence suggests that humans form prototypes while learning concepts?

11. How are brains thought to differ from computers in the way they process information? How might learning occur at the neuron level?

12. What are the fundamental assumptions of neural network models? How do these assumptions differ from those of Pavlov? How do they differ from those of the Rescorla-Wagner model?

13. What is the delta rule? How can it be used to explain the formation of prototypes?

14. Aside from possible differences in personality, how do slugs and humans differ?

15. What is the essential difference between associative and cognitive approaches to learning? What are some of the instances in which associative theorists have provided explanations for evidence that initially seemed irrefutable support for a cognitive analysis? What are the implications of neural network models for this conflict?

16. What is *your* view of the role of associative and cognitive processes in learning?

REFERENCES

Adams, C. D., & Dickinson, A. (1981). Instrumental responding following reinforcer devaluation. *Quarterly Journal of Experimental Psychology, 34B*, 109–121.

Ader, R., & Cohen, N. (1985). CNS-immune system interactions: Conditioning phenomena. *Behavior and Brain Sciences, 8*, 379–394.

Allen, K. E., Hart, B., Buell, J. S., Harris, F. R., & Wolf, M. M. (1964). Effects of social reinforcement on isolate behavior of a nursery school child. *Child Development, 35*, 511–518.

Allison, J. (1989). The nature of reinforcement. In S. B. Klein & R. R. Mowrer (Eds.), *Contemporary learning theories: Instrumental conditioning theory and the impact of biological constraints on learning.* Hillsdale, NJ: Erlbaum.

Allison, M. G., & Ayllon, T. (1980). Behavioral coaching in the development of skills in football, gymnastics, and tennis. *Journal of Applied Behavior Analysis, 13*, 297–314.

Amsel, A. (1962). Frustrative nonreward in partial reinforcement and discrimination learning. *Psychological Review, 69*, 306–328.

Amsel, A. (1972). Partial reinforcement effects on vigor and persistence. In K. W. Spence & J. T. Spence (Eds.), *The psychology of learning and motivation* (Vol. 1). New York: Academic Press.

Amsel, A., & Roussel, J. (1952). Motivational properties of frustration: I. Effect on a running response of the addition of frustration to the motivational complex. *Journal of Experimental Psychology, 43*, 363–368.

Anderson, J. R. (1984). Spreading activation. In J. R. Anderson & S. M. Kosslyn (Eds.), *Essays in learning and memory.* New York: W. H. Freeman.

Anderson, J. R. (1990). *Cognitive psychology and its implications* (3rd ed.). New York: W. H. Freeman.

Anderson, J. R., & Bower, G. H. (1973). *Human associative memory.* Washington, DC: Winston.

Andrews, E. A., & Braveman, N. S. (1975). The combined effects of dosage level and inter-stimulus interval on the formation of one-trial poison-based aversions in rats. *Animal Learning and Behavior, 3,* 287–289.

Annau, Z., & Kamin, L. J. (1961). The conditioned emotional response as a function of intensity of the US. *Journal of Comparative and Physiological Psychology, 54,* 428–432.

Anrep, G. V. (1920). Pitch discrimination in the dog. *Journal of Physiology, 53,* 367–385.

Aronfreed, J. (1968). Aversive control of socialization. In D. Levine (Ed.), *Nebraska symposium on motivation.* Lincoln: University of Nebraska Press.

Astley, S. L., & Wasserman, E. A. (1992). Categorical discrimination and generalization in pigeons: All negative stimuli are not created equal. *Journal of Experimental Psychology: Animal Behavior Processes, 18,* 193–207.

Axelrod, S., & Apsche, J. (1983). *The effects of punishment on human behavior.* New York: Academic Press.

Azrin, N. H., Holz, W. C., & Hake, D. F. (1963). Fixed-ratio punishment. *Journal of the Experimental Analysis of Behavior, 6,* 141–148.

Azrin, N. H., Hutchinson, R. R., & Hake, D. F. (1966). Extinction-induced aggression. *Journal of the Experimental Analysis of Behavior, 9,* 191–204.

Baddeley, A. D. (1990). *Human memory.* Hillsdale, NJ: Erlbaum.

Baker, B. L. (1969). Symptom treatment and symptom substitution in enuresis. *Journal of Abnormal Psychology, 74,* 42–49.

Balsam, P., & Tomie, A. (Eds.). (1985). *Context and learning.* Hillsdale, NJ: Erlbaum.

Bandura, A. (1965). Influence of models' reinforcement contingencies on the acquisition of imitative responses. *Journal of Personality and Social Psychology, 1,* 589–595.

Bandura, A., Blanchard, E. B., & Ritter, B. (1969). Relative efficacy of desensitization and modeling approaches for inducing behavioral, affective, and attitudinal changes. *Journal of Personality and Social Psychology, 13,* 173–199.

Bandura, A., & Perloff, B. (1967). Relative efficacy of self-monitored and externally imposed reinforcement systems. *Journal of Personality and Social Psychology, 7,* 111–116.

Bandura, A., Ross, D., & Ross, D. A. (1963). Imitation of film-mediated aggressive models. *Journal of Abnormal and Social Psychology, 66,* 3–11.

Barber, T. X. (1976). *Hypnosis: A scientific approach.* New York: Psychological Dimensions.

Barber, T. X., & Hahn, K. W., Jr. (1964). Experimental studies in "hypnotic" behavior: Physiological and subjective effects of imagined pain. *Journal of Nervous and Mental Disease, 139,* 416–425.

Bateson, P. (1991). Is imprinting such a special case? In J. R. Krebs & G. Horn (Eds.), *Behavioural and neural aspects of learning and memory.* Oxford: Oxford University Press.

Baum, W. M., & Rachlin, H. C. (1969). Choice as time allocation. *Journal of Comparative and*

Physiological Psychology, 12, 861–874.

Beatty, W. W., & Shavalia, D. A. (1980a). Rat spatial memory: Resistance to retroactive interference at long retention intervals. *Animal Learning & Behavior, 8,* 550–552.

Beatty, W. W., & Shavalia, D. A. (1980b). Spatial memory in rats: Time course of working memory and effects of anesthetics. *Behavioral and Neural Biology, 28,* 454–462.

Beecher, M. D. (1988). Some comments on the adaptationist approach to learning. In R. C. Bolles & M. D. Beecher (Eds.), *Evolution and learning.* Hillsdale, NJ: Erlbaum.

Bellingham, W. P., Gillette-Bellingham, K., & Kehoe, E. J. (1985). Summation and configuration in patterning schedules with the rat and rabbit. *Animal Learning & Behavior, 13,* 152–164.

Berkowitz, L., Cochrane, S., & Embree, M. (1979). Influence of aversive experience and the consequences of one's aggression on aggressive behavior. Reported in L. Berkowitz, *A survey of social psychology* (2nd ed.). New York: Holt, Rinehart & Winston.

Bernstein, I. L. (1978). Learned taste aversions in children receiving chemotherapy. *Science, 200,* 1302–1303.

Bernstein, I. L., & Borson, S. (1986). Learned food aversion: A component of anorexia syndromes. *Psychological Review, 93,* 462–472.

Best, P. J., Best, M. R., & Henggeler, S. (1977). The contribution of environmental noningestive cues in conditioning aversive internal consequences. In L. M. Barker, M. R. Best, & M. Domjan (Eds.), *Learning mechanisms in food selection.* Waco, TX: Baylor University Press.

Biferno, M. A., & Dawson, M. E. (1977). The onset of contingency awareness and electrodermal classical conditioning: An analysis of temporal relationships during acquisition and extinction. *Psychophysiology, 14,* 164–171.

Bilodeau, E. A., & Bilodeau, I. M. (1958). Variation of temporal intervals among critical events in five studies of knowledge of results. *Journal of Experimental Psychology, 55,* 603–612.

Bindra, D. (1972). A unified account of classical conditioning and operant training. In A. H. Black & W. F. Prokasy (Eds.), *Classical conditioning II: Current research and theory.* New York: Appleton-Century-Crofts.

Birch, H. G. (1945). The relation of previous experience to insightful problem-solving. *Journal of Comparative Psychology, 38,* 367–383.

Blanchard, E. B. (1969). *The relative contributions of modeling, informational influences, and physical contact in the extinction of phobic behavior.* Unpublished doctoral dissertation, Stanford University, Stanford, CA.

Blanchard, R. J., Blanchard, D. C., & Takahashi, L. K. (1977). Reflexive fighting in the rat: Aggressive or defensive behavior? *Aggressive Behavior, 3,* 145–155.

Blough, D. S. (1975). Steady state data and a quantitative model of operant generalization and discrimination. *Journal of Experimental Psychology: Animal Behavior Processes, 1,* 3–21.

Boe, E. E., & Church, R. M. (1967). Permanent effects of punishment during extinction. *Journal of Comparative and Physiological Psychology, 63,* 486–492.

Boesch, C., & Boesch, H. (1984). Possible causes of sex differences in the use of natural hammers by wild chimpanzees. *Journal of Human Evolution, 13,* 415–440.

Boland, F. J., Mellor, C. S., & Revusky, S. (1978). Chemical aversion treatment of alcoholism: Lithium as the aversive agent. *Behavior Research and Therapy, 16,* 401–409.

Bolles, R. C. (1970). Species-specific defense reactions and avoidance learning. *Psychological Review, 71,* 32–48.

Bolles, R. C. (1972). Reinforcement, expectancy, and learning. *Psychological Review, 79,* 394–409.

Bolles, R. C. (1975). *Theory of motivation* (2nd ed.). New York: Harper & Row.

Bolles, R. C. (1979). *Learning theory* (2nd ed.). New York: Holt, Rinehart & Winston.

Bolles, R. C. (1989). Acquired behaviors, aversive learning. In R. J. Blanchard, P. F. Brain, D. C. Blanchard, & S. Parmigiani (Eds.), *Ethoexperimental approaches to the study of behavior.* Boston: Kluwer.

Bolles, R. C., Holtz, R., Dunn, T., & Hill, W. (1980). Comparisons of stimulus learning and response learning in a punishment situation. *Learning and Motivation, 11,* 78–96.

Bombace, J. C., Brandon, S. E., & Wagner, A. R. (1991). Modula-

tion of a conditioned eyeblink response by a putative emotive stimulus conditioned with hindleg shock. *Journal of Experimental Psychology: Animal Behavior Processes, 17,* 323–333.

Booth, D. A. (1972). Conditioned satiety in the rat. *Journal of Comparative and Physiological Psychology, 81,* 457–471.

Bootzin, R. R. (1972). Stimulus control treatment for insomnia. *Proceedings of the 80th Annual Convention of the American Psychological Association, 7,* 395–396.

Bootzin, R. R., & Nicassio, P. M. (1978). Behavioral treatments for insomnia. In M. Hersen, R. M. Eisler, & P. M. Miller (Eds.), *Progress in behavior modification* (Vol. 6). New York: Academic Press.

Boring, E. G. (1950). *A history of experimental psychology* (2nd ed.). New York: Appleton-Century-Crofts.

Bower, G. H. (1981). Mood and memory. *American Psychologist, 36,* 129–148.

Braveman, N. S. (1977). Visually guided avoidance of poisonous foods in mammals. In L. M. Barker, M. R. Best, & M. Domjan (Eds.), *Learning mechanisms in food selection.* Waco, TX: Baylor University Press.

Bregman, N. J., & McAllister, H. A. (1982). Motivation and skin temperature biofeedback: Yerkes-Dodson revisited. *Psychophysiology, 19,* 282–285.

Breland, K., & Breland, M. (1961). The misbehavior of organisms. *American Psychologist, 16,* 681–684.

Brewer, W. F. (1974). There is no

convincing evidence for operant or classical conditioning in adult humans. In W. B. Weimer & D. S. Palermo (Eds.), *Cognition and the symbolic processes.* Hillsdale, NJ: Erlbaum.

Broadhurst, P. L. (1957). Emotionality and the Yerkes-Dodson law. *Journal of Experimental Psychology, 54,* 345–352.

Brogden, W. J. (1939). Sensory preconditioning. *Journal of Experimental Psychology, 25,* 323–332.

Brown, J. S., & Jacobs, A. (1949). The role of fear in the motivation and acquisition of responses. *Journal of Experimental Psychology, 39,* 747–759.

Brown, M. F. (1992). Does a cognitive map guide choices in the radialarm maze? *Journal of Experimental Psychology: Animal Behavior Processes, 18,* 56–66.

Brown, P. L., & Jenkins, H. M. (1968). Auto-shaping of the pigeon's key-peck. *Journal of the Experimental Analysis of Behavior, 11,* 1–8.

Brown, R. T. (1975). Following and visual imprinting in ducklings across a wide age range. *Developmental Psychobiology, 8,* 27–33.

Bryan, J. H., & Test, M. A. (1967). Models and helping: Naturalistic studies in aiding behavior. *Journal of Personality and Social Psychology, 6,* 400–407.

Bucher, B., & Lovaas, O. I. (1968). The use of aversive stimulation in behavior modification. In M. R. Jones (Ed.), *Miami symposium on the prediction of behavior: aversive stimulation.* Coral Gables, FL: University of Miami Press.

Buchwald, A. M. (1967). Effects of immediate versus delayed outcomes in associative learning. *Journal of Verbal Learning and Verbal Behavior, 6,* 317–320.

Buchwald, A. M. (1969). Effects of "right" and "wrong" on subsequent behavior: A new interpretation. *Psychological Review, 76,* 132–143.

Butler, R. A. (1954). Incentive conditions which influence visual exploration. *Journal of Experimental Psychology, 48,* 19–23.

Bykov, K. M. (1957). *The cerebral cortex and the internal organs.* New York: Chemical Publishing.

Byrne, J. H. (1985). Neural and molecular mechanisms underlying information storage in *Aplysia:* Implications for learning and memory. *Trends in Neurosciences, 8,* 478–482.

Campbell, D., Sanderson, R. E., & Laverty, S. G. (1964). Characteristics of a conditioned response in human subjects during extinction trials following a single traumatic conditioning trial. *Journal of Abnormal and Social Psychology, 68,* 627–639.

Cantor, M. B., & Wilson, J. F. (1984). Feeding the face: New directions in adjunctive behavior research. In F. R. Brush & J. B. Overmier (Eds.), *Affect, conditioning, and cognition.* Hillsdale, NJ: Erlbaum.

Capaldi, E. D., Hovancik, J. R., & Friedman, F. (1976). Effects of expectancies of different reward magnitudes in transfer from noncontingent pairings to instrumental performance. *Learning and Motivation, 7,* 197–210.

Capaldi, E. J. (1967). A sequential hypothesis of instrumental learning. In K. W. Spence & J. T. Spence (Eds.), *The psychology of learning and motivation* (Vol. 1). New York: Academic Press.

Capaldi, E. J. (1971). Memory and learning: A sequential viewpoint. In W. K. Honig & P. H. R. James (Eds.), *Animal memory*. New York: Academic Press.

Capaldi, E. J., Campbell, D. H., Sheffer, J. D., & Bradford, J. P. (1987). Conditioned flavor preferences based on delayed caloric consequences. *Journal of Experimental Psychology: Animal Behavior Processes, 13,* 150–155.

Capaldi, E. J., & Kassover, K. (1970). Sequence, number of nonrewards, anticipation, and intertrial interval in extinction. *Journal of Experimental Psychology, 84,* 470–476.

Case, D. A., Fantino, E., & Wixted, J. (1985). Human observing: Maintained by negative informative stimuli only if correlated with improvement in response efficiency. *Journal of the Experimental Analysis of Behavior, 43,* 289–300.

Cerella, J. (1980). The pigeon's analysis of pictures. *Pattern Recognition, 12,* 1–6.

Cermak, L. S., & Craik, F. I. M. (1979). *Levels of processing in human memory.* Hillsdale, NJ: Erlbaum.

Champion, R. A., & Jones, J. E. (1961). Forward, backward, and pseudoconditioning of the GSR. *Journal of Experimental Psychology, 62,* 58–61.

Chapuis, N., Thinus-Blanc, C., & Poucet, B. (1983). Dissociation of mechanisms involved in dogs' oriented displacements. *Quarterly Journal of Experimental Psychology, 35B,* 213–220.

Cheyne, J. A. (1969). *Punishment and reasoning in the development of self-control.* Paper presented at the R. H. Walters Memorial Symposium at the Biennial Meeting of the Society for Research in Child Development, Santa Monica, CA.

Cheyne, J. A., Goyeche, J. R. M., & Walters, R. H. (1969). Attention, anxiety, and rules in resistance-to-deviation in children. *Journal of Experimental Child Psychology, 8,* 127–139.

Clark, F. C. (1958). The effect of deprivation and frequency of reinforcement on variable-interval responding. *Journal of the Experimental Analysis of Behavior, 1,* 221–227.

Collins, A. M., & Loftus, E. F. (1975). A spreading-activation theory of semantic processing. *Psychological Review, 82,* 407–428.

Colwill, R. M., & Rescorla, R. A. (1985). Postconditioning devaluation of a reinforcer affects instrumental responding. *Journal of Experimental Psychology: Animal Behavior Processes, 11,* 120–132.

Colwill, R. M., & Rescorla, R. A. (1986). Associative structures in instrumental learning. In G. H. Bower (Ed.), *The psychology of learning and motivation* (Vol. 20). New York: Academic Press.

Comroe, J. H., Jr., & Dripps, R. D. (1977). *The top ten clinical advances in cardiovascular-pulmonary medicine and surgery, 1945–1975. Final report. January 31, 1977.* Bethesda, MD: National Heart, Lung, and Blood Institute.

Conger, R., & Killeen, P. (1974). Use of concurrent operants in small group research. *Pacific Sociological Review, 17,* 399–416.

Cook, E. W., Hodes, R. L., & Lang, P. J. (1986). Preparedness and phobia: Effects of stimulus content on human visceral conditioning. *Journal of Abnormal Psychology, 95,* 195–207.

Cook, M., Mineka, S., Wolkenstein, B., & Laitsch, K. (1985). Observational conditioning of snake fear in unrelated rhesus monkeys. *Journal of Abnormal Psychology, 94,* 591–610.

Couvillon, P. A., & Bitterman, M. E. (1992). A conventional conditioning analysis of "transitive inference" in pigeons. *Journal of Experimental Psychology: Animal Behavior Processes, 18,* 308–310.

Crawford, M., & Masterson, F. (1978). Components of the flight response can reinforce barpress avoidance. *Journal of Experimental Psychology: Animal Behavior Processes, 4,* 144–151.

Crespi, L. P. (1942). Quantitative variation in incentive and performance in the white rat. *American Journal of Psychology, 55,* 467–517.

Culler, E. A. (1938). Recent advances in some concepts of conditioning. *Psychological Review, 45,* 134–153.

Curio, E. K., Ernst, K., & Vieth, W. (1978). The adaptive significance of avia mobbing II. Cultural transmission of enemy recognition in blackbirds: Effectiveness and some constraints. *Zeitschrift für Tierspsychologie, 48,* 184–202.

Daly, H. B., & Daly, J. T. (1982). A mathematical model of reward and aversive nonreward: Its application over 30 appetitive

learning situations. *Journal of Experimental Psychology: General, 6,* 441–480.

D'Amato, M. R., Fazzaro, J., & Etkin, M. (1968). Anticipatory responding and avoidance discrimination as factors in avoidance conditioning. *Journal of Experimental Psychology, 77,* 41–47.

Darwin, C. R. (1859). *On the origin of species by means of natural selection.* London: Murray.

Davey, G. (1989). *Ecological learning theory.* London: Routledge.

Davey, G., Oakley, D., & Cleland, G. G. (1981). Autoshaping in the rat: Effects of omission on the form of the response. *Journal for the Experimental Analysis of Behavior, 36,* 75–91.

Davies, J. C. (1962). Toward a theory of revolution. *American Sociological Review, 27,* 5–19.

Davis, M. (1974). Sensitization of the rat startle response by noise. *Journal of Comparative and Physiological Psychology, 87,* 571–581.

Davison, G. C. (1968). Systematic desensitization as a counterconditioning process. *Journal of Abnormal Psychology, 73,* 91–99.

Davison, M., & McCarthy, D. (1988). *The matching law.* Hillsdale, NJ: Erlbaum.

Dawkins, R. (1989). *The selfish gene.* Oxford: Oxford University Press.

Deaux, E. B., & Patten, R. L. (1964). Measurement of the anticipatory goal response in instrumental runway conditioning. *Psychonomic Science, 1,* 357–358.

Deci, E. L., & Ryan, R. M. (1980). The empirical exploration of intrinsic motivational processes. In L. Berkowitz (Ed.), *Advances in experimental social psychology*

(Vol. 13). New York: Academic Press.

DeNike, L. D., & Spielberger, C. D. (1963). Induced mediating states in verbal conditioning. *Journal of Verbal Learning and Verbal Behavior, 1*, 339–345.

DeRivera, J. (1959). Some conditions governing the use of the cue-producing response as an explanatory device. *Journal of Experimental Psychology, 57*, 299–304.

Descartes, R. (1650). The passions of the soul. In G. T. B. Ross (Trans.), *The philosophical works of Descartes* (Vol. 1). Cambridge: Cambridge University Press.

Deutsch, J. A., & Clarkson, J. K. (1959). Reasoning in the hooded rat. *Quarterly Journal of Experimental Psychology, 11*, 150–154.

DeVito, P. L., & Fowler, H. (1986). Effects of contingency violations on the extinction of a conditioned fear inhibitor and a conditioned fear excitor. *Journal of Experimental Psychology: Animal Behavior Processes, 12*, 99–115.

DiCara, L. V., & Miller, N. E. (1968). Instrumental learning of vasomotor responses by rats: Learning to respond differentially in the two ears. *Science, 159*, 1485–1486.

Dickinson, A. (1980). *Contemporary animal learning theory*. Cambridge: Cambridge University Press.

Dickinson, A., & Dearing, M. F. (1979). Appetitive-aversive interactions and inhibitory processes. In A. Dickinson & R. A. Boakes (Eds.), *Mechanisms of learning and motivation*. Hillsdale, NJ: Erlbaum.

Dickinson, A., Hall, G., & Mackintosh, N. J. (1976). Surprise and the attenuation of blocking. *Journal of Experimental Psychology: Animal Behavior Processes, 2*, 313–322.

Doleys, D. M. (1977). Behavioral treatments for nocturnal enuresis in children: A review of the recent literature. *Psychological Bulletin, 84*, 30–54.

Domjan, M. (1980). Ingestional aversion learning: Unique and general processes. In J. S. Rosenblatt, R. A. Hinde, C. Beer, & M. Busnel (Eds.), *Advances in the study of behavior* (Vol. 11). New York: Academic Press.

Domjan, M. (1983). Biological constraints on instrumental and classical conditioning: Implications for general process theory. In G. H. Bower (Ed.), *The psychology of learning and motivation* (Vol. 17). New York: Academic Press.

Domjan, M., & Burkhard, B. (1986). *The principles of learning and behavior* (2nd ed.). Pacific Grove, CA: Brooks/Cole.

Drabman, R. S., Spitalnik, R., & O'Leary, K. D. (1973). Teaching self-control to disruptive children. *Journal of Abnormal Psychology, 82*, 10–16.

Dweck, C. S., & Licht, B. G. (1980). Learned helplessness and intellectual achievement. In J. Garber & M. E. P. Seligman (Eds.), *Human helplessness: Theory and applications*. New York: Academic Press.

Dweck, C. S., & Repucci, N. D. (1973). Learned helplessness and reinforcement responsibility in children. *Journal of Personality and Social Psychology, 25,* 109–116.

Easterbrook, J. A. (1959). The effect of emotion on cue utilization and the organization of behavior. *Psychological Review, 66,* 183–201.

Eich, J. E. (1980). The cue-dependent nature of state-dependent retrieval. *Memory and Cognition, 8,* 157–173.

Eikelboom, R., & Stewart, J. (1982). Conditioning of drug-induced physiological responses. *Psychological Review, 89,* 507–528.

Eimas, P. D. (1966). Effects of overtraining and age on intradimensional and extradimensional shifts in children. *Journal of Experimental Child Psychology, 3,* 348–355.

Eimas, P. D. (1984). Infant competence and the acquisition of language. In D. Caplan, A. R. Lecours, & A. Smith (Eds.), *Biological perspectives on language.* Cambridge, MA: MIT Press.

Eisenberger, R., Karpman, M., & Trattner, J. (1967). What is the necessary and sufficient condition for reinforcement in the contingency situation? *Journal of Experimental Psychology, 74,* 342–350.

Eldridge, G. D., Pear, J. J., Torgrud, L. J., & Evers, B. H. (1988). Effects of prior response-contingent reinforcement on superstitious behavior. *Animal Learning and Behavior, 16,* 277–284.

Enzle, M. A., & Ross, J. M. (1978). Increasing and decreasing intrinsic interest with contingent rewards: A test of cognitive evaluation theory. *Journal of Experimental and Social Psychology, 14,* 588–597.

Epstein, R., Kirshnit, C. E., Lanza, R. P., & Rubin, L. C. (1984). "Insight" in the pigeon: Antecedents and determinants of an intelligent performance. *Nature, 308,* 61–62.

Eron, L. D., Walder, L. O., Toigo, R., & Lefkowitz, M. M. (1963). Social class, parental punishment for aggression, and child aggression. *Child Development, 34,* 849–867.

Estes, W. K. (1959). The statistical approach to learning theory. In S. Koch (Ed.), *Psychology: A study of a science* (Vol. 2). New York: McGraw-Hill.

Estes, W. K. (1986). Array models for category learning. *Cognitive Psychology, 18,* 500–549.

Estes, W. K., & Skinner, B. F. (1941). Some quantitative properties of anxiety. *Journal of Experimental Psychology, 29,* 390–400.

Falk, J. L. (1961). Production of polydipsia in normal rats by an intermittent food schedule. *Science, 133,* 195–196.

Fanselow, M. S. (1989). The adaptive function of conditioned defensive behavior: An ecological approach to Pavlovian stimulus-substitution theory. In R. J. Blanchard, P. F. Brain, D. C. Blanchard, & S. Parmigiani (Eds.), *Ethoexperimental approaches to the study of behavior.* Boston: Kluwer.

Fanselow, M. S., & Lester, L. S. (1988). A functional behavioristic approach to aversively motivated behavior: Predatory imminence as a determinant of the topography of defensive behavior. In R. C. Bolles & M. D. Beecher (Eds.), *Evolution and learning*. Hillsdale, NJ: Erlbaum.

Fantino, E. (1977). Conditioned reinforcement. In W. K. Honig & J. E. R. Staddon (Eds.), *Handbook of operant behavior*. Englewood Cliffs, NJ: Prentice-Hall.

Farris, H. E. (1967). Classical conditioning of courting behavior in the Japanese quail, *Coturnix coturnix japonica*. *Journal of the Experimental Analysis of Behavior, 10*, 213–217.

Ferster, C. B., & Skinner, B. F. (1957). *Schedules of reinforcement*. New York: Appleton-Century-Crofts.

Flaherty, D. F. (1982). Incentive contrast: A review of behavioral changes following shifts in reward. *Animal Learning and Behavior, 10*, 409–440.

Flanders, J. P. (1968). A review of research on imitative behavior. *Psychological Bulletin, 69*, 316–337.

Fowler, H., & Miller, N. E. (1963). Facilitation and inhibition of runway performance by hind- and forepaw shock of various intensities. *Journal of Comparative Physiological Psychology, 56*, 801–805.

Fowler, H., & Wischner, G. J. (1969). The varied function of punishment in discrimination learning. In B. A. Campbell & R. M. Church (Eds.), *Punishment and aversive behavior*. New York: Appleton-Century-Crofts.

Fox, L. (1966). Effecting the use of efficient study habits. In R. Ulrich, T. Stachnik, & J. Mabry (Eds.), *Control of human behavior*

(Vol. 1). Glenview, IL: Scott, Foresman.

Franks, J. J., & Bransford, J. D. (1971). The abstraction of visual patterns. *Journal of Experimental Psychology, 90*, 65–74.

Fuhrer, M. J., & Baer, P. E. (1980). Cognitive factors and CS–UCS interval effects in the differential conditioning and extinction of skin conductance responses. *Biological Psychology, 10*, 283–298.

Garcia, J. (1981). Tilting at the paper mills of Academe. *American Psychologist, 36*, 149–158.

Garcia, J., Brett, L. P., & Rusiniak, K. W. (1989). Limits of Darwinian conditioning. In S. B. Klein & R. R. Mowrer (Eds.), *Contemporary learning theories: Instrumental conditioning theory and the impact of biological constraints on learning*. Hillsdale, NJ: Erlbaum.

Garcia, J., & Koelling, R. A. (1966). Relation of cue to consequence in avoidance learning. *Psychonomic Science, 4*, 123–124.

Gardner, R. A., & Gardner, B. T. (1969). Teaching sign language to a chimpanzee. *Science, 165*, 664–672.

Gardner, R. A., & Gardner, B. T. (1985). Signs of intelligence in cross-fostered chimpanzees. In L. Weiskrantz (Ed.), *Animal intelligence*. Oxford: Clarendon.

Garlington, W. K., & Dericco, D. A. (1977). The effect of modeling on drinking rate. *Journal of Applied Behavior Analysis, 10*, 207–211.

Geen, R. G. (1985). Test anxiety and visual vigilance. *Journal of Personality and Social Psychology, 49*, 963–970.

Gelperin, A. (1986). Complex associative learning in small neural networks. *Trends in Neurosciences, 9,* 323–328.

Gholson, B. G. (1980). *The cognitive-developmental basis of human learning: Studies in hypothesis testing.* New York: Academic Press.

Gibbon, J., & Balsam, P. (1981). Spreading association in time. In C. M. Locurto, H. S. Terrace, & J. Gibbon (Eds.), *Autoshaping and conditioning theory.* New York: Academic Press.

Gibbon, J., Farrell, L., Locurto, C. M., Duncan, H. J., & Terrace, H. S. (1980). Partial reinforcement in autoshaping with pigeons. *Animal Learning and Behavior, 8,* 45–59.

Gibson, E. J. (1969). *Principles of perceptual learning and development.* New York: Appleton-Century-Crofts.

Gibson, E. J., Walk, R. D., Pick, H. L., Jr., & Tighe, T. J. (1958). The effect of prolonged exposure to visual patterns on learning to discriminate similar and different patterns. *Journal of Comparative and Physiological Psychology, 51,* 584–587.

Gilbert, R. M. (1974). Ubiquity of schedule-induced polydipsia. *Journal for the Experimental Analysis of Behavior, 21,* 277–284.

Glass, D. C., Singer, J. E., & Friedman, L. N. (1969). Psychic cost of adaptation to an environmental stressor. *Journal of Personality and Social Psychology, 12,* 200–210.

Gleitman, H., Nachmias, J., & Neisser, U. (1954). The S–R reinforcement theory of extinction. *Psychological Review, 61,* 23–33.

Gluck, M. A., & Bower, G. H. (1988). From conditioning to category learning: An adaptive network model. *Journal of Experimental Psychology: General, 117,* 227–247.

Gluck, M. A., & Thompson, R. F. (1987). Modeling the neural substrates of associative learning and memory: A computational approach. *Psychological Review, 94,* 176–191.

Glueck, S., & Glueck, E. (1950). *Unraveling juvenile delinquency.* Cambridge, MA: Harvard University Press.

Goldiamond, I. (1965). Self-control procedures in personal behavior problems. *Psychological Reports, 17,* 851–868.

Goldstein, H., Krantz, D. L., & Rains, J. D. (1965). *Controversial issues in learning.* New York: Appleton-Century-Crofts.

Goodall-van Lawick, J. (1968). *My friends the wild chimpanzees.* Washington, DC: National Geographic Society.

Goorney, A. B., & O'Connor, P. J. (1971). Anxiety associated with flying: A retrospective survey of military aircrew psychiatric casualties. *British Journal of Psychiatry, 119,* 159–166.

Gordon, W. C. (1981). Mechanisms for cue-induced retention enhancement. In N. E. Spear & R. R. Miller (Eds.), *Information processing in animals: Memory mechanisms.* Hillsdale, NJ: Erlbaum.

Gorn, G. J. (1982). The effects of music in advertising on choice behavior: A classical conditioning approach. *Journal of Marketing, 46,* 94–101.

Gould, J. L. (1986a). The biology of learning. *Annual Review of Psychology, 37,* 163–192.

Gould, J. L. (1986b). The locale map of honey bees: Do insects have a cognitive map? *Science, 232,* 861–863.

Graham, J. M., & Desjardins, C. (1980). Classical conditioning: Induction of luteinizing hormone and testosterone secretion in anticipation of sexual activity. *Science, 210,* 1039–1041.

Grant, D. S. (1976). Effect of sample presentation time on long-delay matching in the pigeon. *Learning and Motivation, 7,* 580–590.

Grant, D. S., Brewster, R. G., & Stierhoff, K. A. (1983). "Surprisingness" and short-term retention in pigeons. *Journal of Experimental Psychology: Animal Behavior Processes, 9,* 63–79.

Greenspoon, J. (1955). The reinforcing effect of two spoken sounds on the frequency of two responses. *American Journal of Psychology, 68,* 409–416.

Grice, G. R. (1948). The relation of secondary reinforcement to delayed reward in visual discrimination learning. *Journal of Experimental Psychology, 38,* 1–16.

Grice, G. R. (1968). Stimulus intensity and response evocation. *Psychological Review, 75,* 359–373.

Gross, C. G., Bender, D. B., & Rocha-Miranda, C. E. (1969). Visual receptive fields of neurons in infero-temporal cortex of the monkey. *Science, 166,* 1303–1305.

Grossen, N. E., & Kelley, M. J. (1972). Species-specific behavior and acquisition of avoidance behavior in rats. *Journal of Comparative and Physiological Psychology, 81,* 307–310.

Grossen, N. E., Kostansek, D. J., &

Bolles, R. C. (1969). Effects of appetitive discriminative stimuli on avoidance behavior. *Journal of Experimental Psychology, 81,* 340–343.

Groves, P. M., & Thompson, R. F. (1970). Habituation: A dual-process theory. *Psychological Review, 77,* 419–450.

Guiton, P. (1966). Early experience and sexual object-choice in the brown leghorn. *Animal Behaviour, 14,* 534–538.

Gustavson, C. R., Garcia, J., Hankins, W. G., & Rusiniak, K. W. (1974). Coyote predation control by aversive conditioning. *Science, 184,* 581–583.

Guthrie, E. R. (1952). *The psychology of learning* (rev. ed.). New York: Harper & Row.

Guttman, N., & Kalish, H. I. (1956). Discriminability and stimulus generalization. *Journal of Experimental Psychology, 51,* 79–88.

Hall, R. V., Axelrod, S., Tyler, L., Grief, E., Jones, F. C., & Robertson, R. (1972). Modification of behavior problems in the home with a parent as observer and experimenter. *Journal of Applied Behavior Analysis, 5,* 53–64.

Hall, R. V., Lund, D., & Jackson, D. (1968). Effects of teacher attention on study behavior. *Journal of Applied Behavior Analysis, 1,* 1–12.

Hall, S. M., Rugg, D., Tunstall, C., & Jones, R. T. (1984). Preventing relapse to cigarette smoking by behavioral skill training. *Journal of Consulting and Clinical Psychology, 52,* 372–382.

Hammond, L. J. (1980). The effect of contingency upon the appetitive conditioning of free operant behavior. *Journal of the Experi-*

mental Analysis of Behavior, 34, 297–304.

Hanson, H. M. (1959). Effects of discrimination training on stimulus generalization. Journal of Experimental Psychology, 58, 321–333.

Harlow, H. F. (1949). The formation of learning sets. Psychological Review, 56, 51–65.

Harlow, H. F., & Harlow, M. K. (1965). The affectional systems. In A. M. Schrier, H. F. Harlow, & F. Stollnitz (Eds.), Behavior of nonhuman primates (Vol. 2). New York: Academic Press.

Harlow, H. F., Harlow, M. K., & Meyer, D. R. (1950). Learning motivated by a manipulation drive. Journal of Experimental Psychology, 40, 228–234.

Hawkins, R. D., & Kandel, E. R. (1984). Is there a cell-biological alphabet for simple forms of learning? Psychological Review, 91, 375–391.

Hayes, S. C., Rosenfarb, I., Wulfert, E., Munt, E. D., Korn, Z., & Zettle, R. D. (1985). Self-reinforcement effects: An artifact of social standard setting? Journal of Applied Behavior Analysis, 18, 201–214.

Hearst, E., & Jenkins, H. M. (1974). Sign-tracking: The stimulus-reinforcer relation and directed action. Austin, TX: Psychonomic Society.

Hebert, J. A., & Krantz, D. L. (1965). Transposition: A re-evaluation. Psychological Bulletin, 63, 244–257.

Hefferline, R. F., & Keenan, B. (1961). Amplitude-induction gradient of a small operant in an escape-avoidance situation. Journal of the Experimental Analysis of Behavior, 4, 41–43.

Hefferline, R. F., Keenan, B., & Harford, R. A. (1959). Escape and avoidance conditioning in human subjects without their observation of the response. Science, 130, 1338–1339.

Heinemann, E. G., & Rudolph, R. L. (1963). The effect of discriminative training on the gradient of stimulus generalization. American Journal of Psychology, 76, 653–658.

Herbert, E. W., Pinkston, E. M., Hayden, M. L., Sajwaj, T. E., Pinkston, S., Cordua, G., & Jackson, C. (1973). Adverse effects of differential parental attention. Journal of Applied Behavior Analysis, 6, 15–30.

Herrnstein, R. J. (1961). Relative and absolute strength of response as a function of frequency of reinforcement. Journal for the Experimental Analysis of Behavior, 4, 267–272.

Herrnstein, R. J. (1979). Acquisition, generalization, and discrimination reversal of a natural concept. Journal of Experimental Psychology: Animal Behavior Processes, 5, 116–129.

Herrnstein, R. J. (1984). Objects, categories, and discriminative stimuli. In H. L. Roitblat, T. G. Bever, & H. S. Terrace (Eds.), Animal cognition. Hillsdale, NJ: Erlbaum.

Herrnstein, R. J., & Loveland, D. H. (1964). Complex visual concept in the pigeon. Science, 146, 549–551.

Herrnstein, R. J., Loveland, D. H., & Cable, C. (1976). Natural concepts in pigeons. Journal of Experimental Psychology: Animal Behavior Processes, 2, 285–311.

Hess, E. H. (1959). Imprinting. Science, 130, 133–141.

Hilgard, E. R., & Bower, G. H. (1981). *Theories of learning* (5th ed.). Englewood Cliffs, NJ: Prentice-Hall.

Hintzman, D. L. (1978). *The psychology of learning and memory.* San Francisco: W. H. Freeman.

Hintzman, D. L. (1986). "Schema abstraction" in a multiple-trace memory model. *Psychological Review, 93,* 411–428.

Hirst, W., Spelke, E. S., Reaves, C. C., Caharack, G., & Neisser, U. (1980). Dividing attention without alternation or automaticity. *Journal of Experimental Psychology: General, 109,* 98–117.

Hochauser, M., & Fowler, H. (1975). Cue effects of drive and reward as a function of discrimination difficulty: Evidence against the Yerkes-Dodson law. *Journal of Experimental Psychology: Animal Behavior Processes, 1,* 261–269.

Hoffman, H. S. (1978). Experimental analysis of imprinting and its behavioral effects. In G. H. Bower (Ed.), *The psychology of learning and motivation.* New York: Academic Press.

Hoffman, M. L. (1983). Affective and cognitive processes in moral internalization. In E. T. Higgins, D. Ruble, & W. W. Hartup (Eds.), *Social cognition and social development.* Cambridge: Cambridge University Press.

Hogan, J. A. (1974). Responses in Pavlovian conditioning studies. *Science, 186,* 156–157.

Holland, P. C. (1977). Conditioned stimulus as a determinant of the form of the Pavlovian conditioned response. *Journal of Experimental Psychology: Animal Behavior Processes, 3,* 77–104.

Holland, P. C. (1985). The nature of conditioned inhibition in serial and simultaneous feature negative discriminations. In R. R. Miller & N. E. Spear (Eds.), *Information processing in animals: Conditioned inhibition.* Hillsdale, NJ: Erlbaum.

Holland, P. C., & Straub, J. J. (1979). Differential effect of two ways of devaluing the unconditioned stimulus after Pavlovian appetitive conditioning. *Journal of Experimental Psychology: Animal Behavior Processes, 5,* 67–78.

Hollis, K. L. (1982). Pavlovian conditioning of signal-centered action patterns and autonomic behavior: A biological analysis of function. *Advances in the Study of Behavior, 12,* 1–64.

Hollis, K. L. (1984). The biological function of Pavlovian conditioning: The best defense is a good offense. *Journal of Experimental Psychology: Animal Behavior Processes, 10,* 413–425.

Hollis, K. L., ten Cate, C., & Bateson, P. (1991). Stimulus representation: A subprocess of imprinting and conditioning. *Journal of Comparative Psychology, 105,* 307–317.

Homme, L. W., deBaca, P. C., Devine, J. V., Steinhorst, R., & Rickert, E. J. (1963). Use of the Premack principle in controlling the behavior of nursery school children. *Journal of the Experimental Analysis of Behavior, 6,* 544.

Honig, W. K., Boneau, C. A., Burstein, K. R., & Pennypacker, H. S. (1963). Positive and negative generalization gradients obtained after equivalent training conditions. *Journal of Com-*

parative and Physiological Psychology, 56, 111–116.

Honig, W. K., & Slivka, R. M. (1964). Stimulus generalization of the effects of punishment. *Journal of the Experimental Analysis of Behavior, 7,* 21–25.

Hull, C. L. (1920). Quantitative aspects of the evolution of concepts. *Psychological Monographs, 28* (1, Whole No. 123).

Hull, C. L. (1943). *Principles of behavior.* New York: Appleton-Century-Crofts.

Hull, C. L. (1952). *A behavior system.* New Haven, CT: Yale University Press.

Hulse, S. H., Fowler, H., & Honig, W. K. (Eds.). (1978). *Cognitive processes in animal behavior.* Hillsdale, NJ: Erlbaum.

Hunt, G. L., Jr., & Smith, W. J. (1967). Pecking and initial drinking responses in young domestic fowl. *Journal of Comparative and Physiological Psychology, 64,* 230–236.

Ince, L. P., Brucker, B. S., & Alba, A. (1978). Reflex conditioning in a spinal man. *Journal of Comparative and Physiological Psychology, 92,* 796–802.

Iversen, I. H., Ragnarsdottir, G. A., & Randrup, K. I. (1984). Operant conditioning of autogrooming in vervet monkeys (*Cercopithecus aethiops*). *Journal of the Experimental Analysis of Behavior, 42,* 171–189.

Jackson, B., & Van Zoost, B. (1972). Changing study behaviors through reinforcement contingencies. *Journal of Counseling Psychology, 19,* 192–195.

Jackson, R. L., Alexander, J. H., & Maier, S. F. (1980). Learned helplessness, inactivity, and associative deficits: Effects of inescapable shock on response choice escape learning. *Journal of Experimental Psychology: Animal Behavior Processes, 6,* 1–20.

Janis, I. L., Kaye, D., & Kirschner, P. (1965). Facilitating effects of "eating-while-reading" on responsiveness to persuasive communications. *Journal of Personality and Social Psychology, 1,* 181–186.

Jenkins, H. M., Barrera, F. J., Ireland, C., & Woodside, B. (1978). Signal-centered action patterns of dogs in appetitive classical conditioning. *Learning and Motivation, 9,* 272–296.

Jenkins, H. M., & Harrison, R. H. (1960). Effects of discrimination training on auditory generalization. *Journal of Experimental Psychology, 59,* 246–253.

Jenkins, H. M., & Moore, B. R. (1973). The form of the autoshaped response with food or water reinforcers. *Journal of the Experimental Analysis of Behavior, 20,* 163–181.

Jenkins, J. G., & Dallenbach, K. M. (1924). Oblivescence during sleeping and waking. *American Journal of Psychology, 35,* 605–612.

Johnston, T. D. (1981). Contrasting approaches to the theory of learning. *Behavioral and Brain Sciences, 4,* 125–139.

Jones, A., Wilkinson, H. J., & Braden, I. (1961). Information deprivation as a motivational variable. *Journal of Experimental Psychology, 62,* 126–137.

Jones, M. C. (1924). The elimination of children's fears. *Journal of Experimental Psychology, 7,* 382–390.

Kamin, L. J. (1969). Predictability, surprise, attention, and conditioning. In B. A. Campbell & R. M. Church (Eds.), *Punishment and aversive behavior*. New York: Appleton-Century-Crofts.

Kamin, L. J., Brimer, C. J., & Black, A. H. (1963). Conditioned suppression as a monitor of fear of the CS in the course of avoidance training. *Journal of Comparative and Physiological Psychology, 56*, 497–501.

Kandel, H. J., Ayllon, T., & Roberts, M. D. (1976). Rapid educational rehabilitation for prison inmates. *Behavior Research and Therapy, 14*, 323–331.

Kanfer, F. H., & Seidner, M. L. (1973). Self-control: Factors enhancing tolerance of noxious stimulation. *Journal of Personality and Social Psychology, 25*, 381–389.

Katzev, R. D., & Berman, J. S. (1974). Effect of exposure to conditioned stimulus and control of its termination in the extinction of avoidance behavior. *Journal of Comparative and Physiological Psychology, 87*, 347–353.

Kazdin, A. E. (1977). *The token economy: A review and evaluation.* New York: Plenum.

Kazdin, A. E., & Wilcoxon, L. A. (1976). Systematic desensitization and nonspecific treatment effects: A methodological evaluation. *Psychological Bulletin, 83*, 729–758.

Kehoe, E. J. (1988). A layered network model of associative learning: Learning to learn and configuration. *Psychological Review, 95*, 411–433.

Keller, R. J., Ayres, J. J. B., & Mahoney, W. J. (1977). Brief versus extended exposure to truly random control procedures. *Journal of Experimental Psychology: Animal Behavior Processes, 3*, 53–66.

Kemler, D. G., & Shepp, B. E. (1971). Learning and transfer of dimensional relevance and irrelevance in children. *Journal of Experimental Psychology, 90*, 120–127.

Kendler, T. (1979). Toward a theory of mediational development. In H. W. Reese & L. P. Lipsitt (Eds.), *Advances in child development and behavior* (Vol. 13). New York: Academic Press.

Kimble, G. A. (1961). *Hilgard and Marquis' conditioning and learning.* New York: Appleton-Century-Crofts.

Kimble, G. A., Mann, L. I., & Dufort, R. H. (1955). Classical and instrumental eyelid conditioning. *Journal of Experimental Psychology, 49*, 407–417.

Kirschenbaum, D. S., & Flanery, R. C. (1983). Behaviorial contracting: Outcomes and elements. In M. Hersen, R. M. Eisler, & P. M. Miller (Eds.), *Progress in behavior modification.* New York: Academic Press.

Kish, G. B. (1966). Studies of sensory reinforcement. In W. K. Honig (Ed.), *Operant behavior: Areas of research and application.* New York: Appleton-Century-Crofts.

Koch, S. (1954). Clark L. Hull. In W. K. Estes, S. Koch, K. MacCorquodale, P. E. Meehl, C. G. Mueller, Jr., W. N. Schoenfeld, & W. S. Verplanck, *Modern learning theory.* New York: Appleton-Century-Crofts.

Kohlberg, L. (1976). Moral stages and moralization: The cognitive-developmental approach. In T.

Lickona (Ed.), *Moral development and behavior: Theory, research and social issues.* New York: Holt, Rinehart & Winston.

Kohler, W. (1927). *The mentality of apes* (rev. ed.). London: Routledge & Kegan Paul.

Kohler, W. (1939). Simple structural functions in the chimpanzee and in the chicken. In W. D. Ellis (Ed. and Trans.), *A source book of gestalt psychology.* New York: Harcourt, Brace. (Original work published 1918)

Konorski, J. (1948). *Conditioned reflexes and neuron organization.* Cambridge: Cambridge University Press.

Konorski, J. (1967). *Integrative activity of the brain.* Chicago: University of Chicago Press.

Krebs, J. R. (1991). Food-storing in birds: Adaptive specialization in brain and behaviour? In J. R. Krebs & G. Horn (Eds.), *Behavioural and neural aspects of learning and memory.* Oxford: Oxford University Press.

Kremer, E. F. (1971). Truly random and traditional control procedures in CER conditioning in the rat. *Journal of Comparative and Physiological Psychology, 76,* 441–448.

Kruschke, J. K. (1992). ALCOVE: An exemplar-based connectionist model of category learning. *Psychological Review, 99,* 22–44.

Kruse, J. M., Overmier, J. B., Konz, W. A., & Rokke, E. (1983). Pavlovian conditioned stimulus effects upon instrumental choice behavior are reinforcer specific. *Learning and Motivation, 14,* 165–181.

Kuhn, T. S. (1970). *The structure of scientific revolutions.* Chicago: University of Chicago Press.

Kuo, Z. Y. (1937). Forced movement or insight? *University of California Publications in Psychology, 6,* 169–188.

Lamb, M. R. (1991). Attention in humans and animals: Is there a capacity limitation at the time of encoding? *Journal of Experimental Psychology: Animal Behavior Processes, 17,* 45–54.

Lamon, S., Wilson, G. T., & Leaf, R. C. (1977). Human classical aversion conditioning: Nausea versus electric shock in the reduction of target beverage consumption. *Behavior Research and Therapy, 15,* 313–320.

Lane, D. M., & Rabinowitz, F. M. (1979). A rule-based theory of intermediate-size transposition. *Child Development, 48,* 412–426.

Lavin, M. J. (1976). The establishment of flavor-flavor associations using a sensory preconditioning training procedure. *Learning and Motivation, 7,* 173–183.

Lawrence, D. H. (1963). The nature of a stimulus: Some relationships between learning and perception. In S. Koch (Ed.), *Psychology: A study of a science* (Vol. 5). New York: McGraw-Hill.

Lawrence, D. H., & DeRivera, J. (1954). Evidence for relational transposition. *Journal of Comparative and Physiological Psychology, 47,* 465–471.

Lawrence, D. H., & Hommel, L. (1961). The influence of differential goal boxes on discrimination learning involving delay of reinforcement. *Journal of Comparative and Physiological Psychology, 54,* 552–555.

Lazarus, A. A. (1971). *Behavior therapy*

and beyond. New York: McGraw-Hill.

Lazarus, A. A. (1981). *The practice of multimodal therapy.* New York: McGraw-Hill.

Lefcourt, H. M. (1973). The function of the illusions of control and freedom. *American Psychologist, 28,* 417–425.

Lefkowitz, M. M., Blake, R. R., & Mouton, J. S. (1955). Status factors in pedestrian violation of traffic signals. *Journal of Abnormal and Social Psychology, 51,* 704–706.

Leonard, D. W. (1969). Amount and sequence of reward in partial and continuous reinforcement. *Journal of Comparative and Physiological Psychology, 67,* 204–211.

Lepper, M. R. (1981). Intrinsic and extrinsic motivation in children: Detrimental effects of superfluous social controls. In W. A. Collins (Ed.), *Minnesota symposium on child psychology* (Vol. 14). Hillsdale, NJ: Erlbaum.

Lepper, M. R., Greene, D., & Nisbett, R. E. (1973). Undermining children's intrinsic interest with extrinsic rewards: A test of the overjustification hypothesis. *Journal of Personality and Social Psychology, 28,* 129–137.

le Roy Conel, J. P. (1963). *Postnatal development of the human cerebral cortex.* Cambridge, MA: Harvard University Press.

Lett, B. T. (1977). Long delay learning in the T-maze: Effect of reward given in the home cage. *Bulletin of the Psychonomic Society, 10,* 211–214.

Lett, B. T. (1979). Long delay learning: Implications for learning and memory theory. In N.S. Sutherland (Ed.), *Tutorial essays*

in psychology: A guide to recent advances (Vol. 2). Hillsdale, NJ: Erlbaum.

Levine, M. (1959). A model of hypothesis behavior in discrimination learning set. *Psychological Review, 66,* 353–366.

Levine, M. (1965). Hypothesis behavior. In A. M. Schrier, H. F. Harlow, & F. Stollnitz (Eds.), *Behavior of nonhuman primates: Modern research trends* (Vol. 1). New York: Academic Press.

Levine, M. (1971). Hypothesis theory and nonlearning despite ideal S–R reinforcement contingencies. *Psychological Review, 78,* 130–140.

Levine, M. (1975). *A cognitive theory of learning: Research based on hypothesis testing.* Hillsdale, NJ: Erlbaum.

Levis, D. J. (1989). The case for a return to a two-factor theory of avoidance: The failure of non-fear interpretations. In S. B. Klein & R. R. Mowrer (Eds.), *Contemporary learning theories: Pavlovian conditioning and the status of traditional learning theory.* Hillsdale, NJ: Erlbaum.

Lewis, D. J. (1979). Psychobiology of active and inactive memory. *Psychological Bulletin, 86,* 1054–1083.

Lewis, D. J., & Duncan, C. P. (1956). Effect of different percentages of money reward on extinction of a lever pulling response. *Journal of Experimental Psychology, 52,* 23–27.

Leyens, J. P., Camino, L., Parke, R. D., & Berkowitz, L. (1975). Effects of movie violence on aggression in a field setting as a function of group dominance and cohesion. *Journal of Personality* and Social Psychology, 32, 346–360.

Lichtenstein, E., Harris, D. E., Birchler, G. R., Wahl, J. M., & Schmahl, D. P. (1973). Comparison of rapid smoking; warm, smoky air; and attention placebo in the modification of smoking behavior. Journal of Consulting and Clinical Psychology, 40, 92–98.

Lieberman, D. A. (1972). Secondary reinforcement and information as determinants of observing behavior in monkeys (Macaca mulatta). Learning and Motivation, 3, 341–358.

Lieberman, D. A. (1979). Behaviorism and the mind: A (limited) call for a return to introspection. American Psychologist, 34, 319–333.

Lieberman, D. A., McIntosh, D. C., & Thomas, G. V. (1979). Learning when reward is delayed: A marking hypothesis. Journal of Experimental Psychology: Animal Behavior Processes, 5, 224–242.

Lieberman, D. A., & Thomas, G. V. (1986). Marking, memory, and superstition in the pigeon. Quarterly Journal of Experimental Psychology, 38B, 449–459.

Lindsay, P. H., & Norman, D. A. (1977). Human information processing. New York: Academic Press.

Locke, J. (1961). An essay concerning human understanding (J. W. Yolton, Ed.). London: Dent. (Original work published 1690)

Logan, F. A., & Wagner, A. R. (1965). Reward and punishment. Boston: Allyn & Bacon.

Logue, A. W. (1988). A comparison of taste aversion learning in humans and other vertebrates:

Evolutionary pressures in common. In R. C. Bolles & M. D. Beecher (Eds.), Evolution and learning. Hillsdale, NJ: Erlbaum.

LoLordo, V. M., & Droungas, A. (1989). Selective associations and adaptive specializations: Taste aversions and phobias. In S. B. Klein & R. R. Mowrer (Eds.), Contemporary learning theories: Instrumental conditioning theory and the impact of biological constraints on learning. Hillsdale, NJ: Erlbaum.

Lorenz, K. (1937). The companion in the bird's world. Auk, 54, 245–273.

Lorenz, K. (1952). King Solomon's ring. New York: Crowell.

Lovaas, O. I., Schaeffer, B., & Simmons, J. Q. (1965). Experimental studies in childhood schizophrenia: Building social behavior in autistic children by the use of electric shock. Journal of Experimental Research in Personality, 1, 99–109.

Lowe, C. F. (1979). Determinants of human operant behavior. In M. D. Zeiler & P. Harzem (Eds.), Reinforcement and the organization of behavior. New York: Wiley.

Lowitz, G. H., & Suib, M. R. (1978). Generalized control of persistent thumbsucking by differential reinforcement of other behaviors. Journal of Behavior Therapy and Experimental Psychiatry, 9, 343–346.

Lubow, R. E., & Moore, A. U. (1959). Latent inhibition: The effect of nonreinforced preexposure to the conditioned stimulus. Journal of Comparative and Physiological Psychology, 52, 415–419.

Lucas, G. A., & Timberlake, W.

(1992). Negative anticipatory contrast and preference conditioning: Flavor cues support preference conditioning, and environmental cues support contrast. *Journal of Experimental Psychology: Animal Behavior Processes, 18,* 34–40.

Macfarlane, D. A. (1930). The role of kinesthesis in maze learning. *University of California Publications in Psychology, 4,* 277–305.

Mackintosh, N. J. (1965). Selective attention in animal discrimination learning. *Psychological Bulletin, 64,* 124–150.

Mackintosh, N. J. (1973). Stimulus selection: Learning to ignore stimuli that predict no change in reinforcement. In R. A. Hinde & J. Stevenson-Hinde (Eds.), *Constraints on learning.* New York: Academic Press.

Mackintosh, N. J. (1974). *The psychology of animal learning.* New York: Academic Press.

Mackintosh, N. J. (1975). A theory of attention: Variations in the associability of stimuli with reinforcement. *Psychological Review, 82,* 276–298.

Mackintosh, N. J. (1983). *Conditioning and associative learning.* Oxford: Oxford University Press.

Mackintosh, N. J., & Dickinson, A. (1979). Instrumental (Type II) conditioning. In A. Dickinson & R. A. Boakes (Eds.), *Mechanisms of learning and motivation.* Hillsdale, NJ: Erlbaum.

Mackintosh, N. J., & Little, L. (1969). Intradimensional and extradimensional shift learning by pigeons. *Psychonomic Science, 14,* 5–6.

Mackintosh, N. J., & Little, L. (1970). Effects of different patterns of reinforcement on performance under massed or spaced extinction. *Psychonomic Science, 20,* 1–2.

Macphail, E. M. (1982). *Brain and intelligence in vertebrates.* Oxford: Clarendon.

MacQueen, G. M., & Siegel, S. (1989). Conditional immunomodulation following training with cyclophosphamide. *Behavioral Neuroscience, 103,* 638–647.

Madsen, C. H., Becker, W. C., Thomas, D. R., Koser, L., & Plager, E. (1968). An analysis of the reinforcing function of "sit down" commands. In R. K. Parker (Ed.), *Readings in educational psychology.* Boston: Allyn & Bacon.

Maier, S. F. (1989). Learned helplessness: Event covariation and cognitive changes. In S. B. Klein & R. R. Mowrer (Eds.), *Contemporary learning theories: Instrumental conditioning theory and the impact of biological constraints on learning.* Hillsdale, NJ: Erlbaum.

Maier, S. F., & Jackson, R. L. (1979). Learned helplessness: All of us were right (and wrong): Inescapable shock has multiple effects. In G. H. Bower (Ed.), *The psychology of learning and motivation* (Vol. 13). New York: Academic Press.

Maier, S. F., Seligman, M. E. P., & Solomon, R. L. (1969). Pavlovian fear conditioning and learned helplessness: Effects on escape and avoidance behavior of (a) the CS-US contingency and (b) the independence of the US and voluntary responding. In B. A. Campbell & R. M. Church (Eds.), *Punishment and aversive behavior.* New York: Appleton-Century-Crofts.

Maki, W. S. (1979). Pigeon's short-term memories for surprising vs. expected reinforcement and nonreinforcement. *Animal Learning and Behavior, 7,* 31–37.

Mandler, G. (1981). The recognition of previous encounters. *American Scientist, 69,* 211–218.

Marler, P. (1967). Comparative study of song development in sparrows. *Proceedings of the International Ornithological Congress, 14,* 231–244.

Marler, P. (1991). Song learning: The interface between behaviour and neuroethology. In J. R. Krebs & G. Horn (Eds.), *Behavioural and neural aspects of learning and memory.* Oxford: Oxford University Press.

Marler, P., & Richards, S. (1989). Species differences in auditory responsiveness in early vocal learning. In R. Dooling & S. Hulse (Eds.), *The comparative psychology of audition: Perceiving complex sounds.* Hillsdale, NJ: Erlbaum.

Martin, E. (1971). Verbal learning theory and independent retrieval phenomena. *Psychological Review, 78,* 314–332.

Martin, J. A. (1977). Effects of positive and negative adult-child interactions on children's task performance and task preferences. *Journal of Experimental Child Psychology, 23,* 493–502.

Masserman, J. H., & Pechtel, C. (1953). Neurosis in monkeys: A preliminary report of experimental observations. *Annals of the New York Academy of Sciences, 56,* 253–265.

Mathews, A. (1978). Fear-reduction research and clinical phobias. *Psychological Bulletin, 85,* 390–404.

McAllister, W. R. (1953). Eyelid conditioning as a function of the CS–UCS interval. *Journal of Experimental Psychology, 45,* 417–422.

McAllister, W. R., & McAllister, D. E. (1992). Fear determines the effectiveness of a feedback stimulus in aversively motivated instrumental learning. *Learning and Motivation, 23,* 99–115.

McClelland, J. L., & Rumelhart, D. E. (1985). Distributed memory and the representation of general and specific information. *Journal of Experimental Psychology: General, 114,* 159–188.

McClelland, J. L., & Rumelhart, D. E. (1986). A distributed model of human learning and memory. In J. L. McClelland, D. E. Rumelhart, & the PDP Research Group, *Parallel distributed processing: Explorations in the microstructure of cognition: Vol. 1. Psychological and biological models.* Cambridge, MA: MIT Press.

McGraw, K. O., & McCullers, J. C. (1979). Evidence of a detrimental effect of extrinsic incentives on breaking a mental set. *Journal of Experimental Social Psychology, 15,* 285–294.

McGuire, R. J., Carlisle, J. M., & Young, B. G. (1965). Sexual deviations as conditioned behaviour: A hypothesis. *Behaviour Research and Therapy, 2,* 185–190.

McLaren, I. P. L., Kaye, H., & Mackintosh, N. J. (1989). An associative theory of the representations of stimuli: Applications to perceptual learning and latent inhibition. In R. G. M. Morris (Ed.), *Parallel distributed processing.* Oxford: Oxford University Press.

McNamara, H. J., Long, J. B., & Wike, E. L. (1956). Learning without response under two conditions of external cues. *Journal of Comparative and Physiological Psychology, 49,* 477–480.

Medin, D. L. (1977). Memory processes and discrimination learning set formation. In A. M. Schrier (Ed.), *Progress in behavioral primatology.* Hillsdale, NJ: Erlbaum.

Medin, D. L. (1989). Concepts and conceptual structure. *American Psychologist, 44,* 1469–1481.

Meehl, P. E. (1950). On the circularity of the law of effect. *Psychological Bulletin, 47,* 52–75.

Meichenbaum, D., & Cameron, R. (1982). Cognitive-behavior therapy. In G. T. Wilson & C. M. Franks (Eds.), *Contemporary behavior therapy: Conceptual and empirical foundations.* New York: Guilford.

Meltzer, D., & Brahlek, J. A. (1968). Quantity of reinforcement and fixed-interval performance. *Psychonomic Science, 12,* 207–208.

Milgram, S. (1963). Behavioral study of obedience. *Journal of Abnormal and Social Psychology, 67,* 371–378.

Milgram, S. (1974). *Obedience to authority.* New York: Harper & Row.

Mill, J. (1878). *Analysis of the phenomena of the human mind* (J. S. Mill, Ed.). London: Longmans, Green, Reader & Dyer. (Original work published 1829)

Miller, N. E. (1985). The value of behavioral research on animals. *American Psychologist, 40,* 423–440.

Miller, N. E., & DiCara, L. V. (1967). Instrumental learning of heart-rate changes in curarized rats: Shaping and specificity to discriminative stimulus. *Journal of Comparative and Physiological Psychology, 63,* 12–19.

Miller, N. E., & Dworkin, B. R. (1974). Visceral learning: Recent difficulties with curarized rats and significant problems for human research. In P. A. Obrist, A. H. Black, J. Brener, & L. V. DiCara (Eds.), *Cardiovascular psychophysiology: Current issues in response mechanisms, biofeedback, and methodology.* Chicago: Aldine.

Millikan, G. C., & Bowman, R. I. (1967). Observations on Galapagos tool-using finches in captivity. *Living Bird, 6,* 23–41.

Milner, B. (1962). Les troubles de la mémoire accompagnant des lésions hippocampiques bilatérales. In *Physiologie de l'hippocampe.* Paris: Centre National de la Recherche Scientifique.

Milner, B. (1966). Amnesia following operation on the temporal lobes. In C. W. M. Whitty & O. L. Zangwill (Eds.), *Amnesia.* London: Butterworth.

Mineka, S. (1979). The role of fear in theories of avoidance learning, flooding, and extinction. *Psychological Bulletin, 86,* 985–1010.

Mineka, S., & Cook, M. (1986). Immunization against the observational conditioning of snake fear in rhesus monkeys. *Journal of Abnormal Psychology, 95,* 307–318.

Mischel, W., Ebbesen, E. B., & Zeiss, A. R. (1972). Cognitive and attentional mechanisms in delay of gratification. *Journal of Personality and Social Psychology, 21,* 204–218.

Mischel, W., & Grusec, J. (1966). Determinants of the rehearsal and transmission of neutral and aversive behaviors. *Journal of Personality and Social Psychology, 3,* 197–205.

Mischel, W., & Liebert, R. M. (1966). Effects of discrepancies between observed and imposed reward criteria on their acquisition and transmission. *Journal of Personality and Social Psychology, 3,* 45–53.

Mischel, W., & Mischel, H. N. (1977). Self-control and the self. In T. Mischel (Ed.), *The self: Psychological and philosophical issues.* Oxford: Blackwell.

Mitchell, G., & Brandt, E. M. (1972). Paternal behavior in primates. In F. E. Poirier (Ed.), *Primate socialization.* New York: Random House.

Miyadi, D. (1964). Social life of Japanese monkeys. *Science, 143,* 783–786.

Modaresi, H. A. (1990). The avoidance barpress problem: Effects of enhanced reinforcement and an SSDR-congruent lever. *Learning and Motivation, 21,* 199–220.

Moeller, G. (1954). The CS-UCS interval in GSR conditioning. *Journal of Experimental Psychology, 48,* 162–166.

Moltz, H. (1957). Latent extinction and the fractional anticipatory response mechanism. *Psychological Review, 64,* 229–241.

Montgomery, K. C. (1954). The role of the exploratory drive in learning. *Journal of Comparative and Physiological Psychology, 47,* 60–64.

Morgan, M. J. (1974). Resistance to satiation. *Animal Behavior, 22,* 449–466.

Morris, R. G. M. (1981). Spatial localization does not require the presence of local cues. *Learning and Motivation, 12,* 239–260.

Morse, W., & Kelleher, R. (1977). Determinants of reinforcement and punishment. In W. K. Honig & J. E. R. Staddon (Eds.), *Handbook of operant behavior.* Englewood Cliffs, NJ: Prentice-Hall.

Mowrer, O. H. (1947). On the dual nature of learning: A reinterpretation of "conditioning" and "problem-solving." *Harvard Educational Review, 17,* 102–150.

Mowrer, O. H., & Mowrer, W. M. (1938). Enuresis: A method for its study and treatment. *American Journal of Orthopsychiatry, 8,* 436–459.

Munn, N. L. (1961). *Psychology* (4th ed.). Boston: Houghton Mifflin.

Nathan, P. E. (1985). Aversion therapy in the treatment of alcoholism: Success and failure. *Annals of the New York Academy of Science, 443,* 357–364.

Nation, J. R., & Cooney, J. B. (1982). The time course of extinction-induced aggressive behavior in humans: Evidence for a stage model of extinction. *Learning and Motivation, 13,* 95–112.

Nedelman, D., & Sulzbacher, S. I. (1972). Dicky at 13 years of age: A long-term success following early application of operant conditioning procedures. In G. Semb (Ed.), *Behavior analysis and education, 1972.* Lawrence: University of Kansas.

Neil, A. S. (1960). *Summerhill: A radical approach to child rearing.* New York: Hart.

Newell, A., & Simon, H. A. (1963). Computers in psychology. In R. D. Luce, R. R. Bush, & E. Galanter (Eds.), *Handbook of mathematical psychology* (Vol. 1). New York: Wiley.

Nissen, H. W. (1950). Description of the learned response in discrimination behavior. *Psychological Review, 59,* 121–137.

Nosofsky, R. M. (1991). Exemplars, prototypes, and similarity rules. In A. Healy, S. Kosslyn, & R. Shiffrin (Eds.), *Essays in honor of W. K. Estes.* Hillsdale, NJ: Erlbaum.

Notterman, J. M., & Mintz, D. E. (1965). *Dynamics of response.* New York: Wiley.

Odling-Smee, F. J. (1975). Background stimuli and the interstimulus interval during Pavlovian conditioning. *Quarterly Journal of Experimental Psychology, 27,* 387–392.

O'Leary, K. D., Becker, W. C., Evans, M. B., & Saudargas, R. A. (1969). A token reinforcement program in a public school: A replication and systematic analysis. *Journal of Applied Behavior Analysis, 2,* 3–13.

O'Leary, K. D., Poulos, R. W., & Devine, V. T. (1972). Tangible reinforcers: Bonuses or bribes? *Journal of Consulting and Clinical Psychology, 38,* 1–8.

Olton, D. S., & Samuelson, R. J. (1976). Remembrance of places passed: Spatial memory in rats. *Journal of Experimental Psychology: Animal Behavior Processes, 2,* 97–116.

Ono, K. (1987). Superstitious behavior in humans. *Journal of the Experimental Analysis of Behavior, 47,* 261–271.

Orne, M. T. (1962). On the social psychology of the psychological experiment: With particular reference to demand characteristics and their implications. *American Psychologist, 17,* 776–783.

Overmier, J. B., Bull, J. A. III, & Pack, K. (1971). On instrumental response interaction as explaining the influences of Pavlovian CSs upon avoidance behavior. *Learning and Motivation, 2,* 103–112.

Overmier, J. B., & Lawry, J. A. (1979). Pavlovian conditioning and the mediation of behavior. In G. H. Bower (Ed.), *The psychology of learning and motivation* (Vol. 13). New York: Academic Press.

Overmier, J. B., & Seligman, M. E. P. (1967). Effects of inescapable shock upon subsequent escape and avoidance learning. *Journal of Comparative and Physiological Psychology, 63,* 23–33.

Overton, D. A. (1985). Contextual stimulus effects of drugs and internal states. In P. D. Balsam & A. Tomie (Eds.), *Context and learning.* Hillsdale, NJ: Erlbaum.

Paletta, M. S., & Wagner, A. R. (1986). Development of context-specific tolerance to morphine: Support for a dual-process interpretation. *Behavioral Neuroscience, 100,* 611–623.

Parkin, A. J. (1987). *Memory and amnesia: An introduction.* Oxford: Blackwell.

Paul, G. L. (1969). Outcome of systematic desensitization II: Controlled investigations of individual treatment, technique variations, and current status. In C. M. Franks (Ed.), *Behavior therapy: Appraisal and status*. New York: McGraw-Hill.

Paul, G. L., & Lentz, R. J. (1977). *Psychosocial treatment of chronic mental patients: Milieu versus social-learning programs*. Cambridge, MA: Harvard University Press.

Pavlov, I. P. (1927). *Conditioned reflexes* (G. V. Anrep, Trans.). Oxford: Oxford University Press.

Pavlov, I. P. (1928). *Lectures on conditioned reflexes* (W. H. Gantt, Trans.). New York: International Publishers.

Pavlov, I. P. (1941). *Conditioned reflexes and psychiatry*. New York: International Publishers.

Payne, J. W., & Bettman, J. R. (1992). Behavioral decision research: A constructive processing perspective. *Annual Review of Psychology, 43*, 87–131.

Pearce, J. M. (1987). *An introduction to animal cognition*. Hillsdale, NJ: Erlbaum.

Pearce, J. M., Colwill, R. M., & Hall, G. (1978). Instrumental conditioning of scratching in the laboratory rat. *Learning and Motivation, 9*, 255–271.

Pearce, J. M., & Hall, G. (1980). A model for Pavlovian learning: Variations in the effectiveness of conditioned but not of unconditioned stimuli. *Psychological Review, 87*, 532–552.

Pearce, J. M., & Wilson, P. N. (1991). Effects of extinction with a compound conditioned stimulus. *Journal of Experimental Psychology: Animal Behavior Processes, 17*, 151–162.

Peele, D. B., Casey, J., & Silberberg, A. (1984). Primacy of interresponse-time reinforcement in accounting for rate differences under variable-ratio and variable-interval schedules. *Journal of Experimental Psychology: Animal Behavior Processes, 10*, 149–167.

Pendery, M., & Maltzman, I. (1977). Instructions and the orienting reflex in "semantic conditioning" of the galvanic skin response in an innocuous situation. *Journal of Experimental Psychology: General, 106*, 120–140.

Penfield, W. (1958). *The excitable cortex in conscious man*. Liverpool: University of Liverpool Press.

Pepperberg, I. M. (1987). Acquisition of the same/different concept by an African Grey parrot (*Psittacus erithacus*): Learning with respect to categories of color, shape and material. *Animal Learning and Behavior, 15*, 423–432.

Perkins, C. C., Jr. (1947). The relation of secondary reward to gradients of reinforcement. *Journal of Experimental Psychology, 37*, 377–392.

Perkins, C. C., Jr., & Weyant, R. G. (1958). The interval between training and test trials as determiner of the slope of generalization gradients. *Journal of Comparative and Physiological Psychology, 51*, 596–600.

Peterson, G. B., Ackil, J. E., Frommer, G. P., & Hearst, E. S. (1972). Conditioned approach and contact behavior toward signals for food and brain-stimulation reinforcement. *Science, 177*, 1009–1011.

Peterson, L. R., & Peterson, M. J. (1959). Short-term retention of individual verbal items. *Journal* of *Experimental Psychology, 58,* 193–198.

Petrinovich, L., & Bolles, R. C. (1957). Delayed alternation: Evidence for symbolic processes in the rat. *Journal of Comparative and Physiological Psychology, 50,* 363–365.

Petty, R. E., & Cacioppo, J. T. (1981). *Attitudes and persuasion: Classic and contemporary approaches.* Dubuque, IA: Brown.

Pfungst, O. (1965). *Clever Hans: The horse of Mr. von Osten.* New York: Holt, Rinehart and Winston.

Phelps, M. T., & Roberts, W. A. (1991). Pattern tracking on the radial maze: Tracking multiple patterns at different spatial locations. *Journal of Experimental Psychology: Animal Behavior Processes, 17,* 411–422.

Phillips, E. L. (1968). Achievement Place: Token reinforcement procedures in a home-style rehabilitation setting for "pre-delinquent" boys. *Journal of Applied Behavior Analysis, 1,* 213–233.

Podlesny, J. A., & Raskin, D. C. (1977). Physiological measures and the detection of deception. *Psychological Bulletin, 84,* 782–799.

Posner, M. I. (1973). *Cognition: An introduction.* Glenview, IL: Scott, Foresman.

Posner, M. I., & Keele, S. W. (1968). On the genesis of abstract ideas. *Journal of Experimental Psychology, 77,* 353–363.

Postman, L. (1985). Human learning and memory. In G. A. Kimble & K. Schlesinger (Eds.), *Topics in the history of psychology* (Vol. 1). Hillsdale, NJ: Erlbaum.

Postman, L., Stark, K., & Fraser, J. (1968). Temporal changes in interference. *Journal of Verbal Learning and Verbal Behavior, 7,* 672–694.

Poulson, C. L. (1983). Differential reinforcement of other-than-vocalization as a control procedure in the conditioning of infant vocalization rate. *Journal of Experimental Child Psychology, 36,* 471–489.

Powell, D. R., Jr., & Perkins, C. C., Jr. (1957). Strength of secondary reinforcement as a determiner of the effects of duration of goal response on learning. *Journal of Experimental Psychology, 53,* 106–112.

Premack, D. (1965). Reinforcement theory. In D. Levine (Ed.), *Nebraska symposium on motivation* (Vol. 13). Lincoln: University of Nebraska Press.

Premack, D. (1971). Catching up with common sense, or two sides of a generalization: Reinforcement and punishment. In R. Glaser (Ed.), *The nature of reinforcement.* New York: Academic Press.

Premack, D., & Woodruff, G. (1978). Chimpanzee problem solving: A test for comprehension. *Science, 202,* 532–535.

Rabin, B. M., & Rabin, J. S. (1984). Acquisition of radiation- and lithium chloride-induced conditioned taste aversions in anesthetized rats. *Animal Learning and Behavior, 12,* 439–441.

Rachlin, H. (1974). Self-control. *Behaviorism, 2,* 94–107.

Rachlin, H., & Green, L. (1972). Commitment, choice, and self-control. *Journal of the Experimental Analysis of Behavior, 17,* 15–22.

Rachlin, H., Logue, A. W., Gibbon, J., & Frankel, M. (1986). Cognition and behavior in studies of choice. *Psychological Review, 93,* 33–45.

Rachman, S., & Hodgson, R. J. (1968). Experimentally induced "sexual fetishism": Replication and development. *Psychological Record, 18,* 25–27.

Ramachandran, R., & Pearce, J. M. (1987). Pavlovian analysis of interactions between hunger and thirst. *Journal of Experimental Psychology: Animal Behavior Processes, 13,* 182–192.

Raymond, M. J. (1964). The treatment of addiction by aversion conditioning with apomorphine. *Behaviour Research and Therapy, 1,* 287–291.

Reiss, S., & Sushinsky, L. W. (1975). Overjustification, competing responses, and the acquisition of intrinsic interest. *Journal of Personality and Social Psychology, 31,* 1116–1125.

Reiss, S., & Wagner, A. R. (1972). CS habituation produces a "latent inhibition effect" but no active "conditioned inhibition." *Learning and Motivation, 3,* 237–245.

Rescorla, R. A. (1966). Predictability and number of pairings in Pavlovian fear conditioning. *Psychonomic Science, 4,* 383–384.

Rescorla, R. A. (1968). Probability of shock in the presence and absence of CS in fear conditioning. *Journal of Comparative and Physiological Psychology, 66,* 1–5.

Rescorla, R. A. (1970). Reduction in the effectiveness of reinforcement after prior excitatory conditioning. *Learning and Motivation, 1,* 372–381.

Rescorla, R. A. (1973). Evidence for "unique stimulus" account of configural conditioning. *Journal of Comparative and Physiological Psychology, 85,* 331–338.

Rescorla, R. A. (1976). Stimulus generalization: Some predictions from a model of Pavlovian conditioning. *Journal of Experimental Psychology: Animal Behavior Processes, 2,* 88–96.

Rescorla, R. A. (1980). *Pavlovian second-order conditioning.* Hillsdale, NJ: Erlbaum.

Rescorla, R. A. (1981). Simultaneous associations. In P. Harzem & M. D. Zeiler (Eds.), *Predictability, correlation, and contiguity.* New York: Wiley.

Rescorla, R. A. (1982). Simultaneous second-order conditioning produces S–S learning in conditioned suppression. *Journal of Experimental Psychology: Animal Behavior Processes, 8,* 23–32.

Rescorla, R. A. (1985a). Conditioned inhibition and facilitation. In R. R. Miller & N. E. Spear (Eds.), *Information processing in animals: Conditioned inhibition.* Hillsdale, NJ: Erlbaum.

Rescorla, R. A. (1985b). Pavlovian conditioning analogues to Gestalt perceptual principles. In F. R. Brush & J. B. Overmier (Eds.), *Affect, conditioning, and cognition: Essays on the determinants of behavior.* Hillsdale, NJ: Erlbaum.

Rescorla, R. A. (1987). A Pavlovian analysis of goal-directed behavior. *American Psychologist, 42,* 119–129.

Rescorla, R. A. (1988). Pavlovian conditioning: It's not what you think it is. *American Psychologist, 43,* 151–160.

Rescorla, R. A., & Durlach, P. J. (1981). Within-event learning in Pavlovian conditioning. In N. E. Spear & R. R. Miller (Eds.), *Information processing in animals: Memory mechanisms.* Hillsdale, NJ: Erlbaum.

Rescorla, R. A., & Holland, P. C. (1982). Behaviorial studies of associative learning in animals. *Annual Review of Psychology, 33,* 265–308.

Rescorla, R. A., & LoLordo, V. M. (1965). Inhibition of avoidance behavior. *Journal of Comparative and Physiological Psychology, 59,* 406–412.

Rescorla, R. A., & Solomon, R. L. (1967). Two-process learning theory: Relationships between Pavlovian conditioning and instrumental learning. *Psychological Review, 74,* 151–182.

Rescorla, R. A., & Wagner, A. R. (1972). A theory of Pavlovian conditioning: Variations in the effectiveness of reinforcement and nonreinforcement. In A. H. Black & W. F. Prokasy (Eds.), *Classical conditioning II: Current research and theory.* New York: Appleton-Century-Crofts.

Revusky, S. (1971). The role of interference in association over a delay. In W. K. Honig & P. H. R. James (Eds.), *Animal memory.* New York: Academic Press.

Revusky, S. (1977). The concurrent interference approach to delay learning. In L. M. Barker, M. R. Best, & M. Domjan (Eds.), *Learning mechanisms in food selection.* Waco, TX: Baylor University Press.

Revusky, S. (1985). The general process approach to animal learn-

ing. In T. D. Johnston & A. T. Petrewicz (Eds.), *Issues in the ecological study of learning.* Hillsdale, NJ: Erlbaum.

Reynolds, G. S. (1961). Attention in the pigeon. *Journal of the Experimental Analysis of Behavior, 4,* 203–208.

Riley, D. A., & Leith, C. R. (1976). Multidimensional psychophysics and selective attention in animals. *Psychological Bulletin, 83,* 138–160.

Rincover, A., & Koegel, R. L. (1975). Setting generality and stimulus control in autistic children. *Journal of Applied Behavior Analysis, 8,* 235–246.

Risley, T. R. (1968). The effects and side effects of punishing the autistic behaviors of a deviant child. *Journal of Applied Behavior Analysis, 1,* 21–34.

Roberts, W. A. (1979). Spatial memory in the rat on a hierarchical maze. *Learning and Motivation, 10,* 117–140.

Romanes, G. J. (1882). *Animal intelligence.* London: Kegan Paul.

Roper, T. J., Edwards, L., & Crossland, G. (1983). Factors affecting schedule-induced wood-chewing in rats: Percentage and rate of reinforcement, and operant requirement. *Animal Learning and Behavior, 11,* 35–43.

Rosch, E. (1978). Principles of categorization. In E. Rosch & B. Lloyd (Eds.), *Cognition and categorization.* Hillsdale, NJ: Erlbaum.

Rosenfeld, H. M., & Baer, D. M. (1969). Unnoticed verbal conditioning of an aware experimenter by a more aware subject: The double-agent effect. *Psychological Review, 76,* 425–432.

Rosenthal, R. (1966). *Experimenter effects in behavioral research.* New York: Appleton-Century-Crofts.

Rosenthal, T., & Bandura, A. (1978). Psychological modeling: Theory and practice. In S. L. Garfield & A. E. Bergin (Eds.), *Handbook of psychotherapy and behavior change: An empirical analysis* (2nd. ed.). New York: Wiley.

Rosenzweig, M. R. (1984). Experience, memory, and the brain. *American Psychologist, 39,* 365–376.

Ross, R. T., & LoLordo, V. M. (1987). Evaluation of the relation between Pavlovian occasion-setting and instrumental discriminative stimuli: A blocking analysis. *Journal of Experimental Psychology: Animal Behavior Processes, 13,* 3–16.

Roueche, B. (1954). *Eleven blue men.* Boston: Little, Brown.

Rowland, R. F. (1977). Environmental events predicting death for the elderly. *Psychological Bulletin, 84,* 349–372.

Rumelhart, D. E., & McClelland, J. L. (1986). On learning the past tenses of English verbs. In J. L. McClelland, D. E. Rumelhart, & the PDP Research Group, *Parallel distributed processing: Explorations in the microstructure of cognition: Vol. 2. Psychological and biological models.* Cambridge, MA: MIT Press.

Russell, B. (1927). *An outline of philosophy.* London: George Allen & Unwin.

Ryan, R. M. (1982). Control and information in the intrapersonal sphere: An extension of cognitive evaluation theory. *Journal of Personality and Social Psychology, 43,* 450–461.

Saltz, E. (1971). *The cognitive bases of human learning.* Homewood, IL: Dorsey.

Salzen, E. A., & Meyer, C. C. (1968). Reversibility of imprinting. *Journal of Comparative and Physiological Psychology, 66,* 269–275.

Savage-Rumbaugh, E. S. (1986). *Ape language: From conditioned response to symbol.* New York: Columbia University Press.

Schneider, B. A., & Shiffrin, R. M. (1977). Controlled and automatic human information processing: I. Detection, search, and attention. *Psychological Review, 84,* 1–66.

Schull, J. (1979). A conditioned opponent theory of Pavlovian conditioning and habituation. In G. H. Bower (Ed.), *The psychology of learning and motivation* (Vol. 13). New York: Academic Press.

Schusterman, R. J. (1962). Transfer effects of successive discrimination reversal training in chimpanzees. *Science, 137,* 422–423.

Schwarz, N., Bless, H., & Bohner, G. (1991). Mood and persuasion: Affective states influence the processing of persuasive communications. In M. P. Zanna (Ed.), *Advances in Experimental Psychology* (Vol. 24). San Diego, CA: Academic Press.

Scott, W. A. (1959). Attitude change by response reinforcement: Replication and extension. *Sociometry, 22,* 328–335.

Sears, R. R., Maccoby, E. E., & Levin, H. (1957). *Patterns of child rearing.* Evanston, IL: Row, Peterson.

Sejnowski, T. J., & Rosenberg, C. R. (1987). Parallel networks that learn to pronounce English text. *Complex Systems, 1,* 145–168.

Seligman, M. E. P. (1969). Control group and conditioning: A comment on operationalism. *Psychological Review, 76,* 484–491.

Seligman, M. E. P. (1970). On the generality of the laws of learning. *Psychological Review, 77,* 406–418.

Seligman, M. E. P. (1975). *Helplessness.* San Francisco: W.H. Freeman.

Seligman, M. E. P., & Johnston, J. C. (1973). A cognitive theory of avoidance learning. In F. J. McGuigan & D. B. Lumsden (Eds.), *Contemporary approaches to conditioning and learning.* Washington, DC: Winston-Wiley.

Seligman, M. E. P., & Maier, S. F. (1967). Failure to escape traumatic shock. *Journal of Experimental Psychology, 74,* 1–9.

Seward, J. P., & Levy, N. (1949). Sign learning as a factor in extinction. *Journal of Comparative and Physiological Psychology, 39,* 660–668.

Shea, J. B., & Upton, G. (1976). The effects on skill acquisition of an interpolated motor short-term memory task during the KR-delay interval. *Journal of Motor Behavior, 8,* 277–281.

Sheffield, F. D. (1965). Relation between classical conditioning and instrumental learning. In W. F. Prokasy (Ed.), *Classical conditioning.* New York: Appleton-Century-Crofts.

Sheffield, F. D., Wulff, J. J., & Backer, R. (1951). Reward value of copulation without sex drive reduction. *Journal of Comparative and Physiological Psychology, 44,* 3–8.

Sheffield, V. F. (1949). Extinction as a function of partial reinforcement and distribution of practice. *Journal of Experimental Psychology, 39,* 511–526.

Shepp, B. E. (1983). The analyzability of multidimensional objects: Some constraints on perceived structure, the development of perceived structure, and attention. In T. J. Tighe & B. E. Shepp (Eds.), *Perception, cognition and development: Interactional analyses.* Hillsdale, NJ: Erlbaum.

Shepp, B. E., & Schrier, A. M. (1969). Consecutive intradimensional and extradimensional shifts in monkeys. *Journal of Comparative and Physiological Psychology, 67,* 199–203.

Shettleworth, S. J. (1983). Function and mechanism in learning. In M. D. Zeiler & P. Harzem (Eds.), *Advances in analysis of behaviour* (Vol. 3). Chichester, England: Wiley.

Shiffrin, R. M., & Schneider, W. (1977). Controlled and automatic human information processing: II. Perceptual learning, automatic attending, and a general theory. *Psychological Review, 84,* 127–190.

Sidman, M., & Stoddard, L. T. (1967). The effectiveness of fading in programming a simultaneous form discrimination for retarded children. *Journal of the Experimental Analysis of Behavior, 10,* 3–16.

Siegel, S. (1970). The physiology of conditioning. In M. H. Marx (Ed.), *Learning: Interactions.* London: Macmillan.

Siegel, S. (1972). Conditioning of insulin-induced glycemia. *Journal of Comparative and Physiological Psychology, 78,* 233–241.

Siegel, S. (1975). Evidence from rats that morphine tolerance is a learned response. *Journal of Comparative and Physiological Psychology, 89,* 498–506.

Siegel, S. (1978). A Pavlovian conditioning analysis of morphine tolerance. In N. A. Krasnegor (Ed.), *Behavioral tolerance: Research and treatment implications* (NIDA Research Monograph No. 18). Washington, DC: U.S. Government Printing Office.

Siegel, S. (1984). Pavlovian conditioning and heroin overdose: Reports by overdose victims. *Bulletin of the Psychonomic Society, 22,* 428–430.

Siegel, S., Hinson, R. E., Krank, M. D., & McCully, J. (1982). Heroin "overdose" death: Contribution of drug-associated environmental cues. *Science, 216,* 436–437.

Siqueland, E. R., & DeLucia, C. A. (1969). Visual reinforcement of non-nutritive sucking in human infants. *Science, 165,* 1144–1146.

Skinner, B. F. (1938). *The behavior of organisms.* New York: Appleton-Century-Crofts.

Skinner, B. F. (1948a). "Superstition" in the pigeon. *Journal of Experimental Psychology, 38,* 168–172.

Skinner, B. F. (1948b). *Walden two.* New York: Macmillan.

Skinner, B. F. (1953). *Science and human behavior.* New York: Macmillan.

Skinner, B. F. (1955). Freedom and the control of men. *American Scholar, 25,* 47–65.

Skinner, B. F. (1956). A case history in scientific method. *American Psychologist, 32,* 221–233.

Skinner, B. F. (1971). *Beyond freedom and dignity.* New York: Knopf.

Small, W. S. (1901). An experimental study of the mental processes of the rat. *American Journal of Psychology, 12,* 206–239.

Smith, G. H., & Engel, R. (1968). Influence of a female model on perceived characteristics of an automobile. *Proceedings of the 76th Annual Convention of the American Psychological Association, 3,* 681–682.

Smith, S. M. (1979). Remembering in and out of context. *Journal of Experimental Psychology: Human Learning and Memory, 5,* 460–471.

Solomon, R. L., Kamin, L. J., & Wynne, L. C. (1953). Traumatic avoidance learning: The outcomes of several extinction procedures with dogs. *Journal of Abnormal and Social Psychology, 48,* 291–302.

Solomon, R. L., Turner, L. H., & Lessac, M. S. (1968). Some effects of delay of punishment on resistance to temptation in dogs. *Journal of Personality and Social Psychology, 8,* 233–238.

Solomon, R. L., & Wynne, L. (1953). Traumatic avoidance learning: Acquisition in normal dogs. *Psychological Monographs, 67* (4, Whole No. 354).

Spear, N. E. (1978). *The processing of memories: Forgetting and retention.* Hillsdale, NJ: Erlbaum.

Spence, K. W. (1936). The nature of discrimination learning in animals. *Psychological Review, 43,* 427–449.

Spence, K. W. (1937). The differential response in animals to stimuli varying within a single dimension. *Psychological Review, 44,* 430–444.

Spence, K. W. (1947). The role of secondary reinforcement in delayed-reward learning. *Psychological Review, 54,* 1–8.

Spence, K. W. (1956). *Behavior theory and conditioning.* New Haven, CT: Yale University Press.

Spence, K. W. (1966). Cognitive and drive factors in the extinction of the conditioned eye blink in human subjects. *Psychological Review, 73,* 445–458.

Spence, K. W., Homzie, M. J., & Rutledge, E. F. (1964). Extinction of the human eyelid CR as a function of the discriminability of the change from acquisition to extinction. *Journal of Experimental Psychology, 67,* 545–552.

Spence, J. T. (1970). The distracting effects of material reinforcers in the discrimination learning of lower- and middle-class children. *Child Development, 71,* 103–111.

Spielberger, C. D., & DeNike, L. D. (1966). Descriptive behaviorism versus cognitive theory in verbal operant conditioning. *Psychological Review, 73,* 306–326.

Spivey, J. E., & Hess, D. T. (1968). Effect of partial reinforcement trial sequences on extinction performance. *Psychonomic Science, 10,* 375–376.

Squire, L. R. (1987). *Memory and brain.* New York: Oxford University Press.

Staddon, J. E. R. (1983). *Adaptive behavior and learning.* Cambridge: Cambridge University Press.

Staddon, J. E. R., & Simmelhag, V. L. (1971). The "superstition" experiment: A reexamination of its implications for the principles of adaptive behavior. *Psychological Review, 78,* 3–43.

Stokes, T. F., Baer, D. M., & Jackson, R. L. (1974). Programming the generalization of a greeting response in four retarded children. *Journal of Applied Behavior Analysis, 7,* 599–610.

Suedfeld, P., & Landon, P. B. (1970). Motivational arousal and task complexity. *Journal of Experimental Psychology, 83,* 329–330.

Sutherland, N. S., & Mackintosh, N. J. (1971). *Mechanisms of animal discrimination learning.* New York: Academic Press.

Sutton, R. S., & Barto, A. G. (1981). Toward a modern theory of adaptive networks: Expectation and prediction. *Psychological Review, 88,* 135–170.

Suzuki, S., Augerinos, G., & Black, A. H. (1980). Stimulus control of spatial behavior on the eight-arm maze in rats. *Learning and Motivation, 11,* 1–18.

Telegdy, G. A., & Cohen, J. S. (1971). Cue utilization and drive level in albino rats. *Journal of Comparative and Physiological Psychology, 75,* 248–253.

Terrace, H. S. (1966). Stimulus control. In W. K. Honig (Ed.), *Operant behavior: Areas of research and application.* New York: Appleton-Century-Crofts.

Terrace, H. S. (1985). Animal cognition: Thinking without language. In L. Weiskrantz (Ed.), *Animal intelligence.* Oxford: Clarendon.

Testa, T. J. (1975). Effects of similarity of location and temporal intensity pattern of conditioned and unconditioned stimuli on the acquisition of conditioned suppression in rats. *Journal of Experimental Psychology: Animal Behavior Processes, 1,* 114–121.

Thomas, D. R., Mood, K., Morrison, S., & Wiertelak, E. (1991). Peak shift revisited: A test of alterntive interpretations. *Journal* of Experimental Psychology: Animal Behavior Processes, 17, 130–141.

Thomas, D. R., & Sherman, L. (1986). An assessment of the role of handling cues in "spontaneous recovery" after extinction. Journal of the Experimental Analysis of Behavior, 46, 305–314.

Thomas, G. V. (1981). Contiguity, reinforcement rate, and the law of effect. Quarterly Journal of Experimental Psychology, 33B, 33–43.

Thomas, G. V., Robertson, D., & Lieberman, D. A. (1987). Marking effects in Pavlovian trace conditioning. Journal of Experimental Psychology: Animal Behavior Processes, 13, 126–135.

Thorndike, E. L. (1898). Animal intelligence: An experimental study of the associative processes in animals. Psychological Review Monograph Supplement, 2(8).

Thorndike, E. L. (1911). Animal intelligence. New York: Macmillan.

Thorndike, E. L. (1935). The psychology of wants, interests, and attitudes. New York: Appleton-Century-Crofts.

Thorndike, E. L. (1946). Expectation. Psychological Review, 53, 277–281.

Tiffany, S. T., Maude-Griffin, P. M., & Drobes, D. J. (1991). Effect of interdose interval on the development of associative tolerance to morphine in the rat: A dose-response analysis. Behavioral Neuroscience, 105, 49–61.

Timberlake, W. (1984). The functional organization of appetitive behavior: Behavior systems and learning. In M. D. Zeiler & P. Harzem (Eds.), Advances in the analysis of behavior (Vol. 3). New York: Wiley.

Timberlake, W., & Allison, J. (1974). Reponse deprivation: An empirical approach to instrumental performance. Psychological Review, 81, 146–164.

Timberlake, W., & Grant, D. S. (1975). Auto-shaping in rats to the presentation of another rat predicting food. Science, 190, 690–692.

Timberlake, W., & Lucas, G. A. (1989). Behavior systems and learning: From misbehavior to general principles. In S. B. Klein & R. R. Mowrer (Eds.), Contemporary learning theories: Instrumental conditioning theory and the impact of biological constraints on learning. Hillsdale, NJ: Erlbaum.

Timberlake, W., Wahl, G., & King, D. (1982). Stimulus and response contingencies in the misbehavior of rats. Journal of Experimental Psychology: Animal Behavior Processes, 8, 62–85.

Tinbergen, N., & Perdeck, A. C. (1950). On the stimulus situation releasing the begging response in the newly hatched herring gull chick (Larus argentatus argentatus Pont.). Behaviour, 3, 1–39.

Tinklepaugh, O. L. (1928). An experimental study of representative factors in monkeys. Journal of Comparative and Physiological Psychology, 8, 197–236.

Titchener, E. B. (1915). A textbook of psychology. New York: Macmillan.

Toates, F. M. (1980). Animal behavior: A systems approach. New York: Wiley.

Tolman, E. C. (1932). Purposive be-

havior in animals and men. New York: Century.

Tolman, E. C. (1948). Cognitive maps in rats and men. *Psychological Review, 55,* 189–208.

Tolman, E. C., & Honzik, C. H. (1930a). "Insight" in rats. *University of California Publications in Psychology, 4,* 215–232.

Tolman, E. C., & Honzik, C. H. (1930b). Introduction and removal of reward, and maze performance in rats. *University of California Publications in Psychology, 4,* 257–275.

Trabasso, T. (1963). Stimulus emphasis and all-or-none learning of concept identification. *Journal of Experimental Psychology, 65,* 395–406.

Trabasso, T., & Bower, G. H. (1968). *Attention in learning: Theory and research.* New York: Wiley.

Tulving, E., & Psotka, J. (1971). Retroactive inhibition in free recall: Inaccessibility of information available in the memory store. *Journal of Experimental Psychology, 87,* 1–8.

Turner, A. M., & Greenough, W. T. (1985). Differential rearing effects on rat visual cortex synapses: I. Synaptic and neuronal density and synapses per neuron. *Brain Research, 329,* 195–203.

Ulrich, R. E., & Azrin, N. H. (1962). Reflexive fighting in response to aversive stimulation. *Journal of the Experimental Analysis of Behavior, 5,* 511–520.

Underwood, B. J. (1957). Interference and forgetting. *Psychological Review, 64,* 49–60.

Vander Wall, S. B. (1982). An experimental analysis of cache recovery in Clark's nutcracker. *Animal Behavior, 30,* 84–94.

Vaughan, W., Jr. (1988). Formation of equivalence sets in pigeons. *Journal of Experimental Psychology: Animal Behavior Processes, 14,* 36–42.

Visintainer, M. A., Volpicelli, J. R., & Seligman, M. E. P. (1982). Tumor rejection in rats after inescapable versus escapable shock. *Science, 216,* 437–439.

Wagner, A. R. (1959). The role of reinforcement and nonreinforcement in an "apparent frustration effect." *Journal of Experimental Psychology, 57,* 130–136.

Wagner, A. R. (1969). Incidental stimuli and discrimination learning. In R. M. Gilbert & N. S. Sutherland (Eds.), *Animal discrimination learning.* London: Academic Press.

Wagner, A. R. (1981). SOP: A model of automatic memory processing in animal behavior. In N. E. Spear & R. R. Miller (Eds.), *Information processing in animals: Memory mechanisms.* Hillsdale, NJ: Erlbaum.

Wagner, A. R., & Brandon, S. E. (1989). Evolution of a structured connectionist model of Pavlovian conditioning (Aesop). In S. B. Klein & R. R. Mowrer (Eds.), *Contemporary learning theories: Pavlovian conditioning and the status of traditional learning theory.* Hillsdale, NJ: Erlbaum.

Wagner, A. R., Rudy, J. W., & Whitlow, J. W. (1973). Rehearsal in animal conditioning. *Journal of Experimental Psychology Monograph, 97,* 407–426.

Wahlsten, D. L., & Cole, M. (1972). Classical and avoidance training of leg flexion in the dog. In A. H. Black & W. F. Prokasy (Eds.), *Classical conditioning II:*

Current research and theory. New York: Appleton-Century-Crofts.

Walters, G. C., & Grusec, J. E. (1977). *Punishment.* San Francisco: W. H. Freeman.

Warren, J. M. (1954). Perceptual dominance in discrimination learning by monkeys. *Journal of Comparative and Physiological Psychology, 47,* 290–292.

Warren, R. M. (1970). Perceptual restorations of missing speech sounds. *Science, 167,* 392–393.

Warren, V. L., & Cairns, R. B. (1972). Social reinforcement satiation: An outcome of frequency or ambiguity? *Journal of Experimental Child Psychology, 13,* 249–260.

Washburn, D. A., Hopkins, W. D., & Rumbaugh, D. M. (1991). Perceived control in rhesus monkeys (*Macaca mulatta*): Enhanced video-task performance. *Journal of Experimental Psychology: Animal Behavior Processes, 17,* 123–129.

Wasserman, E. A. (1973). Pavlovian conditioning with heat reinforcement produces stimulus-directed pecking in chicks. *Science, 181,* 875–877.

Wasserman, E. A., & Neunaber, D. J. (1986). College students' responding to and rating of contingency relations: The role of temporal contiguity. *Journal of the Experimental Analysis of Behavior, 46,* 15–35.

Watkins, M. J. (1979). Engrams as cuegrams and forgetting as cue overload: A cueing approach to the structure of memory. In C. R. Puff (Ed.), *Memory organization and structure.* New York: Academic Press.

Watkins, M. J., Peynircioglu, Z. F., &

Burns, D. J. (1984). Pictorial rehearsal. *Memory and Cognition, 12,* 553–557.

Watkins, M. J., & Watkins, O. C. (1976). Cue-overload theory and the method of interpolated attributes. *Bulletin of the Psychonomic Society, 7,* 289–291.

Watson, J. B. (1913). Psychology as the behaviorist views it. *Psychological Review, 20,* 158–177.

Watson, J. B., & McDougall, W. (1929). *The battle of behaviorism.* New York: Norton.

Watson, J. B., & Raynor, R. (1920). Conditioned emotional reactions. *Journal of Experimental Psychology, 3,* 1–14.

Weingarten, H. P. (1983). Conditioned cues elicit feeding in sated rats: A role for learning in meal initiation. *Science, 20,* 431–433.

Weinstein, C. E., & Meyer, R. E. (1986). The teaching of learning strategies. In M. Wittrock (Ed.), *The handbook of research on teaching* (3rd ed.). New York: Macmillan.

Wexler, D. B. (1973). Token and taboo: Behavior modification, token economies, and the law. *Behaviorism, 1,* 1–24.

White, N. M., & Milner, P. M. (1992). The psychobiology of reinforcers. *Annual Review of Psychology, 43,* 443–471.

Whitlow, J. W., Jr., & Wagner, A. R. (1984). Memory and habituation. In H. V. S. Peeke & L. Petrinovich (Eds.), *Habituation, sensitization, and behavior.* New York: Academic Press.

Wickens, D. D., & Wickens, C. D. (1942). Some factors related to pseudoconditioning. *Journal of*

Experimental Psychology, 31, 518–526.

Widrow, G., & Hoff, M. E. (1960). Adaptive switching circuits. *Institute of Radio Engineers, Western Electronic Show and Convention, Convention Record, 4*, 96–194.

Wiens, A. N., & Menustik, C. E. (1983). Treatment outcome and patient characteristics in an aversion therapy program for alcoholism. *American Psychologist, 38*, 1089–1096.

Wike, E. L. (1966). *Secondary reinforcement: Selected experiments.* New York: Harper & Row.

Wilcoxon, H. C., Dragoin, W. B., & Kral, P. A. (1971). Illness-induced aversions in rat and quail: Relative salience of visual and gustatory cues. *Science, 171*, 826–828.

Williams, B. A. (1978). Information effects on the response-reinforcer association. *Animal Learning and Behavior, 6*, 371–379.

Williams, C. D. (1959). The elimination of tantrum behaviors by extinction procedures. *Journal of Abnormal and Social Psychology, 59*, 269.

Williams, D. A., Overmier, J. B., & LoLordo, V. (1992). A reevaluation of Rescorla's dictums about Pavlovian conditioned inhibition. *Psychological Bulletin, 111*, 275–290.

Williams, D. R., & Williams, H. (1969). Automaintenance in the pigeon: Sustained pecking despite contingent non-reinforcement. *Journal of the Experimental Analysis of Behavior, 12*, 511–520.

Wilson, G. T. (1982). Adult disorders. In G. T. Wilson & C. M.

Franks (Eds.), *Contemporary behavior therapy: Conceptual and empirical foundations.* New York: Guilford Press.

Winett, R. A., & Winkler, R. C. (1972). Current behavior modification in the classroom: Be still, be quiet, be docile. *Journal of Applied Behavior Analysis, 5*, 499–504.

Wolf, M. M., Risley, T. R., & Mees, H. L. (1964). Application of operant conditioning procedures to the behavior problems of an autistic child. *Behavior Research and Therapy, 1*, 305–312.

Wolfe, J. B. (1934). The effect of delayed reward upon learning in the white rat. *Journal of Comparative Psychology, 17*, 1–21.

Wolfe, J. B. (1936). Effectiveness of token-rewards for chimpanzees. *Comparative Psychology Monographs, 12*(5, Serial No. 60).

Wolpe, J., & Lazarus, A. A. (1966). *Behavior therapy techniques.* London: Pergamon.

Wong, P. T. P. (1978). A behavior field approach to instrumental learning in the rat: II. Training parameters and a stage model of extinction. *Animal Learning and Behavior, 6*, 82–93.

Wood, R., & Flynn, J. M. (1978). A self-evaluation token system versus an external evaluation token system with predelinquent youth. *Journal of Applied Behavior Analysis, 11*, 503–512.

Woodbury, C. B. (1943). Learning of stimulus patterns by dogs. *Journal of Comparative Psychology, 35*, 29–40.

Wright, A. A., Cook, R. G., Rivera, J. J., Sands, S. F., & Delius, J. D. (1988). Concept learning by pigeons: Matching-to-sample with trial-unique video picture stimuli. *Animal Learning and Behavior, 16,* 436–444.

Yerkes, R. M., & Morgulis, S. (1909). The method of Pavlov in animal psychology. *Psychological Bulletin, 6,* 257–273.

Young, H. F., Greenberg, E. R., Paton, W., & Jane, J. A. (1967). A reinvestigation of cognitive maps. *Psychonomic Science, 9,* 589–590.

Zaffy, D. J., & Bruning, J. L. (1966). Drive and the range of cue utilization. *Journal of Experimental Psychology, 71,* 382–384.

Zamble, E. (1967). Classical conditioning of excitement anticipatory to food reward. *Journal of Comparative and Physiological Psychology, 63,* 526–529.

Zamble, E., Hadad, G. M., Mitchell, J. B., & Cutmore, T. R. H. (1985). Pavlovian conditioning of sexual arousal: First- and second-order effects. *Journal of Experimental Psychology: Animal Behavior Processes, 11,* 598–610.

Zamble, E., Mitchell, J. B., & Findlay, H. (1986). Pavlovian conditioning of sexual arousal: Parametric and background manipulations. *Journal of Experimental Psychology: Animal Behavior Processes, 12,* 403–411.

Zeaman, D., & Hanley, P. (1983). Stimulus preferences as structural features. In T. J. Tighe & B. E. Shepp (Eds.), *Perception, cognition, and development: Interactional analyses.* Hillsdale, NJ: Erlbaum.

Zeaman, D., & House, B. J. (1963). The role of attention in retardate discrimination learning. In N. R. Ellis (Ed.), *Handbook of mental deficiency: Psychological theory and research.* New York: McGraw-Hill.

Zeaman, D., & House, B. J. (1979). A review of attention theory. In N. R. Ellis (Ed.), *Handbook of mental deficiency: Psychological theory and research* (2nd ed.). Hillsdale, NJ: Erlbaum.

Zeiler, M. (1977). Schedules of reinforcement: The controlling variables. In W. K. Honig & J. E. R. Staddon (Eds.), *Handbook of operant behavior.* Englewood Cliffs, NJ: Prentice-Hall.

Zener, K. (1937). The significance of behavior accompanying conditioned salivary secretion for theories of the conditoned response. *American Journal of Psychology, 50,* 384–403.

ACKNOWLEDGMENTS

Fig. 1.3 from Premack, D., and Woodruff, G. (1978), "Chimpanzee Problem Solving: A Test for Comprehension," *Science, 202,* 532–535. Copyright 1978 by the AAAS. Reprinted by permission of the American Association for the Advancement of Science and the author.

Fig. 1.4 from Davis, M. (1974), "Sensation of the Rat Startle Response by Noise," *Journal of Comparative and Physiological Psychology, 87,* 571–581. © 1974 by the American Psychological Association. Reprinted by permission of the publisher.

Fig. 4.6 from Rescorla, R. A. (1966), "Predictability and Number of Pairings in Pavlovian Fear Conditioning," *Psychonomic Science, 4,* 383–384. Reprinted by permission of Psychonomic Society Publications and the author.

Fig. 4.8 from Garcia, J., and Koelling, R. A. (1966), "Relation of Cue to Consequence in Avoidance Learning," *Psychonomic Science, 20,* 313–314. Reprinted by permission of Psychonomic Society Publications and the author.

Fig. 5.9 from Jenkins, H. M., and Moore, B. R. (1973), "The Form of the Auto-Shaped Response with Food or Water Reinforcers," *Journal of the Experimental Analysis of Behavior, 20,* 163–181. Reprinted by permission of the publisher and the author.

Fig. 5.10 from Domjan, M., and Burkhard, B. (1986), *The Principles of Learning and Behavior.* © 1986 Brooks/Cole Publishing Company, Pacific Grove, CA 93950. Reprinted by permission of Wadsworth, Inc.

Fig. 5.13 from Pendery, M., and Maltzman, I. (1977), "Instructions and the Orienting Reflex in 'Semantic Conditioning' of the Galvanic Skin Response in an Innocuous Situation," *Journal of Experimental Psychology: General, 106,* 120–140. Reprinted by permission of the publisher and the author.

Fig. 5.14 from Spence, K. W., Homzie, M. J., and Rutledge, E. F. (1964), "Extinction of the Human Eyelid CR as a Function of the Discriminability of the Change from Acquisition to Extinction," *Journal of Experimental Psychology, 67,* 545–552. Reprinted by permission of the publisher and the author.

Fig. 6.3 from Allen, K. E., Hart, B., Buell, J. S., Harris, F. R., and Wolf, M. M. (1964), "Effects of Social Reinforcement on Isolate Behavior of a Nursery School Child," *Child Development, 35,* 511–518. © 1964 The Society for Research in Child Development, Inc. Reprinted by permission.

Fig. 6.8 from Phillips, E. L. (1968), "Achievement Place: Token Reinforcement Procedures in a Home-Style Rehabilitation Setting for 'Pre-Delinquent' Boys," *Journal of Applied Behavior Analysis*, 1, 213–223. Copyright 1968 by the Society for the Experimental Analysis of Behavior. Reprinted by permission of the publisher.

Fig. 6.14 from Clark, F. C. (1958), "The Effect of Deprivation and Frequency of Reinforcement on Variable-Interval Responding," *Journal of the Experimental Analysis of Behavior*, 1, 221–228. Reprinted by permission of the publisher.

Fig. 6.15 from Crespi, L. P. (1942), "Quantitative Variation in Incentive and Performance in the White Rat," *American Journal of Psychology*, 55, 467–517. Reprinted by permission of the University of Illinois Press.

Fig. 6.18 from Stokes, T. F., Baer, D. M., and Jackson, R. L. (1974), "Programming the Generalization of a Greeting Response in Four Retarded Children," *Journal of Applied Behavior Analysis*, 7, 599–610. Copyright 1974 by the Society for the Experimental Analysis of Behavior. Reprinted by permission of the publisher and the author.

Fig. 6.20 from Sidman, M., and Stoddard, L. T. (1967), "The Effectiveness of Fading in Programming a Simultaneous Form Discrimination for Retarded Children," *Journal of Experimental Analysis of Behavior*, 10, 3–15. Reprinted by permission of the publisher.

Fig. 7.1 from Skinner, B. F. (1938), *The Behavior of Organisms*. New York: Appleton-Century-Crofts. Reprinted by permission of B. F. Skinner.

Fig. 7.2 from Boe, E. E., and Church, R. M. (1967), "Permanent Effects of Punishment During Extinction," *Journal of Comparative and Physiological Psychology*, 63, 486–492. © 1967 by the American Psychological Association. Reprinted by permission of the author and the publisher.

Fig. 7.3 from Honig, W. K., and Slivka, R. M. (1964), "Stimulus Generalization of the Effects of Punishment," *Journal of the Experimental Analysis of Behavior*, 7, 21–25. Reprinted by permission.

Fig. 7.4 from Bucher, B., and Lovaas, O. I. (1968), "The Use of Aversive Stimulation in Behavior Modification," in M. R. Jones (Ed.), *Miami Symposium on the Prediction of Behavior: Aversive Stimulation*. Coral Gables, FL: University of Miami Press. Reprinted by permission of the publisher.

Fig. 7.7 from Madsen, C. H., Becker, W. C., Thomas, D. R., Koser, L., and Plager, E. (1970), "An Analysis of the Reinforcing Function of 'Sit Down' Commands," in R. K. Parker (Ed.), *Readings in Educational Psychology*. Reprinted by permission of Allyn & Bacon Publishers.

Fig. 8.1 from Hall, R. V., Lund, D., and Jackson, D. (1968), "Effects of Teacher Attention on Study Behavior," *Journal of Applied Behavior Analysis*, 1, 1–12. © 1968 by the Society for the Experimental Analysis of Behavior. Reprinted by permission of the author and the publisher.

Fig. 8.2 from Allyson, M. G., and Ayllon, T. (1980), "Behavioral Coaching in the Development of Skills in Football, Gymnastics, and Tennis," *Journal of Applied Behavior Analysis*, 13, 297–314. © 1980 by the Society for the Experimental Analysis of Behavior. Reprinted by permission of the author and the publisher.

Fig. 8.3 from Hall, R. V., Axelrod, S., Tyler, L., Grief, E., Jones, F. C., and Robertson, R. (1972), "Modification of Behavior Problems in the Home with a Parent as Observer and Experimenter," *Journal of Applied Behavior Analysis, 5,* 53–64. © 1972 by the Society for the Experimental Analysis of Behavior. Reprinted by permission of the author and the publisher.

Fig. 8.4 from Garlington, W. K., and Dericco, D. A. (1977), "The Effect of Modeling on Drinking Rate," *Journal of Applied Behavior Analysis, 10,* 207–211. © 1977 by the Society for the Experimental Analysis of Behavior. Reprinted by permission of the author and the publisher.

Fig. 8.5 from Bandura, A., Blanchard, E. B., and Ritter, B. (1969), "Relative Efficacy of Desensitization and Modeling Approaches for Inducing Behavioral, Affective, and Attitudinal Changes," *Journal of Personality and Social Psychology, 13,* 173–199. © 1969 by the American Psychological Association. Reprinted by permission of the author and the publisher.

Fig. 8.6 from Drabman, R. S., Spitalnik, R., and O'Leary, K. D. (1973), "Teaching Self-Control to Disruptive Children," *Journal of Abnormal Psychology, 82,* 10–16. © 1973 by the American Psychological Association. Reprinted by permission of the author and the publisher.

Fig. 9.1 from Thomas, G. (1981), "Contiguity, Reinforcement Rate and the Law of Effect," *Quarterly Journal of Experimental Psychology, 33B,* 33–43. Reprinted by permission of the University of Edinburgh.

Fig. 9.2 from Wasserman, E. A., and Neunaber, D. J. (1986), "College Students Responding to and Rating of Contingency Relations: The Role of Temporal Contiguity," *Journal of the Experimental Analysis of Behavior, 46,* 15–35. Reprinted by permission of the publisher.

Fig. 9.3 from DeNike, L. D., and Spielberger, C. D. (1963), "Induced Mediating States in Verbal Conditioning," *Journal of Verbal Learning and Verbal Behavior, 1,* 339–345. Reprinted by permission of the Academic Press and the author.

Fig. 9.4 from Rosenfeld, H. M., and Baer, D. M. (1969), "Unnoticed Verbal Conditioning of an Aware Experimenter by a More Aware Subject: The Double-Agent Effect," *Psychological Review, 76,* 425–432. © 1969 by the American Psychological Association. Reprinted by permission of the author and the publisher.

Fig. 9.5 reprinted by permission of The University of California Press.

Fig. 9.11 from Kamin, L. J., Brimer, C. J., and Black, A. H. (1963), "Conditioned Suppression as a Monitor of Fear of the CS in the Course of Avoidance Training," *Journal of Comparative and Physiological Psychology, 56,* 497–501. © 1963 by the American Psychological Association. Reprinted by permission of the author and the publisher.

Fig. 10.2 from Hess, E. H. (1959), "Imprinting," *Science, 130,* 133ff, July 17, 1959. Copyright 1959 by the AAAS. Reprinted by permission of the American Association for the Advancement of Science.

Fig. 10.3 from Andrews, E. A., and Braverman, N. S. (1975), *Animal Learning and Behavior, 3,* 187–189. Reprinted by permission of Psychonomic Society, Inc., and the author.

Fig. 10.5 from Chapuis, N., Thinus-Blanc, C., and Poucet, B. (1983), "Dissociation of Mechanisms Involved in Dogs' Oriented Displacements," *Quarterly Journal of Experimental Psychology, 35B,* 213–220. Reprinted by permission of the University of Edinburgh.

Fig. 11.5 from Fowler, H., and Miller, N. E. (1963), "Facilitation and Inhibition of Runway Performance by Hind- and Forepaw Shock of Various Intensities," *Journal of Comparative Physiological Psychology, 56,* 801–805. © 1963 by the American Psychological Association. Reprinted by permission of the author and the publisher.

Fig. 11.6 from Colwill, R. M., and Rescorla, R. A. (1985), "Postconditioning Devaluation of Reinforcer Affects Instrumental Responding," *Journal of Experimental Psychology: Animal Behavior Processes, 11,* 120–132. © 1985 by the American Psychological Association. Reprinted by permission of the author and the publisher.

Fig. 12.11 from Reynolds, G. S. (1961), "Attention in the Pigeon," *Journal of the Experimental Analysis of Behavior, 4,* 203–208. Reprinted by permission.

Fig. 12.15 from Grant, D. S. (1976), "Effect of Sample Presentation Time on Long-Delay Matching in the Pigeon," *Learning and Motivation, 7,* 580–590. Reprinted by permission of the Academic Press and the author.

Fig. 12.16 from Shea, J. B., and Upton, G. (1976), "The Effects on Skill Acquisition of an Interpolated Motor Short-Term Memory Task During the KR-Delay Interval," *Journal of Motor Behavior, 8,* 277–281. Reprinted with permission of the Helen Dwight Reid Educational Foundation. Published by Heldref Publications, 4000 Albemarle St., N.W., Washington, DC 20016. © 1976.

Figures 12.18 and 12.19 from Wagner, A. R., Rudy, J. W., and Whitlow, J. W. (1973), "Rehearsal in Animal Conditioning," *Journal of Experimental Psychology Monograph, 97,* 407–426. © 1973 by the American Psychological Association. Reprinted by permission of the author and the publisher.

Fig. 12.20 from Rescorla, R. A. (1985), "Inhibition and Facilitation," in R. R. Miller and N. E. Spear (Eds.), *Information Processing in Animals: Conditioned Inhibition,* 299–326. Reprinted by permission of Lawrence Erlbaum Associates, Inc., and the author.

Fig. 13.1 reprinted by permission of The University of California Press.

Fig. 13.2 from Olton, D. S., and Samuelson, R. J. (1976), "Remembrance of Places Passed: Spatial Memory in Rats," *Journal of Experimental Psychology: Animal Behavior Processes, 2,* 97–116. © 1976 by the American Psychological Association. Reprinted by permission of the author and the publisher.

Fig. 13.3 from Morris, R. G. M. (1981), "Spatial Localization Does Not Require the Presence of Local Cues," *Learning and Motivation, 12,* 239–260. Reprinted by permission of the Academic Press and the author.

Fig. 13.4 from Vander Wall, S. B. (1982), "An Experimental Analysis of Cache Recovery in Clark's Nutcracker," *Animal Behavior, 30,* 84–94. Reprinted by permission of the author.

Fig. 13.5 from Schusterman, R. (1962), "Transfer Effects of Successive Discrimination-Reversal Training in Chimpanzees," *Science, 137,* 422–423. © 1962 by the American Association for the Advancement of Science. Reprinted by permission of the author and the publisher.

Fig. 13.6 from Maier, S. F., Seligman, M. E. P., and Solomon, R. L. (1969), "Pavlovian Fear Conditioning and Learning Helplessness: Effects on Escape and Avoidance Behavior of (a) the CS-US Contingency and (b) the Independence of the US and Voluntary Responding," in B. A. Campbell and R. M. Church (Eds.), *Punishment and Aversive Behavior*, p. 328. © 1969. Reprinted by permission of Prentice Hall, Inc., Englewood Cliffs, New Jersey.

Fig. 13.7 from Trabasso, T. (1963), "Stimulus Emphasis and All-or-None Learning of Concept Identification," *Journal of Experimental Psychology*, 65, 395–406. © 1963 by the American Psychological Association. Reprinted by permission of the author and the publisher.

Fig. 13.8 from Posner, M. I., and Keele, S. W. (1968), "On the Genesis of Abstract Ideas," *Journal of Experimental Psychology*, 77, 353–363. Reprinted by permission of the author.

Author Index

Subject Index

Pages on which terms are defined are indicated by **bold** type.